The Maryland Militia in the Revolutionary War

*By S. Eugene Clements
and F. Edward Wright*

HERITAGE BOOKS
2006

HERITAGE BOOKS
AN IMPRINT OF HERITAGE BOOKS, INC.

Books, CDs, and more—Worldwide

For our listing of thousands of titles see our website
at
www.HeritageBooks.com

Published 2006 by
HERITAGE BOOKS, INC.
Publishing Division
65 East Main Street
Westminster, Maryland 21157-5026

Copyright © 1987 S. Eugene Clements and F. Edward Wright

All rights reserved. No part of this book may be reproduced or transmitted in any form or by any means, electronic or mechanical, including photocopying, recording or by any information storage and retrieval system without written permission from the author, except for the inclusion of brief quotations in a review.

International Standard Book Number: 978-1-58549-003-2

PREFACE

The surviving records of the Maryland Militia of the Revolutionary War can be found primarily in the collections of the Maryland State Archives and the Maryland Historical Society. Some extracts from these records have been published, but there is no overall compilation of the names of the officers and men and no definitive history of Maryland's militia activity during this period.

The term "militia" applies to part time or citizen soldiers to distinguish them from full time or professional soldiers. The soldiers raised by Maryland to meet quotas set by the Continental Congress for the Continental Army are not included in the militia. Such soldiers are usually called "Continentals." Another military group organized outside the militia consisted of "state" troops. These soldiers were raised for full time service in Maryland.

Publication of the names of Maryland's Revolutionary veterans has been generally limited to the rolls of the non-militia groups, i.e. the Continentals and the "state" troops. Documents relating to these men were published in Volume 18 of the 72-volume series, Archives of Maryland. This volume is titled, Muster Rolls and Other Records of Service of Maryland Troops in the American Revolution 1775-1783. Generally the militia was intended for service within the state. For that reason, perhaps, the rolls of the two companies of Maryland militia that were sent into Virginia's Eastern Shore counties in early 1776 were included in Volume 18. Militia units were sent out of the state later in response to requests by the Continental Congress, but rolls listing the men who actually went have not been found. The editors of Volume 18 noted that, "The discipline of the Revolutionary armes was not strict, and many left the ranks, when they were needed at home returning to the service after a few months." A similar situation existed for the militia, and surviving records generally do not provide information as to the individual soldiers who responded to the various calls for active duty.

In addition to the above mentioned Virginia expedition only a few of the militia rolls have been published: The Kent County rolls were listed in a small booklet, Kent County Maryland and Vicinity List of Militia and Oaths of Allegiance June 1775; the rolls of the Talbot County militia were included in Bulletin Number Three of the Maryland Original Research Society of Baltimore published in 1913; and, the rolls of the early companies of the Harford County militia were included in W.W. Preston's History of Harford County, published in 1901.

The purpose of this work is to provide an overview of the Maryland militia in the Revolutionary War and a compilation of the names of the officers and men from surviving records. A summary of the commissioned officers service records is shown as Appendix A Most of this information was extracted from eight different volumes of the Archives of Maryland series for the war years, besides original records and commissions held by the Maryland State Archives. Appendix B is a collection of the rolls of the companies, and sometimes other groups held by the Maryland Historical Society and the State Archives. In a few cases the lists consist of petitions. The names are recorded here in the same order as in the source itself. Both appendices include information from the Calendars of Maryland State Papers. The various sources have been cited with the material. Appendix A has been arranged alphabetically whereas Appendix B has retained the original order. An alphabetical index to Appendix B follows that appendix. In locating an individual militiaman one should check both appendices. In addition one should determine if he also served as a Continental by referring to Volume 18 of the Archives of Maryland, since many of the militia were recruited into Continental service.

The resolutions adopted by the Maryland Convention in January 1776 provided that all officers of the militia be commissioned by the Convention or its executive group, the Council of Safety; and, when the state government was established in March 1777, the State Assembly and State Council assumed that function. The transactions of these agencies have been published in the Proceedings of the Conventions of Maryland, 1774, 1775 and 1776, and in Archives of Maryland, volumes 11, 12, 16, 21, 43, 45, 47, and 48. A number of original commissions issued in early January 1776 and now in the Maryland State Archives are not in the transactions, so there is uncertainty as to the completeness of those records. Prior to the Militia Act of 1777 there was no requirement for furnishing the names of the militia soldiers to the state, so there is a scarcity of information on soldiers before 1777. Lists that may have been submitted under the 1777 Act have not survived for several of the counties.

Pension applications often give considerable information about the men who served, their families, and their military experiences. Applications should be consulted when available. However pension benefits were instituted many years after the war, and after many of the men had died, so few of the Revolutionary veterans actually received them. Pension lists were not used in the preparation of this book, but they are discussed in further detail in the Pensions section of the narrative portion of this book.

The authors are grateful to the Maryland State Archives and to the Maryland Historical Society for the willing assistance given by their staffs.

S. Eugene Clements and F. Edward Wright

CONTENTS

PREFACE iii
Part I BACKGROUND 1
Part II THE EARLY CONVENTIONS 2
Part III HOSTILITIES BEGIN .3
Part IV MARYLAND ORGANIZES ITS MILITIA 5
Part V LORD DUNMORE THREATENS 7
Part VI MARYLAND CONTINUES TO ORGANIZE 9
Part VII THE "OTTER" AND THE "FOWEY" ALERTS 13
Part VIII PERSONNEL PROBLEMS 15
Part IX SUPPLY 17
Part X MARYLAND CONTINENTALS AND THE FLYING CAMP 18
Part XI THE BRITISH FLEET THREATENS THE BAY 19
Part XII MILITIA WITH WASHINGTON'S ARMY 21
Part XIII GENERAL SMALLWOOD AND THE DISAFFECTED 23
Part XIV THE MILITIA ACT OF 1777 24
Part XV THE INVASION OF MARYLAND 26
Part XVI FALSE INVASION THREATS (1778 - 1783) 28
Part XVII RAIDS 31
Part XVIII DISSIDENTS 33
Part XIX GUARDING THE PRISONERS 37
Part XX THE FRONTIERS 39
Part XXI VETERANS' BENEFITS 40
APPENDIX A: COMMISSIONED OFFICERS - MARYLAND REVOLUTIONARY MILITIA . 43
APPENDIX B: MUSTER ROLLS AND OTHER LISTS 143
INDEX TO APPENDIX 260

THE MARYLAND MILITIA IN THE REVOLUTIONARY WAR

Part I - BACKGROUND

The Maryland militia was but one facet of the revolutionary activity of Maryland, and, like the Revolution itself, its roots go back to the beginnings of the Province The concept of having citizens armed for defense of their community came to Maryland with the early English settlers. The Charter given by Charles I in 1632 contained broad military-related sections with nebulous authority to Lord Baltimore and his officers to handle both external and internal threats to the colony. For most of the Colonial period the "trayned bands" were a protection from depredations of hostile Indians. Military operations were usually in pursuit of small groups who had plundered a few houses maybe burning one or two, and occasionally committing a murder The first of these was against Eastern Shore Indians who had done some mischief on Kent Island. A volunteer company of ten men was raised in 1639 to apprehend them.

A century later, on the eve of the French-Indian War, Maryland had a militia that included all able bodied freemen, 16 to 60 years of age excepting ministers and a few government officials. Indentured servants and slaves were excluded. Members were supposed to provide themselves with guns and powder. On muster days, once a month, except during winter months, there were required drills of each company. Officers and muster-masters appointed by the Governor were responsible for training the men and for inspecting their arms. In 1748, Governor Ogle reported that there were 12,500 militiamen in the population of about 94,000 whites.

The French-Indian War brought significant changes to the Maryland militia. Militia units were called into extended periods of duty, whereas previously volunteers or recruits were solicited but the militia companies were not called out. Maryland provincial troops were recruited and were engaged in full-scale actions with British regulars against French regular troops. Full-time provincial troops were raised for garrison on the western frontier. As a legacy, Maryland entered the revolutionary era with a nucleus of experienced officers and men, and with experience in mobilization.

After the Treaty of Paris in 1763 ended the war, England sought more revenue from the colonies. Opposition of the colonies led to recision of several taxes, but that on tea was retained. The drastic action of the Boston Tea party of December 1773 and other opposition to the collection of revenue were countered by strong action of the British government, rather than by recision. They closed the Port of Boston for all commerce and sent General Gage with four regiments of British regulars to enforce the laws.

The militant Bostonians publicized their plight through a network of correspondance committees that had been organized in the provinces. Elements within each province felt some sympathy for Boston because they too had grievances with the British government, and they feared similar treatment. In Maryland, the maritime interests were particularly active. The Baltimore committee, which was in close contact with Bostonians proposed a Maryland-wide meeting, and in June 1774 the 1st Maryland Convention was held in Annapolis. The convention consisted of delegates elected by the freemen of each county and was strictly an extra-legal activity that had no official standing, but as the months passed the Convention became the de facto government of the Province. For the time being though, it existed side by side with the Provincial authorities. In fact many of the delegates of the Convention were also delegates to the Maryland Assembly.

THE MARYLAND MILITIA IN THE REVOLUTIONARY WAR

Part II - THE EARLY CONVENTIONS

The session of the 1st Maryland Convention was not a long one. It passed non-importation and non-exportation resolutions with exhortations for compliance, and it also called upon merchants not to raise prices on stocks of previously imported goods. A subscription campaign was started for the distressed citizens of Boston. The Convention agreed to a Congress of all the Provinces, and named persons to solicit support of such a Congress from the other colonies. The same persons were to be the Maryland delegates to the Congress when it was held. There is no record of military measures having been discussed at the 1st Maryland Convention.

The 1st Continental Congress had no more legal standing than the Maryland Convention that preceded it. After considerable debate the principal items of agreement were a petition to the King and the Continental Association. The petition, as others before, pledged allegiance to the King but denied the authority of Parliament to tax the unrepresented colonies.

An "association" was a document setting forth principles and rules for conduct. Copies were passed around and signed by freemen who agreed to abide by them. The technique was first used extensively in the colonies to counter the Townsend Acts of 1767. The Continental Association of the 1st Continetal Congress contained non-importation and non-exportation provisions similar to those of the Maryland Convention but it incorporated compromises to insure its acceptance by all of the colonies. It also asked people to forego "every species of extravagance and dissipation, especially all horse-racing, and all kinds of gaming, cock-fighting, exhibitions of shows, plays, and other expensive diversions and entertainments." No explanation was offered as to the relationship of horse-racing or cock fighting to the trade barriers with the motherland. Enforcement of the terms of the Association was provided for as follows:

> "That a committee be chosen in each county, city and town...whose business it shall be attentively to observe the conduct of all persons touching this association; and when it shall be made to appear...that any person within the limits of their appointment has violated this association, that [they] cause the truth of the case to be published in the gazette; to the end, that all such foes to the rights of British-America maybe publically known, and universally condemned as the enemies of American liberty."

Further, if any colony did not accept the Association or should violate it, such colony would be held "unworthy of the rights of freedom, and as inimical to the liberties of their country." No mention was made of rioting, burnings, tar and feathering, and harassment that became the ultimate weapons against the individual violators.

The Congress indirectly addressed the matter of military preparations. In September 1774 when General Gage began fortifying the land approaches to Boston, the Suffolk County (Mass.) convention advised the towns to choose their own militia officers. The Continental Congress considered the Suffolk Resolves and incorporated some of them in their actions, but they did not endorse the militia section. Nevertheless they gave stature to all of the Resolves by sending copies to each colony when the report of Congressional actions was distributed.

THE EARLY CONVENTIONS

The 2nd Maryland convention assembled immediately after the Congress to hear reports from its delegates. In addition the Convention delegates had been exposed to circular letters from the other colonies and to newspapers, handbills and other information about affairs around Boston and elsewhere. The Convention record does not recount the debates nor the positions of individual delegates. Nevertheless, whatever the reasons, the Convention exhibited more aggressiveness than the predecessor only six months before.

On 12 December 1774, the Maryland Convention resolved unanimously:

> "That a well regulated militia, composed of the gentlemen, freeholders, and other freemen, is the natural strength and only stable security of a free government, and that such militia will relieve our mother country from any expense in our protection and defense; will obviate the pretence of a necessity for taxing us on that account, and render it unnecessary to keep any standing army (ever dangerous to liberty) in this province..."

The resolution continued with the recommendation that men from 16 to 50 years old form themselves into militia companies, chose officers, drill, arm themselves, and "be in readiness to act on any emergency." Each company was to have a captain, 2 lieutenants, an ensign, 4 sergeants, 4 corporals, 68 privates and a drummer. The same Convention initiated a subscription campaign to raise 10,000 pounds for the purchase of arms and ammunition. No military structure was established over the individual militia companies.

Sentiment was such that several companies were formed by the end of the year. However possibly due to the extra-legal nature only a few related documents survive. A relatively small number of names of militia members before 1 January 1776 were found for inclusion in the Appendices of this work. By the spring of 1775 one of Lord Baltimore's officials in a letter to England wrote that "every appearance indicates approaching hostilities," and that "large sums have been collected for the purchase of arms and ammunition; and persons of all denominations are required to associate under military regulations, on pain of the severest censure."

We know little about the royal militia in Maryland in this period, but certainly there was one. Governor Sharpe had expressed reservations about its loyalty, and there are numerous military titles among the gentlemen of the Province. From the alacrity with which the revolutionary companies were formed, it seems likely that they were reorganized units of the royal militia possibly retaining those officers most sympathetic to the colonial cause. Some support for this theory is given by the fact the one of the artillery companies raised in Annapolis called itself the Royal Artillery Train for a short time.

Part III - HOSTILITIES BEGIN

During the first quarter of 1775 attention still centered on Massachusetts and its plight under the military occupation. Numerous persons in the colonies hoped for a peaceful settlement of the differences with England. There were also those in Parliament who favored repeal of the Intolerable Acts and reconciliation. The matter was settled for many in April 1775 when General Gage sent out a sizeable military force from Boston to seize powder stocks in the hands of

THE MARYLAND MILITIA IN THE REVOLUTIONARY WAR

the militia at Concord. The troops were also expected to capture Samuel Adams and John Hancock, the leaders of the opposition, for trial in England. The previous September, Gage had successfully seized arms and ammunition at Charlestown and at Cambridge, but this time it was different. The people and the troops had endured nine months of mutual harassment since then. The anti-British militia had been training for months, sentries had been posted to detect any unusual movement of the troops from Boston, and tension was high in the entire area. Hostilities broke out at Lexington and Concord on 19 April 1775.

By coincidence the 3rd Maryland Convention was in session and had made some military preparations before news of Lexington and Concord reached Annapolis. On 27 April 1775 they agreed:

> "that it is earnestly recommended to the inhabitants of this province, to continue the regulation of the militia, as recommended by the last provincial convention, and that particular attention be paid to forming and exercising the militia throughout this province, and that the subscription for the purpose by the said convention recommended be forthwith completed and applied."

On the same day a committee of the convention asked the Governor to place some of the arms and ammunition of the Province "in the hands of the people" ostensibly for fear of a servant or slave uprising. Governor Eden later wrote:

> "[I] tried to convince them that they were only going to accelerate the evil they dreaded from their servants and slaves...in vain...and by advice of the Council...I agreed to furnish four counties (whose Colonels made a regular application) with arms, etc., such as they are, and perhaps each county (of those four) will get one hundred stand, which their Colonels give receipts for, and are to share with the counties that have not had time to apply."

The Convention then elected delegates for the previously scheduled meeting of the Continental Congress to be held 10 May. A later Maryland Convention would decide what to do with the arms and ammunition.

The 2nd Continental Congress was a memorable one. Its members had hardly digested the significance of Lexington and Concord when early in the session came news of the successful capture of Ticonderoga and Crown Point through the initiative of the revolutionary militia of Vermont and Connecticut. Before they adjourned they would receive news of Bunker Hill. So despite the hope and desire for reconciliation, albeit on its own terms of representation before taxation, the 2nd Congress was forced by events to prepare for armed conflict. It did draft a petition to the King, and it did table a proposal for a permanent union, but it also organized for military operations. Before adjournment on 2 August it:

- Approved a continental army of 20,000 men.

- Appointed George Washington as commander-in-chief of the army, and selected four Major Generals, four Brigadier Generals and a number of support officers.

- Called for 10 rifle companies from among three of the Middle colonies to go to Boston for one year's service; two of the companies to be raised in Maryland, two in Virginia and six in Pennsylvania. This call was the first in

HOSTILITIES BEGIN

the long series of levies against the Provinces for troops of what would become the Continental army.

- Recommended that each province put its militia in order, proposing a general plan for its organization.

- Recommended each colony make provision for sea coast defense.

- Adopted a plan for a military medical service to support the 20,000 man army.

- Arranged for financing the army by issue of paper money.

- Modified the Association rules to permit the importation of arms and ammunition and the non-exportation rules to permit export of sufficient produce of the colonies to pay for the imported arms and ammunition.

- Recommended each colony appoint a committee of safety to superintend and direct all matters necessary for their safety and security during recesses of their provincial conventionas or assemblies.

Several of these actions directly affected Maryland. The requirement for two rifle companies from Maryland was assigned to the Frederick County Committee on Observation. The Committee selected officers and enlisted volunteers from frontiersmen, hunters, and trappers, some of whom were said to have come hundreds of miles from beyond the western boundaries of the Province. On 18 July 1775 about a hundred men left Frederick for Boston. They arrived there 22 days later after walking 550 miles and joined the troops maintaining the seige. These companies became the first Maryland Continentals. The names of the commissioned officers were published in James McSherry, "History of Maryland," (Baltimore, Md., John Murphy, 1849) and in the Archives of Maryland volume 18. A roster of the men in Capt. Thomas Price's company is in The Maryland Historical Magazine, 22:275,399. A list of Capt. Cresap's company was published in W.F. Horn, "The Horn Papers," (Waynesburg, Pa., 1945), but the authenticity of this list has been questioned.

Part IV - MARYLAND ORGANIZES ITS MILITIA

The Maryland Convention met from 26 July to 14 August 1775 to consider the reports of the delegates from the 2nd Congressional Congress. Once again, the Convention members were probably already well-informed on happenings in the north from other sources. The Convention accepted the principle that it was necessary and justifiable to repel force with force, and approved the opposition by arms to the British troops employed to enforce obedience to acts of the British Parliament. The principle was incorporated into a formal statement, the "Association of the Freemen of Maryland, July 26, 1775" that was to be carried by persons in each parish and hundred to all Freeholders for their signature. The names of persons who would not sign within ten days were to be reported to the next Convention.

To support its acceptance of military force, the Maryland Convention then took action to refine and strengthen the military arrangements made in the prior convention. Resolutions were passed that:

THE MARYLAND MILITIA IN THE REVOLUTIONARY WAR

- Established 40 companies of minutemen to serve to 1 March 1776 "to march to such places, either in this, or the neighbouring colonies, as we may be commanded...and fight...for the preservation of American Liberty..."

-- The companies were to be raised by counties, one each in Worcester, Somerset, Talbot, Caroline, Kent, and Calvert; two each in Dorchester, Queen Anne's, St. Mary's, and Cecil; three each in Charles, Prince George's, and Harford; four in Ann Arundel; five in Baltimore; and eight in Frederick. Company officers were to be elected by the companies. The companies were to drill two days per week and get paid for one of them.

-- Three battalions were set up: one consisting of the Frederick companies; one of the Baltimore and Harford companies; and one battalion of the St. Marys, Charles, Prince George's companies.

-- Each battalion was to have a colonel, a lieutenant colonel, two majors, a quartermaster, and an adjutant each to be commissioned by the Convention or the Council of Safety.

-- The battalions were also to have a light infantry company made up of eight men drawn from each of the battalion's companies; The officers of the light infantry companies were to be appointed by the Convention or the Council of Safety.

Next the Convention established a similar structure for the militia in which all able-bodied Freemen (excepting Clergymen of all denominations, physicians, the Household of the Governor, Minute and Artillery men, and such persons who from their religious principles could not bear arms in any case) were to enroll by 15 September. The militia men were to "...march to such places within this province...and fight..." Note that the ordinary militia was limited to action within the Province, whereas the minutemen could also be sent into neighboring provinces.

-- The companies were to drill one day a week by company; including one day a month as part of the battalion.

-- Assignment of the companies to battalions was to be made by the county committees of observation.

-- Non-enrollers were to be reported to Convention, "...against whom no further proceedings or measures shall be taken, but by the future order of the Convention"

-- By 1 October the Captains were to submit their rolls to their committee of observation, who were to send the names of officers and numbers of men to the Council of Safety.

-- Artillery companies could be formed if enough men volunteered.

The Convention took several steps to support the military organization that it set up. Pay rates were set for militia on active duty and penalties prescribed for discipline. It was decided:

- To purchase 5000 stand of arms.

- To borrow 5900 pounds "...on the credit of this Convention to be laid

MARYLAND ORGANIZES ITS MILITIA

out in the purchase of 48 tons of lead, one hundred pounds value in Gun-flints, two Tons of cannon powder, and the residue of the said sum in Musquetry powder, for the use of this Province..."

- To issue paper money to fund the manufacture of powder. The money was to be redeemed by January 1786.

- To transfer some of the public arms and ammunition in possession of Colonels Joshua Beall, Richard Lloyd, Edward Lloyd, and Henry Hooper to the Minute-men companies.

Then the Convention formally established the Council of Safety and approved procedures for its operation. It formalized the structure and election of the committees of observation in the counties. Also in the political area it divided Frederick County into three districts that later became separate counties.

After the Convention, William Eddis wrote back to England, "Government is now almost totally annihilated, and power transferred to the multitude."

The Fall of 1775, after the August adjournment of the Maryland Convention, was a period of transition and adjustment to operation under the rules set by the Convention. Local elections were held, militia companies formed, and violators of the trading regulations punished. Concurrently the Governor, whose civil power was being steadily eroded, made feeble efforts to stem the tide by appeals to the people on the one hand and by appeals to the authorities in England on the other.

Questions arose about the conduct of some of the elections of officers for militia companies that were appealed to the Council of Safety. Petitions from company members are the sources for some of the names listed in the Appendices of this book. On 21 October the Council reiterated the request for reports from the county committees of the numbers of men enrolled in the militia and the names of the officers so that commissions might be issued. The numerous militia commissions issued in January 1776 undoubtedly resulted from the replies to the Council request, although only a few of the original replies are now in the Maryland State Archives.

Part V - LORD DUNMORE THREATENS

In June 1775, Lord Dunmore, the Royal Governor of Virginia, felt so threatened by the hostility of Williamsburg and the rest of Virginia that he took refuge on the FOWEY, one of the British warships in the lower Chesapeake Bay. He requested troop support and was sent some 140 British regulars from Florida. The fleet has three other British warships, in addition to the FOWEY, as well as a number of smaller armed ships and numerous unarmed supply vessels. The warships, the troops, and Lord Dunmore's aggressiveness combined to be a substantial threat to both Virginia and Maryland. This threat was realized on 24 October 1775 when six tenders shelled Hampton and embarked men in small boats to pillage the town. Local defenders drove off the attackers.

The historian, McSherry, relates:

THE MARYLAND MILITIA IN THE REVOLUTIONARY WAR

"Dunmore was actively at work disseminating the seeds of disaffection by his agents on the Eastern Shore of Maryland. His partizans were partially successful, and raised several companies of men pledged to support the royal cause if arms, ammunition and a small additional force should be furnished them. They even became so bold as openly to tear off the black cockade which the patriots wore at their militia trainings, to replace it with the red cockade, and to parade under officers of their own selection. A party under one of their leaders, in November, seized on a small craft and sailed secretly to obtain the necessary supplies of ammunition: but before the malcontents could mature their plans, the committee of safety of the Eastern Shore, aided by the committees of Somerset and Worcester counties assembled a body of a thousand militia, crushed the attempt and secured the principal conspirators."

The militia units involved in this action have not been further identified, and in retrospect it seems doubtful that under the conditions prevailing in the lower counties that "a body of a thousand militia" could be mobilized in those counties at that time. Doubtless some militia were used to try to overcome loyalist strength there.

As great a factor as the military threat in arousing the Marylanders and Virginians was Lord Dunmore's proclamation of 7 November 1775. He declared all to be rebels who would not immediately come to his standard, and he offered freedom to all servants and slaves of those rebels. The offer of freedom caused much unrest among the slaves and servants; and, many joined the Loyalist militia. A Williamsburg dispatch of 1 December rumored that some 2000 men had been recruited in the two counties around Norfolk, including a regiment of blacks. The proclamation in threatening the economic and social foundations of the area alienated many who had previously been loyal or passively neutral. Nevertheless the Norfolk and the southern Eastern Shore remained heavily Loyalist and under the influence of Dunmore to the extent that the Northampton County Committee of Observation solicited help from the Continental Congress early in December 1775.

Before assistance could come to the peninsula, Lord Dunmore sent a landing force ashore at Norfolk to surpress some of the revolutionary elements there, particularly a printer who was circulating subversive literature. The printer was arrested and his press confiscated. The landing party was driven out by some Virginia militia, who, in turn, were bombarded by the British men-of-war. The bombardment set fires in the town, and the militia before leaving apparently touched off some Tory properties. Consequently much of Norfolk burned with great suffering to its inhabitants. The happening caused anxiety and concern in Maryland, particularly in the exposed towns of Annapolis and Baltimore but also all up and down the bay and its navigable waterways.

The Continental Congress took prompt action on Northampton's request by ordering three Pennsylvania companies to go there; but, before they could get started they were diverted to Albany, N.Y. for possible use in Canada. In their stead Congress on 8 January asked Maryland to send three Minuteman companies from the Eastern Shore, one each from Kent, Queen Anne's, and Dorchester counties. The Kent company marched 29 January under Captain James Kent and arrived at Northampton 12 February; the Queen Anne's company under Captain William Henry left 3 February and arrived at Northampton 14 February; the Dorchester company was not able to get enough guns to respond. In Virginia, the Maryland units recovered a schooner that thirteen slaves had stolen to join the British off shore. Later, in Cheriton Creek, they drove off a tender that was

LORD DUNMORE THREATENS

attempting a landing while accompanying the OTTER on its return down the Bay. In late March the two companies marched back home and passed out of existence with the demise of the Minutemen companies in the state. These were the first Maryland militia units in combat during the war. A considerable number of their officers and men later became senior officers in the militia and in the Flying Camp. The Continental Congress eventually reimbursed Maryland for the expenses of these two companies, although technically, they were not part of the Continental establishment. The rosters of the officers and men of these companies are contained in the Archives of Maryland, volume 18, and consequently were omitted from this book.

Part VI - MARYLAND CONTINUES TO ORGANIZE

Even before Dunmore's proclamation of November, the Maryland Council of Safety in late October issued a call for the Maryland Convention to meet in December. The Convention was in session from 7 December 1775 to 18 January 1776, and it took several significant actions on military matters. Full-time "regular" state troops were authorized; the state was divided into military districts; militia battalions were set up; officers were named for the state troops and for the militia; regulations were drawn up for administration of the forces; and several manufacturing projects were funded for military supplies.

The regular state units were:

- A battalion with eight infantry and one light infantry company. Five of the infantry companies and the light infantry company were to be stationed at Annapolis and the other three infantry companies at Baltimore. William Smallwood and Francis Ware, delegates from Charles County, were elected Colonel and Lieutenant Colonel respectively of the battalion.

- Seven independent infantry companies. Five were to be stationed on the Eastern Shore, one each in Worcestor, Somerset, Dorchester, Talbot, and the other to be half in Queen Annes and half in Kent counties. One was to be stationed in St. Mary's country and the other split one-half in Calvert and half in Charles county. Three Convention delegates were made Captains of independent companies and one was a Lieutenant.

- Two artillery companies, one to be stationed at Annapolis and the other at Baltimore.

- One company of Marines.

Five districts were set up for the militia and Brigadier Generals named for each:

District	Counties	Brigadier General
1	Frederick	Thomas Johnson, Jr.
2	Dorchester, Caroline, Worcester, and Somerset	Henry Hooper
3	St. Mary's, Charles, Calvert, and Prince George's	John Dent
4	Cecil, Kent, Queen Anne's, Talbot	James L. Chamberlaine

THE MARYLAND MILITIA IN THE REVOLUTIONARY WAR

5   Ann Arundel, Baltimore, Harford   Andrew Buchanan

The Convention also established a battalion structure for the militia and assigned battalions to the various counties. Each battalion was to have a staff including a colonel, a lieutenant colonel, a first major, a second major, a quartermaster and an adjutant, with commissions to be issued by the Convention. Later the battalion colonels were given authority to appoint the quartermaster and the adjutant without commissions. Later too the "first" and "second" were dropped from the designation of majors. There was no regimental structure in the militia, so the battalions reported directly to the district brigadier generals.

The Convention approved the field officers for all of the initial battalions except those of Kent county that were deferred to the next Convention. Some thirty-five of the field officers appointed for the militia were from among the sixty-five Convention delegates. Five other delegates were also subsequently appointed field officers. The commissions were issued on a form devised by a committee and 2500 were ordered to be printed.

The battalions were often called by the name of the geographical area in which they were raised, such as the "Lower Battalion" or the "Elk Ridge Battalion". The Militia Act of 1777 resulted in a partial reorganization of the battalions, and the new commnissions issued afterwards used names rather than numbers. Many of these names are identifiable with the prior numbered battalions but a few new ones are not. A list of the known battalion follows:

Number	County	Name
1	Somerset	Upper Battalion
2	Cecil	Elk, Elk River Battalion
3	Dorchester	Upper Battalion
4	Talbot	
5	Queen Anne's	Upper Battalion
6	St. Mary's	Upper Battalion
7	Ann Arundel	Severn Battalion
8	Harford	Lower Battalion
9	Baltimore	(Not used, see unnumbered bns.)
10	Worcester	1st Battalion
11	Prince George's	Lower Battalion
12	Charles	Lower Battalion
13	Kent	Lower Battalion
14	Caroline	East Battalion
15	Calvert	
16	Montgomery	Upper Bn.(former Frederick Lower District)
17	Somerset	Lower Battalion
18	Cecil	Bohemia Battalion
19	Dorchester	Lower Battalion
20	Queen Anne's	Lower Battalion
21	St. Mary's	Lower Battalion
22	Ann Arundel	Elk Ridge Battalion
23	Harford	Upper, Hall's Battalion
24	Worcester	2nd Battalion
25	Prince George's	Upper Battalion
26	Charles	Upper Battalion
27	Kent	Upper Battalion

MARYLAND CONTINUES TO ORGANIZE

28	Caroline	West Battalion
29	Montgomery	Lower Bn.(former Frederick Lower District)
30	Cecil	Susquehanna Battalion
31	Ann Arundel	West River, South River Battalion
32	Washington	1st Bn. (former Frederick Upper District)
33	Frederick	1st Bn. (former Middle District)
34	Frederick	4th Bn. (former Middle District)
35	Frederick	3rd Bn. (former Middle District)
36	Washington	2nd Bn. (former Frederick Upper District)
37	Frederick	2nd Bn. (former Middle District)
38	Talbot	

The following battalions, not numbered in the above listing, also appear in the listings of Appendix A:

Baltimore	Baltimore City, Baltimore Town
Baltimore	Soldier's Delight
Baltimore	Gist's
Baltimore	Gunpowder
Baltimore	Gunpowder Upper
Cecil	Sassafras
Frederick	Catoctin
Frederick	Linganore
Harford	Deer Creek
Prince George's	Middle
Somerset	Princess Ann
Somerset	Salisbury
Washington	3rd Bn, Western
Worcester	Sinapuxent
Worcester	Snow Hill
Worcester	Wicomico

The Brigadier Generals were given authority to form corps of the companies that were in excess of the assigned battalions. The only known use of this authority was by General Hooper in the lower Eastern Shore district where he established a separate corps of four companies in Dorchester. In other cases excess companies were simply assigned to one of the existing battalions.

The Convention record does not show approval of the company grade militia officers, nor are they listed in the Journal of the Council of Safety. Nevertheless a number of surviving commissions are dated during the Convention session, and there are also other indications of commissions issued then. It seems likely that the counties did submit names of the company officers in accordance with the requirement of the prior Convention and that commissions were issued. Unfortunately no such lists have been located, and in the absence of a Convention record the complete initial roster of the company officers of the militia can not be compiled.

Within the militia the relative rank of the Brigadier Generals was established upon their appointment. Initially the battalions were given a relative rank by ballot of the Convention, and the Colonels took that ranking. Subsequent appointees were to rank by date of appointment. The relative rank of regular and militia officers when operating together was established as:

Field officers of regulars,
Brigadier Generals and Colonels of militia,

THE MARYLAND MILITIA IN THE REVOLUTIONARY WAR

> Captains of the regulars,
> Lieutenant Colonels and Majors of militia,
> Lieutenants of the regulars,
> Captains and Lieutenants of the militia,
> Ensigns of the regulars,
> Ensigns of the militia.

The rules adopted "for regulating and governing" the forces comprise sixty-five sections, covering all phases of military life. They were applicable to all troops on active duty with some variations for the militia. For example, militia courts-martial were to consist only of militia officers. Another unique provision for the militia was:

> "That to avoid a needless and insupportable expense, no person after the tenth day of May next, wear any uniform at exercise, either in single companies or in battalion, but hunting shirts, the officers distinguishing themselves from the privates by different feathers, cockades, or the like, as fancy may direct."

A pay scale and rations schedule was approved for all troops while on active duty. These were the same for regulars and the militia. The ration allowance probably reflected typical meals of the time. It called for:

> "...one pound of beef, or three quarters of a pound of pork, one pound of flour or bread per man per day, three pints of beans at six shillings per bushel per week, or other vegetables equivalent; one quart of indian meal per week; a gill of vinegar and a gill of molasses per man per day; a quart of cider, small beer, or a gill of rum, per man per day; three pounds of candles for one hundred men per week, for guards; twenty-four pounds of soft soap, or eight pounds of hard soap for one hundred men per week."

It was decided to discontinue the minutemen companies by 1 March 1776 but the Kent and Queen Anne's companies on duty in Virginia remained there for most of March. By separate action two Annapolis militia companies were made independent companies and the Ann Arundel battalion was left with seven companies.

Although the debate of the Convention was not recorded, it is apparent that non-compliance with previous resolutions on enrollment in the militia was a serious problem. The Convention decided to require all eligible men to enroll by 1 March, and militia officers were permitted to take the firearms away from non-enrollers, except for their pistols. Those who actively advocated non-enrollment were subject to arrest and trial. When brought to trial the violators were usually treated leniently being released under bond for future good behavior.

Part VII - THE "OTTER" AND THE "FOWEY" ALERTS

On the political level in the spring of 1776, Congress struggled with the question of independence versus reconciliation. The more radical Bostonians who had experienced great oppression led a group advocating immediate independence. Maryland on the other hand was not yet ready. The Maryland Convention had instructed its delegates to give first priority to reconciliation and not to agree to independence without coming back for further guidance. Nevertheless, the actions of the Maryland Convention showed that Maryland would be willing to fight if necessary; and thanks to Lord Dunmore, Maryland was acutely aware of the need for defense against the threat from the Bay. The state troops were intended partially for that purpose, and partially for the control of dissidents. Preparations began on a state navy with the construction of the ship, DEFENCE, at Baltimore, and fortifications were commenced at Baltimore and Annapolis. But before the state troops and the DEFENCE were fully ready, the OTTER alert occurred.

On Tuesday evening 5 March, the pilot boat stationed south of Annapolis reported a man-of-war and two tenders on the way up the Bay. The warship, first reported as having 44-guns, turned out to be the OTTER, a 16-gun vessel from Lord Dunmore's fleet. She was accompanied by a 6-gun sloop, and several smaller vessels mounting swivel guns. The Council of Safety immediately commenced to mobilize the defense forces:

- The Severn militia battalion of Ann Arundel county under Colonel Hall was ordered to Annapolis.

- The other two Ann Arundel battalions, Colonel Weems' West River battalion and Colonel Dorsey's Elk Ridge, were alerted to be ready to march on one hour's notice; and a warning sent to Baltimore.

- The state troops in Annapolis were provided with guns from the militia companies there.

The next day, the Calvert militia reported the ships off shore. They planned mobilizing about 100 men to keep watch on the ships and to guard against a landing. They also said that the British had captured a New England vessel in the Bay.

On Thursday, Colonel Weems' battalion was ordered to take stations on each side of the South River. The records show that his battalion mustered 70 officers and 284 men with 246 muskets for this assignment. That would have been about half the number of men expected of a full battalion. Capt. Stone and his state company were ordered to Annapolis. Half of Capt. Rezin Beall's state company was to go to Drum Point on the Bay and the other half to Port Tobacco on the Potomac. When the hostile group passed the mouth of the Severn, it was clear that Baltimore was their goal. The Elk Ridge battalion was ordered to Baltimore; and in Baltimore efforts were hastened to complete the DEFENCE. She was in the water being outfitted, but her main guns did not get to Baltimore until Wednesday evening. By Friday evening they were in place on the ship. Under cover of darkness the DEFENCE, in company with a number of smaller boats carrying troops, was towed out close to where a hostile tender and some smaller ships were trying to salvage the cargo of flour from a large grounded ship. The OTTER itself was several miles off shore.

Saturday morning the weather was so thick and hazy that the hostile ves-

THE MARYLAND MILITIA IN THE REVOLUTIONARY WAR

sels were completely surprised by the DEFENCE. The British tender sailed away leaving behind the smaller ships that had been with them. The tender joined the OTTER, and the group retreated to the south. At Annapolis the OTTER sent two officers ashore under a flag of truce asking the Governor for provisions and for permission to take their New England ship with them. The Governor immediately referred the requests to the Council of Safety which refused them. The OTTER next sent in five prisoners that had been captured previously. The Council was later to report that "The Gentlemen (i.e. the British officers) behaved very politely and on some subjects were free and communicative - they know everything that has transpired here and to the Northward." Later the Council wrote that they had received some prisoners "who said they were treated with great humility and in return it was thought proper to compliment the officer with two quarters of beef." Still later John Wells was paid seven pounds, seven shillings and seven pence for 322 lbs. of beef "given as a compliment...to Captain Boucher he having restored five prisoners."

When the OTTER left Annapolis, the West River battalion was ordered south along the Bay to assist the Calvert militia. Brigadier General Chamberlaine of Talbot was ordered to alert their battalion, and Colonel Murray of Dorchester reported that his battalion was in positions along the Bay shore. Harford, Kent and York, Pennsylvania militia were ready to assist had landings been attempted on the upper Bay. On the way down the Bay, the OTTER is said to have taken some livestock and a small boat from an Eastern Shore island, possibly Sharp's Island. Farther south, they sent small boats into the Hungar River of Northampton county where the landings were repelled by the minutemen on duty from Kent and Queen Anne's counties as related above.

The incident confirmed that there was a real threat on the Bay, and that it could touch Annapolis and Baltimore. It also demonstrated that an aggressive show of force protected against a threat of that size. Afterwards, it was widely expected that the raiders would soon come north again so there were renewed efforts to complete and supplement the defenses.

Another alert, less extensive than the OTTER incident, occurred when the FOWEY went to Annapolis to pick up Governor Eden upon his leaving the province. This was preceded by some interesting political happenings that saw the Maryland Council defy a Continental Congress resolution to take custody of the Governor. About the same time, the British squadron of the warships and some 90 other ships moved north and occupied Gwinn's Island at the mouth of the Rappahannock River in Virginia. The Marylanders suspected a raid would be made either up the Potomac or up the bay from there.

The Maryland Convention, on 24 April, had suggested that Governor Eden leave, and he made the necessary arrangements with the British naval commander. The Governor told the Council of Safety of his plans and received assurances of safe conduct from them. The Council in turn instructed its forces to allow the FOWEY free passage. Nevertheless the Maryland patriots did not quite trust the British naval vessel, nor did the British Captain trust the Marylanders. The trip up to Annapolis went without incident, but at some point the FOWEY picked up nine indentured men who wanted to join the British forces. The Council asked for their release, but the British Captain refused. In retaliation some of the belongings of the Governor and his party were withheld, and the FOWEY departed on 25 June 1776 with the Governor and his party.

Under the strained circumstances, the Council was "...apprehensive that the ship of war on her return down the Bay may make some attempt to land,

THE "OTTER" AND THE "FOWEY" ALERTS

either to procure provisions or to make deprecations." Orders were issued to Capt. Beall of the state company to be on guard, and two Ann Arundel battalion commanders were authorized to call out their units. In each case the instructions gave the dual mission of repelling landings and preventing servants and slaves from going out to the FOWEY. No further incident occurred, and the FOWEY with Governor Eden aboard rejoined the British ships at Gwinn's Island.

Part VIII - PERSONNEL PROBLEMS

During this period personnel problems began to emerge in the militia. Some of these were forerunners of a real shortage of manpower that came later, but at this time they were not serious. Among other complaints, the requirement for all eligible men to drill in the militia was found to be too stringent. Oddly, school masters and their pupils were the first to be exempted from mustering so long as they exercised themselves. Then conflicts arose with maritime needs. Capt. Wells' militia company in Baltimore consisted mainly of ship carpenters and others working on the two continental frigates under construction there. The company was converted to an Artillery company possibly to reduce their militia duties, and in the summer of 1776 ship carpenters were exempted from all militia musters. Later the Governor was authorized to grant an exemption to anyone engaged in manufacturing for use of the state.

In March 1776 the Continental Congress authorized the provinces to license private armed vessels to prey on British shipping. This was a move to get additional force to counter the British control of the seas. It opened up a lucrative occupation inasmuch as the privateers shared in prize money from the captured ships and their cargoes. Consequently, numerous privateers were outfitted in Maryland ports and went to sea. There was some accompanying loss to the militia that grew larger in later years. The privateers also competed for guns and gunpowder bidding up the prices for those items in the scarce market.

Another personnel problem was the behavior of militia members who were not in sympathy with the cause. Those with the strongest Tory convictions left the province or joined Loyalist military units with the British forces. There were also those who stayed home and remained in the militia while opposed to its purpose.

- In Prince George"s county Col. Beall asked for a court martial for two Lieutenants of Capt. Boyd's company who "...while under arms in the field behaved in a very mutinous manner and seemed much inclined to encourage the same disposition among the men of the company they belonged to."

- In Caroline county, Cornelius Hogans, a member of a Dorchester militia company, showed up at the drill of Capt. Stafford's company. After roll call he took over the company, ordered it to march and then dismissed them. Apparently he had also influenced other companies not to drill. The Council of Safety placed him under a bond of 100 pounds sterling for a year to conform to the rules and "conduct himself in all things agreeable." It seems likely that Hogans could not have acted so brazenly without the support or sympathy of the other officers and men who were at the drill.

- In Frederick county at a drill of two militia companies, Robert

THE MARYLAND MILITIA IN THE REVOLUTIONARY WAR

Gassaway, stepped out of ranks and made a speech saying:

> "...that it is better for the Poor People to lay down their Arms, and pay the Duties and Taxes laid upon them by the King and Parliament, than to be brought into Slavery and to be commanded and ordered around as they were..."

He went on to advocate reconciliation through petitions to the King and Parliament. The Council of Safety finding that he had signed the Association papers and was an active militia member let him go free when he made a public apology. His accompaning written apology was:

> "I confess that I am sorry to think that I should have said enni thing that should have given enny purson reson to think that it is my deiser to disunite the peopel and, acknowledge my error in so doing, and do promis for tim to cum to behave myself carfully in the cause of amarear."

There were numerous complaints from members of militia companies about the selection of their officers. In general the company officers were to be elected by the men and the battalion officers by the company officers of the battalion. However, the Convention or the Council of Safety, if the Convention was not in session, issued the commissions to the officers. In practice the results of the elections were treated as recommendations; and, often someone other than the elected person was actually commissioned. Such actions, as might be expected, caused much dissatisfaction:

- In one Prince George's county company officers were appointed who were "disagreeable to the Company in general, and many had declared if those gentlemen were promoted they would not continue in the company." The battalion Colonel effected a compromise in which the unwanted Captain was made First Lieutenant and the company's choice made Captain.

- In Queen Anne's county, Turbutt Betton was fined for not attending militia drills. In his appeal of the fine, he said that when his captain was made the battalion colonel, the Council of Safety appointed new company officers who were not acceptable. Instead the company elected and drilled under a different set of officers. They also would not acknowledge the new battalion field officers and elected their own for those positions. Betton maintained that he should not be fined for failing to drill under the irregular officers.

- In Baltimore, the First Major of the Soldier's Delight Battalion resigned because the men declared they would be commanded only by officers recommended by themselves.

- Prince George's county had an interesting case in which Capt. Andrew Beall resigned as a company Captain and then objected to the Colonel's choice for his replacement because:

> "...is a poor man and has a wife and several children, and no person to work for them, but himself, therefore cannot make the appearance that an Officer ought to make, is a person of no education, neither is he qualified in any respect whatever to keep company with the other Gentlemen Officers..."

A group of the men in the company also objected saying that a majority of the men would not serve under the Colonel's selection, and that they were

PERSONNEL PROBLEMS

"...a free people and have the right to the choice of our own officers under whom we are to risque our lives and fortunes with theirs." The man in question noted that the prior Captain had really resigned to get the appointment for his son, the Second Lieutenant, and had solicited the company petition. He also pointed out his service of nine years in the provincial forces in the French-Indian War and participation in the reduction of Quebec.

- Philip Thomas of Frederick county refused a Captain's commission. He had commanded without a commission "one of the oldest companies in this province" and had been recommended by the Frederick committee to be Colonel of their 4th battalion. Instead the Convention gave the appointment to a Lieutenant of a younger company in another battalion and also appointed the First Lieutenant of Thomas' old company to be the battalion First Major. Thomas did not wish to serve under officers he considered junior to himself and who were not recommended by Frederick committee.

Part IX - SUPPLY

The business of supply for the forces took much time and effort of the Council. There never seemed to be enough firearms for the troops, and many of those that were available needed repair. The Dorchester minuteman company could not go to Virginia primarily because it had only 10 guns, and those had been sent down from Kent county. As the state companies were recruited, guns were transferred to them from the militia. Guns were purchased from individuals, some came in from the West Indies, and some were manufactured locally. The local gunsmiths were overloaded with repairs and not particularly adept at gun making. In February proof tests showed 100 good and 31 bad of the guns made by three Baltimore gunsmiths. By September 1776 guns were in such short supply that the Convention authorized the Council of Safety to contract for "one thousand pike poles, not less than 12 feet in length." No record has been found of a contract nor of their receipt and issue to troops.

Gunpowder was a major problem. It deteriorated if not stored properly, and dispersed military companies did not have the facilities for storing it properly. It also had a way of disappearing. A year earlier, a Prince George's official said:

> "In December last there was a good deal of powder and lead in the store: instead of the people providing themselves with same & keeping it ready, or in the store, it has most shamefully been wasted on Xmas guns, fired away at birds and squirrels but now there is very little in the County and that little growing less every day...Our Committee a few days ago applied to me for what I had to dispose among the people which I refused to part with, well knowing that it will go like the rest fired away at Ducks,&. What I have, I intend to keep, till it is wanted, to defend us against the enemy..."

On giving the powder to the militia Captains, Colonel Beall of Prince George's county said:

> "I think there is some of the Captains on whose undoubted care dependence might be had, but I fear there is some others whose prudence on such occasion might be doubtful, this causes me to think of its being under the

THE MARYLAND MILITIA IN THE REVOLUTIONARY WAR

direction of the committees of observation in each neighborhood where it is lodged as the most proper method."

After the OTTER alarm the Council said:

"Upon the late alarm some powder was given into the hands of the militia on this side of the bay and we fear it will be difficult to collect the greater part of it again and that too much of what may remain with the people will be lost to the public."

Colonel Murray of Dorchester related his experience in the OTTER alarm:

"We were in hopes that when it came to the test we should find many of them prepared with private property in ammunition, but in this we find we were deceived."

Yet, as Colonel Beall pointed out, the easy availability of powder to the men was an important factor in keeping up their readiness and their morale.

Part X - MARYLAND CONTINENTALS AND THE FLYING CAMP

In June 1776 the Continental Congress, apprehensive about the expected return of the British who had left Boston and refurbished their forces in Halifax, concluded that General Washington needed a Continental army. On 3 June they:

"Resolved, That a flying camp be immediately established in the middle colonies; and that it consist of 10000 men; to complete which number,

Resolved, That the colony of Pennsylvania be requested to furnish of their militia 6000, Maryland of their militia 3400, Delaware government, of their militia 600.

Resolved, that the militia be engaged to the first day of December next, unless sooner discharged by Congress."

The Maryland Council upon receiving the request quickly replied that they did not have the authority to order militia out of the province of Maryland, and that they had called a Convention to address the matter. The Maryland Congressional delegates clarified the situation by responding that "It never was intended that any part of the militia was compellable to march out of the Provinces...It was intended that the flying camp should be formed by the voluntary inlistments of the militia." Thus although the term "militia" was used to describe the Flying Camp troops, they were, in fact, short term volunteers in the continental forces. Once they left Maryland they were under the control of General Washington, and they were to be paid and supported by the Continental Congress rather than by Maryland.

The hastily called Maryland Convention decided to send the state troops as the first increment of their quota. General Smallwood's battalion and three Independent companies went to Philadelphia and then towards New York. They were to be joined by the other four Independent companies around Elizabeth, New

MARYLAND CONTINENTALS AND THE FLYING CAMP

Jersey. In August and September these units were in the battles around New York city. They eventually became the Maryland Line of the Continental army.

Then to complete its quota the Convention decided, 25 June, to form four battalions and assigned responsibilities for recruitment among the counties. These battalions are known as the Flying Camp. Their names are included in the Archives of Maryland, Volume 18 as Continentals.

In Philadelphia the Congress continued to debate the question of independence. New England and the Southern colonies supported independence whereas the Middle colonies advocated further attempts at reconciliation. One by one the delegations of Delaware, New Jersey and Pennsylvania were given leeway to concur if others did. Maryland and New York held out. Finally on 25 June the Maryland delegates received instructions to concur. The resolution for independence passed 2 July with New York abstaining. On 4 July, the formal document was signed. In military circles, the Declaration was almost a non-event, because the significant military decisions had already been taken.

Part XI - THE BRITISH FLEET THREATENS THE BAY

At the same time the province was wrestling with the problems of fielding units for Washington's army, military operations at home required attention. The British fleet off Gwinn's Island began a series of raids. In June 1776, Colonel Travers of the Dorchester militia reported that five British tenders were in Hooper's Straits and had raided Hopkin's Island. They took some sixty head of cattle and everything else of value on the island, and had departed a few hours before militia of Hooper's Corps arrived. After seven days the militia were "much fatigued and anxious to go home" so all but forty were discharged.

These ships also pillaged in Somerset county where the militia was called out to limit damage. Colonel Ennalls of Dorchester wrote of that incident:

> "In the evening...there appeared in Nanticoke Sound, one large ship and seven other Vessels supposed to be tenders. This gave the Inhabitants great uneasiness and anxiety, they therefore ordered such part of the Militia as cou'd readily be collected to assemble to prevent the Enemy from committing further damage. I am further informed by them that they found many of the people in that part of the county very lukewarm in the opposition, difficult to be got together, and when collected in such bad discipline they are not to be relied on, paying but little regard to the instructions of their officers...I thought it advisable to order part of the militia under my command to march down to their assistance,& I flatter myself we shall be able to prevent their landing in that quarter, but should the enemy continue there a few days and keep the militia on duty numbers of the inhabitants must unavoidably lose a considerable part of their crops, their wheat being now ready to cut."

The Maryland authorities feared that those lower Bay incidents signalled raids farther north in the Bay and possibly an invasion. They were in the process of training and equipping Smallwood's battalion and the independent companies of the state troops that had been pledged to the Continental army. At the same time they were commencing recruitment, training and equipment for the

THE MARYLAND MILITIA IN THE REVOLUTIONARY WAR

Flying Camp. Further the buildup of those units disrupted the militia organization and preempted their very scarce arms and equipment.

To release General Smallwood's battalion the Baltimore Town militia was ordered on 7 July to place three militia companies on duty in Baltimore; the Ann Arundel Elk Ridge battalion to place two companies in Annapolis; and, the West River and Severn battalions to send three companies to Annapolis.

Then before the militia moves were completed, Colonel Wilkinson of the Calvert militia reported 12 July that about forty square-rigged ships had moved as far north as Point Lookout. He said the St. Mary's militia had been called out, and that he had a Calvert company in readiness. Colonel Barnes of St. Mary's said he had two to three hundred men of the 21st battalion stationed at Point Lookout and at different points along the Potomac. He had also asked the other St. Mary's battalion to send one to two hundred men. Calvert county put six companies on duty. Two state companies that had started north were turned back, and Capt. Beall's state company at Drum Point was split by sending half to aid Colonel Barnes on the Potomac side of the county. A few days later, five Prince George's companies went on duty along the upper Potomac River.

While the Marylanders were mobilizing along the river and bay shores, the Virginia militia drove the British off of Gwinn's Island on 13 July. The British took to their ships and went up the Potomac to the vicinity of St. George's Island which they used as a source of fresh water. On 17 July they landed some 300 men apparently with the intention of setting up a base such as the one they had lost on Gwinn's Island. For several hours on that day Barnes' militia and the British exchanged gunfire. The British withdrew to their ships, but stayed in the vicinity, although several ships went up the Potomac as far as Quantico. By this time the shore defenders had received four cannon from Annapolis that enabled them to harass the war ships. Fire from the ships had practically no effect on the dispersed and entrenched militia. Finally the militia and state troops landed about 100 men on the Island and surprised a British landing party, most of which got away in their boats. The militia filled in the fresh water well that was the main attraction for the British, and by the end of July the British stood down the Bay.

General Hooper in Cambridge had been alerted to the possibility of enemy landings on his side of the Bay, and he stationed militia at various points:

      125 men under Col. Richardson at Cambridge
       90 men under Col. Feddeman and 30 of Colonel Ennalls at Cooke's Point
      130 men under Col. Murray and 30 of the Corps at Hooper Straits
      270 men of the Somerset battalions at various points
       15 men each on four of the off-shore islands
       15 men at Meekin's Neck
       45 men on the Hungar River.

As time passed, partially organized Flying Camp companies moved in to relieve the state troops and militia. All of the militia seemed to have been sent home by 7 August thus ending the incident. The Flying Camp companies were sent north to the Washington's army when each became fully armed and trained.

Once again it was shown that a spirited militia could defend against such landing parties as the British forces were able to make. In fact, the British were having a hard time greatly aggravated by the need to feed and support negroes and the civilian loyalists that accompanied them, many of whom were

THE BRITISH FLEET THREATENS THE BAY

seriously ill. It was estimated that 500 died on Gwinn's Island from smallpox and fever; and each day bodies were washed ashore from the ships when they were off St. George's Island. The defenders on shore did not have quite so difficult a time, but they liked neither the duty nor the area. Major Price, a state officer who was sent down from Annapolis to supervise the operations, wrote:

> "This is a Shocking Country everything scarce Water we are Oblidged to hall three miles no liquor but bad Whiskey to drink every Body is fatigued and Tired of the Place if the Enemy Continue here must Certainly have Fresh troops..."

Part XII - MILITIA WITH WASHINGTON'S ARMY

The next major problem for the Maryland militia came in December 1776 as the result of a crisis in the Continental army. The Flying Camp, which comprised a significant portion of the army, had been enlisted only to 1 December. Congress had foreseen the problem and in September decided on an army of eighty-eight battalions, of which Maryland was to provide eight battalions. Credit was given for the two battalions, the state troops, that Maryland had already provided, but they had suffered losses and were to be brought to full strength. Unsuccessful attempts were made to re-enlist men of the Flying Camp, but the Army had been hard pressed in the battles around New York and in New Jersey, and the men were tired of military life. The Marylanders also had a great dislike for their leader, Brigadier General Rezin Beall. In the case of one Maryland Flying Camp company only seven names of the sixty-eight privates are found in later Continental units, and it is questionable that all seven were the same persons of the Flying Camp company.

The general disillusionment of the winter of 1776 was not confined to the soldiers, but extended to the officers. Brigadier General Chamberlaine, the district commander of the upper eastern shore units, submitted his resignation 26 December 1776 saying:

> "...finding myself disappointed that many of us rather disposed to quarrell with his neighbor than face the Enemy, that a general discontent prevails and unwillingness in the people to do any duty or even attend musters, and a disregard to any sort of order, several Battalions without field officers and others absolutely refusing to obey the commands of those appointed over them, has determined me to resign..."

In mid-December the British were advancing towards Philadelphia with General Washington retreating before them. To reinforce the Continental army Congress called for militia, first from New Jersey and Pennsylvania, and then on 14 December from Baltimore, Cecil, Harford, and Frederick counties of Maryland. Brigadier General Thomas Johnson of Frederick was named commander of the Maryland contingent, and he went to Philadelphia to arrange for arms and equipment that were not available in Maryland. The units were sent to Philadelphia to complete their outfitting. Then they were to join the army in New Jersey. Just after Christmas some 300 men started from Frederick in deep snow, with others scheduled a few days later. In the meanwhile before the Maryland militia units joined him, General Washington was able to stop the British with the victory at Trenton and the battle at Princton. General Howe decided to go

THE MARYLAND MILITIA IN THE REVOLUTIONARY WAR

into winter quarters in New York and Washington in central New Jersey.

In January the militia was called out from Ann Arundel, Prince George's, Kent, Queen Anne's, Frederick, Baltimore, Harford and Cecil counties but the response as before was desultory. In February, General Johnson reported from Philddelphia that numerous men, including entire companies, had gone home from there without approval. He said that 1000 fully equipped men had been sent to New Jersey to join the army. Solomon Wright, Chairman of the Queen Anne's Committee on Observation wrote:

> "We lament the backwardness which has generally appeared on this occasion. The raging of the Small Pox to the northward which has been brought here by the Soldiers of the Flying Camp, and is now spreading fast in this county we have good reason to think has discouraged many, who would otherwise have offerred themselves for this service...The backwardness of men of property was assigned by many as the reason for their declining the present service, who declared that if such men would set an example they would most cheerfully follow it."

The Cecil Committee wrote:

> "The Committee will do every thing in their power to expedite the marching of the militia of this county to reinforce General Washington, but are of opinion that a sum of money must be sent us for the Support of the militia on the road and to advance some poor men who may want necessarys before they can possibly march. We think it necessary to acquaint you that there are very few guns in this county, and we believe not above 40 well fitted. A limited time we think ought to be fixed for the Militia to remain with General Washington, without which we are fearful the men will be backward..."

Very little is known about this period of deployment of the militia. It appears that little action took place as the main armies were in winter quarters. General Johnson reported:

> "We have nothing very material from Camp. I am afraid we can expect no great things from New York. The enemy are pretty close in the Jerseys. The war is carried on pretty much by small scouting parties on our side, and they often take some prisoners, 16 British were brought here on Sunday, taken within about a mile of Brunswick, as they were going out without arms to plunder."

We have neither the names of the Maryland militia men nor of their units in this mobilization except for the 33rd Battalion from Frederick county that was in camp at Basking Ridge, New Jersey.

The squeeze on available manpower became apparent during this period. Recruiting became competitive. The state was trying to get men for the eight battalions in the Continental Army at the same time they were trying to send militia to it. Other recruiters were active in the state for units of other states and for the 16 battalions being recruited across the colonies for the Continentals. One county said that of the 2100 men on its 31 December militia return, probably less than 1500 were available because of those who left for land and sea service. They also recommended that two thirds of the remaining force be left at home for use in the event of Tory troubles or British raids in the Bay.

Part XIII - GENERAL SMALLWOOD AND THE DISAFFECTED

There were two other major undertakings by militia forces in 1777. One was another chapter in the almost continuous effort to keep the lower counties of the Eastern Shore under control, and the other came with the invasion of Maryland by the main British army. The root problem with the Eastern Shore counties of Worcester and Somerset in Maryland and Sussex in Delaware was that a large number of the inhabitants were not in sympathy with the Revolution. The attitude also existed but to a lesser degree in the adjacent counties. The lower shore area, although seemingly isolated from the principal centers of the colonies, posed several threats. It was a good source of men and supplies for the British forces. The British ships in the Chesapeake were regularly supplied from there, and many persons left there to join the Loyalist military units. Beyond that was the fear that British forces might land there and establish a major base. Neither Virginia nor Maryland believed they had the capability to dislodge a major British operation by action from the Western Shore.

General Smallwood described the situation in March 1777:

"I am daily discovering persons who are not only more disaffected but whose conduct has been more criminal & from their influence have injured the common cause much beyond what has been in the power of any excepted persons: yet I've the strongest assurances that without altering their principles will avail themselves of the benefit of the proclamation, & will view it in no other light than as a compulsory act whilst others more conscientious cannot renouce their beloved King, and therefore several have already refused to take the oath of Allegiance to this state. What have you to expect from those who have cut down Liberty poles, and in direct opposition thereto, have erected the King's standard, & in an avowed manner drank his health and success & destruction to Congress and Conventions, of those who have advised and actually signed General Howe's Proclamation, of militia officers who have embodied with & headed the insurgents, of persons under bonds, surety to the State & forfeited the penalty by commission of most of the within mentioned crimes. Of such who have supplied the King's ships with provision, and kept up a constant intercourse with them, of those who knowingly aided and conveyed public prisoners on board, of those enrolling in the King's service,...of those advising the soldiers of this state and the Continent to desert, & not only harboring them, but supplying them with arms to defend themselves against being taken..."

In February 1777, the Continental Congress, having received a number of petitions from residents of the lower counties, directed Maryland to surpress the Tories with militia and also promised regular Continental troops if needed. Congress forwarded a list of fourteen persons to be arrested as ring-leaders of the insurgents. The efforts were spurred by word that some 250 armed insurgents supported by three field guns from the British man-of-war, the ROEBUCK were to invade the lower Eastern Shore. The Maryland legislature issued a Proclamation for use in the area which gave amnesty to anyone who came in with their arms and took the oath of fidelity within forty days. The fourteen wanted persons were the "excepted" ones referred to by General Smallwood in the above quotation.

In addition to the local militia, Colonel William Buchanan's battalion of

THE MARYLAND MILITIA IN THE REVOLUTIONARY WAR

Baltimore militia that was ready to go to New Jersey was diverted; General Smallwood's Continental battalion, two Independent companies, and a detachment of state troops of the Artillery company in Annapolis were sent. General Smallwood was named the commander of the group. In a short time Smallwood had captured 12 of the 14 wanted persons. He also reported picking up a number of deserters "skulking among these people." But he had little success in getting persons to follow the Proclamation. In his reports he seemed to realize that occupying military forces have definite limitations in trying to control an unfriendly population. Early in April Smallwood and the Continentals had to return to the Continental Army, and the local militia was left to contend with the dissidents.

However, the Maryland authorities were able to convince Congress that one of the eight Maryland Continental regiments should be stationed at Salisbury. Congress gave Maryland the choice of the weakest regiment, and Maryland took Colonel Richardson's. This might be considered a dubious honor for Richardson, but the Council told him "We are not sorry that it happened so, as there are many reasons to make it desirable that you should command the Force designed to cover the Eastern Shore." The plan was to fill out his regiment with five companies to be enlisted with service to 10 December. In support of Colonel Richardson the state established a Commission for the trial of treason on the Eastern Shore, i.e. a special court to handle the dissidents. As might have been expected, Colonel Richardson had difficulty in getting volunteers, so he was not in Salisbury until after 7 July. Because Colonel Richardson's battalion was a Continental unit not a Maryland miltia unit, the names of its members are listed in the Archives of Maryland Volume 18 and not included in the Appendices to this work.

Part XIV - THE MILITIA ACT OF 1777

During these military operations, the Maryland Assembly made some important changes in the militia by the Militia Act of 1777:

- A new senior military official, the "County Lieutenant" was named in each county to supervise its military affairs. This arrangement, effective 1 July 1777, replaced the previous military districts. The officers appointed to the new positions were:

St. Mary's	Richard Barnes	(3)
Kent	William Bordley	(4)
Anne Arundel	James Brice	(7)
Calvert	Benjamin Mackall 4th	
Charles	Francis Ware	(11)
Somerset	George Dashiell	(1)
Dorchester	Henry Hooper	(10)
Baltimore	Andrew Buchanan	(9)
Cecil	Charles Rumsey	
Prince George's	Luke Marbury	
Talbot	Christopher Birkhead	(2)
Queen Anne's	William Hemsley	(4)
Worcester	Joseph Dashiell	(5)
Frederick	Charles Beatty	
Harford	Aquilla Hall	

THE MILITIA ACT OF 1777

Caroline	William Whitely	(6)
Washington	Daniel Hughes	
Montgomery	Charles Greenbury Griffith	

(Note: The numbers in parentheses show the relative rank assigned by the State Council on 14 April 1780 after drawing lots from a ballot box. The other officers were appointed later.)

- The County Lieutenants were to divide their counties into battalions and assign companies to them;

- The men in each company were to be divided into eight equal classes, and the company officers of the battalion were assigned to the classes, all to be done by 1 September. In the event of need the militia was to be called out in classes made up as follows:

1st Class of all companies, under the Captain of the 1st Company, the 1st Lieutenant of the 2nd Company, the 2nd Lieutenant of the 3rd Company, and the Ensign of the 4th Company. A class thus consisted of officers and men equal to one full company.

2nd Class of all companies, under the Captain of the 2nd Company, the 1st Lieutenant of the 3rd Company, the 2nd Lieutenant of the 4th Company, and the Ensign of the 5th Company; and so on through the battalion.

This arrangement of classes for duty should not be confused with a later scheme of assigning classes to the taxpayers of a county for drafting soldiers.

- After arranging the classes, muster lists were to be submitted; and the Governor was to appoint commissioned officers as recommended by the Assembly;

- In the event of emergency, half battalions and half companies could be ordered out;

- After two consecutive months of service by a class, it was to be released, and the next class put on active duty;

- No more than one fifth of the militia was to be sent out of the state on duty;

- Substitutes were acceptable both for officers and men, but no bounties were supposed to be paid for the substitutes.

The debate on the Act was not recorded so the reasoning for its various provisions can only be speculated. Certainly it was intended to reconstitute the militia and to make service more palatable. Unfortunately the task of dividing the units into classes, sending in the rosters, and getting commissions squared away took time; time that delayed the units in responding to their next call. Much of the information contained in Appendix B was taken from the original returns that were submitted to comply with this Act.

THE MARYLAND MILITIA IN THE REVOLUIONARY WAR

Part XV - THE INVASION OF MARYLAND

The British having been thwarted in their attempt to get to Philadelphia in the last days of 1776 spent the winter in the vicinity of New York City. There they were watched closely by the Continental Army whose winter headquarters were at Middlebrook, New Jersey. In the spring the question was what the British would do in the summer campaign. In April General Washington warned that the British forces were becoming active, but aside from a few scouting forays, they seemed to concentrate on preparations to leave by ship. Finally they embarked at the end of July, sailing southwards. After a period of conjecture as to whether they were going to South Carolina, up the Delaware River to Philadelphia, or into the Chesapeake, on 21 August the fleet passed Annapolis. Thus began what was probably the largest militia operation of the war for Maryland in the period that was described by the Council as "Every Day is big with great events."

The fleet anchored off Baltimore scaring that town; but, then moved north to the head of the Bay. There the troops commenced landings on 25 August. It was now clear that General Howe's objective was to occupy Philadelphia. At Baltimore the militia was called out and manned the defenses while the fleet was there. About the same time the Governor ordered two companies (i.e. the first two classes) of all battalions to converge on the head of the Bay. McSherry says that "...few could be prevailed upon to march to the head of Elk and leave their families unprotected against a sudden inroad of the enemy or his tory dissidents..." but there were other reasons too, the militia was not yet fully reorganized under the late Militia Act. In some battalions the classing had not been done, and commissions were lacking for many company officers. Worst yet the men often showed up without guns. Colonel Rumsey said later that only 40 men with 5 guns showed up for his first company. The shortage of arms was so serious that the companies from Charles, Calvert, St. Mary's, Washington and Frederick were told not to march, but to go on alert at home and to try to get weapons from the population.

As soon as the British left New York, General Washington commenced moving the Continental Army westward to cover Philadelphia. After some confusion as to who would command the Maryland militia, General Washington detached the two senior officers of the Maryland Continentals, General Smallwood and Colonel Gist, to command the Western Shore and the Eastern Shore militia respectively. Colonel Richardson's Continental battalion on duty on the lower Eastern Shore was ordered north to be part of Col. Gist's group. Delays in assembling the militia probably served to permit the British to land and to march northward without opposition. Local militia did have some effect in preventing British parties from pillaging, and did provide intelligence about the British forces.

When the Eastern and Western Shore militia joined together north of Elkton, General Smallwood was given the task of harassing the British rear and preventing foraging. The militia units were not involved in the early battles along the Brandywine where the relatively poor showing of the Maryland Continentals has been attributed by some as due in part to the absence of General Smallwood and Colonel Gist, their regular commanders. Generals Smallwood and Wayne were supposed to join and attack the British flank near Paoli, but the British made surprise attacks and routed their units separately. At Germantown Smallwood and the New Jersey militia units were supposed to make a deep flanking movement around the British, but they were held up on the way and did not

THE INVASION OF MARYLAND

join the main battle. Howe moved into and occupied Philadelphia on 25 September. A number of officers and men of the Maryland militia were wounded in these actions. Major James Cox of the Baltimore was killed at Germantown.

Early in December Howe sent a large group out of Philadelphia towards Washington's main location. Gist with the Maryland militia and Morgan with his riflemen were assigned to blunt the move. A skirmish developed in which the British advance parties were driven back, but on counter-attack the British drove the Marylanders off. Both the Maryland militia and the riflemen had men wounded in this action. The British did not choose to attack the strong defensive position of Washington's main force and withdrew to Philadelphia where they stayed for the Winter. General Washington kept most of the Army at Valley Forge. General Smallwood and the Maryland Continentals were stationed at Wilmington, Delaware to cover the southern flank. Those Maryland militia that remained on duty were sent home.

Under the circumstances it is difficult to estimate the number of militia soldiers actually on duty during the invasion. McSherry, without attribution as to source, states that General Smallwood had 1150 Western Shore militia and 700 Eastern Shore militia when they first combined. He also says 400 militia remained in early November after the last of the 1st class was discharged. The following is known:

Aug.22	All Western Shore counties ordered to send 2 classes to Head of Elk; Charles, Calvert, St. Mary's, Washington and Frederick counties excepted.
Aug.22	Baltimore: battalion called (fleet off harbor)
Aug.23	Harford: 2 Companies called
	Harford: 8th Battalion called
Aug.27	Cecil: 100 men have arms; 300 more available without arms
	Harford: Raid on Joppa repelled by 8th battalion units
Aug.30	Cecil: "will be out tomorrow"
	Queen Anne's: "out next week"
Sept.6	Kent: 5 companies ready
	Queen Anne's: 3 companies ready
	Talbot: "next week"
	Dorchester: "next week"
Oct.2	Washington: 1st two classes called
Oct.10	Harford: 1st and 2nd classes called
	Frederick: 3rd class called
	Washington: 3rd class called
Oct.22	Cecil: 4 classes called
Oct.23	Queen Anne's, Charles, Calvert, St.Mary's, Dorchester: total of 10 companies called to relieve units on duty for 2 months per Militia Act.

The performance of the militia in the invasion left much to be desired. It was slow to respond when not pre-alerted. It was almost unarmed when it did respond. In engagement with the enemy regulars it performed poorly, often as not being driven off in disorder. There was confusion because the Militia Act had not been promptly carried out in setting up the classes and in issuing commissions. The Governor and Council hastily issued many commissions during this period in an effort to rectify the situation.

With respect to performance, General Smallwood was particularly frank in one of his reports, saying that Colonel Murdoch's battalion was the best, but:

THE MARYLAND MILITIA IN THE REVOLUTIONARY WAR

"I coud have wished that they never stept forth the men from Elk Ridge and some other parts of Ann Arundel will shine more at an Election than in the field their disorder & licentiousness....will even render them contemptable in the field."

Colonel Gist complained of the behavior of Colonel William Hopper of the Caroline militia who he said that in the approach to Germantown:

"On the morning of the 4th the Enemy Pickets began a Scattering fire in front of our Column when the Colonel was immediately attacked with some qualms of sickness that oblig'd him to leave his Regiment and retreat to Maryland...I am credibly informed that he reported on his way down & in his neighborhood at home, that the Maryland Militia was posted in front and was entirely cut off; this with other absurditys propogated by him to the prejudice of the Army has had its tendency to prevent the second Class of Militia from turning out so generally as they otherwise would have done."

Part XVI - FALSE INVASION THREATS (1778 - 1783)

During the remainder of the war, the Maryland militia continued with a repetition of the same kinds of incidents and actions that characterized the first years of the war. There were responding to threats of major invasions; defending against raids from the Bay; maintaining internal order; guarding prisoners of war; and watching the Western frontiers.

Three times perceived threats of invasion from the Bay triggered major mobilizations of the militia although no invasions were actually realized. In fact, information developed after the war showed that the British had not planned an invasion in any of them. The first incident began in mid-May 1779 when a group of large vessels accompanied by several smaller ones was sighted coming up the Bay. A few small warships signified a raid; but large warships were interpreted as threats to Annapolis and Baltimore. The threat was greater when the larger vessels were accompanied by vessels that might be carrying troops for a landing. There was also uncertainty as to the intended point of attack.

Initially, on 16 May 1779, the Ann Arundel, Baltimore, and Harford militia units were alerted; and the next day half of the Severn and half of the South River battalions of Ann Arundel were ordered to Annapolis. The independent companies of Annapolis were also called to assemble. On the second day, battalions were alerted on the Eastern Shore and in St. Mary's, Charles and Calvert counties. The Council delayed calling units to duty because in their words:

"Experience shews us that Men who are drawn from their Occupations, soon grow tired disgusted and uneasy and of Course, are not so alert as when just called together."

Then, still fearing invasion, and noting the response of the militia, Maryland called on the Continental Army for help. On 25 May Col. Gist was sent on loan from the Continental army. By 1 June, three large and two smaller ships had progressed to the mouth of the Patuxent; but, on the same date a report was received that all British ships had left the Bay. Gist on learning that the

FALSE INVASION THREATS (1778 - 1783)

Baltimore militia was actually assembling suggested that only one class go on duty, but that signals should be arranged to summon the remainder if needed. Finally on 3 June the ships were identified as French merchant vessels, and all the militia was discharged.

In October 1780 Maryland made the last major changes of the war to its militia. A Select Militia was organized to have a higher alert status and better training than the militia at large. It was planned to have 20,000 men by 10 December and to train in exercises twice a week until mid-April. The men were supposed to respond fully equipped on a few hours notice. Judging from the surviving records it appears doubtful that the objectives of the Select Militia were realized. The same law also provided for horse troops of about twenty five men each to be organized on a voluntary basis in all of the counties. These mounted units were well suited for patrol work along the bay and the rivers, and for control of dissidents. These changes came when the Southern army under General Gates was being hard pressed by General Cornwallis in the Carolinas and the British had moved about 3000 men under General Leslie from New York to the Norfolk area. Names of persons in the Select Militia and in in the horse troops are included in the Appendices.

In the spring of 1781 British land forces were operating in eastern Virginia. Benedict Arnold, now a British General, had arrived at Hampton Roads in January from New York with about 1600 men. After a raid in which he destroyed public property, and tobacco warehouses of Richmond he settled into winter quarters in Portsmouth. He became active again in April raiding extensively in the Tidewater of Virginia. Meanwhile Lord Cornwallis, having been in Carolinas, moved north. He arrived at Petersburg, Virginia in May, and had about 7000 men including reinforcements from New York. The British had a strategic objective of establishing a naval base in the Norfolk area; and, then starting major land operations in the area to destroy the war-making potential of the region. They also hoped to release a large number of British prisoners around Winchester. In General Arnold's words:

> "If joined by Cornwallis or the reinforcements said to be coming from New York, we shall be in force to operate as we please in Virginia and Maryland."

Meanwhile in February, Marquis de LaFayette was sent south from Washington's army around New York to contain the situation. His force augmented by Virginia militia was not sufficient to oppose the combined British forces. In early June British raiders had ranged as far as Charlottesville burning and plundering at will.

Maryland was justifiably alarmed. On 4 June 1781 the Council stated:

> "We think a large body of troops drawn to a point in this state might in all probability prevent the enemy from invading it and would be very important and acceptable succour to the Marquis De La Fayette, if the enemy should be so successful in Virginia as to encourage them to penetrate our state..."

THE MARYLAND MILITIA IN THE REVOLUTIONARY WAR

They ordered to Georgetown on the Potomac militia as follows:

Frederick	500 men
Prince George's	200 men
Montgomery	250 men
Baltimore, Kent, Frederick	Horse troops

The men were to come from the Select militia and from the militia at large. Two days later the call was cancelled for about half of the troops. But then on 8 June, Colonel Ware of Charles County reported British ships coming up the Bay and that he had ordered the Charles county militia out. The Council reinstated the prior militia orders and added to them such that:

Frederick to send	500 men to Georgetown
Montgomery to send	400 men to Georgetown
Prince George's to send	400 men to Georgetown if needed
Washington to send	400 men to invasion place if needed
Prince George's to send	400 men to invasion place if needed
St. Mary's to take care of any landings there	
St. Mary's to remove tobacco inland from warehouses	
Charles	400 men for Colonel Ware
Queen Anne's to alert all battalions	

On 14 June it was decided that the threat of Cornwallis was not so immediate as to warrant the mobilization, so all the militia was discharged. Actually the report from Colonel Ware was true, a British warship was raiding in the lower Potomac, but no large scale invasion was imminent.

Cornwallis and his main force had remained in the Tidewater without a clear indication of his intentions. La Fayette continued to shadow Cornwallis from a distance but was too weak to attack. He wanted assistance from Maryland, but Maryland was reluctant to commit its militia so far away at the same time Maryland itself was threatened. In late June they did order three horse troops of the militia to join LaFayette. These consisted of about 70 men under the command of Capt. Moore of Baltimore. The horse units returned to Maryland before Yorktown so it appears that no Maryland militia took part in that battle.

The last invasion scare for Maryland occurred in August 1781. In late July, while at Malvern Hill, La Fayette learned that a British contingent had been loaded on ships at Portsmouth and were at anchor in Hampton Roads. On 1 August he sent Governor Lee of Maryland copies of notes both received the preceding day from Commodore Barron, the senior U.S. Navy officer in the Norfolk area:

"The Fleet weighed this morning from Cape Henry and stood up the Bay; tis certain they are bound to Baltimore (40 sail in number with several barges full of troops), remains in the Road 2 men-of-war, 8 sail, other Vessels. By a man from Portsmouth last night am informed Cornwallis is still at Portsmouth with part of his Troops. I think the above fleet must contain near 3000 men and 200 Horse." and,

"The Fleet...stood up the Bay about 15 miles the wind and tide being ahead they anchored off Cherrystones They are certainly bound to Baltimore."

FALSE INVASION THREATS (1778 - 1783)

The next morning a patrol boat was sent down to the mouth of the Patuxent River to cruise back and forth and give warning of the fleet's approach. Steps were taken to gather such regular troops and recruits of the Continental Army as were in Maryland. These were to go to Annapolis and Baltimore.

On 4 August the Council gave orders for various actions:

St. Mary's and Calvert militia were to station lookouts to give warning of the fleet's approach.
Baltimore Town and county militia were to prepare to defend the town, and move all public stores inland; inhabitants were to move their goods and valuable property inland.
Harford militia was alerted to be ready to go to Baltimore.
Prince George's, Montgomery, Charles, Frederick and Washington counties select militia and horse troops were called.
Wagons were to be sent to Annapolis to remove public papers and supplies into the country.
Field pieces and arms were requested from the Continental stores.

By 8 August no British had appeared, and the Council said that late information gave them reason to believe that no invasion of Maryland was intended at that time. Some of the militia was released. Then on 10 August a letter of 6 August was received from La Fayette. In it he reported that the British were then fortifying Yorktown. Apparently the troops initially reported as an invasion threat were just being moved by water in the Yorktown-Hampton area. All the Maryland militia was discharged.

Part XVII - RAIDS

During most of the war the British had warships in the Bay. They were usually frigates of 16 guns and were generally accompanied by smaller armed ships. The naval vessels were intended primarily to interrupt shipping from the Bay to outside destinations. The British hoped to restrict the tobacco and other exports thereby reducing the income of the colonies; and to halt the importation of critical arms and other supplies from the West Indies and Europe, particularly France. The accompanying ships were frequently British privateers who worked both off-shore and in the Bay, sometimes on their own and sometimes with the naval vessels.

The activities of the naval vessels in the Bay also included raids of shore installations that brought them into conflict with the militia. In addition to destroying tobacco these raids took away food supplies such as grain, flour, livestock that were intended for the Continental troops. The captured supplies were useful for British troops, and the naval vessels themselves subsisted on foraging and needed local water and wood. In areas having numerous persons not in sympathy with the revolution such as Somerset and Worcester there was active trading between the vessels and inhabitants. There the British frequently bartered salt for farm products. The vessels also provided the means for Loyalists and slaves to join the British forces or to get to more friendly places like New York. These contacts gave the British excellant intelligence on local conditions and local sympathizers.

Probably the largest raid of the 1778-1783 period was that on Vienna on

THE MARYLAND MILITIA IN THE REVOLUTIONARY WAR

the Nanticoke River in March 1781, about which good reports survive. General Henry Hooper, the County Lieutenant for Dorchester, in his letter to Governor Lee states:

> "A brig and two sloops of the enemy came up to Vienna and began a heavy fire on the town. we had previously collected a party of militia and posted them on the bank to oppose the enemies landing who kept up a brisk fire on one of the enemies barges which was rowing a shore full of men til they were drove from their stations by the hot fires from the shiping & on their retreat the enemy landed, our party killed one and wounded three of the enemy we had one man wounded who is since dead of his wound. When the enemy drew up on shore, they sent in a flagg to inform us that they wanted nothing more than the grain in town and if we would give that up they would leave a part for the inhabitants and would not plunder anything more & would pay the market price for the grain, but if we should not agree to that and still continure hostilities they would burn down the town and destroy every thing in it. As we could defend nothing, the town and grain lying under the command of their vessels we agreed to the terms they offerred except that of receiving a price for the grain..."

His neighbor, Colonel Joseph Dashiell, County Lieutenant for Worcester county, had a different view. He wrote Governor Lee that:

> "We have bin much Infested here this Ten days last past with the Enemys crusars, and I am happy to inform you, that we in this Quarter, made a very formidable & suckesfull resistance, but finding themselves unable to land any whare, but they could do it under Cover of their Cannon, run up to Vienna, on Saturday last whare a very few Militia Under Colonel John Dickinson & Capt. Smoot repulsed their barges in landing three times, abought which time, the Lieutenant of that County arived and ordered the Militia to retreat as I am told and has made a Capulation that in my Oppinion will Disgrace us, & Be attended with the worst of consequences but as I make no Doubt but you are fully advis'd of this matter by Mr. Hooper, I shall say no more upon the Subject."

Possibly the same British group was at Poole's Island in the mouth of the Susquehanna where on 15 March two ships and several small vessels landed some men without opposition. They took 14 head of cattle, all the hogs, corn, and all the overseer's bacon and spoons. They also captured two small schooners with about 100 barrels of flour each that was bound for the Continental Army. The group remained in the upper Bay area for several days and even went up the Susquehanna where they captured a small schooner with its 50 barrels of flour and about the same amount of beer. The Harford County Lieutenant called out two militia companies to oppose any landings, but no landing was attempted other than that on Poole's Island. This was about the same time that troops were being moved from the forces around New York to Virginia by way of the Bay. Colonel Dallam of Harford thought the British vessels may have intended to interdict the troop movements; but, fortunately no troops were being moved while the British ships were there.

Another raid with a different result happened in Prince George's county on the Potomac River in April 1781. Colonel Josias Beall reported, in part:

> "..On Thursday morning Captain William Dent Beall who undertook the command of the men who turned out...Marched with about 20 who formed themself into a body of Light horse to go forward to Assist in opposing

RAIDS

the Enemie in Case of their Landing, as the Enemie were then moved down to the mouth of Piscataway Thursday evening the enemie sent a flag on shore to Coll Lyles demanding a supply of fresh provisions, which being refused, they landed about 100 men under cover of their cannon & burnt all his buildings, in this attempt some of Capn Beall's party, got a fire at them on their landing & those prisoners say wounded five of them 1 or 2 mortily. The Enemie got underway on fryday morning but the wind blowing hard at the north west they all came to again, I ordered the remainder of Capn Beall's company to joyne him, who was stationed with some other militia under Coll Lyles as a guard to Mr.Bond's houses & property. Yesterday some of the enemys boats went a shore at Lyleses fishing landing killing some hogs that had got down about the landing, in the evening 2 of their boats again landed with the Sailing Master of the Hope & ten men in one, the purser & 6 men in the other, who had got on shore strolling about when Lieuts Osborn Williams and Henry Lyles with a party of young men pushed in & cut them off from their boat, & took the Sailing Master, boat and all his crew amounting to eleven in the whole & brought them off in the face of the enemy Notwithstanding the fire of their cannon, in short sir this was as brave an action as was ever performed by men as they were exposed to the fire of three of their vessels at a short distance from them..."

Without further contact, the British on Sunday morning left down the river, and the militia was discharged.

In April 1781 the Act for Defence of the Bay authorized a small group of full-time state troops. This consisted of an infantry company of thirty privates enlisted for one year; a horse troop of twenty four men on the lower Eastern Shore; and an artillery company of 65 privates enlisted for three years to be stationed at Drum Point where they were to build a fort with ten nine-pounders. These troops were, of course, not sufficient to stop the raids, but they were available to support the militia.

The above incidents were selected to illustrate the kind of harassing operations undertaken by the British navy which the militia faced. In many instances the target was the property of militia officers or other prominent revolutionaries. These incidents occurred all through the period and did not stop until the spring of 1783 when all hostilities ceased on 22 April.

Part XVIII - DISSIDENTS

More numerous than British raids were incidents involving the "dissidents" or "disaffected persons" as those not in sympathy with the revolutionary movement were called. A Delaware official has been quoted as saying that one-third of the persons were for the revolution, one-third were Loyalists, and one third were neutral and did not wish to be involved. Overall sentiment in Maryland was probably like that, but there was considerable variation across the state. General Smallwood's report, previously quoted, shows the strong Loyalist sentiments on the lower shore. In contrast the western shore was quite supportive of the revolution, particularly the commercial interests in Baltimore and Annapolis, and the German settlers in northern areas. Besides guarding against the British threat, the militia was the major element providing internal security in the state. In fact, except for the county sheriff who had few if any assistants, the militia performed many duties that would now be done by the police.

THE MARYLAND MILITIA IN THE REVOLUTIONARY WAR

Active opposition took many forms, but it did not escalate into open warfare in Maryland. The only incident that had such potential was the Clows affair. Parties of Tories led by Cheny Clows had been harassing inhabitants of the northern part of Queen Anne's and adjacent areas for some time in 1778. The County Lieutenants in Kent and Queen Anne's were given authority to call out up to 40 men each for one month to work in cooperation with the Delaware militia in apprehending the group. In addition 32 men with two field guns were sent from Annapolis to support the militia.

A militia party found about 100 Tories in a fort that had been built in a swampy, wooded area of Delaware near the Maryland boundary. There the militia party was driven off in a fire fight in which a Tory was killed and a militiaman wounded. The Tories had fled when the militia went back in greater force a few days later. The fort contained arms and goods that had been plundered; and, some 50 Tories were rounded up in the area. Clows himself was not captured until later and was eventually hanged in Delaware for treason.

Many men expressed their opposition by leaving the state to join the British. Numerous escaping slaves and indentured servants were among those who left. In fact, a Loyalist regiment under the command of John Chalmers of Kent county included many Eastern Shore men. The men who were leaving often went aboard British ships that were close to shore in the bay and its tributaries. Others went overland to areas held by the British.

The militia endeavored to cut off this flow as well as stopping the illicit trade with the enemy ships. In April 1778 it was reported that 90 recruits from Worcester and Somerset counties had joined the British fleet there. In May a group of Loyalist recruits from Sussex county is said to have crossed over to British ships at Annemessex on the bay in Maryland. Militia, sent to intercept this group, arrived too late. The militia was often handicapped by the unavailability of sufficent armed ships to pursue in the many waterways of the Eastern Shore. These Tories who left the area gave the British excellant intelligence about Maryland, and their presence in the Loyalists military units gave rise to rumors twice in 1778 that they were planning an invasion of the lower shore.

Frequently raids by British ships were assisted by dissidents in person or by intelligence from them. Thus the possessions of militia officers or revolutionary officials were often the targets of the raids. For example Colonel Lyles of Prince George's and Colonel Barnes of St. Mary's lost property in the Spring of 1781. The Lloyd's Wye House was plundered. At times when the British were close the Tory activity became bolder; and, it was particularly high in 1781 when Cornwallis was in Virginia.

One resident of Annemessix in Somerset county asked the Governor to discharge his recently drafted son to help the family because they had been plundered in the fall of 1780 by British barges and four times again in the spring of 1781. They took all his meat and provisions: his houses with his furniture and Indian corn were burned; and, he was beat and bruised severely.

There were also those who took advantage of conditions to rob and steal from their neighbors. From the records it is not always possible to separate common lawlessness from political opposition. Colonel George Dashiell of Somerset wrote the Governor in part:

"...it has become absolutely necessary to call out a number of our Militia to protect us from the ravages of the enemy. Sundry of the inhabitants

DISSIDENTS

of this county within a few days past have suffered much by parties either from British cruisers or the inhabitants of the larger islands (th' I believe the latter) as a number of them are well known by the persons that they have plundered."

Taxes and other levies to support the war effort created much unrest during this period. Even many of the staunch supporters of independence were weary of the war and hard-pressed financially. Beef cattle, horses, grain, and extra blankets were among those items taken for the troops in return for certificates that were, in effect, promissory notes that could be sold only at a discount because the state was unable to redeem them. The paper Continental currency lacked backing and was also only a promise of future payment. It, too, steadily declined in value, and persons would not accept it in payment. Tobacco, the traditional Maryland medium of exchange, was no longer useful as such because the war interrupted overseas sales.

An additional financial hardship resulted from initiation of the military draft. If a county could not come up with sufficient volunteers to meet its quota of recruits for the Continental army, the property owners were divided into classes for drafting. The classes were equal in number to the number of men needed. Each class was to contain the same amount of assessed property and about the same number of eligible men. Each class was then given five days to come up with a recruit either by persuasion or by financial inducement. If the class could not furnish a body each property holder in it was taxed five percent of the value of his property.

As early as 1778 the militia was used to assist the sheriff in collecting taxes, but the State Council at that time discouraged it. Colonel William Hemsley, the County Lieutenant of Queen Anne's county was told in February:

"We are very sorry that the Conduct of any Set of People should make Protection and Assistance necessary to the Civil Officers, in carrying laws into Execution, but where it is rendered necessary, it must be afforded and we request you give the necessary Aid, of the Militia under your Command, to enable the Sheriff to collect the substitute money. A like opposition was made in Baltimore, and also in St. Mary's but, in both Places, it was quieted by vigorous Measures...If you are apprehensive that the Opposition will be too general for you to go through with it, we would, on being so advised, send you a few Matrosses (i.e.artillerymen) and a Field Piece or two, tho' we much rather chuse not to employ a Regular Soldier in enforcing the Laws, if the Business can be done without them."

In August 1780 William Whiteley, the Caroline County Lieutenant wrote the Governor:

"...we have made a poor hand at Recruiting as we have got but three as yet. I have begun to collect the fifteen or five pounds on the Hundred, but there is many of our People Complains that they should be obliged to pay Money when they have Certificates for Money due them from the State, therefore I should be glad to know of you whether I must take Certificates in discharge of the aforesaid tax or not as there is not the least likelihood of getting the recruits and the Money will of Course go in the Treasury."

In early 1781 tax resistance became so serious in Somerset that the Assembly approved the use of outside militia. A company of one hundred men of the

THE MARYLAND MILITIA IN THE REVOLUTIONARY WAR

Dorchester militia were ordered to Pocomoke and Annemessix Hundreds on 3 February to assist in the collection of public taxes due there. However, word of the law got to Somerset before the militia because Colonel Joseph Dashiell of neighboring Worcester wrote on 2 February:

> "I most sincerely wish that the Law that past to Inforce payment of the Taxes in Somerset County had have bin extended to this County, as we already see the good effects of the Law, those people are runing to see who shall pay first, and I am in hopes, the Tax will be nearly paid in this month & Before the Militia from Dorchester gits down."

He also told of tax collection in Worcester county:

> "...there is sundry People in this County that seem determind to give all the opposition they Can, to the Collection of the Taxes, a Certain Benj. Shockley an old offender, Tryed all in his power to kill the Sheriff, the other Day in the Execution of his office, the Sheriff resigned his Commission, I realy beleave for fear of Losing his Life..."

The discontent was not limited to the Eastern Shore because in April 1781 Colonel Samuel S. Smith of Baltimore wrote the Governor:

> "There are a great number of dissaffected & others who refuse to bear arms, Indeed to whom it would be dangerous to trust arms & whose situation Capable & willing to do every injury gives great Discontent to those worthy's who turn out on all & every occasion, they demand that such persons (where there is a real danger) be order'd at least 30 miles from the Town, this is the general opinion & I imagine if your Excellency cannot take such step, that it will be done in an illegal manner."

The dissident incidents usually involved few persons, such as the destruction of Isaac Perkins' flour mills by arson in June 1780. Most of the County Lieutenants on occasion received alerts from the State to apprehend individuals known to be active in opposition. Many persons were arrested by militia detachments and brought to trial. For the most part justice was tempered and punishment mild. The guilty might be fined or banished from sensitive areas, but usually they were released under bond for future good behavior.

One person joining the British; a few bushels of produce sent out to a ship; a kidnapping or a plundering of a farm as isolated incidents would have been of little concern. But the number and frequency of such incidents was serious. They had a chilling effect on the population, and they reduced the support to the Revolutionary military forces. The hundreds who left to join the British reduced the manpower pool for the Revolutionary forces, and for the production of needed food and supplies. Those who stayed but shirked militia duty were not available to repel raids. Those who did not pay taxes eroded the financial base of the state. Militia members and supporters of the revolution were reluctant to leave their locale for fear of harm to their families and possessions during their absence. Thus the overall impact of the disaffected was serious, and the militia despite its inadequacies was the main bulwark against it.

Part XIX - GUARDING THE PRISONERS

The guarding of prisoners of war became a constant problem for Maryland after the surrender of General Burgoyne in October 1777. Overall the Continental Congress and its Board of War were responsible for the prisoners; however, they turned custody of the prisoners to the several states, particularly Maryland, Virginia, Pennsylvania and Connecticut. Often militia companies were called upon to assist in guarding at the prison sites and in transferring prisoners across the state.

Before 1778 the small numbers of prisoners in Maryland were kept in Frederick itself. In December 1777 the Assembly decided to repair Fort Frederick, west of Hagerstown, in anticipation of receiving some of the 3500 men surrendered at Saratoga. These were known as "Convention" prisoners from the name of the paper, or "Convention" that formalized the surrender. The prisoners held under the Convention were sometimes called "Conventioners" to distinguish them from the "unconditional" prisoners taken elsewhere. The state also decided to form a guard company of 60 men for both the prisoners and the newly constructed magazine at Frederick. Recognizing the difficulty of recruitment in the face of bounties being offered for enlistments in the Continental Army, a bounty of $5 was sought for enlistment in the guard company but the Governor had no authority to pay it. He suggested raising the bounty money by contribution and sent $40 to start the fund. The Frederick militia was instructed to assist in the guard duty as needed, and it was frequently called on to do so.

In February 1778 the Frederick County Lieutenant reported that the militia would not stay much longer and recommended that prisoners on good behavior be put to work on local farms. The Continental Congress disapproved the work proposal and decreed close confinement until the American prisoners in British hands were treated better. So the State Council called out 60 men from the Frederick and 50 from the Washington county militia for guard duty.

By April 1778 Fort Frederick was ready to receive prisoners. For the next year militia companies from Washington and Frederick counties were used periodically to supplement the guard company. In the Spring of 1779 the situation was relieved somewhat by the decision of the Continental Board of War to permit prisoners of good behavior to work for patriotic persons. This permitted release of the militia guards for the moment.

There was considerable confusion in the fall of 1779 over the transfer of 400 prisoners of war from Philadelphia. Initially Maryland was warned to expect them at Fort Frederick by 28 September and militia units from Washington, Frederick and Montgomery were ordered to duty for five weeks. A sucession of militia units were alerted in relief of the initial men, but the prisoners did not arrive until after February 1780.

Concern arose in the fall of 1780 when it was learned that Cornwallis and Arnold intended to secure the freedom of prisoners held in the Winchester area of Virginia. After a warning, Governor Jefferson of Virginia, in early November, wrote that 800 British prisoners were being marched towards Frederick. He said that about 1500 Germans would be sent later. Maryland reacted with the callup of two more Washington county militia companies in addition to the one Washington company and the Guard company already on duty at Fort Frederick. Apparently some of the Virginia militia stayed on to help because on 5 February

THE MARYLAND MILITIA IN THE REVOLUTIONARY WAR

1781 a Montgomery county militia company was alerted to relieve the Virginia Guard. The guard situation did not improve. The same month a resident of Frederick wrote Governor Lee:

> "The Guard to the prisoners at Frederick are by no means adequate to the purpose should the prisoners be vicously inclined; they are about 150 but such banditry you never see collected, they have been pilfering & robing for several miles around the Town, Steers, hogs, behives and geas - one of their Lieuts was broak the other day for being concerned in stealing the latter they carried away 22 from me in one night which is all I've suffered by them as yet - those stationed at the magazines have broak it open, what quantity of lead and powder has been carryed away is uncertain..."

The state then called up a militia company each from Ann Arundel, Prince George's, Baltimore and Frederick counties. It also planned to send an Artillery detachment from Annapolis and several companies of the Continental German battalion that were wintering in Maryland; but, before they could move, the Continental forces were ordered to join the Southern Army. The guard problem was back in the hands of the militia.

In March 1781 there were 810 British Convention prisoners at Frederick including a Brigadier General and 47 other officers. Thirty four had escaped and 28 had been exchanged since the prior return. The 1500 Germans mentioned by Governor Jefferson remained in Virginia. In May, Col. Rawlings, the Guard commander at Fort Frederick reported that 435 men, 145 women, 206 children and 70 sailors had been transferred from Frederick, and that Fort Frederick was "pretty full." The report of October 1781 showed 750 officers and 5953 others at Fort Frederick before receipt of any prisoners from Yorktown. The Guard commander had great difficulty in getting adequate food for the prisoners and the guards because of the unwillingness of the local providers to accept his depreciated Continental money. One problem of the militia is highlighted by the letter from the County Lieutenant to Governor Lee:

> "I have to inform you that I have applied to Colonel Thomas Price for Either Rum or whiskey for my select Company of Militia when in Actual Service and the Colonel says he has no orders to issue any and my men now on Guard over the State prisoners in Frederick Town Goal do murmer most of being clipt of their jill per day..."

The last major prisoner of war episode began with the surrender of Lord Cornwallis at Yorktown 17 October 1781 where over 7000 men were taken. The prisoners were to be divided among Virginia, Maryland and Pennsylvania, and the Maryland Council planned for 2000 of them. Arrangements were made for the Frederick militia to guard the prisoners until companies of 80 men each could arrive from Washington and Montgomery counties. One Frederick company was also to remain on duty in addition to the regular Guard company. It is not known how many prisoners were received from Yorktown nor their date of arrival. In mid-November Col. Rawlings reported he had 1500 at Frederick, and Col. Price reported that 300 head of beef had been received from Washington and Prince George's counties that would be sufficient for about five weeks.

The State continued to have problems with providing guards from the miltia to assist the Guard company, which itself could not be maintained at strength. In December units were called for two months duty to replace the Select Militia companies on duty at Frederick. Baltimore was to send 100 men, Montgomery and

GUARDING THE PRISONERS

Frederick 50 men each. Buchanan, the Baltimore County Lieutenant wrote that he had 100 men marching but had to promise them but one month's duty rather than the two that were prescribed. Then there was the problem of wood for heating. The new Commandant of Guards, Mountjoy Bayly, wrote:

> "I am sorry to inform your Honorable Counsel (sic) that it is with the greatest difficulty I can supply the Prisoners which are Quartered at this post with Wood I have done it heretofore by Fatigue parties from the Militia Guards - but that mode I find I can no longer pursue - the Guards refuse to Cut Wood - they say they are Soldiers And not Wood Cutters - the officers who Command the Militia in this County has not the least Idea of discipline or indeed even distinction."

He received the obvious reply:

> "As we cannot possibly furnish money for Wood Cutters,...we request that the Prisoners themselves may be made to cut their own wood; a Guard should be turned out with the Fatigue parties of the prisoners, to prevent their escaping."

By February 1782 when the Baltimore militia was due to be released, only 75 of the original 100 were still on duty; and the county was instructed to send in a relief unit. In three months Montgomery county had not sent one man to meet the December call, so the call was reiterated. By 5 April only 29 men were available to the guard commander, so 100 men were called to immediate duty from the Frederick militia. Negotiations with General Smallwood to use Continental troops failed.

In early summer 1782 the guard problem was solved for the militia when arrangements were made to use the Corps of Invalids, i.e. injured or disabled Continental troops awaiting recovery or discharge. In January 1783 the duties were taken over by regular Continental troops. Finally the Peace Treaty signed 3 September 1783 provided that "all prisoners on both sides shall be set at Liberty."

Part XX - THE FRONTIERS

The western frontiers of Maryland were quiet during the Revolution compared with the situation during the French-Indian war a quarter of a century earlier. This was probably due to conditions distant from Maryland rather than actions of Maryland. The British did not succeed in getting the support of Indians to the extent the French had previously done. Also the British did not control the invasion routes from Canada. Nevertheless there was constant apprehension among the isolated settlers of western Maryland.

Militia companies were organized in what was then the Upper District of Frederick county in 1775 and 1776 at the same period as in the other parts of the province. The Upper District became Washington county in 1776, and the militia west of Hagerstown became the 3rd, or Western, battalion of the new county.

Early in 1776, Lord Dunmore devised a plan that involved getting Indians and Tories to attack down the Potomac River valley from Cumberland to Alexandria

THE MARYLAND MILITIA IN THE REVOLUTIONARY WAR

in concert with his coming up the Potomac and taking Alexandria. He thought that Alexandria could be a base for dividing the northern and southern colonies. John Conolly, a Pennsylvania Tory who may have proposed the concept, together with two associates, one from Virginia and one from Maryland were sent up the river to mobilize the Tories and Indians. The plan was foiled when the conspirators were arrested near Hagerstown and sent to Philadelphia for trial. Conolly who was a Loyalist military officer was jailed, but released in an exchange for a captured American officer.

In 1778 there were Indian disturbances in the north, and General Washington initiated a three-pronged attack, one of which was an expedition from Fort Pitt northwards up the Allegany River. Meanwhile the 3rd battalion was furnished with additional arms and powder. It was authorized to act with the militia of Virginia and Pennsylvania, and to call on the other Washington county militia if needed. Scharf states that the Washington and Montgomery county militia under Colonel Beatty did assist the Continental units in defeating the Indians; but no record has been found that identifies those Maryland units.

In 1779, a militia company of the Western battalion was assigned to patrol duty on the frontier to encourage the inhabitants to remain there rather than fleeing to the east. The next year three Continental companies of Colonel Rawlings' Maryland Continental regiment were stationed at Fort Pitt to stabilize the Maryland-Virginia-Pennsylvania frontier area.

Then in 1781 when the British General Leslie was sent to Virginia a modified Dunmore-Conolly plan of 1776 appeared. This time, instead of trying to get Indians to move in from the frontier, the plan was to foment insurrection among Tories in Washington and Frederick counties. It is said that Colonel Conally himself was secretly organizing British Convention prisoners in Frederick to assist. Captain Orndorff, a Frederick militia officer, was solicited to join a group of the Tories. He found out enough about the plans to initiate the arrest of seven persons who were tried for treason in July. All were convicted, and three were hanged. The British took no further action to pursue the plan.

Part XXI - VETERANS' BENEFITS

For over one hundred years after 1776 laws were enacted giving benefits to Revolutionary war veterans and their spouses. These benefits may be grouped in several different categories:

- Payments to the wounded or disabled veterans and to the families of those killed in action.

- Benefits promised during the war as inducements for service.

- Payments to needy veterans

- Pensions for service.

From the early days of the province persons disabled in the service and unable to make a living for themselves and family were, in effect, public wards and as such given public support. This benefit was extended to the widows and

VETERANS' BENEFITS

minor children of those killed in action. Such a policy was approved by the Convention of Maryland 14 January 1776:

> "That if any officer or soldier of the regular forces, minute men or militia, in the service of this province, shall loose a limb, or be otherwise maimed or hurt, so as to be rendered incapable of earning a livelihood, this province will make provision for the comfortable support of such officer or soldier."

The Continental Congress in August 1776 provided half pay for disabled Continental veterans incapable of earning a living. Some years after the war in 1789 the federal government assumed responsibility for paying all the state commitments for disabled veterans. In 1806 Congress revised the laws pertaining to invalid veterans and extended the eligibility for pensions to all invalid state troops and the militia.

Inducements to enlist or to remain in the service were another kind of benefit. These benefits applied only to Continental service. They took the form of bounties paid at the time or promises of future payments or grants of land. For example in May 1778 Congress promised those officers who would remain in the Continental service to the end of the war half pay for seven years. Each enlisted man who did likewise was promised a one-time payment of eighty dollars. In 1780 this benefit was extended to cover payments to widows and orphans of officers. Later in 1780 half pay for life was granted to officers who agreed to stay for the duration of the war. Continentals also received other promises that caused controversy and political problems before they were settled. Among these were the option of full pay for life, land grants, and certificates issued to make up the losses suffered from currency depreciation.

In 1777 and again in 1779, Maryland in order to meet its quotas for the Continental army offerred its own inducements over and above those of the Congress. These were money payments and 50 acres of land after the war for persons enlisting for three years.

During the early 1800s as the veterans aged, an increasing number were unable to support themselves. Many sought and received relief through private bills of the Congress and the state legislatures. This created political pressure, and in 1818 Congress approved pensions for all Continental veterans in need rather than only for war-connected disabilities. Nine months service was required, and the pensions were for life.

Finally in 1832 Congress approved pensions for service without regard to need. Militia and Continental veterans who had served more than two years received full pay for life. Those who had served less than two years but more than six months received lesser amounts. Eligibility was periodically extended to widows commencing in 1836 to any widow who had married during the war service of the spouse. In 1855 date of marriage was removed as a requirement for the widows and in 1878 the service requirement was reduced to more than 14 days or participation in one battle. An additional benefit was granted in 1855 of 160 acres of land to anyone who served more than 14 days or who participated in one battle.

Applications for benefits often contain valuable information for the genealogist and historian because they include sworn statements of military service, need (in the years when inability to earn a living was a qualifying

THE MARYLAND MILITIA IN THE REVOLUTIONARY WAR

requirement), and relationship (particularly in the case of widows and orphans). Regretfully the earlier War Office records were lost in the fire of 1801 and the British raid of 1814. The applications after that time are in the National Archives and are indexed in "Index of Revolutionary War Pension Applications in the National Archives, Special Publication No.40," (Washington, D.C.: National Genealogical Society, 1976.)

Information on Maryland state pensioners is contained in Harry Wright Newman, "Records of the Revolutionary War," (Baltimore, Md.: Genealogical Publishing Co., 1967.) Information on lots in Western Maryland that were distributed to veterans under the Maryland provisions is contained in John M. Brewer and Lewis Mayer, "The Laws and Rules of the Land Office of Maryland," (Baltimore, Md.: Kelly, Piet and Co. 1871.)

APPENDIX A

COMMISSIONED OFFICERS OF THE MARYLAND REVOLUTIONARY MILITIA

Abbreviations and Notes

Names (Column 1): Names are given as spelled in the references with a few corrections for obvious errors. In using the tables, alternate spellings should be checked.

Grades (Column 2):

Adj — Adjutant: The clerical officer of a battalion.

BrigGen — Brigadier General: The highest grade in the Maryland militia during the Revolutionary War. Commander of a brigade, also commander of a military district.

B1st Lt — Brevet First Lieutenant: An acting First Lieutenant.

Capt — Captain: Commanding officer of a company or a horse troop.

Col — Colonel: Commander of a battalion.

Cornet — The junior officer of a horse troop.

Cty Lt — County Lieutenant: Senior military officer of a county.

Ensign — The junior officer of a company of infantry in a battalion.

Lt Col — Lieutenant Colonel: Second in command of battalion.

Maj — Major: Third ranking officer of a battalion.

QM — Quartermaster: The supply officer of a battalion.

Surgeon — Medical officer.

1st Lt — First Lieutenant: Second in command of a company or a horse troop.

1st Maj — First Major: Third ranking officer of a battalion. This grade was abandoned in 1777.

2nd Lt — Second Lieutenant: Third ranking officer of a company or a horse troop.

2nd Maj — Second Major: Fourth ranking officer of a battalion. This grade was abandoned in 1777.

3rd Lt — The junior officer of an independent infantry company, also the junior officer of an artillery company.

Date (Column 3): - The date as given by the source. This may differ from the date of the event. Dates on original commissions differ slightly from the dates in the Journals. Dates indicated for resignations, deaths, etc. may be months after the event.

THE MARYLAND MILITIA IN THE REVOLUTIONARY WAR

County (Column 4):

AA	Ann Arundel
AN	Annapolis City
BA	Baltimore
CA	Caroline
CE	Cecil
CH	Charles
CV	Calvert
FR	Frederick
HA	Harford
KE	Kent
MO	Montgomery
QA	Queen Anne's
SM	Saint Mary's
SO	Somerset
WA	Washington
WO	Worcestor

Battalion (Column 5):

Bohe	Bohemia Battalion, Cecil County
Cato	Catocin, Frederick County
Corp	Corps, separate unit not part of a battalion
Deer	Deer Creek, Harford County
ES	Eastern Shore Battalion (Col. Wm. Richardson)
ElkR	Elk Ridge, Ann Arundel County
Gist	Gist's Battalion, Baltimore County
GP	Gunpowder, Baltimore County
GPUp	Gunpowder Upper Battalion, Baltimore County
Hall	Hall's Battalion, Harford County
Ling	Lingamore Battalion, Frederick County
Lwr	Lower
MdDt	Middle District, Frederick County
Mid	Middle
PrAn	Princess Ann, Somerset County
Salb	Salisbury Battalion, Somerset County
Sass	Sassafras Battalion, Cecil County
SD	Soldier's Delight, Baltimore County
SelM	Unit of the Select Militia
SnHl	Snow Hill, Worcester County
Snpx	Sinapuxent Battalion, Worcesetr County
Susq	Susquehanna, Cecil County
Svrn	Severn, Severn River, Ann Arundel County
Town	Baltimore, Frederick,
Up	Upper
UpDt	Upper District, Frederick County, now Washington County
Wico	Wicomico Battalion, Worcester County
WstR	West River, Ann Arundel County
1stW	First Battalion, Washington County
2ndW	Second Battalion, Washington County
3rdW	Third Battalion, Washington County

Company (Column 6): Usually known by name of the commanding officer.
In the case of a new Captain, the prior Captain is listed here.

APPENDIX A - COMMISSIONED OFFICERS

Reference (Column 7):

- AM   Maryland Historical Society, "Archives of Maryland," 72 vols. (Baltimore, Md.: 1883-1973)

- BL   "Calendar of Maryland State Papers, The Blue Books," (Annapolis, Md.)

- BR   Roger Thomas, "Calendar of Maryland State Papers, The Brown Books" (Annapolis, Md.: Hall of Records Commission, 1948)

- DO   Elias Jones, "New Revised History of Dorchester County Maryland," (Cambridge, Md.: Tidewater Publishing Co., 1966)

- FP   "Maryland Revolutionary War Commissions - Militia Officers," (Md.Soc. Daughters of Founders and Patriots of America, 1935) Photostat copies of original documents.

- MH1 Maryland Historical Society, Typescript "Original Commissions in the Maryland Historical Society". These commissions are no longer in the Maryland Historical Society, but were apparently transferred to the Maryland State Archives. Those found in the Archives are indicated by OC in the note column. Those given reference "MH1" were not found at either location.

- MH2 Maryland Historical Society, Typescript of letters from Colonel Wheatley of Caroline County to the Governor 12 June and 21 June 1781 contained in refernce MH3 below. Originals were not found.

- MH5 Margaret Roberts Hodges "Unpublished Revolutionary Records of Maryland," A six volume, bound, typescript at the Maryland Historical Society.

- MM   "Maryland Historical Magazine"

- PA   "The Pennsylvania Magazine," 25:583, 1901

- PC   "Proceedings of the Conventions of Maryland 1774-1775-1776," (Annapolis, Md.: Jonas Green, 1834)

- PR   Walter W. Preston, "History of Harford County," (Baltimore, Md.: Press of the Sun Book Office, 1901)

- RB   The Red Books, Maryland State Archives, Annapolis, Md.

- RC   "Calendar of Maryland State Papers, The Red Books," (Annapolis, Md.: Hall of Records Commission, 1955)

- SC   Scharf Collection, Maryland State Archives, Annapolis, Md.

- SP   Edward Papenfuse, et al "An Inventory of Maryland State Papers, vol.1 " (Annapolis, Md.: Maryland Hall of Records, 1977)

- ST   Rieman Steuart, "The Maryland Line in the Revolutionary War," (Towson, Md.: The Society of the Cincinnati of Maryland, 1969)

THE MARYLAND MILITIA IN THE REVOLUTIONARY WAR

Notes (Column 8):

- CM Court Martial
- Dec Deceased. Note that this indicates the officer had died by the date shown; it is not the actual date of death. The latter is not found in the records.
- Dis Dismissed
- Kil Killed in action.
- Mn Mentioned. Indicates the reference mentions the officer on the date given. Used when no commissioning date found.
- Mov Moved from the county
- OC Original commission in Maryland State Archives.
- POW Prisoner of war.
- Rec Recommended for promotion from grade shown. Used when it is the only information of service in that grade.
- Ref Refused to accept commission. In some instances the reason is given in the reference.
- Rep Replacement issued for a lost commission.
- Res Resigned. Indicates officer had resigned by the date shown; it may or may not be the exact date of the resignation.
- Suc Successor for the officer was appointed on date shown. Used when it is the only information that the officer vacated his position.

General Notes

An effort was made to locate the beginning and termination dates for the service of each officer in each grade that he held. For most officers this objective was not achieved. For numerous officers the only information found was an indication that he was in a particular grade on a certain date, not the dates of entering or leaving a grade. In many cases there is no indication of the officer vacating his commission. Some officers were carried on muster rolls and apparently served many months before their official commissions were issued. No record of a formal commission was found for some officers carried on muster rolls.

In the reconstitution of the militia prescribed by the Militia Act of 1777, many officers were reissued commissions in the same grade they previously had. Thus the records show two commissions in the same grade apparently for the same individual. Many of these second commissions were issued in 1777 and 1778. Nevertheless care should be exercised in assuming identities. There are, for example, cases of father and son or cousins with the same name as well as duplication of common names in apparently unrelated families.

APPENDIX A - COMMISSIONED OFFICERS

Name	Rank	Date	Cty	Bn	Company	Ref.	Notes
Aaron, John	Ensign	23-08-81	DO	Lwr	Capt.J.Robinson	AM 45-577	
Abbott, Samuel	Capt	13-05-76	TA	4th		PC 132	
Abbott, Samuel	Capt	09-04-78	TA	4th	Bullinbrook	AM 21-24	
Abbott, Samuel	Capt	03-12-79	TA	38th		AM 43-28	Suc
Abell, Barton	2nd Lt	26-08-77	SM	Lwr	Capt.I.Abell	AM 16-346	
Abell, Barton	Capt	22-06-80	SM	Lwr	Capt.I.Abell	AM 43-201	
Abell, Enock	1st Lt	26-08-77	SM	Lwr	Capt.I.Abell	AM 16-346	
Abell, Henry	Ensign	07-05-81	SM	Lwr	Capt.B.Abell	AM 45-426	
Abell, Ignatius	Capt	26-08-77	SM	Lwr		AM 16-346	
Abell, Ignatius	Capt	22-06-80	SM	Lwr		AM 43-201	Suc
Abell, Ignatius	Ensign	07-05-81	SM	Lwr	Capt.I.Abell	FP 1-124	Mn
Abell, John	1st Lt	26-08-77	SM	Lwr	Capt.S.Jenifer	AM 16-346	
Abell, John Horn	Capt	26-08-77	SM	Lwr		AM 16-346	
Abell, Jonathan	1st Lt	23-05-76	TA	38th		AM 11-438	
Abell, Jonathan	Capt	09-04-78	TA	38th	Miles River	AM 21-25	
Abell, Jonathan	Capt	12-04-80	TA	38th		AM 43-139	Suc
Abell, Samuel	2nd Maj	12-01-76	SM	21st		PC 78	
Ackerman, George	Capt	04-09-77	BA	Town		AM 16-362	
Ackermann, ---	Capt	19-01-81	BA	Town		AM 47-29	Dec
Acton, Francis	2nd Lt	09-05-78	CH	26th	Capt.S.Smallwood	AM 21-72	
Adams, Alexander	Ensign	22-09-77	SO	PrAn	Capt.J.Jones	AM 16-381	
Adams, Andrew	Capt	24-02-76			Eden School	AM 11-182	Mn
Adams, Charles	Ensign	23-08-81	DO	Up	Capt.L.Kirkman	AM 45-577	
Adams, Charles	Ensign	02-11-81	DO	Up	Capt.L.Kirkham	AM 47-541	Res
Adams, Francis	1st Lt	09-05-78	CH	26th	Capt.G.Dent Jr	AM 21-72	
Adams, Martin	Ensign	29-11-75	FR	3rd	Capt.N.Bruce	MM 11:50	
Adams, Peter	2nd Lt	29-11-75	FR	1st	Capt.P.Mantz	MM 11:50	
Adams, Peter	2nd Lt	26-03-76	FR	MdDt	Capt.Mantz	AM 11-287	
Adams, Peter	2nd Lt	28-12-76	FR	33rd		AM 12-557	Ref
Adams, Samuel	Ensign	04-02-77	BA	Gist	Capt.R.Lemmon	AM 16-114	
Adamson, John	Ensign	04-08-80	MO	Mid	Capt.Lodowick Yost	AM 43-248	
Addison, John	Capt	15-03-76	PG			AM 11-252	Mn
Addison, John	Capt	07-08-76	PG			AM 12-185	Res
Addison, John	Lt Col	01-05-78	PG	Mid		AM 21-63	
Addison, John	Colonel	13-11-79	PG	Mid		AM 43-13	
Adlum, John	2nd Lt	29-11-75	FR	1st	Capt.C.Beatty	MM 11:50	
Adlum, John	Capt	26-03-76	FR	MdDt		AM 11-287	
Adlum, John	Capt	12-05-79	FR	Town		AM 21-387	Suc
Airey, John Pitt	Ensign	10-02-76	DO		New Market Blues	AM 11-147	
Aldridge, Nicholas	Ensign	30-03-79	AA	22nd	Capt.B.Burgess	AM 21-333	
Aldridge, Nicholas	Ensign	18-05-79	AA	22nd	Capt.B.Burgess	AM 21-398	
Aldridge, Nicholas	1st Lt	01-07-80	AA	ElkR	Capt.B.Gassaway	AM 43-209	
Alexander, Arthur	Ensign	03-01-82	CE	Susq	Capt.F.Boyd	AM 48-38	
Alexander, Caleb	Capt	07-06-81	CE	Elk	Capt.S.Gilpin	AM 45-466	
Alexander, George	1st Lt	07-06-81	CE	Elk	Capt.H.South	AM 45-466	
Alexander, Mark	Ensign	03-09-77	BA	Town	Capt.Richardson	AM 16-359	
Alexander, Mark Jr.	Ensign	18-04-81	BA	Town	Capt.R.Ridgeley	AM 45-402	
Alexander, Matthew	Ensign	15-09-75	HA		#5	PR 110	
Alexander, Robert	Ensign	19-12-75	BA		Capt.A.Buchanan	RB 13-37	
Alexander, Robert	2nd Lt	-04-76	BA	Town	Capt.Wm.Buchanan	RB 13-74	
Alexander, Robert	1st Lt	06-06-76	BA	Town	Capt. Smith	AM 11-457	

47

APPENDIX A - COMMISSIONED OFFICERS

Name	Rank	Date	Cty	Bn	Company	Ref.	Notes
Alexander, William	1st Lt	13-06-77	QA	5th		RC 2-1119	Mn
Alexander, William	1st Lt	09-04-78	TA	4th	72nd Volunteer	AM 21-24	
Allen, Archibald	Capt	12-09-77	MO	16th		AM 16-373	
Allen, Charles	Ensign	30-08-77	BA	Up	Capt.R.Lemmon	AM 16-350	
Allen, John	2nd Lt	09-04-78	HA	8th	Capt.T.Hutchens	AM 21-24	
Allen, William	QM	06-01-76	CV	15th		PC 79	
Allengham, Joseph	2nd Lt	17-05-76	AA		Capt.Weems	AM 11-336	
Allison, James	2nd Lt	26-12-74	HA		#2-Lwr Cross Rds	PR 107	
Allnut, Lawrence	Ensign	25-03-80	MO	Up	Capt.C.Gassaway	AM 43-120	
Ambrose, Jacob	Capt	29-11-75	FR	2nd		MM 11:50	
Amos, Benjamin	Capt	26-01-77	HA	8th		AM 16-77	
Amos, Benjamin	Capt	09-04-78	HA	8th		AM 21-24	
Amos, Joseph	Ensign	26-05-76	HA	8th	Capt.Bussey	AM 11-387	
Amos, Joshua	1st Lt	26-01-77	HA	8th	Capt.B.Amos	AM 16-77	
Amos, Joshua	1st Lt	09-04-78	HA	8th	Capt.B.Amos	AM 21-24	
Amos, Mordecai of James	2nd Lt	09-04-78	HA	8th	Capt.A.Norris	AM 21-24	
Amos, Nicholas	Ensign	14-05-76	HA	8th	Capt.Baker	AM 11-424	
Amos, Nichols	Ensign	09-04-78	HA	8th	Capt.C.Baker	AM 21-24	
Amos, Robert	QM	06-01-76	HA	8th		PC 80	
Amos, William	Capt	17-11-79	HA	Deer	Capt.G.Vaughan	AM 43-17	
Amoss, Nicholas	Ensign	27-01-76	HA		#15-Jarrettsb'g	PR 119	
Anderson, Abraham	Ensign	22-02-76	AA		Capt.T.Mulliken	MH 5	
Anderson, Abraham	1st Lt	02-03-78	AA	Svrn	Capt.V.Gaither	AM 16-575	
Anderson, Alexander	Colonel	18-09-77	QA	5th		MH 1	
Anderson, Alexander	Colonel	04-08-79	QA	5th		FP 1-138	Res
Anderson, Charles	Capt	23-09-75	HA		#3	PR 108	
Anderson, Edward	2nd Lt	09-05-78	CH	12th	Capt.W.Wilkinson	AM 21-72	
Anderson, John	2nd Lt	09-09-78	CE	30th	Capt.Robt.Porter	AM 21-196	
Anderson, Joshua	Ensign	20-11-76	BA		Capt.J.Talbott	AM 12-541	
Anderson, Joshua	2nd Lt	23-10-81	BA	GPUp	Capt.J.Talbot	AM 45-650	
Anderson, Thomas	Ensign	- -	TA	4th	Capt.Wm.Stevens	FP 1-80	Mn
Anderson, Absalom	Ensign	22-02-76	AA	Svrn	Capt.T.Mulliken	AM 11-178	
Andrew, Beatchum	2nd Lt	17-12-81	CA	14th	Capt.J.Andrew	AM 48-27	
Andrew, Bromwell	Ensign	17-12-81	CA	14th	Capt.A.Waddle	AM 48-27	
Andrew, James	Capt	17-12-81	CA	14th	Capt.N.Andrew	AM 48-27	
Andrew, Jeremiah	Ensign	17-12-81	CA	14th	Capt.J.Andrew	AM 48-27	
Andrew, Nehemiah	Capt	09-04-78	CA	14th		AM 21-23	
Andrew, Nehemiah	Capt	12-06-81	CA	14th		MH 2	Res
Andrew, Samuel	2nd Lt	29-03-76	CA			SP 1232	Mn
Andrew, Samuel	2nd Lt	14-05-76	CA	14th	Capt.Andrew	AM 11-424	
Andrews, Reubin	Ensign	22-06-78	DO		Capt.J.Todd	AM 21-148	
Andrews, Richard	Capt	29-03-76	CA			SP 1232	Mn
Andrews, Richard	Capt	14-05-76	CA	14th		AM 11-424	
Andrews, Richard	Capt	12-06-81	CA	14th		MH 2	Dec
Archer, Dr.John	2nd Maj	06-01-76	HA	23rd		PC 80	
Archer, John	Capt	26-12-74	HA		#2-Lwr Cross Rds	PR 107	
Archer, John	2nd Maj	01-09-76				SP 2249	Res
Armstrong, John	Capt	26-08-77	SM	Lwr		AM 16-346	
Armstrong, Robert	1st Lt	26-08-77	SM	Lwr	Capt.J.Abell	AM 16-346	
Armstrong, Robert	1st Lt	16-04-78	SM	Up	Capt.Hyland	MH 5	Res
Arrants, Nathan	Ensign	23-05-76	CE			AM 11-438	
Arrats, Harmon	Ensign	09-09-78	CE	2nd	Capt.A.Cazier	MH 1	
Arrents, Harman	1st Lt	28-06-81	CE	Elk	Capt.T.L.Savin	AM 45-489	
Arrints, Harman	2nd Lt	07-06-81	CE	Elk	Capt.A.Cazier	AM 45-466	

APPENDIX A - COMMISSIONED OFFICERS

Name	Rank	Date	Cty	Bn	Company	Ref.	Notes
Ashford, John	Ensign	09-05-78	CH	26th	Capt.G.Dent Jr	AM 21-72	
Ashmead, John	Capt	12-02-77	HA	Hall		AM 16-131	
Ashmead, Samuel	Capt	09-04-78	HA	Deer		AM 21-22	
Ashmead, Samuel	Capt	17-11-79	HA	Deer		AM 43-13	Suc
Asquith, George	Ensign	26-08-77	SM	Lwr	Capt.S.Jenifer	AM 16-346	
Asquith, John	1st Lt	26-08-77	SM	Lwr	Capt.H.Hopewell	AM 16-346	
Atkinson, Angelo	Ensign	21-06-76	WO		Capt.Dennis	AM 11-506	
Atkinson, Thomas	Ensign	06-07-76	WO		Capt.Quinton	AM 11-553	
Atkinson, Thomas	Ensign	28-06-77	WO		Capt.P.Quinton	RC 2-1156	Dis
Attwood, James	1st Lt	07-05-81	SM	Lwr	Capt.J.Mackall	AM 45-426	
Aubock, Lawrence	Ensign	29-11-75	FR	3rd	Capt.M.McGuire	MM 11:50	
Austin, James	Ensign	05-04-80	QA	20th	Capt.C.Cooke	AM 43-130	
Ayres, Henry	1st Lt	30-08-77	WO	SnH1	Capt.J.Paramor	AM 16-351	
Ayres, John	Ensign	30-08-77	WO	SnH1	Capt.S.Smyley	AM 16-351	
Ayton, Henry	2nd Lt	28-08-77	AA	22nd	Capt.B.Warfield	AM 16-347	
Ayton, Henry	1st Lt	02-03-78	AA	ElkR	Capt.B.Warfield	AM 16-525	
		- -					
		- -					
Baden, Benjamin	Ensign	03-07-80	PG	Lwr	Capt.A.H.Magruder	AM 43-210	
Baden, Robert	2nd Lt	01-09-77	PG	Lwr	Capt.R.Bowie	AM 16-356	
Baden, Robert	1st Lt	01-05-78	PG	11th	Capt.R.Bowie	AM 21-62	
Baden, Robert	1st Lt	24-05-79	PG	11th	Capt.J.Beanes	AM 21-414	
Baden, Thomas	Ensign	01-05-78	PG	11th	Capt.A.Magruder	AM 21-62	
Baden, Thomas	2nd Lt	03-07-80	PG	Lwr	Capt.A.H.Magruder	AM 43-210	
Baggs, James	2nd Lt	09-04-78	CA	28th	Capt.S.Jackson	AM 21-23	
Bailey, Benjamin	2nd Lt	20-05-78	DO	3rd	Capt.J.Henry	AM 21-98	
Bailey, Elam	1st Lt	19-12-75	BA		Capt.Z.McCubbin	RB 13-37	
Bailey, Elam	Capt	29-08-77	BA	Town		AM 16-348	OC
Bailey, Elam	Capt	19-03-79	BA	Town		AM 21-324	Suc
Bailey, Elexis	Ensign	01-02-82	FR	Town	Capt.R.Lemmon	AM 48-65	
Bailey, John Jr.	Ensign	19-12-75	BA		Capt.Z.McCubbin	RB 13-37	
Bailey, Robert	2nd Lt	07-12-78	SO	PrAn	Capt.T.King	AM 21-260	
Bailey, Samuel	2nd Lt	26-04-76	HA		Capt.Patrick	AM 11-387	
Bailey, Thomas	Ensign	16-03-76	QA		Capt.Ringgold	AM 11-253	
Bailey, Thomas	2nd Lt	19-06-77	QA	20th	Capt.J.R.Emory	AM 16-295	
Bailey, Thomas	1st Lt	05-04-80	QA	20th	Capt.C.Cooke	AM 43-130	
Bailey, William	Capt	29-08-77	FR	29th		AM 16-348	
Bailiss, Samuel	Capt	17-11-79	HA	Deer	Capt.J.Patrick	AM 43-17	
Baker, Abraham	1st Lt	20-05-76	FR	UpDt	Capt. Reynolds	AM 11-356	
Baker, Charles	Capt	27-01-76	HA		#15-Jarrettsb'g	PR 119	
Baker, Charles	Capt	14-05-76	HA	8th		AM 11-424	
Baker, Charles	Capt	09-04-78	HA	8th		AM 21-24	
Baker, Evan	Capt	22-06-78	WA	3rdW		AM 21-145	
Baker, Francis	1st Lt	16-05-76	TA	4th	Capt.Daugherty	AM 11-428	
Baker, Francis	1st Lt	13-08-76	TA	4th	Capt.J.Daugherty	SP 2108	Res
Baker, Henry	Capt	29-11-75	FR			MM 11:50	
Baker, Henry	Capt	28-11-76	FR			AM 12-555	
Baker, Henry	Capt	17-01-77	FR	Ling		AM 16- 54	
Baker, Isaac	Capt	17-11-80	WA			FP 1-129	Mov
Baker, Jeremiah	Capt	01-08-75	CE			RB 13-40	Mn
Baker, Jeremiah	Capt	06-07-76	CE	30th		AM 11-553	
Baker, Jeremiah	Capt	21-04-78	CE	Susq		AM 21-48	
Baldwin, Elijah	Ensign	29-11-75	FR	3rd	Capt.A.Hayter	MM 11:50	
Baley, Archibald	2nd Lt	09-04-78	HA	23rd	Capt.J.Rogers	AM 21-23	

APPENDIX A - COMMISSIONED OFFICERS

Name	Rank	Date	Cty	Bn	Company	Ref.	Notes
Ball, Jacob	1st Lt	11-05-76	SO	1st	Hitch	AM 11-327	
Ball, John	Ensign	28-06-77	WO			RC 2-1156	Mn
Balsell, Charles	1st Lt	29-11-75	FR	2nd	Capt.Jas.Johnson	MM 11:50	
Balsell, Richard	Capt	15-05-76	FR	37th		AM 11-427	
Banks, William	Ensign	31-07-78	QA	20th	Capt.N.Noble	MH 2	Mn
Banks, William	2nd Lt	31-07-78	QA	20th	Capt.N.Noble	AM 21-172	
Banning, Assa	Ensign	26-07-80	CA	28th	Capt.A.Jump	AM 43-230	
Banning, Henry	Capt	13-05-76	TA	38th		PC 132	Bn
Banning, Henry	Lt Col	08-09-76	TA	38th		SC 48-118	OC
Banning, Henry	Lt Col	26-02-77	TA	30th		SC 48-118	Res
Banning, Henry	Capt	09-04-78	TA	38th	Hearts of Oak	AM 21-25	
Banning, Jeremiah	Capt	21-11-75	TA		Hearts of Oak	BL 217	Mn
Banning, Jeremiah	1st Maj	12-01-76	TA	4th		PC 78	
Banning, Jeremiah	Colonel	09-04-78	TA	38th		AM 21-24	
Barker, William	Ensign	07-03-76	CH		Capt.Winteser	AM 11-206	
Barker, William	Ensign	19-01-81	CH	12th	Capt.J.Gardner	AM 45-280	
Barlett, James	1st Lt	19-06-77	QA	20th	Capt.Noble	AM 16-295	
Barnes, Bennett	Ensign	09-04-78	HA	23rd	Capt.J.Rogers	AM 21-23	OC
Barnes, James	1st Lt	03-01-76	QA		Capt.T.Elliott	SC 48-119	OC
Barnes, James	Ensign	06-06-76	BA	SD	Capt.Owings	AM 11-467	
Barnes, James	2nd Maj	08-05-77	QA	20th		AM 16-244	
Barnes, James	2nd Lt	08-05-77	QA	20th		AM 16-295	
Barnes, James	Maj	29-08-77	QA	20th		SC 48-116	OC
Barnes, James	1st Lt	27-05-79	BA	SD	Capt.E.Dorsey	AM 21-422	
Barnes, James	Maj	13-11-79	QA	20th		SC 48-116	Res
Barnes, Joseph	Ensign	04-08-80	MO	Up	Capt.Benj.Ray	AM 43-248	
Barnes, Joshua	1st Lt	22-06-78	WA	2ndW	Capt.B.Williams	AM 21-145	
Barnes, Nathan	2nd Lt	30-03-79	AA	22nd	Capt.V.Stevens	AM 21-333	
Barnes, Richard	Colonel	12-01-76	SM			PC 78	
Barnes, Richard	Cty Lt	01-07-77	SM			AM 16-303	
Barnes, Thomas	Capt	16-07-76				AM 12-60	Mn
Barnes, Thomas	Capt	31-07-78	QA	20th		MH 2	Res
Barnes, William	2nd Lt	31-10-75	HA		Co.8	PR 114	
Barnes, William	2nd Lt	27-07-76	CH			AM 12-127	
Barns, James	Ensign	09-04-78	TA	38th	Broad Creek	AM 21-25	
Barr, David	Ensign	07-07-81	CE	Elk	Capt.Wm.Scott	AM 45-466	OC
Barr, David	Ensign	03-10-82	CE	ElkR		AM 48-274	
Barrett, Samuel	Capt	22-01-76	FR			AM 11-120	Mn
Barrett, Samuel	Capt	10-02-76	FR			AM 11-152	Res
Barrick, John of Handeal	Ensign	28-04-79	FR	37th	Capt.V.Creager	AM 21-369	
Barrick, John of Handiel	1st Lt	29-06-82	FR	Cato	Capt.P.Barrick	AM 48-203	
Barrick, Peter	1st Lt	29-11-75	FR	2nd	Capt.V.Creager	MM 11:50	
Barrick, Peter	Capt	29-06-82	FR	Cato	Capt.V.Cregar	AM 48-203	
Barrick, Philip	2nd Lt	29-11-75	FR	2nd	Capt.V.Creager	MM 11:50	
Barritt, Lemuel	Colonel	16-05-78	WA	3rdW		AM 21-86	
Barrow, Samuel	Ensign	12-04-80	TA	4th	Capt.R.Bruff	AM 43-139	
Bartlett, James	2nd Lt	14-05-76	QA		Capt.Swett-Ind Co.	AM 11-424	
Bartlett, James	1st Lt	19-06-77	QA	20th	Capt.Noble	AM 16-295	
Bassford, Stephen	2nd Lt	02-03-78	AA	Svrn	Capt.V.Gaither	AM 16-575	
Bassford, Thomas Fowler	Ensign	02-03-78	AA	Svrn	Capt.V.Vachel	AM 16-575	
Bateler, Henry	Capt	04-06-76	FR	UpDt		AM 11-546	
Bateman, Henry	Capt	19-09-78	AA	7th		AM 21-208	
Bateman, Henry Jr.	1st Lt	19-06-77	AA	7th	Capt.Worthington	AM 16-294	
Bateman, Henry Jr.	1st Lt	02-03-78	AA	Svrn	Capt.N.Worthington	AM 16-525	

APPENDIX A - COMMISSIONED OFFICERS

Name	Rank	Date	Cty	Bn	Company	Ref.	Notes
Batey, Archibald	2nd Lt	09-04-78	HA	23rd	Capt.J.Rogers	SC 48-114	OC
Battee, Ferinando	Ensign	02-05-81	AA	WstR	Capt.B.Harrison	AM 45-422	
Baxley, John	QM	03-06-77	BA	SD		AM 16-271	
Bayard, George	Maj	31-07-78	QA	5th		AM 21-172	
Bayard, George	Lt Col	20-04-80	QA	5th		AM 43-146	
Bayard, Samuel	1st Lt	21-04-78	CE	Sass	Capt.S.Veazey	AM 21-47	
Bayard, William	2nd Lt	18-11-79	SM	Up	Capt.J.Shanks	AM 43-18	
Bayles, Nathan	2nd Lt	23-09-75	HA	#3		PR 108	
Bayley, Benjamin	2nd Lt	18-10-77	DO	3rd	Vienna	RC 2-1356	Rec
Bayley, Esme	Maj	30-08-77	SO	Salb		AM 16-351	
Baylis, Samuel	2nd Lt	01-04-76	HA	#17		PR 122	
Baylis, Samuel	2nd Lt	09-04-78	HA	Deer		AM 21-23	
Baynard, George	Capt	02-01-76	QA	5th		MH 1	Mn
Baynard, James	Ensign	07-06-81	QA	5th	Capt.J.Y.Keene	AM 45-465	
Bayne, Samuel Hawkins	Capt	01-09-77	PG	Lwr		AM 16-356	
Baynes, ---	Capt	07-08-76	PG			SP 2062	Mn
Beacham, Stephen	2nd Lt	28-06-77	WO			RC 2-1156	Mn
Beall Jr, Andrew	Capt	23-08-76				AM 12-232	
Beall, Andrew	Capt	31-07-75	PG	25th		AM 11-49	
Beall, Andrew	Capt	18-04-76				AM 11-351	Res
Beall, Basil	2nd Lt	29-11-75	FR	4th	Capt.W.Luckett	MM 11:50	
Beall, Basil	1st Lt	11-06-76	FR	34th	Capt.Frazier	AM 11-476	
Beall, Elisha	2nd Lt	29-11-75	FR	1st	Capt.S.Plummer	MM 11:50	
Beall, George	1st Maj	21-06-77	MO	29th		AM 16-296	
Beall, George	Maj	12-09-77	MO	Mid		AM 16-373	
Beall, George 3rd	1st Lt	01-05-78	PG	Mid	Capt.W.Berry	AM 21-63	
Beall, John	1st Lt	09-04-78	HA	Deer	Capt.T.Hope	AM 21-22	
Beall, Joshua	Colonel	31-07-75	PG	25th		AM 11-49	Mn
Beall, Joshua	Colonel	13-01-76	PG	25th		PC 86	OC
Beall, Joshua	2nd Maj	08-07-76	PG	25th		AM 12-14	Res
Beall, Joshua	Cty Lt	29-11-77	PG			AM 16-429	
Beall, Joshua	Cty Lt	08-04-81	PG			AM 47-172	Mn
Beall, Levin	Ensign	12-09-77	MO	Mid	Capt.A.Orme	AM 16-373	
Beall, Levin	Ensign	- -	MO	Up		MH 5	Mov
Beall, Mordecai	1st Lt	29-11-75	FR	2nd	Capt.R.Wood	MM 11:50	
Beall, Mordecai	Capt	15-05-76	FR	37th		AM 11-427	
Beall, Peter	Capt	15-01-77	WA			AM 16-50	
Beall, R.	Capt	23-08-76				AM 12-233	Mn
Beall, Rezin	Lt Col	10-03-78	PG	Mid		AM 16-532	OC
Beall, Richard	Ensign	12-09-77	MO	29th	Capt.T.Beall	AM 16-373	
Beall, Richard	Ensign	- -	MO	Up		MH 5	Mov
Beall, Richard	Capt	01-05-78	PG	25th		AM 21-62	
Beall, Robert	Capt	12-09-77	MO	29th		AM 16-373	
Beall, Robert	Capt	04-08-80	MO	Lwr		AM 43-248	Suc
Beall, Samuel	Colonel	06-01-76	FR	36th		PC 79	
Beall, Samuel	Colonel	20-04-76	FR			AM 11-356	Res
Beall, Samuel of Saml.	1st Lt	25-03-80	MO	Lwr	Capt.Swearingham	AM 43-120	
Beall, Thaddeus	1st Lt	21-06-77	MO	29th	Capt.J.Gaither	AM 16-296	
Beall, Thadeous	Capt	12-09-77	MO	29th		AM 16-373	
Beall, Thadeus	Capt	- -	MO	Up		MH 5	Mov
Beall, Thomas	1st Lt	01-05-78	PG	25th	Capt.T.Richardson	AM 21-62	
Beall, Thomas	Capt	24-05-79	PG	25th	Capt.T.Richardson	AM 21-414	
Beall, Thomas	Ensign	04-08-80	MO	Lwr	Capt.A.Harris	AM 43-248	
Beall, William D.	1st Lt	18-03-76	PG	25th	Capt.Waring	AM 11-260	

APPENDIX A - COMMISSIONED OFFICERS

Name	Rank	Date	Cty	Bn	Company	Ref.	Notes
Beall, William Dent	Capt	14-04-81	PG			AM 47-188	Mn
Beall, Zephaniah	Ensign	25-06-76	MO	16th	Capt.Orme	AM 11-515	
Beall, Zephaniah	2nd Lt	12-09-77	MO	Mid	Capt.A.Orme	AM 16-373	
Beall, Zephaniah	2nd Lt	12-09-77	MO	29th	Capt.J.Gaither	AM 16-373	
Beall, Zephaniah	Capt	21-04-79	MO	Mid	Capt.A.Orme	AM 21-357	
Beall, Zephaniah	Capt	25-03-80	MO	Mid		AM 43-120	Suc
Beanes, John H.	Capt	24-05-79	PG	11th	Capt.R.Bowie	AM 21-414	
Beanes, John H.	Capt	12-06-81	PG	Lwr		AM 45-472	Suc
Beanes, Samuel H.	Capt	01-09-77	PG	Mid		FP 1-73	Mn
Beans, Colmore	Ensign	03-07-76	PG	11th		AM 11-544	
Beans, John	1st Lt	01-05-78	PG	Mid	Capt.Saml.H.Beans	AM 21-63	
Beans, William, Dr.	Surgeon	04-09-77			Marching militia	AM 16-362	
Beaton, Samuel	Ensign	19-06-77	QA	20th	Capt.Bordley	AM 16-295	
Beatty, Charles	Capt	29-11-75	FR	1st		MM 11:50	
Beatty, Charles	Colonel	06-01-76	FR	33rd		PC 79	
Beatty, Charles	Cty Lt	01-07-77	FR			AM 16-304	
Beatty, James	2nd Lt	29-11-75	FR	1st	Capt.Wm.Beatty	MM 11:50	
Beatty, Robert	Capt	29-11-75	FR	3rd		MM 11:50	
Beatty, Thomas	Ensign	26-03-76	FR	MdDt	Capt.Adlam	AM 11-287	
Beatty, Thomas	Capt	12-05-79	FR	Town	Capt.J.Adlum	AM 21-387	
Beatty, Thomas	Capt	03-08-81	FR	SelM		AM 45-538	
Beatty, William	Capt	29-11-75	FR	1st		MM 11:50	
Beatty, William	Lt Col	06-01-76	FR	33rd		PC 79	
Beavan, Benjamin	1st Lt	- -	CH	26th	Capt.B.Cawood	FP 1-102	Mn
Beck, James	1st Lt	01-05-78	PG	25th	Capt.R.Beall	AM 21-78	
Beck, Samuel	2nd Lt	22-06-76	KE		Capt.St.Clair	AM 11-506	
Beck, Samuel	2nd Lt	04-06-78	KE	13th	Capt.S.Wickes	AM 21-122	
Beckley, Henry	1st Lt	04-12-78	BA	Up	Capt.V.Shroad	AM 21-257	
Beckwith, George	Ensign	29-11-75	FR		Capt.D.Moore	MM 11:50	
Beckwith, George	Capt	22-06-78	FR	Ling		AM 21-145	
Beedle, Noble	Ensign	22-06-78	CE	Bohe	Capt.T.Bouldin Jr	AM 21-145	
Bell, John	2nd Lt	03-01-76	HA			SC 48-112	OC
Bell, Samuel	Colonel	03-01-76	FR	36th		SC 48-111	OC
Bellwood, William	Ensign	07-05-81	SM	Lwr	Capt.J.Chesley	AM 45-426	
Bellwood, Benjamin	Ensign	07-05-81	SM	Lwr	Capt.Hopewell	FP 1-104	Mn
Belmire, Martin	1st Lt	- -	WA	3rdW	Capt.C.Nichodemus	FP 1-35	Mn
Belmire, Martin	Capt	02-11-80	WA	3rdW		FP 1-82	Mn
Belt, Basil	Ensign	01-05-78	PG	25th	Capt.H.Magruder	AM 21-62	
Belt, Basil	1st Lt	24-05-79	PG	25th	Capt.J.Jones	AM 21-414	
Belt, Carlton	Ensign	12-09-77	MO	16th	Capt.J.Harwood	AM 16-373	
Belt, Humphrey	Lt	23-08-76				AM 12-233	Mn
Belt, Humphrey	Capt	01-05-78	PG	Mid		AM 21-63	
Belt, Humphrey	Capt	24-05-79	PG	25th		AM 21-414	Suc
Belt, Josiah	Ensign	24-05-79	PG	25th	Capt.J.Jones	AM 21-414	
Belt, Josias	2nd Lt	24-06-80	PG	Up	Capr.B.Harwood	AM 43-203	
Bennet, James	2nd Lt	30-08-77	WO	Wico	Capt.C.Bennett	AM 16-351	OC
Bennett, Charles	Capt	30-08-77	WO	Wico		AM 16-351	
Bennett, James	Capt	27-05-79	SO	Salb	Capt.W.Winder	AM 21-423	
Bennett, John	Capt	15-05-76	FR	UpDt	Lt.Inf.	AM 11-426	
Bennett, Richard	Capt	23-05-76	PG	25th		AM 11-440	Mn
Bennett, Richard		06-06-76				AM 11-553	CM
Bennett, William	2nd Lt	26-08-77	SM	Lwr	Capt.J.Abell	AM 16-346	
Bennett, William	1st Lt	16-04-78	SM	21st	Capt.J.H.Abell	AM 21-37	
Benny, Charles Walker	2nd Lt	04-11-82	TA	4th	Capt.S.Thomas	AM 48-298	

APPENDIX A - COMMISSIONED OFFICERS

Name	Rank	Date	Cty	Bn	Company	Ref.	Notes
Benny, William	Ensign	09-04-78	TA	4th	Sword In Hand	AM 21-24	
Benson, James	Capt	03-01-76	TA		Miles River Neck	MH 1	
Benson, James	Capt	13-05-76	TA	38th		PC 132	
Benson, Perry	Ensign	07-02-76	TA		Heart of Oak	AM 11-140	
Benson, Perry	2nd Lt	23-05-76	TA	38th		AM 11-438	
Benson, Perry	1st Lt	13-06-77	QA	5th		RC 2-1119	Mn
Benson, Perry	Ensign	03-12-79	TA	38th	Capt.Henry Banning	AM 43-28	
Benson, Perry of Jas.	Ensign	01-07-76	TA	4th	Capt.Goldsborough	AM 11-539	
Bentley, Solomon	2nd Lt	27-04-79	FR	37th	Capt.W.Carmack	AM 21-368	
Bentley, Solomon	1st Lt	16-08-81	FR	Cato	Capt.J.Collins	AM 45-566	
Benton, Mark	1st Lt	13-06-77	QA	5th		RC 2-1119	Mn
Benton, Vincent	Capt	29-08-77		5th		PA	
Benton, Vincent	Capt	07-06-81	QA	5th		AM 45-465	Suc
Berry, Benjamin	Ensign	01-05-78	PG	Mid	Capt.W.Berry	AM 21-63	
Berry, Benjamin	Ensign	09-05-78	CH	26th	Capt.S.Smallwood	AM 21-72	
Berry, Elisha	Ensign	13-11-79	PG	Mid	Capt.C.Clagett	AM 43-13	
Berry, William	Capt	01-05-78	PG	Mid		AM 21-63	
Berry, William	Ensign	11-05-78	TA	4th	Capt.L.Spedding	AM 21-73	
Berry, Zachariah	1st Lt	01-05-78	PG	Mid	Capt.C.Wheeler	AM 21-63	
Berry, Zachariah	Capt	24-06-80	PG	Mid	Capt.C.Wheeler	AM 43-203	
Bestpitch, Levin	1st Lt	20-05-78	DO	3rd	Capt.J.Langfitt	AM 21-98	
Bestpitch,---	Ensign	16-12-79	DO	Lwr	Capt.E.Staplefort	AM 43-37	
Betton, Samuel Dyer	2nd Lt	31-07-78	QA	20th	Capt.Jas.Bordley	AM 21-172	
Betts, Solomon	2nd Lt	03-01-76	QA		Capt.J.Thompson	SC 48-108	OC
Bevins, Roland	1st Lt	30-08-77	WO	Wico	Capt.C.Bennett	AM 16-351	
Biddle, Andrew	1st Lt	22-06-78	FR	Ling	Capt.Winchester	AM 21-144	
Bierly, Michael	2nd Lt	15-04-78	FR	37th	Capt.J.Crist	AM 21-35	
Billmire, Martin	1st Lt	22-06-78	WA	2ndW	Capt.C.Nichodemus	AM 21-145	
Bilsel, Henry	2nd Lt	29-11-75	FR	2nd	Capt.J.Ambrose	MM 11:50	
Bird, Thomas	2nd Lt	21-04-78	CE	Sass	Capt.J.Knight	AM 21-47	
Birde, Richard	2nd Lt	13-06-77	QA	5th		RC 2-1119	Mn
Birkhead, Christopher	Colonel	12-01-76	TA	4th		PC 78	
Birkhead, Christopher	Cty Lt	01-07-77	TA			AM 16-304	
Birkhead, John	2nd Lt	02-05-81	AA	WstR	Capt.S.Chew	AM 45-422	
Bishop, Elijah	Capt	03-01-76	QA			SC 48-107	OC
Bishop, Elijah	2nd Maj	08-05-77	QA	5th		AM 16-243	
Bishop, Elijah	2nd Maj	29-05-77	QA	5th		RC 2-673	
Bishop, William	Ensign	30-08-77	WO	Wico	Capt.G.Spence	AM 16-351	
Bishop, William	Ensign	02-03-78	AA	Svrn	Capt.C.Boone	AM 16-525	
Bitesele, Henry	1st Lt	-- --	FR	Cato	Capt.J.Crist	FP 1-108	Mn
Blackiston, John	1st Lt	18-11-79	SM	Up	Capt.J.Shanks	AM 43-18	
Blacklock, Richard	Ensign	04-08-80	MO	Lwr	Capt.J.Willcoxen	AM 43-248	
Blacklock, Thomas	Ensign	03-07-80	PG	Lwr	Capt.H.Hill Jr	AM 43-210	
Blackmore, Samuel	2nd Lt	12-09-77	MO	16th	Capt.A.Allen	AM 16-373	
Blackmore, Samuel	1st Lt	04-08-80	MO	Up	Capt.Archd.Allen	AM 43-248	
Blackmore, William	1st Lt	12-09-77	MO	16th	Capt.S.Simpson	AM 16-373	
Blackmore, William	Capt	07-10-77	MO	16th	Capt.S.Simpson	AM 16-392	
Blackmore, William	Capt	25-03-80	MO	Up		AM 43-120	Suc
Blair, William	Capt	29-11-75	FR	3rd		MM 11:50	
Blair, William	Lt Col	03-01-76	FR	35th		SC 48-106	OC
Blair, William	Lt Col	07-10-76	FR	35th		PC 266	
Blake, Charles	1st Lt	31-07-78	QA	20th	Capt.J.S.Blake	MH 2	Mn
Blake, Jno.Sawyer	Capt	31-07-78	QA	20th		MH 2	Mn
Blake, Joseph	Ensign	16-04-78	CV	15th	Capt.F.Skinner	AM 21-37	

53

APPENDIX A - COMMISSIONED OFFICERS

Name	Rank	Date	Cty	Bn	Company	Ref.	Notes
Blake, Joseph	Lt	01-09-81	CV	SelM		AM 45-596	
Blunt, Benjamin	1st Lt	03-01-76	CA		Bridgetown Vol.	Sc 48-105	OC
Boarman, Edward	Ensign	19-01-81	CH	12th	Capt.H.Boarman	AM 45-280	
Boarman, Edward Jr.	Ensign	05-07-77	CH	12th	Capt.A.Macpherson	RC 2-1170	Rec
Boarman, Henry	1st Lt	30-07-76	CH			AM 12-141	
Boarman, Henry	Capt	22-10-77	CH	Lwr		AM 16-401	
Boarman, Henry	Capt	09-02-81	CH	12th	Capt.A.McPherson	AM 45-307	
Boarman, Raphael Jr.	Ensign	07-03-76	CH		Capt.Yates	AM 11-206	
Boarman, Richard Bennett	1st Lt	07-03-76	CH		Capt.Winter	AM 11-206	
Boarman, Richard Bennett	Capt	09-02-81	CH	12th	Capt.Winters	AM 45-307	
Boge, James	2nd Lt	28-06-81	CE	Elk	Capt.J.Oglevie	AM 45-489	
Boggass, Samuel	1st Lt	03-01-76	FR		Capt.Maynard	SC 48-103	OC
Boggass, Samuel	1st Lt	- -			Capt.N.Maynard	SC 48-103	Ref
Boggs, James	Ensign	21-04-78	CE	Elk	Capt.J.Oglevee	AM 21-47	OC
Bogs, James	Ensign	07-06-81	CE	Elk	Capt.J.Oglevie	AM 45-466	
Bonchill, Slyter	Ensign	22-06-78	CE	Bohe	Capt.S.Lankaster	AM 21-145	
Bond, Benjamin	Capt	16-04-78	CV	15th		AM 21-37	
Bond, Gerard	Capt	26-08-77	SM	Up		AM 16-345	
Bond, Gerald	Capt	18-11-79	SM	Up		AM 43-18	Suc
Bond, Jacob	Capt	09-12-75	HA		#11	PR 116	
Bond, James	2nd Lt	09-04-78	HA	8th	Capt.D.Scott	AM 21-24	
Bond, Richard Jr.	1st Lt	21-04-78	CE	Elk	Capt.S.Gilpin	AM 21-47	OC
Bond, Richard Jr.	1st Lt	07-06-81	CE	Elk	Capt.J.Oglevie	AM 45-466	
Bond, Thomas	Lt Col	06-01-76	HA	8th		PC 80	
Bond, Thomas	1st Lt	20-11-76	BA		Capt.S.Gill	AM 12-542	
Bond, Wiliam	Capt	26-08-77	SM	Up		AM 16-346	
Boone, Alextious	Ensign	01-05-78	PG	11th	Capt.R.Bowie	AM 21-62	
Boone, Alextious	Ensign	24-05-79	PG	11th	Capt.J.Beanes	AM 21-414	
Boone, Charles	Capt	02-03-78	AA	Svrn		AM 16-525	OC
Boone, Charles	Capt	30-07-81	AA	Svrn		AM 45-467	Suc
Boone, James	Ensign	09-04-78	CA	28th	Capt.T.Hughlet	AM 21-23	
Boone, John	Capt	08-02-76	AA			AM 11-141	
Boone, John	Capt	02-03-78	AA	Svrn		AM 16-575	OC
Boone, John	Capt	23-04-81	AA	Svrn		AM 45-411	Suc
Boone, Stephen	1st Lt	02-03-78	AA	Svrn	Capt.C.Boone	AM 16-525	
Boone, Stephen	1st Lt	30-07-81	AA	Svrn	Capt.G.Pecker	AM 45-527	
Booth, Ebenezer	1st Lt	07-06-81	CE	Elk	Capt.D.Ricketts	AM 45-465	
Booth, Jonathan	Capt	21-04-78	CE	Elk		AM 21-47	OC
Booth, Jonathan	Capt	07-06-81	CE	Elk		AM 45-466	Suc
Bordley, James	Capt	16-03-76	QA			AM 11-254	
Bordley, William	Colonel	08-05-77	KE	13th		AM 16-243	
Bordley, William	Cty Lt	01-07-77	KE			AM 16-303	
Boroughs, James	Ensign	18-11-79	SM	Up	Capt.E.Mattingley	AM 43-18	
Bose, Henry	Ensign	04-12-78	BA	Up	Capt.Lemmon	AM 21-257	
Boseley, Charles	Capt	07-01-77	BA			SP 3409	Mn
Bosley, James	Capt	19-12-75	BA			RB 13-37	
Bosley, James	Capt	25-05-76	BA	GP		AM 11-444	
Bosley, James	1st Lt	23-10-81	BA	GPUp	Capt.Wm.Lane	AM 45-650	
Bosley, Walter	2nd Lt	20-11-76	BA		Capt.L.Wiley	AM 12-542	
Bosley, Walter	1st Lt	31-10-80	BA	GPUp	Capt.R.Cromwell	SC 48-97	OC
Bosley, Zebulon	Ensign	04-09-77	BA	GP	Capt.J.Bosley	AM 16-362	
Bosman, Balland	2nd Lt	- -	SO	PrAn	Capt.Wm.Waters	FP 1-11	Mn
Boteler, Henry	Capt	10-05-78	WA			SP 6907	Res
Bouchell, Slyter	Ensign	- -	CE	Sass	Capt.StC.Lancaster	FP 1-36	Mn

APPENDIX A - COMMISSIONED OFFICERS

Name	Rank	Date	Cty	Bn	Company	Ref.	Notes
Boucher, John Thomas	Capt	30-08-76				SP 2236	Res
Boulden, Thomas Jr.	1st Lt	21-04-78	CE	Sass	Capt.T.Brevard	AM 21-47	
Boulden, Thomas Sr.	2nd Lt	21-04-78	CE	Sass	Capt.T.Brevard	AM 21-47	
Bouldin, Lewis	2nd Lt	07-06-81	CE	Elk	Capt.C.Alexander	AM 45-466	
Bouldin, Thomas Jr.	Capt	22-06-78	CE	Bohe	Capt.Brevard	AM 21-145	
Boulton, James	Ensign	22-06-78	FR	Ling	Capt.Pebble	AM 21-145	
Bourke, Dr. Thomas	Capt	10-02-76	DO		Cambridge Blues	AM 11-147	
Bourne, Jesse Jacob	Ensign	16-04-78	CV	15th	Capt.R.Parran	AM 21-37	
Boven, Josias	Capt	---05-76	BA			RB 13-53	
Bowdle, Henry	Ensign	14-08-79	CA	14th	Capt.J.Mitchell	AM 21-493	
Bowen, Josiah	Capt	25-05-76	BA	GP	Capt.Mercer	AM 11-444	
Bowie, Allen	1st Lt	14-05-76	MO	29th	Capt.Harden	AM 11-424	
Bowie, Allen	1st Lt	12-09-77	MO	29th	Capt.E.Harding	AM 16-373	
Bowie, Fielder	Capt	20-02-76	PG	11th	Nottingham	AM 11-173	
Bowie, Robert	1st Lt	16-03-76	PG			AM 11-253	
Bowie, Robert	Capt	01-09-77	PG	Lwr		AM 16-356	
Bowie, Robert	Capt	01-05-78	PG	11th		AM 21-62	
Bowie, Robert	Capt	24-05-79	PG	11th		AM 21-414	Suc
Bowie, Robert	Capt	12-06-81	PG	Lwr	Capt.J.H.Beanes	AM 45-472	
Bowie, Robert	Lt	01-09-81	PG		Horse troop	AM 45-596	
Bowie, Walter	1st Lt	05-09-77	PG	25th		AM 16-363	
Bowie, Walter	1st Lt	01-05-78	PG	25th	Capt.M.Duvall	AM 21-62	
Bowie, William 3rd	1st Lt	01-05-78	PG	Mid	Capt.J.Burgess	AM 21-63	
Bowie, William Sprigg	2nd Lt	05-01-76				PA	
Bowley, Daniel	2nd Lt	25-09-80	BA	Town	Capt.T.Yeates	AM 43-303	
Boyce, Roger	1st Lt	09-04-78	HA	8th	Capt.J.Sewall	AM 21-24	
Boyd, Abraham	Capt	23-05-76	PG	25th		AM 11-440	
Boyd, Abraham	Maj	10-03-78	PG	25th		AM 16-532	
Boyd, Abraham	Lt Col	01-05-78	PG	25th		AM 21-63	
Boyd, Archibald	2nd Lt	21-02-76	FR		Capt.Young	AM 11-178	Mn
Boyd, Francis	1st Lt	21-04-78	CE	Susq	Capt.P.Cole	AM 21-48	
Boyd, Francis	Capt	03-01-82	CE	Susq	Capt.P.Cole	AM 48-38	
Boyd, Thomas	Ensign	01-05-78	PG	25th	Capt.J.Carlton	AM 21-62	
Boyd, Thomas Jr.	2nd Lt	24-05-79	PG	25th	Capt.J.Shaw	AM 21-414	
Bozman, Ballard	2nd Lt	19-09-76	SO	17th		AM 12-285	
Bozman, Ballard	2nd Lt	22-09-77	SO	PrAn	Capt.W.Waters	AM 16-381	
Bozman, Ballard	1st Lt	07-12-78	SO	PrAn	Capt.I.Handy	AM 21-260	
Bradford, William	Capt	30-09-75	HA		#13	PR 119	
Bradford, William	Capt	09-04-78	HA	23rd		AM 21-24	
Bradford, William	Capt	17-11-79	HA	23rd		AM 43-17	Suc
Brady, John	Ensign	14-06-77				AM 16-289	Res
Bragden, William	Capt	09-03-76	AA	WstR		AM 11-231	Mn
Brambell, John	1st Lt	20-05-78	DO	19th	Capt.R.Jones	AM 21-97	
Brannock, Edward	Ensign	03-01-76	DO		Church Creek	SC 48-96	OC
Brannock, Thomas	2nd Lt	03-01-76	DO		Church Creek	SC 48-95	OC
Brasford, Stephen	2nd Lt	17-06-76	AA	Svrn	Capt.Gaither	AM 11-495	
Brasford, Thomas Foster	Ensign	17-06-76	AA	Svrn	Capt.Gaither	AM 11-495	
Brashears, Jonathan	Ensign	02-05-81	AA	WstR	Capt.A.Welsh	AM 45-422	
Brashears, Rezin	2nd Lt	28-11-76	FR		Capt.W.Brashears	AM 12-555	
Brashears, Rezin	2nd Lt	17-01-77	FR	Ling	Capt.Wm.Brashears	AM 16-55	
Brashears, William	Capt	28-11-76	FR			AM 12-555	
Brashears, William	Capt	17-01-77	FR	Ling		AM 16-54	
Brashears, William	Capt	10-06-78	FR			AM 21-128	Suc
Brayton, Jesse	2nd Lt	27-05-79	WO	Wico	Capt.J.Perdue	AM 21-423	

APPENDIX A - COMMISSIONED OFFICERS

Name	Rank	Date	Cty	Bn	Company	Ref.	Notes
Breem, John	1st Lt	26-08-77	SM	Up	Capt.T.Reeder	AM 16-346	
Breese, Samuel	2nd Lt	31-07-78	QA	5th	Capt.I.Scriviner	AM 21-172	
Brerdah, Peter	Ensign	15-05-76	FR	UpDt		AM 11-426	
Brereton, John		04-06-81	SO			AM 47-278	CM
Breshears, William Jr.	Capt	13-10-77	FR			SC 48-94	OC
Breshears, William Jr.	Capt	10-06-78	FR			SC 48-94	Res
Bretherd, Daniel Coe	Ensign	16-03-81	WO	Snpx	Capt.I.Evans	AM 45-353	
Brevard, ---	Capt	22-06-78	CE	Bohe		AM 21-145	Suc
Brevard, John	Ensign	30-08-77	WO	Snpx	Capt.E.Briddell	AM 16-350	
Brevard, John	2nd Lt	27-05-79	WO	Snpx	Capt.J.Dashiell	AM 21-423	
Brevard, Thomas	Capt	21-04-78	CE	Sass		AM 21-47	
Breveard, Thomas	Capt	03-01-76	CE	18th		PA	
Breveard, Thomas	Capt	05-02-76	CE	18th		PA	Res
Brice, Howard	Capt	03-01-76	AA			SC 48	153
Brice, James	Cty Lt	01-07-77	AA			AM 16-303	
Brice, John	3rd Lt	15-02-77	AN			AM 16-138	
Brice, John	1st Lt	06-10-77	AN		Capt.N.Maccubbin	AM 16-392	
Brice, John	Capt	20-03-79	AN		Independent	AM 21-325	OC
Briddell, Elihu	Capt	30-08-77	WO	Snpx		AM 16-350	
Briddle, Elisha	Capt	- -	WO			MH 5	Mov
Bridles, ---	Capt	27-05-79	WO	Snpx		AM 21-423	Suc
Bright, Francis	Ensign	31-07-78	QA	20th	Capt.J.Ringgold	AM 21-172	
Briscoe, Gerard	Capt	20-06-77	MO			RC 2-1142	Mn
Briscoe, Gerrard	Maj	12-09-77	MO	Mid		AM 16-373	
Briscoe, John Hanson	2nd Maj	12-01-76	SM	6th		PC 78	
Briscoe, John Hanson	Maj	18-11-79	SM	Up		AM 43-18	
Briscoe, Robert	Ensign	18-11-79	SM	Up	Capt.John Mills	AM 43-18	
Brittain, Nicholas	1st Lt	04-02-77	BA		Capt.J.Cockey	AM 16-114	
Brittingham, Beletha	Ensign	30-08-77	WO	Snpx	Capt.W.Purnal	AM 16-350	
Brittingham, Beletha	2nd Lt	13-06-82	WO	Snpx	Capt.L.Robins	AM 48-190	
Brittingham, Joseph	Ensign	27-05-79	WO	Wico	Capt.J.Perdue	AM 21-423	
Brittingham, Samuel	1st Lt	28-06-77	WO		Capt.W.Holland	RC 2-1156	Mn
Brogden, Samuel	2nd Lt	12-09-77	AA	31st	Capt.Wm.Brogden	AM 16-372	
Brogden, Samuel	1st Lt	02-03-78	AA	WstR	Capt.T.Watkins	AM 16-525	
Brogden, William	Capt	23-08-76				AM 12-233	Mn
Brogden, William	Maj	02-03-78	AA	WstR		AM 16-525	
Bromwell, Jonathan	1st Lt	11-06-77	DO	19th	Capt.Jones	AM 16-282	
Brooke, Basil		17-09-76				AM 12-276	Mn
Brooke, John	Maj	16-04-78	CV	15th		AM 21-37	
Brooke, John Smith	1st Lt	01-09-77	PG	Lwr		AM 16-356	
Brooke, Jonathan S.	Lt	23-08-76				AM 12-233	Mn
Brooke, Richard	1st Maj	06-01-76	MO	29th		PC 79	
Brooke, Richard	Maj	15-08-76	FR			AM 12-206	Res
Brooke, Richard	Colonel	12-09-77	MO	Mid		AM 16-373	
Brooke, Richard		15-10-77	BA			SP 5166	
Brooke, Roger	Capt	12-09-77	MO	Mid		AM 16-373	
Brookes, Benjamin	1st Lt	03-07-76	PG	11th	Capt.Bowie	AM 11-544	
Brookes, Francis	Ensign	22-06-80	SM	Lwr	Capt.Zach.Forrest	AM 43-201	
Brookes, Jonathan Smith	Capt	24-06-80	PG	Mid		AM 43-203	Suc
Brookes, Nicholas	Ensign	24-05-79	PG	11th	Capt.H.Hill	AM 21-414	
Brooks, John Smith	Capt	01-05-78	PG	Mid		AM 21-63	
Brooks, Nicholas	2nd Lt	03-07-80	PG	Lwr	Capt.H.Hill Jr	AM 43-210	
Broome, John Hooper	Capt	18-11-79	SM	Up	Capt.T.A.Reeder	AM 43-18	
Brossleday, ---	Capt	24-12-76	FR			AM 12-550	Mn

APPENDIX A - COMMISSIONED OFFICERS

Name	Rank	Date	Cty	Bn	Company	Ref.	Notes
Broton, Joseph	Ensign	16-03-81	WO	Snpx	Capt.J.Tull	AM 45-353	
Brough, Peter	Ensign	- -	WA			FP 1-129	Suc
Broughton, John	Ensign	23-08-81	WO	SelM	Capt.S.Rounds	Am 45-577	
Brown, Charles	1st Lt	20-05-78	DO	3rd	Capt.Jas.Wright	AM 21-98	OC
Brown, Elie	Ensign	25-08-77	AA	22nd	Capt.Walker	AM 16-343	
Brown, George	Ensign	28-11-76	FR	37th		AM 12-555	
Brown, George	2nd Lt	20-05-78	DO	3rd	Capt.J.Langfitt	AM 21-98	
Brown, George	1st Lt	16-08-81	FR	Cato	Capt.D.Sheilor	AM 45-566	
Brown, George	2nd Lt	23-08-81	DO	Up		DO 230	
Brown, George	Capt	30-11-82	FR	Cato	Capt.D.Sheilor	AM 48-311	
Brown, Henry	1st Lt	05-11-81	BA	Up		AM 45-662	
Brown, Jacob	1st Lt	25-09-80	BA	Town	Capt.B.Bickinson	SC 48-91	
Brown, Jacob	2nd Lt	24-04-81	BA	Town	Capt.B.Dickinson	AM 45-412	
Brown, Joel	2nd Lt	03-01-76	QA		Capt.S.Wickes	SC 48-86	OC
Brown, John	2nd Lt	11-05-78	TA	4th	Capt.L.Spedding	AM 21-73	
Brown, Peter	2nd Lt	03-01-76	PG			SC 48-90	OC
Brown, Samuel	2nd Lt	02-03-78	AA	ElkR	Capt Hammond	AM 16-525	
Brown, William	Capt	31-07-78	QA	5th		AM 21-172	
Brown, William	Capt	20-04-80	QA	5th		AM 43-146	Suc
Browne, Nathan	Ensign	16-03-76	QA		Capt.Bordley	AM 11-254	
Browne, Nathan	2nd Lt	19-06-77	QA	20th	Capt.Bordley	AM 16-295	
Browne, Nathan	1st Lt	31-07-78	QA	20th	Capt.Jas.Bordley	AM 21-172	
Bruboi, Rudolph	1st Lt	29-11-75	FR	3rd	Capt.M.McGuire	MM 11:50	
Bruce, Andrew	Lt Col	16-05-78	WA	3rdW		AM 21-86	
Bruce, Charles	Ensign	12-09-77	MO	Mid	Capt.B.Gaither	AM 16-373	
Bruce, Charles	Capt	21-04-79	MO	Mid		AM 21-357	
Bruce, John	2nd Lt	30-08-77	MO	16th	Capt.Owings	AM 16-350	
Bruce, John	Capt	12-09-77	MO	Mid		AM 16-373	
Bruce, John	Capt	25-03-80	MO	Mid		AM 43-120	Suc
Bruce, Norman	Capt	29-11-75	FR	3rd		MM 11:50	
Bruce, Norman	Colonel	07-10-76	FR	35th		PC 266	
Bruce, Norman	Cty Lt	24-04-79	FR			AM 21-364	
Bruce, Peter	Capt	17-11-80	WA		Capt.I.Baker	FP 1-129	Mn
Bruff, Joseph	Capt	13-05-76	TA	4th		PC 132	Bn
Bruff, Joseph	Maj	09-04-78	TA	4th		AM 21-24	
Bruff, Richard	Capt	11-05-78	TA	4th		AM 21-73	
Bruff, Thomas	1st Maj	06-01-76	SO			PC 80	
Bruff, Thomas	Maj	30-08-77	SO	PrAn		AM 16-351	
Bruff, Thomas	Lt Col	28-10-80	SO	PrAn		AM 43-342	Suc
Bruff, William	QM	03-01-76	QA	5th		SC 48-87	OC
Bruff, William	QM	12-06-76	QA	5th		PC 78	
Bruff, William	QM	08-05-77	QA	5th		AM 16-343	Suc
Bruner, Elias	Ensign	29-11-75	FR	1st	Capt.J.Haass	MM 11:50	
Bucham, Stephen	2nd Lt	15-05-76	WO		Capt.Shockley	AM 11-427	
Buchanan, Andrew	Capt	19-12-75	BA			RB 13-37	
Buchanan, Andrew	BrigGen	06-01-76				PC 78	
Buchanan, Andrew	Cty Lt	01-07-77	BA			AM 16-304	
Buchanan, William	1st Lt	19-12-75	BA		Capt.A.Buchanan	RB 13-37	
Buchanan, William	Capt	-04-76	BA	Town		RB 13-74	
Buchanan, William	Colonel	25-05-76	BA	Town		AM 11-443	
Buchanan, William	Ensign	21-04-78	CE	Elk	Capt.A.Miller	AM 21-47	
Buck, Benjamin	1st Lt	25-05-76	BA	GP	Capt.Mercer	AM 11-444	
Buck, Benjamin	Capt	30-08-77	BA	GP		AM 16-350	
Buck, Joshua	1st Lt	30-08-77	BA	GP	Capt.B.Buck	AM 16-350	

57

APPENDIX A - COMMISSIONED OFFICERS

Name	Rank	Date	Cty	Bn	Company	Ref.	Notes
Budd, John	Ensign	24-05-76	DO		Capt. Hicks	AM 11-441	
Budd, John	Ensign	20-05-78	DO	19th	Capt.J.Robinson	AM 21-97	
Budd, John	1st Lt	23-08-81	DO	Lwr	Capt.J.Robinson	AM 45-577	
Bullock, Samuel	1st Lt	09-09-78	KE	13th	Capt.D.Crane	AM 21-196	
Bunbury, Benjamin	1st Lt	07-06-81	QA	20th	Capt.H.Coursey	AM 45-465	
Burch, Benjamin	Ensign	05-07-77	CH	12th		RC 2-1170	Rec
Burch, Jonathan	Ensign	19-01-81	CH	12th	Capt.T.A.Dyson	AM 45-280	
Burch, Oliver	Ensign	01-05-78	PG	Mid	Capt.Saml.H.Beans	AM 21-63	
Burckhart, Peter	Ensign	29-11-75	FR	4th	Capt.Wm.Duvall	MM 11:50	
Burge, William	Capt	26-06-76	FR	29th		SP 1646	Mn
Burgess, Basil	2nd Lt	04-04-76			Capt.Burgess	AM 11-308	
Burgess, Basil	1st Lt	27-08-77	AA	22nd	Capt.C.Hammond	AM 16-347	
Burgess, Basil	Capt	30-03-79	AA	22nd		AM 21-333	
Burgess, Basil	Capt	01-07-80	AA	ElkR		AM 43-209	Suc
Burgess, Caleb	Ensign	19-06-77	AA	7th	Capt.N.Worthington	AA 16-294	
Burgess, Caleb	Ensign	02-03-78	AA	Svrn	Capt.N.Worthington	AM 16-525	
Burgess, Edward	Capt	26-06-76	MO	29th		AM 11-522	Mn
Burgess, Edward	Capt	18-06-77	MO	29th		RC 2-1133	Dec
Burgess, Edward	Capt	11-08-79	MO		Capt.J.Gaither	SC 48-85	OC
Burgess, Henry	Ensign	17-06-77	TA	4th	Volunteer-2nd	RC 2-1130	Rec
Burgess, John	Capt	- -74	AA			AM 11-433	Mn
Burgess, John	Capt	04-04-76	AA			AM 11-308	
Burgess, John	Capt	02-03-78	AA	ElkR		AM 16-525	
Burgess, John	Capt	01-05-78	PG	Mid		AM 21-63	
Burgess, John	Lt Col	02-11-78	AA	22nd		AM 21-229	
Burgess, John Magruder	Ensign	01-09-77	PG	Lwr	Capt.Belt	AM 16-356	
Burgess, John Magruder	Maj	13-11-79	PG	Mid		AM 43-13	
Burgess, Joseph	1st Lt	13-04-76	AA		Capt.Howard	AM 11-329	
Burgess, Joshua	Ensign	30-03-79	AA	22nd	Capt.V.Stevens	AM 21-333	
Burgess, Matthias	Ensign	23-01-82	FR	Town	Capt.J.Shellman	AM 48-53	OC
Burgess, Mitchl.	Ensign	30-03-79	AA	22nd	Capt.N.Warfield	AM 21-333	
Burgess, Mordecai	2nd Lt	01-05-78	PG	Mid	Capt.C.Wheeler	AM 21-63	
Burgess, Mordecai	1st Lt	24-06-80	PG	Mid	Capt.Z.Berry	AM 43-203	
Burgess, Philemo.	Ensign	01-07-80	AA	ElkR	Capt.V.Stevens	AM 43-209	
Burgess, Richard Jr.	Ensign	01-05-78	PG	Mid	Capt.J.Brooks	AM 21-63	
Burgess, Richard Jr.	2nd Lt	24-06-80	PG	Mid	Capt.S.Hepburn	AM 43-203	
Burgess, Vachel	1st Lt	01-07-80	AA	ElkR	Capt.V.Stevens	AM 43-209	
Burk, Thomas	Capt	09-04-78	CA	28th		AM 21-23	
Burnes, David	2nd Lt	01-05-78	PG	25th	Capt.J.Weight	AM 21-78	
Burnes, James	2nd Lt	01-05-78	PG	11th	Capt.J.Perry	AM 21-62	
Burroughs, James	Ensign	26-08-77	SM	Up		SC 48-83	OC
Burtis, Samuel	2nd Lt	25-09-80	BA	Town	Capt.B.Dickinson	SC 48-82	OC
Burtis, Samuel	Ensign	08-02-81	BA	Town	Capt.B.Dickinson	AM 47-61	Dec
Busco, Ralph	1st Lt	11-06-76	FR	34th	Capt.Mackall	AM 11-476	
Busey, Charles	Ensign	03-03-77	FR	33rd	Capt.R.Hilleary	MM 4:379	Mn
Busey, Charles	1st Lt	21-04-79	MO	Up	Capt.Wm.Norris	AM 21-357	
Bush, John	2nd Lt	09-05-78	CH	26th	Capt.W.Winter	AM 21-72	
Bush, Lewis	Ensign	29-11-75	FR	4th	Capt.P.Thomas	MM 11:50	
Bush, Lewis	QM	26-03-76	FR	33rd		AM 11-287	
Bussey, Bennett	Capt	26-04-76	HA	8th		AM 11-387	
Bussey, Edward	2nd Lt	09-04-78	HA	Deer	Capt.S.Ashmead	AM 21-22	
Bussey, Jesse Jr.	Cornet	27-02-82	HA		Horse troop	AM 48-87	
Busy, Charles	2nd Lt	12-09-77	MO	16th	Capt.F.Sprigg	AM 16-373	
Busy, Edward	2nd Lt	12-02-77	HA	Hall		AM 16-131	

APPENDIX A - COMMISSIONED OFFICERS

Name	Rank	Date	Cty	Bn	Company	Ref.	Notes
Butler, Abraham	2nd Lt	05-11-81	BA	Up		AM 45-662	
Butler, Henry	Ensign	30-08-77	BA	Up	Capt.Murray	AM 16-350	
Butler, Richard	QM	28-11-76	FR	37th		AM 12-555	
Byas, Joseph	3rd Lt	04-09-77	BA	Town	Arty	AM 16-362	
Byng, William	Ensign	27-05-79	SO	Salb	Capt.J.Bennett	AM 21-423	
Byng, William	2nd Lt	22-08-81	SO	Salb	Capt.J.Bennett	AM 45-575	
Byns, James	Capt	16-12-79	DO	Lwr	Capt.Jos.Byns	AM 43-37	
Byns, Joseph	Capt	26-10-76	DO			SP 2596	Mn
Byns, Joseph	Capt	16-12-79	DO	Lwr		AM 43-37	Suc
Byus, James	Capt	16-12-79	DO	Lwr		DO 233	Res
Byus, Joseph	Capt	20-05-78	DO	19th		AM 21-97	OC
Byus, Joseph	Capt	23-06-79	DO		Castle Haven	FP 2-70	Dec
Cain, James	Ensign	16-05-76	HA	23rd	Capt.Smith	AM 11-428	
Cain, Patrick	1st Lt	11-04-78	HA	Deer		SC 48-197	Rec
Caldwell, John	Ensign	19-03-79	BA	Town	Capt.J.Merryman	AM 21-324	
Caldwell, John	Ensign	19-05-79	BA	Town	Capt.Merryman	AM 21-401	
Caldwell, Samuel	1st Lt	09-09-75	HA	#7		PR 113	
Caldwell, Samuel	Maj	09-04-78	HA	8th		AM 21-24	
Calgrove, John	Adj	15-09-75	HA		#5	PR 110	
Calhoun, James	QM	25-05-76	BA	Town		AM 11-443	
Calhoun, James	Ensign	25-09-80	BA	Town	Capt.T.Yeates	AM 43-303	
Callahan, John	3rd Lt	06-10-77	AN		Capt.B.Harwood	AM 16-392	
Callahan, John	1st Lt	20-03-79	AN		Middleton-Ind	AM 21-325	
Callison, Richard	2nd Lt	09-04-78	CA	14th	Capt.J.Mitchel	AM 21-23	
Calson, Charles	Capt	03-12-76	WA			AM 12-501	
Calwell, Samuel	Capt	26-04-76	HA	8th		AM 11-387	OC
Calwell, Samuel	Capt	28-09-76	HA			AM 12-310	Res
Campbell, Eneas	Maj	12-09-77	MO	16th		AM 16-373	
Campbell, Eneas	Lt Col	07-10-77	MO	16th		AM 16-392	
Campbell, Eneas Jr.	2nd Lt	12-09-77	MO	16th	Capt.J.Harwood	AM 16-373	
Campbell, George	2nd Lt	06-06-76	BA	Town	Capt.Dean	AM 11-467	
Campbell, James	Capt	05-01-76			Vienna	SP 957	Dis
Campbell, John Corry	Ensign	07-06-81	CE	Elk	Capt.C.Alexander	AM 45-466	
Campbell, Robert	Capt	13-06-77	QA	5th		RC 2-1119	Dec
Campbell, William	Capt	27-01-76	CH			AM 11-111	Mn
Campbell, Zachariah	Capt	10-02-76	DO		Transquaking	AM 11-147	
Cannon, J.	1st Lt	19-01-81	BA	Town	Capt.Dickinson	AM 47-29	Res
Cannon, John	Ensign	29-08-77	BA	Town	Capt.B.Dickinson	AM 16-348	
Cannon, John	2nd Lt	19-03-79	BA	Town	Capt.B.Dickinson	AM 21-324	
Cannon, John	2nd Lt	19-05-79	BA	Town	Capt.J.Smith	AM 21-401	
Cannon, John	2nd Lt	08-02-81	BA	Town	Capt.B.Dickinson	AM 47-61	Res
Carbine, Charles	Ensign	19-05-79	BA	Town	Capt.G.Douglass	AM 21-401	
Carey, Hezekiah	Ensign	28-06-77	WO			RC 2-1156	Mn
Carey, John Due	Capt	18-09-80	FR	Town	Capt.P.Grosh	AM 43-295	
Carey, John Due	Capt	23-01-82	FR	Town		AM 48-54	Suc
Carey, Joshua	2nd Lt	- -	BA	Town		FP 1-44	Mn
Carleton, Joseph	Ensign	25-03-76	PG	25th	Waring	AM 11-285	
Carleton, Joseph	2nd Lt	09-06-77	PG		Capt.B.Waring	RC 2-1103	Rec
Carline, Charles	Ensign	19-03-79	BA	Town	Capt.G.Douglass	AM 21-324	
Carlton, Joseph	Capt	01-05-78	PG	25th		AM 21-62	
Carlton, Joseph	Capt	24-05-79	PG	25th		AM 21-414	Suc
Carmach, William	1st Lt	15-05-76	FR	37th	Capt.Smith	AM 11-427	

APPENDIX A - COMMISSIONED OFFICERS

Name	Rank	Date	Cty	Bn	Company	Ref.	Notes
Carmack, John	Capt	29-11-75	FR	2nd		MM 11:50	
Carmack, John	Capt	16-08-81	FR	Cato		AM 45-566	Suc
Carmack, William	Capt	27-04-79	FR	37th	Capt.P.Smith	AM 21-368	
Carmack, William Jr.	Ensign	29-11-75	FR	2nd	Capt.J.Wood	MM 11:50	
Carmichael, Richard	1st Lt	31-07-78	QA	20th	Capt.J.Dawes	MH 2	Mn
Carmichael, Richard B.	Capt	05-04-80	QA	20th	Capt.J.Dames	AM 43-130	
Carmichael, Richard B.	Capt	19-06-80	QA	20th		PA	Res
Carmichael, Richard B.	Capt	07-06-81	QA	20th		AM 45-465	Suc
Carn, John	Ensign	- -	FR	34th		FP 1-107	Mn
Carnan, Charles	Capt	06-06-76	BA	SD	5th	AM 11-467	
Carnan, Charles	1st Maj	03-06-77	BA	SD		AM 16-271	
Carnan, Charles	Lt Col	10-09-77	BA	SD		AM 16-368	
Carnan, Charles	Lt	04-06-81	BA		Horse troop	AM 45-459	
Carnan, Charles	Lt Col	-11-81	BA	SD		AM 47-560	Res
Carradine, William	Ensign	-09-77	QA	20th		FP 1-75	Mn
Carter, Daniel	1st Lt	02-12-75	HA		#12	PR 118	
Carter, Edward	Ensign	17-12-81	CA	28th	Capt.T.Knotts	AM 48-27	
Carter, James E.	2nd Lt	29-06-80	QA	20th	Capt.J.Rowles	AM 43-208	
Carter, Thomas	Ensign	22-06-78	WA	2ndW	Capt.G.Swingle	AM 21-145	
Carter, William	Ensign	12-09-77	MO	29th	Capt.A.McFadon	AM 16-373	
Carter, William	Capt	04-08-80	MO	Lwr		AM 43-248	Suc
Cartrop, William Marsh	2nd Lt	16-05-76	TA	4th	Capt.Daugherty	AM 11-429	
Cartwright, John	2nd Lt	26-08-77	SM	Up	Capt.T.Reeder	AM 16-346	
Cartwright, John	1st Lt	12-09-77	MO	16th	Capt.A.Allen	AM 16-373	
Cartwright, John	1st Lt	18-11-79	SM	Up	Capt.J.H.Broome	AM 43-18	
Cartwright, William	Ensign	26-08-77	SM	Up	Capt.W.Bond	AM 16-346	
Cartwright, William	2nd Lt	18-11-79	SM	Up	Capt.E.Mattingley	AM 43-18	
Carwan, John	Ensign	20-03-76	DO		Capt.McNemara	AM 11-267	
Cary, Joshua	2nd Lt	29-08-77	BA	Town	Capt.E.Bailey	AM 16-348	
Cary, William	2nd Lt	09-04-78	CA	14th	Capt.P.Rich	AM 21-23	
Casadine, William	Ensign	31-07-78	QA	20th	Capt.J.Bordley	MH 2	Mn
Casey, Elijah	Ensign	15-06-76	WO		Capt.Shockley	AM 11-427	
Casey, John	Capt	01-05-78	PG	Midd		AM 21-63	
Cassey, John	Capt	24-05-79	PG	Midd		AM 21-414	Suc
Casson, Henry Jr.	Capt	05-01-76	CA			SP 2740	
Casson, Henry Jr.	1st Lt	13-08-77	CA	28th	Capt.W.Hopper	SC 49-154	Mn
Casson, James	2nd Lt	09-04-78	CA	28th	Capt.T.Casson	AM 21-23	
Casson, James	1st Lt	26-07-80	CA	28th	Capt.A.Jump	AM 43-230	
Casson, Thomas	Capt	09-04-78	CA	28th		AM 21-23	
Casson, Thomas	Capt	26-07-80	CA	28th		AM 43-230	Suc
Casson, Thomas	1st Lt	07-06-81	QA	5th	Capt.J.Y.Keene	AM 45-465	
Casson, Thomas	Capt	17-12-81	CA	28th		AM 48-27	Suc
Caswell, Robert	2nd Lt	17-11-79	HA	Deer	Capt.S.Bayliss	AM 43-17	
Catheel, Daniel	Ensign	28-06-77	WO			RC 2-1156	Rec
Catheel, John	1st Lt	28-06-77	WO			RC 2-1156	Mn
Catheel, Jonathan	Ensign	30-08-77	WO	Wico	Capt.E.Shockley	AM 16-351	
Cather, George	1st Lt	21-04-78	CE	Susq	Capt.J.Baker	AM 21-48	
Catrop, William Marsh	2nd Lt	09-04-78	TA	4th	Volunteer	AM 21-24	
Caughran, James	2nd Lt	07-06-81	CE	Elk	Capt.H.South	SC 48-79	OC
Caulk, John	Ensign	06-07-76	DO		Capt.Waters	AM 11-553	
Causey, Frederick	Ensign	14-05-76	CA	14th	Andrews	AM 11-424	
Causin, Gerard Blackstone	Ensign	28-05-79	CH	12th	Capt.W.Hansen	AM 21-427	
Cawood, Benjamin	Capt	- -	CH	26th		FP 1-102	Mn
Cawsey, William	Ensign	14-08-79	CA	14th	Capt.R.Andrews	AM 21-493	

APPENDIX A - COMMISSIONED OFFICERS

Name	Rank	Date	Cty	Bn	Company	Ref.	Notes
Cawsey, William	Capt	12-06-81	CA	14th	Capt.R.Andrew	MH 2	Rec
Cazier, Abraham	1st Lt	21-04-78	CE	Elk	Capt.T.Savin	AM 21-47	
Cazier, Abraham	Capt	09-09-78	CE	2nd	Capt.T.Savin	AM 21-196	OC
Cazier, Abraham	Capt	07-06-81	CE	Elk		AM 45-466	OC
Cazier, Abraham	Capt	28-06-81	CE	Elk		AM 45-489	Suc
Cellars, George	Ensign	- -	WA			FP 1-129	Mn
Cellars, John	Capt	- -	WA			FP 1-129	Mn
Certain, Robert	Capt	03-01-76	QA	5th		SC 48-78	OC
Certain, Robert	Capt	03-10-82	QA	5th		SC 48-78	Mn
Chadwick, Thomas	2nd Lt	04-09-77	BA	Town		AM 16-362	
Chaffinch, James	2nd Lt	09-04-78	CA	14th	Capt J.Douglass	AM 21-23	
Chaffinch, James	2nd Lt	- -79				FP 1-48	Res
Chaille, Moses	Lt	03-01-76				SP 967	
Chaille, Moses		27-08-76	WO			AM 12-243	Res
Chaille, Peter	Colonel	06-01-76	WO	10th		PC 80	
Chaille, Peter	Colonel	04-08-80	WO	10th		RC 3-664	Mn
Chalmers, John	1st Lt	19-08-77	DO	ES	Capt.Noel	AM 16-337	
Chamberlain, Phillip	Ensign	-05-76	BA		Capt.J.Gittings	RB 13-53	
Chamberlaine, James Lloyd	BrigGen	06-01-76				PC 78	
Chamberlaine, James Lloyd	BrigGen	26-12-76	TA			AM 12-552	Res
Chamberlaine, Philip	2nd Lt	25-05-76	BA	GP	Capt.Onion	AM 11-444	
Chambers, Benjamin	Lt Col	30-08-77	AA	7th		SC 48-77	OC
Chambers, Benjamin		03-04-78	AN			SP 6462	Res
Chambers, John Campbell	1st Lt	21-04-78	CE	Elk	Capt.A.Miller	AM 21-47	OC
Chambers, John Campbell	1st Lt	- -	CE	Elk	Capt.A.Miller	SC 48-78	Res
Chancey, John	Capt	09-09-75	HA	#4		PR 109	
Chansey, John	2nd Lt	09-04-78	HA	23rd	Capt.J.Forwood	AM 21-23	
Chaplain, ---	Capt	06-12-81	FR			AM 47-568	Mn
Chapline, James	QM	06-01-76	FR	36th		PC 79	
Chapline, James	1st Lt	04-07-76	FR	UpDt	Capt.Chapline	AM 11-546	
Chapline, James	1st Lt	22-06-78	WA	2ndW	Capt.J.Chapline	AM 21-145	
Chapline, James	Lt	30-03-81	WA	SelM	Capt.J.Chapline	AM 45-368	
Chapline, James	Lt	04-06-81	WA	SelM	Capt.Chapline	AM 47-271	Ref
Chapline, Joseph	Capt	04-07-76	FR	UpDt		AM 11-546	
Chapline, Joseph	Capt	22-06-78	WA	2ndW		AM 21-145	
Chapline, Joseph	Capt	30-03-81	WA	SelM		AM 45-368	
Chapman, John	2nd Lt	13-05-76	BA	Gist	Capt.T.Philips	RB 13-69	
Chapman, John	2nd Lt	06-06-76	BA	SD	Capt.Phillips	AM 11-467	
Chapman, John	1st Lt	30-08-77	BA	SD	Capt.Philips	AM 16-350	
Chapman, John	1st Lt	27-05-79	BA	SD	Capt.B.Tevis	AM 21-422	
Chapman, Joshua	2nd Lt	30-08-77	BA	SD	Capt.Philip	AM 16-350	
Chapman, Joshua	2nd Lt	27-05-79	BA	SD	Capt.B.Tevis	AM 21-422	
Charlton, John	1st Lt	- -	WA			FP 1-129	Mn
Charlton, John Usher	2nd Lt	29-11-75	FR	4th	Capt.P.Thomas	MM 11:50	
Charlton, John Usher	Capt	15-05-76	FR	34th		AM 11-426	
Chatham, James	Capt	03-01-76	QA		Capt.C.C.Ruth	SC 48-75	OC
Chatham, James	Capt	15-02-76	QA		Capt.C.C.Ruth	SC 48-75	Ref
Chenoweth, Arthur	2nd Lt	23-10-81	BA	GPUp		FP 1-90	Suc
Chenoweth, Arthur	1st Lt	08-02-82	BA	SD		FP 1-92	
Chenoweth, Thomas	2nd Lt	23-10-81	BA	GPUp		FP 1-91	Suc
Chenoweth, Thomas	Capt	08-02-82	BA	SD		FP 1-41	Mn
Chenoweth, William	Ensign	13-05-76	BA	Gist	Capt.I.Hammond	RB 13-69	
Chenoweth, William	2nd Lt	06-06-76	BA	SD		AM 11-468	
Chenoworth, Thomas	Ensign	27-05-79	BA	SD	Capt.M.Gosnell	AM 21-422	

APPENDIX A - COMMISSIONED OFFICERS

Name	Rank	Date	Cty	Bn	Company	Ref.	Notes
Chesley, John	2nd Lt	26-08-77	SM	Lwr	Capt.H.Hopewell	AM 16-346	
Chesley, John	Capt	07-05-81	SM	Lwr	Capt.H.Hopewell	AM 45-426	
Chew, John	Ensign	02-03-78	AA	WstR	Capt.R.Weems	AM 16-526	
Chew, John	1st Lt	02-05-81	AA	WstR	Capt.B.Harrison	AM 45-422	
Chew, Nathaniel	2nd Lt	02-05-81	AA	WstR	Capt.B.Harrison	AM 45-422	
Chew, Richard	Capt	09-03-76	AA	WstR		AM 11-231	Mn
Chew, Richard	Capt	02-03-78	AA	WstR		AM 16-526	
Chew, Richard	Capt	02-05-81	AA	WstR		AM 45-422	Suc
Chew, Samuel	B1st Lt	12-09-77	AA	31st	Capt. Dare	AM 16-372	
Chew, Samuel	2nd Lt	02-03-78	AA	WstR	Capt.R.Chew	AM 16-526	
Chew, Samuel of Richard	Capt	02-05-81	AA	WstR	Capt.Rich.Chew	AM 45-422	
Chew, William	1st Lt	02-03-78	AA	WstR	Capt.R.Chew	AM 16-526	
Chiezum, Jno	Ensign	- -	CA	14th		FP 1-48	Dec
Chiezum, John	Ensign	09-04-78	CA	14th	Capt.J.Mitchel	AM 21-23	
Chilcoat, Humphry	2nd Lt	04-02-77	BA	Gist	Capt.T.Moore	AM 16-114	
Chilcott, Humphry	1st Lt	30-08-77	BA	Up	Capt.N.Merryman	AM 16-350	
Childs, Gabriel	Ensign	16-04-78	CV	15th	Capt.T.Cleland	AM 21-37	
Chilton, John S.	2nd Lt	26-02-76	CH		Capt.W.Harrison	RC 2-142	Res
Chilton, John Steuart	Ensign	06-12-79	CH	26th		FP 1-102	Mn
Chilton, Thomas	Ensign	12-09-77	MO	16th	Capt.A.Allen	AM 16-373	
Chilton, Thomas	2nd Lt	04-08-80	MO	Up	Capt.Archd.Allen	AM 43-248	
Chinworth, Arthur	2nd Lt	23-10-81	BA	GpUp	Capt.J.Marsh	AM 45-650	
Chinworth, Arthur	1st Lt	07-02-82	BA	SD	Capt.C.Chinworth	AM 48-71	
Chinworth, Charles	Capt	07-02-81	BA	SD	Capt.B.Tevis	AM 48-71	
Chinworth, Thomas	2nd Lt	23-10-81	BA	GpUp	Capt.B.Talbot	AM 45-651	
Chinworth, William	1st Lt	07-02-82	BA	SD	Capt.W.Kelly	AM 48-71	
Chipley, John	2nd Lt	17-12-81	CA	14th	Capt.J.Mitchell	AM 48-27	
Chipley, William	2nd Lt	19-06-77	CA	28th	Capt.Hughlett	AM 16-294	
Chipley, William	Capt	14-08-79	CA	28th		AM 21-493	
Chipley, William	Capt	21-06-81	CA	28th		MH 2	Mov
Chippy, Joshua	2nd Lt	18-04-80	CA	8th	Capt.Hughlett	AM 43-144	
Chippy, Joshua	1st Lt	17-12-81	CA	28th	Capt.R.Hardcastle	AM 48-27	
Choate, Richard	Ensign	07-02-82	BA	SD	Capt.C.Chinworth	AM 48-71	
Chunn, Zachariah	2nd Lt	05-07-77	CH	12th		RC 2-1170	Mn
Clagett, Charles	2nd Lt	01-05-78	PG	Midd	Capt.J.Burgess	AM 21-63	
Clagett, Charles	Capt	13-11-79	PG	Midd	Capt.J.M.Burgess	AM 43-13	
Clagett, Richard	Ensign	24-05-79	PG	11th	Capt.H.Wheeler	AM 21-414	
Clagget, Joseph White	Capt	24-05-79	PG	Midd	Capt.H.Belt	AM 21-414	
Claggett, Alexander	1st Lt	12-09-77	MO	Midd	Capt.A.Orme	AM 16-373	
Claggett, Joseph White	2nd Lt	01-05-78	PG	Midd	Capt.H.Belt	AM 21-63	
Claggett, Thomas	Capt	- -	PG	Midd		FP 1-121	Res
Clandenin, James	Capt	17-11-79	HA	Deer	Capt.Ashmead	AM 43-17	
Clapsaddle, Daniel	Capt	26-09-76	WA			AM 12-301	
Clare, Edmund	Lt	05-07-76				RB 11	Mn
Clare, Edmund	2nd Lt	16-04-78	CV	15th	Capt.R.Parran	AM 21-37	
Clare, John	2nd Lt	10-04-76	CV		Capt.Smith	AM 11-320	
Clare, John	2nd Lt	16-04-78	CV	15th	Capt.W.Smith	AM 21-37	
Clark, Elijah	Ensign	09-04-78	CA	14th	Capt.T.Lockerman	AM 21-23	
Clark, Elijah	2nd Lt	26-07-80	CA	14th	Capt.V.Price	AM 43-230	
Clark, Elijah	1st Lt	17-12-81	CA	14th	Capt.A.Waddle	AM 48-27	
Clark, Josiah	1st Lt	01-05-78	PG	Midd	Capt.H.Belt	AM 21-63	
Clark, Samuel	1st Lt	21-04-78	CE	Susq	Capt.J.Dougharty	AM 21-48	
Clark, William	2nd Lt	25-05-76	BA	GP	Capt.Mercer	AM 11-444	
Clark, William	2nd Lt	09-04-78	HA	23rd	Capt.J.Wheeler	AM 21-24	

APPENDIX A - COMMISSIONED OFFICERS

Name	Rank	Date	Cty	Bn	Company	Ref.	Notes
Clark, William	2nd Lt	09-04-78	TA	4th	Bullinbrook	AM 21-24	
Clark, William	1st Lt	03-12-79	TA	38th	Capt.R.Johnson	AM 43-28	
Clarke, Caleb	Ensign	09-06-77	PG		Capt.M.M.Duvall	RC 2-1103	Rec
Clarkson, Henry	Capt	- -	CH	12th		MH 3	Mov
Clarkson, Henry	Capt	19-01-81	CH	12th		AM 45-280	Suc
Clarkson, Richard	2nd Lt	- -	PG	Midd		FP 1-73	Mn
Claubaugh, John	Ensign	16-08-81	FR			FP 1-108	Suc
Claxon, Richard	Ensign	01-05-78	PG	Midd	Capt.J.Casey	AM 21-63	
Claxon, Richard	2nd Lt	24-05-79	PG	Midd	Capt.E.Lanham	AM 21-414	
Clayton, Dr. Joshua	2nd Maj	06-01-76	CE	18th		PC 80	
Clayton, Joshua	Lt.Col	21-04-78	CE	Sass		AM 21-47	
Clayton, William	Capt	23-05-76	TA	4th	Capt.Joseph Bruff	AM 11-438	
Cleland, Thomas		05-07-76				RB 11	Mn
Cleland, Thomas	Capt	16-04-78	CV	15th		AM 21-37	
Cleland, Thomas	Capt	01-09-81	CV	SelM		AM 45-596	
Clem, William	2nd Lt	18-04-81	BA	Town	Capt.R.Ridgeley	AM 45-402	
Cline, Peter	1st Lt	22-06-78	FR	Ling	Capt.Collyberger	AM 21-144	
Clinton, Charles	Capt	27-07-76	FR			AM 12-127	
Clinton, Charles	Capt	13-05-78	WA		On frontier	AM 21-78	
Clinton, Charles	Capt	22-06-78	WA	3rdW		AM 21-145	
Closser, Michael	2nd Lt	22-06-78	WA	2ndW	Capt.C.Nichodemus	AM 21-145	
Coale, John	2nd Lt	19-03-79	BA	Town	Capt.J.Smith	AM 21-324	
Coale, John	2nd Lt	19-05-79	BA	Town	Capt.J.Smith	AM 21-401	
Coale, William	1st Lt	26-04-76	HA	8th	Capt. Harris	AM 11-387	
Cobble, George	1st Lt	17-01-77	FR	Ling	Capt.Henry Baker	AM 16-54	
Cochran, James	2nd Lt	21-04-78	CE	Elk	Capt.H.South	AM 21-47	
Cochran, John	Ensign	10-04-76	CE		Capt.Dobson	AM 11-320	
Cock, John	1st Lt	22-06-76	FR	37th	Capt.Snodenberry	AM 11-509	Res
Cock, Samuel	1st Lt	02-11-82	FR	Town	Capt.Edw.Salmon	AM 48-296	OC
Cockayne, Carter	Ensign	09-04-78	TA	38th	Miles River	AM 21-25	
Cockey, Edward	Colonel	12-10-76	BA	GP		AM 12-337	
Cockey, John	Capt	20-11-76	BA			AM 12-542	
Cockey, John	Capt	31-10-80	BA	GPUp		AM 43-345	Suc
Cockey, John of Thomas	1st Lt	23-10-81	BA	GPUp	Capt.W.Harvey	AM 45-650	
Cockey, Joshua	Ensign	19-12-75	BA		Capt.B.Nicholson	RB 13-37	
Cockey, Joshua	Ensign	13-05-76	BA	Gist		RB 13-69	
Cockey, Joshua of Edw.	2nd Lt	06-06-76	BA	SD	Capt.Owings	AM 11-467	
Cockey, Peter	2nd Lt	27-06-76	QA			AM 11-523	
Cockey, Thomas	2nd Lt	23-10-81	BA	GpUp	Capt.N.Kelly	AM 45-650	
Cockin, Jonathan	2nd Lt	04-11-82	TA	4th	Capt.Dorhorty	AM 48-298	
Cockran, John	Ensign	21-04-78	CE	Elk	Capt.S.Gilpin	AM 21-47	OC
Coe, Assa	2nd Lt	16-03-81	WO	Snpx	Capt.J.Tull	AM 45-353	
Coe, John	Capt	16-03-81	WO	Snpx		AM 45-353	Suc
Cole, Abraham Sr.	2nd Lt	30-08-77	BA	Up	Capt.N.Merryman	AM 16-350	
Cole, Elijah	1st Lt	10-04-76	CE		Capt.Ogleby	AM 11-320	
Cole, George	2nd Lt	07-05-81	SM	Lwr	Capt.B.Smoot	AM 45-426	
Cole, Mordecai	1st Lt	04-02-77	BA	Gist	Capt.R.Lemmon	AM 16-114	
Cole, Philip	Capt	21-04-78	CE	Susq		AM 21-48	
Cole, Philip	Capt	03-01-82	CE	Susq		AM 48-38	Suc
Cole, Thomas	1st Lt	30-03-79	AA	22nd	Capt.C.White	AM 21-333	
Cole, Thomas	1st Lt	18-05-79	AA	22nd	Capt.C.White	AM 21-398	
Cole, William	Capt	09-04-78	HA	8th		AM 21-24	
Colegate, Thomas	Ensign	20-03-79	BA	GP	Capt.W.Maccubbin	AM 21-325	
Coleson, Henry	Ensign	09-04-78	TA	38th	Hearts of Oak	AM 21-25	

APPENDIX A - COMMISSIONED OFFICERS

Name	Rank	Date	Cty	Bn	Company	Ref.	Notes
Coleston, Henry	2nd Lt	03-12-79	TA	38th	Capt.Henry Banning	AM 43-28	
Colgate, Richard	2nd Lt	19-12-75	BA		Capt.B.Nicholson	RB 13-37	
Colgate, Richard	1st Lt	06-06-76	BA	SD	Capt.Owings	AM 11-467	
Collins, Jacob	Capt	16-08-81	FR	Cato	Capt.Wm.Cormack	AM 45-566	
Collison, Richard	1st Lt	14-08-79	CA	14th	Capt.J.Mitchell	AM 21-493	
Collyburger, John	Capt	22-06-78	FR	Ling		AM 21-144	
Colvin, Philip	2nd Lt	25-06-76	BA	GP	Capt.Young	AM 11-444	
Combs, Bennett	Ensign	23-02-76	SM		Leonardtown	AM 11-181	
Combs, Bennett	2nd Lt	07-03-76	SM			AM 11-205	
Combs, Bennett	2nd Lt	26-08-77	SM	Lwr	Capt.J.Greenwell	AM 16-346	
Combs, Bennett	Capt	22-06-80	SM	Lwr	Capt.J.Greenwell	AM 43-201	
Combs, George	2nd Lt	16-04-78	SM	21st	Capt.A.H.Watts	AM 21-37	
Combs, Ignatius	2nd Lt	26-08-77	SM	Lwr	Capt.J.Armstrong	AM 16-346	
Commack, John	Capt	19-01-76	FR			SP 1596	Mn
Commegys, Cornelius	2nd Lt	20-04-80	QA	5th	Capt.J.Walters	AM 43-146	
Commegys, Samuel	1st Lt	18-09-79	KE	27th	Capt.J.Cosden	AM 21-532	
Compton, John	2nd Lt	12-05-79	FR	Town	Capt.Keepheart	AM 21-387	
Compton, John	1st Lt	18-09-80	FR	Town	Capt.G.Harding	AM 43-295	
Comyges, Jesse	2nd Lt	22-06-78	CE	Bohe	Capt.J.W.Veazey	AM 21-145	
Conner, Thomas	Ensign	20-05-76	MO	16th	Capt.Owen	AM 11-432	
Conner, Thomas	Ensign	12-09-77	MO	Midd	Capt.R.Owen	AM 16-373	
Conner, Thomas	1st Lt	21-04-79	MO	Up	Capt.N.Ray	AM 21-357	
Conner, Thomas	Capt	25-03-80	MO	Midd	Capt.N.Ray	AM 43-120	
Connerly, Jeremiah	Ensign	16-12-79	DO	Up	Capt.Jas.Wright	AM 43-37	
Connerly, Jeremiah	Ensign	23-08-81	DO	Up	Capt.W.Russum	AM 45-577	
Connolly, John	2nd Lt	09-04-78	TA	4th	Third Haven	AM 21-24	OC
Conoway, Vachel	Capt	18-10-82	AA	Svrn	Capt.J.Gray	AM 48-288	
Conrod, William	Ensign	15-01-77	WA		Capt.Peter Beall	AM 16-50	
Constable, Thomas	Ensign	23-05-81	BA	Town	Capt.J.Tool	AM 45-443	
Contee, Benjamin	1st Lt	01-05-78	PG	11th	Capt.A.Magruder	AM 21-62	
Contee, Richard	Ensign	01-05-78	PG	Midd	Capt.J.Burgess	AM 21-78	
Contee, Thomas	Lt Col	13-01-76	PG	11th		PC 86	
Conway, John Span	Capt	22-09-77	SO	Salb	Nanicoke Pt	AM 16-381	
Conway, John Span	Capt	22-08-81	SO	Salb		AM 45-575	Suc
Cook, Charles	1st Lt	16-03-76	QA		Capt.Reynolds	AM 11-253	
Cook, John	1st Lt	22-06-76		37th	Capt.Snodenbery	SP 1613	Mn
Cook, John	2nd Lt	12-09-77	MO	Midd	Capt.J.Bruce	AM 16-373	
Cook, Stanley	Lt	26-10-76		19th		SP 2633	Mn
Cooke, Charles	1st Lt	31-07-78	QA	20th	Capt.J.R.Emory	MH 2	Mn
Cooke, Charles	Capt	05-04-80	QA	20th	Capt.J.R.Emory	AM 43-130	
Cooke, John	2nd Lt	- -	MO	Up		MH 5	Dec
Cooper, Nathaniel	Capt	13-05-76	TA	4th		PC 132	
Cooper, Nathaniel	Capt	09-04-78	TA	4th	Hand in Hand	AM 21-24	
Cooper, Nathaniel	Capt	04-11-82	TA	4th		AM 48-298	Suc
Cooper, Thomas	2nd Lt	21-04-78	CE	Sass	Capt.J.Porter	AM 21-47	
Coppage, Philip	1st Lt	20-04-80	QA	5th	Capt.J.Walters	AM 43-146	
Corbet, James	Ensign	09-04-78	HA	Deer	Capt.G.Voghan	AM 21-23	OC
Corbet, William	2nd Lt	09-09-78	CE	30th	Capt.Saml.Miller	AM 21-196	
Corbitt, David	Ensign	21-04-78	CE	Susq	Capt.J.Pritchard	AM 21-48	
Cork, John	1st Lt	09-04-78	TA	38th	Broad Creek	AM 21-25	
Cormack, William	Capt	16-08-81	FR	Cato		AM 45-566	Suc
Cormacks, John	Capt	22-06-76	FR	37th		AM 11-509	
Cornall, Benjamin	1st Lt	29-11-75	FR	3rd	Capt.S.Shaw	MM 11:50	
Corner, Thomas	Ensign	- -	MO	Midd		FP 1-69	

APPENDIX A - COMMISSIONED OFFICERS

Name	Rank	Date	Cty	Bn	Company	Ref.	Notes
Corry, Benjamin Lesly	1st Lt	05-07-77	CH	12th		RC 2-1170	Rec
Corse, Barney	2nd Lt	03-01-76	KE	13th		SC 48-68	OC
Corse, Barney	2nd Lt	27-04-76	KE	13th		SC 48-68	Mov
Cosden, James	Ensign	21-04-78	CE	Sass	Capt.J.Porter	AM 21-47	
Cosden, Jesse	Capt	13-06-77	QA	5th		RC 2-1119	Mn
Cosden, Jesse	Capt	18-09-79	KE	27th		AM 21-532	
Costin, John	2nd Lt	03-01-76	QA	20th	Capt.C.Cross	SC 48-48	
Costin, John	2nd Lt	15-02-76	QA	20th	Capt.C.Cross	SC 48-48	Ref
Costin, John	Capt	16-03-76	QA		Capt.C.Ruth	AM 11-253	
Costin, John	Capt	19-06-77	QA	20th		AM 16-295	
Costin, John	Capt	31-07-78	QA	20th		MH 2	Mn
Cother, Robert	1st Lt	09-09-78	CE	30th	Capt.Saml.Miller	AM 21-196	
Cotman, Joseph	Capt	22-08-81	SO	Salb	Capt.G.Wilson	AM 45-575	
Cotman, William	2nd Lt	22-08-81	SO	Salb	Capt.J.Cotman	AM 45-575	
Cottman, Joseph	1st Lt	22-09-77	SO	Salb	Capt.G.Wilson	AM 16-382	
Cottrell, Burford	2nd Lt	07-03-76	CH		Capt.Philpot	AM 11-206	
Coughran, James	2nd Lt	07-06-81	CE	Elk	Capt.H.South	AM 45-466	
Coughran, John	Ensign	07-06-81	CE	Elk	Capt.S.Gilpin	AM 45-466	
Coulston, Charles	Capt	13-05-78	WA		On frontier	AM 21-80	
Coulter, Samuel	2nd Lt	21-04-78	CE	Susq	Capt.J.Pritchard	AM 21-48	
Coursey, Henry	2nd Lt	31-07-78	QA	20th	Capt.J.Dawes	MH 2	Mn
Coursey, Henry	1st Lt	05-04-80	QA	20th	Capt.R.Carmichael	AM 43-130	
Coursey, Henry	Capt	07-06-81	QA	20th	Capt.R.Carmichael	AM 45-465	
Coursey, William	Capt	17-12-81	CA	14th	Capt.R.Andrews	AM 48-27	
Coursey, William	1st Lt	17-12-81	CA	28th	Capt.T.Knotts	AM 48-27	
Courtnay, Hercules	Ensign	25-09-80	BA	Town	Capt.B.Griffith	AM 43-303	
Courts, Richard Hendly	1st Lt	07-03-76	CH		Capt.Yates	AM 11-206	
Courts, Richard Hendley	1st Lt	24-01-79	MO			RC 2-1714	Mn
Covington, Edward	Ensign	20-04-80	QA	5th	Capt.S.Ridgeway	AM 43-146	
Covington, Henry	2nd Lt	20-04-80	QA	5th	Capt.W.Falconer	AM 43-146	
Covington, L.	Capt	19-09-76	PG			AM 12-285	Mn
Cowan, Alexander	1st Lt	16-09-75	HA		#6	PR 112	.
Cowan, Alexander	Colonel	09-04-78	HA	8th		AM 21-24	
Coward, Thomas	1st Lt	16-05-76	TA	4th	Capt.Lloyd	AM 11-428	
Cowen, Alexander	Capt	26-04-76	HA			AM 11-267	
Cox, Abraham	2nd Lt	20-11-76	BA		Capt.D.Shaw	AM 12-541	
Cox, Abraham	2nd Lt	16-05-78	WA	3rdW	Capt.P.Pindell	AM 21-86	
Cox, Asa	Ensign	30-08-77	WO	Snpx	Capt.J.Cox	AM 16-350	
Cox, Ezekial	2nd Lt	27-07-76	FR			AM 12-127	
Cox, James	Capt	19-12-75	BA			RB 13-37	
Cox, James	Capt	02-03-76	BA			AM 11-197	
Cox, James	Maj	12-09-77	BA	SD		AM 16-372	
Cox, James	Maj	04-10-77	BA	SD		ST 69	Kil
Cox, John	1st Lt	29-11-75	FR	2nd	Capt.Snowdenburger	MM 11:50	
Cox, John	Capt	30-08-77	WO	Snpx		AM 16-350	
Cox, John	Capt	21-04-78	CE	Sass		AM 21-47	
Cox, Thomas	2nd Lt	23-10-81	BA	GPUp	Capt.S.Gill	AM 45-651	
Crabb, Ralph	2nd Lt	09-06-77	PG		Capt.T.Richardson	RC 2-1103	Suc
Crabb, Richard	2nd Maj	06-01-76	MO	16th		PC 79	
Crabb, Richard	1st Lt	18-03-76	PG	25th	Capt.Richardson	AM 11-260	
Crabs, Christian	Ensign	28-11-76	FR	35th	Capt.Hawkersmith	AM 12-555	
Cradock, John	1st Maj	25-05-76	BA	SD		AM 11-443	
Cradock, John	1st Maj	01-07-76	BA	SD		AM 11-539	Res
Craford, James	Ensign	09-09-78	CE	30th	Capt.Wm.Ewing	AM 21-196	

APPENDIX A - COMMISSIONED OFFICERS

Name	Rank	Date	Cty	Bn	Company	Ref.	Notes
Craige, Adam	Ensign	24-06-80	PG	Up	Capt.W.Moore	AM 43-203	
Cramphin, Richard	Ensign	24-05-79	PG	25th	Capt.J.Shaw	AM 21-414	
Cramphin, Richard	1st Lt	24-06-80	PG	Up	Capt.W.Moore	AM 43-203	
Cramplim, Thomas	Ensign	30-03-81	WA	SM	Capt.J.Campline	AM 45-368	
Crampton, James	2nd Lt	04-07-76	FR	UpDt	Capt.Chapline	AM 11-546	
Crampton, Thomas	2nd Lt	22-06-78	WA	2ndW	Capt.J.Chapline	AM 21-145	
Crampton, Thomas	Lt	04-06-81	WA	SelM	Capt.J.Chapline	AM 45-458	
Crandel, William	2nd Lt	02-03-78	AA	WstR	Capt.J.Deale	AM 16-526	
Crane, David	Capt	09-09-78	KE	13th		AM 21-196	
Crane, Michael	Capt	16-03-79	BA	Town		FP 1-93	
Crawford, David	Capt	23-08-76				AM 12-233	Mn
Crawford, Nathaniel	2nd Lt	12-09-77	MO	Midd	Capt.S.West	AM 16-373	
Crawford, Nathaniel	1st Lt	21-04-79	MO	Midd	Capt.John Ray	AM 21-357	
Creagar, Lawrence	Ensign	15-04-78	FR	Town	Capt.J.Crist	AM 21-35	
Creagar, Valentine	Capt	03-10-76	FR			AM 12-317	
Creager, Adam	Ensign	29-11-75	FR	2nd	Capt.V.Creager	MM 11:50	
Creager, Michael	Ensign	15-04-78	FR	37th	Capt.J.Crist	AM 21-35	
Creager, Valentine	Capt	29-11-75	FR	2nd		MM 11:50	
Creekpaum, Conrad	1st Lt	27-04-79	FR	37th	Capt.J.Trout	AM 21-368	
Cregar, Valentine	Capt	29-06-82	FR	Cato		AM 48-203	Suc
Cresap, Daniel	Capt	27-07-76	FR			AM 12-127	
Cresap, Daniel	Capt	13-05-78	WA		On frontier	AM 21-80	
Cresap, Daniel	Capt	22-06-78	WA	3rdW		AM 21-145	
Creton, James	Ensign	17-11-79	HA	Deer	Capt.J.Clandenin	AM 43-17	
Crickbone, Conrad	Ensign	29-11-75	FR	1st	Capt.C.Stull	MM 11:50	
Crist, Jacob	Capt	15-04-78	FR	37th		AM 21-35	
Crist, Philip	Ensign	27-04-79	FR	37th		AM 21-368	
Crockett, Samuel	2nd Lt	21-04-78	CE	Susq	Capt.P.Cole	AM 21-48	
Cromwell, Francis	1st Lt	02-03-78	AA	Svrn	Capt.Maccubbin	AM 16-575	
Cromwell, Francis	Capt	22-05-79	AA	7th	Capt.J.McCubbin	AM 21-410	
Cromwell, Francis	Capt	18-10-82	AA	Svrn		AM 48-288	Suc
Cromwell, Joshua	Ensign	22-02-76	AA	Svrn	Capt.Watts	AM 11-178	
Cromwell, Joshua	2nd Lt	11-04-76	AA	Svrn	Capt.Watts	AM 11-327	
Cromwell, Rd	1st Lt	12-06-77	AA	7th	Capt.Owens	AM 16-286	
Cromwell, Richard	1st Lt	20-11-76	BA		Capt.L.Wiley	AM 12-542	
Cromwell, Richard	1st Lt	02-03-78	AA	Svrn	Capt.C.Owings	AM 16-525	
Cromwell, Richard	Capt	31-10-80	BA	GPUp	Capt.L.Wylie	AM 43-345	
Cromwell, Richard	Capt	23-10-81	BA	GPUp		AM 45-650	Suc
Cromwell, Stephen	2nd Maj	12-10-76	BA	GP		AM 12-337	
Cromwell, William	Capt	19-12-75	BA			RB 13-37	
Cromwell, William	Capt	25-05-76	BA	GP		AM 11-444	Mn
Cross, Joseph	Lt	15-06-81	PG	SelM	Capt.O.Williams	AM 45-475	
Crouch, Azel	Ensign	- -	AA	Svrn		FP 1-38	Mn
Crouse, Jacob	2nd Lt	17-01-77	FR	Ling	Capt.B.Dorsey	AM 16-55	
Crouse, John	2nd Lt	22-06-78	FR	Ling	Capt.Gobble	AM 21-145	
Crow, Edward	1st Lt	20-05-76	MO	16th	Capt.Owens	AM 11-432	
Crow, Edward Jr	1st Lt	12-09-77	MO	Midd	Capt.R.Owen	AM 16-373	
Crow, John	2nd Lt	24-05-79	PG	25th	Capt.T.Beall	AM 21-414	
Crow, Samuel	2nd Lt	21-04-79	MO	Midd	Capt.N.Ray	AM 21-357	
Crow, Samuel	1st Lt	25-03-80	MO	Midd	Capt.T.Conner	AM 43-120	
Crow, Thomas	1st Lt	04-06-78	KE	13th	Capt.S.Wickes	AM 21-122	
Crush, Adam	1st Lt	28-12-76	FR	33rd		AM 12-557	Ref
Cullem, George	1st Lt	26-03-76	MO		Capt.Riggs	AM 11-287	
Cullom, George	1st Lt	04-09-77	MO	16th	Capt.T.Wilcoxen	AM 16-362	

APPENDIX A - COMMISSIONED OFFICERS

Name	Rank	Date	Cty	Bn	Company	Ref.	Notes
Cullom, George	1st Lt	12-09-77	MO	Midd	Capt.A.Riggs	AM 16-373	
Cullom, George	Capt	21-04-79	MO	Midd	Capt.A.Riggs	AM 21-357	
Cullum, George	Capt	25-03-80	MO	Up		AM 43-120	Suc
Cummins, Anthony	1st Lt	04-12-78	BA	Up	Capt.B.Merryman	AM 21-257	
Cummins, James	Ensign	21-04-78	CE	Susq	Capt.J.Maxwell	AM 21-48	
Cummins, Robert	Capt	30-08-77	BA	Up		AM 16-350	
Cunningham, John	Ensign	09-04-78	HA	Deer	Capt.J.Jolly	AM 21-23	
Curtis, Isaac	Ensign	07-12-78	SO	PrAn	Capt.T.King	AM 21-260	
Curtis, Isaac	Lt	23-08-81	SO	SelM	Capt.J.Williams	AM 45-577	
Curtis, James	Ensign	19-09-76	SO	17th		AM 12-285	
Curtis, James	Ensign	22-09-77	SO	PrAn	Capt.W.Waters	AM 16-381	OC
Curtis, James	Ensign	07-12-78	SO	PrAn	Capt.I.Handy	AM 21-260	
Curtis, James	2nd Lt	07-01-78	SO	Salb	Capt.W.Waters	AM 16-457	OC
Daffin, Charles	Cornet	15-06-81	CA		Horse troop	AM 45-475	
Daffin, Joseph	Capt	20-05-78	DO	3rd		AM 21-98	
Daffin, Joseph	Maj	28-07-80	DO	Up		AM 43-236	
Daffon, Robert	2nd Lt	07-05-81	SM	Lwr	Capt.J.Chesley	AM 45-426	
Dail, William	1st Lt	20-05-78	DO	19th	Capt.A.Wheatley	AM 21-97	
Dail, William	1st Lt	16-12-79	DO	Lwr	Capt.A.Wheatly	AM 43-37	
Dale, Thomas	2nd Lt	16-03-81	WO	Snpx	Capt.I.Evans	AM 45-353	
Dallam, Richard	Cty Lt	29-11-77	HA			AM 16-429	
Dallam, Winston	1st Lt	01-04-76	HA		#17	PR 122	
Dallam, Wm. Stone	1st Lt	09-04-78	HA	Deer	Capt.J.Patrick	AM 21-23	
Dallum, Richard	QM	06-01-76	HA	23rd		PC 80	
Dallum, Winston	1st Lt	26-04-76	HA		Capt.Patrick	AM 11-387	
Dames, James	Capt	05-04-80	QA	20th		AM 43-130	Suc
Dare, Gideon	1st Lt	17-04-76	AA		Capt.Weems	AM 11-336	
Dare, Gideon	1st Lt	02-03-78	AA	WstR	Capt.R.Weems	AM 16-525	
Dare, William	1st Lt	16-06-78	CV		Capt.Fred.Skinner	AM 21-137	
Darnall, Henry	2nd Maj	06-01-76	FR	34th		PC 79	
Dashiell, Arthur	1st Lt	19-08-76	SO	1st	Capt. J.Philips	AM 12-220	
Dashiell, George	Colonel	06-01-76	SO			PC 80	
Dashiell, George	Cty Lt	01-07-77	SO			AM 16-304	
Dashiell, John	2nd Lt	19-08-76	SO	1st		AM 12-220	
Dashiell, John	1st Lt	22-09-77	SO	PrAn	Capt.T.Irving	AM 16-381	
Dashiell, John	2nd Lt	22-09-77	SO	Salb	Capt.R.Dashiell	AM 16-382	
Dashiell, John	1st Lt	20-04-78	SO	Salb	Salisbury	AM 21-42	
Dashiell, John	1st Lt	27-05-79	WO	Wico	Capt.R.Hands	AM 21-423	
Dashiell, Joseph	Lt Col	06-01-76	WO	10th		PC 80	
Dashiell, Joseph	Colonel	03-02-77	WO			AM 16-110	
Dashiell, Joseph	Cty Lt	01-07-77	WO			AM 16-304	
Dashiell, Josiah	Capt	22-09-77	SO	Salb	Wicomico	AM 16-382	
Dashiell, Josiah	Capt	27-05-79	WO	Snpx	Capt.Bridles	AM 21-423	
Dashiell, Robert	Capt	22-09-77	SO	Salb	Salisbury	AM 16-382	OC
Dashiell, Robert	Capt	- -	SO	Salb		SC 48-151	Res
Dashiell, Robert	Ensign	22-09-77	SO	Salb	Capt.H.Gale	AM 16-381	
Dashiell, Wm. Francis	Ensign	22-08-81	SO	Salb	Capt.J.McCloster	AM 45-575	
Daugherty, John	Capt	13-05-76	TA	4th		AM 11-429	
Daugherty, John	Capt	13-05-76	TA	4th		PC 132	Mn
Davidge, Robert	Ensign	19-09-78	AA	7th	Capt.H.Bateman	AM 21-208	
Davidson, John	3rd Lt	06-10-77	AN		Capt.N.Maccubbin	AM 16-392	
Davidson, John	2nd Lt	20-03-79	AN		Capt.Brice-Ind.	AM 21-325	

APPENDIX A - COMMISSIONED OFFICERS

Name	Rank	Date	Cty	Bn	Company	Ref.	Notes
Davidson, John	1st Lt	12-02-80	AN		Capt.S.Howard-Ind	AM 43-84	
Davidson, Samuel	2nd Lt	06-07-76	DO	3rd	Capt.McBridge	AM 11-553	
Davis, Alexander	Ensign	29-08-77	BA	SD	Capt.W.Hudson	AM 16-348	
Davis, Amos	Asst QM	01-09-77			marching troops	AM 16-356	
Davis, Amos	1st Lt	22-06-78	WA	2ndW	Capt.J.Spires	AM 21-145	
Davis, Griffith	Ensign	21-04-79	MO	Up	Capt.C.Bruce	AM 21-357	
Davis, Griffith	1st Lt	04-08-80	MO	Midd	Capt.Lodowick Yost	AM 43-248	
Davis, James	1st Lt	13-08-76			Capt.J.Todd	SP 299	Mn
Davis, James	1st Lt	24-06-78	DO		Capt.J.Todd	AM 21-148	
Davis, Jesse	1st Lt	15-05-76	WO	10th	Capt.Gray	AM 11-426	
Davis, John	Ensign	28-06-77	WO			RC 2-1156	Rec
Davis, John	1st Lt	30-08-77	WO	Wico	Capt.I.Houston	AM 16-351	
Davis, John	Capt	27-05-79	WO	Wico	Capt.I.Houston	AM 21-423	
Davis, Lodwick	2nd Lt	21-04-79	MO	Midd	Capt.C.Bruce	AM 21-357	
Davis, Nixon	2nd Lt	30-08-77	WO	SnH1	Capt.J.Stewart	AM 16-351	
Davis, Philemon	2nd Lt	31-07-78	QA	20th	Capt.John Costin	AM 21-172	
Davis, Philip	Capt	04-06-78	KE	13th		AM 12-122	
Davis, Rezin	Ensign	21-02-76	FR		Capt.Young	AM 11-178	Mn
Davis, Richard	1st Maj	06-01-76	FR	36th		PC 79	
Davis, Richard	Lt Col	20-04-76	FR	36th		AM 11-356	
Davis, Richard	2nd Lt	06-06-76	BA	SD	Capt.Hammond	AM 11-467	
Davis, Richard	1st Lt	29-08-77	BA	SD	Capt.M.Gosnell	AM 16-348	
Davis, Robert Pain	1st Lt	17-03-81	AA	WstR	Capt.S.Watkins	AM 45-354	
Davis, Robert Pain	1st Lt	21-04-81	AA	WstR	Capt.S.Watkins	AM 47-182	Res
Davis, Robert Paine	Ensign	17-08-79	AA	WstR	Capt.T.Watkins	AM 21-496	
Davis, William	Ensign	04-02-77	BA	Gist	Capt.J.Hall	AM 16-114	
Davis, William	2nd Lt	30-08-77	BA	Up	Capt.T.Marshall	AM 16-350	
Davis, William	Ensign	02-03-78	AA	WstR	Capt.T.Watkins	AM 16-525	
Davis, William	1st Lt	05-11-81	BA	Up	Capt.P.Stilts	AM 45-662	
Dawes, John	Capt	31-07-78	QA	20th		MH 2	Mn
Dawes, John	Maj	05-04-80	QA	20th		AM 43-130	
Dawson, George	Capt	09-04-78	TA	38th	Bay Side	AM 21-24	
Dawson, George	Capt	04-11-82	TA	38th		AM 48-298	Suc
Dawson, John	Ensign	14-05-76	CA	14th	Capt.Douglass	AM 11-424	
Dawson, John	2nd Lt	09-04-78	CA	14th	Capt.H.McBride	AM 21-23	
Dawson, John Impey	2nd Lt	23-05-76	TA	38th	Capt.Haddaman	AM 11-438	
Dawson, Joseph	1st Lt	09-04-81	AN		Capt.S.H.Howard	AM 45-355	
Dawson, Robert	Ensign	05-04-80	QA	20th	Capt.R.Carmichael	AM 43-130	
Dawson, Thomas		14-08-77	TA			AM 16-334	Mn
Day, John	Ensign	09-04-78	HA	8th	Capt.S.G.Osburn	AM 21-24	
Day, John	Capt	11-03-79	KE	27th		AM 21-319	
Day, John Jr.	Capt	04-04-81	HA	8th	Capt.S.G.Osborne	AM 45-375	
Deakins, Francis	1st Maj	06-01-76	MO	16th		PC 79	
Deakins, Francis	Capt	20-02-76	MO			SP 1105	Suc
Deakins, Francis	Lt Col	12-09-77	MO	16th		AM 16-373	
Deakins, Francis	Colonel	07-10-77	MO	16th		AM 16-392	OC
Deakins, Francis	Colonel	20-12-77	MO	16th		SP 5488	Res
Deakins, William 2nd	2nd Maj	06-01-76	MO	29th		PC 79	
Deakins, William Jr.	Lt Col	21-06-77	MO	29th		AM 16-296	
Deakins, William	Lt Col	12-09-77	MO	29th		AM 16-373	OC
Deakins, William	Lt Col	-05-82	MO	29th		SC 48-150	Res
Deal, Josiah	2nd Lt	30-08-77	WO	Snpx	Capt.E.Briddell	AM 16-350	
Deal, Joshua	1st Lt	23-05-79	WO	Sinx	Capt.Brindel	RC 3-415	Mov
Deale, John	Capt	09-03-76	AA	WstR		AM 11-231	Mn

APPENDIX A - COMMISSIONED OFFICERS

Name	Rank	Date	Cty	Bn	Company	Ref.	Notes
Deale, John	Capt	02-03-78	AA	WstR		AM 16-526	
Deames, Frederick	Capt	12 04-81	BA	Town	Capt.G.Ackerman	AM 45-393	
Deams, Frederick	Capt	27-05-76				AM 11-448	Mn
Dean, John	Capt	03-01-76	QA	5th		SC 48-148	OC
Deans, Frederick	Capt	06-06-76	BA	Town		AM 11-467	
Death Jacob	Ensign	09-09-78	CE	30th	Capt.Robt.Porter	AM 21-196	
Deaver, John	2nd Lt	---04-76	BA		Capt.W.Galbraith	RB 13-74	
Deaver, John	2nd Lt	06-06-76	BA	Town	Capt.Galbraith	AM 11-467	
Deaver, John	1st Lt	05-09-77	BA	Town	Capt.W.Galbraith	AM 16-363	
Deaver, John	Capt	19-03-79	BA	Town	Capt.Wm.Galbreath	AM 21-324	
Deaver, John	Capt	24-04 81	BA	Town		AM 45-416	Dis
Deaver Richard Jr.	2nd Lt	02-12-75	HA		#12	PR 118	
Deavor, John	Capt	19-05-79	BA	Town	Capt.W.Gailbreath	AM 21-401	
Decker, Frederick	Lt Col	04-02-77	BA	Gist		AM 16-114	
Deems, Frederick	Capt	25-09-80	BA	Town		SC 48-147	OC
Delahay, James	2nd Lt	09-04-78	TA	38th	Oxford	AM 21-25	
Delaplain, Joshua	Ensign	29-11-75	FR	2nd	Capt.J.Carmack	MM 11:50	
Delihay, Thomas	2nd Lt	16-05-76	TA	38th	Capt.Martin	AM 11-428	
Delophain Joshua	Ensign	19-06-76	FR		Capt.Commack	SP 1596	Ref
Demmick, William	Ensign	19-08-76	SO	1st		AM 12-220	
Demmitt, John	Ensign	06-06-76	BA	Town	Capt.Dean	AM 11-467	
Dennis, Benjamin	Capt	21-06-76	WO			AM 11-506	
Dennis, Benjamin	Capt	30-08-77	WO	Wico		AM 16-351	
Dennis, Daniel	1st Lt	23-05-81	BA	Town	Capt.J.Tool	AM 45-443	
Dennis, Daniel	Capt	20-08-81	BA	Town	Capt.J.Toole	AM 45-572	
Dennis, Henry	2nd Lt	30-08-77	WO	SnH1	Capt.T.Marshall	AM 16-351	
Dennis, William	Ensign	30-08-77	WO	Wico	Capt.I.Houston	AM 16-351	
Dennis, William	2nd Lt	27-05-79	WO	Wico	Capt.J.Davis	AM 21-423	
Dennis, William	2nd Lt	09-05-81	BA	Town	Capt.J.Tool	AM 45-429	OC
Denny, Peter	Ensign	19-06-77	QA	20th	Capt.Noble	AM 16-295	
Dent, George	1st Lt	07-03-76	CH		Capt.Marshall	AM 11-206	
Dent, George Jr.	1st Lt	07-03-76	CH		Capt.Winters	AM 11-206	
Dent, George Jr.	Capt	09-05-78	CH	26th		AM 21-72	
Dent, George of John	Capt	09-05-78	CH	26th		AM 21-72	
Dent, Henry	1st Lt	07-03-76	CH			AM 11-206	
Dent, Henry	Capt	09-02-81	CH	12th	Capt.B.Philpot	AM 45-307	
Dent, Hezekiah	2nd Lt	05-07-77	CH	12th		RC 2-1170	Mn
Dent, Hezekiah	1st Lt	22-10-77	CH	Lwr		AM 16-401	
Dent, Hezekiah	Capt	28-05-79	CH	12th		AM 21-427	
Dent, John	Capt	06-01-76	CH			AM 11-186	Mn
Dent, John	BrigGen	06-01-76				PC 78	OC
Dent, Joseph Manning	Ensign	28-05-79	CH	12th	Capt.H.Dent	AM 21-427	
Dent, Thomas	Capt	01-08-77	PG	Lwr		AM 16-356	
Dent, Thomas	Capt	01-05-78	PG	11th		AM 21-62	
Denwood, John	1st Lt	22-09-77	SO	PrAn	Capt.J.Jones	AM 16-381	
Derbin, Thomas	1st Lt	28-11-76	FR	35th	Capt.Little	AM 12-555	
Derr, John Martin	Capt	- -	FR			FP 1-108	Mn
Devilbiss, Frederick	Ensign	29-06-82	FR	Cato	Capt.P.Barrick	AM 48-203	
Devorix, Valentine	2nd Lt	22-10-77	QA	5th	Capt.G.Findley	AM 16-403	
Dew, Andrew	2nd Lt	03-12-76	WA		Capt.G.Johnson	AM 12-501	
Diamond, William	Ensign	07-06-81	QA	20th	Capt.H.Coursey	AM 45-465	
Dickerson, John	Ensign	12-09-77	MO	Midd	Capt.N.Pigman	AM 16-373	
Dickinson, Brittingham	Capt Lt	27-09-75	BA		Artillery	RB 13-36	
Dickinson, Brittingham	1st Lt	06-06-76	BA	Town	Capt.Sheaf	AM 11-467	

APPENDIX A - COMMISSIONED OFFICERS

Name	Rank	Date	Cty	Bn	Company	Ref.	Notes
Dickinson, Brittingham	Capt	29-08-77	BA	Town		AM 16-348	
Dickinson, Henry	Lt Col	12-01-76	CA	14th		PC 78	
Dickinson, Henry	Lt Col	24-06-77	CA	14th		AM 16-299	Suc
Dickinson, Henry	Capt	15-06-81	CA		Horse troop	AM 45-475	
Dickinson, John	Lt Col	10-02-76	DO	3rd		AM 11-147	
Dickinson, John	Colonel	20-05-78	DO	3rd		AM 21-97	
Dickinson, John	Capt	20-05-78	DO	Up		DO 229	Mn
Dickinson, John	1st Lt	21-04-79	MO	Midd	Capt.B.Gaither	AM 21-357	
Dickinson, John	Capt	25-03-80	MO	Midd	Capt.B.Gaither	AM 43-120	
Dickinson, William	Ensign	09-04-78	CA	28th	Capt.J.Reynolds	AM 21-23	
Dickinson, William	1st Lt	14-08-79	CA	28th	Capt.D.Robertson	AM 21-493	
Dickinson, Zadock	Ensign	25-03-80	MO	Midd	Capt.J.Dickinson	AM 43-120	
Diggs, Joseph	Surgeon	04-09-77			Marching militia	AM 16-362	
Dimmit, John	Ensign	- -	BA	Town		FP 1-93	Mn
Dixon, Benjamin	1st Lt	09-04-78	CA	14th	Capt.P.Rich	AM 21-23	
Dixon, Isaac	Ensign	27-05-79	WO	Wico	Capt.Horsey	AM 21-423	
Dixon, Joseph	Ensign	18-04-80	CA	8th	Capt.Postlewait	AM 43-144	Mn
Dixon, Nixon	1st Lt	16-03-81	WO	SnHl	Capt.B.Townsend	AM 45-353	
Dixon, Samuel	2nd Lt	19-09-76	SO	17th	Capt B.Schoolfield	AM 12-285	
Dixon, Samuel	1st Lt	22-09-77	SO	PrAn	Capt.W.Waters	AM 16-381	OC
Dixon, Samuel	2nd Lt	07-01-78	SO	PrAn	Capt.W.Waters	AM 16-457	
Dixon, Thomas	2nd Lt	07-12-78	SO	PrAn		AM 21-260	
Dixon, William	Ensign	22-09-77	SO	PrAn	Capt.H.Miles	AM 16-381	
Dobson, ----	Capt	10-04-76	CE			AM 11-320	
Doll, Conrod	1st Lt	12-05-79	FR	Town	Capt.T.Beatty	AM 21-387	
Doll, Conrod	Lt	03-08-81	FR	SelM	Capt.T.Beatty	AM 45-538	
Doll, Joseph	2nd Lt	- -	FR	Town		FP 1-106	Mn
Done, John	1st Maj	06-01-76	WO	10th		PC 80	
Done, John	Lt Col	03-02-77	WO			AM 16-110	
Done, John	Colonel	30-08-77	WO	SnHl		AM 16-350	OC
Done, John	Colonel	29-09-78	WO	SnHl		AM 21-256	Res
Done, John	Colonel	22-08-81	SO	PrAn		AM 45-575	
Done, Robert	2nd Maj	06-01-76	WO	10th		PC 80	
Done, Robert	1st Maj	03-02-77	WO			AM 16-110	
Done, Robert	Lt Col	30-08-77	WO	SnHl		AM 16-350	
Done, Robert	Colonel	03-12-78	WO	SnHl		AM 21-256	
Dor, John Martin	2nd Lt	29-11-75	FR	2nd	Capt.Jas.Johnson	MM 11:50	
Dorhorty, John	Capt	09-04-78	TA	4th	Volunteer	AM 21-24	
Dornbough, John	Ensign	29-08-77	BA	SD	Capt.M.Gosnell	AM 16-348	
Dorner, Michael	Ensign	- -	WA			FP 1-129	Suc
Dorsen, Benoni	Ensign	25-03-80	MO	Up	Capt.B.Mockby	AM 43-120	
Dorsett, William N.	2nd Lt	16-03-76	PG			AM 11-253	
Dorsey, Basil	Capt	29-11-75	FR			MM 11:50	
Dorsey, Basil	Capt	28-11-76	FR			AM 12-555	
Dorsey, Basil	Capt	17-01-77	FR	Ling		AM 16-55	
Dorsey, Basil	Capt	11-03-77	FR			RC 2-938	Res
Dorsey, Caleb	2nd Lt	28-02-76	AA	ElkR	Capt.Stringer	AM 11-191	
Dorsey, Daniel	Capt	24-07-76				AM 12-109	Mn
Dorsey, Elias	Maj	27-11-81	BA	SD		AM 48-5	
Dorsey, Elie	Capt	27-05-79	BA	SD	Capt.R.Owings	AM 21-422	
Dorsey, Elie	Capt	07-02-82	BA	SD		AM 48-71	Suc
Dorsey, Elisha	1st Lt	11-09-77	BA	SD	Capt.C.Owing	AM 16-369	
Dorsey, Greenbury	Capt	31-10-75	HA		Co.8	PR 114	
Dorsey, Greenbury	Capt	19-12-77	HA	23rd		PA	Res

APPENDIX A - COMMISSIONED OFFICERS

Name	Rank	Date	Cty	Bn	Company	Ref.	Notes
Dorsey, Henry of Joshua	2nd Lt	08-10-82	AA	E1kR	Capt.C.White	AM 48-276	
Dorsey, John	Lt Col	12-06-76	AA	E1kR		PC 78	
Dorsey, John	Lt Col	02-03-78	AA	E1kR		AM 16-525	OC
Dorsey, John	Capt	02-03-78	AA	E1kR		AM 16-525	OC
Dorsey, John	Lt Col	11-06-78	AA	E1kR		SC 48-143	Res
Dorsey, John	Capt	05-09-78	AA	E1kR		SC 48-142	Res
Dorsey, John Worthington	2nd Lt	06-06-76	BA	SD	Capt.Stinchcomb	AM 11-467	
Dorsey, John Worthington	Capt	02-03-78	AA	E1kR		AM 16-525	
Dorsey, Joshua	1st Lt	06-06-76	BA	SD	Capt.Phillip	AM 11-467	
Dorsey, Lacon	Ensign	22-06-78	WA	2ndW	Capt.J.Spires	AM 21-145	
Dorsey, Thomas	Capt	- -75	AA			AM 11-433	Mn
Dorsey, Thomas	Colonel	12-01-76	AA	E1kR		PC 78	
Dorsey, Thomas	Colonel	02-03-78	AA	E1kR		AM 16-525	
Dorsey, Thomas	Colonel	11-06-78	AA	E1kR		PA	Res
Douden, John	2nd Lt	21-04-79	MO	Up	Capt.Wm.Blackmore	AM 21-356	
Dougharty, James	Capt	21-04-78	CE	Susq		AM 21-48	
Douglas, George Sewall	2nd Lt	06-06-76	BA	Town	Capt.W.Richardson	AM 11-467	
Douglass, George Sewall	Capt	19-03-79	BA	Town	Capt.Wm.Richardson	AM 21-324	
Douglass, James	Capt	09-04-78	CA	14th		AM 21-23	
Douglass, James	Capt	28-06-80	CA	14th		AM 43-207	Suc
Douglass, Joseph	Capt	14-05-76	CA	14th		AM 11-424	
Douglass, Joseph	Capt	14-08-79	CA	14th	Capt.H.McBride	AM 21-493	
Douglass, Joseph	Capt	17-12-81	CA	14th		AM 48-27	Suc
Douglass, Robert	2nd Lt	23-06-78	WA	1stW	Capt.Saml.Hughes	AM 21-147	
Dowden, John	1st Lt	25-03-80	MO	Up	Capt.G.Hoskinson	AM 43-120	
Dowden, Michael	2nd Lt	12-09-77	MO	16th	Capt.S.Simpson	AM 16-373	
Dowley, Daniel	Ensign	-04-76	BA	Town	Capt.J.Sterrett	RB 13-74	
Downes, Aaron	Ensign	14-08-79	CA	28th	Capt.D.Robertson	AM 21-493	
Downes, Aaron	2nd Lt	17-12-81	CA	28th	Capt.D.Robinson	AM 48-27	
Downes, Charles	Capt	31-07-78	QA	20th		AM 21-172	
Downes, George	1st Lt	30-08-77	WO	Wico	Capt.B.Dennis	AM 16-351	
Downes, Henry	Capt	02-08-75	CA			AM 11-48	Mn
Downes, Henry	2nd Maj	12-01-76	CA	28th		PC 78	OC
Downes, Henry	Adj	30-08-76	CA	28th		AM 12-248	
Downes, Henry	Capt	13-08-77	CA	28th		SC 49-154	Mn
Downes, Henry	Maj	09-04-78	CA	28th		AM 21-23	
Downes, Henry	2nd Maj	29-09-78				MH 5	Res
Downes, Henry	Lt Col	17-12-81	CA	28th		AM 48-27	
Downes, Levin	2nd Lt	31-07-78	QA	20th	Capt.N.Noble	MH 2	Mn
Downes, Levin	1st Lt	31-07-78	QA	20th	Capt.N.Noble	AM 21-172	
Downes, Philemon	Ensign	31-07-78	QA	20th	Capt.J.Dawes	MH 2	Mn
Downes, Philemon	Capt	17-12-81	CA	28th	Capt.T.Casson	AM 48-27	
Downes, Vachel	Capt	20-04-80	QA	5th		AM 43-146	Suc
Downes, Vachel	Maj	21-06-80	QA	5th		AM 43-200	
Downes, William	2nd Lt	26-04-76	HA	8th	Capt.Harris	AM 11-387	
Downes, William	1st Lt	09-04-78	HA	8th	Capt.W.Cole	AM 21-24	
Downey, Thomas	2nd Lt	01-02-82	BA	Uppr	Capt.R.Lemmon	AM 48-65	
Dowry, James	2nd Lt	09-04-78	TA	38th	Broad Creek	AM 21-25	
Doyle, Thomas	Ensign	06-06-76	BA	SD	Capt.Carnan	AM 11-467	
Drane, James Jr.	2nd Lt	13-11-79	PG	Midd	Capt.C.Clagett	AM 43-13	
Driver, Christopher	Ensign	09-03-76	CA		Capt.Haslet	AM 11-230	
Driver, Christopher	1st Lt	10-04-76	CA		Capt.Haslet	AM 11-320	
Driver, Matthew	2nd Maj	12-01-76	CA	14th		PC 78	
Driver, Matthew	Lt Col	24-06-77	CA	14th		AM 16-299	

APPENDIX A - COMMISSIONED OFFICERS

Name	Rank	Date	Cty	Bn	Company	Ref.	Notes
Driver, Matthew	Colonel	09-04-78	CA	14th		AM 21-23	
Drury, Charles	Ensign	02-03-78	AA	WstR	Capt.W.Simmons	AM 16-526	
Drury, Charles	1st Lt	02-05-81	AA	WstR	Capt.A.Welsh	AM 45-422	
Ducker, Jeremiah	2nd Lt	21-06-77	MO	29th	Capt.J.Gaither	AM 16-296	
Ducker, Jeremiah	1st Lt	12-09-77	MO	29th	Capt.J.Gaither	AM 16-373	
Duckett, Baruch	Ensign	03-01-76	PG	25th		SC 48-139	OC
Duckett, Baruch	2nd Lt	25-03-76	PG	25th	Capt.Waring	AM 11-285	
Duckett, Baruch	1st Lt	09-06-77	PG		Capt.B.Waring	RC 2-1103	Rec
Duckett, Baruch	2nd Lt	01-05-78	PG	25th	Capt.J.Mullican	AM 21-63	
Duckett, Richard	Ensign	01-05-78	PG	25th	Capt.J.Mullican	AM 21-63	
Duckett, Richard	2nd Lt	24-06-80	PG	Up	Capt.J.Mulliken	AM 43-203	
Duckett, Thomas	1st Lt	01-05-78	PG	25th	Capt.J.Mullican	AM 21-63	
Dudley, William	2nd Lt	07-06-81	QA	5th	Capt.M.Hawkins	AM 45-465	
Duer, Joshua	Ensign	30-08-77	WO	SnHl	Capt.W.Holland	AM 16-351	OC
Duer, Joshua	Ensign	03-08-81	WO	SnHl		SC 48-138	Res
Duffey, Thomas	Ensign	14-05-76	QA		Capt.Swat-Ind.Co.	AM 11-424	
Duffey, Thomas	2nd Lt	19-06-77	QA	20th	Capt.Noble	AM 16-295	
Duffey, Thomas	Ensign	31-07-78	QA	20th	Capt.N.Noble	AM 21-172	
Duitt, Thomas	1st Lt	18-04-81	BA	Town	Capt.R.Ridgeley	AM 45-402	
Duncan, John	2nd Lt	20-04-80	QA	5th	Capt.R.Holding	AM 43-146	
Dunn, James of Ezekiah	2nd Lt	18-09-79	KE	13th	Capt.Williamson	AM 21-532	
Dunnington, George	Ensign	06-04-81	CH	26th	Capt.S.Luckett	AM 45-379	
Dunnock, John	1st Lt	20-11-76	BA		Capt.J.Talbott	AM 12-541	
Duvall, Jacob	Ensign	07-02-76	PG		Capt.J.Macgill	AM 11-139	
Duvall, Jacob	1st Lt	24-05-79	PG	25th	Capt.M.Duval	AM 21-414	
Duvall, Jacob of John	2nd Lt	01-05-78	PG	25th	Capt.M.Duvall	AM 21-62	
Duvall, Marsh Mareen	Capt	05-09-77	PG	25th	Capt.J.Macgill	AM 16-363	
Duvall, Marsh Mareen	Capt	01-05-78	PG	25th		AM 21-62	
Duvall, Samuel	QM	06-01-76	MO	16th		PC 79	
Duvall, William	Capt	29-11-75	FR	4th		MM 11:50	
Dwiggins, James	Ensign	19-06-77	CA	28th	Capt.Price	AM 16-294	
Dwiggins, Nathan	Ensign	09-04-78	CA	28th	Capt.T.Burk	AM 21-23	
Dwiggins, Robert	2nd Lt	17-06-77	TA	4th	Wye	RC 2-1130	Mn
Dwigons, James	1st Lt	09-04-78	CA	28th	Capt.J.Reynolds	AM 21-23	
Dyer, Francis	Ensign	01-05-78	PG	11th	Capt.T.Dent	AM 21-78	
Dyer, George	2nd Lt	01-05-78	PG	11th	Capt.R.Stonestreet	AM 21-62	
Dyer, Giles	1st Lt	01-05-78	PG	11th	Capt.R.Stonestreet	AM 21-62	
Dyer, John	Ensign	01-05-78	PG	11th	Capt.H.Wheeler	AM 21-62	
Dyer, John	2nd Lt	24-05-79	PG	11th	Capt.H.Wheeler	AM 21-414	
Dyer, John	Lt	25-05-81	PG	SelM	Capt.H.Wheeler	AM 45-445	
Dyer, Thomas	2nd Lt	01-05-78	PG	11th	Capt.T.Dent	AM 21-62	
Dyson, Bennett	1st Lt	05-07-77	CH	12th		RC 2-1170	Mn
Dyson, Bennett	Capt	06-04-81	CH	12th	Capt.J.Parnham	AM 45-379	
Dyson, George	2nd Lt	19-01-81	CH	12th	Capt.T.A.Dyson	AM 45-280	
Dyson, Samuel	2nd Lt	25-03-80	MO	Up	Capt.C.Gassaway	AM 43-120	
Dyson, Thomas	1st Lt	05-07-77	CH	12th	Capt.H.Clarkson	RC 2-1170	Mn
Dyson, Thomas A.	Capt	19-01-81	CH	12th	Capt.H.Clarkson	AM 45-280	
Dyson, Thomas Andrew	2nd Lt	22-10-77	CH	Lwr		AM 16-401	
	- -						
	- -						
Earickson, William	Ensign	29-08-77	QA	20th	Capt.T.Elliott	SC 48-137	OC
Earickson, William	Ensign	30-08-81	QA	20th		SC 48-137	Res
Earle, James	2nd Lt	16-03-76	QA		Capt.Bordley	AM 11-254	
Earle, John	QM	19-06-77	QA	20th		AM 16-295	

APPENDIX A - COMMISSIONED OFFICERS

Name	Rank	Date	Cty	Bn	Company	Ref.	Notes
Earle, Joseph		03-08-76				AM 12-168	Ref
Earle, Richard T.	Colonel	12-01-76	QA	5th		PC 78	
Earle, Richard T.	Colonel	08-05-77	QA	5th		AM 16-243	Suc
Eastbun, Benjamin	1st Lt	11-06-76	FR	34th	Capt.Poe	AM 11-476	
Eastburn, Benjamin	Capt	22-08-82	FR			AM 48-248	Mn
Eaton, Thomas	1st Lt	14-05-76	CA	14th	Capt.Douglass	AM 11-424	
Eaton, Thomas	1st Lt	09-04-78	CA	14th	Capt.H.McBride	AM 21-23	
Eaton, Thomas	Capt	17-12-81	CA	14th	Capt.J.Douglass	AM 48-27	
Eavens, Henry	2nd Lt	01-05-78	PG	11th	Capt.H.Wheeler	AM 21-62	
Eccleston, Thomas	Capt	20-05-78	DO	19th		AM 21-97	OC
Eccleston, Thomas	Capt	28-02-79	DO	19th		SC 48-134	Res
Eccleston, Thomas Firmin	2nd Lt	10-02-76	DO		Cambridge Blues	AM 11-147	
Eccleston, Thomas Firmin	1st Lt	12-09-76	DO	19th	Capt.E.Vickars	AM 12-266	
Echson, Nicholas	2nd Lt	09-04-78	HA	8th	Capt.S.G.Osburn	AM 21-24	
Eckle, Christian	2nd Lt	22-06-78	WA	2ndW	Capt.J.Smith	AM 21-145	
Eden, James	1st Maj	12-01-76	SM	6th		PC 78	
Eden, John	1st Lt	26-08-77	SM	Up	Capt.C.Jordan	AM 16-345	
Edison, Thomas	Adj	28-11-76	FR	37th		AM 12-555	
Edmonson, James	Ensign	01-05-78	PG	25th	Capt.R.Beall	AM 21-62	
Edmonston, Thomas	1st Lt	12-09-77	MO	29th	Capt.T.Beall	AM 16-373	
Edmonston, Thomas	Capt	19-06-81	MO			AM 47-304	Mn
Edwards, Benjamin	2nd Lt	26-08-77	SM	Up	Capt.W.Kilgour	AM 16-346	
Edwards, John	1st Lt	26-08-77	SM	Up	Capt.W.Kilgour	AM 16-346	
Edwards, Jonathan	2nd Lt	26-08-77	SM	Up	Capt.W.Bond	AM 16-346	
Edwards, Jonathan	1st Lt	18-11-79	SM	Up	Capt.E.Mattingley	AM 43-18	
Eichelburger, Barnet	1st Lt	-04-76	BA	Town	Capt.J.Sterrett	RB 13-74	
Elder, Francis	Ensign	01-02-77	FR	37th		AM 16-106	
Elder, Ignatius	Ensign	15-05-76	FR	37th	Capt.Ogle	AM 11-426	
Elder, Ignatius	Ensign	01-02-77	FR	37th		AM 16-106	
Elder, Thomas	2nd Lt	13-10-77	FR	Cato	Capt.Simpkin	SC 48-130	OC
Elicot, Andrew	Capt	02-03-78	AA	ElkR		AM 16-525	
Eliot, Thomas	Capt	29-09-77	QA	20th		SC 48-131	OC
Eliot, Thomas	Capt	30-07-78	QA	20th		SC 48-131	Res
Ellicot, Jonathan	2nd Lt	30-03-79	AA	22nd	Capt.C.Fox	AM 21-333	
Ellicott, Andrew	Maj	02-11-78	AA	22nd		AM 21-229	
Elliott, Benjamin	Ensign	03-01-76	QA	5th	Capt.S.Wickes	SC 48-135	OC
Elliott, Benjamin	1st Lt	22-10-77	QA	5th	Capt.G.Findley	AM 16-403	
Elliott, Jacob	2nd Lt	04-08-80	MO	Midd	Capt.B.Ricketts	AM 43-248	
Elliott, John	1st Lt	03-01-76	DO		Friendship	SC 48-132	OC
Elliott, Thomas	Capt	16-07-76				AM 12-60	Mn
Ellis, Richard	Capt	23-12-75	CE		Delaware	PC 58	Del
Ellis, Zachariah	Lt	20-06-77	MO			SP 4562	Mn
Elsbury, Lambert	Ensign	21-04-78	CE	Sass	Capt.J.Knight	AM 21-47	
Elzey, James	Ensign	22-09-77	SO	PrAn	Capt.D.Wilson	AM 16-381	
Elzey, James	2nd Lt	07-01-78	SO	PrAn	Capt.D.Wilson	AM 16-457	
Elzey, James	Capt	07-12-78	SO	PrAn		AM 21-260	
Emory, Arthur	2nd Maj	12-01-76	QA	20th		PC 78	
Emory, Arthur	Lt Col	08-05-77	QA	20th		AM 16-244	
Emory, Arthur	Colonel	31-07-78	QA	20th		MH 2	Mn
Emory, Gideon	1st Lt	13-06-77	QA	5th		RC 2-1119	Mn
Emory, John Register	Capt	19-06-77	QA	20th		AM 16-295	
Emory, Richard	Capt	13-06-77	QA	5th		RC 2-1119	Mn
Emory, Thomas	2nd Lt	16-03-76	QA		Capt.Wright	AM 11-254	
Emory, Thomas	1st Lt	19-06-77	QA	20th	Capt. Hanson	AM 16-295	

APPENDIX A - COMMISSIONED OFFICERS

Name	Rank	Date	Cty	Bn	Company	Ref.	Notes
Emory, Thomas	1st Lt	31-07-78	QA	20th		MH 2	Res
Ennalls, Bartholomew	2nd Lt	10-02-76	DO		Transquaking	AM 11-147	
Ennalls, Bartholomew	1st Lt	20-05-78	DO	3rd	Capt.J.LeCompt	AM 21-98	
Ennalls, Bartholomew	Capt	01-03-79	DO	Up	Capt.John LeCompt	AM 21-310	
Ennalls, Bartholomew	Capt	23-08-81	DO	SelM		AM 45-577	
Ennalls, John	Lt Col	10-02-76	DO	Lwr		AM 11-147	
Ennalls, John	Colonel	23-10-76	DO	Lw		AM 12-393	
Ennalls, John	Colonel	14-03-78				SP 6284	Dec
Ennalls, Joseph	1st Maj	10-02-76	DO	3rd		AM 11-147	
Ennalls, Joseph	Lt Col	20-05-78	DO	3rd		AM 21-97	
Ennalls, Joseph	Lt Col	13-04-80	DO	Up		AM 43-470	Dec
Ennalls, Thomas	Colonel	10-02-76	DO	19th		AM 11-147	
Ennis, Jesse	2nd Lt	30-08-77	WO	SnHl	Capt.G.Spence	AM 16-351	
Ennis, Joseph	2nd Lt	30-08-77	WO	Snpx	Capt.WW.Purnal	AM 16-350	
Ennis, Joseph	1st Lt	13-06-82	WO	Snpx	Capt.L.Robins	AM 48-190	
Ensor, William	2nd Lt	20-11-76	BA		Capt.H.Howard	AM 12-541	
Ensor, William	1st Lt	23-10-81	BA	GPUp	Capt.J.Marsh	AM 45-650	
Ephraim, John	2nd Lt	27-05-79	WO	SnHl		FP 1-86	Mn
Eppard, Andrew	1st Lt	22-06-78	FR	Ling	Capt.Gobble	AM 21-145	
Eppart, Andrew	Ensign	17-01-77	FR	Ling	Capt.Henry Baker	AM 16-54	
Erreckson, Charles	Ensign	29-06-80	QA	20th	Capt.J.Rowles	AM 43-208	
Erreckson, James	2nd Lt	19-06-77	QA	20th	Capt.Elliott	AM 16-295	
Errickson, James	Ensign	27-06-76	QA			AM 11-523	
Errickson, William	Ensign	31-07-78	QA	20th	Capt.T.Elliott	MH 2	Res
Estep, Richard	Ensign	27-07-76	CH			AM 12-127	
Estep, Richard	2nd Lt	19-01-81	CH	12th	Capt.J.Gardner	AM 45-280	
Evans, Griffith	1st Lt	17-11-79	HA	Deer	Capt.Wm.Amos	AM 43-17	
Evans, Henry	2nd Lt	01-09-77	PG	Lwr	Capt.Wheeler	AM 16-356	
Evans, Isaac	1st Lt	30-08-77	WO	Snpx	Capt.W.Purnal	AM 16-350	
Evans, Isaac	Capt	09-08-80	WO	Snpx	Capt.J.Postley	AM 43-251	
Evans, Isaac	Lt	23-08-81	WO	SelM	Capt.S.Rounds	AM 45-577	
Evans, John	Ensign	20-09-76	PG		Capt.M.Lowe	AM 12-287	
Evans, John	2nd Lt	07-01-78	SO	Salb	Capt.J.S.Conway	AM 14-457	
Evans, John	Ensign	07-06-81	CE	Elk	Capt.H.South	AM 45-466	
Evans, John	2nd Lt	03-10-82	CE	ElkR	Capt.H.South	AM 48-274	
Evans, Joseph	1st Lt	02-03-78	AA	ElkR	Capt.A.Elicot	AM 16-525	
Evans, Philip	Ensign	26-08-77	SM	Lwr	Capt.J.Mackall	AM 16-346	OC
Evans, Robert	2nd Lt	21-04-78	CE	Susq	Capt.J.Maxwell	AM 21-48	
Evans, Samuel	Capt	21-04-78	CE	Elk		AM 21-47	OC
Evans, Samuel	Lt Col	07-06-81	CE	Elk		AM 45-465	
Everhard, George	2nd Lt	04-12-78	BA	Up	Capt.V.Shroad	AM 21-257	
Everitt, Joseph	2nd Lt	09-04-78	CA	28th	Capt.Postlethwait	AM 21-23	
Evertson, Jacob	2nd Lt	21-04-78	CE	Sass	Capt.C.Heath	AM 21-47	
Evitt, Seth	Ensign	24-06-77	CA	14th	Capt.S.Lighton	AM 16-299	
Evitts, Seth	Ensign	09-04-78	CA	14th	Capt.J.Liden	AM 21-23	
Ewing, James	Ensign	28-06-80	CA	14th	Capt.J.Greyless	AM 43-207	
Ewing, John	Ensign	22-09-77	SO	PrAn	Capt.W.Waters	AM 16-381	
Ewing, William	Ensign	10-10-76	HA	8th	Capt.B.Norriss	AM 12-326	
Ewing, William	Ensign	09-04-78	HA	8th	Capt.T.Hutchens	AM 21-24	
Ewing, William	Capt	21-04-78	CE	Susq		AM 21-48	
Ewing, William	Capt	03-01-82	CE	Susq		AM 48-38	Suc
§§		- -					

APPENDIX A - COMMISSIONED OFFICERS

Name	Rank	Date	Cty	Bn	Company	Ref.	Notes
Fackler, Michael	Capt	- -	WA			FP 1-129	Suc
Falcon, Birket	Capt	13-06-77	QA	5th		RC 2-1119	Res
Falconer, William	Capt	20-04-80	QA	5th	Capt.Wm.Clarkson	AM 43-146	
Fallen, Daniel	Maj	16-05-76		Corp		AM 11-419	
Fallen, Daniel	Maj	20-05-78	DO	Corp		DO 234	Mn
Falton, William	2nd Lt	10-05-76	CE		Capt.Mackey	AM 11-319	
Farmer, John	1st Lt	22-05-76	HA		Capt.Morgan	AM 11-436	
Farmer, John	1st Lt	09-04-78	HA	Deer	Capt.W,Morgan	AM 21-23	
Farmer, John	Capt	17-11-79	HA	Deer	Capt.Wm.Morgan	AM 43-17	
Farnandis, James	1st Lt	26-02-76	CH		Capt.R.Sennett	RC 2-142	Res
Farnandis, Peter	1st Lt	27-07-76	CH			AM 12-127	
Fasset, James	1st Lt	27-05-78	WO	Snpx	Capt.J.Dashiell	AM 21-423	
Fassitt, James	1st Lt	30-08-77	WO	Snpx	Capt.E.Briddell	AM 16-350	
Fauntleroy, John	Capt	17-09-76	CA			SP 2372	Mn
Fauntleroy, John	Capt	16-11-76	CA			AM 12-505	CM
Fenalt, Edmund	1st Lt	07-06-81	QA	5th	Capt.M.Hawkins	AM 45-465	
Fenwick, Ignatius Jr.	1st Maj	12-01-76	SM	21st		PC 78	
Fenwick, Ignatius	Maj	22-08-76				AM 12-232	Mn
Fenwick, Ignatius	Colonel	26-08-77	SM	Lwr		AM 16-346	
Fenwick, Philip	1st Lt	26-08-77	SM	Lwr	Capt.J.Greenwell	AM 16-346	
Ferguson, John	Ensign	29-11-75	FR	1st	Capt.C.Beatty	MM 11:50	
Ferguson, John	1st Lt	26-03-76	FR	MdDt		AM 11-287	
Ferguson, Philip	Ensign	10-02-76	DO		Plymouth Greens	AM 11-147	
Ferguson, Philip	Ensign	16-05-76		Corp	Capt.M.Traverse	AM 11-429	
Ferguson, Philip	2nd Lt	24-06-78	DO		Capt.M.Traverse	AM 21-147	
Ferguson, William	2nd Lt	23-08-76			Capt.A.Beall Jr	AM 12-232	
Fiddeman, Philip	Colonel	12-01-76	CA	28th		PC 78	
Findley, George	Capt	23-10-77	QA	5th		AM 16-403	
Finley, Ebenezer	2nd Lt	24-02-76	SO	17th	Capt.Williams	AM 11-182	
Finley, Richard	2nd Lt	15-03-76	KE		Capt.Frisby	AM 11-246	
Firthhunt, Henry	2nd Lt	28-11-76	FR	35th	Capt.Little	AM 12-555	
Fischer, Adam	Surgeon	10-01-77	FR	33rd		AM 16-33	
Fish, Benjamin	Ensign	12-06-77	AA	7th	Capt.Boone	AM 16-286	
Fish, Benjamin	Ensign	02-03-78	AA	Svrn	Capt.J.Boone	AM 16-575	
Fish, Benjamin	2nd Lt	19-09-78	AA	7th	Capt.John Boone	AM 21-208	
Fish, Benjamin	1st Lt	23-04-81	AA	Svrn	Capt.C.Boone	AM 45-411	
Fisher, George	Ensign	04-12-78	BA	Up	Capt.V.Shroad	AM 21-257	
Fisher, John	1st Lt	16-03-76	QA		Capt.Costin	AM 11-253	OC
Fisher, William	2nd Lt	14-10-75	CE		Capt.Webb	AM 11-537	Mn
Fisher, William	2nd Lt	26-04-76	HA	8th	Capt.Webb	AM 11-387	
Fisher, William	Capt	09-04-78	HA	Deer		AM 21-22	
Fister, James	Ensign	---04-76	BA		Capt.G.Wells	RB 13-74	
Fitzhugh, Peregrine	1st Lt	24-09-77	CV		Capt.J.Grahame	AM 16-384	
Fitzhugh, William Jr.	Ensign	16-04-78	CV	15th	Capt.J.Graham	AM 21-37	
Fleming, James	1st Lt	29-11-75	FR	4th	Capt.M.Troutman	MM 11:50	
Flemming, James	1st Lt	13-10-77	FR	Cato	Capt.Simpkins	SC 48-125	OC
Flemming, John	Ensign	07-01-78	SO	PrAn	Capt.D.Wilson	AM 16-457	OC
Flemming, John	Ensign	07-12-78	SO	PrAn	Capt.J.Elzey	AM 21-260	
Flemming, Thomas	1st Lt	15-05-76	FR	34th	Capt.Charlton	AM 11-426	
Fletcher, ---	Capt	20-06-77	MO			RC 2-1142	Dec
Fletcher, Jacob	2nd Lt	10-01-77	FR	33rd	Capt. Watson	AM 16-33	
Fletcher, John	Capt	28-07-80	DO	Lwr	Capt.A.Wheatley	AM 43-236	
Floary, Robert	Ensign	27-07-76	FR			AM 12-127	
Foble, Jacob	2nd Lt	04-12-78	BA	Up	Capt.Lemmon	AM 21-257	

75

APPENDIX A - COMMISSIONED OFFICERS

Name	Rank	Date	Cty	Bn	Company	Ref.	Notes
Fogwell, Aquila	Ensign	07-06-81	QA	5th	Capt.J.Thompson	AM 45-465	
Forbes, John	2nd Lt	30-07-76	CH			AM 12-141	
Ford, ---	Capt	22-06-78	CE	Bohe		AM 21-145	Suc
Ford, James	1st Lt	09-04-78	HA	23rd	Capt.J.Rogers	AM 21-23	
Ford, John	Capt	21-04-78	CE	Sass		AM 21-47	
Ford, Robert	2nd Lt	22-06-80	SM	Lwr	Capt.B.Combs	AM 43-201	
Forepaugh, William	Ensign	04-09-77	BA	Town	Capt.W.Richardson	AM 16-362	
Forepaugh, William	1st Lt	19-03-79	BA	Town	Capt.G.Douglass	AM 21-324	
Forepaugh, William	1st Lt	25-09-80	BA	Town	Capt.Lemmon	SC 48-123	OC
Forrest, Zachariah	1st Lt	26-08-77	SM	Lwr	Capt.J Smith	AM 16-346	
Forrest, Zachariah	Capt	22-06-80	SM	Lwr	Capt.John Smith	AM 43-201	
Forrest, Zephaniah	2nd Lt	26-08-77	SM	Lwr	Capt.J.Smith	AM 16-346	
Forrest, Zephaniah	1st Lt	22-06-80	SM	Lwr	Capt.Z.Forrest	AM 43-201	
Forrester,	Ensign	31-05-76	QA	20th	Capt.Wilson	AM 11-454	
Forris, John	1st Lt	28-11-76	FR	35th	Capt.J.Shields	AM 12-555	
Forster, James	Ensign	06-06-76	BA	Town	Capt.Wells	AM 11-467	
Forwood, Jacob	2nd Lt	09-09-75	HA		#4	PR 109	
Forwood, Jacob	Capt	09-04-78	HA	23rd		AM 21-23	
Forwood, Jacob	Capt	17-11-79	HA	23rd		AM 43-17	Suc
Foster, John	Capt	20-06-77	BA			RC 2-1141	Mn
Founger, ---	Lt	06-12-81	FR			AM 47-568	Mn
Fountain, Collin	Ensign	24-02-76	SO	17th	Capt.Fountain	AM 11-182	
Fountain, Thomas	Ensign	22-09-77	SO	Salb	Capt.J.Dashiell	AM 16-382	
Fountain, William	Capt	24-02-76	SO	17th		AM 11-182	
Fountleroy, John	1st Lt	09-04-78	TA	4th	Wye	AM 21-24	
Fowke, Gerrard	Ensign	30-07-76	CH			AM 12-141	
Fowke, Roger	2nd Lt	09-05-78	CH	26th	Capt.G.Dent Jr	AM 21-72	
Fowler, John	2nd Lt	17-01-77	FR	Ling	Capt.Wm.Winchester	AM 16-54	
Fowler, John	2nd Lt	22-06-78	WA	2ndW	Capt.J.Spires	AM 21-145	
Fox, Charles	2nd Lt	28-08-77	AA	22nd	Capt.Ellicott	AM 16-347	
Fox, Charles	Capt	30-03-79	AA	22nd		AM 21-333	
Fox, Jeremiah	1st Lt	23-01-82	FR	Town	Capt.J.Shellman	AM 48-54	OC
Frampton, Richard	2nd Lt	09-04-78	CA	14th	Capt.T.Lockerman	AM 21-23	
Franklin, Benjamin	2nd Lt	04-09-77	BA	GP	Capt.J.Bosley	AM 16-362	
Frantum, Richard	2nd Lt	24-06-77	CA	14th	Capt.T.Lockerman	AM 16-299	
Frasher, John	2nd Lt	11-06-76	FR	34th	Capt.Frazier	AM 11-476	
Frazer, Thomas	1st Lt	29-11-75	FR	4th	Capt.W.Luckett	MM 11:50	
Frazier, Solomon	Capt	21-03-83			Barge"Fearnought"	AM 48-386	
Frazier, Thomas	Capt	11-06-76	FR	34th	Capt Luckett	AM 11-476	
Frazier, William	1st Lt	13-06-77	QA	5th		RC 2-1119	Mn
Freeland, Frisbee	Capt	10-05-76	CV			AM 11-320	
Freeland, Frisbie	Capt	16-04-78	CV	15th		AM 21-37	
Freeman, Isaac	1st Lt	11-03-79	KE	27th	Capt.J.Day	AM 21-320	
Fringer, Nicholas	2nd Lt	22-06-78	FR	Ling	Capt.Winchester	AM 21-144	
Frisby, James	2nd Lt	07-06-76	KE		Capt.Wm.Frisby	AM 11-470	OC
Frisby, Richard	1st Lt	07-06-76	KE		Capt.Wm.Frisby	AM 11-470	
Frisby, William	Capt	07-06-76	KE			AM 11-246	Mn
Frisby, William	Maj	04-06-78	KE	13th		AM 21-122	
Fulton, William	1st Lt	21-04-78	CE	Elk	Capt.J.Macky	AM 21-47	
Funk, John	Capt	22-06-78	WA	2ndW		AM 21-145	
Funk, John	Capt	23-01-81	WA	2ndW		AM 47-34	Mn
Furny, Michael	Ensign	28-11-76	FR	35th	Capt.Peppel	AM 12-555	

APPENDIX A - COMMISSIONED OFFICERS

Name	Rank	Date	Cty	Bn	Company	Ref.	Notes
Gabert, Daniel	1st Lt	29-11-75	FR	4th	Capt.P.Rodenbieler	MM 11:50	
Gafford, Joseph	Ensign	07-06-81	QA	5th	Capt.R.Holding	AM 45-465	
Gailbreath, William	Capt	19-03-79	BA	Town		AM 21-324	Suc
Gaither, Basil	1st Lt	30-08-77	MO	16th	Capt.Briscoe	AM 16-350	
Gaither, Basil	Capt	12-09-77	MO	Mid		AM 16-373	
Gaither, Basil	Capt	- -	MO	Up		MH 5	Mov
Gaither, Benjamin	1st Lt	14-05-76	MO	29th	Capt.Pigman	AM 11-424	
Gaither, Benjamin	1st Lt	12-09-77	MO	Mid	Capt.N.Pigman	AM 16-373	
Gaither, Benjamin	Capt	21-04-79	MO	Mid		AM 21-357	
Gaither, Benjamin	Capt	25-03-80	MO	Mid		AM 43-120	Suc
Gaither, Burgess	Ensign	12-09-77	MO	Mid	Capt.J.Bruce	AM 16-373	
Gaither, Edward	Maj	02-03-78	AA	ElkR		AM 16-525	
Gaither, Edward	Colonel	02-11-78	AA	22nd		AM 21-229	
Gaither, Edward Jr.	2nd Maj	12-01-76	AA	ElkR		PC 78	
Gaither, George	1st Lt	26-08-77	SM	Lwr	Capt.W.Smoot	AM 16-346	
Gaither, Greenbury	QM	30-08-77	MO	16th		AM 16-350	
Gaither, Greenbury	1st Lt	12-09-77	MO	Mid	Capt.B.Gaither	AM 16-373	
Gaither, Greenbury	1st Lt	- -	MO	Up		MH 5	Mov
Gaither, Henry	Ensign	23-01-81	WA			AM 47-34	Mn
Gaither, John	Capt	21-06-77	MO	29th		AM 16-296	
Gaither, John	Capt	11-08-79	MO			MH 1	Suc
Gaither, Vachel	1st Lt	15-05-76	AA	Svrn	Capt.Mulliken	AM 11-450	Mn
Gaither, Vachel	Capt	17-06-76	AA	Svrn		AM 11-495	
Gaither, Vachel	Capt	02-03-78	AA	Svrn		AM 16-575	
Gaither, William	Ensign	14-05-76	MO	29th	Capt.Pigman	AM 11-424	
Gaither, William	2nd Lt	12-09-77	MO	Mid	Capt.N.Pigman	AM 16-373	
Gaither, Zachariah	Ensign	30-03-79	AA	ElkR	Capt.B.Burgess	SC 48-183	OC
Gaither, Zachariah	Ensign	18-05-79	AA			MH 5	Res
Galbraith, William	Capt	06-06-76	BA	Town		AM 11-467	
Galbraith, William	Capt	25-04-81		39th		AM 47-211	Mn
Gale, Edward	Ensign	20-04-76	FR	LwDt	Capt.Richardson	AM 11-356	
Gale, George	Ensign	22-08-81	SO	Salb	Capt.H.Gale	AM 45-575	
Gale, Henry	Capt	22-09-77	SO	Salb	Quantico	AM 16-381	
Gale, William	1st Lt	22-08-81	SO	Salb	Capt.J.Cotman	AM 45-575	
Galloway, Benjamin	Capt	10-08-76	AA	31st		AM 12-192	OC
Galloway, Joseph	2nd Maj	22-01-76	AA	WstR		AM 11-103	
Galloway, William	Ensign	---05-76	BA		Capt.J.T.Young	RB 13-53	
Galloway, William	Ensign	25-05-77	BA	GP	Capt.Young	AM 11-444	
Gandy, Samuel	Ensign	22-06-78	FR	Ling	Capt.Meridith	AM 21-144	
Gantt, Erasmus	Cornet	25-04-81			Bay Cav Co.	AM 45-414	
Gantt, George Jr	2nd Lt	01-05-78	PG	11th	Capt.A.Magruder	AM 21-62	
Gantt, George	1st Lt	03-07-80	PG	Lwr	Capt.A.H.Magruder	AM 43-210	
Gardiner, Charles	Ensign	27-07-76	CH			AM 12-127	
Gardiner, Charles	Capt	12-04-80	TA	38th	Capt.J.Abell	AM 43-139	
Gardiner, John	1st Lt	27-07-76	CH			AM 12-127	
Gardner, Clement	2nd Lt	26-08-77	SM	Up	Capt.M.Lock	AM 16-345	
Gardner, Francis	Ensign	05-07-77	CH	12th	Capt.A.Macpherson	RC 2-1170	Mn
Gardner, Francis J.	2nd Lt	19-01-81	CH	12th	Capt.H.Boarman	AM 45-280	
Gardner, John	Capt	19-01-81	CH	12th	Capt.John Thomas	AM 45-280	
Gardner, William	2nd Lt	29-08-77	BA	SD	Capt.N.Stinchcomb	AM 16-348	
Garland, Jeremiah	Ensign	09-04-78	TA	4th	Wye	AM 21-24	
Garland, William	Ensign	31-07-78	TA		Drafted militia	AM 21-172	
Garner, Hugh	2nd Lt	12-03-77			Capt.J.Marbury	AM 16-170	Ref
Garnett, Thomas	2nd Lt	13-06-77	QA	5th		RC 2-1119	Res

APPENDIX A - COMMISSIONED OFFICERS

Name	Rank	Date	Cty	Bn	Company	Ref.	Notes
Garretson, Cornelius	2nd Lt	09-04-78	HA	8th	Capt.J.Tolbott	AM 21-24	
Garretson, Job	Capt	---05-76	BA			RB 13-53	
Garretson, Job	Capt	25-05-77	BA	GP		AM 11-444	
Garretson, Job	Colonel	24-07-80	BA	GP		AM 43-227	
Gassaway, Brice	1st Lt	30-03-79	AA	22nd	Capt.B.Burgess	AM 21-333	
Gassaway, Brice	Capt	01-07-80	AA	ElkR	Capt.B.Burgess	AM 43-209	
Gassaway, Charles	Capt	25-03-80	MO	Up	Capt.W.Vearse	AM 43-120	
Gassaway, George	1st Lt	12-09-77	MO	16th	Capt.W.Vearse	AM 16-373	
Gatro, Joseph	1st Lt	19-05-79	BA	Town	Capt.J.Deavor	AM 21-401	
Gauden, Prestin	Ensign	24-06-77	CA	14th	Capt.Stafford	AM 16-299	
Gault, William	Ensign	30-08-77	WO	Snpx	Capt.T.Purnal	AM 16-350	
Gautt, Thomas Jr.	1st Lt	24-05-79	PG	11th	Capt.A.McGuden	AM 21-414	
Geoghan, George	Ensign	28-08-77	AA	22nd	Capt.R.Stringer	AM 16-347	
Geoghan, Robert	Ensign	28-08-77		22nd	Capt.R.Stringer	PA	
Geoghan, Robert	Ensign	13-04-81		22nd	Capt.R.Stringer	PA	Res
Geoghegan, Robert		21-04-81	AA			AM 47-182	Res
George, Joshua	Maj	09-09-78	CE	18th		RC 1-679	Mn
German, John	1st Lt	---05-76	BA		Capt.J.T.Young	RB 13-53	
German, John	1st Lt	25-05-77	BA	GP	Capt.Young	AM 11-444	
Gettings, James	Capt	---05-76	BA			RB 13-53	
Gevans, George	2nd Lt	30-08-77	WO	Wico	Capt.I.Houston	AM 16-351	
Ghiselin, John	Capt	04-01-77	FR			SP 3390	Res
Gibbons, Joseph	1st Lt	17-11-79	HA	Deer	Capt.Wm.Rigdon	AM 43-17	
Gibbons, Nehemiah	Ensign	07-03-76	CH		Capt.Winter	AM 11-206	
Gibbs, John Harris	Ensign	12-06-81	PG	Lwr	Capt.R.Stonestreet	AM 45-472	
Gibson, Jacob	Capt	13-05-76	TA	4th	Wye	PC 132	
Gibson, James	Ensign	16-05-76	TA	4th	Capt.Daugherty	AM 11-429	OC
Gibson, Jonathan	Ensign	23-05-76	TA	38th		AM 11-438	
Gibson, Jonathan	2nd Lt	13-06-77	QA	5th		RC 2-1119	Mn
Gibson, Woolman	2nd Lt	09-04-78	TA	38th	Miles River	AM 21-25	
Gibson, Woolman 3rd	Capt	09-04-78	TA	4th	Wye	AM 21-24	
Gibson, Woolman IV	1st Lt	17-06-77	TA	4th	Wye	RC 2-1130	Mn
Gibson, Woolman of Jno.	1st Lt	01-07-76	TA	4th	Goldsbourough	AM 11-539	Mn
Gilbert, Michael	Ensign	23-09-75	HA		#3	PR 108	
Gilbert, Michael	2nd Lt	17-11-79	HA	23rd	Capt.Hugh Smith	AM 43-17	
Gilbert, Michael of Chas.	Ensign	09-04-78	HA	23rd	Capt.G.Patterson	AM 21-24	
Giles, James	2nd Lt	15-09-75	HA		#5	PR 110	
Giliss, Ezekiel	1st Lt	22-09-77	SO	PrAn	Capt.D.Wilson	AM 16-381	OC
Gill, Nicholas	Ensign	20-11-76	BA		Capt.S.Gill	AM 12-542	
Gill, Stephen	Capt	20-11-76	BA			AM 12-542	
Gilleland, Thomas	1st Lt	07-06-81	CE	Elk	Capt.J.Mackey	AM 45-466	
Gillis, George	Ensign	22-09-77	SO	Salb	Capt.J.Vennables	AM 16-381	
Gillis, William	QM	06-01-76	SO	17th		PC 80	
Gillispie, David	Capt	- -	WA		Capt.S.Hughes	FP 1-129	Mn
Gilliss, Ezekiel	2nd Lt	22-09-77	SO	PrAn	Capt.D.Wilson	MH 1	
Gilliss, Joseph	2nd Lt	22-09-77	SO	Salb	Capt.J.Dashiell	AM 16-382	
Gilman, Wm	Ensign	17-01-77	FR	Ling	Capt.Meredith	AM 16-54	
Gilmor, Robert	QM	10-02-76	DO	3rd		AM 11-147	
Gilpin, Samuel	Capt	21-04-78	CE	Elk		AM 21-47	OC
Gilpin, Samuel	Capt	07-06-81	CE	Elk	Capt.J.Oglevie	AM 45-466	Suc
Gist, David	2nd Lt	30-08-77	BA	Up	Capt.Murray	AM 16-350	
Gist, Joseph	Maj	13-05-76	BA	Gist		RB 13-69	Rec
Gist, Joseph	QM	25-05-77	BA	SD		AM 11-443	
Gist, Joseph	1st Lt	06-06-76	BA	SD	Capt.Stinchcomb	AM 11-467	

APPENDIX A - COMMISSIONED OFFICERS

Name	Rank	Date	Cty	Bn	Company	Ref.	Notes
Gist, Joseph	2nd Maj	03-06-77	BA	SD		AM 16-271	
Gist, Joseph	Maj	10-09-77	BA	SD		AM 16-368	
Gist, Joseph	Maj	-11-81	BA			AM 47-560	Res
Gist, Joshua	1st Maj	04-02-77	BA	Gist		AM 16-114	
Gist, Thomas	Colonel	13-05-76	BA	Gist		RB 13-69	
Gist, Thomas,Jr.	Colonel	04-02-77	BA	Gist		AM 16-114	
Gittings, James	1st Maj	25-05-76	BA	GP		AM 11-449	
Gittings, James	Lt Col	30-08-77	BA	GP		AM 16-350	
Gittings, James	Lt Col	17-02-80	BA	GP		PA	Res
Gitzadanner, Baltzer	1st Lt	12-05-79	FR	Town	Capt.J.Stones	AM 21-387	
Glascow, Patrick	Ensign	25-05-76	WO	10th	Capt.Martin	AM 11-444	
Glassgow, Patrick	1st Lt	30-08-77	WO	Snpx	Capt.W.Handy	AM 16-350	
Glen, Robert	Capt	10-02-77	HA			AM 16-129	Mn
Glen, Robert	Maj	09-04-78	HA	Deer		AM 21-22	
Glenvill, Stephen	Ensign	11-03-79	KE	13th	Capt.S.Wicks	AM 21-320	
Gobble, George	Capt	22-06-78	FR	Ling		AM 21-145	
Godfrey, Samuel	Ensign	30-03-79	AA	22nd	Capt.C.Fox	AM 21-333	
Godman, Samuel	1st Lt	07-02-76	AA			AM 11-139	
Godsgrace, William	1st Lt	15-09-75	HA		#5	PR 110	
Godsgrace, William	1st Lt	22-05-76	HA		Capt.W.Morgan	BK 341	Mov
Gohs, Joseph	Ensign	-04-76	BA		Capt.W.Galbraith	RB 13-74	
Goldsborough, Greenbury	Capt	13-05-76	TA	4th	Sword in Hand	PC 132	Mn
Goldsborough, Greensbury	Capt	17-06-77	TA	4th	Sword in Hand	RC 2-1130	Res
Goldsborough, Robert IV	Lt	03-01-76				SP 955	
Goldsborough, Robert IV	Lt	10-06-77				RC 2-63	Res
Goldsborough, William		07-02-76				SP 1050	Ref
Goldsborough, William	Capt	09-04-78	TA	4th	Union	AM 21-24	
Goldsborough, William	2nd Lt	09-04-78	TA	4th	Sword in Hand	AM 21-24	
Goldsmith, William	2nd Lt	20-03-79	AN		Middleton-Ind	AM 21-325	
Good, ---	Capt	10-02-76	FR		Minuteman	AM 11-165	
Good, Jacob	Capt	29-11-75	FR			MM 11:50	
Good, Jacob	Colonel	06-01-76	FR	35th		PC 79	OC
Good, Jacob	Colonel	07-10-76	FR	35th		PC 266	Suc
Goodhan, James	2nd Lt	31-07-78	QA	20th	Capt.J.Ringgold	AM 21-172	
Goodhand, Jones	Ensign	31-07-78	QA	20th	Capt.T.Barnes	MH 2	Mn
Goodhand, Jones	2nd Lt	31-07-78	QA	20th	Capt.T.Barnes	MH 2	Rec
Goodwin, Lyde	Surg	09-06-81			Horse troops	AM 45-467	Mn
Gordon, Thomas	Capt	13-05-76	TA	4th		PC 132	Mn
Gordon, Thomas	2nd Maj	17-06-77	TA	4th		RC 2-1130	Rec
Gormon, Abraham	1st Lt	28-02-77			"Conqueror"	AM 16-154	
Gorsuch, Loveless	Ensign	23-10-81	BA	GpUp	Capt.J.Marsh	AM 45-650	
Gorsuch, Norman	Ensign	23-10-81	BA	GpUp	Capt.N.Kelly	AM 45-650	
Gosnell, Mordecai	Capt	29-08-77	BA	SD		AM 16-348	
Gotro, Joseph	2nd Lt	19-03-79	BA	Town	Capt.J.Deaver	AM 21-324	
Gould, James	Ensign	13-06-77	QA	5th		RC 2-1119	Mn
Gould, Joseph	Ensign	07-07-81	QA	5th	Capt.M.Hawkins	AM 45-465	
Grable, Philip	Capt	25-09-80	BA	Town		AM 43-303	
Grace, Aaron	Ensign	09-04-78	HA	23rd	Capt.J.Wood	AM 21-23	
Grace, Aaron	Capt	04-04-81	HA	23rd	Capt.S.Osborne	AM 45-375	
Grace, Abel	Ensign	09-04-78	TA	4th	Volunteer	AM 21-24	
Grace, Abell	1st Lt	04-11-82	TA	4th	Capt.J.Dorhorty	AM 48-298	
Grace, Aron	Capt	04-04-81	HA	23rd		AM 47-139	Mn
Graham, James	Capt	16-04-78	CV	15th		AM 21-37	
Grahame, James	Capt	24-09-77	CV			AM 16-384	

APPENDIX A - COMMISSIONED OFFICERS

Name	Rank	Date	Cty	Bn	Company	Ref.	Notes
Grahame, John	2nd Lt	16-04-78	CV	15th	Capt.J.Graham	AM 21-37	
Gramer, Jacob	1st Lt	22-06-78	FR	Ling	Capt.Miers	AM 21-145	
Grant, John	Ensign	07-03-76	CH		Capt.Marshall	AM 11-206	
Grant, John	1st Lt	09-05-78	CH	26th	Capt.G.Dent	AM 21-72	
Grash, Adam	1st Lt	26-03-76	FR	MdDt	Capt.Mantz	AM 11-287	
Grason, Richard	1st Lt	03-01-76	TA		Miles River Neck	SC 48-176	OC
Grason, Richard	1st Lt	11-05-76	QA		Capt.Benson	AM 11-420	Res
Grason, Richard	Ensign	29-08-77		20th	Capt.J.Blake	PA	Mn
Grason, Richard	Ensign	17-06-80		20th	Capt.J.Blake	PA	Res
Grason, Thomas	Comdore	08-06-78				AM 21-125	
Grasson, Richard	Ensign	31-07-78	QA	20th	Capt.J.S.Blake	MH 2	Mn
Graves, James Hudson	1st Lt	21-06-80	QA	5th	Capt.J.Walters	AM 43-200	
Graves, Richard	1st Maj	08-05-77	KE	13th		AM 16-243	
Graves, William	2nd Lt	25-05-77	BA	GP	Capt.Garretson	AM 11-444	
Gray, Benjamin	Ensign	21-04-79	MO	Mid	Capt.J.Bruce	AM 21-357	
Gray, Benjamin	2nd Lt	25-03-80	MO	Mid	Capt.H.Griffith	AM 43-120	
Gray, Benjamin	1st Lt	04-08-80	MO	Mid	Capt.B.Ricketts	AM 43-248	
Gray, James W.	1st Lt	13-06-77	QA	5th		RC 2-1119	Mn
Gray, Jesse	Capt	15-05-76	WO	10th		AM 11-426	
Gray, John	Capt	02-09-77	AA	Svrn		AM 16-358	
Gray, John	Capt	18-10-82	AA	Svrn		AM 48-288	
Gray, John of Joshua	2nd Lt	18-10-82	AA	Svrn	Capt.V.Conoway	AM 48-288	
Gray, Joshua Jr.	2nd Lt	12-06-77	AA		Capt.Boone	AM 16-286	
Gray, Thomas	2nd Lt	10-04-76	CV		Capt.Williamson	AM 11-320	
Gray, Thomas	2nd Lt	16-04-78	CV	15th	Capt.C.Williamson	AM 21-37	
Greaves, John	Ensign	18-11-79	SM	Up	Capt.R.Rapier	AM 43-18	
Greaves, Robert	Ensign	16-04-78	SM	21st	Capt.A.H.Watts	AM 21-37	
Green, John	2nd Lt	30-03-79	AA	22nd	Capt.N.Warfield	AM 21-333	
Green, John	Ensign	14-08-79	CA	28th	Capt.W.Chipley	AM 21-493	
Green, Peter	1st Lt	07-03-76	CH		Capt.McPherson	AM 11-206	
Green, Shadrack	Ensign	25-05-76	BA	GP	Capt.Standiford	AM 11-444	
Green, Thomas	2nd Lt	07-03-76	CH		CaptMcPherson	AM 11-206	
Green, Valentine	2nd Lt	19-06-77		ES		AM 16-294	
Green, Vincent	2nd Lt	25-05-76	BA	GP	Capt.Bowen	AM 11-444	
Green, Vincent	1st Lt	20-03-79	BA	GP	Capt.W.Maccubbin	AM 21-325	
Greenfield, Thos.Trueman	Capt	10-04-76	CV		Capt.Williamson	AM 11-320	
Greenfield, Thos.Trueman	Capt	16-04-78	CV	15th		AM 21-37	
Greenfield, Walter Truman	Ensign	01-05-78	PG	11th	Capt.J.Hellen	AM 21-78	
Greenwell, Bennett	Ensign	21-04-79	MO	Mid	Capt.Z.Beall	AM 21-357	
Greenwell, Bennett	2nd Lt	04-08-80	MO	Mid	Capt.Benj.Ray	AM 43-248	
Greenwell, John	Capt	26-08-77	SM	Lwr		AM 16-346	
Greenwell, John	Capt	22-06-80	SM	Lwr		AM 43-201	Suc
Greenwell, Robert	2nd Lt	07-05-81	SM	Lwr	Capt.B.Abell	AM 45-426	
Greenwood, Thomas	2nd Lt	27-05-79	BA	SD	Capt.J.Hurd	AM 21-422	
Gresham, Richard	3rd Lt	26-06-76	KE	13th	Capt.Smyth-Lt.Inf.	AM 11-520	
Gresham, Richard	1st Lt	09-09-78	KE	13th	Capt.D.Crane	RC 1-678	Res
Greyless, Jesse	1st Lt	09-04-78	CA	14th	Capt.J.Douglass	AM 21-23	
Greyless, Jesse	Capt	28-06-80	CA	14th	Capt.J.Douglass	AM 43-207	
Griest, Isaac	QM	29-08-77			Militia on duty	AM 16-347	
Griffin, Charles G.	Cty Lt	27-02-81	MO			AM 47-90	Res
Griffin, John	Ensign	07-03-76	CH		Capt.J.Hanson	AM 11-206	
Griffis, John	Ensign	30-08-77	BA	GP	Capt.S.Pryor	AM 16-350	
Griffis, Kinsey	2nd Lt	30-08-77	BA	GP	Capt.S.Pryor	AM 16-350	
Griffith, ---	Col	17-01-77	FR			SP 3483	

APPENDIX A - COMMISSIONED OFFICERS

Name	Rank	Date	Cty	Bn	Company	Ref.	Notes
Griffith, Benjamin	1st Lt	01-02-77	BA		Capt.John Smith	AM 16-106	
Griffith, Benjamin	1st Lt	02-09-77	BA	Town	Capt.Smith	AM 16-358	
Griffith, Benjamin	Capt	25-09-80	BA	Town		AM 43-303	
Griffith, Charles G.	Lt Col	06-01-76	MO	16th		PC 79	
Griffith, Chas.Greenbury	Cty Lt	01-07-77	MO			AM 16-304	OC
Griffith, Chas.Greenbury	Cty Lt	02-03-81	MO			AM 45-334	Suc
Griffith, Henry	1st Lt	28-08-77	AA	22nd	Capt.B.Warfield	AM 16-346	
Griffith, Henry Jr.	Lt Col	12-09-77	MO	Mid		AM 16-373	
Griffith, Hezekiah	1st Lt	12-09-77	MO	Mid	Capt.J.Bruce	AM 16-373	
Griffith, Hezekiah	Capt	25-03-80	MO	Mid	Capt.J.Bruce	AM 43-120	
Griffith, Hezekiah	Capt	04-08-80	MO	Mid		AM 43-248	Suc
Griffith, Howard	Ensign	12-09-77	MO	16th	Capt.F.Sprigg	AM 16-373	
Griffith, James	2nd Lt	29-08-77	BA	SD	Capt.W.Hudson	AM 16-348	
Griffith, John	Ensign	30-11-75	DO		The Bucks	DO 212	Mn
Griffith, John	Ensign	20-03-76	DO		Capt.Keene	AM 11-267	
Griffith, John	Ensign	12-09-77	MO	Mid	Capt.R.Brooke	AM 16-373	
Griffith, John	Ensign	20-05-78	DO	19th	Capt.B.Keene	AM 21-97	
Griffith, John	2nd Lt	23-08-81	DO	Lwr	Capt.J.Keene	AM 45-577	
Griffith, John	1st Lt	17-12-81	CA	14th	Capt.J.Andrew	AM 48-27	
Griffith, Samuel	1st Lt	09-09-75	HA		#4	PR 109	
Griffith, Samuel	1st Lt	15-03-76	KE		Capt.Wm.Frisby	AM 11-246	
Griffith, Samuel	1st Lt	13-05-76	KE		Capt.Frisby	AM 11-423	Dec
Griffith, Samuel	Capt	16-05-76	HA	23rd		AM 11-428	
Grimes, Edward	2nd Lt	03-12-76	WA		Capt.C.Calson	AM 12-501	
Grindle, William	Ensign	24-05-79	PG	11th	Capt.B.Wales	AM 21-414	
Grosch, Michael	2nd Lt	29-11-75	FR	1st	Capt.J.Haass	MM 11:50	
Grosch, Peter	1st Lt	21-02-76	FR		Capt.Young	AM 11-178	Mn
Grosh, Adam	1st Lt	29-11-75	FR	1st	Capt.P.Mantz	MM 11:50	
Grosh, Peter	Capt	18-09-80	FR	Town		AM 43-295	Suc
Grover, William	2nd Lt	-05-76	BA		Capt.J.Garretson	RB 13-53	
Groves, Thomas	Capt	02-08-81			Barge "Wye"	AM 45-533	
Gudgeon, Sutton	2nd Lt	-05-76	BA		Capt.J.Gittings	RB 13-53	
Gudgeon, Sutton	1st Lt	25-05-76	BA	GP	Capt.Onion	AM 11-444	
Guthro, Joseph	Ensign	06-06-76	BA	Town	Capt.Galbraith	AM 11-467	
Gwin, James	2nd Lt	28-06-77	WO			RC 2-1156	Mn
Gwinn, John	1st Lt	07-03-76	CH		Capt.Swann	AM 11-206	
Gwins, George	1st Lt	27-05-79	WO	Wico	Capt.J.Davis	AM 21-423	
		- -					
		- -					
Haass, John	Capt	29-11-75	FR	1st		MM 11:50	
Hackett, James	1st Lt	23-10-77	QA	5th	Capt.S.Wickes	AM 16-403	
Hackett, James	Capt	20-04-80	QA	5th	Capt.Simon Wicks	AM 43-146	
Hackett, John	2nd Lt	23-10-77	QA	5th	Capt.S.Wickes	AM 16-403	
Hackett, John	1st Lt	20-04-80	QA	5th	Capt.Jas.Hackett	AM 43-146	
Hackett, Thomas	Ensign	03-01-76	QA	5th	Capt.J.Thompson	SC 48-174	OC
Hackett, William	Ensign	19-06-77	QA	20th	Capt.Hanson	AM 16-295	
Hackett, William	2nd Lt	31-07-78	QA	20th	Capt.C.Downes	AM 21-172	
Hadaway, William Webb	Capt	13-05-76	TA	38th		PC 132	Mn
Haddaman,---	Capt	23-05-76	TA	38th		AM 11-438	
Haddaway, John	Ensign	09-04-78	TA	38th	Bay Side	AM 21-25	
Haddaway, John	Ensign	15-06-80	TA	38th	Capt.Dawson	PA	Res
Haddaway, Robert	1st Lt	09-04-78	TA	38th	Bay Side	AM 21-24	
Haddaway, William Webb	Lt Col	09-04-78	TA	38th		AM 21-24	
Haff, Abraham	1st Lt	29-11-75	FR	1st	Capt.Wm.Beatty	MM 11:50	

APPENDIX A - COMMISSIONED OFFICERS

Name	Rank	Date	Cty	Bn	Company	Ref.	Notes
Haff, Abraham	Maj	12-05-79	FR	Town		AM 21-387	
Haff, Abraham	Capt	16-08-79	FR	Town		AM 21-494	Suc
Haff, Richard	1st Lt	29-11-75	FR		Capt.L.Kemp	MM 11:50	
Hahn, John	2nd Lt	22-06-78	WA	2ndW	Capt.G.Swingle	AM 21-145	
Hail, Richard	Ensign	04-12-78	BA	Up	Capt.Murray	AM 21-257	
Haile, Tilley	1st Lt	23-10-81	BA	GPUp	Capt.S.Gill	AM 45-651	
Haill, Nicholas(son Geo)	Ensign	04-02-77	BA		Capt.J.Cockey	AM 16-114	
Hale, Neale Jr	Ensign	23-10-81	BA	GPUp	Capt.B.Talbot	AM 45-651	
Haley, John	Ensign	18-09-79	KE	29th	Capt.J.Cosden	AM 21-532	
Hall, Acquila	Capt	09-09-75	HA		#4	PR 109	
Hall, Acquila	Colonel	06-01-76	HA	23rd		PC 80	
Hall, Acquila	Cty Lt	01-07-77	HA			AM 16-304	
Hall, Acquila	Cty Lt	29-11-77	HA			AM 16-429	Res
Hall, Basil	Ensign	18-11-79	SM	Up	Capt.J.H.Broome	AM 43-18	
Hall, Benjamin	Maj	10-03-77	PG	Mid		SC 48-172	OC
Hall, Benjamin	Maj	10-03-77	PG	Mid		AM 16-532	
Hall, Benjamin	Maj	20-03-78	PG			SP 6347	Ref
Hall, Cuthbert	2nd Lt	18-09-79	KE	29th	Capt.J.Cosden	AM 21-532	
Hall, Elihu	2nd Maj	06-01-76	CE	30th		PC 80	
Hall, Elihu	Lt Col	09-09-78	CE	30th		AM 21-196	OC
Hall, Elihu	Lt Col	04-10-79	CE			SC 48-197	Res
Hall, Elihu Jr.	Maj	21-04-78	CE	Susq		AM 21-48	
Hall, Elihu of Elisha	Lt Col	09-09-78	CE	30th		RC 1-679	Mn
Hall, Henry	Capt	22-02-76	AA	Svrn		AM 11-178	OC
Hall, Isaac	Ensign	07-06-81	CE	Elk	Capt.J.Mackey	AM 45-466	
Hall, James White	Capt	09-04-78	HA	23rd		AM 21-23	
Hall, John	Colonel	12-01-76	AA	Svrn		PC 79	OC
Hall, John	Colonel	13-12-76	AA	7th		SC 48-169	Res
Hall, John	Capt	04-02-77	BA	Gist		AM 16-114	
Hall, John Beadle	2nd Lt	12-09-75	HA		#1	PR 105	
Hall, John Beadle	Maj	09-04-78	HA	23rd		AM 21-23	OC
Hall, John(son of Josa)	2nd Maj	04-02-77	BA	Gist		AM 16-114	
Hall, Joseph	Surgeon	04-09-77	MO	29th		AM 16-362	
Hall, Josiah Carvill	1st Maj	06-01-76	HA	23rd		PC 80	
Hall, Josias Carvil	Capt	12-09-75	HA		#1	PR 105	
Hall, Lawrence	Ensign	31-07-78	QA	20th	Capt.John Costin	AM 21-172	
Hall, Nicholas	Capt	10-06-78	FR		Capt.Wm.Brashears	AM 21-128	
Hall, Richard	Capt	16-06-77	PG			SP 4538	
Hall, Richard Bennett	Capt	23-08-76	PG			AM 12-233	CM
Hall, Richard Bennett	Capt	10-06-77	PG			RC 2-1126	Res
Hall, Robert	1st Lt	03-01-76	QA	5th	Capt.Wm.Pryor	SC 48-167	OC
Hall, Robert	Ensign	23-05-76	TA	4th	Capt.J.Gibson	AM 11-438	
Hall, Robert	2nd Lt	09-04-78	TA	4th	Wye	AM 21-24	
Hall, Thomas	Ensign	12-09-75	HA		#1	PR 105	
Hambleton, John	QM	06-01-76	CE	30th		PC 80	
Hambleton, William	Capt	13-05-76	TA	38th		PC 132	
Hamilton, Burdit	2nd Lt	07-03-76	CH		Capt.Winter	AM 11-206	
Hamilton, Burdit	1st Lt	09-05-78	CH	26th	Capt.W.Winter	AM 21-72	
Hamilton, George	1st Lt	13-06-77	QA	5th		RC 2-1119	Mn
Hamilton, James	BrigGen	30-10-81	FR			AM 47-41	Mn
Hamilton, John	2nd Lt	09-04-78	TA	38th	United	AM 21-25	
Hamilton, John G.	1st Lt	09-05-81	BA	Town	Capt.B.Dickinson	AM 45-429	OC
Hamilton, Leonard	Ensign	07-03-76	CH		Capt.McPherson	AM 11-206	
Hamilton, William	1st Lt	18-04-76	PG	25th	Capt.Beall	AM 11-350	

APPENDIX A - COMMISSIONED OFFICERS

Name	Rank	Date	Cty	Bn	Company	Ref.	Notes
Hamilton, William	Capt	09-04-78	TA	38th	Broad Creek	AM 21-25	
Hamkins, John	Cornet	01-09-81	PG		Horse troop	AM 45-596	
Hammett, Zachariah	Ensign	26-08-77	SM	Up	Capt.T.Reeder	AM 16-346	
Hammett, Zachariah	2nd Lt	18-11-79	SM	Up	Capt.J.H.Broome	AM 43-18	
Hammond, Charles(son Jno)	Capt	28-08-77	AA	22nd		AM 16-347	
Hammond, George	Ensign	12-06-77	AA	7th	Capt.Owens	AM 16-286	
Hammond, George	Ensign	02-03-78	AA	Svrn	Capt.C.Owings	AM 16-525	
Hammond, Isaac	Capt	13-05-76	BA	Gist		RB 13-69	
Hammond, Isaac	2nd Maj	25-05-76	BA	SD		AM 11-443	
Hammond, Isaac	Colonel	10-09-77	BA	SD		AM 16-368	
Hammond, Jas.	Lt Col	03-06-77	BA	SD		AM 16-271	
Hammond, John	Capt	15-08-76				AM 12-205	Mn
Hammond, John	Ensign	04-08-79	QA	20th	Capt.J.Bordley	AM 21-488	
Hammond, Matthias	QM	12-01-76	AA	Svrn		PC 78	
Hammond, Mordecai	Capt	06-06-76	BA	SD	7th	AM 11-467	
Hammond, Rezin	Lt Col	12-01-76	AA	Svrn		PC 78	OC
Hammond, Rezin	Lt Col	12-12-76	AA	Svrn		SC 48-165	Res
Hammond, William	QM	30-08-77	AA	ElkR		AM 16-351	
Hammond, William	Capt	30-08-77	AA			AM 16-351	
Hance, Samuel	Ensign	10-04-76	CV		Capt.Freeland	AM 11-320	
Hance, Samuel	Ensign	16-04-78	CV	15th	Capt.F.Freeland	AM 21-37	OC
Hance, Samuel	Ensign	21-04-80	CV		Capt.Freeland	SC 48-164	Res
Hancock, Wm. (of Wm)	Ensign	02-09-77	AA	Svrn	Capt.J.Gray	AM 16-356	
Hancock, Wm. (of Wm)	Ensign	- -	AA	Svrn		FP 1-38	Dec
Handley, Handy	Ensign	18-10-77	DO	3rd	Transqusaking	RC 2-1356	Rec
Handy, Ebenezer	Capt	15-06-76	WO	10th		AM 11-426	
Handy, Ebenezer	Maj	30-08-77	WO	Wico		AM 16-351	
Handy, Ebenezer	Lt Col	27-05-79	WO	Wico		AM 21-423	
Handy, Ebenezer	Colonel	12-06-82	WO	Wico		AM 48-189	
Handy, George	2nd Lt	22-09-77	SO	Salb	Capt.J.Conway	AM 16-381	
Handy, Handly	1st Lt	16-12-79	DO	Up		DO 230	Mn
Handy, Henry	Ensign	20-04-78	SO	Salb	Salisbury	AM 21-42	
Handy, Isaac	1st Lt	22-09-77	SO	PrAn	Capt.W.Waters	AM 16-381	
Handy, Isaac	Capt	07-12-78	SO	PrAn		AM 21-260	
Handy, Isaac	Capt	22-08-81	SO	PrAn		AM 45-575	Suc
Handy, Levin	Capt	13-06-77	QA	5th		RC 2-1119	Mn
Handy, Levin	Ensign	07-01-78	SO	Salb	Capt.H.Gale	AM 16-457	OC
Handy, Levin	Ensign	12-05-78	SO	1st	Capt.Gale	SC 48-163	Res
Handy, Levin	Capt	28-07-80	DO	Up		AM 43-236	Suc
Handy, Robert	Capt	30-08-77	WO	Wico		AM 16-351	
Handy, Samuel	1st Maj	06-01-76	WO	24th		PC 80	
Handy, Samuel	Lt Col	30-08-77	WO	Snpx		AM 16-350	
Handy, Samuel	Colonel	23-03-78	WO	Snpx		AM 16-547	
Handy, Thomas	Ensign	07-12-78	SO	PrAn		AM 21-260	
Handy, William	Capt	30-08-77	WO	SnHl		AM 16-350	
Handy, William Jr.	1st Lt	25-05-76	WO	10th	Capt. Martin	AM 11-444	
Hankins, Jno	Capt	13-06-77	QA	5th		RC 2-1119	Mn
Hanley, Levin	Capt	20-05-78	DO	3rd		AM 21-98	
Hanly, Handley	2nd Lt	20-05-78	DO	3rd	Capt.J.LeCompt	AM 21-98	
Hanly, Handley	1st Lt	01-03-79	DO	Up	Capt.B.Ennalls	AM 21-310	
Hann, Paul	Capt	05-11-81	BA	Up	Capt.J.Showers	AM 45-662	
Hanskins, George	Ensign	30-08-77	MO	16th	Capt.Simpson	AM 16-350	
Hanson, George	1st Lt	16-03-76	QA		Capt.Wright	AM 11-254	
Hanson, George	Capt	19-06-77	QA	20th		AM 16-295	

APPENDIX A - COMMISSIONED OFFICERS

Name	Rank	Date	Cty	Bn	Company	Ref.	Notes
Hanson, George	Capt	04-06-78	KE	13th		AM 21-122	
Hanson, George	Capt	31-07-78	QA	20th	Capt.J.Dawes	MH 2	Mov
Hanson, George	Lt	30-05-81	KE		Horse troop	AM 45-449	
Hanson, Haskins	2nd Lt	28-05-79	CH	12th	Capt W.Hansen	AM 21-427	
Hanson, Henry Massey	1st Lt	07-03-76	CH		Capt.J.Hanson	AM 11-206	
Hanson, Jas.	Ensign	31-07-78	QA	20th	Capt.J.R.Emory	MH 2	Mn
Hanson, John	Capt	26-07-76	CH			AM 12-125	Mn
Hanson, John(youngest)	Capt	07-03-76	CH			AM 11-206	
Hanson, Peter	Lt	23-07-76			Capt Hardman	AM 12-108	Mn
Hanson, Samuel	Capt	- -75	CH			RC 2-142	Mn
Hanson, Samuel	Surgeon	04-09-77	FR	34th		AM 16-362	
Hanson, Samuel	2nd Maj	17-06-78	CH	26th		AM 21-138	Res
Hanson, Samuel	Ensign	13-11-79	PG	Mid	Capt.C.Wheeler	AM 43-13	
Hanson, Samuel Jr.	2nd Maj	06-01-76	CH	26th		PC 78	
Hanson, Samuel of Samuel	Lt Col	06-01-76	CH	26th		PC 78	
Hanson, Walter	QM	06-01-76	CH	26th		PC 78	
Hanson, Walter (of John)	Capt	07-03-76	CH			AM 11-206	
Harbaugh, Christian	Ensign	29-03-79	FR	34th	Capt.C.Smith	AM 21-331	
Harbin, Edward	2nd Lt	05-09-77	PG	25th	Capt.J.Shaw	AM 16-363	
Harbin, Edward Vellis	1st Lt	01-05-78	PG	25th	Capt.J.Weight	AM 21-62	
Hardcastle, John	Ensign	09-04-78	TA	4th	Hand in Hand	AM 21-24	
Hardcastle, John	2nd Lt	09-04-78	CA	28th	Capt.T.Burk	AM 21-23	
Hardcastle, Robert	1st Lt	19-06-77	CA	28th	Capt.T.Hughlett	AM 16-294	
Hardcastle, Robert	1st Lt	09-04-78	CA	28th	Capt.T.Hughlett	AM 21-23	
Hardcastle, Robert	Capt	17-12-81	CA	28th	Capt.T.Hughlett	AM 48-27	
Hardcastle, Thomas	QM	12-01-76	CA	28th		PC 78	
Hardcastle, Thomas	2nd Lt	13-08-77	CA	28th	Capt.H.Downes	SC 49-154	Mn
Harden, Elias	Capt	14-05-76	MO	29th		AM 11-424	
Hardican, Robert	2nd Lt	20-05-78	DO	3rd	Capt.J.Wright	AM 21-98	OC
Harding, Elias	Capt	12-09-77	MO	29th		AM 16-373	
Harding, Elias	Capt	11-08-79	MO	Up		MH 5	Suc
Harding, Gray	Capt	18-09-80	FR	Town	Capt.P.Keepheart	AM 43-295	
Harding, Walter	Ensign	21-04-79	MO	Up	Capt.Wm.Blackmore	AM 21-356	
Harding, Walter	2nd Lt	25-03-80	MO	Up	Capt.G.Hoskinson	AM 43-120	
Hardman, Henry	2nd Lt	15-05-76	FR	34th	Capt.Charlton	AM 11-426	
Hardy, Anthony	1st Lt	24-05-79	PG	Mid	Capt.E.Lanham	AM 21-414	
Hargadine, Edward	Ensign	31-07-78	QA	20th	Capt.C.Downes	AM 21-172	
Harper, William	2nd Lt	09-04-78	CA	28th	Capt.R.Keen	AM 21-23	
Harper, William	1st Lt	17-12-81	CA	28th	Capt.R.Keene	AM 48-27	
Harrington, Peter	Ensign	13-08-77	CA	28th	Capt.T.Hughlett	SC 49-154	Mn
Harrington, Peter	2nd Lt	09-04-78	CA	28th	Capt.T.Hughlet	AM 21-23	
Harrington, Richard	Ensign	12-04-80	TA	38th	Capt.C.Gardiner	AM 43-140	
Harrington, Richard	1st Lt	04-11-82	TA	38th	Capt.C.Gardiner	AM 48-298	
Harris, Aaron	1st Lt	12-09-77	MO	29th	Capt.R.Beall	AM 16-373	
Harris, Aaron	Capt	04-08-80	MO	Lwr	Capt.R.Beall	AM 43-248	
Harris, David	1st Lt	25-09-80	BA	Town	Capt.B.Griffith	AM 43-303	
Harris, David	Capt	25-11-80	BA	Town	Capt.Thos.Yates	AM 45-223	
Harris, John	Ensign	12-09-77	MO	16th	Capt.T.Sprigg	AM 16-373	
Harris, John	2nd Lt	04-21-79	MO	Up	Capt.Thos.Spriggs	AM 21-356	
Harris, John 2nd	2nd Maj	06-01-76	CH	12th		PC 78	
Harris, Robert	Capt	19-12-75	HA		Minuteman	PC 54	Mn
Harris, Robert	Capt	26-04-76	HA	8th		AM 11-387	
Harris, Thomas	Capt	- -75	CH			RC 2-142	Mn
Harris, Thomas	Maj	26-02-76	CH			AM 11-186	

APPENDIX A - COMMISSIONED OFFICERS

Name	Rank	Date	Cty	Bn	Company	Ref.	Notes
Harris, Thomas	Capt	29-08-77	QA	5th		SC 48-161	OC
Harris, Thomas	Capt	04-08-79	QA	5th		SC 48-161	Res
Harris, Thomas	Lt Col	19-01-81	CH	12th		AM 45-280	
Harris, Zadock	2nd Lt	12-09-77	MO	29th	Capt.R.Beall	AM 16-373	
Harris, Zadock	1st Lt	04-08-80	MO	Lwr	Capt.A.Harris	AM 43-248	
Harrison, Benjamin	Ensign	17-04-76	AA		Capt.Weems	AM 11-336	
Harrison, Benjamin	2nd Lt	02-03-78	AA	WstR	Capt.R.Weems	AM 16-526	
Harrison, Benjamin	Capt	02-05-81	AA	WstR	Capt.R.Weems	AM 45-422	
Harrison, Jonathan C.	Ensign	12-09-76	DO	19th	Capt.E.Vickars	AM 12-266	
Harrison, Joseph	2nd Lt	16-05-76	TA	38th	Capt.Rothe	AM 11-428	
Harrison, Joseph W.	2nd Lt	07-03-76	CH		Capt.W.Hanson	AM 11-206	
Harrison, Richard	Ensign	02-03-78	AA	WstR	Capt.R.Weems	AM 16-526	
Harrison, Richard	Capt	11-05-81			"Decoy"	AM 45-432	
Harrison, Richard of Rich	1st Lt	02-05-81	AA	WstR	Capt.S.Chew	AM 45-422	
Harrison, Robert	1st Maj	10-02-76	DO	19th		AM 11-147	
Harrison, Robert	1st Lt	16-05-76	TA	38th	Capt.Rothe	AM 11-428	
Harrison, Robert	Lt Col	23-10-76	DO	Lw		AM 12-393	
Harrison, Robert	Colonel	20-05-78	DO	19th		AM 21-97	
Harrison, Robert	Colonel	08-02-81	DO			AM 47-59	Res
Harrison, Thomas	Ensign	16-05-76	TA	38th	Capt.Rothe	AM 11-428	
Harrison, Thomas	Ensign	09-04-78	TA	38th	United	AM 21-25	
Harrison, William	Capt	- -75	CH			RC 2-142	Mn
Harrison, William	Colonel	06-01-76	CH	26th		PC 78	
Hart, Joseph	Ensign	20-11-76	BA		Capt.B.Owings	AM 12-541	
Hart, Joseph	2nd Lt	30-08-77	BA	GPUp	Capt.W.Harvey	AM 16-350	
Hart, Robert	2nd Lt	09-09-78	CE	30th		AM 21-196	
Hart, Robert Jr.	Ensign	21-04-78	CE	Susq	Capt.S.Hyland	AM 21-48	
Hart, Robert Jr.	1st Lt	03-01-82	CE	Susq		AM 48-38	
Hartestiom, Joshua	Ensign	27-05-79	BA	SD	Capt.W.Hudson	AM 21-422	
Hartshorn, George	Capt	11-03-79	KE	13th		AM 21-320	
Hartshorn, John	1st Maj	06-01-76	CE	30th		PC 80	
Harvey, Nicholas	2nd Lt	23-10-76	BA	GPUp	Capt.W.Harvey	AM 45-650	
Harvey, William	1st Lt	20-11-76	BA		Capt.B.Owings	AM 12-541	
Harvey, William	Capt	30-08-77	BA	GPUp		AM 16-350	
Harvy, David	2nd Lt	26-09-76	WA		Capt.D.Clapsaddle	AM 12-301	
Harwood, Benjamin	1st Lt	15-02-77	AN			AM 16-138	
Harwood, Benjamin	Capt	06-10-77	AN		Independent	AM 16-392	
Harwood, Benjamin	2nd Lt	01-05-78	PG	25th	Capt.H.Magruder	AM 21-62	
Harwood, Benjamin	Capt	24-06-80	PG	Up	Capt.Jos.Jones	AM 43-203	
Harwood, Benjamin	Capt	27-06-81	PG	Up		AM 47-320	Res
Harwood, John	2nd Lt	30-08-77	MO	16th	Capt.Simpson	AM 16-350	
Harwood, John	Capt	12-09-77	MO	16th		AM 16-373	
Harwood, Richard Jr.	Lt Col	06-01-76	AA	WstR		PC 79	
Harwood, Richard	Lt Col	02-03-78	AA	WstR		AM 16-525	
Harwood, Thomas	Capt	01-09-81	PG		Horse troop	AM 45-596	
Harwood, William	Ensign	12-02-76	AA	WstR	Capt. Watkins	AM 11-158	
Harwood, William	Ensign	02-03-78	AA	WstR	Capt.T.Watkins	AM 16-525	
Harwood, William	2nd Lt	17-08-79	AA	WstR	Capt.T.Watkins	AM 21-496	
Haskins, Josiah	Colonel	06-01-76	CH	12th		PC 78	
Haslet, William	Capt	09-03-76	CA			AM 11-230	Mn
Haslet, William	Colonel	09-04-78	CA	28th		AM 21-23	
Hasslett, William	Colonel	17-12-81	CA	28th		AM 48-27	Suc
Hatton, Jacon	Ensign	20-05-78	DO	Up	Capt.J.Henry	AM 21-98	
Haward, James	2nd Lt	28-08-77	AA	22nd	Capt.J.Dorsey	AM 16-347	

APPENDIX A - COMMISSIONED OFFICERS

Name	Rank	Date	Cty	Bn	Company	Ref.	Notes
Hawkersmith, George	Capt	28-11-76	FR	35th		AM 12-555	
Hawkersmith, Jacob	2nd Lt	28-11-76	FR	35th	Capt.Hawkersmith	AM 12-555	
Hawkersmith, Michael	2nd Lt	28-11-76	FR	35th	Capt.J.Shields	AM 12-555	
Hawkins, James	1st Lt	01-05-78	PG	11th	Capt.H.Wheeler	AM 21-78	
Hawkins, Josiah	Capt	-75	CH			RC 2-142	Mn
Hawkins, Josiah	Colonel	03-01-76	CH	12th		PA	Mn
Hawkins, Josiah	Colonel	23-09-83	CH	12th		PA	Res
Hawkins, Matthew	Capt	07-06-81	QA	5th	Capt.V.Benton	AM 45-465	
Hay, James	1st Lt	31-05-81	BA	Town	Capt.B.Dickinson	AM 45-452	
Haye, Thomas	Ensign	16-03-76	PG			AM 11-253	
Hayes, Thomas	1st Lt	12-09-77	MO	16th	Capt.R.Smith	AM 16-373	
Hayman, John	2nd Lt	06-06-76	BA	Town	Capt.Wells	AM 11-467	
Hayner, James	2nd Lt	22-09-77	SO	Salb	Capt.L.Irving	AH 16-381	
Hays, John	Ensign	27-07-76	FR			AM 12-127	
Hays, Thomas	Ensign	26-03-76	MO		Capt.Smith	AM 11-287	
Hays, Thomas	Capt	21-04-79	MO	Up	Capt.R.Smith	AM 21-356	
Hays, Thomas	Capt	25-03-80	MO	Up		AM 43-120	Suc
Hayter, Abraham	Capt	29-11-75	FR	3rd		MM 11:50	
Hayward, Thomas	Colonel	06-01-76	SO	17th		PC 80	
Hayward, Thomas	Colonel	30-08-77	SO	PrAn		AM 16-351	OC
Hayward, Thomas	Colonel	29-01-81	SO	PrAn		AM 47-40	Res
Hayward, William	2nd Lt	22-09-77	SO	PrAn	Capt.G.Waters	AM 16-381	
Hazard, Elihu	Ensign	15-05-76	WO	10th	Capt.Gray	AM 11-426	
Hazle, Caleb	2nd Lt	02-03-78	AA	Svrn	Capt.Maccubbin	AM 16-575	
Hazle, Caleb	1st Lt	22-05-79	AA	7th	Capt.F.Cromwell	AM 21-410	
Hazle, Caleb	Capt	18-10-82	AA	Svrn	Capt.F.Cromwell	AM 48-288	
Head, Bigger	Ensign	29-11-75	FR	2nd	Capt.R.Wood	MM 11:50	
Head, Bigger	2nd Lt	15-05-76	FR	37th	Capt.Beall	AM 11-426	
Head, Bigger	1st Lt	28-11-76	FR	37th	Capt.W.B.Head	AM 12-555	
Head, William Beckwith	2nd Lt	29-11-75	FR	2nd	Capt.R.Wood	MM 11:50	
Head, William Beckwith	1st Lt	15-05-76	FR	37th	Capt.Beall	AM 11-426	
Head, William Beckwith	Capt	28-11-76	FR	37th		AM 12-555	
Heagle, Jacob	Ensign	27-07-76	FR			AM 12-127	
Heard, Jonathan	Ensign	22-06-80	SM	Lwr	Capt.B.Combs	AM 43-201	
Heath, Charles	Capt	21-04-78	CE	Sass		AM 21-47	
Heath, William	1st Lt	02-09-77	AA	Svrn	Capt.J.Gray	AM 16-358	
Hebb, Vernon	Lt Col	26-08-77	SM	Lwr		AM 16-346	
Heddington, Abel	QM	01-09-77	BA			AM 16-355	
Hedge, Joseph	Ensign	29-11-75	FR	4th	Capt.M.Troutman	MM 11:50	
Hedge, William	1st Lt	29-11-75	FR	1st	Capt.C.Stull	MM 11:50	
Hedge, William	1st Lt	03-03-77	FR	33rd	Capt.C.Stull	MM 4:379	Mn
Heighe, James	1st Lt	10-04-76	CV		Capt.Freeland	AM 11-320	
Heighe, James	1st Lt	16-04-78	CV	15th	Capt.F.Freeland	AM 21-37	
Hellen, Jesse	Capt	01-05-78	PG	11th		AM 21-62	
Hemsley, William	1st Maj	12-01-76	QA	20th		PC 78	
Hemsley, William	Colonel	08-05-77	QA	20th		AM 16-244	
Hemsley, William	Cty Lt	01-07-77	QA			AM 16-304	
Hench, John	2nd Lt	22-06-78	WA	3rdW	Capt.D.Cresap	AM 21-145	
Henderson, Richard	Officer	04-08-75	PG			AM 11-49	Mn
Henet, John	2nd Lt	27-07-76	FR			AM 12-127	
Henry, Hugh	Ensign	31-07-78	QA	5th	Capt.I.Scriviner	AM 21-172	
Henry, Hugh	2nd Lt	20-04-80	QA	5th	Capt.S.Ridgeway	AM 43-146	
Henry, Isaac	Ensign	22-09-77	SO	Salb	Capt.L.Irving	AM 16-381	
Henry, James	Capt	13-06-77	QA	5th		RC 2-1119	Mn

APPENDIX A - COMMISSIONED OFFICERS

Name	Rank	Date	Cty	Bn	Company	Ref.	Notes
Henry, John	Capt	20-05-78	DO	3rd	Vienna	AM 21-98	
Henry, John	Capt	15-07-80	DO	3rd		FP 2-71	Mn
Henry, William	Lt Col	08-05-77	KE	27th		AM 16-243	
Henson, Jonathan	Ensign	30-08-77	WO	SnH1	Capt.J.Patterson	AM 16-351	
Henton, John	2nd Lt	21-04-79	MO	Up	Capt.Wm.Norris	AM 21-357	
Hepburn, Samuel	1st Lt	01-05-78	PG	Mid	Capt.J.Brooks	AM 21-63	
Hepburn, Samuel	Capt	24-06-80	PG	Mid	Capt.J.Brookes	AM 43-203	
Herbert, William	Ensign	16-04-78	SM	21st	Capt.J.Mackall	AM 21-37	
Herrington, Peter	Ensign	19-06-77	CA	28th	Capt.Hughlett	AM 16-294	
Hickman, Charles	2nd Lt	15-05-76	SO	1st	Capt.McClester	AM 11-426	
Hickman, Matthias	Ensign	26-09-76	WA		Capt.D.Clapsaddle	AM 12-301	
Hickman, William	2nd Lt	25-03-80	MO	Up	Capt.G.Walter	AM 43-120	
Hicks, Abraham	1st Lt	30-08-77	BA	Up	Capt.R.Cummins	AM 16-350	
Hicks, Denwood	Capt	24-05-76	DO			AM 11-441	
Hicks, William Ennalls	2nd Lt	01-03-79	DO	Up	Capt.Smoot	AM 21-310	
Hicks, William Ennalls	1st Lt	02-07-81	DO	Up	Capt.L.Kirkman	AM 45-492	
Hill, Abell	Ensign	15-02-76	AA	WstR	Capt.Simmons	AM 11-161	
Hill, Abel	Ensign	02-03-78	AA	WstR	Capt.A.Simmons	AM 16-525	
Hill, Abrahamn	1st Lt	29-11-75	FR	3rd	Capt.A.Hayter	MM 11:50	
Hill, Clement 3rd	2nd Lt	01-05-78	PG	Mid	Capt.W.Berry	AM 21-63	
Hill, Edward	1st Lt	15-05-76	FR	31st	Lt.Inf.Co.	AM 11-426	
Hill, Frederick	Ensign	19-02-77	SO		Capt. Handy	AM 16-144	
Hill, Frederick	Ensign	30-08-77	WO	Wico	Capt.R.Handy	AM 16-351	
Hill, Frederick	1st Lt	22-09-77	SO	PrAn	Capt.R.Handy	AM 16-381	
Hill, Henry	Capt	01-05-78	PG	11th		AM 21-78	
Hill, Henry Jr.	2nd Lt	01-08-77	PG	Lwr	Capt.T.Dent	AM 16-356	
Hill, John	Ensign	10-04-76	CE		Capt.Mackey	AM 11-319	
Hill, John	2nd Lt	21-04-78	CE	Elk	Capt.J.Macky	AM 21-47	
Hill, Joseph	2nd Lt	09-11-76	FR		Capt.Mackall	AM 12-432	
Hill, Levin	Ensign	30-08-77	WO	SnH1	Capt.J.Paramor	AM 16-351	
Hill, Philip	Lt	25-04-81			Bay Cav Co.	AM 45-414	
Hill, Richard	2nd Lt	24-06-80	PG	Mid	Capt.Z.Berry	AM 43-203	
Hill, Thomas	Ensign	18-09-80	FR	Town	Capt.G.Harding	AM 43-295	
Hill, William	1st Lt	- -	WA			FP 1-129	Suc
Hillary, Henry	1st Lt	21-04-79	MO	Mid	Capt.C.Bruce	AM 21-357	
Hillary, Ralph	1st Lt	29-11-75	FR	1st	Capt.S.Plummer	MM 11:50	
Hilleary, Ralph	Capt	03-03-77	FR	33rd		MM 4:379	Mn
Hilleary, Ralph	Capt	16-08-81	FR	SelM		AM 45-566	
Hilleary, Thomas	Ensign	16-08-81	FR	SelM		AM 45-566	
Hinckel, John	Ensign	29-11-75	FR		Capt.H.Baker	MM 11:50	
Hinckell, John	Ensign	28-11-76	FR		Capt.H.Baker	AM 12-555	
Hindman, William	1st Lt	17-06-77	TA	4th	Union	RC 2-1130	Rec
Hinds, Henry	2nd Lt	16-08-79	FR	Town	Capt.E.Salmon	AM 21-494	
Hinson, James	2nd Lt	30-08-77	WO	SnH1	Capt.J.Patterson	AM 16-351	
Hisler, Nicholas	2nd Lt	12-05-79	FR	Town	Capt.T.Beatty	AM 21-387	
Hitch, Robert	Capt	11-04-76	SO	1st		AM 11-327	
Hitch, Severn	QM	06-01-76	SO	1st		PC 80	
Hitchcock, Azael	2nd Lt	26-04-76	HA	8th	Capt.Bussey	AM 11-387	
Hitchcock, Josiah	Ensign	26-01-77	HA	8th	Capt.B.Amos	AM 16-77	
Hitchcock, Josias	2nd Lt	09-04-78	HA	8th	Capt.B.Amos	AM 21-24	
Hobbs, Joseph	1st Lt	29-11-75	FR		Capt.B.Dorsey	MM 11:50	
Hobbs, Joseph	1st Lt	28-11-76	FR		Capt.B.Dorsey	AM 12-555	
Hobbs, Nicholas	2nd Lt	29-11-75	FR		Capt.B.Dorsey	MM 11:50	
Hobbs, Nicholas	2nd Lt	28-11-76	FR		Capt.B.Dorsey	AM 12-555	

APPENDIX A - COMMISSIONED OFFICERS

Name	Rank	Date	Cty	Bn	Company	Ref.	Notes
Hobbs, Nicholas	Ensign	30-03-79	AA	22nd	Capt.R.Warfield	AM 21-333	
Hobbs, Samuel	1st Lt	27-07-76	FR			AM 12-127	
Hockersmith, George	1st Lt	29-11-75	FR	3rd	Capt.W.Blair	MM 11:50	
Hockersmith, Jacob	Ensign	29-11-75	FR	3rd	Capt.W.Blair	MM 11:50	
Hockersmith, Michael	2nd Lt	29-11-75	FR	3rd	Capt.W.Shields	MM 11:50	
Hockey, Nicholas	Lt	30-03-81	WA	SM	Capt.A.Ott	AM 45-368	
Hodgson, Richard	Cornet	14-06-81	CE		Horse troop	AM 45-474	
Hodgson, Robert	2nd Lt	21-04-78	CE	Sass	Capt.J.Ford	AM 21-47	
Hodgson, Robert	1st Lt	22-06-78	CE	Bohe	Capt.S.Lankaster	AM 21-145	
Hodson, James	Ensign	01-03-79	DO	Up	Capt.B.Ennalls	AM 21-310	
Hoffman, Francis	Ensign	29-11-75	FR		Capt.L.Kemp	MM 11:50	
Hoffstadler, Henry	Ensign	03-08-81	FR	SelM	Capt.T.Beatty	AM 45-538	
Hoge, Thomas	2nd Lt	01-05-78	PG	11th	Capt.R.Bowie	AM 21-62	
Hoggy, ---	Lt	06-12-81	FR			AM 47-568	Mn
Hogmire, Conrad	Capt	03-01-76	FR	32nd		SC 48-159	OC
Hogmire, Conrad		10-10-76	WA			SP 2523	Res
Holding, James	Ensign	31-07-78	QA	5th	Capt.Tho.Harris	AM 21-172	
Holding, James	2nd Lt	20-04-80	QA	5th	Capt.Seager	AM 43-146	
Holding, James	1st Lt	07-06-81	QA	5th	Capt.J.Thompson	AM 45-465	
Holding, Richard	Capt	20-04-80	QA	5th	Capt.Wm.Brown	AM 43-146	
Holland, Francis	Colonel	09-04-78	HA	23rd		AM 21-23	
Holland, John	Ensign	16-03-81	WO	Snpx	Capt.J.Dale	AM 45-353	
Holland, Stephen	Ensign	21-04-79	MO	Mid		AM 21-357	
Holland, Stephen	2nd Lt	25-03-80	MO	Mid	Capt.J.Dickinson	AM 43-120	
Holland, William	Capt	30-08-77	WO	SnHl		AM 16-351	
Holland, William	Maj	27-05-79	WO	SnHl		AM 21-423	
Hollingsworth, Henry	Lt Col	06-01-76	CE	2nd		PC 80	
Hollingsworth, Henry	Colonel	07-06-81	CE	Elk		AM 45-465	
Hollingsworth, Jacob	2nd Lt	21-04-78	CE	Elk	Capt.J.Booth	AM 21-47	
Hollyday, Robert	QM	12-10-76	BA	GP		AM 12-337	
Holmes, William	1st Lt	05-09-77	PG	25th	Capt.J.Shaw	AM 16-363	
Holmes, William	1st Lt	17-12-77	PG	25th	Capt.J.Shaw	PA	Res
Holmes, William	1st Lt	13-01-78				SP 5817	Res
Holt, Isaac	Ensign	07-06-81	CE	Elk	Capt.A.Cazier	AM 45-466	OC
Holton, William	Ensign	16-04-78	SM	21st	Capt.J.H.Abell	AM 21-37	
Hood, Benjamin	Ensign	25-08-77	AA		Capt.Ellicot	AM 16-343	
Hood, John	1st Lt	03-01-76	AA			MH 1	Com
Hooe, Robert T.	1st Maj	06-01-76	CH	12th		PC 78	
Hook, James	1st Lt	09-04-78	TA	4th	Volunteer	AM 21-24	OC
Hooke, John	Ensign	05-11-81	BA	Up	Capt.N.Merryman	AM 45-662	
Hooke, Joseph	2nd Lt	20-08-81	BA	Town	Capt.F.Deems	AM 45-572	
Hooker, Aquila	1st Lt	06-06-76	BA	SD	Capt.Hammond	AM 11-467	
Hooper, Ennalls		23-06-79	DO	Up		FP 2-73	Dis
Hooper, Henry	Colonel	14-08-75				AM 11-14	Mn
Hooper, Henry	BrigGen	06-01-76				PC 78	
Hooper, Henry	Cty Lt	01-07-77	DO			AM 16-304	
Hooper, James	2nd Lt	20-05-78	DO	3rd	Capt.L.Hanley	AM 21-98	
Hooper, James	Ensign	16-08-79	FR	Town	Capt.E.Salmon	AM 21-494	
Hooper, James	1st Lt	16-12-79	DO	Up		DO 231	Mn
Hooper, James	1st Lt	02-07-81	DO	Up	Capt.J.Hooper	AM 45-492	
Hooper, John	1st Lt	09-04-78	CA	14th	Capt.S.Liden	AM 21-23	
Hooper, John	1st Lt	20-05-78	DO	3rd	Capt.L.Hanley	AM 21-98	
Hooper, John	Capt	28-06-80	CA	14th	Capt.S.Lyden	AM 43-207	
Hooper, John	Capt	02-04-81	DO	Up		DO 231	Mn

APPENDIX A - COMMISSIONED OFFICERS

Name	Rank	Date	Cty	Bn	Company	Ref.	Notes
Hooper, John	Capt	12-06-81	CA	14th		MH 2	Res
Hooper, John	Capt	02-07-81	DO	Up	Capt.W.E.Hooper	AM 45-492	
Hooper, John	Capt	17-12-81	CA	14th		AM 48-27	Suc
Hooper, John Ascum	1st Lt	24-06-77	CA	14th	Capt.S.Lighton	AM 16-299	
Hooper, Joseph	Ensign	16-12-79	DO	Up		DO 230	Mn
Hooper, Roger	2nd Lt	16-04-78	CV	15th	Capt.T.Cleland	AM 21-37	
Hooper, Roger	1st Lt	03-05-80	CV		Capt.Thos.Cleland	AM 43-162	
Hooper, Roger A	Capt	20-05-78	DO	3rd		AM 21-98	
Hooper, Roger Askom	Capt	15-07-80	DO	3rd		FP 2-71	Mn
Hooper, Samuel	1st Lt	11-06-77	DO	19th	Capt.Stapleford	AM 16-282	
Hooper, Samuel	2nd Lt	20-05-78	DO	19th	Capt.C.Stappleford	AM 21-97	
Hooper, Samuel	1st Lt	16-12-79	DO	Up	Capt.R.Hooper	AM 43-37	
Hooper, Samuel	2nd Lt	31-08-81	DO		Capt.R.Hooper	AM 47-462	Res
Hooper, Samuel A	Ensign	20-05-78	DO	3rd	Capt.R.Hooper	AM 21-98	
Hooper, Samuel A	Ensign	28-07-80	DO	Up	Capt.R.Hooper	AM 43-236	
Hooper, William	Lt	31-05-81	DO		Horse troop	AM 45-452	
Hooper, William Ennalls	Capt	28-07-80	DO	Up	Capt.Levin Handy	AM 43-236	
Hooper, William Ennalls	Capt	02-07-81	DO	Up		AM 45-492	Suc
Hope, Thomas	Capt	09-04-78	HA	Deer		AM 21-22	OC
Hopewell, George	1st Lt	07-05-81	SM	Lwr	Capt.J.Chesley	AM 45-426	
Hopewell, Hugh	QM	12-01-76	SM	21st		PC 78	
Hopewell, Hugh	Capt	26-08-77	SM	Lwr		AM 16-346	
Hopewell, Hugh	Capt	07-05-81	SM	Lwr		AM 45-426	Suc
Hopewell, William	Colonel	30-08-77	WO	Wico		AM 16-351	OC
Hopewell, William	Colonel	03-06-81	WO	Wico		AM 47-269	Res
Hopewell,Polard	2nd Lt	07-05-81	SM	Lwr	Capt.S.Jenifer	AM 45-426	
Hopkins, Thomas	Capt	09-04-78	TA	38th	United	AM 21-25	
Hopper, William	Capt	13-08-77	CA	28th		SC 49-154	Mn
Hopper, William	Col	31-10-77				SP 5241	Mn
Horsey, John	1st Lt	22-09-77	SO	PrAn	Capt.H.Miles	AM 16-381	
Horsey, John	Ensign	23-08-81	SO	SelM	Capt.J.Williams	AM 45-577	
Horsey, Outerbridge	Capt	- -78	DO			SP 5581	Mn
Horsey, Samuel	Capt	30-08-77	WO	Wico		AM 16-351	
Horsey, William	2nd Maj	06-01-76	SO	1st		PC 80	
Horsgadrie, Edward	Ensign	31-07-78	QA	20th	Capt.C.Downes	MH 2	Rec
Horskins, George	Ensign	12-09-77	MO	16th	Capt.S.Simpson	AM 16-373	
Horskinson, George	1st Lt	21-04-79	MO	Up	Capt.Wm.Blackmore	AM 21-356	
Hoskinson, George	Capt	25-03-80	MO	Up	Capt.Wm.Blackmore	AM 43-120	
Hoskinson, Hugh	Ensign	25-03-80	MO	Up	Capt.J.Sommers	AM 43-120	
House, John	2nd Lt	27-07-76	FR			AM 12-127	
House, John	2nd Lt	22-06-78	WA	3rdW	Capt.C.Clinton	AM 21-145	
Houston, Isaac	1st Lt	28-06-77	WO			RC 2-1156	Mn
Houston, Isaac		13-08-77	WO	Wico		SC 48-154	Res
Houston, Isaac	Capt	30-08-77	WO	Wico		AM 16-351	
Houston, Isaac	Capt	08-05-78	WO			MH 5	Res
Houston, James	Ensign	28-06-77	WO		Capt.J.Patterson	RC 2-1156	Dec
Houston, William	Cornet	13-06-82	KE		Horse troop	AM 48-190	
Howard, Benjamin	QM	12-01-76	AA	ElkR		PC 78	
Howard, Brice	Capt	03-01-76	AA			SC 48-153	OC
Howard, Brice	Capt	- -	AA			SC 48-153	Res
Howard, Charles Wallace	1st Lt	06-10-77	AN		Capt.B.Harwood	AM 16-392	
Howard, Ephraim	1st Lt	29-11-75	FR		Capt.D.Moore	MM 11:50	
Howard, Ephraim	2nd Maj	28-11-76	FR			AM 12-555	OC
Howard, Ephraim	2nd Maj	02-01-77	FR	Ling		AM 16-8	Ref

APPENDIX A - COMMISSIONED OFFICERS

Name	Rank	Date	Cty	Bn	Company	Ref.	Notes
Howard, Ephraim	Surgeon	03-09-77	AA	Svrn		AM 16-359	
Howard, Henry	Capt	20-11-76	BA			AM 12-541	
Howard, Henry	Capt	31-10-80	BA	GPUp		AM 43-345	
Howard, James	2nd Lt	24-07-76			Capt Danl Dorsey	AM 12-109	Mn
Howard, James	2nd Lt	18-04-81	BA	Town	Capt.M.Crane	AM 45-401	
Howard, John Beale	2nd Lt	16-09-75	HA		#6	PR 112	
Howard, John Beale	1st Lt	26-04-76	HA		Capt.Caven	AM 11-387	
Howard, John Beale	1st Lt	29-06-76	HA		Capt.A.Cowen	AM 11-538	
Howard, John Edgar	2nd Lt	19-12-75	BA		Capt.T.Rutter	RB 13-37	
Howard, Samuel Harvey	2nd Lt	06-10-77	AN		Capt.N.Maccubbin	AM 16-392	
Howard, Samuel Harvey	Capt	12-02-80	AN		Independent	AM 43-84	
Howard, Samuel Harvy	1st Lt	20-03-79	AN		Capt.Brice-Ind	AM 21-325	
Howard, Thomas Cornelius	Ensign	13-04-76	AA		Capt.Howard	AM 11-329	
Howard, Thomas Henry	AstSurg	20-01-77			to Dr.Tootell	AM 16-63	
Howard, Thomas Henry	2nd Lt	09-04-81	AN		Capt.S.H.Howard	AM 45-385	
Howard, Thomas Henry	1st Lt	18-06-81	AN		Capt.S.H.Howard	AM 45-479	
Hoy, Paul	1st Lt	12-09-77	MO	Mid	Capt.R.Brooke	AM 16-373	
Hoye, Thomas	2nd Lt	24-05-79	PG	11th	Capt.J.Beanes	AM 21-414	
Hubbard, Joseph	2nd Lt	16-12-79	DO	Lwr	Capt.J.Byns	AM 43-37	
Hubbard, Joseph	Capt	28-07-80	DO	Lwr		DO 233	Mn
Hubbard, Levin	Capt	16-12-79	DO	Lwr	Capt.J.Woolford	AM 43-37	
Hubbard, Samuel	Ensign	16-12-79	DO	Lwr	Capt.J.Byus	AM 43-37	
Hubbard, Thomas	Ensign	20-05-78	DO	19th	Capt.J.Woolford	AM 21-97	
Hubbard, Thomas	Ensign	16-12-79	DO	Lwr	Capt.L.Hubbard	AM 43-37	
Hubberd, Joseph	Capt	28-07-80	DO	Lwr	Capt.James Byus	AM 43-236	
Hubberd, Samuel	2nd Lt	28-07-80	DO	Lwr	Capt.J.Fletcher	AM 43-236	
Hubbert, Joseph	2nd Lt	11-06-76	DO	19th	Capt.Stapleford	AM 16-283	
Hubbert, Joseph	2nd Lt	20-05-78	DO	19th	Capt.J.Byus	AM 21-97	
Hubbert, Samuel	Ensign	11-06-77	DO	19th	Capt.Staplefort	AM 16-283	
Hubbert, Samuel	Ensign	20-05-78	DO	19th	Capt.J.Byus	AM 21-97	
Hubbs, Samuel	1st Lt	22-06-78	WA	3rdW	Capt.D.Cresap	AM 21-145	
Hudson, Robert	Ensign	09-10-77	AA	E1kR	Capt.Hammond	AM 16-387	
Hudson, William	1st Lt	06-06-76	BA	SD	Capt.Carnan	AM 11-467	
Hudson, William	Capt	29-08-77	BA	SD		AM 16-348	
Huggins, Thomas	QM	06-01-76	CE	2nd		PC 80	
Hughes, Daniel	Cty Lt	01-07-77	WA			AM 16-304	
Hughes, John Hall	1st Lt	16-05-76	HA	23rd	Capt.Griffith	AM 11-428	
Hughes, Samuel	Capt	- -	WA			FP 1-129	Suc
Hughes, Thomas	Lt Col	06-01-76	CE	30th		PC 80	
Hughlet, Thomas	Capt	09-04-78	CA	28th		AM 21-23	
Hughlett, ---	Capt	19-06-77	CA	28th		AM 16-294	
Hughlett, Thomas	Maj	17-12-81	CA	28th		AM 48-27	
Hughlett, Thomas	Capt	17-12-81	CA	28th		AM 48-27	Suc
Hugo, Thomas B.	2nd Lt	13-06-77	QA	5th		RC 2-1119	Mn
Humphreys, Thomas	1st Lt	16-05-78	WA	3rdW	Capt.J.Prather	AM 21-86	
Humphries, Thomas	2nd Lt	11-04-76	DO	1st	Capt.Hitch	AM 11-327	
Hunt, Benjamin	Ensign	19-03-79	BA	Town	Capt.B.Dickinson	AM 21-324	
Hunt, Benjamin	Ensign	19-05-79	BA	Town	Capt.B.Dickinson	AM 21-401	
Hunt, John Wilkinson	2nd Lt	16-04-78	CV	15th	Capt.F.Skinner	AM 21-37	
Hunt, Morgan	1st Lt	04-06-78	KE	13th	Capt.J.Williamson	AM 21-122	
Hupington, Jonathan	Ensign	19-08-76	SO	1st	Capt.J.Philips	AM 12-220	
Hupstadler, Henry	Ensign	12-05-79	FR	Town	Capt.T.Beatty	AM 21-387	
Hurd, Joshua	Ensign	29-08-77	BA	SD	Capt.T.Owings	AM 16-348	
Hurd, Joshua	Capt	27-05-79	BA	SD	Capt.T.Owings	AM 21-414	

APPENDIX A - COMMISSIONED OFFICERS

Name	Rank	Date	Cty	Bn	Company	Ref.	Notes
Hurd, Joshua	Capt	07-02-82	BA	SD		AM 48-71	Suc
Hutchens, Richard	2nd Lt	09-04-78	HA	8th	Capt.C.Baker	AM 21-24	
Hutchens, Thomas	Capt	09-04-78	HA	8th		AM 21-24	
Hutchings, Richard	2nd Lt	14-05-76	HA	8th	Capt.Baker	AM 11-424	
Hutchings, Thomas	1st Lt	16-04-78	CV	15th	Capt.E.Wood	AM 21-37	
Hutchins, Richard	2nd Lt	27-01-76	HA		#15-Jarrettsb'g	PR 119	
Hutchins, Thomas	1st Lt	09-09-75	HA		#7	PR 113	
Hutchins, Thomas	1st Lt	26-04-76	HA	8th	Capt.Calwell	AM 11-387	
Hutchinson, Samuel	1st Lt	22-06-78	CE	Bohe	Capt.T.Bouldin Jr	AM 21-145	
Hutchison, Samuel	Ensign	21-04-78	CE	Sass	Capt.T.Brevard	AM 21-47	
Hyland, John	2nd Lt	03-01-82	CE	Susq		AM 48-38	
Hyland, Lambert	2nd Lt	22-09-77	SO	Salb	Capt.G.Wilson	AM 16-382	
Hyland, Lambert	Capt	22-08-81	SO	PrAn	Capt.I.Handy	AM 45-575	
Hyland, Stephen	Capt	23-05-76	CE			AM 11-438	
Hyland, Stephen	Capt	21-04-78	CE	Susq		AM 21-48	
Hyland, Stephen	Colonel	09-09-78	CE	30th		AM 21-196	
Hyland, Stephen	Capt	09-09-78	CE	30th		AM 21-196	Suc
Hynes, Andrew	Capt	27-07-76	FR			AM 12-127	
Hynes, Henry	Ensign	26-05-78	FR	Town	Capt.A.Haff	AM 21-111	
Hynes, Thomas	1st Lt	16-05-78	WA	3rdW	Capt.P.Pindell	AM 21-86	
Hynson, John	Ensign	03-01-76	CA	28th		SC 48-152	OC
	- -						
	- -						
Iiams, John	Ensign	12-09-77	AA	31st	Capt.W.Brogden	AM 16-372	
Ijams, John Jr	2nd Lt	02-03-78	AA	WstR	Capt.T.Watkins	AM 16-525	
Inslow, Joseph	Ensign	16-05-78	WA	3rdW	Capt.Cresap	AM 21-86	
Ireland, Gilbert	2nd Lt	16-04-78	CV	15th	Capt.J.Leach	AM 21-37	
Ireland, Joseph	1st Lt	16-04-78	CV	15th	Capt.T.Cleland	AM 21-37	
Irving, John	Ensign	22-09-77	SO	PrAn	Capt.Waters	SC 48-184	OC
Irving, John	1st Lt	07-01-78	SO	PrAn	Capt.W.Waters	AM 16-457	OC
Irving, John	1st Lt	07-12-78	SO	PrAn	Capt.J.Elzey	AM 21-260	
Irving, Levin	Capt	22-09-77	SO	PrAn	Black Water	AM 16-381	
Irving, Thomas	Capt	22-09-77	SO	PrAn	Monie	AM 16-381	
Irving, Thomas	Maj	28-10-80	SO	PrAn		AM 43-342	
Israel, Basil	Ensign	28-08-77	AA	22nd	Capt.J.Dorsey	AM 16-347	
Isreal, Bazil	1st Lt	30-03-79	AA	22nd	Capt.N.Warfield	AM 21-333	
	- -						
	- -						
Jackson, Archibald	Ensign	17-12-81	CA	28th	Capt.A.Robertson	AM 48-27	
Jackson, Edward	2nd Lt	03-01-82	CE	Susq	Capt.F.Boyd	AM 48-38	
Jackson, George	Ensign	22-06-76	KE		Capt.St.Clair	AM 11-506	
Jackson, Henry	1st Lt	22-09-77	SO	PrAn	Capt.D.Wilson	AM 16-381	OC
Jackson, Peter	2nd Lt	17-12-81	CA	28th	Capt.A.Robertson	AM 48-27	
Jackson, Samuel	Capt	09-04-78	CA	28th		AM 21-23	
Jackson, Samuel	Capt	17-12-81	CA	28th		AM 48-27	Suc
Jackson, William	Ensign	09-04-78	CA	28th	Capt.S.Jackson	AM 21-23	
Jackson, William	Ensign	01-05-78	PG	25th	Capt.J.Selby	AM 21-78	
Jackson, William	1st Lt	17-12-81	CA	28th	Capt.A.Robertson	AM 48-27	
Jacob, John Jeremiah	Ensign	15-05-76	FR		Capt.Waring	AM 11-427	
Jacob, Samuel	1st Lt	09-09-77	AA	7th	Capt.Boon	AM 16-367	
Jacob, Samuel	Capt	23-04-81	AA	Svrn	Capt.J.Boone	AM 45-411	
Jacob, William	1st Lt	25-09-80	BA	Town	Capt.J.Young	AM 43-303	
Jacob, Zacharius	2nd Lt	23-04-81	AA	Svrn	Capt.C.Boone	AM 45-411	
Jacobs, Mordecai	Ensign	24-05-79	PG	25th	Capt.M.Duvall	AM 21-414	

APPENDIX A - COMMISSIONED OFFICERS

Name	Rank	Date	Cty	Bn	Company	Ref.	Notes
Jacobs, William	Ensign	07-02-77	BA		Capt.Rutter	AM 16-121	
Jacobs, Zacharius	Ensign	19-09-78	AA	7th	Capt.John Boone	AM 21-208	
James, George	Ensign	22-08-81	SO	Salb	Capt.W.Turpin	AM 45-575	
James, Sedwick	Ensign	09-04-78	HA	Deer	Capt.W.Fisher	AM 21-22	
James, Solomon	Ensign	16-05-76	TA	4th	Capt.Lloyd	AM 11-428	
Jarboe, Robert	Ensign	26-08-77	SM	Lwr	Capt.H.Hopewell	AM 16-346	
Jarrett, Abraham	Capt	19-12-75	HA		Minuteman	PC 54	
Jarrett, Abraham	1st Maj	06-01-76	HA	8th		PC 80	
Jarrett, Jesse	Ensign	09-04-78	HA	8th	Capt.B.Amos	AM 21-24	
Jarrett, Jesse	Lt	27-02-82	HA		Horse troop	AM 48-87	
Jeane, William	Ensign	30-08-77	BA	GPUp	Capt.W.Harvey	AM 16-350	
Jenifer, Saml	Capt	26-08-77	SM	Lwr		AM 16-346	
Jenkins, Thomas	1st	26-08-77	SM	Lwr	Capt.J.Mackall	AM 16-346	
Jenkins, Thomas	2nd Lt	09-04-78	TA	4th	72nd Volunteer	AM 21-24	
Jenkins, Walter	Ensign	03-12-79	TA	38th	Capt.R.Johnson	AM 43-28	
Job, Daniel	2nd Lt	07-06-81	CE	Elk	Capt.J.Mackey	AM 45-466	
Johns, Richard	1st Lt	09-04-78	TA	4th	Hand in Hand	AM 21-24	
Johns, Richard	Capt	04-11-82	TA	4th	Capt.N.Cooper	AM 48-298	
Johns, Thomas	Lt Col	06-01-76	MO	29th		PC 79	
Johnson, ---	Capt	28-06-77	WO			RC 2-1156	Dec
Johnson, Baker	1st Lt	29-11-75	FR	1st	Capt.C.Beatty	MM 11:50	
Johnson, Baker	Colonel	06-01-76	FR	34th		PC 79	
Johnson, Baker	Colonel	06-09-77	FR	34th		AM 16-364	Rep
Johnson, Baker	Cty Lt	15-05-80	FR			AM 43-175	
Johnson, Baker	Cty Lt	20-02-81	FR			AM 45-318	Res
Johnson, Benjamin	1st Maj	06-01-76	FR	33rd		PC 79	
Johnson, Benjamin	Maj	21-06-77	FR			AM 16-297	Mn
Johnson, Benjamion	Colonel	06-12-81	FR			AM 47-568	Mn
Johnson, Charles	2nd Lt	20-03-76	DO		Friends to America	AM 11-267	
Johnson, Charles	2nd Lt	24-06-78	DO		Capt.T.McNemara	AM 21-148	
Johnson, Cornelius	1st Lt	26-07-80	CA	14th	Capt.J.Richardson	AM 43-230	
Johnson, Cornelius	Capt	17-12-81	CA	14th	Capt.J.Hooper	AM 48-27	
Johnson, Eliacam	2nd Lt	27-05-78	WO	SnH1	Capt,F.Waltam	AM 21-423	
Johnson, George	Colonel	06-01-76	CE	30th		PC 80	OC
Johnson, Griffin	Capt	03-12-76	WA			AM 12-501	
Johnson, Griffith	Capt	22-06-78	WA	3rdW		AM 21-145	
Johnson, Horatio	Ensign	07-01-76	AA			AM 11-139	
Johnson, Horatio	1st Lt	25-08-77	AA	22nd	Capt.Walker	AM 16-343	
Johnson, James	Capt	18-10-75	FR		Minuteman	AM 11-84	Mn
Johnson, James	Capt	29-11-75	FR	2nd		MM 11:50	
Johnson, James	Colonel	06-01-76	FR	37th		PC 79	
Johnson, James	1st Lt	15-05-76	WO		Capt.Shockley	AM 11-426	
Johnson, James	2nd Lt	07-06-81	CE	Elk	Capt.Wm.Scott	AM 45-466	OC
Johnson, James	2nd Lt	23-08-81	CE	Elk	Capt.Wm.Scott	SC 48-214	Res
Johnson, James	2nd Lt	03-10-82	CE	ElkR		AM 48-274	
Johnson, John	1st Lt	03-01-76	QA	5th	Capt.R.Certain	SC 48-213	OC
Johnson, John	Capt	07-12-76	MO			AM 12-511	
Johnson, John	3rd Lt	12-02-80	AN		Capt.S.Harvey-Ind	AM 43-84	
Johnson, John	2nd Lt	18-09-80	FR	Town	Capt.G.Harding	AM 43-295	
Johnson, Jonathan	2nd Lt	30-08-77	WO	Spnx	Capt.W.Purnal	AM 16-350	
Johnson, Joseph	2nd Lt	29-11-75	FR	4th	Capt.M.Troutman	MM 11:50	
Johnson, Josiah	Ensign	29-06-76	KE	13th	Capt.Smyth	AM 11-534	
Johnson, Josiah	Capt	13-06-77	QA	5th		RC 2-1119	Mn
Johnson, Lemuel	1st Lt	28-06-77	WO			RC 2-1156	Dis

APPENDIX A - COMMISSIONED OFFICERS

Name	Rank	Date	Cty	Bn	Company	Ref.	Notes
Johnson, Moses	1st Lt	27-01-76	HA		#15-Jarrettsb'g	PR 119	
Johnson, Moses	1st Lt	14-05-76	HA	8th	Capt.Baker	AM 11-424	
Johnson, Moses	1st Lt	09-04-78	HA	8th	Capt.C.Baker	AM 21-24	
Johnson, Randolph	1st Lt	09-04-78	TA	4th	Bullinbrook	AM 21-24	
Johnson, Randolph	Capt	03-12-79	TA	38th	Capt.Saml.Abbott	AM 43-28	
Johnson, Roger	2nd Maj	06-01-76	FR	37th		PC 79	
Johnson, Thomas	1st Lt	09-12-75	HA		#11	PR 116	
Johnson, Thomas	Ensign	10-04-76	CV		Capt.Smith	AM 11-320	
Johnson, Thomas	Ensign	16-04-78	CV	15th	Capt.W.Smith	AM 21-37	
Johnson, Thomas	Ensign	21-04-78	CE	Susq	Capt.S.Miller	AM 21-48	OC
Johnson, Thomas Jr.	BrigGen	06-01-76				PC 78	
Johnson, William	Capt	12-09-77	MO	29th		AM 16-373	
Johnson, William	1st Lt	21-04-78	CE	Susq	Capt.J.Maxwell	AM 21-48	
Johnson, William	Capt	04-08-80	MO	Lwr		AM 43-248	Suc
Johnson, William	Ensign	25-09-80	BA	Town	Capt.B.Dickinson	SC 48-211	OC
Johnson, William	Ensign	19-01-81	BA	Town	Capt.Dickinson	AM 47-29	Res
Jolley, John	Capt	26-04-76	HA			AM 11-387	
Jolly, John	Capt	09-04-78	HA	Deer		AM 21-23	
Jones, ---	Ensign	06-12-81	FR			AM 47-568	Mn
Jones, David	2nd Lt	- -	WA			FP 1-129	Res
Jones, George	Ensign	15-05-76	SO	1st	Capt.McClester	AM 11-426	
Jones, Gilbert	1st Lt	09-04-78	HA	8th	Capt.A.Norris	AM 21-24	
Jones, Jacob	Ensign	13-06-77	QA	5th		RC 2-1119	Mn
Jones, James	Ensign	11-11-82	DO	Up	Capt.L.Kirkman	AM 48-301	
Jones, Jesse	2nd Lt	30-08-77	WO	Snpx	Capt.J.Purnal	AM 16-350	
Jones, Jesse	1st Lt	14-08-79	WO	Snpx	Capt.E.Purnall	AM 21-493	
Jones, John	2nd Lt	11-06-77	DO	19th	Capt.Jones	AM 16-283	
Jones, John	2nd Lt	13-06-77	QA	5th		RC 2-1119	Mn
Jones, John	Ensign	30-08-77	WO	Snpx	Capt.M.Purnal	AM 16-350	
Jones, John	Capt	22-09-77	SO	PrAn	Princess Ann	AM 16-381	
Jones, John	2nd Lt	21-04-78	CE	Elk	Capt.S.Gilpin	AM 21-47	OC
Jones, John	2nd Lt	20-05-78	DO	19th	Capt.R.Jones	AM 21-97	
Jones, John	Ensign	13-04-81	MO	SM	Capt.J.H.Nicholls	AM 45-396	
Jones, John	2nd Lt	07-06-81	CE	Elk	Capt.S.Gilpin	AM 45-466	
Jones, John	2nd Lt	23-10-81	BA	GpUp	Capt.Wm.Lane	AM 45-650	
Jones, John G.C.	Ensign	22-09-77	SO	Salb	Capt.G.Wilson	AM 16-382	
Jones, John of Robert	2nd Lt	22-09-77	SO	PrAn	Capt.T.Irving	AM 16-381	
Jones, Joseph	Ensign	03-01-76	PG	25th		SC 49-109	Mn
Jones, Joseph	Capt	24-05-79	PG	25th	Capt.H.Magruder	AM 21-414	
Jones, Joseph	Capt	24-06-80	PG	Up		AM 43-203	Suc
Jones, Mitchel	2nd Lt	19-08-76	SO	1st	Capt. J.Philips	AM 12-220	
Jones, Robinson	Ensign	30-08-77	BA	Up	Capt.N.Merryman	AM 16-350	
Jones, Robinson	2nd Lt	05-11-81	BA	Up	Capt.N.Merryman	AM 45-662	
Jones, Roger	Capt	11-06-77	DO	19th		AM 16-282	
Jones, Roger	Capt	20-05-78	DO	19th	Capt.L.Hubbard	AM 21-97	
Jones, Solomon	Ensign	17-06-77	TA	4th	Third Haven	RC 2-1130	Mn
Jones, Solomon	1st Lt	20-05-78	DO	19th	Capt.J.Byus	AM 21-97	
Jones, Solomon	1st Lt	16-12-79	DO	Lwr	Capt.J.Byus	AM 43-37	
Jones, Thomas	QM	10-02-76	DO	19th		AM 11-147	
Jones, Thomas	1st Maj	11-05-76	DO	19th		AM 11-282	
Jones, Thomas	2nd Maj	25-05-76	BA	Town		AM 11-443	
Jones, Thomas	1st Lt	19-09-76	SO	17th	Capt B.Schoolfield	AM 12-285	
Jones, Thomas	2nd Maj	23-10-76	DO	Lw		AM 12-393	
Jones, Thomas	Ensign	13-06-77	QA	5th		RC 2-1119	Mn

APPENDIX A - COMMISSIONED OFFICERS

Name	Rank	Date	Cty	Bn	Company	Ref.	Notes
Jones, Thomas	2nd Lt	24-09-77	CV		Capt.J.Grahame	AM 16-384	
Jones, Thomas	1st Lt	16-04-78	CV	15th	Capt.J.Graham	AM 21-37	
Jones, Thomas	Lt Col	20-05-78	DO	19th		AM 21-97	
Jones, Thomas	Ensign	14-08-79	WO	Snpx	Capt.E.Purnall	AM 21-493	
Jones, Thomas	Colonel	15-01-83	DO	Lwr		AM 48-344	
Jones, William	Ensign	02-12-75	HA		#12	PR 118	
Jones, William	Ensign	15-05-76	CH	26th	Capt.Mastin	AM 11-426	
Jones, William	2nd Lt	07-12-78	SO	PrAn	Capt.J.Elzey	AM 21-260	
Jones, William	2nd Lt	17-11-79	HA	Deer	Capt.Wm.Rigdon	AM 43-17	
Jordan, Charles	Capt	26-08-77	SM			AM 16-345	
Jordan, Jeremiah	Colonel	12-01-76	SM	6th		PC 78	
Jordan, Jeremiah	Colonel	26-08-77	SM	Up		AM 16-345	
Juet, Nathaniel	2nd Lt	22-09-77	SO	PrAn	Capt.H.Miles	AM 16-381	
Jump, Allensby	1st Lt	09-04-78	CA	28th	Capt.T.Casson	AM 21-23	
Jump, Allensby	Capt	26-07-80	CA	28th	Capt.T.Casson	AM 43-230	
Kaiger, James	Ensign	09-04-78	HA	23rd	Capt.S.Smith	AM 21-23	
Kane, John	Ensign	17-01-77	FR	33rd	Capt.Van Sweareng.	AM 16-54	
Kankey, John Jr	Ensign	03-01-82	CE	Susq		AM 48-38	
Keene, Benjamin	Capt	16-12-75	DO			AM 11-258	Mn
Keene, Benjamin	Capt	20-03-76	DO			AM 11-268	
Keene, Benjamin	Capt	20-05-78	DO	19th		AM 21-97	
Keene, Benjamin	Ensign	23-08-81	DO	Lwr	Capt.J.Keene	AM 45-577	
Keene, Benjamin	Capt	23-08-81	DO	Lwr		AM 45-577	Suc
Keene, Henry	Lt	15-01-76	DO		Minuteman	SP 974	
Keene, Henry	Lt	23-01-76	DO			SP 997	Res
Keene, Henry	2nd Lt	24-05-76	DO		Capt.Hicks	AM 11-441	
Keene, Henry	2nd Lt	20-05-78	DO	19th	Capt.J.Robinson	AM 21-97	
Keene, John Jr.	1st Lt	30-11-75	DO		The Bucks	DO 212	Mn
Keene, John Jr.	1st Lt	20-03-76	DO		Capt.Keene	AM 11-267	
Keene, John	1st Lt	20-05-78	DO	19th	Capt.B.Keene	AM 21-97	
Keene, John	Capt	23-08-81	DO	Lwr	Capt.B.Keene	AM 45-577	
Keene, John Young	1st Lt	31-07-78	QA	5th	Capt.I.Scrivener	AM 21-172	
Keene, John Y.	1st Lt	20-04-80	QA	5th	Capt.S.Ridgeway	AM 43-146	
Keene, John Young	Capt	07-06-81	QA	5th	Capt.S.Ridgeway	AM 45-465	
Keene, Richard	Capt	09-04-78	CA	28th		AM 21-23	
Keene, Richard of Wm.	Ensign	09-04-78	CA	28th	Capt.Fountleroy	AM 11-428	
Keene, Young	2nd Lt	13-08-77	CA	28th	Capt.J.Fauntleroy	SC 49-154	Mn
Keene, Young	1st Lt	09-04-78	CA	28th	Capt.R.Keen	AM 21-23	
Keepheart, Peter	Capt	18-09-80	FR	Town		AM 43-296	Suc
Kellam, Edward	2nd Lt	07-01-78	SO	Salb	Capt.W.Turpin	AM 16-457	
Kellam, Edward	1st Lt	22-08-81	SO	Salb	Capt.Wm.Turpin	AM 45-575	
Kelly, John	2nd Lt	21-04-78	CE	Susq	Capt.J.Baker	AM 21-48	
Kelly, Joshua	2nd Lt	07-02-82	BA	SD	Capt.W.Kelly	AM 48-71	
Kelly, Nicholas	Ensign	29-08-77	BA	Gp	Capt.I.Cockey	AM 16-348	
Kelly, Nicholas	Capt	23-10-81	BA	GpUp	Capt.J.Owings	AM 45-650	
Kelly, Thomas	Ensign	21-04-78	CE	Susq	Capt.P.Cole	AM 21-48	
Kelly, Thomas	1st Lt	03-01-82	CE	Susq	Capt.F.Boyd	AM 48-38	
Kelly, William	Capt	07-02-82	BA	SD	Capt.E.Dorsey	AM 48-71	
Kelly. William	Ensign	29-08-77	BA	SD	Capt.C.Owings	AM 16-348	
Kelty, William	Ensign	24-09-77	CV		Capt.J.Grahame	AM 16-384	
Kemp, Ludowick	Capt	29-11-75	FR			MM 11:50	
Ken, John	1st Lt	31-05-76	QA	20th	Capt.Wilson	AM 11-454	

APPENDIX A - COMMISSIONED OFFICERS

Name	Rank	Date	Cty	Bn	Company	Ref.	Notes
Kenderdine, Cooper	Ensign	14-08-79	CA	28th	Capt.T.Hughlett	AM 21-493	
Kennedy, John	2nd Lt	15-05-76	FR	37th	Capt.Smith	AM 11-426	
Kent, Daniel	Ensign	10-05-76	CV		Capt.Williamson	AM 11-320	
Kent, Daniel	Ensign	16-04-78	CV	15th	Capt.C.Williamson	AM 21-37	
Kent, Jacob	2nd Lt	03-03-77	FR	33rd	Capt.C.Stull	MM 4:379	Mn
Kent, James	2nd Maj	12-01-76	QA	5th		PC 78	OC
Kent, James	Capt	31-07-78	QA	20th		MH 2	Mn
Kent, John	1st Lt	16-03-76	QA		Capt.Bordley	AM 11-254	
Kent, John	1st Lt	19-06-77	ES			AM 16-294	
Kenting, Solomon	Ensign	13-08-77	CA	28th	Capt.W.Hopper	SC 49-154	Mn
Kenting, Solomon	1st Lt	09-04-78	CA	28th	Capt.T.Burk	AM 21-23	
Kenting, Solomon	Ensign	09-04-78	CA	28th	Capt.T.Casson	AM 21-23	
Kenting, Solomon	2nd Lt	17-12-81	CA	28th	Capt.P.Downes	AM 48-27	
Kenton, Solomon	2nd Lt	26-07-80	CA	28th	Capt.A.Jump	AM 43-230	
Kern, John	Ensign	03-03-77	FR	33rd	Capt.VanSwearingen	MM 4:379	Mn
Kerr, ---	Ensign	06-12-81	FR	SelM	Capt.Winchester	AM 47-568	CM
Kerr, ---	Ensign	14-12-81	FR	SelM	Capt.Winchester	AM 48-23	Dis
Kerr, David	1st Lt	22-02-76	AA	Svrn	Capt.G.Watts	AM 11-327	
Kerr, David	1st Lt	02-04-76	AA	Svrn	Capt.G.Watts	FP 1-133	Res
Kerr, Hugh	Ensign	29-11-75	FR		Capt.J.Good	MM 11:50	
Kerr, John	1st Lt	21-05-76	QA	20th	Capt.T.Wilson	PA	
Kerr, John	1st Lt	-08-76	QA	20th	Capt.T.Wilson	PA	Res
Kershner, Jacob	Ensign	- -	WA			FP 1-129	Mn
Kershner, John	Capt	20-03-79	FR		Guard	AM 21-325	Mn
Keser, Stophel	2nd Lt	29-08-77	FR	29th	Capt.W.Bailey	AM 16-348	
Ketzendanner, Baltis	2nd Lt	29-11-75	FR	1st	Capt.J.Stoner	MM 11:50	
Key, Job	2nd Lt	14-09-75	HA		#10	PR 115	
Key, John Ross	Capt	28-11-76	FR	35th		AM 12-555	
Key, John Ross	Lt	02-02-81	FR		Horse troop	AM 45-299	
Key, John R.	Capt	25-06-81	FR		Horse troop	AM 47-313	Mn
Kilgour, James	Ensign	03-10-82	CE	ElkR	Capt.H.South	AM 48-274	
Kilgour, William	Capt	26-08-77	SM	Up		AM 16-346	
King, James	2nd Lt	15-05-76	WO	10th	Capt.Gray	AM 11-426	
King, John	Ensign	24-06-78	DO		Capt.M.Traverse	AM 21-148	
King, Levin	Ensign	13-06-77	QA	5th		RC 2-1119	Mn
King, Nehemiah	Ensign	07-01-78	SO	PrAn	Capt.W.Waters	AM 16-457	OC
King, Richard	2nd Lt	26-08-77	SM	Lwr	Capt.S.Jenifer	AM 16-346	
King, Richard	1st Lt	07-05-81	SM	Lwr	Capt.S.Jenifer	AM 45-426	
King, Robert Jenkins	Ensign	22-09-77	SO	PrAn	Capt.G.Waters	AM 16-381	
King, Thomas	1st Lt	22-09-77	SO	PrAn	Capt.J.Williams	AM 16-381	
King, Thomas	Capt	07-12-78	SO	PrAn		AM 21-260	
King, Thomas	Capt	22-08-81	SO	PrAn	Capt.W.Waters	AM 45-575	
King, William	2nd Lt	20-09-76	PG		Capt.M.Lowe	AM 12-287	
King, William	QM	09-06-81			Horse troops	AM 45-467	
Kinley, Samuel	2nd Lt	17-11-79	HA	Deer	Capt.J.Farmer	AM 43-17	
Kinnard, Nathaniel Jr.	2nd Lt	29-06-76	KE	13th	Capt.Smyth	AM 11-534	
Kinton, Solomon	Ensign	19-06-77	CA	28th	Capt.Hooper	AM 16-294	
Kirk, Abner	2nd Lt	21-04-78	CE	Susq	Capt.J.Dougharty	AM 21-48	
Kirk, Thomas	Ensign	29-11-75	FR	1st	Capt.S.Plummer	MM 11:50	
Kirk, Thomas	1st Lt	03-03-77	FR	33rd	Capt.R.Hilleary	MM 4:379	Mn
Kirk, Thomas	1st Lt	12-09-77	MO	16th	Capt.F.Sprigg	AM 16-373	
Kirkman, James	2nd Lt	20-05-78	DO	3rd	Capt.J.Smoot	AM 21-98	
Kirkman, Levin	1st Lt	20-05-78	DO	3rd	Capt.J.Smoot	AM 21-98	
Kirkman, Levin	Capt	02-07-81	DO	Up	Capt.J.Smoot	AM 45-492	

APPENDIX A - COMMISSIONED OFFICERS

Name	Rank	Date	Cty	Bn	Company	Ref.	Notes
Kirkpatrick, Hugh	2nd Lt	30-09-75	HA		#13	PR 119	
Kirkpatrick, Hugh	2nd Lt	09-04-78	HA	23rd	Capt.W.Bradford	AM 21-24	OC
Kirts, Peter	2nd Lt	- -	MO	Up		MH 5	Mov
Kirts, Peter	2nd Lt	12-09-77	MO	29th	Capt.A.McFadon	AM 16-373	
Kirwan, John	Ensign	30-11-75	DO		Friends to America	DO 212	Mn
Kirwan, John	Ensign	24-06-78	DO		Capt.T.McNemara	AM 21-148	
Kleinhoff, John	1st Lt	29-11-75	FR		Capt.J.Good	MM 11:50	
Knight, John Leach	Capt	21-04-78	CE	Sass		AM 21-47	
Knock, William	Capt	09-09-78	KE	27th	Capt.Little	AM 21-196	
Knot, Thomas	Ensign	19-03-79	BA	Town	Capt.J.Deaver	AM 21-324	
Knotts, Thomas	2nd Lt	13-08-77	CA	28th	Capt.Wm.Chipley	SC 49-154	Mn
Knotts, Thomas	Capt	17-12-81	CA	28th	Capt.W.Chiply	AM 48-27	
Kraner, Michael	1st Lt	06-02-77	BA		Capt.Rutter	AM 16-120	
Kranor, Michael	Ensign	19-12-75	BA		Capt.T.Rutter	RB 13-37	
Kurtz, Peter	2nd Lt	21-06-77	MO	29th	Capt.Mcfadon	AM 16-296	
Kyger, John	2nd Lt	30-03-81	WA	2ndW	Capt.John Funk	AM 45-368	
		- -					
		- -					
Lackland, James	2nd Lt	14-05-76	MO	29th	Capt.Harden	AM 11-424	
Lackland, James	2nd Lt	12-09-77	MO	29th	Capt.E.Harding	AM 16-373	
Lackland, James	2nd Lt	- -	MO	Up		MH 5	Mov
Lafever, Christian	2nd Lt	01-02-77	FR	37th		AM 16-106	
Lafield, George	2nd Lt	30-08-77	WO	SnH1	Capt.W.Holland	AM 16-351	
Lafield, Isaac	Capt	30-08-77	WO	SnH1		AM 16-351	
Lake, Henry	Capt	16-05-76		Corp		AM 11-429	
Lake, Henry	Capt	24-06-78	DO			AM 21-148	
Laman, William	Ensign	07-03-76	CH		Capt.Swann	AM 11-206	
Lambden, Daniel	1st Lt	04-11-82	TA	4th	Capt.R.Johns	AM 48-298	
Lambden, Robert	Ensign	03-03-76	TA		Bayside	PA	Mn
Lambden, William	Capt	04-11-82	TA	38th	Capt.G.Dawson	AM 48-298	
Lancaster, John Jr.	Ensign	05-07-77	CH	12th	Capt.J.Yates	RC 2-1170	Mn
Lancaster, John Jr.	1st Lt	28-05-79	CH	12th	Capt.J.Yeates	AM 21-427	
Lancaster, John	Capt	19-01-81	CH	12th	Capt.J.Yates	AM 45-280	
Lancaster, Samuel Clair	1st Lt	21-04-78	CE	Sass	Capt.J.Ford	AM 21-47	
Lane, Ja	1st Lt	17-11-80	WA			FP 1-129	Mn
Lane, William	Capt	23-10-81	BA	GpUp	Capt.R.Cromwell	AM 45-650	
Lang, John Peter	Ensign	04-08-80	MO	Lwr	Capt.D.Rhintzell	AM 43-248	
Langfitt, John	Capt	20-05-78	DO	3rd		AM 21-98	
Langfitt, John	Capt	23-08-81	DO	Up		DO 230	Mn
Langley, Joseph	2nd Lt	26-08-77	SM	Lwr	Capt.W.Smoot	AM 16-346	
Lanham, Edward	Capt	24-05-79	PG	Mid	Capt.J.Cassey	AM 21-414	
Lankaster, Sinclair	Capt	22-06-78	CE	Bohe	Capt.Ford	AM 21-145	
Lantz, Leonard	1st Lt	02-11-82	FR	Town	Capt.N.White	SC 48-205	OC
Lasaver, Christian	2nd Lt	17-01-77	FR	37th	Capt.Martindear	AM 16-54	
Lawes, James	2nd Lt	30-08-77	WO	Snpx	Capt.J.Cox	AM 16-350	
Lawrence, Benjamin	2nd Lt	06-06-76	BA	SD	Capt.R.Owings	AM 11-467	
Laws, John	1st Lt	16-03-81	WO	Snpx	Capt.J.Tull	AM 45-353	
Layfield, George	1st Lt	27-05-79	WO	SnH1	Capt.F.Waltam	AM 21-423	
Layfield, George	Lt	23-08-81	FR	SelM	Capt.Parramore	AM 45-577	
Layfield, Isaac	Capt	28-06-77	WO			RC 2-1156	Mn
Layton, James	Ensign	20-05-78	DO	Up	Capt.J.Smoot	AM 21-98	
Layton, James	Ensign	23-06-79	DO	Up		FP 2-74	Res
Layton, James	Ensign	02-07-81	DO	Up	Capt.L.Kirkman	AM 45-492	
Lazinbey, Elias	Ensign	10-04-76	PG	25th	Capt.Richardson	AM 11-320	

APPENDIX A - COMMISSIONED OFFICERS

Name	Rank	Date	Cty	Bn	Company	Ref.	Notes
LeCompte, Charles	2nd Lt	18-04-80	CA	8th	Capt.Postlewait	AM 43-144	
LeCompte, John	Capt	20-05-78	DO	3rd		AM 21-98	
LeCompte, John	2nd Lt	20-05-78	DO	19th	Capt.J.Woolford	AM 21-97	
LeCompte, John	Capt	01-03-79	DO	Up		AM 21-310	Suc
LeCompte, John	2nd Lt	16-12-79	DO	Lwr	Capt.L.Hubbard	AM 43-37	
LeCompte, Moses Jr	2nd Lt	26-01-76	DO		Capt.Robson (M/M)	AM 11-110	
LeCompte, Moses Jr	1st Lt	12-02-76	DO		Minuteman	AM 11-153	
LeCompte, Moses	1st Lt	24-05-76	DO		Capt.Robson	AM 11-441	
LeCompte, Moses	1st Lt	24-05-76	DO		Capt.Hicks	AM 11-441	
LeCompte, Moses	1st Lt	20-05-78	DO	19th	Capt.J.Robinson	AM 21-97	
LeFrance, C		21-04-78				SP 6671	Res
Leach, James	Capt	16-04-78	CV	15th		AM 21-37	
Leach, Thomas	2nd Lt	16-04-78	CV	15th	Capt.E.Wood	AM 21-37	
Leatherbury, John	2nd Lt	22-09-77	SO	Salb	Capt.H.Gale	AM 16-381	
Leatherman, Godfrey	2nd Lt	29-11-75	FR	4th	Capt.P.Rodenbieler	MM 11:50	
Lee, George	2nd Maj	13-01-76	PG	25th		PC 86	OC
Lee, George	2nd Maj	30-01-76	PG	25th		AM 11-126	Ref
Lee, James of Samuel	Ensign	09-04-78	HA	23rd	Capt.J.Wheeler	AM 21-24	
Lee, John	Ensign	09-04-78	CA	28th	Capt.R.Keen	AM 21-23	
Lee, John	2nd Lt	17-12-81	CA	28th	Capt.R,Keene	AM 48-27	
Lee, Thomas Sim	1st Maj	13-01-76	PG	11th		PC 86	
Lee, Thomas Sim	Colonel	04-02-77	PG	Lwr		AM 16-113	
Lee, Thomas Sim	Colonel	26-03-77	PG	Lwr		AM 16-189	Res
Leigh, George Howel	Ensign	26-08-77	SM	Lwr	Capt.J.Armstrong	AM 16-346	
Lemaster, Albert	Capt	27-04-81				AM 45-417	Mn
Lemmon, Alexis	Capt	04-02-77	BA	Gist		AM 16-114	
Lemmon, Joshua	Ensign	25-09-80	BA	Town	Capt.R.Lemmon	SC 49-201	OC
Lemmon, Richard	1st Lt	27-09-75	BA		Artillery	RB 13-36	
Lemmon, Richard	Capt	25-09-80	BA	Town	Capt.G.S.Douglas	SC 48-200	OC
Lemmon, Robert	Capt	04-02-77	BA	Gist		AM 16-114	
Lessar, Christian	Ensign	15-05-76	FR	37th	Capt.Balsell	AM 11-426	
Letchworth, Leonard	2nd Lt	05-07-77	CH	12th		RC 2-1170	Rec
Letherbury, Peregrine	Maj	12-12-81	KE	13th		AM 48-19	
Levan, ---	Capt	07-08-76	PG			SP 2062	Mn
Lewis, Aaron	1st Lt	17-12-81	CA	14th	Capt.T.Eaton	AM 48-27	
Lewis, Charles	2nd Lt	07-02-82	BA	SD	Capt.Stinchicomb	AM 48-71	
Lewis, Job	1st Lt	07-02-82	BA	SD	Capt.Stinchicomb	AM 48-71	
Lewis, John	1st Lt	19-03-79	BA	Town	Capt.J.Smith	AM 21-324	
Lewis, Joseph	2nd Lt	26-04-76	HA	8th	Capt.S.Calwell	AM 11-387	
Lewis, Joseph	Capt	27-02-82	HA		Horse troop	AM 48-87	
Liden, Richard	2nd Lt	26-07-80	CA	14th	Capt.J.Hooper	AM 43-230	
Liden, Richard	1st Lt	17-12-81	CA	14th	Capt.C.Johnson	AM 48-27	
Liden, Shadrack	Capt	09-04-78	CA	14th		AM 21-23	
Lighton, Shadrick	Capt	24-06-77	CA	14th		AM 16-299	
Linderberger, George	2nd Lt	19-12-75	BA		Capt.J.Cox	RB 13-37	
Lindsay, Anthony	2nd Lt	17-01-77	FR	Ling	Capt.Henry Baker	AM 16-54	
Lindsey, David	Ensign	20-04-80	QA	5th	Capt.Jas.Hackett	AM 43-146	
Lingan, James Maccubbin	Capt	25-04-81			Bay Cav Co.	AM 45-414	
Link, John	Ensign	29-11-75	FR	1st	Capt.Wm.Beatty	MM 11:50	
Link, John	2nd Lt	26-05-78	FR	Town	Capt.A.Haff	AM 21-111	
Link, John	1st Lt	16-08-79	FR	Town	Capt.E.Salmon	AM 21-494	
Linthecum, John	Ensign	23-04-81	AA	Svrn	Capt.V.Gaither	AM 45-411	
Linthecum, Nathan	Ensign	26-03-76	MO		Capt.Riggs	AM 11-287	
Linthecum, Nathan	Ensign	12-09-77	MO	Mid	Capt.A.Riggs	AM 16-373	

APPENDIX A - COMMISSIONED OFFICERS

Name	Rank	Date	Cty	Bn	Company	Ref.	Notes
Linthecum, Nathan	2nd Lt	21-04-79	MO	Mid	Capt.G.Cullam	AM 21-357	
Linthecum, Nathan	1st Lt	25-03-80	MO	Mid	Capt.B.Mockby	AM 43-120	
Linton, Isaiah	Ensign	16-09-75	HA	#6		PR 112	
Little, ---	Capt	09-09-78	KE	27th		RC 1-678	Dec
Little, William	1st Lt	09-09-78	KE	27th	Capt.W.Knock	AM 21-196	
Little,---	Capt	28-11-76	FR	35th		AM 12-555	
Livingston, Stephen Horsy	2nd Lt	30-08-77	WO	Wico	Capt.S.Horsey	AM 16-351	
Lloyd, Edward	Colonel	14-08-75				AM 11-14	Mn
Lloyd, James	Capt	16-05-76	TA	4th		AM 11-428	
Lloyd, James	2nd Lt	11-09-76	KE		Capt.Frisby	AM 12-265	
Lloyd, Richard	Colonel	14-08-75				AM 11-14	Mn
Lock, Meveral	Ensign	26-08-77	SM	Up	Capt.C.Jordan	AM 16-345	
Locke, Merveral	2nd Lt	18-11-79	SM	Up	Capt.C.Jordan	AM 43-18	
Lockerman, Thos. Wm.	Capt	24-06-77	CA	14th		AM 16-299	
Lockerman, Thomas	Capt	09-04-78	CA	14th		AM 21-23	
Lockerman, Thomas	Capt	26-07-80	CA	14th		AM 43-230	Suc
Logan, Thomas	1st Lt	10-02-76	DO		New Market Blues	AM 11-147	
Logan, Thomas	1st Lt	20-05-78	DO	3rd	Capt.J.Daffin	AM 21-98	
Logan, Thomas	Capt	28-07-80	DO	Up	Capt.Jos.Daffin	AM 43-236	
Logan, Thomas	Capt	02-07-81	DO	Up		AM 45-492	
Logenby, Elias	2nd Lt	09-06-77	PG		Capt.T.Richardson	RC 2-1103	Rec
Long, John	1st Lt	-05-76	BA		Capt.J.Garretson	RB 13-53	
Long, John	1st Lt	11-04-78	HA	Deer		SC 48-197	Ref
Long, John Jr.	1st Lt	09-04-78	HA	Deer	Capt.G.Vanhorne	AM 21-22	OC
Long, John Jr.	1st Lt	11-04-78	HA	Deer	Capt.G.Vanhorne	SC 48-197	Ref
Long, Jonathan	1st Lt	25-05-76	BA	GP	Capt.Garretson	AM 11-444	
Long, Littleton	Ensign	30-08-77	WO	SnH1	Capt.T.Marshall	AM 16-351	
Long, Solomon	Maj	27-05-79	WO	Wico		AM 21-423	
Long, Solomon	Lt Col	13-06-82	WO	Wico		AM 48-190	
Long, Thomas	Ensign	18-09-80	FR	Town	Capt.John Stoner	AM 43-295	
Lontz, Leonard	1st Lt	02-11-82	FR	Town	Capt.N.White	AM 48-296	
Lorah, John	1st Lt	25-09-80	BA	Town	Capt.P.Grable	AM 43-303	
Loutz, Leonard	2nd Lt	15-04-78	FR	Town	Capt.White	AM 21-35	
Love, John	Capt	14-09-75	HA	#10		PR 115	
Love, John	Lt Col	06-01-76	HA	23rd		PC 80	OC
Love, Robert	1st Lt	21-04-78	CE	Susq	Capt.W.Ewing	AM 21-48	
Loveall, William	Ensign	05-11-81	BA	Up		AM 45-662	
Loveday, Nicholas	2nd Lt	04-11-82	TA	4th	Capt.R.Johns	AM 48-298	
Low, Andrew	Ensign	23-01-82	FR	Town	Capt.J.Shellman	AM 48-54	OC
Low, Isaac	Ensign	23-08-81	DO	Up		DO 230	Mn
Lowe, Isaac	Ensign	20-05-78	DO	3rd	Capt.J.Wright	AM 21-98	
Lowe, James	Ensign	23-05-76	TA	38th	Capt.Haddaman	AM 11-438	
Lowe, John	1st Lt	04-11-82	TA	38th	Capt.Wm.Lambden	AM 48-298	
Lowe, John Hawkins	Maj	01-05-78	PG	Mid		AM 21-63	
Lowe, John Hawkins	Lt.Col	31-11-79	PG	Mid		AM 43-13	
Lowe, Michael	Capt	04-09-77	PG			AM 16-362	
Lowe, William	1st Lt	20-05-78	DO	3rd	Capt.J.Wright	AM 21-98	
Lowe, William	1st Lt	23-08-81	DO	Up		DO 230	Mn
Lucas, Barton	Colonel	10-03-78	AA	25th		AM 16-532	
Luckett, ---	Capt	11-06-76	FR	34th		AM 11-476	Suc
Luckett, Samuel	Capt	19-01-81	CH	26th	Capt.F.Mastin	AM 45-280	
Luckett, William Jr.	Capt	29-11-75	FR	4th		MM 11:50	
Luckett, William	Lt Col	06-01-76	FR	33rd		PC 79	
Lucus, David	2nd Lt	17-06-77	TA	4th	Volunteer-2nd	RC 2-1130	Rec

APPENDIX A - COMMISSIONED OFFICERS

Name	Rank	Date	Cty	Bn	Company	Ref.	Notes
Ludwick, Young	2nd Lt	- -	WA			FP 1-129	Mn
Lum, Jacob	Ensign	21-04-78	CE	Elk	Capt.T.Savin	AM 21-47	
Lum, Jacob	2nd Lt	09-09-78	CE	2nd	Capt.A.Cazier	AM 21-196	
Lunley, Leonard	Ensign	11-06-76	FR	34th	Capt.Mackall	AM 11-476	
Lunn, Jacob	1st Lt	07-06-81	CE	Elk	Capt.A.Cazier	AM 45-466	OC
Lusby, Robert	2nd Lt	19-09-78	AA	7th	Capt.H.Bateman	AM 21-208	
Lux, Darby	Lt Col	25-05-76	BA	GP		AM 11-443	
Lux, Darby	Colonel	30-08-77	BA	GP		AM 16-350	
Lux, George	1st Lt	25-09-80	BA	Town	Capt.F.Deems	SC 48-193	OC
Lux, George	1st Lt	26-04-81	BA	Town	Capt.F.Deems	AM 45-416	
Lyden, Shadrack	Capt	28-06-80	CA	14th		AM 43-207	Suc
Lyles Jr., William	Colonel	15-01-81	PG			AM 47-16	Mn
Lyles, Richard	2nd Lt	24-05-79	PG	25th	Capt.J.Jones	AM 21-414	
Lyles, Richard	1st Lt	24-06-80	PG	Up	Capt.B.Harwood	AM 43-203	
Lyles, Thomas	Ensign	05-09-77	PG	25th	Capt.M.Duvall	AM 16-363	
Lyles, Thomas	Ensign	01-05-78	PG	25th	Capt.M.Duvall	AM 21-62	
Lyles, Thomas	2nd Lt	24-05-79	PG	25th	Capt.M.Duvall	AM 21-414	
Lyles, William Jr.	2nd Maj	04-02-77	PG	Lwr		AM 16-113	
Lyles, William Jr.	Maj	01-09-77	PG	Up		AM 16-356	
Lyles, William	Lt Col	07-10-80	PG	Lwr		AM 43-318	
Lynch, Jno	Capt	13-06-77	QA	5th		RC 2-1119	Mn
Lyon, Henry	2nd Lt	27-07-76	CH			AM 12-127	
Lyon, Henry	1st Lt	19-01-81	CH	12th	Capt.J.Gardner	AM 45-280	
Lyon, Henry Jr.	Ensign	05-07-77	CH	12th		RC 2-1170	Rec
Lytle, George	Ensign	09-04-78	HA	23rd	Capt.J.Forwood	AM 21-23	
		- -					
		- -					
Macamson, Joseph	Ensign	09-04-78	HA	Deer	Capt.T.Hope	AM 21-22	OC
Macamson, Robert	2nd Lt	09-04-78	HA	Deer	Capt.G.Vanhorne	AM 21-22	
Macbee, Brock	2nd Lt	12-09-77	MO	Mid		AM 16-373	
Maccamson, John	1st Lt	17-11-79	HA	Deer	Capt.G.Vanhorn	AM 43-17	
Maccamson, William	Ensign	17-11-79	HA	Deer	Capt.G.Vanhorn	AM 43-17	
Maccubbin, Joseph	Capt	02-03-77	AA	Svrn		AM 16-525	OC
Maccubbin, Joseph	Capt	22-05-79	AA	Svrn		SC 48-188	Res
Maccubbin, Nicholas	2nd Lt	15-02-77	AN			AM 16-138	
Maccubbin, Nicholas	Capt	06-10-77	AN		Independent	AM 16-392	
Maccubbin, Nicholas	Capt	19-05-81				AM 45-439	Mn
Maccubbin, William	Capt	20-03-79	BA	GP		AM 21-325	
Macgruder, Joseph	Capt	12-09-77	MO	29th		AM 16-373	
Mackall, Benjamin 4th	Colonel	06-01-76	CV	15th		PC 79	
Mackall, Benjamin 4th	Cty Lt	01-07-77	CV			AM 16-303	
Mackall, Benjamin 4th	Cty Lt	12-01-81	CV			AM 45-272	Suc
Mackall, James	Ensign	10-04-76	CV		Capt.Greenfield	AM 11-320	
Mackall, James	Capt	11-06-76	FR	34th		AM 11-476	
Mackall, James	Ensign	16-04-78	CV	15th	Capt.T.Greenfield	AM 21-37	
Mackall, John	Lt	05-07-76	CV			SP 1715	Mn
Mackall, John	Capt	26-08-77	SM	Lwr		AM 16-346	
Mackall, John Jr.	Capt	02-11-76				SP 2667	Res
Mackey, James	Capt	10-04-76	CE			AM 11-319	Mn
Mackey, James	Capt	07-06-81	CE	Elk	Capt.H.South	AM 45-466	
Mackie, William	1st Lt	09-11-76	FR		Capt.Mackall	AM 12-432	
Mackubbin, William	1st Lt	25-05-76	BA	GP	Capt.Bowen	AM 11-444	
Macky, James	Capt	21-04-78	CE	Elk		AM 21-47	OC

APPENDIX A - COMMISSIONED OFFICERS

Name	Rank	Date	Cty	Bn	Company	Ref.	Notes
Madding, Joseph	Lt	16-08-81	FR	SelM		AM 45-566	
Maddon, Lazarus	2nd Lt	07-12-78	SO	PrAn	Capt.I.Handy	AM 21-260	
Maddox, Samuel	2nd Lt	26-08-77	SM	Up	Capt.C.Jordan	AM 16-345	
Maddux, Daniel	1st Lt	24-02-76	SO	17th	Capt.Fountain	AM 11-182	
Maddux, Samuel	1st Lt	18-11-79	SM	Up	Capt.C.Jordan	AM 43-18	
Maddux, Stoughlin	2nd Lt	24-02-76	SO	17th	Capt.Fountain	AM 11-182	
Maddux, Thomas Jr.	2nd Lt	22-09-77	SO	PrAn	Capt.J.Jones	AM 16-381	
Maffet, Samuel	Capt	07-06-81	CE	Elk		AM 45-466	Suc
Maffet, Samuel	Major	07-07-81	CE	Elk		AM 45-465	
Maffitt, Samuel	Capt	21-04-78	CE	Elk		AM 21-47	OC
Magruder, Alex. Howard	Capt	01-05-78	PG	11th		AM 21-62	
Magruder, Dennis	1st Lt	01-05-78	PG	Mid	Capt.J.Casey	AM 21-63	
Magruder, Henderson	Capt	03-01-76	PG	25th		SC 49-109	Mn
Magruder, Henderson	Capt	01-05-78	PG	25th		AM 21-62	
Magruder, Henderson	Capt	24-05-79	PG	25th		AM 21-414	Suc
Magruder, Henry	Capt	23-08-76				AM 12-233	Mn
Magruder, Hezekiah	1st Lt	29-08-77	FR	29th	Capt.W.Bailey	AM 16-348	OC
Magruder, Hezekiah	1st Lt	-05-82	FR	29th		SC 48-250	Res
Magruder, Joseph	Capt	21-06-77	MO	29th		AM 16-296	
Magruder, Josiah	Ensign	29-08-77	FR	29th	Capt.W.Bailey	AM 16-348	
Magruder, Nathaniel Beall	Ensign	22-04-80			State Inf.co.	AM 43-149	
Magruder, Samuel B.	Ensign	12-09-77	MO	29th	Capt.W.Johnson	AM 16-373	
Magruder, Samuel B.	1st Lt	04-08-80	MO	Lwr	Capt.J.Willcoxen	AM 43-248	
Magruder, Samuel Wade	Capt	20-11-76	MO	29th		AM 12-464	Ref
Magruder, Samuel Wade	2nd Maj	21-06-77	MO	29th		AM 16-296	
Magruder, Wade	Capt	26-06-76	MO	29th		AM 11-522	Mn
Magruder, Zadock	Colonel	06-01-76	MO	16th		PC 79	
Magruder, Zadock	Colonel	12-09-77	MO	16th		AM 16-373	
Mainship, Aaron	1st Lt	09-04-78	CA	14th	Capt.N.Andrew	AM 21-23	
Majors, Robert	2nd Lt	07-02-82	BA	SD	Capt.C.Chinworth	AM 48-71	
Manard, Nathan	Ensign	28-11-76	FR		Capt.B.Dorsey	AM 12-555	
Maniard, Nathan	1st Lt	17-01-77	FR	Ling	Capt.B.Dorsey	AM 16-55	
Manning, Anthony	Ensign	20-05-78	DO	3rd	Capt.J.LeCompt	AM 21-98	
Manning, Anthony	2nd Lt	01-03-79	DO	Up	Capt.B.Ennalls	AM 21-310	
Manning, Nathaniel	Ensign	10-02-76	DO		Cambridge Blues	AM 11-147	
Manning, Nathaniel	2nd Lt	12-09-76	DO	19th	Capt.E.Vickars	AM 12-266	
Manning, Nathaniel	1st Lt	20-05-78	DO	19th	Capt.T.Eccleston	AM 21-97	
Manning, Nathaniel	Capt	16-12-79	DO	Lwr		DO 232	Mn
Manning, Nathaniel	Capt	15-07-80	DO	19th		FP 2-71	Mn
Manning, Nicholas	Capt	16-12-79	DO	Lwr	Capt.T.Eccleston	AM 43-37	
Manship, Nathan	2nd Lt	09-04-78	CA	14th	Capt.N.Andrew	AM 21-23	
Mantch, Adam	1st Lt	03-03-77	FR	33rd	Capt.J.H.Yost	MM 4:379	Mn
Mantz, Peter	Capt	29-11-75	FR	1st		MM 11:50	
Mantz, Peter	QM	02-03-76	FR	33rd		AM 11-198	Ref
Mantz, Peter	Capt	26-03-76	FR	33rd		AM 11-287	
Mantz, Peter	Maj	10-12-76	MO	16th		SC 48-245	OC
Mantz, Peter	Capt	28-12-76	FR	33rd		AM 12-557	Ref
Manyard, Nathan	Capt	13-10-77	FR			SC 48-248	OC
Marbury, Luke	Capt	15-03-76	PG			AM 11-252	Mn
Marbury, Luke	Lt Col	04-02-77	PG	Lwr		AM 16-113	
Marbury, Luke	Cty Lt	01-07-77	PG			AM 16-304	
Marbury, Luke	Colonel	01-09-77	PG	Lwr		AM 16-356	
Marbury, Luke	Cty Lt	29-11-77	PG			AM 16-422	Res
Marbury, Luke	Colonel	03-09-81	PG			AM 18-616	POW

100

APPENDIX A - COMMISSIONED OFFICERS

Name	Rank	Date	Cty	Bn	Company	Ref.	Notes
Marquiss, John	2nd Lt	21-06-77	MO	29th	Capt.J.Magruder	AM 16-296	
Marriott, John	1st Lt	07-02-76	AA	E1kR		AM 11-139	
Marriott, John	1st Lt	29-03-76	AA	E1kR		AM 11-299	Dec
Marriott, John	Ensign	19-09-78	AA	7th	Capt.P.Warfield	AM 21-208	
Marsh, Joshua	Capt	31-10-80	BA	GPUp	Capt.H.Howard	AM 43-345	
Marsh, Richard	2nd Lt	06-06-76	BA	SD	Capt.Carnan	AM 11-467	
Marshall	Colonel	17-07-76	CV			AM 12-67	Mn
Marshall, Benjamin 7th	Lt	01-07-77	CA			PA	Mn
Marshall, Benjamin 7th	Lt	02-10-80	CA			PA	Res
Marshall, John	Capt	- -75	CH			RC 2-142	Mn
Marshall, John	1st Maj	06-01-76	CH	12th		PC 78	
Marshall, John	Maj	26-02-76				AM 11-186	Mn
Marshall, John	Ensign	20-05-78	DO	3rd	Capt.L.Hanley	AM 21-98	
Marshall, John	Ensign	02-07-81	DO	Up	Capt.J.Hooper	AM 45-492	
Marshall, John Jr.	Capt	04-07-76	CV	15th		AM 11-548	Mn
Marshall, Philip	Ensign	07-03-76	CH		Capt.Philpot	AM 11-206	
Marshall, Thomas	1st Lt	04-02-77	BA	Gist	Capt.J.Hall	AM 16-114	
Marshall, Thomas	Capt	30-08-77	BA	Up		AM 16-350	
Marshall, Thomas	1st Lt	30-08-77	WO	SnH1	Capt.T.Marshall	AM 16-351	
Marshall, Thomas	Ensign	24-06-80	PG	Mid	Capt.Z.Berry	AM 43-203	
Marshall, Thomas	Capt	05-11-81	BA	Up		AM 45-662	Suc
Marshall, Thomas Hanson	Capt	07-03-76	CH			AM 11-206	
Martin, George	QM	06-01-76	WO	10th		PC 80	
Martin, James	Capt	25-05-76	WO	10th		AM 11-444	
Martin, James	Lt Col	30-08-77	WO	Wico		AM 16-351	
Martin, James	Lt Col	27-05-79	WO	SnH1		AM 21-423	
Martin, Nicholas	Capt	16-05-76	TA	38th		AM 11-428	
Martindear, John	1st Lt	15-05-76	FR	37th	Capt.Balsell	AM 11-426	
Martindear, John	Capt	17-01-77	FR	37th		AM 16-104	
Martindear, John	Capt	01-02-77	FR	37th		AM 16-106	
Martz, Balzer	Ensign	26-05-78	FR	Town	Capt.N.White	AM 21-111	
Mason, Richard	1st Maj	12-01-76	CA	28th		PC 78	
Mason, Richard	1st Lt	13-08-77	CA	28th	Capt.Wm.Chipley	SC 49-154	Mn
Mason, Richard	1st Lt	14-08-79	CA	28th	Capt.W.Chipley	AM 21-493	
Mason, Solomon	2nd Lt	19-06-77	CA	28th	Capt.Jackson	AM 16-294	
Mason, Thomas	2nd Lt	13-06-77	QA	5th		RC 2-1119	Mn
Massey, Daniel Tres.	2nd Lt	09-09-78	KE	27th	Capt.W.Knock	AM 21-196	
Massey, Eliazer	Ensign	07-06-81	QA	5th	Capt.W.Falconer	AM 45-465	
Massey, James	Ensign	20-04-80	QA	5th	Capt.W.Falconer	AM 43-146	
Massey, James	2nd Lt	07-06-81	QA	5th	Capt.W.Falconer	AM 45-465	
Mastin, Francis	Capt	15-05-76	CH	26th		AM 11-426	
Mastin, Francis	Capt	19-01-81	CH	26th		AM 45-280	Suc
Mathews, Henry	1st Lt	15-05-76	FR	37th	Capt.Ogle	AM 11-426	
Matthews, Henry	1st Lt	29-11-75	FR	2nd	Capt.B.Ogle	MM 11:50	
Matthews, William	Ensign	30-08-77	BA	Up	Capt.T.Marshall	AM 16-350	
Mattingley, Edward	Capt	18-11-79	SM	Up	Capt.Wm.Bond	AM 43-18	
Mattingly, Edward	1st Lt	26-08-77	SM	Up	Capt.W.Bond	AM 16-346	
Mauldin, William	2nd Lt	23-05-76	CE		Capt.Hyland	AM 11-438	
Maxwell, James	Capt	21-04-78	CE	Susq		AM 21-48	
Maxwell, James	Maj	15-08-81	CE	30th		AM 45-560	
Maxwell, William Jr.	2nd Maj	08-05-77	KE	27th		AM 16-243	
Maybury, Beriah	Ensign	09-04-81	AN		Capt.S.H.Howard	AM 45-385	
Maybury, Beriah	2nd Lt	18-06-81	AN		Capt.Howard-Indep.	AM 45-479	
Maynadier, William	Capt	09-04-78	TA	4th	Third Haven	AM 21-24	OC

101

APPENDIX A - COMMISSIONED OFFICERS

Name	Rank	Date	Cty	Bn	Company	Ref.	Notes
Maynard, Nathan	Ensign	29-11-75	FR		Capt.B.Dorsey	MM 11:50	
Mayo, Joseph Jr.	Ensign	18-10-82	AA	Svrn	Capt.J.Merrikin	AM 48-288	
Mayo, Thomas	2nd Lt	08-02-76	AA		Capt.J.Boone	AM 11-141	
McAllister, James	Ensign	28-07-80	DO	Up	Capt.W.E.Hooper	AM 43-236	
McAllister, James	2nd Lt	02-04-81	DO	Up		DO 231	Mn
McBride, Henry	2nd Lt	02-09-77	BA	Town	Capt.Galbraith	AM 16-359	
McBride, Henry	1st Lt	19-03-79	BA	Town	Capt.J.Deaver	AM 21-324	
McBride, Henry	1st Lt	19-05-79	BA	Town	Capt.J.Deavor	AM 21-401	
McBride, Hugh	Capt	06-07-76	DO	3rd		AM 11-553	Mn
McBride, Hugh	Capt	09-04-78	CA	14th		AM 21-23	
McBride, Hugh	Capt	14-08-79	CA	14th		AM 21-493	Suc
McBryde, William	Ensign	22-09-77	SO	Salb	Capt.R.Dashiell	AM 16-382	
McCabe, John	1st Lt	06-06-76	BA	Town	Capt.Richardson	AM 11-467	
McCallister, James	2nd Lt	02-07-81	DO	Up	Capt.J.Hooper	AM 45-492	
McCallister, James	Lt	23-08-81	DO	SelM	Capt.Ennalls	AM 45-577	
McCallum, William	2nd Lt	09-04-78	TA	4th	Union	AM 21-24	OC
McCaslin, Elisha	Ensign	19-12-75	BA		Capt.J.Bosley	RB 13-37	
McClellan, David	Ensign	19-12-75	BA		Capt.J.Cox	RB 13-37	
McClellan, David	Ensign	02-03-76	BA		Capt.Cox	AM 11-197	Dis
McClellan, John	1st Lt	19-12-75	BA		Capt.J.Cox	RB 13-37	
McClentick, Matthew	1st Lt	09-04-78	HA	23rd	Capt.S.Smith	AM 21-23	
McClester, John	Capt	15-05-76	SO	1st		AM 11-426	
McClester, John	1st Lt	22-09-77	SO	Salb	Capt.J.Conway	AM 16-381	
McClinton, Matthew	1st Lt	12-02-77	HA	Hall		AM 16-131	
McCloser, John	Capt	22-08-81	SO	Salb	Capt.J.Conway	AM 45-575	
McCloster, Samuel	Ensign	06-04-76	DO	3rd	Capt.McBridge	AM 11-553	OC
McCloster, Samuel	Ensign	30-08-76	DO	3rd		SC 48-190	Res
McCollister, James	Lt	- -81	DO	SelM	Capt.B.Ennalls Jr	DO 244	Mn
McColloch, John	Ensign	21-04-78	CE	Susq	Capt.J.Baker	AM 21-48	
McComas, Edward	Ensign	30-09-75	HA		#13	PR 119	
McComas, Edward	Ensign	09-04-78	HA	23rd	Capt.W.Bradford	AM 21-24	
McComas, Edward Day	Capt	17-11-79	HA	23rd	Capt.Wm.Bradford	AM 43-17	
McComas, James	2nd Lt	09-12-75	HA		#11	PR 116	
McComas, James	Capt	26-04-76	HA	8th		AM 11-387	
McComas, James	Lt Col	09-04-78	HA	8th		AM 21-24	OC
McComas, James	Lt Col	07-10-78	HA	8th		SC 48-189	Res
McComas, James	2nd Lt	17-11-79	HA	Deer	Capt.Wm.Amos	AM 43-17	
McConchie, William	2nd Lt	07-03-76	CH	26th	Capt.Sinnett	AM 11-206	
McCondree, William	2nd Lt	17-10-77	CH	26th	Capt.R.Sinnett	AM 16-399	
McCown, Samuel	1st Lt	07-06-81	CE	Elk	Capt.S.Gilpin	AM 45-466	
McCoy, Perry	Ensign	22-06-78	WA	2ndW	Capt.J.Walling	AM 21-145	
McCubbin, Joseph	2nd Lt	22-02-76	AA	Svrn	Capt.Watts	AM 11-178	
McCubbin, Joseph	1st Lt	11-04-76	AA	Svrn	Capt.Watts	AM 11-327	
McCubbin, Joseph	Capt	22-05-79	AA	7th		AM 21-410	Res
McCubbin, William	Lt Col	24-07-80	BA	GP		AM 43-227	
McCubbin, Zach	Capt	19-12-75	BA			RB 13-37	
McCune, Thomas	2nd Lt	29-11-75	FR	3rd	Capt.A.Hayter	MM 11:50	
McDonal, John	1st Lt	09-04-78	HA	Deer	Capt.G.Voghan	AM 21-23	
McFadon, Alexander	1st Lt	20-04-76	FR	LrDt	Capt.Richardson	AM 11-356	
McFadon, Alexander	Capt	12-09-77	MO	29th		AM 16-373	
McFadon, Alexander	Capt	11-08-79	MO	Up		MH 5	Mov
McGill, John	Capt	08-07-76	PG	25th		AM 12-14	Mn
McGuire, Hugh	1st Lt	20-05-78	DO	19th	Capt.E.Staplefort	AM 21-97	
McGuire, James	2nd Lt	07-06-81	CE	Elk	Capt.D.Ricketts	AM 45-465	

APPENDIX A - COMMISSIONED OFFICERS

Name	Rank	Date	Cty	Bn	Company	Ref.	Notes
McGuire, John	Ensign	20-05-78	DO	19th	Capt.E.Staplefort	AM 21-97	
McGuire, Michael	Capt	29-11-75	FR	3rd		MM 11:50	
McIlroy, Fergus	Ensign	06-06-76	BA	Town	Capt.Richardson	AM 11-467	
McInheimer, John	2nd Lt	25-09-80	BA	Town	Capt.P.Grable	AM 43-303	
McKeown, Samuel	2nd Lt	21-04-78	CE	Elk	Capt.S.Maffitt	AM 21-47	OC
McKillip, Joseph	QM	06-01-76	FR	35th		PC 79	OC
McKillip, Joseph	QM	07-10-76	FR	35th		PC 266	
McLachlan, Thomas	Lt.	14-06-81	CE		Horse troop	AM 45-474	
McNamara, Timothy	Capt	15-07-80	DO			FP 2-73	Mn
McNemara, John Stewart	1st Lt	20-03-76	DO		Friends to America	AM 11-267	
McNemara, John Stewart	1st Lt	24-06-78	DO		Capt.T.McNemara	AM 21-148	
McNemara, Timothy	Capt	20-03-76	DO		Friends to America	AM 11-267	
McNemara, Timothy	Capt	24-06-78	DO			AM 21-148	
McPherson	Capt	26-07-76	CH			AM 12-125	Mn
McPherson, Alexander	Capt	09-02-81	CH	12th		AM 45-307	Suc
McPherson, William	Capt	07-03-76	CH	26th		AM 11-206	
McSwain, David	2nd Lt	09-04-78	HA	Deer	Capt.J.Jolly	AM 21-23	
Mead, Thomas	Ensign	20-04-80	QA	5th	Capt.J.Walters	AM 43-146	
Meads, Thomas	Ensign	17-12-81	CA	28th	Capt.P.Downes	AM 48-27	
Mears, Zadock	Ensign	26-07-80	CA	14th	Capt.V.Price	AM 43-230	
Meeds, Thomas	2nd Lt	12-06-81	CA	28th	Capt.Burk	MH 2	Rec
Mefford, John	2nd Lt	29-11-75	FR	2nd	Capt.J.Carmack	MM 11:50	
Melott, Peter	Ensign	22-06-78	WA	2ndW	Capt.J.Smith	AM 21-145	
Menger, ---	Lt	21-05-78	SM			AM 21-104	Mn
Mensh, Adam	2nd Lt	29-11-75	FR	1st	Capt.H.Yost	MM 11:50	
Mercer, John	Capt	25-05-76	BA	GP		AM 11-444	
Meredith, Simon	Capt	28-11-76	FR			AM 12-555	
Meredith, Simon	Capt	17-01-77	FR	Ling		AM 16-54	
Merikan, Joshua	Capt	19-09-78	AA	7th		AM 21-208	
Merikin, Joshua	2nd Lt	02-03-78	AA	Svrn	Capt.C.Owings	AM 16-525	
Merkrekin, Isaac	1st Lt	27-07-76	FR			AM 12-127	
Merony, Henry	2nd Lt	15-05-76	FR	34th	Capt.Merony	AM 11-426	
Merony, Philip	Capt	15-05-76	FR	34th		AM 11-426	
Merony, Phil	Capt	24-12-76	FR	34th		AM 12-550	Dis
Merony, Philip	Cornet	20-02-81	FR		Horse troop	AM 45-318	
Merriken, Joseph	Capt	26-08-76				AM 12-240	Mn
Merriken, Joseph	Maj	02-03-78	AA	Svrn		AM 16-525	
Merrikin, Joshua	2nd Lt	12-06-77	AA	7th	Capt.Owens	AM 16-286	Mn
Merrill, John	2nd Lt	28-06-77	WO		Capt.I.Layfield	RC 2-1156	Suc
Merryman, Benjamin	Capt	04-12-78	BA	Up		AM 21-257	
Merryman, John	Capt	15-03-79	BA	Town		SC 48-247	Suc
Merryman, Micajah	1st Maj	12-10-76	BA	GP		AM 12-337	
Merryman, Nicholas	Capt	30-08-77	BA	Up		AM 16-350	
Merryman, Nicholas Jr.	1st Lt	04-02-77	BA	Gist	Capt.T.Moore	AM 16-114	
Merryman, Samuel Jr.	2nd Lt	13-05-76	BA	Gist	Capt.I.Hammond	RB 13-69	
Merryman, Samuel Jr.	1st Lt	06-06-76	BA	SD	Capt.C.Owings	AM 11-467	
Merryman, Samuel Jr.	1st Lt	11-09-77	BA	SD	Capt.C.Owing	AM 16-369	Suc
Messick, Nehemiah	2nd Lt	16-09-76	DO		Friendship	AM 12-274	
Messick, Nehemiah	2nd Lt	20-05-78	DO	3rd	Capt.S.Waters	AM 21-98	
Middleton, Gilbert	2nd Lt	06-10-77	AN		Capt.B.Harwood	AM 16-392	
Middleton, Gilbert	Capt	20-03-79	AN		Ind	AM 21-325	
Middleton, Horatio	Ensign	09-05-78	CH	26th	Capt.G.Dent	AM 21-72	
Middleton, Isaac S.	1st Lt	09-05-78	CH	26th	Capt.S.Smallwood	AM 21-72	
Middleton, Theodore	2nd Lt	01-05-78	PG	Mid	Capt.Saml.H.Beans	AM 21-63	

103

APPENDIX A - COMMISSIONED OFFICERS

Name	Rank	Date	Cty	Bn	Company	Ref.	Notes
Middleton, Theodore	Capt	27-04-81			Inf.for Bay def.	AM 45-418	
Miers, Henry	Capt	22-06-78	FR	Ling	Capt.Barr	AM 21-145	
Mikesell, Martin	Ensign	22-06-78	FR	Ling	Capt.Collyberger	AM 21-144	
Miles, Henry	Capt	22-09-77	SO	PrAn	Little Annamessex	AM 16-381	
Miles, John	1st Lt	16-12-79	DO	Up	Capt.Jas.Wright	AM 43-37	
Miles, John	1st Lt	23-08-81	DO	Up	Capt.W.Russum	AM 45-577	
Miles, John	Ensign	23-08-81	DO	SelM	Capt.Ennalls	AM 45-577	
Miles, Joshua	1st Lt	26-04-76	HA	8th	Capt.Bussey	AM 11-387	
Miles, Nicholas	Ensign	01-05-78	PG	11th	Capt.H.Hill	AM 21-62	
Miles, Nicholas	2nd Lt	24-05-79	PG	11th	Capt.H.Hill jr.	AM 21-414	
Miles, Richard	2nd Lt	27-05-79	WO	Wico	Capt.Horsey	AM 21-423	
Miles, Thomas	2nd Lt	19-12-75	BA		Capt.Wm.Cromwell	RB 13-37	
Miles, Thomas	1st Lt	30-08-77	BA	GunP	Capt.S.Prior	AM 16-350	
Millard, Francis	1st Lt	26-08-77	SM	Up	Capt.J.Thomas	AM 16-346	
Millard, Francis	Capt	18-11-79	SM	Up	Capt.J.Thomas	AM 43-18	
Miller, Abraham	1st Lt	01-02-77	FR	37th		AM 16-106	
Miller, Andrew	Capt	21-04-78	CE	Elk		AM 21-47	OC
Miller, Andrew	Capt	07-06-81	CE	Elk		AM 45-466	Suc
Miller, Benjamin	1st Lt	07-06-81	CE	Elk	Capt.C.Alexander	AM 45-466	
Miller, Isaac	Ensign	15-05-76	FR	37th	Capt.Beall	AM 11-426	
Miller, Isaac	2nd Lt	28-11-76	FR	37th	Capt.W.B.Head	AM 12-555	
Miller, Jacob	1st Lt	29-11-75	FR	4th	Capt.P.Thomas	MM 11:50	
Miller, Jacob	1st Maj	06-01-76	FR	34th		PC 79	
Miller, John	2nd Lt	30-08-77	BA	Up	Capt.R.Cummins	AM 16-350	
Miller, Joseph	2nd Lt	19-03-79	BA	Town	Capt.J.Merryman	AM 21-324	
Miller, Philip	2nd Lt	17-01-77	FR	33rd	Capt.Van Sweareng.	AM 16-54	
Miller, Samuel	Capt	21-04-78	CE	Susq		AM 21-48	
Miller, William	2nd Lt	12-05-79	FR	Town	Capt.J.Stones	AM 21-387	
Mills, Benjamin	2nd Lt	30-08-77	WO	Snpx	Capt.M.Purnal	AM 16-350	
Mills, Cornelius	3rd Lt	20-03-79	AN		Middleton	AM 21-325	
Mills, James	QM	12-01-76	SM	6th		PC 78	
Mills, John	Capt	26-08-77	SM	Up		AM 16-346	
Mills, John	Ensign	26-08-77	SM	Lwr	Capt.I.Abell	Am 16-346	
Mills, John	Ensign	16-04-78	CV	15th	Capt.B.Bond	AM 21-37	
Mills, John	2nd Lt	02-02-79	CV		Capt.N.Wilson	AM 21-290	
Mills, John	1st Lt	07-05-81	SM	Lwr	Capt.B.Abell	AM 45-426	
Mills, Leavin	Adj	07-03-76	CV	15th		AM 16-24	
Mills, Levin		05-07-76	CV			SP 1715	CM
Mills, Richard	Ensign	30-08-77	WO	Wico	Capt.S.Horsey	AM 16-351	
Milward, William	2nd Lt	17-06-77	TA	4th	Union	RC 2-1130	Rec
Milward, William	1st Lt	09-04-78	TA	4th	Union	AM 21-24	OC
Mires, Stephen	Ensign	09-09-78	KE	27th	Capt.W.Knock	AM 21-196	
Mitchell, J.P.	Capt	27-05-79	WO	Wico		AM 21-423	Suc
Mitchell, John	Capt	16-11-76	CA			SP 2740	Mn
Mitchell, John	Capt	09-04-78	CA	14th		AM 21-23	
Mitchell, John	Lt	11-05-81			"Decoy"	AM 45-432	
Mitchell, John Pope	Capt	30-08-77	WO	Wico		AM 16-351	
Mitchell, Josias	QM	06-01-76	WO	24th		PC 80	
Mitchell, Richard B.	Capt	27-07-76	CH			AM 12-127	
Mitchell, Richard Bennet	Capt	19-07-76	CH	26th		AM 12-83	Mn
Moale, John	Lt Col	25-05-76	BA	Town		AM 11-443	
Moale, John	Lt Col	17-03-80	BA	Town		AM 43-452	Res
Mobberly, Lewis	Ensign	13-10-77			Capt.Maynard	SC 48-243	OC
Mobberly, Lewis	Ensign	- -				SC 48-243	Ref

104

APPENDIX A - COMMISSIONED OFFICERS

Name	Rank	Date	Cty	Bn	Company	Ref.	Notes
Mockbee, Brock	2nd Lt	26-03-76	MO		Capt.Riggs	AM 11-287	
Mockby, Brock	1st Lt	21-04-79	MO	Mid	Capt.G.Cullam	AM 21-357	
Mockby, Brock	Capt	25-03-80	MO	Mid	Capt.Geo.Cullum	AM 43-120	
Molton, William	2nd Lt	01-09-77	PG	Lwr	Capt.Helen	AM 16-356	
Money, John	2nd Lt	29-03-79	FR	34th	Capt.D,Smith	AM 21-331	
Money, Robert	2nd Lt	21-04-78	CE	Sass	Capt.J.Veazey	AM 21-47	
Monohan, Thomas	Ensign	22-06-78	FR	Ling	Capt.Gobble	AM 21-145	
Montgomery, John	1st Lt	26-04-76	HA		Capt.Jolley	AM 11-387	
Montgomery, John	1st Lt	09-04-78	HA	Deer	Capt.J.Jolly	AM 21-23	
Moody, Balfour	2nd Lt	17-11-80	WA			FP 1-129	Mn
Moor, Alexander	2nd Lt	22-06-78	FR	Ling	Capt.Collyberger	AM 21-144	
Moore, Abraham	2nd Lt	28-11-76	FR		Capt.H.Baker	AM 12-555	
Moore, Abraham	2nd Lt	17-01-77	FR	Ling	Capt.Meredith	AM 16-54	
Moore, David	Capt	29-11-75	FR			MM 11:50	
Moore, David	1st Maj	28-11-76	FR			AM 12-555	
Moore, David	1st Maj	05-01-77	FR	Ling		AM 16-22	Ref
Moore, John W.	1st Lt	25-03-80	MO	Mid	Capt.J.Dickinson	AM 43-120	
Moore, Jonathan William	2nd Lt	21-04-79	MO	Mid	Capt.B.Gaither	AM 21-357	
Moore, N.R.	Capt	25-06-81	BA		Horse Troop	AM 47-313	Mn
Moore, Nicholas Rauxton	Lt	08-07-76	BA			AM 12-9	Mn
Moore, Nicholas Ruxton	Capt	26-07-80	BA		Light Horse	AM 43-230	
Moore, Robert	2nd Lt	27-09-75	BA		Artillery	RB 13-36	
Moore, Robert	2nd Lt	06-06-76	BA	Town	Capt.Shaef	AM 11-467	
Moore, Robert	1st Lt	29-08-77	BA	Town	Capt.B.Dickinson	AM 16-348	OC
Moore, Robert	1st Lt	10-05-79	BA	Town	Capt.B.Dickinson	SC 48-241	Res
Moore, Smith	2nd Lt	13-06-77	QA	5th		RC 2-1119	Res
Moore, Thomas	Capt	04-02-77	BA	Gist		AM 16-114	
Moore, Thomas	Capt	20-06-77	BA			RC 2-1141	Mov
Moore, William	Ensign	03-12-76	WA		Capt.G.Johnson	AM 12-501	
Moore, William	2nd Lt	01-05-78	PG	25th	Capt.J.Carlton	AM 21-78	
Moore, William	1st Lt	24-05-79	PG	25th	Capt.J.Shaw	AM 21-414	
Moore, William	Capt	24-06-80	PG	Up	Capt.Josiah Shaw	AM 43-203	
Moore, William		27-06-81	PG			AM 47-320	Mov
Moore, William	Capt	02-07-81	PG	Up		AM 45-492	
Moran, William	1st Lt	05-07-77	CH	12th		RC 2-1170	Rec
Moran, William	1st Lt	09-05-78	CH	12th	Capt.W.Wilkinson	AM 21-72	
More, Abraham	2nd Lt	29-11-75	FR		Capt.H.Baker	MM 11:50	
More, William	Ensign	22-06-78	WA	3rdW	Capt.E.Baker	AM 21-145	
Morgan, Benjamin	2nd Lt	26-08-77	SM	Lwr	Capt.J.Mackall	AM 16-346	
Morgan, James	1st Lt	-04-76	BA		Capt.G.Wells	RB 13-74	
Morgan, Robert	1st Lt	09-04-78	HA	23rd	Capt.A.Paca	AM 21-24	
Morgan, William	Capt	22-05-76	HA			AM 11-436	
Morgan, William	Capt	09-04-78	HA	Deer		AM 21-23	OC
Morgan, William	Capt	17-11-79	HA	Deer		AM 43-17	Suc
Morgan, William	Ensign	16-12-79	DO	Up	Capt.J.Henry	AM 43-37	
Morningstar, Adam	2nd Lt	28-11-76	FR	37th		AM 12-555	
Morris, William	2nd Maj	06-01-76	WO	24th		PC 80	
Morris, William	1st Lt	22-06-76	KE		Capt.St.Clair	AM 11-506	
Morris, William	Maj	30-08-77	WO	SnHl		AM 16-350	
Morris, William	Lt Col	27-03-78	WO	Snpx	Capt.S.Handy	AM 16-547	
Morse, Thomas	Maj	28-11-76				SP 2833	Dec
Mort, John	Ensign	30-11-82	FR	Cato	Capt.G.Brown	AM 48-311	
Morton, Thomas	2nd Lt	15-02-76	AA	WstR	Capt.Simmons	AM 11-161	
Morton, Thomas Jr.	2nd Lt	02-03-78	AA	WstR	Capt.A.Simmons	AM 16-525	

APPENDIX A - COMMISSIONED OFFICERS

Name	Rank	Date	Cty	Bn	Company	Ref.	Notes
Morton, William	2nd Lt	01-05-78	PG	11th	Capt.J.Hellen	AM 21-78	
Moss, Nathan	Ensign	23-04-81	AA	Svrn	Capt.J.Gray	AM 45-411	
Moss, Robert	Ensign	30-07-81	AA	Svrn	Capt.G.Pecker	AM 45-527	
Mouldin, William	Ensign	21-04-78	CE	Susq	Capt.S.Hyland	AM 21-48	
Mouldin, William	1st Lt	09-09-78	CE	30th		AM 21-196	
Mourer, Nicholas	1st Lt	22-06-78	WA	2ndW	Capt.G.Swingle	AM 21-145	
Moxley, John	1st Lt	12-09-77	MO	16th	Capt.J.Harwood	AM 16-373	
Mucker, George	Ensign	29-11-75	FR	4th	Capt.P.Rodenbieler	MM 11:50	
Muir, Charles	1st Lt	06-07-76	DO	3rd	Capt.H.McBride	SC 48-252	OC
Muir, Charles	1st Lt	30-08-76	DO	3rd	Capt.H.McBride	SC 48-252	Ref
Muir, John	1st Lt	06-07-76	DO	3rd	Capt.McBride	AM 11-553	
Muir, John	1st Lt	20-05-78	DO	3rd	Capt.J.Henry	AM 21-98	
Muir, John	3rd Lt	20-03-79	AN		Brice-Ind.	AM 21-325	
Muir, John	2nd Lt	12-02-80	AN		Capt.S.Howard-Ind	AM 43-84	
Mullican, James	Capt	01-05-78	PG	25th		AM 21-62	
Mullikan, Joseph	2nd Lt	14-08-79	CA	14th	Capt.J.Mitchell	AM 21-493	
Mulliken, Thomas	Capt	22-02-76	AA	Svrn		AM 11-178	OC
Mulliken, Thomas	Capt	15-05-76	AA	Svrn		AM 11-450	Res
Mulliken, Wm.Belt	2nd Lt	15-05-76	AA	Svrn	Capt T.Mulliken	AM 11-450	Res
Mullikin, James		18-06-76				SP 1589	Mn
Murdock, Addison	1st Maj	13-01-76	PG	25th		PC 86	
Murdock, Addison	1st Maj	23-01-76	PG	25th		AM 11-109	Ref
Murdock, John	Colonel	06-01-76	MO	29th		PC 79	
Murdock, John	Colonel	12-09-77	MO	29th		AM 16-373	
Murdock, John	Cty Lt	02-03-81	MO			AM 45-334	
Murphey, Philemon	2nd Lt	31-07-78	QA	20th	Capt.James KE	AM 21-172	
Murphy, William	2nd Lt	29-08-77	BA	SD	Capt.T.Owings	AM 16-348	
Murray, James	Colonel	10-02-76	DO	3rd		AM 11-147	
Murray, James		27-11-76				SP 2825	
Murray, John	Capt	04-02-77	BA	Gist		AM 16-114	
Muschett, John	1st Lt	07-03-76	CH		Capt.Sinnett	AM 11-206	
Muse, Thomas	2nd Maj	10-02-76	DO	19th		AM 11-147	
Muse, Thomas	1st Maj	23-10-76	DO	Lw		AM 12-393	
Muse, Thomas	Major	28-11-76	DO			AM 12-487	Dec
Musgrove, Samuel	Ensign	21-04-79	MO	Mid	Capt.N.Ray	AM 21-357	
Myers, Christopher	2nd Lt	13-10-77	FR	Ling	Capt.Winchester	SC 48-233	OC
Myers, Christopher	2nd Lt	- -78	FR	Ling	Capt.Winchester	RC 2-233	Res
Myers, Henry	2nd Lt	28-11-76	FR		Capt.H.Stephenson	AM 12-555	
Myers, Henry	2nd Lt	17-01-77	FR	Ling	Capt.H. Stevenson	AM 16-54	
Nace, Peter	Ensign	04-02-77	BA	Gist	Capt.A. Lemmon	AM 16-114	
Nailer, John	1st Lt	01-05-78	PG	11th	Capt.H.Hill	AM 21-62	
Narkland, John	Ensign	09-04-78	TA	38th	Oxford	AM 21-25	
Neal, John	2nd Lt	07-03-76	CH		Capt.Yates	AM 11-206	
Neal, Raphael	Ensign	18-11-79	SM	Up	Capt.C.Jordan	AM 43-18	
Neale, John	1st Lt	19-01-81	CH	12th	Capt.J.Lancaster	AM 45-280	
Neale, Winfield	2nd Lt	26-08-77		Up		SC 48-234	OC
Need, Christopher	Ensign	16-08-81	FR	Cato	Capt.D.Sheilor	AM 45-566	
Need, Christopher	2nd Lt	30-11-82	FR	Cato	Capt.G.Brown	AM 48-311	
Neet, George	2nd Lt	15-05-76	FR	37th	Capt.Ogle	AM 11-426	
Neit, George	2nd Lt	03-10-76	FR		Capt.V.Creagar	AM 12-317	
Nelms, Edward Nothorn	2nd Lt	22-09-77	SO	PrAn	Capt.R.Handy	AM 16-381	
Nelson, Harry	Ensign	04-08-80	MO	Mid	Capt.T.Conner	AM 43-248	

APPENDIX A - COMMISSIONED OFFICERS

Name	Rank	Date	Cty	Bn	Company	Ref.	Notes
Nelson, William	1st Lt	21-04-78	CE	Sass	Capt.C.Heath	AM 21-47	
Nett, George	2nd Lt	29-11-75	FR	2nd	Capt.B.Ogle	MM 11:50	
Nevil, James	Ensign	21-06-80	QA	5th	Capt.John Seney	AM 43-200	
Nevil, John	1st Lt	03-01-76	QA	5th	Capt.Dean	SC 48-235	OC
Newman, Bexley	Capt	07-06-81	QA	5th	Capt.Thos.Price	AM 45-465	
Newman, Bixby	1st Lt	20-04-80	QA	5th	Capt.T.Price	AM 43-146	
Newton, Willis	Ensign	01-03-79	DO	Up	Capt.Daffin	AM 21-310	
Newton, Willis	2nd Lt	16-12-79	DO	Up		DO 231	Suc
Newton, Willis	2nd Lt	28-07-80	DO	Up	Capt.Thos.Logan	AM 43-236	
Newton, Willis	1st Lt	02-07-81	DO	Up	Capt.J.Sullivan	AM 45-492	
Nichodemus, Conrad	Capt	22-06-78	WA	2ndW		AM 21-145	
Nichodemus, Conrad	Capt	02-11-80	WA	2ndW		MH 4	Res
Nicholls, ---	Capt	06-12-81	FR			AM 47-568	Mn
Nicholls, John H.	Capt	13-04-81	MO	SelM		AM 45-396	
Nicholls, Joseph	2nd Lt	14-05-76	CA	14th	Capt.Douglass	AM 11-424	
Nicholls, Thomas	1st Lt	26-08-77	SM	Up	Capt.J.Mills	AM 16-346	
Nicholls, Thomas	Ensign	21-04-79	MO	Up	Capt.G.Cullam	AM 21-357	
Nicholls, Thomas	2nd Lt	25-03-80	MO	Mid	Capt.B.Mockby	AM 43-120	
Nicholls, Thomas	Lt	13-04-81	MO	SelM	Capt.J.H.Nicholls	AM 45-396	
Nicholls, William	Ensign	01-05-78	PG	Mid	Capt.H.Belt	AM 21-63	
Nicholls, William	1st Lt	24-05-79	PG	Mid	Capt.J.Clagget	AM 21-414	
Nichols, Jeremiah	QM	08-05-77	KE	13th		AM 16-243	
Nichols, John	2nd Lt	04-07-76	FR	UpDt	Capt.Bateler	AM 11-546	
Nichols, Robert Lloyd	2nd Maj	12-01-76	TA	4th		PC 78	
Nichols, Robert Lloyd	1st Maj	17-06-77	TA	4th		RC 2-1130	Rec
Nichols, Robert Lloyd	Lt Col	09-04-78	TA	4th		AM 21-24	
Nicholson, Benjamin	Capt	19-12-75	BA			RB 13-37	
Nicholson, Benjamin	Capt	13-05-76	BA			AM 11-423	Res
Nicholson, Benjamin	1st Maj	25-05-76	BA	Town		AM 11-443	
Nicholson, Benjamin	Lt Col	12-09-77	BA	Town		AM 16-372	
Nicholson, Benjamin	Capt	04-06-81	BA		Horse troop	AM 45-459	
Nicodemus, Frederick	1st L	26-09-76	WA		Capt.D.Clapsaddle	AM 12-301	
Noble, Nehemiah	1st Lt	14-05-76	QA		Capt.Sweat-Ind.Co.	AM 11-424	
Noble, Nehemiah	Capt	19-06-77	QA	20th		AM 16-295	
Noel, Edward	Capt	16-11-77	ES			SP 5302	Res
Noel, Edward Jr.	Capt	18-08-77	DO	ES		AM 16-337	
Nolan, Elias	Ensign	21-04-78	CE	Sass	Capt.C.Heath	AM 21-47	
Nollart, Philip	Capt	19-04-81	FR	34th	Capt.VanSwearingen	AM 45-405	
Nollert, Philip	2nd Lt	03-03-77	FR	33rd	Capt.VanSwearingen	MM 4:379	Mn
Noots, Thomas	2nd Lt	14-08-79	CA	28th	Capt.W.Chipley	AM 21-493	
Norman, Benjamin	1st Lt	02-03-78	AA	WstR	Capt.J.Deale	AM 16-526	
Norris, Aquila of Edward	Capt	09-04-78	HA	8th		AM 21-24	
Norris, George	2nd Lt	26-03-76	MO		Capt.Smith	AM 11-287	
Norris, George	2nd Lt	12-09-77	MO	16th	Capt.T.Sprigg	AM 16-373	
Norris, James	2nd Lt	20-11-76	BA		Capt.J.Talbott	AM 12-541	
Norris, John	1st Lt	29-11-75	FR		Capt.H.Baker	MM 11:50	
Norris, John	2nd Lt	03-01-76	TA		Bayside	SC 48-236	OC
Norris, John	1st Lt	28-11-76	FR		Capt.H.Baker	AM 12-555	
Norris, John	2nd Lt	12-09-77	MO		Capt.J.Macgruder	AM 16-373	
Norris, John	1st Lt	09-04-78	HA	8th	Capt.T.Hutchens	AM 21-24	
Norris, Martin	1st Lt	16-04-78	CV	15th	Capt.J.Leach	AM 21-37	
Norris, William	1st Lt	12-09-77	MO	16th	Capt.T.Sprigg	AM 16-373	
Norris, William	Capt	21-04-79	MO	Up	Capt.T.Sprigg	AM 21-356	
Norriss, Benj.Bradford	Capt	08-10-76	HA	8th		AM 12-326	

APPENDIX A - COMMISSIONED OFFICERS

Name	Rank	Date	Cty	Bn	Company	Ref.	Notes
Norwood, Edward	Capt	07-02-76	AA			AM 11-139	
Norwood, John	2nd Lt	13-04-76	AA		Capt.Howard	AM 11-329	
Norwood, John	2nd Lt	02-03-78	AA	E1kR	Capt.J.W.Dorsey	AM 16-525	OC
Norwood, John	2nd Lt	11-06-78	AA	E1kR		SC 48-237	Res
Norwood, Saml	2nd Lt	25-08-77	AA	22nd	Capt.Walker	AM 16-343	
Null, Michael	Ensign	10-01-77	FR	33rd	Capt. Watson	AM 16-33	
Nuller, ---	Lt	06-12-81	FR			AM 47-568	Mn
Nutter, Huet	1st Lt	31-07-78	SO		Capt.W.Turpin	AM 21-173	Mn
Nutter, Huet	1st Lt	24-09-78	SO		Capt.W.Turpin	RC 2-1672	Res
Nutter, Huit	1st Lt	22-09-77	SO	Salb	Capt.W.Turpin	AM 16-382	
O'Bryan, James	Capt	03-01-76	QA	20th		SC 48-238	OC
O'Bryan, Jas.	1st Maj	08-05-77	QA	20th		AM 16-244	
O'Bryan, Jas.	Lt Col	31-07-78	QA	20th		MH 2	Mn
O'Hara, John	2nd Lt	24-07-76			Capt Danl Dorsey	AM 12-109	Res
O'Neal, John	2nd Lt	22-06-78	FR	Ling	Capt.Beckwith	AM 21-145	
ONeal, Henry	Ensign	12-09-77	MO	Mid	Capt.S.West	AM 16-373	
Oakley, John	Bvt Maj	17-04-81	PG			AM 47-193	Mn
Odd, Hugh	1st Lt	09-04-78	TA	38th	United	AM 21-25	
Odle, Thomas	1st Lt	04-07-76	FR	UpDt	Capt.Bateler	AM 11-546	
Offutt, Nathaniel	Capt	18-06-77	MO	29th		RC 2-1133	Dec
Offutt, Samuel	2nd Lt	21-04-79	MO	Mid	Capt.Z.Beall	AM 21-357	
Offutt, Samuel	1st Lt	04-08-80	MO	Mid	Capt.Benj.Ray	AM 43-248	
Ogden, Benjamin	Ensign	09-05-78	CH	12th	Capt.W.Wilkinson	AM 21-72	
Ogle, ---	Maj	10-09-77				SP 4979	Mn
Ogle, Benjamin	1st Maj	06-01-76	FR	37th		PC 79	
Ogle, Benjamin	3rd Lt	18-06-81	AN		Capt.Howard	AM 45-479	
Ogle, Benjamin Jr.	Capt	29-11-75	FR	2nd		MM 11:50	
Ogle, James	Ensign	29-11-75	FR	2nd	Capt.B.Ogle	MM 11:50	
Ogle, James	Capt	15-05-76	FR	37th		AM 11-426	
Ogleby, John	Capt	10-04-76	CE			AM 11-320	Mn
Oglevee, John	Capt	21-04-78	CE	Elk		AM 21-47	OC
Oglevie, James	2nd Lt	25-06-76	BA	GP	Capt.Standiford	AM 11-444	
Oglevie, John	Capt	07-06-81	CE	Elk		AM 45-466	Suc
Oglevie, John	Capt	07-06-81	CE	Elk	Capt.J.Booth	AM 45-466	
Oldham, Edward	1st Lt	25-06-76	BA	GP	Capt.Standiford	AM 11-444	
Oldham, Richard	Ensign	28-06-81	CE	Elk	Capt.J.Oglevie	AM 45-489	
Oler, Peter	2nd Lt	29-11-75	FR	3rd	Capt.R.Beatty	MM 11:50	
Omansetter, John	2nd Lt	16-03-79	BA	Town	Capt.J.Merryman	SC 48-228	OC
Onion, Zachariah	Capt	25-06-76	BA	GP		AM 11-444	
Onion, Zacheus	1st Lt	-05-76	BA		Capt.J.Gittings	RB 13-53	
Orendoff, Christopher Jr.	1st Lt	22-06-78	WA	2ndW	Capt.J.Rennolds	AM 21-145	
Orendoff, Christopher	Maj	22-06-78	WA	2ndW		AM 21-145	
Orendorff, Christian	Capt	20-04-76	FR			AM 11-356	Mn
Orendorff, Christian	2nd Maj	20-04-76	FR	36th		AM 11-326	
Orendorff, Christopher	2nd Lt	20-04-76	FR	UpDt	Capt.Reynolds	AM 11-356	
Orme, ---	Capt	25-06-76	MO	16th		AM 11-515	Mn
Orme, Archibald	Capt	12-09-77	MO	Mid		AM 16-373	
Orme, Archibald	Colonel	01-03-79	MO	Mid		AM 21-310	
Orme, Moses	Ensign	01-05-78	PG	11th	Capt.J.Perry	AM 21-62	
Orme, Moses	1st Lt	24-05-79	PG	11th	Capt.B.Wales	AM 21-414	
Orrick, Charles	Ensign	25-09-80	BA	Town	Capt.J.Young	AM 43-303	OC
Orrick, Charles	Ensign	12-04-81	BA	Town		FP 1-93	Res

APPENDIX A - COMMISSIONED OFFICERS

Name	Rank	Date	Cty	Bn	Company	Ref.	Notes
Orrick, Thomas	2nd Lt	23-04-81	AA	Svrn	Capt.V.Gaither	AM 45-411	
Osborn, Cyrus	Ensign	31-10-75	HA	#8		PR 114	
Osborn, Cyrus	1st Lt	09-04-78	HA	23rd	Capt.J.Wood	AM 21-23	
Osborn, Cyrus	Capt	17-11-79	HA	23rd	Capt.John Wood	AM 43-17	
Osborn, Cyrus	Capt	04-04-81	HA	23rd		AM 47-139	Mov
Osborn, Samuel Groome	2nd Lt	26-04-76	HA		Capt.Cowen	AM 11-387	
Osborn, Samuel Groome	Capt	09-04-78	HA	8th		AM 21-24	
Osborn, Samuel Groome	Capt	21-03-81	HA	8th		AM 47-139	Res
Ott, Adam	Capt	30-03-81	WA	SelM		AM 45-368	
Ott, Jacob	1st Lt	15-01-77	WA		Capt.Peter Beall	AM 16-50	
Outten, Thomas	2nd Lt	21-06-76	WO		Capt.Dennis	AM 11-506	
Outton, Levin	Ensign	30-08-77	WO	Wico	Capt.B.Dennis	AM 16-351	
Owen, Robert	Capt	20-05-76	MO	16th		AM 11-432	
Owen, Robert	Capt	12-09-77	MO	Mid		AN 16-373	
Owen, Robert	Maj	01-03-79	MO	Mid		AM 21-310	
Owen, Thomas	2nd Lt	04-08-80	MO	Mid	Capt.T.Conner	AM 43-248	
Owens, John Lockey	1st Lt	19-12-75	BA		Capt.B.Nicholson	RB 13-37	
Owings, Beal	Capt	20-11-76	BA			AM 12-541	
Owings, Caleb	Capt	28-01-77	AA	Svrn		AM 16-82	
Owings, Caleb	Capt	02-03-78	AA	Svrn		AM 16-525	
Owings, Christopher	1st Lt	13-05-76	BA	Gist	Capt.I.Hammond	RB 13-69	
Owings, Christopher	Capt	06-06-76	BA	SD		AM 11-467	
Owings, Christopher	Capt	24-09-77	BA	SD		AM 16-384	
Owings, John C.	Capt	23-10-81	BA	GPUp		AM 45-650	Suc
Owings, John Cockey	1st Lt	13-05-76	BA	Gist		RB 13-69	
Owings, John Cockey	Capt	06-06-76	BA	SD		AM 11-467	
Owings, John Cockey	Capt	19-03-81	BA	SD		PA	Res
Owings, Joshua	1st Lt	29-08-77	BA	SD	Capt.N.Stinchcomb	AM 16-348	
Owings, Joshua of John	Ensign	13-05-76	BA	Gist	Capt.N.Stincomb	RB 13-69	
Owings, Joshua of John	Ensign	06-06-76	BA	SD	Capt.Stinchcomb	AM 11-467	
Owings, Nathaniel	Ensign	30-03-76	AA	ElkR		AM 11-299	
Owings, Nathaniel	1st Lt	02-03-78	AA	ElkR	Capt.J.Dorsey	AM 16-525	
Owings, Richard	Capt	13-05-76	BA	Gist		RB 13-69	
Owings, Richard	Capt	27-05-79	BA	SD		AM 21-422	Suc
Owings, Richard of Samuel	Capt	06-05-76	BA	SD	3rd Co.	AM 11-467	
Owings, Samuel	Lt Col	25-05-76	BA	SD		AM 11-443	
Owings, Samuel	Colonel	03-06-77	BA	SD		AM 16-271	
Owings, Thomas	2nd Lt	13-05-76	BA	Gist	Capt.S.Owings	RB 13-69	
Owings, Thomas	1st Lt	06-06-76	BA	SD	Capt.Wells	AM 11-467	
Owings, Thomas	Capt	29-08-77	BA	SD		AM 16-348	OC
Owings, Thomas	Capt	13-04-78	BA			SP 6563	Res
Ozment, Richard	Ensign	09-04-78	CA	14th	Capt.H.McBride	AM 21-23	
Paca, Aquila Jr.	Capt	09-04-78	HA	23rd		AM 21-24	OC
Paca, Aquila	Lt Col	09-04-78	HA	23rd		AM 21-23	
Page, John	2nd Maj	08-05-77	KE	13th		AM 16-243	
Page, John	Capt	30-05-81	KE		Horse troop	AM 45-449	
Parish, Edward	2nd Lt	29-08-77	BA	SD	Capt.M.Gosnell	AM 16-348	
Parish, Edward of Edward	Ensign	06-06-76	BA	SD	Capt.Hammond	AM 11-467	
Parish, William	Ensign	03-09-77	BA	GP	Capt.Standiford	AM 16-359	
Parker, Edward	1st Maj	06-01-76	CE	2nd		PC 80	
Parker, Edward	Colonel	21-04-78	CE	Elk		AM 21-47	OC
Parker, Edward	Colonel	07-06-81	CE	Elk		AM 45-465	Suc

109

APPENDIX A - COMMISSIONED OFFICERS

Name	Rank	Date	Cty	Bn	Company	Ref.	Notes
Parker, Levin	QM	16-05-76		Corp		AM 11-429	
Parker, Scarborough	2nd Lt	16-03-81	WO	SnH1	Capt.B.Townsend	AM 45-353	
Parker, Scarborough	Ensign	23-08-81	WO	Se1M	Capt.Parramore	AM 45-577	
Parker, Selby	Ensign	02-06-81	WO	Wico	Capt.B.Townsend	AM 45-457	
Parker, Walter Smith	1st Lt	29-08-77	BA	Town	Capt.E.Bailey	AM 16-348	
Parker, William	2nd Lt	19-12-75	BA		Capt.Z.McCubbin	RB 13-37	
Parker, William	Ensign	30-08-77	WO	SnH1	Capt.J.Stewart	AM 16-351	
Parker, William	Ensign	27-05-79	BA	SD	Capt.J.Hurd	AM 21-422	
Parker, William	Ensign	21-04-81	WO	SnH	Capt.Stewart	PA	Res
Parkinson, John	Ensign	15-05-76	FR	37th	Capt.Smith	AM 11-426	
Parkinson, John	Ensign	03-10-76	FR		Capt.V.Creagar	AM 12-317	
Parkinson, John	1st Lt	27-04-79	FR	37th	Capt.W.Carmack	AM 21-368	
Parmer, James	Ensign	09-04-78	CA	14th	Capt.P.Rich	AM 21-23	
Parnham, ---	Capt	26-07-76	CH			AM 12-125	Mn
Parnham, John	Capt	13-09-76				AM 12-269	Mn
Parnham, John	Capt	20-03-81	CH	12th		AM 47-136	Res
Parramore, John	Capt	30-08-77	WO	SnH1		AM 16-351	
Parramore, John	Capt	23-08-81	WO	Se1M		AM 45-577	
Parran, Robert	Capt	16-04-78	CV	15th		AM 21-37	
Parrott, Christo.		17-06-77			Capt.Beall	AM 16-291	Mn
Parrott, Richard	1st Lt	09-04-78	TA	38th	Miles River	AM 21-25	
Parsons, George	1st Lt	15-05-76	WO	10th	Capt.Handy	AM 11-426	
Parsons, George	1st Lt	30-08-77	WO	Wico	Capt.R.Handy	AM 16-351	
Parsons, George	1st Lt	27-05-79	WO			MH 5	Suc
Patrick, John	Capt	01-04-76	HA		#17	PR 122	
Patrick, John	Capt	26-04-76	HA			AM 11-387	
Patrick, John	Capt	10-02-77	HA			AM 16-129	Mn
Patrick, John	Capt	09-04-78	HA	Deer		AM 21-23	
Patrick, John	Capt	17-11-79	HA	Deer		AM 43-17	Suc
Patterson, George	1st Lt	23-09-75	HA		#3	PR 108	
Patterson, George	Capt	16-05-76	HA	23rd		AM 11-428	
Patterson, George	Capt	09-04-78	HA	23rd		AM 21-23	OC
Patterson, George	Capt	17-11-79	HA	23rd		AM 43-17	Suc
Patterson, James	Capt	30-08-77	WO	SnH1		AM 16-351	
Patterson, James	1st Lt	22-06-78	WA	2ndW	Capt.J.Walling	AM 21-145	
Patterson, John	2nd Lt	21-04-78	CE	Susq	Capt.S.Miller	AM 21-48	
Patterson, John	1st Lt	09-09-78	CE	30th	Capt.Robt.Porter	AM 21-196	
Patterson, William	Ensign	29-11-75	FR	3rd	Capt.R.Beatty	MM 11:50	
Patterson, William	Capt	06-02-77			"Dolphin"	AM 16-121	Mn
Peckham, John	1st Lt	04-06-77			"The Chester"	AM 16-273	
Peckham, John	1st Lt	18-09-78			"The Chester"	AM 21-207	Res
Pecker, Charles	Ensign	23-04-81	AA	Svrn	Capt.C.Boone	AM 45-411	
Pecker, George	Capt	30-07-81	AA	Svrn	Capt.C.Boone	AM 45-527	
Peckly, Henry	Ensign	30-08-77	Up		Capt.J.Showers	AM 16-350	
Penn, Charles	2nd Lt	20-05-76	MO	16th	Capt.Owens	AM 11-432	
Peppel, ---	Capt	28-11-76	FR	35th		AM 12-555	
Pepples, William	Capt	28-11-76	FR			AM 12-555	
Perdue, James	2nd Lt	15-05-76	WO	10th	Capt.Handy	AM 11-426	
Perdue, James	Capt	27-05-79	WO	Wico	Capt.J.Mitchell	AM 21-423	
Perine, Samuel	1st Lt	19-12-75	BA		Capt.Wm.Cromwell	RB 13-37	
Perkins, Isaac	Capt	15-05-76	KE			AM 11-426	
Perkins, Isaac	Lt Col	04-06-78	KE	13th		AM 21-122	
Perkins, William	Ensign	09-04-78	HA	23rd	Capt.J.W.Hall	AM 21-23	OC
Perry, John	Capt	01-05-78	PG	11th		AM 21-62	

APPENDIX A - COMMISSIONED OFFICERS

Name	Rank	Date	Cty	Bn	Company	Ref.	Notes
Perry, John	Capt	24-05-79	PG	11th		AM 21-414	Suc
Perry, William	QM	13-08-76	TA	4th		AM 12-198	
Peter, John	2nd Lt	20-04-76	FR	LrDt	Capt.Richardson	AM 11-356	
Peter, John	1st Lt	12-09-77	MO	29th	Capt.A.McFadon	AM 16-373	
Phares, John	1st Lt	29-11-75	FR	3rd	Capt.W.Shields	MM 11:50	
Philip,---	2nd Lt	23-02-76	SM	21st	Leonardtown	AM 11-181	Res
Philips, Charles	Ensign	21-06-77	MO	29th	Capt.R.Beall	AM 16-296	
Philips, James	Ensign	22-08-81	SO	Salb	Capt.Wm.Turpin	AM 45-575	
Philips, John	Capt	19-08-76	SO	1st		AM 12-220	
Philips, John	2nd Lt	22-09-77	SO	Salb	Capt.W.Turpin	AM 16-382	
Philips, John	1st Lt	31-07-78	SO		Capt.W.Turpin	AM 21-173	Mn
Philips, Thomas	Capt	13-05-76	BA	Gist		RB 13-69	
Philips, Thomas	Capt	27-05-79	BA	SD		AM 21-422	Suc
Philips, William	Ensign	20-05-78	DO	3rd	Capt.J.Langfitt	AM 21-98	
Phillips, Charles	Ensign	12-09-77	MO	29th	Capt.R.Beall	AM 16-373	
Phillips, John	1st Lt	07-01-78	SO	Salb	Capt.W.Turpin	AM 16-457	
Phillips, Nathan	Ensign	28-06-81	CE	Elk	Capt.T.L.Savin	AM 45-489	
Phillips, Thomas	Capt	06-06-76	BA	SD	4th	AM 11-467	
Phillips, William	Ensign	18-10-77	DO	3rd	Chickamacamico	RC 2-1356	Rec
Phillips, William	Ensign	23-08-81	DO	Up		DO 230	Mn
Philpot, Barton	Ensign	04-07-76	FR	UpDt	Capt.Bateler	AM 11-546	
Philpot, Benjamin	Capt	07-03-76	CH			AM 11-206	
Philpot, Benjamin	Capt	09-02-81	CH	12th		AM 45-307	Suc
Philpot, John	Ensign	30-08-77	BA		Capt.Sterrett	AM 16-351	
Phipps, Roger	Ensign	02-03-78	AA	WstR	Capt.J.Deale	AM 16-526	
Pigman, Nathaniel	Capt	14-05-76	MO	29th		AM 11-424	
Pigman, Nathaniel	Capt	12-09-77	MO	Mid		AM 16-373	
Pigman, Nathaniel	Lt Col	01-03-79	MO	Mid		AM 21-310	
Piles, William	Lt	22-04-80			State Inf co.	AM 43-149	
Piles, William	Lt	01-07-80	FR		Guard Inf Co	AM 45-1	Ref
Pindell, Philip	Capt	16-05-78	WA	3rdW		AM 21-86	
Pindell, Philip	1st Lt	23-10-81	BA	GPUp	Capt.N.Kelly	AM 45-650	
Piper, Joseph	Ensign	22-09-77	SO	Salb	Capt.W.Turpin	AM 16-382	
Piper, Joseph	2nd Lt	22-08-81	SO	Salb	Capt.Wm.Turpin	AM 45-575	
Pittany, John	Ensign	20-05-78	DO	3rd	Capt.J.Daffin	AM 21-98	
Plowden, Edmund	Capt	26-08-77	SM	Up		AM 16-346	
Plowden, Edward	Capt	17-08-76				AM 12-215	Mn
Plowman, Richard	Ensign	07-02-82	BA	SD	Capt.W.Kelly	AM 48-71	
Plummer, Samuel	Capt	29-11-75	FR	1st		MM 11:50	
Poe, George	Capt	11-06-76	FR	34th		AM 11-476	
Polk, Gilliss	1st Lt	22-09-77	SO	PrAn	Capt.L.Irving	AM 16-381	
Polk, James	1st Lt	22-09-77	SO	Salb	Capt.H.Gale	AM 16-381	
Porter, Andrew	1st Lt	14-05-77			Capt.Gosden	AM 16-254	Ref
Porter, Andrew	1st Lt	13-06-77	QA	5th		RC 2-1119	Res
Porter, Andrew	2nd Lt	21-04-78	CE	Susq	Capt.W.Ewing	AM 21-48	
Porter, Andrew	Capt	03-01-82	CE	Susq	Capt.Wm.Ewing	AM 48-38	
Porter, Benjamin	Ensign	21-04-78	CE	Sass	Capt.J.Veazey	AM 21-47	
Porter, Benjamin	1st Lt	22-06-78	CE	Bohe	Capt.J.W.Veazey	AM 21-145	
Porter, Francis	Ensign	15-06-80	TA	38th	Capt.Dawson	AM 43-195	
Porter, James	Capt	14-06-77				SP 4534	Mn
Porter, James	Capt	21-04-78	CE	Sass		AM 21-47	
Porter, Joshua	1st Lt	06-05-76	BA	SD	Capt.Owings	AM 11-467	
Porter, Joshua	1st Lt	13-05-76	BA	Gist	Capt.R.Owings	RB 13-69	
Porter, McKimmey	Ensign	22-08-81	SO	Salb	Capt.J.Venable	AM 45-575	

111

APPENDIX A - COMMISSIONED OFFICERS

Name	Rank	Date	Cty	Bn	Company	Ref.	Notes
Porter, Robert	Capt	21-04-78	CE	Susq		AM 21-48	
Posey, Belain	Capt	30-07-76	CH			AM 12-141	
Posey, Belam	Capt	27-01-76	CH			AM 11-111	Mn
Posey, Francis	Ensign	05-07-77	CH	12th		RC 2-1170	Mn
Posey, Francis	1st Lt	28-05-79	CH	12th	Capt.H.Dent	AM 21-427	
Posey, Humphrey	Ensign	24-03-81	CH	26th	Capt.S.Luckett	AM 45-361	
Postlewait, Robert	Ensign	10-04-76	CA			AM 11-320	
Postlewait, Robert	Capt	09-04-78	CA			AM 21-23	
Postley, John	Capt	30-08-77	WO	Snpx		AM 16-350	
Postley, John	Maj	09-08-80	WO	Snpx		AM 43-251	
Postley, John	Colonel	13-06-82	WO	Snpx		AM 48-190	
Potter, Andrew	Ensign	22-06-78	WA	3rdW	Capt.E.Baker	AM 21-145	
Potter, Libdial	Ensign	15-05-76	CA	14th		SP 1457	Mn
Potter, Nathaniel	Capt	24-05-76	CA	14th		AM 11-442	Mn
Potter, Nathaniel	1st Maj	24-06-77	CA	14th		AM 16-299	
Potter, Nathaniel	Lt Col	09-04-78	CA	14th		AM 21-23	
Potter, Zebdiah	Ensign	15-05-76	CA		Capt.J.Richardson	AM 11-427	Res
Potter, Zebdiah	Surg	15-05-76	CA	14th		AM 11-427	Mn
Pottorff, Andrew	2nd Lt	- -	WA			FP 1-129	Mn
Potts, Richard	Ensign	15-05-76	FR	34th	Capt.Charlton	AM 11-426	
Powel, Brittain	Ensign	19-09-76	SO	17th		AM 12-285	
Power, Clement	Ensign	26-08-77	SM	Up	Capt.J.Thomas	AM 16-346	OC
Power, Clement	2nd Lt	18-11-79	SM	Up	Capt.F.Millard	AM 43-18	
Pownall, Thomas	1st Lt	03-01-76	AA	31st		SC 48-219	Com
Pownall, Thomas	1st Lt	09-08-76	AA	31st		AM 12-191	Res
Prall, Edward	1st Lt	26-12-74	HA		#2-Lwr Cross Rds	PR 107	
Prather, Charles	Ensign	16-05-78	WA	3rdW	Capt.J.Prather	AM 21-86	
Prather, James	1st Lt	15-05-76	FR		Capt.Warring	AM 11-427	
Prather, James	Capt	16-05-78	WA	3rdW		AM 21-86	
Pratt, Henry	Ensign	16-03-76	QA		Capt.Costin	AM 11-253	
Pratt, Henry	2nd Lt	31-07-78	QA	20th	Capt.J.Costin	MH 2	Res
Presbury, George B.	1st Lt	04-04-81	HA	8th	Capt.J.Day	AM 45-375	
Presbury, Joseph Jr.	Ensign	04-04-81	HA	8th	Capt.J.Day	AM 45-375	
Preston, Crafton	1st Lt	14-09-75	HA		#10	PR 115	
Preston, Grafton	1st Lt	09-04-78	HA	Deer	Capt.S.Ashmead	AM 21-22	
Preston, Grafton	1st Lt	17-11-79	HA	Deer	Capt.J.Clandenin	AM 43-17	
Preston, James	2nd Lt	17-11-79	HA	Deer	Capt.J.Clandenin	AM 43-17	
Preston, Martin	Ensign	09-12-75	HA		#11	PR 116	
Preston, Martin	2nd Lt	26-04-76	HA	8th	Capt.McComas	AM 11-387	
Preston, Martin	1st Lt	09-04-78	HA	8th	Capt.D.Scott	AM 21-24	
Price, Absalom	1st Lt	06-05-78	BA	Town	Capt Dean	AM 11-467	
Price, Hyland	Ensign	21-04-78	CE	Sass	Capt.J.Ford	AM 21-47	
Price, Hyland	2nd Lt	22-06-78	CE	Bohe	Capt.S.Lankaster	AM 21-145	
Price, Josiah	1st Lt	22-06-78	WA	3rdW	Capt.E.Baker	AM 21-145	
Price, Neale	1st Lt	17-12-81	CA	28th	Capt.P.Downes	AM 48-27	
Price, Thomas	2nd Lt	21-04-78	CE	Elk	Capt.T.Savin	AM 21-47	
Price, Thomas	1st Lt	09-09-78	CE	2nd	Capt.A.Cazier	AM 21-196	
Price, Thomas	Capt	20-04-80	QA	5th	Capt.V.Downes	AM 43-146	
Price, Thomas	Capt	07-06-81	QA	5th		AM 45-465	Suc
Price, Thomas Lane	2nd Lt	09-04-78	TA	4th	Hand in Hand	AM 21-24	
Price, Timothy	2nd Lt	17-06-77	TA	4th	Hand in Hand	RC 2-1130	Mn
Price, Vincent	Capt	16-11-76		28th		SP 2740	Mn
Price, Vincent	Lt Col	09-04-78	CA	28th		AM 21-23	
Price, Vincent	Capt	26-07-80	CA	14th	Capt.T.Lockerman	AM 43-230	

APPENDIX A - COMMISSIONED OFFICERS

Name	Rank	Date	Cty	Bn	Company	Ref.	Notes
Price, Vincent	Lt	15-06-81	CA		Horse troop	AM 45-475	
Price, Vincent	Colonel	17-12-81	CA	28th		AM 48-27	
Price, Vincent	Ensign	04-11-82	TA	4th	Capt.Dorhorty	AM 48-298	
Prigg, Edward	1st Lt	09-04-78	HA	23rd	Capt.J.Wheeler	AM 21-24	
Prigg, William	Ensign	22-05-76	HA		Capt.Morgan	AM 11-436	
Prigg, William	Ensign	09-04-78	HA	Deer	Capt.W.Morgan	AM 21-23	OC
Priggs, John F.A.	QM	13-01-76	PG	11th		PC 86	
Pringle, Mark	Cornet	26-07-80	BA		Light Horse	AM 43-230	
Pringle, Mark	Cornet	25-06-81	BA		Capt.N.R.Moore	AM 47-313	Mn
Prior, Emory	1st Lt	31-07-78	QA	5th	Capt.J.Sudler	AM 21-172	
Pritchard, James	Capt	21-04-78	CE	Susq		AM 21-48	
Pritchard, Jesse	Ensign	- -75	HA		#9	PR 115	
Pritchard, Jesse	Ensign	03-01-76	HA	8th		SC 48-223	OC
Pritchard, Obediah	2nd Lt	09-04-78	HA	23rd	Capt.G.Patterson	AM 21-24	
Pritchard, Obediah	1st Lt	17-11-79	HA	23rd	Capt.Hugh Smith	AM 43-17	
Pritchett, Edward	2nd Lt	20-06-78	DO	19th	Capt.E.Staplefort	AM 21-97	
Pryor, Simon	Capt	30-08-77	BA	GP		AM 16-350	
Pryor, William	Capt	03-01-76	QA	5th		SC 48-221	OC
Purday, William	1st Lt	29-11-75	FR	4th	Capt.Wm.Duvall	MM 11:50	
Purdue, James	2nd Lt	30-08-77	WO	Wico	Capt.R.Handy	AM 16-351	
Purnal, Benjamin	Ensign	30-08-77	WO	Snpx	Capt.J.Purnal	AM 16-350	
Purnal, Elisha	1st Lt	30-08-77	WO	Snpx	Capt.J.Purnal	AM 16-350	
Purnal, John	Capt	30-08-77	WO	Snpx		AM 16-350	
Purnal, Matthew	Capt	30-08-77	WO	Snpx		AM 16-350	
Purnal, Thomas	Capt	30-08-77	WO	Snpx		AM 16-350	
Purnal, William	Capt	30-08-77	WO	Snpx		AM 16-350	
Purnall, Benjamin	2nd Lt	14-08-79	WO	Snpx	Capt.E.Purnall	AM 21-493	
Purnall, Elisha	Capt	14-08-79	WO	Snpx	Capt.John Purnall	AM 21-493	
Purnall, John	Capt	14-08-79	WO	Snpx		AM 21-493	Suc
Purnell, John	Capt	14-08-79	WO			MH 5	Dec
Purnell, Thomas	2nd Lt	17-12-81	CA	28th	Capt.T.Knotts	AM 48-27	
Purnell, Thomas	Lt Col	13-06-82	WO	Snpx		AM 48-190	
Purnell, William	Colonel	06-01-76	WO	24th		PC 80	
Purnell, William	Colonel	04-08-80	WO	24th		RC 3-664	Mn
Purnell, William	Maj	13-06-82	WO	Snpx		AM 48-190	
Purnell, Zadock	Lt Col	06-01-76	WO	24th		PC 80	
Purnell, Zadock	Colonel	30-08-77	WO	Snpx		AM 16-350	OC
Purnell, Zadock	Colonel	23-03-78	WO	Snpx		AM 16-547	Res
Pusety, Dennis	1st Lt	27-07-77	WA		Capt.Renblin	RC 2-1186	Rec
Pye, Walter	2nd Lt	09-05-78	CH	26th	Capt.G.Dent	AM 21-72	
Queen, Francis	2nd Lt	05-07-77	CH	12th	Capt.A.Macpherson	RC 2-1170	Rec
Queen, Joseph	Ensign	01-05-78	PG	25th	Capt.J.Weight	AM 21-62	
Queen, Joseph	Ensign	15-06-81	PG	SelM	Capt.O.Williams	AM 45-475	
Queen, Walter	Adj	29-08-77	FR	29th		AM 16-348	
Quinton, Philip	Capt	30-08-77	WO	Wico		AM 16-351	
Quinton, Philip	Maj	13-06-82	WO	Wico		AM 48-190	
Quinton, William		15-05-81	WO			AM 47-244	Res
Quinton,---	Capt	06-07-76	DO			AM 11-553	Mn
Quntan, James	2nd Lt	30-08-77	WO	Snpx	Capt.T.Purnal	AM 16-350	
Raisin, Thomas	Cornet	30-05-81	KE		Capt.J.Page	SC 49-71	Com

APPENDIX A - COMMISSIONED OFFICERS

Name	Rank	Date	Cty	Bn	Company	Ref.	Notes
Raisin, Thomas	Cornet	-05-82	KE		Capt.J.Page	SC 49-71	Res
Ramsberg, Jacob	2nd Lt	27-04-79	FR	37th	Capt.J.Trout	AM 21-368	
Ramsburgh, Christian	Ensign	29-11-75	FR	1st	Capt.J.Stoner	MM 11:50	
Ramsey, Andrew	Ensign	17-11-79	HA	Deer	Capt.S.Bayliss	AM 43-17	
Ramsey, Nathaniel	Capt	01-08-75	CE			RB 13-40	Mn
Rancher, James	Ensign	17-11-79	HA	Deer	Capt.J.Farmer	AM 43-17	
Randall, Aquila	Blst Lt	24-09-77	BA		Capt.R.Owings	AM 16-384	
Randall, George	Blst Lt	19-09-77	BA		Capt.Garretson	AM 16-380	
Randel, Aquila	2nd Lt	30-03-76	AA	ElkR	Capt.Riggs	AM 11-299	
Raper, James	1st Lt	26-08-77	SM	Up	Capt.J.Roach	AM 16-346	OC
Raper, William	2nd Lt	26-08-77	SM	Up	Capt.J.Roach	AM 16-346	OC
Rapier, Robert James	Capt	18-11-79	SM	Up	Capt.James Roach	AM 43-18	
Rapier, William	1st Lt	18-11-79	SM	Up	Capt.R.Rapier	AM 43-18	
Rasin, Thomas	Cornet	30-05-81	KE		Horse troop	AM 45-449	
Ratcliffe,---	Capt	12-06-76	WO	24th		AM 11-286	Mn
Ratliff, John	Capt	30-08-77	WO	Snpx		AM 16-350	
Ratliff, John	Capt	09-08-80	WO	Snpx		AM 43-251	Suc
Ratliff, Nathaniel	1st Lt	30-08-77	WO	Snpx	Capt.T.Purnal	AM 16-350	
Rawley, Walter	Ensign	16-12-79	DO	Up	Capt.R.Hooper	AM 43-37	
Rawley, Walter	Ensign	31-08-81	DO		Capt.R.Hooper	AM 47-462	Res
Rawling, Aaron	2nd Lt	02-05-81	AA	WstR	Capt.S.Watkins	AM 45-422	
Rawlings, Andrew	Ensign	17-03-81	AA	WstR	Capt.S.Watkins	AM 45-354	
Rawlings, Robert Jr.	1st Lt	16-04-78	CV	15th	Capt.R.Parran	AM 21-37	
Ray, Benjamin	1st Lt	21-04-79	MO	Mid	Capt.Z.Beall	AM 21-357	
Ray, Benjamin	Capt	25-03-80	MO	Mid	Capt.Zeph.Beall	AM 43-120	
Ray, John	Ensign	26-08-77	AA	22nd	Capt.J.Burgess	AM 16-346	
Ray, John	1st Lt	12-09-77	MO	Mid	Capt.S.West	AM 16-373	
Ray, John	2nd Lt	30-03-79	AA	22nd	Capt.B.Burgess	AM 21-333	
Ray, John	Capt	21-04-79	MO	Mid	Capt.Saml.West	AM 21-357	
Ray, John	Ensign	04-11-82	TA	38th	Capt.C.Gardiner	AM 48-298	
Ray, Nicholas	2nd Lt	12-09-77	MO	Mid	Capt.R.Owen	AM 16-373	
Ray, Nicholas	Capt	21-04-79	MO	Mid	Capt.R.Owen	AM 21-357	
Ray, Nicholas	Capt	25-03-80	MO	Mid		AM 43-120	Suc
Read, Andrew	Ensign	21-04-78	CE	Elk	Capt.S.Maffitt	AM 21-47	OC
Read, Joseph	2nd Lt	16-05-78	WA	3rdW	Capt.J.Prather	AM 21-86	
Rease, Frederick	2nd Lt	22-06-78	FR	Ling	Capt.Miers	AM 21-145	
Reed, Ezekiel	Capt	27-04-78	DO	Up		DO 230	Mn
Reed, Ezekiel	Capt	27-04-80	DO	Up	Capt.S.Waters	AM 43-154	
Reed, Isaac	1st Lt	20-05-78	DO	3rd	Capt.S.Waters	AM 21-98	
Reed, John	Capt	22-04-80			Inf.co.	AM 43-149	
Reed, John	2nd Lt	28-07-80	DO	Up	Capt.E.Reed	AM 43-236	
Reed, John Hatton	Lt Col	12-01-76	SM	21st		PC 78	
Reed, Philip	Lt	23-09-77	FR			SP 1112	Res
Reed, Philip	Ensign	13-06-77	QA	5th		RC 2-1119	Mn
Reeder, John	Lt Col	26-08-77	SM	Up		AM 16-345	
Reeder, John Jr.	1st Lt	16-04-78	SM	21st	Capt.A.H.Watts	AM 21-37	
Reeder, Thomas Attaway	Capt	26-08-77	SM	Up		AM 16-346	
Reeder, Thomas Attaway	Capt	18-11-79	SM	Up		AM 43-18	Suc
Reid, Isaac	1st Lt	16-09-76	DO		Friendship	AM 12-274	
Reid, John	Capt	01-07-80	FR		Guard Inf Co	AM 45-1	Mn
Reider, John Jr.	Lt Col	12-01-76	SM	6th		PC 78	
Reily, John	2nd Lt	19-12-75	BA		Capt.J.Bosley	RB 13-37	
Reily, William	1st Lt	19-12-75	BA		Capt.J.Bosley	RB 13-37	
Reisten, Thomas	2nd Lt	05-11-81	BA	Up	Capt.P.Stilts	AM 45-662	

APPENDIX A - COMMISSIONED OFFICERS

Name	Rank	Date	Cty	Bn	Company	Ref.	Notes
Renblin, Jacob	Capt	27-07-77	WA			RC 2-1186	Rec
Rench, Andrew	Lt Col	06-01-76	FR	32nd		PC 79	OC
Rennolds, Joseph of John	Ensign	22-06-78	WA	2ndW	Capt.J.Rennolds	AM 21-145	
Rennolds, William	Capt	22-06-78	WA	2ndW		AM 21-145	
Renshaw, Joshua	Ensign	26-04-76	HA	8th	Capt.Harris	AM 11-387	
Reswick, Wilfred	Ensign	26-08-77	SM	Up	Capt.E.Plowden	AM 16-346	
Reyner, Ebenezer	2nd Lt	15-05-76	KE		Capt.Perkins	AM 11-426	
Reynolds, Edward	2nd Lt	10-04-76	CV		Capt.Freeland	AM 11-320	
Reynolds, Edward	2nd Lt	16-04-78	CV	15th	Capt.F.Freeland	AM 21-37	
Reynolds, James	2nd Lt	18-10-82	AA	Svrn	Capt.J.Merrikin	AM 48-288	
Reynolds, John	Capt	20-04-76	FR	UpDt		AM 11-356	
Reynolds, John	Lt	25-06-76	CA			SP 1640	
Reynolds, John	1st Lt	19-06-77	CA	28th	Capt.Price	AM 16-294	
Reynolds, John	Capt	09-04-78	CA	28th		AM 21-23	
Reynolds, John	Capt	14-08-79	CA	28th		AM 21-493	Suc
Rhea, George	Ensign	09-09-78	CE	30th	Capt.Saml.Miller	AM 21-196	
Rhintzell, Anthony	2nd Lt	04-08-80	MO	Lwr	Capt.D.Rhintzell	AM 43-248	
Rhintzell, Daniel	Capt	04-08-80	MO	Lwr	Capt.Wm.Carter	AM 43-248	
Rhodes, Jacob	Ensign	21-04-79	MO	Up	Capt.Wm.Norris	AM 21-357	
Rice, Thomas	2nd Lt	29-11-75	FR	3rd	Capt.M.McGuire	MM 11:50	
Rich, Peter	2nd Lt	19-06-77	QA	20th	Capt.Hanson	AM 16-295	
Rich, Peter	Capt	09-04-78	CA	14th		AM 21-23	
Rich, Peter	1st Lt	31-07-78	QA	20th	Capt.C.Downes	AM 21-172	
Richardon, William	1st Lt	30-08-77	WO	SnHl	Capt.S.Smyley	AM 16-351	
Richards, Harry	1st Lt	29-03-76	CA		Capt R.Andrews	SP 1232	Mn
Richards, Henry	1st Lt	14-05-76	CA	14th	Capt.Andrews	AM 11-424	
Richards, Joseph	Ensign	30-08-77	WO	Wico	Capt.C.Bennett	AM 16-351	
Richardson, Daniel	Ensign	26-07-80	CA	14th	Capt.J.Hooper	AM 43-230	
Richardson, Daniel	2nd Lt	17-12-81	CA	14th	Capt.C.Johnson	AM 48-27	
Richardson, George	1st Lt	03-12-76	WA		Capt.C.Calson	AM 12-501	
Richardson, John	2nd Lt	30-08-77	WO	Wico	Capt.E.Shockley	AM 16-351	
Richardson, Joseph	2nd Maj	10-02-76	DO	3rd		AM 11-147	
Richardson, Joseph	Capt	16-11-76	CA			SP 2740	Mn
Richardson, Joseph	2nd Maj	24-06-77	CA	14th		AM 16-299	
Richardson, Joseph	Maj	09-04-78	CA	14th		AM 21-23	
Richardson, Joseph	Maj	20-05-78	DO	19th		AM 21-97	
Richardson, Joseph	Lt Col	27-04-80	DO	Up		AM 43-154	
Richardson, Peter	1st Lt	09-04-78	CA	14th	Capt.J.Mitchel	AM 21-23	
Richardson, Peter	1st Lt	- -	CA	14th		FP 1-48	Dec
Richardson, Thomas	Capt	18-03-76	PG	25th		AM 11-260	
Richardson, Thomas	Capt	01-05-78	PG	25th		AM 21-78	
Richardson, Vincent	Ensign	09-09-75	HA	#7		PR 113	
Richardson, William	Colonel	12-01-76	CA	14th		PC 78	
Richardson, William	Capt	06-06-76	BA	Town		AM 11-467	
Richardson, William	Capt	19-03-79	BA	Town		AM 21-324	Suc
Ricker, Conrad	Ensign	11-06-76	FR	34th	Capt.Frazier	AM 11-476	
Ricketts, Benjamin	2nd Lt	21-04-79	MO	Mid	Capt.J.Bruce	AM 21-357	
Ricketts, Benjamin	1st Lt	25-03-80	MO	Up	Capt.H.Griffith	AM 43-120	
Ricketts, Benjamin	Capt	04-08-80	MO	Mid	Capt.H.Griffith	AM 43-248	
Ricketts, Benjamin	Ensign	07-06-81	CE	Elk	Capt.D.Ricketts	AM 45-466	
Ricketts, Benjamin	2nd Lt	03-10-82	CE	ElkR	Capt.D.Ricketts	AM 48-274	
Ricketts, David	1st Lt	21-04-78	CE	Elk	Capt.J.Booth	AM 21-47	
Ricketts, David	Capt	07-06-81	CE	Elk	Capt.Saml.Evans	AM 45-465	
Ricketts, Joseph	Ensign	04-08-80	MO	Mid	Capt.B.Ricketts	AM 43-248	

APPENDIX A - COMMISSIONED OFFICERS

Name	Rank	Date	Cty	Bn	Company	Ref.	Notes
Ricketts, Thomas	1st Lt	02-03-78	AA	E1kR	Capt.J.W.Dorsey	AM 16-525	OC
Ricketts, Thomas	1st Lt	05-09-78	AA			MH 5	Res
Riddle, Samuel	1st Lt	21-04-78	CE	Susq	Capt.S.Miller	AM 21-48	
Ridenour, Martin	Capt	- -	WA		Capt.Hogmire	FP 1-129	Mn
Ridge, William	Ensign	28-11-76	FR	37th	Capt.W.B.Head	AM 12-555	
Ridgeley, Richard	Capt	18-04-81	BA	Town		AM 45-402	
Ridgely, Frederick	Surgeon	10-01-77	FR	34th		AM 16-33	
Ridgely, Nicholas	Ensign	28-02-76	AA	E1kR	Capt.Stringer	AM 11-191	
Ridgely, Nicholas	2nd Lt	28-08-77	AA	22nd	Capt.R.Stringer	AM 16-347	OC
Ridgely, Nicholas	2nd Lt	13-04-81	AA	22nd		SC 49-66	Res
Ridgely, Westal	1st Lt	29-11-75	FR	1st	Capt.H.Yost	MM 11:50	
Ridgeway, John	2nd Ly	09-06-77	PG		Capt.H.Magruder	RC 2-1103	Rec
Ridgeway, Samuel	Capt	20-04-80	QA	5th	Capt.I.Scrivener	AM 43-146	
Ridgeway, Samuel	Capt	07-06-81	QA	5th		AM 45-465	Suc
Ridley, Matthew	Adj	09-06-81			Horse troops	AM 45-467	
Rigdon, Alexander	Capt	02-12-75	HA	#12		PR 118	
Rigdon, Alexander	Capt	10-02-77	HA			AM 16-129	Mn
Rigdon, Alexander	Lt Col	09-04-78	HA	Deer		AM 21-22	
Rigdon, Benjamin	Ensign	17-11-79	HA	Deer	Capt.Wm.Rigdon	AM 43-17	
Rigdon, William	Capt	09-04-78	HA	Deer		AM 21-23	
Riggs, Aaron	Capt	- -	MO	Up		MH 5	Res
Riggs, Amon	Capt	26-03-76	MO			AM 11-287	
Riggs, Amon	Capt	12-09-77	MO	Mid		AM 16-373	
Riggs, Amon	Capt	21-04-79	MO	Mid		AM 21-357	Suc
Riggs, Amos	Capt	04-09-77	MO	16th		AM 16-362	
Riggs, Elisha	Capt	07-02-76	AA			AM 11-139	
Riggs, Samuel	2nd Lt	14-05-76	MO	29th	Capt.Pigman	AM 11-424	
Riley, Jeremiah	Lt	23-05-76	PG	25th	Capt.Boyd	AM 11-440	Mn
Riley, Jeremiah		06-07-76				AM 11-553	CM
Ringgold, Jacob	1st Lt	06-09-77	QA	20th	Capt.T.Barnes	SC 49-64	OC
Ringgold, Jacob	Capt	31-07-78	QA	20th		AM 21-172	
Ringgold, William	Capt	16-03-76	QA		Capt.J.O'Bryan	AM 11-253	
Ringgold, William Jr.	Lt Col	08-05-77	KE	13th		AM 16-243	
Rinshaw, Joseph Jr.	2nd Lt	09-04-78	HA	8th	Capt.W.Cole	AM 21-24	
Rippath, James	2nd Lt	29-06-80	QA	5th	Capt.John Seney	AM 43-208	
Rister, Philip	1st Lt	29-08-77	BA	SD	Capt.W.Hudson	AM 16-348	
Riston, Henry	Ensign	08-10-82	AA	E1kR	Capt.C.White	AM 48-276	
Ritch, Peter	Ensign	16-03-76	QA		Capt.Wright	AM 11-254	
Ritchie, William	QM	26-03-76	FR	33rd		AM 11-287	
Roach, James	Capt	26-08-77	SM	Up		AM 16-346	
Roach, Stephen	2nd Lt	28-06-77	WO			RC 2-1156	Mn
Robboson, Vachel	2nd Lt	18-10-82	AA	Svrn	Capt.C.Hazle	AM 48-288	
Roberts, Allen	2nd Lt	16-04-78	CV	15th	Capt.B.Bond	AM 21-37	
Roberts, Allen	1st Lt	02-02-79	CV		Capt.N.Wilson	AM 21-290	
Roberts, James	1st Lt	03-01-76	QA	5th	Capt.J.Thompson	SC 49-61	OC
Roberts, James	Capt	29-08-77	QA	5th		SC 49-62	OC
Roberts, Thomas	2nd Lt	31-07-78	QA	5th	Capt.W.Brown	AM 21-172	
Roberts, Thomas	1st Lt	20-04-80	QA	5th	Capt.R.Holding	AM 43-146	
Robertson, Alexander	Capt	17-12-81	CA	28th	Capt.S.Jackson	AM 48-27	
Robertson, David	2nd Lt	09-04-78	CA	28th	Capt.J.Reynolds	AM 21-23	
Robertson, David	Capt	14-08-79	CA	28th	Capt.J.Reynolds	AM 21-493	
Robertson, William	2nd Lt	12-09-77	MO	Mid	Capt.R.Brooke	AM 16-373	
Robertson, William	2nd Lt	14-08-79	CA	28th	Capt.D.Robertson	AM 21-493	
Robey, Thomas	Ensign	04-12-78	BA	Up	Capt.B.Merryman	AM 21-257	

APPENDIX A - COMMISSIONED OFFICERS

Name	Rank	Date	Cty	Bn	Company	Ref.	Notes
Robins, John Purnal	Maj	30-08-77	WO	Snpx		AM 16-350	
Robins, Littleton	1st Lt	30-08-77	WO	Snpx	Capt.W.Purnal	AM 16-350	
Robins, Littleton	Capt	13-06-82	WO	Snpx	Capt.Wm.Purnell	AM 48-190	
Robinson jr., David	1st Lt	09-04-78	TA	38th	Oxford	AM 21-25	
Robinson, Alexander	1st Lt	19-06-77	CA	28th	Capt.Jackson	AM 16-294	
Robinson, Charles	Ensign	28-11-76	FR	35th	Capt.J.Shields	AM 12-555	
Robinson, David	Ensign	16-05-76	TA	38th	Capt.Martin	AM 11-428	
Robinson, David	Ensign	19-06-77	CA	28th	Capt.Price	AM 16-294	
Robinson, Elijah	Maj	28-08-76				AM 12-245	Mn
Robinson, Ezekial	1st Lt	09-04-78	CA	28th	Capt.S.Jackson	AM 21-23	
Robinson, James	Ensign	15-03-76	KE		Capt.Wm.Frisby	AM 11-246	
Robinson, John	2nd Lt	13-08-76	DO		Capt J.Todd	SP 299	Mn
Robinson, Joseph	Capt	20-05-78	DO	19th		AM 21-97	
Robinson, Luke	2nd Lt	16-05-76		Corp	Capt.H.Lake	AM 11-429	
Robinson, Luke	2nd Lt	24-06-78	DO		Capt.H.Lake	AM 21-148	
Robinson, Solomon	Ensign	09-04-78	TA	4th	Bullinbrook	AM 21-24	
Robinson, Solomon	2nd Lt	03-12-79	TA	38th	Capt.R.Johnson	AM 43-28	
Robinson, William	Ensign	28-05-79	CH	12th	Capt.B.Philpot	AM 21-427	
Roboson, Charles	2nd Lt	22-05-79	AA	7th	Capt.F.Cromwell	AM 21-410	
Robosson, Charles	1st Lt	18-10-82	AA	Svrn	Capt.C.Hazle	AM 48-288	
Robosson, Elijah	2nd Maj	12-01-76	AA	Svrn		PC 78	
Robosson, Elijah	Lt Col	26-01-77	AA	Svrn		AM 16-77	
Robosson, Elijah	Colonel	02-03-78	AA	Svrn		AM 16-525	
Robosson, Richard	Ensign	02-03-78	AA	Svrn	Capt.Maccubbin	AM 16-525	
Robson, Joseph	Capt	24-05-76	DO			AM 11-441	
Robson, Joseph	Capt	15-07-80	DO	19th		DO 235	Mn
Rodenbieler, Philip	Capt	29-11-75	FR	4th		MM 11:50	
Rodgers, John	Capt	15-09-75	HA		#5	PR 110	
Rogers, Benjamin	QM	25-05-76	BA	GP		AM 11-449	
Rogers, Elisha	Ensign	10-04-76	CE		Capt.Ogleby	AM 11-320	
Rogers, Elisha	2nd Lt	21-04-78	CE	Elk	Capt.J.Oglevee	AM 21-47	
Rogers, Elisha	2nd Lt	07-06-81	CE	Elk	Capt.J.Oglevie	AM 45-466	OC
Rogers, Elisha	1st Lt	28-06-81	CE	Elk	Capt.J.Oglevie	AM 45-489	
Rogers, John	2nd Maj	13-01-76	PG	11th		PC 86	
Rogers, John	Capt	09-04-78	HA	23rd		AM 21-23	
Rogers, John	Ensign	01-07-80	AA	ElkR	Capt.B.Gassaway	AM 43-209	
Role, John	Maj	09-04-78	TA	38th		AM 21-24	
Rolle, John	Capt	13-05-76	TA	38th		PC 132	Mn
Rollison, James	1st Lt	11-03-79	KE	13th	Capt.G.Hartshorn	AM 21-320	
Root, Daniel	2nd Lt	22-05-76	HA		Capt.Morgan	AM 11-436	
Root, Daniel	2nd Lt	09-04-78	HA	Deer	Capt.W.Morgan	AM 21-23	OC
Rose, Joseph	1st Lt	30-09-75	HA		#13	PR 119	
Rose, Joseph	1st Lt	09-04-78	HA	23rd	Capt.W.Bradford	AM 21-24	OC
Rose, William	2nd Lt	04-11-82	TA	4th	Capt.R.Bruff	AM 48-298	
Ross, Joseph	Lt	25-06-81	PG	SM		AM 45-488	
Ross, Stephen	Ensign	20-05-78	DO	19th	Capt.A.Wheatley	AM 21-97	OC
Ross, Stephen	Ensign	23-06-79	DO	Lwr	Fishing Creek	MH 4-70	Res
Rothe, John	Capt	16-05-76	TA	38th		AM 11-428	
Round, Samuel Hopkins	1st Lt	30-08-77	WO	Snpx	Capt.J.Ratliff	AM 16-350	
Round, Samuel H.	Capt	09-08-80	WO	Snpx	Capt.J.Ratliff	AM 43-251	
Rounds, Samuel Hopkins	Capt	23-08-81	WO	SelM		AM 56-577	
Rowles, John	Capt	29-06-80	QA	20th		AM 43-208	
Rozer, Henry	2nd Lt	01-05-78	PG	Mid	Capt.J.Casy	AM 21-63	
Ruff, John	1st Lt	09-04-78	HA	23rd	Capt.J.Forwood	AM 21-23	

APPENDIX A - COMMISSIONED OFFICERS

Name	Rank	Date	Cty	Bn	Company	Ref.	Notes
Ruff, John	Capt	17-11-79	HA	23rd	Capt.J.Forwood	AM 43-17	
Rumney, Edgar	Ensign	09-04-78	CA	28th	Capt.Postlethwait	AM 21-23	
Rumney, Edgar	1st Lt	18-04-80	CA	8th	Capt.Postlewait	AM 43-144	
Rumsey, Benjamin	Capt	16-09-75	HA	#6		PR 112	
Rumsey, Benjamin	Colonel	12-01-76	HA	8th		PC 78	
Rumsey, Benjamin	Colonel	15-01-77	HA	8th		PA	Res
Rumsey, Charles	Colonel	06-01-76	CE	2nd		PC 80	
Rumsey, Charles	Cty Lt	01-07-77	CE			AM 16-304	
Rumsey, Charles	Cty Lt	25-03-80	CE			AM 43-119	Dec
Rumsey, William	1st Maj	06-01-76	CE	10th		PC 80	
Rush, Lewis		02-03-76				AM 11-198	Ref
Russel, Thomas	Lt	25-06-81	BA		Capt.N.R.Moore	AM 47-313	Mn
Russell, James	2nd Lt	07-03-76	CH		Capt.J.Hanson	AM 11-206	
Russell, Thomas	Lt	26-07-80	BA		Light Horse	AM 43-230	
Russum, Robert	2nd Lt	16-12-79	DO	Up	Capt.Jos.Wright	AM 43-37	
Russum, Robert	2nd Lt	23-08-81	DO	Up		DO 230	Mn
Russum, William	Capt	23-08-81	DO	Up		AM 45-577	
Ruth, Christopher Cross	Capt	03-01-76	QA	20th		SC 49-56	OC
Rutter, Henry	2nd Lt	06-02-77	BA		Capt.Rutter	AM 16-120	
Rutter, John	2nd Lt	22-06-78	WA	2ndW	Capt.J.Walling	AM 21-145	
Rutter, John	1st Lt	05-11-81	BA	Up	Capt.P.Hann	AM 45-662	
Rutter, Thomas	Capt	19-12-75	BA			RB 13-37	
Rutter, Thomas	Capt	06-06-76	BA	Town		AM 11-467	Mn
Ryley, Thomas	Ensign	30-08-77	WO	Snpx	Capt.J.Ratliff	AM 16-350	
Sadler, Samuel	1st Lt	26-04-81	BA	Town	Capt.J.Tool	AM 45-416	OC
Sadler, ---		19-05-81	BA	Town		AM 47-247	Ref
Safford, John	Capt	10-06-76	CA	14th		AM 11-481	Mn
Salmon, Edward	1st Lt	15-04-78	FR	Town	Capt.Haff	AM 21-35	
Salmon, Edward	Capt	16-08-79	FR	Town	Capt.A.Haff	AM 21-494	
Sands, John	Ensign	07-06-81	QA	5th	Capt.B.Newman	AM 45-465	
Sank, George	2nd Lt	30-07-81	AA	Svrn	Capt.G.Pecker	AM 45-527	
Sansbury, Isaac	2nd Lt	01-05-78	PG	25th	Capt.R.Beall	AM 21-62	
Satterfield, Andrew	Ensign	17-12-81	CA	14th	Capt.C.Johnson	AM 48-27	
Savin, Richard	1st Lt	21-04-78	CE	Sass	Capt.J.Porter	AM 21-47	
Savin, Thomas	Capt	21-04-78	CE	Elk		AM 21-47	
Savin, Thomas	Maj	09-09-78	CE	2nd		AM 21-196	
Savin, Thomas	Maj	07-05-81	CE	2nd		AM 47-234	Res
Savin, Thomas Littleton	Capt	28-06-81	CE	Elk	Capt.A.Cazier	AM 45-489	
Sawyer, John	Capt	- -	QA	20th		FP 1-75	Mn
Scarf, John	Ensign	09-04-78	HA	8th	Capt.J.Tolbott	AM 21-24	
Scarf, William	1st Lt	30-08-77	BA	GPUp	Capt.W.Harvey	AM 16-350	
Scarff, William	2nd Lt	20-11-76	BA		Capt.B.Owings	AM 12-541	
Schley, Jacob	1st Lt	29-11-75	FR	1st	Capt.J.Haass	MM 11:50	
Schoolfield, Benjamin	1st Lt	24-02-76	SO	17th	Capt.Williams	AM 11-182	
Schoolfield, Benjamin	Capt	19-09-76	SO	17th		AM 12-285	
Schoolfield, Benjamin	2nd Lt	22-09-77	SO	PrAn	Capt.J.Williams	AM 16-381	OC
Schoolfield, Benjamin	1st Lt	07-12-78	SO	PrAn	Capt.T.King	AM 21-260	
Schoolfield, Bozman	1st Lt	30-08-77	WO	Wico	Capt.P.Quinton	AM 16-351	OC
Schoolfield, Bozman	1st Lt	20-05-78	WO	Wico		SC 49-54	Res
Schoolfield, George	2nd Lt	19-09-76	SO	17th		AM 12-285	
Schoolfield, George	1st Lt	17-06-77		17th		AM 16-291	
Schoolfield, William	Ensign	03-01-76	SO	17th		SC 49-52	OC

APPENDIX A - COMMISSIONED OFFICERS

Name	Rank	Date	Cty	Bn	Company	Ref.	Notes
Schoolfield, William	1st Lt	19-09-76	SO	17th		AM 12-285	
Scott, Aquila	Ensign	09-04-78	HA	8th	Capt.D.Scott	AM 21-24	
Scott, Benjamin	1st Lt	26-04-76	HA	8th	Capt.McComas	AM 11-387	
Scott, Daniel	Capt	09-04-78	HA	8th		AM 21-24	
Scott, George Day	Lt Col	06-01-76	SO	1st		PC 80	
Scott, George Day	Colonel	30-08-77	SO	Salb		AM 16-351	
Scott, John	Ensign	30-08-77	WO	Wico	Capt.P.Quinton	AM 16-351	
Scott, John	2nd Lt	21-04-78	CE	Elk	Capt.S.Evans	AM 21-47	
Scott, John	1st Lt	20-05-78	DO	19th	Capt.C.Stappleford	AM 21-97	
Scott, John	1st Lt	13-06-82	WO	Wico	Capt.S.Long	AM 48-190	
Scott, John	Capt	03-10-82	CE	ElkR		AM 48-274	
Scott, Thomas	Ensign	21-06-77	MO	29th	Capt.J.Magruder	AM 16-296	
Scott, Thomas	Ensign	12-09-77	MO	29th	Capt.J.Macgruder	AM 16-373	
Scott, William	Capt	07-06-81	CE	Elk	Capt.S.Maffet	AM 45-466	OC
Scott, William	Capt	23-08-81	CE	Elk		SC 49-51	Res
Scotten, Edward	2nd Lt	16-12-79	DO	Up		DO 230	Mn
Scotton, Edward	2nd Lt	20-05-78	DO	3rd	Capt.R.Hooper	AM 21-98	
Scottow, Edward	1st Lt	28-07-80	DO	Up	Capt.R.Hooper	AM 43-236	
Scriviner, Isaac	1st Lt	03-01-76	QA	5th	Capt.G.Baynard	SC 49-50	OC
Scriviner, Isaac	Capt	31-07-78	QA	5th		AM 21-172	
Scriviner, Isaac	Capt	20-04-80	QA	5th		AM 43-146	Suc
Scroggin, Philip	Ensign	16-03-81	WO	Wico	Capt.R.Handy	AM 45-353	
Seager, John	1st Lt	31-07-78	QA	5th	Capt.J.Sency	AM 21-172	
Seager, Thomas	Capt	20-04-80	QA	5th		AM 43-146	
Seager, Thomas	Capt	07-06-81	QA	5th		AM 45-465	Suc
Sears, John	2nd Lt	02-03-78	AA	Svrn	Capt.N.Worthington	AM 16-525	
Sears, John	1st Lt	19-09-78	AA	7th	Capt.H.Bateman	AM 21-208	
Sears, William	2nd Lt	04-11-82	TA	38th	Capt.Wm.Lambden	AM 48-298	
Selby, Henry	2nd Lt	02-09-77	AA	Svrn	Capt.J.Gray	AM 16-358	
Selby, Henry	2nd Lt	- -	AA	Svrn		FP 1-38	Res
Selby, John	2nd Lt	30-08-77	WO	SnH1	Capt.J.Paramor	AM 16-351	
Selby, Joseph	Capt	23-08-76				AM 12-233	Mn
Selby, Joshua Wilson	Capt	20-07-76				AM 12-84	Mn
Selby, Josiah Wilson	Capt	01-05-78	PG	25th		AM 21-62	
Selby, Thomas	Ensign	16-03-81	WO	Snpx	Capt.S.H.Rounds	AM 45-353	
Selby, William Wilson	1st Lt	01-05-78	PG	25th	Capt.J.Selby	AM 21-62	
Selby, William of William	2nd Lt	25-05-76	WO	10th	Capt.Martin	AM 11-444	
Sellman, Johnny	2nd Lt	27-05-79	BA	SD	Capt.E.Dorsey	AM 21-422	
Selman, Johnsey	2nd Lt	25-09-80	BA	Town	Capt.J.Young	AM 43-303	
Semmes, Robert Doyne	Ensign	09-05-78	CH	26th	Capt.W.Winter	AM 21-72	
Semmes, Thomas	1st Lt	07-03-76	CH		Capt.W.Hanson	AM 11-206	
Semms, Edward	1st Lt	19-01-81	CH	12th	Capt.H.Boarman	AM 45-280	
Seney, John	1st Maj	12-01-76	QA	5th		PC 78	OC
Seney, John	Lt Col	08-05-77	QA	5th		AM 16-243	
Seney, John	Lt Col	13-05-77				RC 2-1041	Ref
Seney, John	Capt	31-07-78	QA	5th		AM 21-172	
Seth, James	2nd Lt	13-08-77	CA	28th	Capt.W.Hopper	SC 49-154	Mn
Sewall, John	Capt	09-04-78	HA	8th		AM 21-24	
Sewell, Basil	2nd Lt	09-04-78	TA	38th	Bay Side	AM 21-24	
Shadrack, John	1st Lt	07-05-81	SM	Lwr	Capt.B.Smoot	AM 45-426	
Shanks, John	1st Lt	26-08-77	SM	Up	Capt.M.Lock	AM 16-345	
Shanks, John	Capt	18-11-79	SM	Up	Capt.G.Bond	AM 43-18	
Shannahan, John	1st Lt	09-04-78	TA	38th	Hearts of Oak	AM 21-25	
Sharer, George	2nd Lt	23-01-81	WA	2nd	Capt.J.Funk	AM 47-34	Res

APPENDIX A - COMMISSIONED OFFICERS

Name	Rank	Date	Cty	Bn	Company	Ref.	Notes
Sharer, George	1st Lt	26-03-81	WA	2ndW	1st	AM 47-150	Res
Sharp, John	1st Lt	20-11-76	BA		Capt.D.Shaw	AM 12-541	
Sharrer, George	2nd Lt	22-06-78	WA	2ndW	Capt.J.Funk	AM 21-145	
Shaver, Adam	1st Lt	29-11-75	FR		Capt.L.Kemp	MM 11:50	
Shaver, John	Ensign	05-11-81	BA	Up	Capt.P.Hann	AM 45-662	
Shaw, Daniel	Capt	20-11-76	BA			AM 12-541	
Shaw, James	1st Lt	03-01-76	DO		Vienna	SC 49-47	OC
Shaw, James	1st Lt	17-06-76			Vienna	SC 49-47	Res
Shaw, James	Cornet	31-05-81	DO		Horse troop	AM 45-452	
Shaw, John	2nd Lt	19-09-78	AA	7th	Capt.J.Merikan	AM 21-208	
Shaw, Jonias	1st Lt	23-08-76			Capt.A.Beall Jr	AM 12-232	
Shaw, Joseph	Ensign	19-01-81	CH	12th	Capt.J.Lancaster	AM 45-280	
Shaw, Josiah	Capt	05-09-77	PG	25th		AM 16-363	
Shaw, Josiah	1st Lt	01-05-78	PG	25th	Capt.J.Carlton	AM 21-78	
Shaw, Josiah	Capt	24-05-79	PG	25th	Capt.J.Carlton	AM 21-414	
Shaw, Josiah	Capt	24-06-80	PG	Up		AM 43-203	Suc
Shaw, Samuel	Capt	29-11-75	FR	3rd		MM 11:50	
Shaw, Samuel	1st Maj	06-01-76	FR	35th		PC 79	OC
Shaw, Samuel	2nd Maj	07-10-76	FR	35th		PC 266	
Sheaff, Henry	Capt	27-09-75	BA		Artillery	RB 13-36	
Sheaff, Henry	Capt	---04-76	BA			RB 13-74	Mn
Sheaff, Henry	Capt	06-06-76	BA	Town		AM 11-467	
Sheckells, Samuel	Capt	02-07-81	PG	Up	Capt.Wm.Moore	AM 45-492	
Sheckle, John	Ensign	12-09-77	MO	29th	Capt.J.Gaither	AM 16-373	
Sheckles, John	Ensign	21-06-77	MO	29th	Capt.J.Gaither	AM 16-296	
Sheckles, Samuel	2nd Lt	24-06-80	PG	Up	Capt.W.Moore	AM 43-203	
Sheilor, Daniel	Capt	16-08-81	FR	Cato	Capt.J.Carmack	AM 45-566	
Sheilor, Daniel	Capt	30-11-82	FR	Cato		AM 48-311	Mov
Shellman, John	1st Lt	18-09-80	FR	Town	Capt.J.Carey	AM 43-295	
Shellman, John	Capt	23-01-82	FR	Town	Capt.J.D.Carey	AM 48-54	
Shelmerden, Stephen	2nd Lt	25-04-81	BA	39th	Capt.Dickinson	AM 47-214	Res
Shelmerdine, Stephen	1st Lt	12-04-81	BA	Town	Capt.F.Deames	AM 45-393	
Shelor, David	1st Lt	29-11-75	FR	2nd	Capt.J.Carmack	MM 11:50	
Shepherd, Nichs	2nd Lt	02-03-78	AA	Svrn	Capt.C.Boone	AM 16-525	
Sheredine, Upton	2nd Lt	29-11-75	FR		Capt.D.Moore	MM 11:50	
Sheredine, Upton	Colonel	28-11-76	FR			AM 12-555	
Sheridine, Upton	Colonel	01-01-77	FR	Ling		AM 16-6	Ref
Sherwood, Charles	2nd Lt	12-04-80	TA	38th	Capt.C.Gardiner	AM 43-140	
Sherwood, Edward	Capt	09-04-78	TA	38th	Oxford	AM 21-25	
Shields, Archibald	1st Lt	21-04-78	CE	Sass	Capt.J.Veazey	AM 21-47	
Shields, Caleb	Ensign	06-06-76	BA	Town	Capt.Sheaf	AM 11-467	
Shields, Caleb	2nd Lt	29-08-77	BA	Town	Capt.B.Dickinson	AM 16-348	
Shields, Caleb	1st Lt	19-03-79	BA	Town	Capt.B.Dickinson	AM 21-324	
Shields, Caleb	1st Lt	08-02-81	BA	Town	Capt.B.Dickinson	AM 47-61	Dis
Shields, John	Ensign	29-11-75	FR	3rd	Capt.W.Shields	MM 11:50	
Shields, John	Capt	28-11-76	FR			AM 12-555	
Shields, William	Capt	29-11-75	FR	3rd		MM 11:50	
Shields, William	2nd Maj	06-01-76	FR	35th		PC 79	OC
Shields, William	1st Maj	07-10-76	FR	35th		PC 266	
Shielor, Caleb	Ensign	---04-76	BA		Capt.H.Sheaff	RB 13-74	
Shingletaker, Andrew	2nd Lt	28-11-76	FR	35th	Capt.Peppel	AM 12-555	
Shipley, John	Ensign	15-05-76	AA	ElkR	Capt.Howard	AM 11-424	
Shipley, John	Ensign	02-03-78	AA	ElkR	Capt.J.W.Dorsey	AM 16-525	
Shipley, John	1st Lt	30-03-79	AA	22nd	Capt.V.Stevens	AM 21-333	

APPENDIX A - COMMISSIONED OFFICERS

Name	Rank	Date	Cty	Bn	Company	Ref.	Notes
Shipley, Richard	Ensign	06-06-76	BA	SD	Capt.Phillips	AM 11-467	
Shircliff, William	Ensign	08-06-81	PG	SelM	Capt.H.Wheeler	AM 45-466	
Shistaker, John	2nd Lt	15-05-76	FR	37th	Capt.Balsell	AM 11-426	
Shockley, Elijah	Capt	15-05-76	WO			AM 11-466	
Shockley, Elijah	Capt	30-08-77	WO	Wico		AM 16-351	
Shockley, John	1st Lt	27-05-79	WO	Wico	Capt.J.Perdue	AM 21-423	
Shoemaker, John	2nd Lt	16-08-81	FR	Cato	Capt.D.Sheilor	AM 45-566	
Shoemaker, John	1st Lt	30-11-82	FR	Cato	Capt.G.Brown	AM 48-311	
Sholly, Peter	Capt	03-01-76	FR	36th		SC 49-48	OC
Sholly, Peter	Capt	07-06-76				SP 1587	Res
Shover, Peter	1st Lt	29-11-75	FR	2nd	Capt.J.Ambrose	MM 11:50	
Showers, John	Capt	04-02-77	BA	Gist		AM 16-114	
Showers, John	Capt	05-11-81	BA	Up		AM 45-662	Suc
Shroad, Stophel	1st Lt	30-08-77	BA	Up	Capt.J.Showers	AM 16-350	
Shroad, Valentine	Capt	04-12-78	BA	Up		AM 21-257	
Shryock, Henry	1st Maj	06-01-76	FR	32nd		PC 79	
Shryock, John	1st Lt	- -	WA			FP 1-129	Suc
Shryock, Leonard	2nd Lt	15-01-77	WA			AM 16-50	
Shryock, Leonard	2nd Lt	- -	WA			FP 1-129	Suc
Shytacre, John	Ensign	29-11-75	FR	2nd	Capt.Jas.Johnson	MM 11:50	
Shytaker, John	1st Lt	17-01-77	FR	37th	Capt.Martindear	AM 16-54	
Sibell, Conrod	Ensign	28-11-76	FR	35th	Capt.Little	AM 12-555	
Silvester, And.	1st Lt	31-07-78	QA	20th	Capt.J.Costin	MH 2	Mn
Sim, Joseph	Colonel	13-01-76	PG	11th		PC 86	OC
Sim, Joseph	Colonel	23-09-76	PG	11th		AM 12-296	Res
Sim, Patrick	Colonel	10-03-78	PG	Mid		AM 16-532	
Simkins, Dickson	1st Lt	27-07-76	FR			AM 12-127	
Simkins, John	Capt	19-04-78				SP 6652	Ref
Simmons, Abraham	Capt	15-02-76	AA	WstR		AM 11-161	
Simmons, Abraham	Capt	02-03-78	AA	WstR		AM 16-525	
Simmons, William	Capt	02-03-78	AA	WstR		AM 16-526	
Simmons, William	Capt	04-08-80	AA	WstR		PA	Res
Simpkins, Dickerson	1st Lt	22-06-78	WA	3rdW	Capt.C.Clinton	AM 21-145	
Simpkins, John	Ensign	30-03-81	WA	SelM	Capt.A.Ott	AM 45-368	
Simpson, John	1st Lt	01-09-77	PG	Lwr	Capt.T.Dent	AM 16-396	
Simpson, John	1st Lt	01-05-78	PG	11th	Capt.T.Dent	AM 21-78	
Simpson, Soloman	Maj	07-10-77	MO	16th		AM 16-392	
Simpson, Solomon	Capt	12-09-77	MO	16th		AM 16-373	
Simpson, William	Ensign	04-04-76			Capt.Burgess	AM 11-308	
Singleton, John	1st Lt	16-05-76	TA	38th	Capt.Martin	AM 11-428	
Sinnett, Robert	Capt	07-03-76	CH			AM 11-206	Mn
Sinnett, Samuel	Ensign	13-06-77	QA	5th		RC 2-1119	Res
Sinnett, Samuel	2nd Lt	04-06-78	KE	13th	Capt.P.Davis	AM 21-122	
Skinner, Frederick	Capt	16-04-78	CV	15th		Am 21-37	
Skinner, Mordecai	2nd Lt	09-04-78	TA	38th	Hearts of Oak	AM 21-25	
Skinner, Mordecai	1st Lt	03-12-79	TA	38th	Capt.Henry Banning	AM 43-28	
Skinner, Robert	2nd Lt	10-04-76	CV		Capt.Greenfield	AM 11-320	
Skinner, Robert	2nd Lt	16-04-78	CV	15th	Capt.T.Greenfield	AM 21-37	
Skinner, Thomas	Capt	23-08-76				AM 12-233	Mn
Skinner, Thomas	2nd Lt	13-06-77	QA	5th		RC 2-1119	Mn
Skinner, Thomas	1st Lt	27-05-79	SO	Salb	Capt.J.Bennett	AM 21-423	
Skinner, Trueman	Lt Col	24-05-79	PG	11th		AM 21-414	
Skinner, Trueman	Lt Col	07-10-80	PG	Lwr		AM 43-318	Dec
Skinner, Truman	1st Maj	04-02-77	PG	Lwr		AM 16-113	

APPENDIX A - COMMISSIONED OFFICERS

Name	Rank	Date	Cty	Bn	Company	Ref.	Notes
Skinner, Truman	Lt Col	01-09-77	PG	Up		AM 16-356	
Skinner, Truman	Lt Col	01-04-78	PG	11th		AM 21-62	
Slatony, Bartholomew	Ensign	27-05-79	WO	Wico	Capt.J.Davis	AM 21-423	
Sliney, James	Ensign	29-06-80	QA	5th	Capt.J.Ringgold	AM 43-208	
Slocum, Job Jr.	Capt	15-07-80	DO	Corp		MH 4-73	Mn
Smallwood, Heabord	2nd Lt	15-05-76	CH	26th	Capt.Maston	AM 11-426	
Smallwood, Samuel	Capt	09-05-78	CH	26th		AM 21-72	
Smith, Archibald	Ensign	22-09-77	SO	PrAn	Capt.R.Handy	AM 16-381	
Smith, Archibald	Ensign	12-03-81	WO	Wico	Capt.R.Handy	PA	
Smith, Charles	Ensign	25-05-81	PG	SelM	Capt.H.Wheeler	AM 45-445	OC
Smith, Charles	Ensign	08-06-81	PG			SC 49-43	Res
Smith, Chas.Sommerset	Capt	03-03-76	CH	12th		PA	
Smith, Charles S.	Capt	09-09-76	CH			SP 2314	Res
Smith, Christian	2nd Lt	13-05-78	FR	Cato	Capt.Simkins	AM 21-79	
Smith, Christian	1st Lt	29-03-79	FR	34th	Capt.D.Smith	AM 21-331	
Smith, Christian	2nd Lt	16-08-81	FR	Cato	Capt.J.Collins	AM 45-566	
Smith, Clement	SurgMt	16-01-77			Ship"Defence"	AM 16-50B	
Smith, Daniel	1st	13-05-78	FR	Cato	Capt.Simkins	AM 21-79	
Smith, Daniel	Capt	29-03-79	FR	34th		AM 21-331	
Smith, Ezekiel	Ensign	17-12-81	CA	14th	Capt.W.Coursey	AM 48-27	
Smith, Forgus	1st Lt	21-04-78	CE	Elk	Capt.H.South	AM 21-47	OC
Smith, George	1st Lt	12-06-81	CA	28th	Capt.W.Chipley	MH 2	Rec
Smith, Gibert Hamilton	Ensign	02-05-81	AA	WstR	Capt.S.Chew	AM 45-422	
Smith, Hugh	1st Lt	09-04-78	HA	23rd	Capt.G.Patterson	AM 21-24	
Smith, Hugh	Capt	17-11-79	HA	23rd	Capt.G.Patterson	AM 43-17	
Smith, James	Capt	22-06-78	WA	2ndW		AM 21-145	
Smith, Job	Ensign	25-05-76	BA	GP	Capt.Bowen	AM 11-444	
Smith, Job	2nd Lt	20-03-79	BA	Gp	Capt.W.Maccubbin	AM 21-325	
Smith, John	2nd Lt	19-12-75	BA		Capt.A.Buchanan	RB 13-37	
Smith, John	1st Lt	-04-76	BA	Town	Capt.Wm.Buchanan	RB 13-74	
Smith, John	Capt	06-06-76	BA	Town		AM 11-467	
Smith, John	Capt	26-08-77	SM	Lwr		AM 16-346	
Smith, John	Ensign	26-08-77	SM	Lwr	Capt.J.Smith	AM 16-346	
Smith, John	2nd Lt	09-04-78	HA	Deer	Capt.T.Hope	AM 21-22	
Smith, John	Capt	19-03-79	BA	Town	Capt.E.Bailey	AM 21-324	
Smith, John	Capt	22-06-80	SM	Lwr		AM 43-201	Suc
Smith, John Jr.	2nd Lt	22-06-80	SM	Lwr	Capt.Zach.Forrest	AM 43-201	
Smith, Joseph	Lt Col	06-01-76	FR	36th		PC 79	
Smith, Joseph	Colonel	20-04-76	FR	36th		AM 11-356	
Smith, Joseph	Colonel	22-06-78	WA	2ndW		AM 21-145	
Smith, Matthew	2nd Lt	02-07-81	DO	Up	Capt.L.Kirkman	AM 45-492	
Smith, Nathan	Ensign	16-04-78	CV	15th	Capt.J.Leach	AM 21-37	
Smith, Nathan	2nd Lt	- -81	DO	Up		DO 230	
Smith, Patrick Sim	2nd Maj	06-01-76	CV			PC 79	
Smith, Patrick	Lt Col	16-04-78	CV	15th		AM 21-37	
Smith, Philip	Capt	15-05-76	FR	37th		AM 11-426	
Smith, Philip	1st Lt	03-10-76	FR		Capt.V.Creagar	AM 12-317	
Smith, Philip Jr.	Maj	27-04-79	FR	37th		AM 21-368	
Smith, Ralph	1st Lt	17-11-79	HA	Deer	Capt.J.Farmer	AM 43-17	
Smith, Richard	Capt	26-03-76	MO			AM 11-287	
Smith, Richard	Capt	12-09-77	MO	16th		AM 16-373	
Smith, Richard	Colonel	01-03-79	MO	Up		AM 21-310	
Smith, Robert	1st Lt	22-06-78	WA	2ndW	Capt.J.Smith	AM 21-145	
Smith, Robert	2nd Lt	17-03-81	AA	WstR	Capt.S.Watkins	AM 45-354	

APPENDIX A - COMMISSIONED OFFICERS

Name	Rank	Date	Cty	Bn	Company	Ref.	Notes
Smith, Robert	1st Lt	02-05-81	AA	WstR	Capt.S.Watkins	AM 45-422	
Smith, Samuel	Ensign	26-12-74	HA		#2-Lwr Cross Rds	PR 107	
Smith, Samuel	Capt	08-03-76	BA			AM 11-220	Mn
Smith, Samuel	Capt	09-04-78	HA	23rd		AM 21-23	
Smith, Samuel	Colonel	25-09-80	BA	Town		AM 43-303	
Smith, Thomas Jr.	Ensign	18-08-77	DO	ES	Capt.Noel	AM 16-337	
Smith, Walter	Capt	10-04-76	CV			AM 11-320	
Smith, Walter	Capt	16-04-78	CV	15th		AM 21-37	
Smith, William	2nd Lt	08-10-76	HA	8th	Capt.B.Norriss	AM 12-326	
Smith, William	1st Lt	30-08-77	WO	SnH1	Capt.J.Patterson	AM 16-351	
Smith, William	2nd Lt	09-04-78	HA	Deer	Capt.W.Fisher	AM 21-22	
Smith, William	2nd Lt	17-12-81	CA	14th	Capt.T.Eaton	AM 48-27	
Smith, William Jr.	1st Lt	29-11-75	FR	2nd	Capt.J.Wood	MM 11:50	
Smithson, Nathaniel	Ensign	09-04-78	HA	8th	Capt.A.Norris	AM 21-24	
Smoot, Hendley	Ensign	28-05-79	CH	12th	Capt.J.Parnham	AM 21-427	
Smoot, Isaac	Ensign	22-10-77	CH	Lwr	Capt.A.McPherson	AM 16-401	
Smoot, Isaac	2nd Lt	28-05-79	CH	12th	Capt.H.Dent	AM 21-427	
Smoot, John	Capt	20-05-78	DO	3rd		AM 21-97	
Smoot, John	Capt	23-06-79	DO	Up		MH 4-74	Dis
Smoot, John	Capt	31-05-81	DO		Horse Troop	AM 45-452	
Smoot, John	Capt	02-07-81	DO	Up		AM 45-492	Suc
Smoot, John Nathan	QM	06-01-76	CH	12th		PC 78	
Smoot, William Barton	Capt	26-08-77	SM	Lwr		AM 16-346	
Smyley, Samuel	Capt	30-08-77	WO	SnH1		AM 16-351	
Smyth, Simon	2nd Lt	11-03-78	KE	13th	Capt.G.Hartshorn	AM 21-320	
Smyth, Thomas	1st Lt	12-02-76	FR		Capt.Stricker	AM 11-155	
Smyth, Thomas Jr.	Capt	26-06-76	KE		Light Inf.Co.	AM 11-534	
Smyth, William	Surgeon	23-10-77	QA	20th		AM 16-403	
Snap, Peter	2nd Lt	04-02-77	BA	Gist	Capt.R.Lemmon	AM 16-114	
Snider, Peter	Ensign	29-11-75	FR	2nd	Capt.Snowdenburger	MM 11:50	
Snider, Peter	Ensign	22-06-76	FR	37th	Capt.Snodenberry	AM 11-509	Dis
Snodenberry, John	Capt	22-06-76	FR	37th		AM 11-509	Mn
Snowden, Thomas	2nd Maj	18-03-76	PG	25th		AM 11-260	
Snowdenberger, Jacob	Capt	29-11-75	FR	2nd		MM 11:50	
Sollers, Sabrit	1st Lt	04-02-77	BA		Capt.W.Wilkinson	AM 16-114	
Sollers, Thomas	2nd Maj	25-05-76	BA	GP		AM 11-443	
Sollers, Thomas	Maj	30-08-77	BA	GP		AM 16-350	
Somervell, Alexander	Lt Col	06-01-76	CV			PC 79	OC
Somervell, Alexander	Lt Col	03-01-77	CV			AM 16-13	Res
Somervill, William	Capt	07-05-81	SM	Lwr	Capt.A.H.Watts	AM 45-426	
Sommers, Benjamin	2nd Lt	12-09-77	MO	16th	Capt.W.Vearse	AM 16-373	
Sommers, Benjamin	1st Lt	25-03-80	MO	Up	Capt.C.Gassaway	AM 43-120	
Sommers, John	2nd Lt	12-09-77	MO	16th	Capt.R.Smith	AM 16-373	
Sommers, John	1st Lt	21-04-79	MO	Up	Capt.T.Hay	AM 21-356	
Sommers, John	Capt	25-03-80	MO	Up	Capt.Thos.Hays	AM 43-120	
Sommers, William	Ensign	21-04-79	MO	Up	Capt.Thos.Spriggs	AM 21-356	
Sothern, John Johnson	Ensign	26-08-77	SM	Up	Capt.W.Kilgour	AM 16-346	
South, Hezekiah	Capt	21-04-78	CE	Elk		AM 21-47	OC
South, Hezekiah	Capt	07-07-81	CE	Elk	Capt.A.Miller	AM 45-466	
Sower, Philip	2nd Lt	29-11-75	FR	2nd	Capt.Snowdenburger	MM 11:50	
Sower, Philip	1st Lt	28 11-76	FR	37th		AM 12-555	
Speak, Richard	1st Lt	15-05-76	CH	26th	Capt.Mastin	AM 11-426	
Speck, Henry	Ensign	25-09-80	BA	Town	Capt.P.Grable	AM 43-303	
Spedding, Levin	1st Lt	09-04-78	TA	4th	Third Haven	AM 21-24	OC

APPENDIX A - COMMISSIONED OFFICERS

Name	Rank	Date	Cty	Bn	Company	Ref.	Notes
Spedding, Levin	Capt	11-05-78	TA	4th		AM 21-73	
Spence, George	Capt	30-08-77	WO	SnH1		AM 16-351	
Spence, John	1st Lt	30-08-77	WO	SnH1	Capt.G.Spence	AM 16-351	
Spencer, Isaac	Colonel	08-05-77	KE	27th		AM 16-243	
Spickernall, John	1st Lt	10-04-76	CV		Capt.Williamson	AM 11-320	
Spicknall, John	1st Lt	16-04-78	CV	15th	Capt.C.Williamson	AM 21-37	
Spink, William	1st Lt	26-08-77	SM	Up	Capt.E.Plowden	AM 16-346	
Spires, Jeremiah	Capt	22-06-78	WA	2ndW		AM 21-145	
Spires, Zephaniah	2nd Lt	22-06-78	WA	2ndW	Capt.B.Williams	AM 21-145	
Spreden, Levin	2nd Lt	16-05-76	TA	4th	Capt.Lloyd	AM 11-428	
Sprigg, Frederick	Maj	01-03-79	MO	Up		AM 21-310	
Sprigg, Frederick	Capt	21-04-79	MO	Up		AM 21-356	Suc
Sprigg, John Clark	2nd Lt	01-05-78	PG	Mid	Capt.J.Brooks	AM 21-63	
Sprigg, John Clarke	1st Lt	24-06-80	PG	Mid	Capt.S.Hepburn	AM 43-203	
Sprigg, Philip	1st Lt	13-11-79	PG	Mid	Capt.C.Clagett	AM 43-13	
Sprigg, Thomas	Capt	12-09-77	MO	16th		AM 16-373	
Sprigg, Thomas	Cty Lt	21-12-79	WA			AM 43-39	
Spriggs, Thomas	Cty Lt	23-01-81	WA			AM 47-34	Mn
Springer, Charles	2ns Lt	29-11-75	FR	2nd	Capt.J.Wood	MM 11:50	
Spurior, Aaron	2nd Lt	30-03-79	AA	22nd	Capt.R.Warfield	AM 21-333	
Spurrier, William	1st Lt	28-02-76	AA	ElkR	Capt.Stringer	AM 11-191	
Spurrier, William	1st Lt	02-03-78	AA	ElkR	Capt.R.Stringer	AM 16-525	
St.Clair, James	2nd Lt	26-04-76	HA	8th	Capt.McComas	AM 11-387	
St.Clair, William	Capt	22-06-76	KE			AM 11-506	
Stack, Joseph	2nd Lt	06-07-76	DO		Capt.Waters	AM 11-553	
Stack, Joseph	2nd Lt	20-05-78	DO	3rd	Capt.Jas.Wright	AM 21-98	
Stafford, James	Ensign	14-08-79	CA	14th	Capt.Jas.Douglass	AM 21-493	
Stafford, James	2nd Lt	28-06-80	CA	14th	Capt.J.Greyless	AM 43-207	
Stafford, John	Capt	08-06-76	CA	14th		RB 12	Mn
Stainton, Benson	Lt Col	12-01-76	CA	28th		PC 78	
Stainton, Benson	Colonel	12-03-77	CA			SP 3918.	Res
Stample, Frederick	1st Lt	17-01-77	FR	33rd	Capt Van Sweareng.	AM 16-54	
Standiford, John	Capt	25-05-77	BA	GP		AM 11-444	
Stanford, John	Ensign	20-05-78	DO	3rd	Capt.Jas.Wright	AM 21-98	OC
Stansbury, Benjamin	Ensign	25-05-76	BA	GP	Capt.Mercer	AM 11-444	
Stansbury, Edmond	1st Lt	03-09-77	BA	GP	Capt.Standiford	AM 16-359	
Stansbury, Joseph	Ensign	25-05-77	BA	GP	Capt.Garretson	AM 11-444	
Stansbury, Thomas	1st Lt	04-12-78	BA	Up	Capt.Lemmon	AM 21-257	
Stansbury, Thomas,Jr.	2nd Lt	04-02-77	BA	Gist	Capt.A.Lemmon	AM 16-114	
Stapleford, Charles	Capt	11 06-77	DO	19th		AM 16-283	
Staplefort, Charles	Capt	15-07-80	DO	19th		DO 235	Mn
Staplefort, Charles	Capt	23-08-81	DO	SelM		AM 45-577	
Staplefort, Edward	Capt	20-05-78	DO	19th		AM 21-97	
Staplefort, Edward	Capt	15-07-80	DO	19th		DO 235	Mn
Stapplefort, Charles	Capt	20-05-78	DO	19th		AM 21-97	
Stark, Joseph	2nd Lt	23-08-81	DO	Up	Capt.W.Russum	AM 45-577	
Start, Richard	2nd Lt	04-11-82	TA	38th	Capt.C.Gardiner	AM 48-298	
Start, William	1st Lt	12-04-80	TA	38th	Capt.C.Gardiner	AM 43-140	
Statton, Jacob	Ensign	20-05-78	DO	Up	Capt.J.Henry	SC 49-101	OC
Statton, Jacob	Ensign	21-06-79				MH 5	Res
Steaker, Lehr	2nd Lt	13-06-77	QA	5th		RC 2-1119	Mn
Steal, John	Ensign	25-03-80	MO	Up		AM 43-120	
Steel, James	Ensign	26-04-76	HA	8th	Capt.McComas	AM 11-387	
Steel, James	Ensign	09-04-78	HA	Deer	Capt.G.Vanhorne	AM 21-22	OC

APPENDIX A - COMMISSIONED OFFICERS

Name	Rank	Date	Cty	Bn	Company	Ref.	Notes
Steel, James	Ensign	14-04-78	HA	Deer		SC 49-38	Res
Steel, John	2nd Lt	04-09-77	BA	Town	Arty	AM 16-362	
Stelly, Peter	1st Lt	29-11-75	FR	1st	Capt.J.Stoner	MM 11:50	
Stemple, Frederick	1st Lt	03-03-77	FR	33rd	Capt.VanSwearingen	MM 4:379	Mn
Stenson, James	Ensign	19-06-77	QA	20th	Capt.J.R.Emory	AM 16-295	
Stephens, Chas.Crouch	1st Lt	28-11-76	FR		Capt.W.Brashears	AM 12-555	
Stephens, Edward	Ensign	20-05-78	DO	19th	Capt.C.Stappleford	AM 21-97	
Stephens, Edward	Ensign	23-06-79	DO	Lwr	Capt.Stapleford	MH 4-70	Res
Stephenson, Charles	1st Lt	28-11-76	FR		Capt.H.Stephenson	AM 12-555	
Stephenson, Henry	Capt	28-11-76	FR			AM 12-555	
Stephenson, William	Ensign	28-11-76	FR		Capt.H.Stephenson	AM 12-555	
Stephenson, William	Ensign	17-01-77	FR	Ling	Capt.H.Stevenson	AM 16-54	
Stephenson, William	2nd Lt	30-08-77	WO	Snpx	Capt.J.Ratliff	AM 16-350	
Sterrett, John	Capt	---04-76	BA	Town		RB 13-74	
Steuard, James	Ensign	04-07-76	FR	UpDt	Capt.Chapline	AM 11-546	
Stevens, Bentol	Ensign	09-04-78	CA	14th	Capt.J.Douglass	AM 21-23	
Stevens, Bentol	2nd Lt	14-08-79	CA	14th	Capt.Jas.Douglass	AM 21-493	
Stevens, Bentol	1st Lt	28-06-80	CA	14th	Capt.J.Greyless	AM 43-207	
Stevens, Charles	1st Lt	17-01-77	FR	Ling	Capt.Wm Brashears	AM 16-55	
Stevens, Edward	Ensign	09-04-78	TA	4th	Third Haven	AM 21-24	OC
Stevens, Edward	1st Lt	11-05-78	TA	4th	Capt.L.Spedding	AM 21-73	
Stevens, Ephraim	1st Lt	22-09-77	SO	Salb	Capt.J.Dashiell	AM 16-382	
Stevens, John	2nd Lt	15-05-76	CA		Capt.J.Richardson	AM 11-427	Res
Stevens, John	1st Lt	15-05-76	CA		Capt.J.Richardson	AM 11-427	
Stevens, Vachel	Capt	30-03-79	AA	22nd		AM 21-333	
Stevens, Vachel	Capt	20-06-81	AA	ElkR		AM 47-304	Mn
Stevens, William	1st Lt	22-09-77	SO	PrAn	Capt.G.Waters	AM 16-381	
Stevens, William	Capt	09-04-78	TA	4th	72nd Volunteer	AM 21-24	
Stevenson, Charles	1st Lt	17-01-77	FR	Ling	Capt.H.Stevenson	AM 16-54	
Stevenson, Henry	Capt	17-01-77	FR	Ling		AM 16-54	
Stevenson, James	2nd Lt	28-06-77	WO		Capt.J.Patterson	RC 2-1156	Mn
Stevenson, John	1st Lt	16-05-76	HA	23rd	Capt.Smith	AM 11-428	
Stevenson, John	LtM	25-01-77			"Independance"	AM 16-75	OC
Stevenson, John	LtM	19-03-79			"Independence"	AM 21-324	Res
Stevenson, John	Ensign	03-01-82	CE	Susq	Capt.S.Miller	AM 48-33	
Stevenson, Jonathan	Ensign	28-06-77	WO		Capt.J.Patterson	RC 2-1156	Rec
Stevenson, Joshua	Lt Col	12-10-76	BA	GP		AM 12-557	
Stevenson, William	1st Lt	09-08-80	WO	Snpx	Capt.S.Round	AM 43-231	
Steward, John	2nd Lt	23-05-81	BA	Town	Capt.J.Tool	AM 45-443	
Steward, Robert	Ensign	02-05-81	AA	WstR	Capt.S.Watkins	AM 45-422	
Steward, Stephen	2nd Lt	25-09-80	BA	Town	Capt.B.Griffith	AM 43-303	
Stewart, Charles	Ensign	15-07-80	DO	Lwr		MH 4-75	Mn
Stewart, Charles	Ensign	02-04-81	DO	Lwr	Capt.N.Manning	AM 45-490	
Stewart, Charles	Ensign	23-08-81	DO	SelM	Capt.C.Staplefort	AM 45-577	
Stewart, David	2nd Lt	01-02-77	BA		Capt.John Smith	AM 16-106	
Stewart, David	1st Lt	25-09-80	BA	Town	Capt.T.Yeates	AM 43-303	
Stewart, Elisha	2nd Lt	17-06-77	TA	4th	Sword in Hand	RC 2-1130	Rec
Stewart, Elisha	1st Lt	04-11-82	TA	4th	Capt.S.Thomas	AM 48-298	
Stewart, James	Capt	- -75	HA		#9	PR 115	
Stewart, James	Ensign	22-06-78	WA	2ndW	Capt.J.Chapline	AM 21-145	
Stewart, John	1st Maj	06-01-76	SO	1st		PC 80	
Stewart, John	Capt	30-08-77	WO	SnH1		AM 16-351	
Stewart, John	Lt Col	30-08-77	SO	Salb		AM 16-351	
Stewart, John	Capt	23-02-81	WO	SnH1		PA	Res

125

APPENDIX A - COMMISSIONED OFFICERS

Name	Rank	Date	Cty	Bn	Company	Ref.	Notes
Stewart, John	1st Lt	20-08-81	BA	Town	Capt.D.Dennis	AM 45-572	
Stewart, William	Ensign	22-09-77	SO	Salb	Capt.J.Conway	AM 16-381	
Stewart, William	1st Lt	21-04-78	CE	Elk	Capt.S.Evans	AM 21-47	
Stewart, William	1st Lt	22-08-81	SO	Salb	Capt.J.McCloster	AM 45-575	
Stewart, William	Ensign	17-12-81	CA	28th	Capt.D.Robinson	AM 48-27	
Stewart,---	Capt	07-03-76	HA	8th		AM 11-212	Mn
Stewart,---	Capt	02-04-76	HA	8th		AM 11-303	Mn
Stilts, Philip	2nd Lt	04-02-77	BA	Gist	Capt.J.Hall	AM 16-114	
Stilts, Philip	1st Lt	30-08-77	BA	Up	Capt.T.Marshall	AM 16-350	
Stilts, Philip	Capt	05-11-81	BA	Up	Capt.T.Marshall	AM 45-662	
Stinchcomb, Nathaniel	Capt	06-06-76	BA	SD		AM 11-467	
Stinchcomb, Nathaniel	Lt Col	27-11-81	BA	SD		AM 48-5	
Stinchcomb, Thomas	Ensign	29-08-77	BA	SD	Capt.N.Stinchcomb	AM 16-348	
Stinchicomb, Thomas	Capt	07-02-82	BA	SD	Capt.J.Hurd	AM 48-71	
Stinson, James	2nd Lt	16-03-76	QA		Capt.Ringgold	AM 11-253	OC
Stinson, James	2nd Lt	05-04-80	QA	20th	Capt.C.Cooke	AM 43-130	
Stinson, William	2nd Lt	13-06-77	QA	5th		RC 2-1119	Mn
Stinton, John	Ensign	22-06-78	FR	Ling	Capt.Barr	AM 21-145	
Stoakes, Peter	2nd Lt	13-06-77	ES			AM 16-288	
Stockett, Thomas Noble	1st Lt	12-02-76	AA	WstR	Capt.Watkins	AM 11-231	
Stockton, John	1st Lt	13-06-77	QA	5th		RC 2-1119	Mov
Stockton, Thomas Noble	1st Lt	02-03-78	AA	WstR	Capt.T.Watkins	AM 16-525	OC
Stoddert, Kenelin Trueman	1st Maj	26-01-76	CH	26th		PC 78	
Stokes, Robert	1st Lt	09-04-78	HA	23rd	Capt.J.W.Hall	AM 21-23	
Stone, John Hoskins	Capt	- -75	CH			RC 2-142	Mn
Stone, Joseph	2nd Lt	26-08-77	SM	Up	Capt.E.Plowden	AM 16-346	
Stone, Michael	2nd Lt	07-03-76	CH		Capt.Swann	AM 11-206	
Stone, Samuel	Ensign	07-03-76	CH		Capt.Sinnett	AM 11-206	
Stoner, John	Capt	29-11-75	FR	1st		MM 11:50	
Stonestreet, John	Ensign	01-05-78	PG	11th	Capt.R.Stonestreet	AM 21-62	
Stonestreet, Richard	2nd Lt	01-09-77	PG	Lwr	Capt.S.Bayne	AM 16-356	
Stonestreet, Richard	Capt	01-05-78	PG	11th		AM 21-62	
Story, Henry	1st Lt	31-07-78	QA	20th	Capt.J.Kent	MH 2	Mn
Story, Ralph	1st Lt	04-09-77	BA	Town	Artillery	AM 16-362	
Stratton, Jacob	Ensign	- -	DO	Up		DO 231	Mn
Strawbridge, John	2nd Maj	06-01-76	CE	2nd		PC 80	
Strawbridge, John	Lt Col	21-04-78	CE	Elk		AM 21-47	OC
Stricker, George	Capt	02-09-75	FR			AM 11-78	Mn
Stricker, George	Capt	04-10-75	FR		Minuteman	AM 11-82	
Stricker, George	Capt	22-01-76	FR		Light Inf.co.	AM 11-120	Mn
Stricker, George	Lt Col	09-04-77				AM 16-205	Mn
Stringer, Richard	Capt	28-02-76	AA	ElkR		AM 11-191	
Stringer, Richard	Capt	02-03-78	AA	ElkR		AM 16-525	
Stull, Christian	Capt	27-04-79	FR	37th		AM 21-368	Suc
Stull, Christopher	Capt	29-11-75	FR	1st		MM 11:50	
Stull, Christopher	Capt	03-03-77	FR	33rd		MM 4:379	Mn
Stull, John	Colonel	06-01-76	FR	32nd		PC 79	OC
Stump, Henry Jr	2nd Lt	09-04-78	HA	23rd	Capt.J.W.Hall	AM 21-23	
Sturgis, John	1st Lt	30-08-77	WO	Wico	Capt.S.Horsey	AM 16-351	
Sturgis, John Otten	2nd Lt	30-08-77	WO	SnHl	Capt.S Smyley	AM 16-351	
Sturgis, William	Ensign	04-06-78	KE	13th	Capt.P.Davis	AM 21-122	
Sudler, Emory	Capt	19-12-75	KE			SP 236	Mn
Sudler, Emory	Capt	03-01-76	KE	13th		SC 49-93	OC
Sudler, Emory	Capt	06-06-76	KE			SP 1548	Res

APPENDIX A - COMMISSIONED OFFICERS

Name	Rank	Date	Cty	Bn	Company	Ref.	Notes
Sudler, James	1st Lt	29-06-80	QA	20th	Capt.J.Rowles	AM 43-208	
Sudler, John	Capt	31-07-78	QA	5th		AM 21-172	
Sudler, John	Capt	20-04-80	QA	5th		AM 43-146	Suc
Sudler, Benjamin	1st Lt	29-08-77				SP 4877	
Sulivane, James	2nd Lt	10-02-76	DO		New Market Blues	AM 11-147	
Sullivan, James	Capt	02-04-81	DO	Up	Capt.Thos.Logan	AM 45-492	
Sullivane, James	2nd Lt	20-05-78	DO	3rd	Capt.J.Daffin	AM 21-98	
Sullivane, James	1st Lt	28-07-80	DO	Up	Capt.Thos.Logan	AM 43-236	
Suter, John	2nd Lt	12-09-77	MO	Mid	Capt.B.Gaither	AM 16-373	
Suter, Joshua	2nd Lt	25-09-80	BA	Town	Capt.R.Lemmon	SC 49-92	OC
Sutherland, David	Ensign	13-05-76	BA	Gist	Capt.S.Owings	RB 13-69	
Sutherland, David	1st Lt	29-08-77	BA	SD	Capt.T.Owings	AM 16-348	
Sutherland, Richard	2nd Lt	06-06-76	BA	SD	Capt.Wells	AM 11-467	
Sutton, Joseph	Ensign	23-10-81	BA	GPUp	Capt.J.Talbot	AM 45-650	
Swan, Edward	Ensign	07-05-81	SM	Lwr	Capt.S.Jenifer	AM 45-426	
Swan, Jonathan	2nd Lt	05-07-77	CH	12th	Capt.H.Clarkson	RC 2-1170	Mn
Swank, David	Ensign	16-05-78	WA	3rdW	Capt.Clinton	AM 21-86	
Swank, Peter	Ensign	22-06-78	WA	2ndW	Capt.C.Nichodemus	AM 21-145	
Swann, George	Capt	07-03-76	CH	26th		AM 11-206	
Swann, Henry	Ensign	26-08-77	SM	Up	Capt.J.Mills	AM 16-346	
Swearengen, Samuel	Ensign	12-09-77	MO	29th	Capt.E.Harding	AM 16-373	
Swearingan, Benone	Ensign	04-06-81	WA	SelM	Capt.J.Chapline	AM 45-459	
Swearingen, Charles	2nd Maj	06-01-76	FR	36th		PC 79	
Swearingen, Charles	1st Maj	20-04-76	FR	36th		AM 11-356	
Swearingen, Charles	Lt Col	22-06-78	WA	2ndW		AM 21-145	
Swearingen, Samuel	Ensign	14-05-76	MO	29th	Capt.Harden	AM 11-424	
Swett, George Noble	Capt	14-05-76	QA		Independent	AM 11-424	
Swingle, George	Capt	22-06-78	WA	2ndW		AM 21-145	
Sybert, John	Ensign	22-06-78	WA	1stW	Capt.Saml.Hughes	AM 21-147	
Sybert, John	2nd Lt	23-01-81	WA			AM 47-34	Mn
Sybert, John	Capt	- -	WA			FP 1-129	Suc
Sylvester, Andrew	2nd Lt	16-03-76	QA		Capt.Costin	AM 11-253	
		- -					
		- -					
Talbot, Benjamin	2nd Lt	04-02-77	BA		Capt.J.Cockey	AM 16-114	
Talbot, Benjamin	1st Lt	23-04-81	AA	Svrn	Capt.V.Gaither	AM 45-411	
Talbot, Tobias	Ensign	24-05-79	BA	SD	Capt.E.Dorsey	AM 21-422	
Talbott, Benjamin	Capt	31-10-80	BA	GPUp	Capt.John Cockey	AM 43-345	
Talbott, James	1st Lt	- -75	HA		#9	PR 115	
Talbott, John	Capt	20-11-76	BA			AM 12-541	
Talbott, Matthew	Ensign	02-04-76	HA		Capt.Stewart	AM 11-303	
Talbott, Matthew	1st Lt	09-04-78	HA	8th	Capt.J.Tolbott	AM 21-24	
Talbott, Vincent	1st Lt	23-10-81	BA	GPUp	Capt.V.Talbot	AM 45-651	
Talbott, William	2nd Lt	04-08-80	MO	Lwr	Capt.J.Willcoxen	AM 43-248	
Tamer, Michael	Ensign	15-01-77	WA			AM 16-50	
Taney, Joseph	Ensign	02-02-79	CV		Capt.N.Wilson	AM 21-290	
Taney, Michael	1st Lt	16-04-78	CV	15th	Capt.T.Greenfield	AM 21-37	
Tannehill, Carlton	1st lt	15-05-76	FR	34th	Capt.Merony	AM 11-426	
Tanner, Joseph	2nd Lt	10-04-76	CE		Capt.Ogleby	AM 11-320	
Tanner, Joseph	1st Lt	21-04-78	CE	Elk	Capt.J.Oglevee	AM 21-47	OC
Tanyhill, Carlton	Capt	28-11-76	FR			AM 12-555	
Tarlton, Joshua	Ensign	26-08-77	SM	Lwr	Capt.W.Smoot	AM 16-346	
Tarlton, Stephen	Ensign	26-08-77	SM	Up	Capt.M.Lock	AM 16-345	
Tate, Robert	2nd Lt	31-05-76	QA	20th	Capt.Wilson	AM 11-454	

APPENDIX A - COMMISSIONED OFFICERS

Name	Rank	Date	Cty	Bn	Company	Ref.	Notes
Tawney, Michael	1st Lt	10-04-76	CV		Capt.Greenfield	AM 11-320	
Tawney, Michael	2nd Lt	22-06-78	FR	Ling	Capt.Pebble	AM 21-145	
Taylor, Asa	2nd Lt	09-04-78	HA	23rd	Capt.J.Wood	AM 21-23	
Taylor, Ignatius	Maj	26-08-77	SM	Lwr		AM 16-346	
Taylor, Jeremiah	2nd Lt	21-04-78	CE	Elk	Capt.A.Miller	AM 21-47	
Taylor, John	Capt	09-09-75	HA	#7		PR 113	
Taylor, John	2nd Maj	06-01-76	HA	8th		PC 80	
Taylor, Joseph	Ensign	31-07-78	QA	20th	Capt.J.Kent	MH 2	Mn
Taylor, Robert	1st Lt	24-03-81	CH	26th	Capt.S.Luckett	AM 45-361	
Taylor, William	Ensign	21-04-78	CE	Sass	Capt.S.Veazey	AM 21-47	
Taylor, William	2nd Lt	16-03-81	WO	Snpx	Capt.S.H.Rounds	AM 45-353	
Tennison, Samuel	Ensign	18-11-79	SM	Up	Capt.J.Shanks	AM 43-18	
Teves, Robert	Ensign	30-08-77	BA	SD	Capt.Philips	AM 16-350	
Tevis, Benjamin	Capt	27-05-79	BA	SD	Capt.T.Philips	AM 21-422	
Tevis, Benjamin	Capt	07-02-82	BA	SD		AM 48-71	Suc
Tevis, Robert	Ensign	27-05-79	BA	SD	Capt.B.Tevis	AM 21-422	
Thad, Wm.Edw.	1st Lt	29-11-75	FR	3rd	Capt.N.Bruce	MM 11:50	
Thomas, Benjamin	2nd Lt	11-06-76	FR	34th		AM 11-476	
Thomas, Edward	2nd Lt	07-06-81	QA	20th	Capt.H.Coursey	AM 45-465	
Thomas, James	Ensign	26-04-76	HA		Capt.Jolley	AM 11-387	
Thomas, James	Ensign	18-11-79	SM	Up	Capt.F.Millard	AM 43-18	
Thomas, John	1st Maj	06-01-76	AA	WstR		PC 79	
Thomas, John		12-01-76	AA	WstR		PC 85	Ref
Thomas, John	Capt	27-07-76	CH			AM 12-127	
Thomas, John	Ensign	09-11-76	FR		Capt.Mackall	AM 12-432	
Thomas, John	1st Lt	17-06-77	TA	4th	Sword in Hand	RC 2-1130	Rec
Thomas, John	Capt	26-08-77	SM	Up		AM 16-346	
Thomas, John	Capt	18-11-79	SM	Up		AM 43-18	Suc
Thomas, John	Lt Col	18-11-79	SM			AM 43-18	
Thomas, John	Capt	19-01-81	CH	12th		AM 45-280	Suc
Thomas, John Allen	Maj	26-08-77	SM			AM 16-345	
Thomas, John Jr.	Ensign	03-01-76	TA	4th	Wye	SC 49-96	OC
Thomas, John Jr.	2nd Lt	01-07-76	TA	4th	Capt.Goldsborough	AM 11-539	Mn
Thomas, John Jr.	Capt	09-04-78	TA	4th	Sword in Hand	AM 21-24	
Thomas, John Jr.	Capt	04-11-82	TA	4th		AM 48-298	Suc
Thomas, Jonathan	2nd Lt	07-03-76	CH		Capt.Winter	AM 11-206	
Thomas, Nicholas	QM	12-01-76	TA	4th		PC 78	OC
Thomas, Nicholas	QM	08-08-76	TA	4th		AM 12-188	Res
Thomas, Philip	Capt	29-11-75	FR	4th		MM 11:50	
Thomas, Philip	Capt	07-03-76	FR	34th		AM 11-210	Ref
Thomas, Philip	Capt	02-02-81	FR		Horse troop	AM 45-299	
Thomas, Philip	Cty Lt	20-02-81	FR			AM 45-318	
Thomas, Philip	2nd Lt	20-08-81	BA	Town	Capt.D.Dennis	AM 45-572	
Thomas, Samuel	Capt	13-06-77	QA	5th		RC 2-1119	Res
Thomas, Samuel	1st Lt	09-04-78	TA	4th	Sword in Hand	AM 21-24	
Thomas, Samuel	Ensign	20-04-80	QA	5th	Capt.T.Price	AM 43-146	
Thomas, Samuel	Capt	04-11-82	TA	4th	Capt.J.Thomas	AM 48-298	
Thomas, Samuel W.	2nd Lt	05-04-80	QA	20th	Capt.R.Carmichael	AM 43-130	
Thomas, Samuel Wright		25-12-76				SP 3055	Res
Thomas, William	2nd Lt	26-08-77	SM	Up	Capt.J.Thomas	AM 16-346	OC
Thomas, William	1st Lt	20-05-78	DO	19th	Capt.J.Woolford	AM 21-97	
Thomas, William	1st Lt	18-11-79	SM	Up	Capt.F.Millard	AM 43-18	
Thomas, William	1st Lt	16-12-79	DO	Lwr	Capt.L.Hubbard	AM 43-37	
Thompson, Alexander	Ensign	09-04-78	HA	8th	Capt.W.Cole	AM 21-24	

APPENDIX A - COMMISSIONED OFFICERS

Name	Rank	Date	Cty	Bn	Company	Ref.	Notes
Thompson, David	1st Lt	04-04-81	HA	23rd	Capt.A.Grace	AM 45-375	
Thompson, David	Lt	04-04-81	HA	23rd	Capt.A.Grace	AM 47-139	Mn
Thompson, Ephraim Jr.	1st Lt	21-04-78	CE	Sass	Capt.J.Knight	AM 21-47	
Thompson, James	1st Lt	30-08-77	WO	Wico	Capt.E.Shockley	AM 16-351	
Thompson, James	2nd Lt	31-07-78	QA	5th	Capt.J.Sency	AM 21-172	
Thompson, James	Capt	07-06-81	QA	5th	Capt.T.Seager	AM 45-465	
Thompson, John	Capt	03-01-76	QA	5th		SC 49-88	OC
Thompson, John	1st Lt	20-04-80	QA	5th	Capt.Seager	AM 43-146	
Thompson, John	Colonel	20-04-80	QA	5th		AM 43-146	
Thompson, John Dockery	Colonel	21-04-78	CE	Sass		AM 21-47	
Thompson, John Dockery	Cty Lt	25-03-80	CE			AM 43-119	
Thompson, Nathaniel Jr.	Lt Col	12-01-76	QA	5th		PC 78	
Thompson, Nathaniel Jr.	Lt Col	08-05-76	QA	5th		AM 16-343	Suc
Thompson, Richard	QM	06-01-76	MO	29th		PC 79	
Thompson, Samuel	Lt Col	03-01-76	QA	5th		SC 49-89	OC
Thompson, Samuel		13-05-77	QA			SP 4333	Ref
Thompson, Samuel Jr.	Colonel	08-05-77	QA	5th		AM 16-243	
Thompson, William	Ensign	20-04-80	QA	5th	Capt.Seager	AM 43-146	
Thompson, William	2nd Lt	07-06-81	QA	5th	Capt.J.Thompson	AM 45-465	
Thomson, John D.	Lt Col	06-01-76	CE	18th		PC 80	
Thorn, Barton	Ensign	23-10-77	CH		Capt.A.McPherson	AM 16-403	Dis
Thorn, Barton	1st Lt	19-01-81	CH	12th	Capt.T.A.Dyson	AM 45-280	
Thrasher, John	Ensign	29-11-75	FR	4th	Capt.W.Luckett	MM 11-50	
Tibbels, Thomas	Ensign	17-06-77	TA	4th	Capt.J.Bruff	RC 2-1130	Mn
Tibbels, Thomas	2nd Lt	12-04-80	TA	4th	Capt.R.Bruff	AM 43-139	
Tibbett, James	Comdore	11-11-80				AM 43-358	
Tibble, Thomas	Ensign	11-05-78	TA	4th	Capt.R.Bruff	AM 21-73	
Tibbles, Thomas	Ensign	09-04-78	TA	4th	Union	AM 21-24	
Tice, Nicholas	QM	06-01-76	FR	34th		PC 79	
Tilghman, James	QM	12-01-76	QA	20th		PC 78	
Tilghman, James	QM	08-05-76	QA	20th		AM 16-244	Suc
Tilghman, Peregrine	Lt Col	12-01-76	TA	4th		PC 78	
Tilghman, Peregrine	Colonel	09-04-78	TA	4th		AM 21-24	
Tilghman, Rd(son of Ma)	1st Maj	08-05-77	QA	5th		AM 16-243	OC
Tilghman, Richard	Lt Col	12-01-76	QA	20th		PC 78	
Tilghman, Richard	1st Maj	08-05-77	QA	20th		AM 16-243	
Tilghman, Richard	1st Maj	13-05-77	QA	20th		RC 2-1041	Ref
Tillard, Edward	QM	06-01-76	AA	WstR		PC 79	
Tillard, Edward	Capt	09-03-76	AA	WstR		AM 11-231	Mn
Tillard, Edward	Capt	09-08-76	AA	31st		AM 12-191	Res
Tillard, Thomas	2nd Maj	06-01-76	AA	WstR		PC 79	
Tillard, Thomas	1st Maj	22-01-76	AA	WstR		AM 11-103	OC
Tillard, Thomas	Maj	18-12-76				SP 3005	Res
Tillard, Thomas	1st Maj	18-12-76	TA	4th		SC 49-75	Res
Tinnerly, John	Ensign	01-05-78	PG	Mid	Capt.Lowe	AM 21-63	
Tinnerly, John	2nd Lt	24-05-79	PG	Mid	Capt.M.Lower	AM 21-414	
Tipton, Aquila	2nd Lt	20-11-76	BA		Capt.S.Gill	AM 12-542	
Tipton, Samuel	Ensign	30-08-77	BA	Up	Capt.R.Cummins	AM 16-350	
Todd, Job	Ensign	30-11-75	DO		Capt.H.Lake	DO 213	Mn
Todd, Job	Ensign	31-07-76				AM 12-151	Mn
Todd, Job	Ensign	19-09-76			Capt.H.Lake	AM 12-285	Mn
Todd, Job	Ensign	20-05-78	DO	Corp		DO 233	Mn
Todd, John	Ensign	16-05-76		Corp	Capt.H.Lake	AM 11-429	
Todd, John	Capt	13-08-76	DO			SP 299	Mn

APPENDIX A - COMMISSIONED OFFICERS

Name	Rank	Date	Cty	Bn	Company	Ref.	Notes
Todd, John	Capt	20-05-78	DO	Corp		DO 233	Mn
Todd, John	Ensign	24-06-78	DO		Capt.H.Lake	AM 21-148	
Todd, John	Capt	24-06-78	DO			AM 21-148	
Todd, John	Capt	15-07-80	DO	Corp		FP 2-71	Mn
Todd, Michael	2nd Lt	24-06-78	DO		Capt.J.Todd	AM 21-148	
Tolbott, James	Capt	09-04-78	HA	8th		AM 21-24	
Tolly, Alexander	2nd Lt	10-02-76	DO		Plymouth Greens	AM 11-147	
Tolly, Alexander	2nd Lt	16-05-76		Corp	Capt.M.Traverse	AM 11-429	
Tolly, Walter Jr.	Colonel	25-05-76	BA	GP		AM 11-443	
Tolson, John	Ensign	18-04-80	CA	28th	Capt.Hughlett	AM 43-144	
Tolson, John	2nd Lt	17-12-81	CA	28th	Capt.R.Hardcastle	AM 48-27	
Tongue, Thomas	1st Lt	15-02-76	AA	WstR	Capt.Simmons	AM 11-161	
Tongue, Thomas	1st Lt	02-03-78	AA	WstR	Capt.A.Simmons	AM 16-525	
Tool, James	Capt	26-04-81	BA	Town	Capt.J.Deaver	AM 45-416	
Toole, James	1st Lt	06-06-76	BA	Town	Capt.Galbraith	AM 11-467	
Toole, James	Capt	20-08-81	BA	Town		AM 45-572	Suc
Tootel, James	Lt Col	02-03-78	AA	Svrn		AM 16-525	
Tootell, James	Capt	22-02-76	AA	Svrn		AM 11-178	
Tootell, James	Major	25-01-77	AA	Svrn		AM 16-77	
Towney, John	2nd Lt	22-06-78	FR	Ling	Capt.Barr	AM 21-145	
Townsend, Barkeley	1st Lt	30-08-77	WO	SnHl	Capt.J.Stewart	AM 16-351	
Townsend, Bartlet	Capt	16-03-81	WO	SnHl	Capt.J.Stewart	AM 45-353	
Townsend, Benjamin	Capt	14-06-81	CE		Horse troop	AM 45-474	
Townsend, James	2nd Lt	06-07-76	WO		Capt.Quinton	AM 11-553	
Townsend, James	2nd Lt	30-08-77	WO	Wico	Capt.P.Quinton	AM 16-351	
Townsend, James	Capt	13-06-82	WO	Wico	Capt.P.Quinton	AM 48-190	
Townsend, John	1st Lt	21-06-76	WO		Capt.Dennis	AM 11-506	
Townsend, Joshua	2nd Lt	30-08-77	WO	SnHl	Capt.W.Handy	AM 350	
Townsend, Samuel	1st Lt	15-05-76	SO	1st	Capt.McClester	AM 11-426	
Towson, Ezekiel	1st Lt	19-12-75	BA		Capt.T.Rutter	RB 13-37	
Towson, Ezekiel	Lt	26-09-76	BA			AM 12-302	Mn
Trapnel, James	2nd Lt	30-08-77	BA	GP	Capt.Step.Giles	AM 16-350	
Trapnell, James	2nd Lt	21-10-81	BA		Capt.S.Gale	AM 47-530	Res
Travers	Capt	30-07-76				AM 12-144	Mn
Travers, William	Colonel	16-05-76		Corp		AM 11-429	
Travers, William	Capt	20-05-78	DO	Corp		DO 234	
Traverse, John	1st Lt	24-06-78	DO		Capt.M.Traverse	AM 21-147	
Traverse, John Askon	1st Lt	10-02-76	DO		Plymouth Greens	AM 11-147	
Traverse, Levin	1st Lt	20-05-78	DO	3rd	Capt.R.Hooper	AM 21-98	OC
Traverse, Matt	Capt	16-05-76		Corp		AM 11-429	
Traverse, Matthias	2nd Lt	12-02-76	DO		Minuteman	AM 11-153	
Traverse, Matthias	Capt	24-06-78	DO			AM 21-147	
Traverse, William	Capt	10-02-76	DO		Plymouth Greens	AM 11-147	
Traverse, William		17-09-76				AM 12-276	Mn
Travey, Jno Askom	1st Lt	16-05-76		Corp	Capt.M.Traverse	AM 11-429	
Treyferd, Jonathan	Ensign	16-09-76	DO		Friendship	AM 12-274	
Tripp, John	Capt	21-10-76			Castle Haven	AM 12-390	Mn
Trout, Jacob	2nd Lt	29-11-75	FR	1st	Capt.C.Stull	MM 11-50	
Trout, Jacob	Capt	27-04-79	FR	37th	Capt.C.Stull	AM 21-368	
Troutman, Michael	Capt	29-11-75	FR	4th		MM 11-50	
Troutman, Michael	Capt	22-08-82	FR			AM 48-248	Mn
Truelock, Henry	Ensign	13-06-77	QA	5th		RC 2-1119	Mn
Truelock, Henry	2nd Lt	09-09-78	KE	13th	Capt.D.Crane	AM 21-196	
Trundell, John	2nd Lt	04-08-80	MO	Lwr	Capt.A.Harris	AM 43-248	

APPENDIX A - COMMISSIONED OFFICERS

Name	Rank	Date	Cty	Bn	Company	Ref.	Notes
Tubeman, Richard	2nd Lt	20-05-78	DO	19th	Capt.B.Keene	AM 21-97	
Tubman, Richard	2nd Lt	20-03-76	DO		Capt.Keene	AM 11-267	
Tubman, Richard	1st Lt	23-08-81	DO	Lwr	Capt.J.Keene	AM 45-577	
Tubman, Richard	Lt	23-08-81	DO	SelM	Capt.C.Staplefort	AM 45-577	
Tull, George	Ensign	11-04-76	SO	1st	Capt.Hitch	AM 11-327	
Tull, John	1st Lt	30-08-77	WO	Snpx	Capt.J.Cox	AM 16-350	
Tull, John	Capt	16-03-81	WO	Snpx	Capt.J.Coe	AM 45-353	
Turnbell, John	QM	08-04-81	PG	Up		AM 47-172	Mn
Turner, John	1st Lt	10-04-76	CV		Capt.Smith	AM 11-320	
Turner, John	1st Lt	16-04-78	CV	15th	Capt.W.Smith	AM 21-37	
Turner, John Beal	Ensign	07-03-76	CH		Capt.W.Hanson	AM 11-206	
Turner, Philip	Ensign	28-11-76	FR		Capt.W.Brashears	AM 12-555	
Turner, Philip	Ensign	17-01-77	FR	Ling	Capt.Wm.Brashears	AM 16-55	
Turner, Philip	Ensign	24-06-80	PG	Up	Capt.J.Mulliken	AM 43-203	
Turpin, Francis	Ensign	28-07-80	DO	Up	Capt.E.Reed	AM 43-236	
Turpin, John	1st Lt	07-12-78	SO	PrAn	Capt.J.Williams	AM 21-260	
Turpin, William	Capt	22-09-77	SO	Salb	Rewastico	AM 16-382	
Turpin, William	Capt	31-07-78	SO			AM 21-173	Mn
Twyford, John	Ensign	20-05-78	DO	3rd	Capt.S.Waters	AM 21-98	
Tyler, Robert	Lt Col	13-01-76	PG	25th		PC 86	
Tyler, Robert	Colonel	11-09-77	PG	25th		AM 16-369	Mn
Tyler, Robert B.	Capt	02-07-81	PG	Up	Capt.B.Harwood	AM 45-492	
Ulrey, Christopher	Ensign	22-06-78	FR	Ling	Capt.Winchester	AM 21-145	
Urnges, Michael	Ensign	28-11-76	FR	37th		AM 12-555	
Van Swearingen,---	Capt	17-01-77	FR	33rd		AM 16-54	
Van Swearingen,---	Capt	03-07-77	FR	33rd		MM 4:379	Mn
Van Swearingen,---	Capt	19-04-81	FR	34th		AM 45-405	Suc
Vance, David	2nd Lt	27-05-79	SO	Salb	Capt.J.Bennett	AM 21-423	
Vanhorn, Aaron	2nd Lt	17-11-79	HA	Deer	Capt.G.Vanhorn	AM 43-17	
Vanhorn, Gabriel Peterson	Colonel	29-06-80	HA	Deer		AM 43-207	
Vanhorne, Gabriel	Capt	09-04-78	HA	Deer		AM 21-22	
Vaughan, Christopher	1st Lt	04-02-77	BA	Gist	Capt.J.Murray	AM 16-114	
Vaughan, George	Capt	17-11-79	HA	Deer		AM 43-17	Suc
Vaughan, Gist	2nd Maj	04-02-77	BA	Gist		AM 16-114	
Veach, Hezekiah	Ensign	12-09-77	MO	16th	Capt.R.Smith	AM 16-373	
Vearse, William	Capt	12-09-77	MO	16th		AM 16-373	
Vearse, William	Lt Col	01-03-79	MO	Up		AM 21-310	
Vearse, William	Capt	25-03-80	MO	Up		AM 43-120	Suc
Veatch, Hezekiah	2nd Lt	21-04-79	MO	Up	Capt.T.Hay	AM 21-356	
Veatch, Hezekiah	1st Lt	25-03-80	MO	Up	Capt.J.Sommers	AM 43-120	
Veazey, John	Colonel	06-01-76	CE	18th		PC 80	
Veazey, John Ward	Capt	21-04-78	CE	Sass		AM 21-47	
Veazey, Noble	2nd Lt	22-06-78	CE	Bohe	Capt.T.Bouldin Jr	AM 21-145	
Veazey, Samuel	Capt	21-04-78	CE	Sass		AM 21-47	
Veazey, William	1st Lt	21-04-78	CE	Susq	Capt.S.Hyland	AM 21-48	
Veazey, William	2nd Lt	21-04-78	CE	Sass	Capt.S.Veazey	AM 21-47	
Veazey, William	Capt	09-09-78	CE	30th	Capt.S.Hyland	AM 21-196	
Veazy, William	1st Lt	23-05-76	CE		Capt.Hyland	AM 11-438	
Venables, William	Ensign	07-01-78	SO	Salb	Capt.R.Dashiell	AM 16-457	
Venables, William	2nd Lt	20-04-78	SO	Salb	Salisbury	AM 21-42	

APPENDIX A - COMMISSIONED OFFICERS

Name	Rank	Date	Cty	Bn	Company	Ref.	Notes
Vennables, Bejamin	1st Lt	22-09-77	SO	Salb	Capt.J.Vennables	AM 16-381	
Vennables, Joseph	Capt	22-09-77	SO	Salb	Barron Creek	AM 16-381	
Vickars, Ezekiel	Lt Col	15-01-83	DO	Lwr		AM 48-344	
Vickars, Ezekiel	Capt	12-09-76	DO	19th		AM 12-266	
Vickars, Ezekiel	Maj	20-05-78	DO	19th		AM 21-97	
Vickars, Thomas	Ensign	16-12-79	DO	Lwr	Capt.A.Wheatly	AM 43-37	
Vickars, Wm. of John	Ensign	28-07-80	DO	Lwr	Capt.J.Hubberd	AM 43-236	
Vickers, Ezekiel	1st Lt	10-02-76	DO		Cambridge Blues	AM 11-147	
Victor, John	2nd Lt	30-08-77	WO	Wico	Capt.B.Dennis	AM 16-351	
Vincent, John	2nd Lt	19-01-81	CH	12th	Capt.J.Lancaster	AM 45-280	
Voghan, George	Capt	09-04-78	HA	Deer		AM 21-22	
Waddell, Alexander	Ensign	24-05-76	CA		Capt.J.Richardson	AM 11-442	
Waddell, Alexander	1st Lt	24-06-77	CA	14th	Capt.T.Lockerman	AM 16-299	
Waddell, Alexander	1st Lt	09-04-78	CA	14th	Capt.T.Lockerman	AM 21-23	
Waddle, Alexander	Capt	17-12-81	CA	14th	Capt.V.Price	AM 48-27	
Waddy, William	Capt	22-08-81	SO	PrAn	Capt.J.Williams	AM 45-575	
Wade, ---	Capt	07-08-76	PG			SP 2062	Mn
Wagoner, John	Ensign	22-06-78	WA	2ndW	Capt.J.Funk	AM 21-145	
Wahlager, Jacob	2nd Lt	- -	WA			FP 1-129	Mn
Wailes, Edward Lloyd	2nd Lt	24-05-79	PG	11th	Capt.B.Wales	AM 21-414	
Wailes, George	Capt	10-02-76	SO			SP 1061	Res
Wailes, Samuel Perri	Ensign	03-07-80	PG	Lwr	Capt.Benj.Wailes	AM 43-210	
Wails, George	Capt	11-05-76	SO	1st		AM 11-327	Res
Wales, Benjamin	2nd Lt	01-09-77	PG	Lwr	Capt.W.Wilkenson	AM 16-356	
Wales, Benjamin	1st Lt	01-05-78	PG	11th	Capt.J.Perry	AM 21-62	
Wales, Benjamin	Capt	24-05-79	PG	11th	Capt.J.Perry	AM 21-414	
Walker, Isaac	Ensign	05-09-77	PG	25th	Capt.J.Shaw	AM 16-363	
Walker, Isaac	2nd Lt	01-05-78	PG	25th	Capt.T.Richardson	AM 21-62	
Walker, Isaac	1st Lt	24-05-79	PG	25th	Capt.T.Beall	AM 21-414	
Walker, James	2nd Lt	07-02-76	AA			AM 11-139	
Walker, James	2nd Lt	12-04-77	HA	Hall		AM 16-131	
Walker, James	Capt	25-08-77	AA	22nd		AM 16-343	
Walker, James	2nd Lt	09-04-78	HA	23rd	Capt.S.Smith	AM 21-23	
Walker, John	Ensign	03-01-76	QA	20th	Capt.C.C.Cross	SC 49-78	OC
Walker, John	1st Lt	19-06-77	QA	20th	Capt.Costin	AM 16-295	
Walker, John	1st Lt	19-09-78	AA	7th	Capt.J.Merikan	AM 21-208	
Walker, Joseph Jr.	2nd Lt	07-02-76	AA	ElkR	Capt.Riggs	AM 11-139	
Walker, Joseph Jr.	1st Lt	30-03-76	AA	ElkR		AM 11-299	
Walker, Moses	2nd Lt	17-12-81	CA	14th	Capt.A.Waddle	AM 48-27	
Walker, Richard	Ensign	24-05-79	PG	25th	Capt.T.Beall	AM 21-414	
Walker, William	2nd Lt	22-06-78	WA	2ndW	Capt.J.Rennolds	AM 21-145	
Wallace, David	1st Lt	21-04-78	CE	Elk	Capt.S.Maffitt	AM 21-47	OC
Wallace, David	Lt	- -78	CE			SP 5659	Res
Wallace, James	Lt	20-11-76	MO	29th		AM 12-464	Ref
Waller, William	Ensign	19-09-76	SO	17th		AM 12-285	
Waller, William	Ensign	02-04-81	DO	Up	Capt.E.Reed	AM 45-492	
Waller, William	2nd Lt	22-08-81	SO	Salb	Capt.J.McCloster	AM 45-575	
Walling, James	Capt	22-06-78	WA	2ndW		AM 21-145	
Walls, Jno. N.	Ensign	13-06-77	QA	5th		RC 2-1119	Mn
Walls, Samuel	2nd Lt	20-04-80	QA	5th	Capt.T.Price	AM 43-146	
Walls, Samuel	1st Lt	07-06-81	QA	5th	Capt.B.Newman	AM 45-465	
Walsh, George	Ensign	01-03-76	BA		Capt.James Cox	AM 11-197	

APPENDIX A - COMMISSIONED OFFICERS

Name	Rank	Date	Cty	Bn	Company	Ref.	Notes
Walsten, Ben	Ensign	16-02-77	WO		Capt.Handy	AM 16-140	Mn
Walston, Boaz	Ensign	15-05-76	WO	10th	Capt.Hardy	AM 11-426	
Waltam, Fisher	Capt	27-05-79	WO	SnHl	Capt.W.Holland	AM 21-423	
Walter, David	Capt	12-09-77	MO	16th		AM 16-373	
Walter, David	Ensign	12-09-77	MO	16th	Capt.J.Walter	AM 16-373	
Walter, George	1st Lt	12-09-77	MO	16th	Capt.J.Walter	AM 16-373	
Walter, George	Capt	25-03-80	MO	Up	Capt.J.Walter	AM 43-120	
Walter, John	Capt	12-09-77	MO	16th	Capt.Fletcher	AM 16-373	
Walter, Jonathan	Capt	25-03-80	MO	Up		AM 43-120	Suc
Walters, George	Capt	- -76	DO			DO 213	Mn
Walters, Jacob	Capt	20-04-80	QA	5th	Capt.J.Sudler	AM 43-146	
Walters, Robert	2nd Lt	31-07-78	QA	20th	Capt.T.Barnes	MH 2	Mn
Walters, Robert	1st Lt	31-07-78	QA	20th	Capt.J.Ringgold	AM 21-172	
Walters, William	Ensign	- -	DO	Up		DO 230	Mn
Walton, Fisher	1st Lt	30-08-77	WO	SnHl	Capt.W.Holland	AM 16-351	
Walton, William	2nd Lt	26-08-77	SM	Up	Capt.J.Mills	AM 16-346	
Wamsley, Benjamin	Ensign	21-04-78	CE	Sass	Capt.J.Cox	AM 21-47	
Ward, Henry	2nd Lt	07-03-76	CH		Capt.Marshall	AM 11-206	
Ward, John Jr.	2nd Lt	21-04-78	CE	Sass	Capt.J.Cox	AM 21-47	
Ward, John Sr	1st Lt	21-04-78	CE	Sass	Capt.J.Cox	AM 21-47	
Ward, Richard	Ensign	01-04-76	HA	23rd	Capt.Patrick	AM 11-537	
Ward, Richard	Ensign	09-04-78	HA	Deer	Capt.J.Patrick	AM 21-23	
Ward, Richard	1st Lt	17-11-79	HA	Deer	Capt.S.Bayliss	AM 43-17	
Ware, Francis	Capt	- -75	CH			RC 2-142	Mn
Ware, Francis	Colonel	28-02-76	CH			AM 11-186	Mn
Ware, Francis	Cty Lt	01-07-77	CH			AM 16-304	
Ware, John	2nd Lt	- -75	HA		#9	PR 115	
Warfield, Benjamin	Capt	02-03-78	AA	ElkR		AM 16-525	
Warfield, Benjamin	Capt	05-09-78	AA			MH 5	Res
Warfield, C.A.	1st Maj	12-01-76	AA	ElkR		PC 78	
Warfield, Charles	QM	28-11-76	FR			AM 12-555	
Warfield, Charles	1st Lt	17-01-77	FR	Ling	Capt.Meredith	AM 16-54	
Warfield, Charles	Ensign	02-03-78	AA	ElkR	Capt.B.Warfield	AM 16-525	
Warfield, Davidge	1st Lt	04-04-76			Capt.Burgess	AM 11-308	Mn
Warfield, Ephraim	1st Lt	30-03-79	AA	22nd	Capt.R.Warfield	AM 21-333	
Warfield, Joseph	Ensign	28-01-77	AA	Svrn	Capt.P.Warfield	AM 16-83	
Warfield, Joseph	2nd Lt	13-06-77	QA	5th		RC 2-1119	Mn
Warfield, Joseph	Ensign	02-03-78	AA	Svrn	Capt.P.Warfield	AM 16-575	
Warfield, Joseph	2nd Lt	19-09-78	AA	7th	Capt.P.Warfield	AM 21-208	
Warfield, Lancelot	2nd Lt	22-02-76	AA	Svrn	Capt.Tootell	AM 11-178	
Warfield, Lancelot	1st Lt	28-01-77	AA	Svrn	Capt.P.Warfield	AM 16-83	
Warfield, Lancelot	1st Lt	02-03-78	AA	Svrn	Capt.P.Warfield	AM 16-575	
Warfield, Nicho.Ridgeley	Capt	30-03-79	AA	22nd		AM 21-333	
Warfield, Philemon	1st Lt	22-02-76	AA	Svrn	Capt.Tootell	AM 11-178	
Warfield, Philemon	Lt	20-07-76				AM 12-84	Mn
Warfield, Philemon	Capt	28-01-77	AA	Svrn		AM 16-83	
Warfield, Philemon	Capt	02-03-78	AA	Svrn		AM 16-575	
Warfield, Richard	1st Lt	22-06-78	FR	Ling	Capt.Beckwith	AM 21-145	
Warfield, Robert	2nd Lt	02-03-78	AA	ElkR	Capt.B.Warfield	AM 16-525	
Warfield, Robert	Capt	30-03-79	AA	22nd		AM 21-333	
Warfield, Thomas	Ensign	22-02-76	AA	Svrn	Capt.Tootell	AM 11-178	
Warfield, Thomas	2nd Lt	28-01-77	AA	Svrn	Capt.P.Warfield	AM 16-83	
Warfield, Thomas	2nd Lt	02-03-78	AA	Svrn	Capt.P.Warfield	AM 16-575	
Warfield, Walter	AstSurg	03-09-77	AA	Svrn		AM 16-359	

APPENDIX A - COMMISSIONED OFFICERS

Name	Rank	Date	Cty	Bn	Company	Ref.	Notes
Warham, Henry	1st Lt	04-02-77	BA	Gist	Capt.R.Lemmon	AM 16-114	
Waring, Basil 3rd	Capt	18-03-76	PG	25th		AM 11-260	
Waring, Leonard	1st Lt	01-05-78	PG	11th	Capt.J.Hellen	AM 21-78	
Warley, Thomas	2nd Lt	22-06-78	WA	3rdW	Capt.E.Baker	AM 21-145	
Warrell, William	1st Lt	04-06-78	KE	13th	Capt.P.Davis	AM 21-122	
Warren, Edward	Ensign	28-05-79	CH	12th	Capt.J.Yates	AM 21-427	
Warring, Thomas	Capt	15-05-76	FR			AM 11-427	
Waters, Azel	QM	06-01-76	FR	37th		PC 79	
Waters, Azel	QM	23-12-76				SP 3036	Res
Waters, George	Capt	06-07-76	DO			AM 11-553	
Waters, George	Capt	22-09-77	SO	PrAn	Pocomoke	AM 16-381	
Waters, Jacob	2nd Lt	31-07-78	QA	5th	Capt.J.Sudler	AM 21-172	
Waters, Peter	Lt Col	06-06-76	SO	17th		PC 80	
Waters, Peter	Lt Col	24-10-80	SO	PrAn		PA	Res
Waters, Richard	2nd Lt	18-09-80	FR	Town	Capt.J.Carey	AM 43-295	
Waters, Samuel Wright	Ensign	29-08-77	BA	Town	Capt.E.Bailey	AM 16-348	
Waters, Spencer	Capt	20-05-78	DO	3rd		AM 21-98	
Waters, Spencer	Capt	27-04-80	DO	Up		AM 43-154	
Waters, Thomas	Ensign	22-08-81	SO	Salb	Capt.J.Cotman	AM 45-575	
Waters, William of John	Capt	22-09-77	SO	PrAn	Great Annamesex	AM 16-381	OC
Waters, William of Wm.	2nd Maj	06-01-76	SO	17th		PC 80	
Waters, William of Wm.	Capt	22-09-77	SO	PrAn	St.Asaph	AM 16-381	
Waters, William of Wm.	Lt Col	28-10-80	SO	PrAn		AM 43-342	
Waters, William of Wm.	Capt	22-08-81	SO	PrAn		AM 45-575	Suc
Watkins, John	Lt	27-08-76				AM 12-242	Mn
Watkins, John	Ensign	12-09-77	MO	16th	Capt.W.Vearse	AM 16-373	
Watkins, Nicholas	1st Lt	28-08-77	AA	22nd	Capt.J.Dorsey	AM 16-347	OC
Watkins, Nicholas	1st Lt	05-09-78	AA			MH 5	Res
Watkins, Samuel	2nd Lt	12-02-76	AA	WstR	Capt.Watkins	AM 11-158	
Watkins, Samuel	2nd Lt	02-03-78	AA	WstR	Capt.T.Watkins	AM 16-525	
Watkins, Samuel	2nd Lt	09-04-78	HA	Deer	Capt.G.Voghan	AM 21-23	
Watkins, Samuel	1st Lt	17-08-79	AA	WstR	Capt.T.Watkins	AM 21-496	
Watkins, Samuel	Capt	17-03-81	AA	WstR	Capt.T.Watkins	AM 45-354	
Watkins, Thomas	Capt	12-02-76	AA	WstR		AM 11-158	
Watkins, Thomas	Capt	09-12-76				AM 12-514	Res
Watkins, Thomas	Capt	06-09-77	AA	31st		AM 16-364	
Watkins, Thomas	Capt	02-03-78	AA	WstR		AM 16-525	
Watkins, Thomas	Capt	30-06-80	AA	SoR		PA	Res
Watson, Joseph	Ensign	03-10-82	CE	ElkR	Capt.D.Ricketts	AM 48-274	
Watson, Patrick		24-03-76	FR	35th		RC 2-171	Mn
Watson, Patrick	Capt	10-01-77	FR	33rd		AM 16-33	
Watson, Patt.	2nd Lt	29-11-75	FR	3rd	Capt.S.Shaw	MM 11:50	
Watson, Samuel	Ensign	20-06-77	MO			RC 2-1142	Mn
Watson, Samuel	2nd Lt	12-09-77	MO	16th		AM 16-373	
Watson, Samuel	1st Lt	25-03-80	MO	Up	Capt.G.Walter	AM 43-120	
Watts, Alexander	1st Lt	26-08-77	SM	Lwr	Capt.J.Armstrong	AM 16-346	
Watts, Alexander Hawkins	Capt	16-04-78	SM	21st		AM 21-37	
Watts, Alexander H.	Capt	07-05-81	SM	Lwr		AM 45-426	Suc
Watts, George	Capt	22-02-76	AA	Svrn		AM 11-178	
Watts, John	Ensign	17-12-81	CA	28th	Capt.R.Keene	AM 48-27	
Weatherby, John	2nd Lt	22-09-77	SO	Salb	Capt.J.Vennables	AM 16-381	
Weaver, Christian	2nd Lt	26-03-76	FR	MdDt	Capt.Adlum	AM 11-287	
Webb, John	Ensign	16-05-78	WA	3rdW	Capt.P.Pindell	AM 21-86	
Webb, John Jr.	Ensign	14-10-75	HA		#16	PR 121	

APPENDIX A - COMMISSIONED OFFICERS

Name	Rank	Date	Cty	Bn	Company	Ref.	Notes
Webb, Samuel	Ensign	14-10-75	HA		Capt.Webb	AM 11-537	Mn
Webb, Samuel	Capt	26-04-76	HA			AM 11-387	
Webb, Samuel	Ensign	26-04-76	HA		Capt.Webb	AM 11-387	
Webb, Samuel	1st Lt	09-04-78	HA	Deer	Capt.W.Fisher	AM 21-22	
Webb, William	Capt	14-10-75	HA		#16	PR 121	
Webb, William	Capt	26-04-76	HA			AM 11-387	
Wedderstat, Theodr.	2nd Lt	31-07-78	QA	20th	Capt.J.S.Blake	MH 2	Mn
Weeks, Robert	Ensign	18-09-79	KE	13th	Capt.Tilden	AM 21-532	
Weems, John	Colonel	06-01-76	AA	WstR		PC 79	
Weems, John	Colonel	02-03-78	AA	WstR		AM 16-525	
Weems, Richard	Capt	17-04-76	AA			AM 11-336	
Weems, Richard	Capt	02-03-78	AA	WstR		AM 16-525	
Weems, Richard	Capt	02-05-81	AA	WstR		AM 45-422	Suc
Weight, John	Capt	01-05-78	PG	25th		AM 21-62	
Wells, Alexander	1st Lt.	13-05-76	BA	Gist	Capt.S.Owings	RB 13-69	
Wells, Alexander	Capt	06-06-76	BA	SD	2nd	AM 11-467	
Wells, George	Capt	06-06-76	BA	Town		AM 11-467	
Wells, James	Lt Col	28-11-76	FR			AM 12-555	
Wells, James	Colonel	17-01-77	FR	Ling		AM 16-54	
Wells, James		10-09-81				AM 47-484	Res
Wells, John	Ensign	24-06-80	PG	Up	Capt.B.Harwood	AM 43-203	
Wells, Richard	2nd Lt	03-01-76	AA			SC 49-84	OC
Wells, William	Ensign	13-11-79	PG	Mid	Capt.J.W.Clagett	AM 43-13	
Wells, Richard	2nd Lt	12-07-77	AA			MH 5	Res
Welsh, Aaron	1st Lt	10-08-76	AA	31st		AM 12-192	
Welsh, Aaron	2nd Lt	12-09-77	AA	31st	Capt.Dare	AM 16-372	
Welsh, Aaron	1st Lt	02-03-78	AA	WstR	Capt.W.Simmons	AM 16-526	
Welsh, Aaron	Capt	02-05-81	AA	WstR	Capt.Wm.Simmons	AM 45-422	
Welsh, Joshua	Ensign	20-11-76	BA		Capt.H.Howard	AM 12-541	
Welsh, Robert	2nd Lt	02-03-78	AA	WstR	Capt.W.Simmons	AM 16-526	
Welsh, Robert	2nd Lt	02-05-81	AA	WstR	Capt.A.Welsh	AM 45-422	
Welsh, William	Ensign	19-12-75	BA		Capt.Wm.Cromwell	RB 13-37	
Weltner, Ludwick	1st Maj	06-01-76	FR	33rd		PC 79	
Welty, John	1st Lt	29-11-75	FR	3rd	Capt.R.Beatty	MM 11:50	
West, Nathaniel	Ensign	14-09-75	HA		#10	PR 115	
West, Nathaniel	Ensign	12-02-77	HA	Hall		AM 16-131	
West, Nathaniel	Ensign	09-04-78	HA	Deer	Capt.S.Ashmead	AM 21-22	
West, Samuel	Capt	12-09-77	MO	Mid		AM 16-373	
West, Samuel	Capt	21-04-79	MO	Mid		AM 21-357	
Weston, John	2nd Lt	30-08-77	BA	GP	Capt.B.Buck	AM 16-350	
Wetler, John	Ensign	29-11-75	FR	2nd	Capt.J.Ambrose	MM 11:50	
Wetsel, Peter	1st Lt	28-11-76	FR	35th	Capt.Peppel	AM 12-555	
Wharton, ---	Capt	07-08-76	PG			SP 2062	Mn
Wheatley, Arthur	Capt	20-05-78	DO	19th		AM 21-97	OC
Wheatley, Arthur	Capt	16-12-79	DO	Lwr		AM 43-37	Suc
Wheatley, Augustus	Capt	16-12-79	DO	Lwr	Capt.Artr.Wheatly	AM 43-37	
Wheatley, Augustus	Capt	28-07-80	DO	Lwr		AM 43-236	Suc
Wheatly	Capt	30-07-76				AM 12-144	Mn
Wheatly, William	Colonel	24-06-77	CA	14th		AM 16-299	
Wheeler, ---	1st Lt	19-01-81	BA	Town	Capt.Ackerman	AM 47-29	Dec
Wheeler, Clement	Capt	01-05-78	PG	Mid		AM 21-63	
Wheeler, Clement	Capt	24-06-80	PG	Mid		AM 43-203	Suc
Wheeler, Edward	2nd Lt	12-09-77	MO	29th	Capt.T.Beall	AM 16-373	
Wheeler, Ezekial	Ensign	09-04-78	CA	14th	Capt.N.Andrew	AM 21-23	

APPENDIX A - COMMISSIONED OFFICERS

Name	Rank	Date	Cty	Bn	Company	Ref.	Notes
Wheeler, Hezekiah	Capt	15-03-76	PG			AM 11-252	
Wheeler, Hezekiah	Capt	01-05-78	PG	11th		AM 21-78	
Wheeler, Hezekiah	Capt	25-05-81	PG	SelM		AM 45-445	
Wheeler, Ignatius	1st Lt	26-04-76	HA		Capt.Webb	AM 11-387	
Wheeler, Ignatius	Colonel	09-04-78	HA	Deer		AM 21-22	OC
Wheeler, Ignatius	2nd Lt	01-05-78	PG	Mid	Capt.Lowe	AM 21-63	OC
Wheeler, Ignatius	Colonel	29-06-80	HA	Deer		AM 43-207	Suc
Wheeler, Ignatius Jr.	1st Lt	14-10-75	HA		#16	PR 121	
Wheeler, Isaac	1st Lt	04-09-77	BA	Town	Capt.G.Ackerman	AM 16-362	
Wheeler, Joseph	Capt	09-04-78	HA	23rd		AM 21-24	
Wheeler, Thomas	2nd Lt	20-05-78	DO	19th	Capt.A.Wheatley	AM 21-97	
White, Abraham	Ensign	29-11-75	FR	3rd	Capt.S.Shaw	MM 11:50	
White, Abraham	1st Lt	10-01-77	FR	33rd	Capt.Watson	AM 16-33	
White, Benjamin	2nd Lt	13-11-79	PG	Mid	Capt.J.W.Clagett	AM 43-13	
White, Charles	Capt	30-03-79	AA	22nd		AM 21-333	
White, Charles	Capt	20-06-81	AA	ElkR		AM 47-304	Mn
White, James	2nd Lt	24-06-77	CA	14th	Capt.S.Lighton	AM 16-299	
White, James	2nd Lt	09-04-78	CA	14th	Capt.S.Liden	AM 21-23	
White, John	QM	12-01-76	CA	14th		PC 78	
White, John	1st Lt	09-04-78	CA	28th	Capt.Postlethwait	AM 21-23	
White, John	Ensign	02-07-81	DO	Up	Capt.J.Sullivan	AM 45-492	
White, Joseph	1st Lt	21-06-77	MO	29th	Capt.J.Magruder	AM 16-296	
White, Joseph	1st Lt	12-09-77	MO	29th	Capt.J.Macgruder	AM 16-373	
White, Nicholas	Ensign	29-11-75	FR	1st	Capt.P.Mantz	MM 11:50	
White, Nicholas	Ensign	26-03-76	FR	MdDt	Capt.Mantz	AM 11-287	
White, Nicholas	Capt	10-01-77	FR	33rd		AM 16-33	
White, Otho	Ensign	07-02-82	BA	SD	Capt.Stinchicomb	AM 48-71	
White, Thomas	2nd Lt	16-12-79	DO	Up		DO 231	Mn
White, Thomas	Ensign	28-07-80	DO	Up	Capt.Thos.Logan	AM 43-236	
White, Thomas	2nd Lt	02-07-81	DO	Up	Capt.J.Sullivan	AM 45-492	
White, Thomas	Ensign	17-12-81	CA	14th	Capt.J.Guyless	AM 48-27	
White, Walter	1st Lt	26-03-76	MO		Capt.Smith	AM 11-287	
White, Walter	Ensign	21-04-79	MO	Up	Capt.T.Hay	AM 21-356	
White, Walter	2nd Lt	25-03-80	MO	Up	Capt.J.Sommers	AM 43-120	
White, William	1st Lt	30-08-77	WO	Snpx	Capt.M.Purnal	AM 16-350	
Whiteley, Arthur	Capt	23-06-79	DO	Lwr	Fishing Creek	MH 4-70	Res
Whiteley, William	1st Maj	12-01-76	CA	14th		PC 78	
Whiteley, William	Cty Lt	01-07-77	CA			AM 16-304	
Whittingham, John	2nd Lt	20-04-80	QA	5th	Capt.Jas.Hackett	AM 43-146	
Whittington, John	Ensign	23-10-77	QA	5th	Capt.S.Wickes	AM 16-403	
Wickes, Samuel	Capt	03-01-76	QA	5th		SC 49-77	OC
Wickes, Samuel	QM	08-05-77	QA	5th		AM 16-243	
Wickes, Simon	Capt	23-10-77	QA	5th		AM 16-403	
Wickes, Simon	Capt	04-06-78	KE	13th		AM 21-122	
Wicks, Joseph	2nd Lt	11-03-79	KE	13th	Capt.S.Wicks	AM 21-320	
Wicks, Simon	Capt	20-04-80	QA	5th		AM 43-146	
Wiggans, Thomas	Ensign	20-04-80	QA	5th	Capt.R.Holding	AM 43-146	
Wilcoxen, Jesse	1st Lt	07-12-76	MO		Capt.J.Johnson	AM 12-511	
Wilcoxen, Jesse	Capt	-05-82	MO	Lwr		SC 49-123	Res
Wilcoxen, Thomas	1st Lt	04-09-77	PG		Capt.M.Lowe	AM 16-362	
Wilcoxen, Thomas	1st Lt	01-05-78	PG	Mid	Capt.Lowe	AM 21-63	
Wilcoxen, Thos.of Jacob	Ensign	13-11-79	PG	Mid	Capt.M.Lowe	AM 43-13	
Wilcoxon, Thomas	1st Lt	20-09-76	PG		Capt.M.Lowe	AM 12-287	
Wiley, James	Capt	04-10-79	FR	35th		AM 21-546	

APPENDIX A - COMMISSIONED OFFICERS

Name	Rank	Date	Cty	Bn	Company	Ref.	Notes
Wiley, John	Ensign	20-11-76	BA		Capt.D.Shaw	AM 12-541	
Wiley, Luke	Capt	20-11-76	BA			AM 12-542	
Wilkenson, William	Capt	01-09-77	PG	Lwr		AM 16-356	
Wilkinson, Joseph	1st Maj	06-01-76	CV			PC 79	
Wilkinson, Joseph	Colonel	16-04-78	CV	15th		AM 21-37	
Wilkinson, Joseph	Cty Lt	12-01-81	CV			AM 45-272	
Wilkinson, William	Capt	04-02-77	BA			AM 16-114	
Wilkinson, William	Capt	09-05-78	CH	12th		AM 21-72	
Willcoxen, Anthony	2nd Lt	25-03-80	MO	Lwr	Capt.Swearingham	AM 43-120	
Willcoxen, George	Ensign	25-03-80	MO	Lwr	Capt.Swearingham	AM 43-120	
Willcoxen, Jesse	1st Lt	12-09-77	MO	29th	Capt.W.Johnson	AM 16-373	
Willcoxen, Jesse	Capt	04-08-80	MO	Lwr	Capt.W.Johnson	AM 43-248	OC
Willcoxen, Thomas	2nd Lt	03-01-76	PG	11th	Light Inf	SC 49-125	OC
Willen, Levi	1st Lt	16-05-76		Corp	Capt.H.Lake	AM 11-429	
Willen, Levi	1st Lt	19-09-76			Capt.H.Lake	AM 12-285	Mn
Willet, Edward	Ensign	24-06-80	PG	Mid	Capt.S.Hepburn	AM 43-203	
Williahr, Elias	2nd Lt	11-06-76	FR	34th	Capt.Poe	AM 11-476	
Williahr, Theobold	Ensign	11-06-76	FR	34th	Capt.Poe	AM 11-476	
Williams, Abraham	2nd Lt	26-01-77	HA	8th	Capt.B.Amos	AM 16-77	
Williams, Baruch	Capt	03-03-76				SP 1143	Mn
Williams, Baruch	Capt	24-03-76				SP 1220	Res
Williams, Baruch	Capt	10-05-76	CE	30th		AM 11-419	Mn
Williams, Baruch	Maj	09-09-78	CE	30th		AM 21-196	
Williams, Baruch	Lt Col	15-08-81	CE	30th		AM 45-560	
Williams, Basil	Capt	22-06-78	WA	2ndW		AM 21-145	
Williams, Bazil	1st Lt	21-04-78	CE	Susq	Capt.J.Pritchard	AM 21-48	
Williams, Benjamin	Ensign	26-08-77	SM	Lwr	Capt.J.Abell	AM 16-346	
Williams, Benjamin	2nd Lt	16-04-78	SM	21st	Capt.J.H.Abell	AM 21-37	
Williams, Benjamin	Capt	16-10-80			"Independence"	AM 43-330	
Williams, David	2nd Lt	17-06-77		17th		AM 16-291	
Williams, David	Ensign	22-09-77	SO	PrAn	Capt.J.Williams	AM 16-381	OC
Williams, Elie	QM	06-01-76	FR	32nd		PC 79	
Williams, Esau	Ensign	30-08-77	WO	Snpx	Capt.W.Purnal	AM 16-350	
Williams, Esau	1st Lt	16-03-81	WO	Snpx	Capt.I.Evans	AM 45-353	
Williams, Henry	2nd Lt	29-11-75	FR	3rd	Capt.W.Blair	MM 11:50	
Williams, Henry	1st Lt	28-11-76	FR	35th	Capt.Hawkersmith	AM 12-555	
Williams, James	Ensign	07-03-76	SM			AM 11-205	
Williams, James	Ensign	26-08-77	SM	Lwr	Capt. J.Greenwell	AM 16-346	
Williams, James	1st Lt	22-06-80	SM	Lwr	Capt.B.Combs	AM 43-201	
Williams, John	Capt	22-09-77	SO	PrAn	Watkin's Point	AM 16-381	
Williams, John	Ensign	09-09-78	KE	13th	Capt.D.Crane	AM 21-196	
Williams, John	Capt	22-08-81	SO	PrAn		AM 45-575	Suc
Williams, John	Capt	23-08-81	SO	SelM		AM 45-577	
Williams, Osborn	Lt	17-04-81	PG			AM 47-193	Mn
Williams, Osborne	Capt	15-06-81	PG	SelM		AM 45-475	
Williams, Otho H.	Colonel	23-07-76	FR			BR 15	
Williams, Peter	Ensign	03-12-76	WA		Capt.C.Calson	AM 12-501	
Williams, Planner	Capt	24-02-76	SO	17th		AM 11-182	
Williams, Robert	1st Lt	21-04-78	CE	Susq	Capt.S.Miller	AM 21-48	
Williams, Thomas	Ensign	24-02-76	SO	17th	Capt.Williams	AM 11-182	
Williams, Thomas	1st Maj	18-03-76	PG	25th		AM 11-260	
Williams, Thomas	2nd Lt	22-09-77	SO	PrAn	Capt.W.Waters	AM 16-381	OC
Williams, Thomas	Ensign	07-01-78	SO	PrAn	Capt.J.Williams	AM 16-458	OC
Williams, Thomas	Lt Col	10-03-78	PG	25th		AM 16-532	OC

137

APPENDIX A - COMMISSIONED OFFICERS

Name	Rank	Date	Cty	Bn	Company	Ref.	Notes
Williams, Thomas	Lt Col	20-03-78	PG	25th		RC 2-1538	Res
Williams, Thomas Owen	Ensign	09-06-77	PG		Capt.B.Waring	RC 2-1103	Rec
Williams, Thomas Owens	Maj	01-05-78	PG	25th		AM 21-63	
Williams, William Jr.	2nd Lt	04-08-80	MO	Mid	Capt.Lodowick Yost	AM 43-248	
Williams, Zadock	Ensign	22-06-78	WA	2ndW	Capt.B.Williams	AM 21-145	
Williamson, Charles	Capt	10-04-76	CV			AM 11-320	
Williamson, Charles	Capt	16-04-78	CV	15th		AM 21-37	
Williamson, James	Capt	04-06-78	KE	13th		AM 21-122	
Willin, Henry	1st Lt	24-06-78	DO			AM 21-148	
Willin, Levi	Lt	31-07-76				AM 12-151	Mn
Willin, Levi	Lt	19-09-76				SP 2386	Mn
Willin, Levin	1st Lt	20-05-78	DO	Corp		DO 233	Mn
Willis, Andrew	2nd Lt	12-06-81	CA	14th	Capt.J.Andrew	MH 2	Rec
Willis, Ioel	Ensign	11-03-79	KE	13th	Capt.G.Hartshorn	AM 21-320	
Willis, Richard	Ensign	11-09-76	KE		Capt.Frisby	AM 12-265	
Willison, Cornelius	1st Lt	03-12-76	WA		Capt.G.Johnson	AM 12-501	
Willison, Jeremiah	1st Lt	22-06-78	WA	3rdW	Capt.G.Johnson	AM 21-145	
Willson, Alexander	Ensign	21-04-78	CE	Elk	Capt.S.Evans	AM 21-47	
Willson, Andrew	2nd Lt	19-03-79	BA	Town	Capt.G.Douglass	AM 21-324	
Willson, Henry	Capt	16-05-76	HA	23rd		AM 11-429	OC
Willson, James	2nd Lt	03-05-80	DO		Capt.Thos.Cleland	AM 43-162	
Willson, William	Ensign	15-05-76	FR	34th	Capt.Merony	AM 11-426	
Wilmer, Lambert	Ensign	26-04-76	HA		Capt.Cowen	AM 11-387	
Wilmer, Lambert	1st Lt	09-04-78	HA	8th	Capt.S.G.Osburn	AM 21-24	
Wilmot, Robert	2nd Lt	05-06-77	BA		Arty	AM 16-278	
Wilmott, John	Ensign	20-11-76	BA		Capt.L.Wiley	AM 12-542	
Wilson, Alexander	1st Lt	07-06-81	CE	Elk	Capt.Wm.Scott	AM 45-466	OC
Wilson, Alexander	1st Lt	03-10-82	CE	ElkR		AM 48-474	
Wilson, Andrew	2nd Lt	19-05-79	BA	Town	Capt.G.Douglass	AM 21-401	
Wilson, David	Capt	22-09-77	SO	PrAn	Back Creek	AM 16-381	OC
Wilson, Edward	2nd Lt	29-11-75	FR	4th	Capt.Wm.Duvall	MM 11:50	
Wilson, George	Ensign	03-01-76				SC 49-116	OC
Wilson, George	Capt	22-09-77	SO	Salb	White Haven	AM 16-382	
Wilson, George	Capt	22-08-81	SO	Salb		AM 45-575	Suc
Wilson, Gittings	2nd Lt	03-09-77	BA	GP	Capt.Standiford	AM 16-359	
Wilson, James	2nd Lt	26-04-76	HA		Capt.Jolley	AM 11-387	
Wilson, John	Ensign	03-01-76	PG	11th		SC 49-114	OC
Wilson, John	1st Lt	20-11-76	BA		Capt.H.Howard	AM 12-541	
Wilson, Joseph S.	Ensign	23-08-76			Capt.A.Beall Jr	AM 12-232	
Wilson, Mathew	Ensign	25-03-80	MO	Up	Capt.G.Hoskinson	AM 43-120	
Wilson, Nathan	1st Lt	16-04-78	CV	15th	Capt.B.Bond	AM 21-37	
Wilson, Nathaniel	Capt	02-02-79	CV			AM 21-290	
Wilson, Nathaniel	Ensign	19-05-79	BA	Town	Capt.J.Smith	AM 21-401	
Wilson, Nathaniel Jr.	Ensign	24-05-79	PG	Mid	Capt.E.Lanham	AM 21-414	
Wilson, Richard	Capt	03-01-76	QA	20th		SC 49-113	OC
Wilson, Samuel	2nd Lt	29-11-75	FR		Capt.J.Good	MM 11:50	
Wilson, Thomas	2nd Lt	29-11-75	FR	3rd	Capt.N.Bruce	MM 11:50	
Wilson, Thomas	Capt	31-05-76	QA	20th		AM 11-454	OC
Wilson, William	2nd Lt	01-05-78	PG	25th	Capt.J.Selby	AM 21-62	
Wilson, William	Ensign	11-03-79	KE	27th	Capt.J.Day	AM 21-320	
Wilson,---	Ensign	11-04-76	SO	1st		AM 11-327	Res
Wilton, Nathaniel	Ensign	19-03-79	BA	Town	Capt.J.Smith	AM 21-324	
Winchester, ---	Capt	06-12-81	FR			AM 47-568	Mn
Winchester, ---	Capt	14-12-81	FR	SelM		AM 48-23	Mn

APPENDIX A - COMMISSIONED OFFICERS

Name	Rank	Date	Cty	Bn	Company	Ref.	Notes
Winchester, Jacob	1st Lt	27-06-76	QA			AM 11-523	
Winchester, Jacob Jr.	1st Lt	29-08-77	QA	20th	Capt.T.Elliott	SC 49-111	OC
Winchester, Jacob Jr.	1st Lt	30-07-78	QA	20th	Capt.T.Elliott	MH 1	Res
Winchester, Jacob Sr.	Ensign	19-06-77	QA	20th	Capt.Elliott	AM 16-295	
Winchester, Jacob Sr.	2nd Lt	29-08-77	QA	20th	Capt.T.Elliott	SC 49-110	OC
Winchester, Jacob Sr.	2nd Lt	30-07-78	QA	20th	Capt.T.Elliott	SC 49-110	Res
Winchester, James	1st Lt	17-01-77	FR	Ling	Capt.Wm Winchester	AM 16-54	
Winchester, William	Capt	17-01-77	FR	Ling		AM 16-54	
Winder, William	1st Lt	22-09-77	SO	Salb	Capt.R.Dashiell	AM 16-382	
Winder, William	Capt	27-05-79	SO	Salb		AM 21-423	Suc
Winder, William Jr.	Capt	20-04-78	SO	Salb	Salisbury	AM 21-42	
Window, Thomas	2nd Lt	18-10-77	DO	3rd	Transqusaking	RC 2-1356	Rec
Winson, James	1st Lt	29-06-76	KE	13th	Capt.Smyth	AM 11-534	
Winter, Walter	Capt	07-03-76	CH			AM 11-206	
Winter, William	Capt	07-03-76	CH		Capt.W.Harrison	AM 11-206	
Wire, Thomas	1st Lt	27-05-79	BA	SD	Capt.J.Hurd	AM 21-422	
Wise, Adam	Ensign	- -	WA			FP 1-129	Mn
Wise, William	Ensign	30-08-77	WO	SnH1	Capt.W.Handy	AM 16-351	
Woltz, George	2nd Maj	06-01-76	FR	33rd		PC 79	
Wood, Edward	Capt	10-04-76	CV			AM 11-320	
Wood, Edward	Capt	17-04-78	CV	15th		AM 21-37	
Wood, John	1st Lt	31-10-75	HA		Co.8	PR 114	
Wood, John	Ensign	10-04-76	CV		Capt.Wood	AM 11-320	
Wood, John	Capt	09-04-78	HA	23rd		AM 21-23	OC
Wood, John	Ensign	16-04-78	CV	15th	Capt.E.Wood	AM 21-37	
Wood, John	Ensign	27-04-79	FR	37th	Capt.W.Carmack	AM 21-368	
Wood, John	Capt	17-11-79	HA	23rd		AM 43-17	Suc
Wood, John	Ensign	16-08-81	FR	Cato	Capt.J.Collins	AM 45-566	
Wood, Jonathan	Ensign	22-06-78	FR	Ling	Capt.Beckwith	AM 21-145	
Wood, Joseph	Lt Col	06-01-76	FR	37th		PC 79	
Wood, Joseph	Ensign	17-12-81	CA	28th	Capt.R.Hardcastle	AM 48-27	
Wood, Joseph Jr.	Capt	29-11-75	FR	2nd		MM 11:50	
Wood, Peter	2nd Lt	05-07-77	CH	12th		RC 2-1170	Mn
Wood, Robert	Capt	29-11-75	FR	2nd		MM 11:50	
Wood, William	Ensign	03-01-76	CV	15th	Capt.E.Wood	SC 49-104	OC
Wood, William	1st Lt	21-03-83			Barge"Defence"	AM 48-386	
Woodal, Edward	Ensign	03-01-76	QA	5th	Capt.Wm.Pryor	SC 49-103	OC
Woodland, James	2nd Lt	11-03-79	KE	27th	Capt.J.Day	AM 21-320	
Woodward, Benjamin	Ensign	20-05-78	DO	19th	Capt.T.Eccleston	AM 21-97	
Woodward, Benjamin	2nd Lt	16-12-79	DO	Lwr	Capt.N.Manning	AM 43-37	
Woodward, Joseph	Ensign	26-08-77	SM	Up	Capt.J.Roach	AM 16-346	
Woodward, Joseph	2nd Lt	18-11-79	SM	Up	Capt.R.Rapier	AM 43-18	
Woodward, William Jr	Ensign	22-02-81	AA	Svrn	Capt.P.Warfield	AM 45-322	
Woolford, James	Ensign	11-06-77	DO	19th	Capt.Jones	AM 11-282	
Woolford, James	Capt	20-05-78	DO	Lwr		AM 21-97	OC
Woolford, James	Ensign	20-05-78	DO	Lwr	Capt.R.Jones	AM 21-97	
Woolford, James	Capt	23-06-79	DO	Lwr	Fishing Creek	MH 4-70	Res
Woolford, Levin	2nd Lt	20-05-78	DO	19th	Capt.T.Eccleston	AM 21-97	
Woolford, Levin	1st Lt	16-12-79	DO	Lwr	Capt.N.Manning	AM 43-37	
Woolford, Stephen	QM	01-06-77	DO	19th		AM 11-282	
Woolford, Stephens	Capt	30-07-76				AM 12-144	Mn
Woolford, Thomas	2nd Lt	18-08-77	DO	ES	Capt.Noel	AM 16-337	
Woolhide, Henry	Ensign	01-02-77	FR	37th		AM 16-106	
Woollick, Henry	Ensign	10-01-77	FR	37th	Capt.Martindear	AM 16-54	

APPENDIX A - COMMISSIONED OFFICERS

Name	Rank	Date	Cty	Bn	Company	Ref.	Notes
Woolrich, Philip	Ensign	04-02-77	BA		Capt.W.Wilkinson	AM 16-114	
Woolsey, George	Ensign	---04-76	BA	Town	Capt.Wm.Buchanan	RB 13-74	
Woolsey, George	2nd Lt	06-06-76	BA	Town	Capt.Smith	AM 11-467	
Woolsey, George		07-11-76	BA			SP 2694	Ref
Wootton, Richard	1st Lt	03-01-76	PG	25th	Capt.H.Magruder	SC 49-109	OC
Wootton, Richard		25-09-76				AM 12-299	Res
Wootton, Singleton	2nd Lt	03-01-76	PG	25th		SC 49-109	Mn
Wootton, Singleton	1st Lt	01-05-78	PG	25th	Capt.H.Magruder	AM 21-62	
Wootton, Wm.Turner	QM	13-01-76	PG	25th		PC 86	
Worley, Thomas	1st Lt	- -	WA			FP 1-129	Mn
Worth, Jonathan	1st Maj	08-05-77	KE	27th		AM 16-243	
Worthington, John	1st Lt	22-02-76	AA	Svrn	Capt.Hall	AM 11-178	
Worthington, Nicholas Jr.	2nd Lt	22-02-76	AA	Svrn	Capt.Hall	AM 11-178	
Worthington, Nicholas Jr.	Capt	19-06-77	AA	7th		AM 16-294	
Worthington, Nicholas	1st Maj	12-01-76	AA	Svrn		PC 78	
Worthington, Nicholas	Colonel	26-01-77	AA	Svrn		AM 16-77	
Worthington, Nicholas	Capt	02-03-78	AA	Svrn		AM 16-525	
Worthington, Thos.of Nich	2nd Lt	19-09-77	AA	ElkR	Capt.Burgess	AM 16-380	
Worthington, William	1st Lt	18-10-82	AA	Svrn	Capt.V.Conoway	AM 48-288	
Wright, Benjamin	Ensign	11-04-76	AA	7th	Capt.Watts	AM 11-327	
Wright, Gavin	Ensign	22-09-77	SO	PrAn	Capt.T.Irving	AM 16-381	
Wright, Isaac	Ensign	17-12-81	CA	14th	Capt.T.Eaton	AM 48-27	
Wright, Jacob	Capt	20-05-78	DO	3rd		AM 21-98	
Wright, Jacob	Capt	23-08-81	DO	Up		DO 230	Mn
Wright, James	1st Lt	06-07-76	DO		Capt.Waters	AM 11-553	
Wright, James	Capt	20-05-78	DO	3rd		AM 21-98	
Wright, James	Capt	23-06-79	DO	Up		FP 2-73	Mov
Wright, Jonathan	Lt	06-06-76	PG	25th		AM 11-553	CM
Wright, Nathaniel	Capt	16-03-76	QA			AM 11-254	
Wright, Robert	2nd Lt	03-01-76	AA	5th	Capt.G.Baynard	SC 49-108	Com
Wright, Thomas	Colonel	12-01-76	QA	20th		PC 78	
Wright, Thomas	Colonel	18-03-76	QA	20th		PC 260	Ref
Wroth, James	Ensign	22-06-78	CE	Bohe	Capt.J.W.Veazey	AM 21-145	
Wylie, Luke	Capt	31-10-80	BA	GPUp		AM 43-345	Suc
Wyly, Greenbury	Ensign	23-10-81	BA	GPUp	Capt.Wm.Lane	AM 45-650	
		- -					
Yates, Jonathan	Capt	07-03-76	CH			AM 11-206	
Yates, Jonathan	Maj	19-01-81	CH	12th		AM 45-280	
Yates, Thomas	Capt	25-09-80	BA	Town		AM 43-303	
Yates, Thomas	Capt	18-10-80	BA	Town		FP 1-93	Res
Yates,---	Capt	28-01-77	BA			AM 16-86	Mn
Yieldhall, Gilbert	Ensign	22-02-76	AA	Svrn	Capt.Hall	SC 49-107	OC
Yieldhall, Gilbert	Ensign	14-06-76	AA	Svrn	Capt.Hall	SC 49-107	Res
Yost, Henry	1st Lt	22-06-78	WA	2ndW	Capt.J.Funk	AM 21-145	
Yost, Herman	Capt	29-11-75	FR	1st		MM 11:50	
Yost, John Hd.	Capt	03-03-77	FR	33rd		MM 4:379	Mn
Yost, Tobias	Capt	04-08-80	MO	Lwr	Capt.D.Rhintzell	AM 43-248	
Young, Abraham	2nd Lt	12-09-77	MO	29th	Capt.W.Johnson	AM 16-373	
Young, Abraham	2nd Lt	07-12-76	MO		Capt.J.Johnson	AM 12-511	
Young, George	Ensign	17-11-80	WA			FP 1-129	Mn
Young, Hugh	2nd Lt	-04-76	BA	Town	Capt.J.Sterrett	RB 13-74	
Young, Jacob	Capt	16-02-76	FR		Minuteman	AM 11-165	Mn
Young, James	Capt	25-09-80	BA	Town		AM 43-303	OC

APPENDIX A - COMMISSIONED OFFICERS

Name	Rank	Date	Cty	Bn	Company	Ref.	Notes
Young, James	Capt	17-04-81	BA	Town		SC 49-106	Res
Young, John Tully	Capt	25-05-76	BA	GP		AM 11-444	
Young, Samuel	QM	06-01-76	CE	18th		PC 80	
Young, William	1st Lt	12-09-75	HA		#1	PR 105	
Youns, David	2nd Lt	15-05-76	FR	UpDt	Light Inf Co	AM 11-426	
Yudi, Philip	Ensign	29-11-75	FR	1st	Capt.H.Yost	MM 11:50	

APPENDIX B: MUSTER ROLLS AND OTHER LISTS

ANNE ARUNDEL COUNTY

6 Mar 1776/At a meeting of several inhabitants of the neighbourhood of Herring Creek Church in Ann Arundel County in the Province of Maryland on Wednesday the sixth Day of March Anno Domini 1776 The following persons resolved to form themselves into a company of militia, agreeable to a Resolve of the Convention of said Province held at the City of Annapolis on the (blank) day of December then last. And thereupon severally subscribed their names to the form of enrolment directed by a former Convention of the said Province held at the City of Annapolis aforesaid on the 26th Day of July Anno Domini 1775, in the following order to wit.
Adam Allen; Benjamin Harrison; Joseph Allengham; John Chew; John Dowell; John Franklin; Joseph Deale; Richard Weems; Thomas Mace; James Medcalf; William Medcalf; Benjamin Ward; Horatio Harrison; Henry Wilson; Richard Wells; Edward Fox; James Hutton; Thomas Neale; William Tucker; Gedeon Dare; Joseph Hill; William Arnold; Jacob Franklin; Fardenando Battee Senior; Jonathan Jones; Nathaniel Chew; Ezekiel Gott; Thomas Larkin; Thomas Crutchley; Benjamin Wells; Benjamin Battee Shearbut; Benjamin Attwell Junior; George Morrison; John Chaffey; John Coale; William Eaton; Moses Williams; Robert Atwell; John Pibus; Thomas Deale; John Crandall; Thomas Lane; Richard Shearbut; Abraham Burkhead; Thomas Shearbut; John Battee; Thomas Laughlin; Samuel Atwell; Jacob Welsh; Joseph Gott; William Selman; Kinsey Johns; Fardenando Battee Junr. Immediately after which enrolment the(y) proceeded to a choice of Officers by Ballot. And the choice falling on the following persons they were declared duly elected. Vizt. Richard Weems Captain. Messrs. Gideon Dare and Joseph Allengham Lieutenants. Benjamin Harrison Ensign. Messrs John Chew, Jacob Franklin, John Franklin and Nathaniel Chew Sergants, Messrs. John Dowell, Fardenando Battee Sen(i)or, Jonathan Jones, and Joseph Hill Corporals. And Edward Fox appointed Clerk. [Md. Hist. Society, MS. 1814]

5 Oct 1776/Petition of Capt. Richard Chew's Company of Col. John Weem's Battalion, Anne Arundel County. Asking "for a new choice of commissioned officers," first, because after the election for second lieutenant held on August 9 a candidate was denied sight of the poll; second, the officers offered to cancel the fines of those who would vote for Richard Harrrison; third, the captain and ensign have spoken against poor people in general, as in the attached deposition of Gilbert Hamilton Smith.
Signed: Francis Birckhead, Francis Birckhead, Jr., John Birckhead, John Birckhead, Jr., Joseph Birckhead, Matthew Birckhead, Nehemiah Birckhead, Nehemiah Birckhead of Samuel, William Fisher, Benjamin French (M), Richard Joice, Morgan Jones (M), Thomas Lane, William Larkins (M), Abraham Janquary (M), Richard Joice, Morgan Jones (M), Thomas Lane, William Larkins (M), Samuel Lewin, Richard Randall, Daniel Searles, Gideon Shoemaker, John Skinner, Gilbert Hamilton Smith, Lancelot Stallings (M), Lewis Stevens, Isaac Tucker (M), Seaborn Tucker (M), Abraham Turner (M), Thomas Turner (M), William Turner (M), West [?] Ward, Francis Whittington, Jr., Francis Whittington, Sr., William Whittington, Hopewell Wood (M), John Wood (M), Morgan Wood (M), William Wood (M), and Robert Young. [p. 95 of Calendar of Maryland State Papers - The Red Books. Also printed in Archives of Md., XII, pp. 322-3.]

APPENDIX B: MUSTER ROLLS AND OTHER LISTS

21 Oct 1776/A list of men enrold by Capt. Watkins [Anne Arundel County] and his officers for the Service of this State.
Edward Hall; Richd. Hall; James Warfield; Isaac Dycus; Henry Riston; Benj. Simpson; Gedion Gary; William Whithim; Michl. Hughs; Henry Shiply; Henry Cook; Charl. Hern; Machl. Hawk; Silvanus Potee; Charles Lowery; William Davis; Mark Ryly; Aquila Dorsey; Sam. Crowe; Gilbert Dorsey; Beal Gaither; Jon.(?) Harley; John Lappe; Michl Maller; Thos. North; Isaac Barton; William Gorwood; Robert Harris; Robert Smithe; Edward Hensley; Isaac Clivey; William Robuck; Benj. Palmorne; John Williams; Michl. Green; Thos. Burton; Cornialus ODonaly; George May; Nathaniel Macmani; Edward Gale; Robert Stewart; Gassy Watkins of Jno.; John Cross; Gasy Chambers Watkins; John Lee; Nicholas Pindell; John Swan; Jerre Thomas; Joseph Richardson; John Brewer; Ray Vinem; John Smith; Aaron Watkins; Thomas Bagnall; Nicholas Knighton; Hugh Chaplin; Benj. Gravel; Saml. Brogdan; William Williams; James Reed; Thos. Franklin; John Perkinson; Richd. Vinall; Thomas Philpott; Stephen Nicholson; John Elliott; Robert Hawkes; Mathew Elliott; John Marr; Anthony Smith; John Onion; John Rhodes; Vachal Ijams; Cele Tydings; Caleb Stewart; John Jervis; Vacey Butler; Edward Powell; Nath. Worthington; John Gray. [Md. Hist. Soc., MS 1814]

15 Aug 1778/Severn Battalion [7th Battalion] - Anne Arundel County. Lists names, viz: Henry Ballman, Nicholas Worthington, John Sears, Robert Lusby, Robert Davidge, Benjamin Fish, Zachariah Jacobs, John Walker, John Boone, Joshua Merriken, Joseph Warfield, Philomen Warfield, Thomas Warfield, John Marriott, Joseph Warfield, Joshua Gray, Caleb Owings, John Shaw. [Calendar of Maryland State Papers - The Red Books. Also see Archives of Maryland, XXI, p. 207]

20 March 1779/An Independent Company of militia of Annapolis, Md.
Gilbert Middleton Captn.; John Callahan, 1st Lt; Wm Goldsmith, 2d Lt; Cor's Mills, 3d Lt; John Howard 1st Sgt; John Chalmbners, 2d Sgt; Thos. Sparrow, 3d Sgt; Nichs. Hannah, 4th do.; Wm Middleton, 1st Corpl; James Freeland, 2d Corpl; Wm Howard, 3d Corpl; John Ball Ju'r, 4th Corpl; Archd. Chisholme; Justice Siebert; Robt. Johnson; Wm Tuck; Chas. Maccubbin; Joseph Middleton; Daniel Fowler; Jonathan Parker; Edwd. Sefton; John Green; Daniel Wells; Richd. Tompson; John Wells; Oliver Whedon; Wm Fowler; Jubb Fowler; Nichs. Brewer; Robt. Reynolds; Absalom Ridgley; Christian Lybrant; Wm Caldwell; Chas. Ratclift; Robt. Clarke; Robt. Berry; Wm Sands; Henry Dawson; Daniel Coalter; Thos. Hammond; Wm Maw; Edward Maw; Cha' Barbor; Thos. Lewis; John Allen; Zachariah Norris; Adam Richardson; Jonathan Wiltshire; Thos. Graham; Elisha Hall; John Peaboddy; Thos. Copper Larson; Edward McGrill; Thos. Sands; Nichs. Valliant; James Taylor; Gabriel Duvall; Alexander Tompson.
[Vol. 21, Arch. of Md., p. 325]

BALTIMORE COUNTY

3 Dec 1774/The Baltimore Independent Cadets
Mordecai Gist; A. McLure; James Clarke; Barnet Eichelburger; Rich'd Cary, Jr.; Christ'r Hughes; Wm. Beard; Henry Sheaf; Robert McKim; Alex. Donaldson; Walter Roe; William Sterett; John McLure; Samuel Smith; John Smith, Jr.; J. Kennedy; G. McCall; J. Hudson; Thomas Lansdale; J. Govane; William McCreery;

BALTIMORE COUNTY

Hugh Young; Wm. Hammond; William Stone; Abm. Risteau; Moses Darley; Robert Buchanan; George Lux; N. Ruxton Moore; David Plunket; Matt'w Scott; John Spear; Philip Graybell; Thos. Russell; David Hopkins; John Lanavan; A. McKim; J. Riddle; Brian Philpot; Charles McConnell; Christ'r Johnston; Thomas Ewing; Robert Portteous; Christ'r Leon; Caleb Shields; David Evans; Simon Vashon; David McMechon; George Peter Keeports; John Weatherburn; Matthew Patton; Robert Long; Robert Brown; Hez. Waters; Wm. Geaton; John Deitch; Thomas Jones; James Somervell; Joseph Magoffin; George Mathews. Baltimore Committee off Observation, 1774-6. Signed 3 Dec 1774. [Maryland Historical Magazine, Vol. 4, p. 372]

16 June 1777/Muster roll of Capt. Henry Sheaff's Company.
Captain Henry Sheaff; Lieutenants Brittingham Dickeson and Robert Moore; Ensign Caleb Shields; Sergeants William Adams, John Brown, and John Cannon; Corporals John Gordon, William Jacobs, and Abraham Jackson; Privates Edward Allen, John Bodden, Dennis Brian, Samuel Burtis, William Clower, William Davey, Lewis D'Sheild, Henry Evans, Alexander Finlater, Peter Frick, John Gibbons, Andrew Granger Andrew Grayble, Christopher Grisler, Caleb Hall, Patrick Hannon, William Hays, William Hobbs, Andrew Hooke, William Johnson, Michael Kripps, Philip Littig, Yost Littig, George Litzinger, Arthur McCarter, Rowland McQuillan, Alexander Munro, William OHay, Henry Philips, George Prestman, John Proctor, Christian Rees, Hammond Richards, John Sheller (drummer), John Sigler, Francis Smith, Valentine Sneider, William Spencer (clerk), John Storke, John Wale, George Warner, Simon Sedge, William Wilson, Henry Worthington. [Calendar of Md. State Papers - The Red Books]

7 June 1781/[Colo. Benj. Nicholson, Baltimore, to Gov. Lee]
Inclosed is a roll of a Troop of Horse wch. I have embodied in the forest. They have agreed to equip themselves, but the scarcity of cash will prevent their compleating it quickly indeed some of them are scarcely able. The Holster Caps and sword belts I believe are ready. Pistols are to be had in this Place but I know not where to get swords unless we get them made, whc. was the intention of the Troops. If the State could furnish pistols & Swords the Troop might be greatly enlarged and would be in immediate readiness. It was at the solicitation of the youth in my Neighborhood that I undertook the embodying and comd. of the Troop. It is my wish to detain my rank as Lt. Colo. If your exly. can consistanly encorporate Horse enough to give me that Comd. If not tis the desire of the Troop to be annexed to the Batln. to wch. I belong & should it be enabled to go on duty wou'd wish to go wth. them. If this should be improper - I can't be worse than my word & must resign my rank & take the comd. as Captain of Troop I will use my endeavour to get them equiped as soon as posible & flatter myself when so will be useful - You'l find among our number some Veteran Officers, who have left the Continental Service & whilst in served wth. reputation.
    Benjamin Nicholson; Charles Carnan; Thos. Cromwell; Robt. Lyon; Stephen Shelmerdine; John Colegate; John Cockey; Robt. Carnan; Joshua Gist; Thos. Nicholson; Benja. Todd; Richd. Colegate; Bazil Tracey; Walter Bosley; Richd. Britton; Edwd. Ford; John Dodd; Roger Boyce; Thos. Risteau; John Summers; John Gist; Joshua Cockey; Benja Bond; Christian Gore; Jas. Howard; Fredk. Counselman; Jno. Worthington; James Trapnell; Joseph Butler; Ephrm. Owings; Richd. Johns; Thos. Cradock; John Bryson. NB - Since the writing the above Colo. Smith informs me he has order to equip us. [Calendar of Maryland State Papers. Also see Archives of Maryland, p. 274]

APPENDIX B: MILITIA ROLLS AND OTHER LISTS

25 June 1781/Baltimore Troops of Horses Commanded by Capt. [Nicholas] R. More as Appraised by Bernard O'Niell; Leonard M. Deakins; Thos. Beall of Geo. [The following persons were credited with possessing one or more horses which were described as to color, age and value. Only the names of the individuals are presented here.]
Catp. [N.] R. Moore; Thos. Russel, Lt.; Mark Pringle, Cornet; Doctr. Gooding; Wm. King, Q.M.; Francis Grant; John Steuart; John McColester; Alexr. McCim; Major T. Yates; Danl. Carroll Ball.; David Reese; Robert Harris; Nathan Levie; Joseph Lemon; James Jaffrey; George Turnbull; Saml. Hollingsworth; Will. Taylor; Chas. [Myers?]; Jno. Spear; Joseph Foster; Danl. Hopkins; Abraham Vanbibber; John Kirwin; Jno. Jeffers; Thorogood Smith; James Stirling; Will Buchanan; George Hamond; James Ryan; Matthew Ridley; Thos. Hollingsworth; Mathew Patten; Bryan Philpott; Luther Martin. [Calendar of Maryland State Papers - The Red Books. Also see Archives of Maryland, XLVII, pp. 312-313.]

CALVERT COUNTY

1777 Aug 10/Petition from William Disney, John Howard, and others, Calvert County. To Gov. Thoms. Johnson. Protest the "unhappy removal" of Capt. James Patterson as commander of county militia; Pattersons's successor is "totally obnoxious" to the county.
Signed: Disney, Howard and Henry Askey, Joseph Blake, Jr., James Brown, [Orton?] Chambers, William Deale, Henry Dorsett, Joseph Edes, Samual Freeman, Alby Gipson, Edward Griffen, John Griffen, Edward Hansin ([Elisha?] Hardesty, John Hardesty, Sr., Jorge Hardesty, Thomas Hardesty, Jr., Thomas Hardesty of John, Thomas Hardesty of Joseph, James Hargney, Hugh Hemsworth, Richard [Hollendshead?], Henry Hunt, John King, Henry King, James Lisbey, George Mackon, Mark Marshall, Richard Marshall, Thomas Marshall, James Mules, John Norris, William [Nowrie?], William Peacocke, Robert Peters, Tayman Philpotts, James Puskim, Daniel Roff, Jr., Jobe Roughtten, Isaac Simmons, Isak Stalling, Thomas Stone, Jr., William Stone, Benjamin Sunderland, John Sunderland, Daniel Prout, Thomas Sunderland, Josias Sunderlane, Thomas Sunderlane, Thomas Sunderling, William Watson, Henry Wattson, William Weems, Daniel Wenner, Jr., John [Wilkinson?], Benjamin Wilson. Two signatures illegible. [p. 111 of Calendar of Maryland State Papers - The Blue Books].

1778 June 12/Petition of Capt. John MacKall's Company. [15th Battalion] Members of Col. Joseph Wilkinson's battalion ask to be commanded by Lt. William Dare.
Signed: Philip Hunt, Benjamin Ware, Tayman Philpot, Thomas Sunderland, Thomas Wilson, Benjamin Wilson, Benjamin Askew, Samuel Lyles, Samuel Lyles, Jr., Thomas Lyles, Bartholomew Gibson, Henry Dowell, Henry Harrison, Samuel Dare, John Norris, Joseph Sunderland, James Ware, Richard Allsop, George Hardesty, John Sunderland, Daniel Prout, Daniel Fibbens, William Watson, William Hardesty, Rezin Sunderland, William Smith, William Parker of William, William Disney, John Gallerway, Thomas Isacke, James Nowel, Thomas Marshall, Thomas Sulivant, Richard Harrison, Thomas Hardesty (his mark), William Barber of George, William Deale, Thomas Lyles, Jr., Richard Halanhead, James Marquess, Samuel Deale, Fealder Parker, John Smith, Jacob Benton, William Sulivant, John Howard, William Lyles. [Calendar of Md. State Papers - The Red Books]

CALVERT COUNTY

1777/A Return of the militia of Calvert County. Edward Wood Capt.; Thoms. Hutchings, 1 Lieut; Thoms. Leach, 2 ditto; John Wood Ensigne
Francis Hutchings; David Bowin; John Robinson; Benjn. Jefferson Junr; Henry Jefferson; John H. Hollandshead; Edward Charlton; James Dotson; John Williams; Bazil Bowen for Bazl.; Talbott Williams; Winmar Ramsey; Richd. Everitt for Wm.; William Hornby; Israel Freeman; David Young; Edward Blackburn; Lorrewell Lawrence; Jona Winfield; John Hudson; Joseph Hutchings; William Younger; Bazil Bowen; John Bowen; Young Bowen; Thom. Gray; Wm. Gray B.C.; Patience Sly; Ignatious Hutchings; William Fryer; George Younger; James Brinkley; John Cullumber; John Buckingham; Edward Burkett; James Kent Burn; Sabret Wood; Leven Mackall; John Sly; Stephen Hutchings; Wm. Cullumber; John Stennett Junr; John Wood Junr; John Tucker; John Younger for Margarett; David Younger for John; Clement Hutchings; Jeremiah Cox; John Denton; Parker Bowen; Wm. Ramsey; John Younger Junr; James Bowen; Henry Gray; Isaac Bowen; Lunard Wood; Bazil Jefferson; James Wood; Joseph Younger; Wm. Gray H.P.; Samuel Sly; Peter Parker; Benjn. Stallings; Benj. H. Young; Abraham Bowen; John Hutchings; William Winnel; James Charlton; Thomas Bourn; Charles Bowen; Benjn. Dotson; Benj. Jefferson; Isaac Bowen; Walter Bowen; John Bowen for Bazil; Thomas Denton. [Md. Hist. Soc., MS 1146, Box 1]

1777/Thomas Cleland, Capt.; Joseph Ireland, 1 Liet.; Roger Hooper, 2 Liet.; Gabriel Childs, Ensign
Thomas Hardesty; John Norfolk for James; George Parker; Francis Holt; John Strickland Junr; Wm. Harris (the fifth); John Weems Junr; Richd. Isaacks; Nathan Cranford; James Scarfe; Wm. Cranford Junr; Samuel Owens; Daniel Talbott; Benj. Harris (the third); Benj. Talbott; Edward Randle; Ellis Slater; Thomas Eades; Thoms. Norfolk Junr; Leonard Barns; Joseph Strickland; James Whiley; Wm. Harris (the third); Richard Skinner; William Huntt; Henry Harrison; Benjamin Hance; Philip Dorsey; Daniel Dorsey; Benj. Dorsey; Wm. Hollandshead; Benj. Johns for Benj.; John Norfolk for John; James Cranford; Saml. Dorsey; Joseph Harris Junr; Sabrett Ruff; Henry Watson; Richard Hance; William Peacock; John Wilson Junr; John Talbott for Jos.; Jacob Eades; Richd. Harris; Robert Harrison; Wm. Allnutt Junr; Elisha Haner; Francis Dorsey; John Stanforth Junr; Wm. Strickland; Wm. Norfolk; John Dorsey Junr; James Dorsey Junr; Jacob Deale Junr; Joseph Barrs; John Conner; Wm. Harris for Wm.; Thomas Dowell; Lemuel Cranford Junr; James Wilson; Francis Hollandshead; Thomas Talbott; Richd. Turner; John Nowell Junr; Wm. Harrison (son Henry); Joseph Dorsey; John Taylor; Elisha Hall; Joseph Yates; Arther Prout; Richd. Stevens Junr. [Md. Hist. Soc., MS 1146, Box 1]

1777/Charles Williamson, Capt.; John Specknall, 1 Lieut.; Thomas Gray, 2 ditto; Daniel Kent, Ensign
Martin Wells; Lewis Cheney; Thomas Cheney; Henry Lyles; Richd. Stallings; Absolem Stallings; Newman Stallings; Bazil Specknall; Thomas Stone; Bazil Williamson; Henry Williamson; John Grahame; Gavin H.Smith; Thomas Stamp; Stephen B. Balch; Benj. Harrison; Elisha Harrison; Alexd. Williamson; Alexd. Fraizer; Edward Gantt Junr; Thomas Loyd; John Dowell; Thomas Henton Junr; John Brassar(?) Junr; Richd. Marshall; Samuel Galloway; John Jones; Elisha Hall; Martin Wells for Thom.; James Williamson; James Weems (of Jas.); Littleton Chilton; Robert Tyler; Thomas Marr; Joseph David; James Lyon; Richd. Johnson; Leonard Specknell; Wm. Johnson; John Tawneyhill; Thoms. Hinton; John Turner; Richd. Winfield; William Turner; Thomas Heathman; Benj.

APPENDIX B: MUSTER ROLLS AND OTHER LISTS

Jones; John Dockett; Danmund Crampher; Slater Britain; Edward McDaniel;
Robert Specknall; John Cox; William Wood of Edward; William Marshall;
Gilbert Nowell; Henry Seares; Richd. Gibson; James Austin; Sam. Austin; Wm.
Austin; Richd. Turner; John H. Smith. [Md. Hist. Soc., MS 1146, Box 1]

1777/Frisby Freeland, Capt; James Hughs, 1 Liut.; Edward Reynolds, 2 ditto;
Samuel Hance, Ensign
George Watson; Joseph Hardesty Junr; James Skinner; Richd. Talbott; Nemiah
Birkhead; Wm. Edmondson; Wm. Edmonds; Kinsey Hance; Moses Jones; John
Lavielle; Jacob Freeland; Benj. Harris; Charles Downing; Richard Downing;
Richd. Hardesty; Zacheus Allnutt; John Miller; Dunbar Williams; Young Cox;
Charles Owens; Benj. Wood; James King; Sabrett Card; James Norfolk; Jesse
Fowler; Benj. Holt; John Elliot; Wm. Wood; George Mackfarland; Francis
Williams; John Sumervill; Benj. Harris Junr; Leonard Wood; Joseph Essex;
Joshua Leach; John Stanforth; Sampson Crane; Wm. Ireland; Asahel Leach;
William Hunter; Gideon Dare; Isaac Essex; John Hance; Richd. Smith; Alexd.
Ogg; Jeremiah Maulding; Philip Dorsey Junr; Philip Talbott; James Weems
Junr; Richd. Evans; John Dorsey (lined through); Thomas Tucker; James
Mackall; John Barns; Isaac Miller; Jonathan Wood; John Ireland; Wm. Sergant
Johnson; James Sewell; Benj. Hance; Peregrin Freeland; James Aulnutt;
Abraham Rhodes; John Strickland; John Lawrance; John Tucker; John Woolf;
Thomas Lyon; John Norfolk of James; Hugh Ryan; Samuel Skinner; Robert
Skinner Junr; Wm. McDaniel Joseph Wood. [Md. Hist. Soc., MS 1146, Box 1]

1777/Walter Smith, Capt.; John Turner, 1 Lieut.; John Clara, 2 ditto; Thoms.
Johnson, Ensign; John Manning; James Mills; John Gray; Charles Dawkins;
James Owens; William Dawkins Junr; Thomas Freeman; George Young; Wm. A.
Hellen; Nathan Blackburn; Zach. Blackburn; Charles Blackburn; Arthur
Conwill; Moses Milley; Dawkins Hellen; John Broom Junr; William Hall; Jesse
Dawkins; Benj. Mackall of John; John McDowell; Thomas Willen; David
Wilkinson; Nathaniel Dare; Edward Willen; Richd Day; Jos. Vansweringen Junr;
Wm. D. Broome; John Mackall; Alexd. Dawkins; Joseph Dawkins; Jesse
Dorremple; Thomas Somervell; George Denton; John Denton; Thos. Blackburn;
Moses P. Duke; Charles Flowers; Bryan Taylor; Edmund Hellen; William
Barefoot; Joseph Gardiner; William White; John Cullumber; Samuel Johnson;
Michl. Culpepper; John Sedwick; Isaac Hooper; Isac Monnett; Wm. Barber;
Abraham Hooper; Robert Gardener; John Carter; Daniel Lavielle; Francis
Hutchings; William Dawkins; Henry Tanner; John Wilkinson; Peter Hellen Junr;
William Dorremple; Christian Panter; Joseph Hance; Thomas Broome; William
Pattison; Jacob Hellen; James Rigby; Jeremiah Cullember; Benj. Dixon; John
Cotton; Abraham Lavielle; John Freeman; Benj. Blackburn; David Blackburn;
James Gray; John Conwill; John Bond. [Md. Hist. Soc., MS 1146, Box 1]

1777/James Grahame, Capt.; Peregreine Fitzhugh, 1 Liet.; Thoms. Jones, 2
ditto; William Kelty, Ensign; Elisha Hardesty; Wm. Weems; John Durumple;
Joseph Cowman; Wm. Peace(?); Wm. Scott; Saml. Trott; Thomas Hardesty; Robert
McKay; Richard Deale; Henry Marshall Benj. Stallings; William Stephens;
Henry Hardesty; David Weems; Wm. Stone; Wm. Turner Junr; Peter Creedy;
Richard. Hinton; Saml. Whittington; William Stallings; Thomas Charlton; John
Gibson of Peter; John Gibson of John; Jacob Eades; Wm. Nowell; John
Robinson; James Jones; Stephen Allingham; George Donaldson; Richd.
Stallings; Saml. Freeman; Martin Marshall; James Weems (of David); Leonard

CALVERT COUNTY

Piles; John Stallings; Henry King; James Brown; James Deale; Henry Deale; Dennis Sulivant; Hugh Warner; John Rode; Thomas Hardesty; John Gibson; Richard Hinton; William King; John King Junr; Richd. Scrivener; John Whittington; Benj. Leach; Thomas Ireland; Joseph Smith; Levin Ballard; John Shean; Saml. Trott of Thoms.; Daniel Febbins; Dr. Thos. Gantt. [Md. Hist. Soc., MS 1146, Box 1]

1777/Richd. Parran, Capt.; Daniel Rawlings Jur(?), Lieut.; Edmund Clare, 2 ditto; Jesse Jacob Bourne, Ensign
Gideon Ireland; Benj. Ellt; Benj. Parran; Alexd. Parran; John Hungerford; Wm. Stallings; Dower Greve; David Avis; David Platford; Wm. Scott; Andrew Duke; Wm. Powell; Robert Day Junr; David Hunter Junr; Nathan Baker Senr; Nathan Baker Junr; Jeremiah Cotton; Robert Day; Isaac Oystin Baker; Wm. Baker; Ortor(?) Huntt; Wm. Allen; Jesse Day; James Walker; John Patterson; James Poole Junr; Wm. Crane; James Ward; James Davis; Benj. Benyon; John Parran Junr; John Avis; Benj. Hellen; Richd. Conwell; Richard. Poole; Daniel Smith; Wm. Johnson; Obid Dixon; Fielder Parker; George Wheeler; Jesse Wood; Henry Stallings; John Grover Junr; Alex. Somervell; Daniel Rawlings; Scarth Hellen; Charles Som. Parran; Isaac Baker Junr; Thomas Simmons; Abraham Low; Nathan Day; John Parran; James Dixon; Ward Nuton; Charles Somers. Parran; James Stallings; Thomas Benyon; Richd. Allen; Jesse Bourne; Jos. Breden; John Rawlings; James Ivey; Isaac Baker; John Baker; Charles Allen; Daniel Day; John Clara Junr; James Hendly; Robert Greves; George Moore; Isaac Gardener; Wm. Hunter; Thomas Parran; John Lusby; John Ivey; John Allen. [Md. Hist. Soc., MS 1146, Box 1]

1777/Benjamin Bond, Capt; Nathan Willson, 1 Lieut.; Allien [Allen] Roberts, 2 ditto; John Mills, Ensign; Jonathan Wedge; Jesse Dixon; Thomas Denton; James Lawrence; Matthew Current; Robert Games; Jesse Cullumber; John Gardener Junr; Absolem Games; James Kirshaw Junr; Benj. Tucker; John Pantry; Kinsey Gardener; Benj. Cullumber; James McKinney; John McKinney; John Rigby; Jeremiah Pattison; Benj. Younger; James Dawkins; William Miller; John Williams; John Yoe; Thomas Pattison; Charles Cullumber; John Avis; Richd. Wilkinson; Thomas Tucker for Derrimple; William Brinkley; Daniel Young; John Asgrue; William Conwell; Edward Truman; Francis Spencer; John Pards; Francis Panter(?); John Melly; Isaac Kent; William Gardener Junr; Easom Edmons; John Tucker; Bazil Brooke; Thoms. Mackall; Thomas Tawney; John R. Eagan; William Wats; John Dare; Jervis Avis; John Willson; Thomas Sedwick; James Melly; Thoms. Tucker for John; Howerton Games; Edward Bradie; Richd Cullumber; Guideon Dare; William Card; Thomas Everett; Edward Denton; Nathaniel Cullumber; Jeremiah Wood; Richd. Everett; Richrd Pattison; Charles Dawkins; James Stewart; James Sollers; Wm. Gardener Senr.; Joseph Tawney; Patison Freeman; Joseph Johnson; Joseph Johnson (Clifts); Leonard Mills; James Hellen; William Yoe; Richard Gray. [Md. Hist. Soc., MS 1146, Box 1]

1777/Richard Lane, Captain; James Leach, 1 Liet.; Martin Norris, 2 ditto; Gilbert Ireland, Ensign
Joseph Camden; John Dicks; George Smith; Samuel Wood; Thomas Smith; Leonard Tawneyhill; Nathan Smith; Samuel Griffin; Daniel Busey; Burdin Crosby; Lewis Jones; Jacob Carr; John Due; Philip Davis; Marmaduke Dove; John Elisha; William Fowler; William Gover; William Hammond; Seaborn Carr; Wm. Johnson for Jerem.; William Lyles Junr; William Lambath; James Whittington; Samuel

APPENDIX B: MUSTER ROLLS AND OTHER LISTS

Northey; James Pybus; Joseph Smith (Crownes); Jeremiah Smith; John Smith (son Jos.); Thomas Simpson; Abraham Sandsbery; Joseph Stricklin; Joseph Tayman; Daniel Wash (?); Joseph Wilkinson; Thomas Wills Junr; George Whiley; William Whittington; John Watson; David Watson; Thomas Woodfield; William Allien; George Bayfield; William Beausey; Charles Beausey Junr; Joseph Crosbey; John Crosbey; John Baptis Deli Frany; Lewis Griffith son John; Henry Johnson; John King; Benjamin Lane for Richd. William Peace; Mordicay Smith; Daniel Smith; John Smith; Jesse Smith; Marshal Stone; William Tayman; James Tawnyhill; Alex. Turner; Zacharia Turner; Francis Whittington Junr; Henry Whiley; Marshal Griffith; Acquilla Hammond; Alex. Wilson Magruder; Samuel Carr; John Johnson. [Md. Hist. Soc., MS 1146, Box 1]

1777/Frederick Skinner, Capt.; Wm. Dare, first a Captain (lined through); James Pattison, 1 Lieut.; John Wilkinson Huntt, 2 ditto; Joseph Blake, Ensign; John Norris; Thomas Sunderland; William Disney; George Hardesty; Thomas Marshall; Bartholemew Gibson; Benjamin Ward; William Sullivant; Wm. Parker son Wm.; Mickal Peign; William Lyles; Tayman Philpott; Joseph Blake; Thomas Sulivant; Thomas Lyles; Thomas Wilson; Thoms. Hardesty son Jos.; John Sunderland; James Ward; Hugh Hensworth; Josiah Sunderland; Daniel Prout; Thomas Blake Junr; Thomas Isaac; Henry Watson; Benjamin Asque; John Griffen; Samuel Deale; Sam. Lyles Junr; James Marquis; Benj. Wilson; Richd. Harrison; George Mackey; Wm. Hardesty; Thomas Lyles Junr; Michal Catterton; Joseph Hardesty; Henry Harrison; Richd. Ward Junr; John Howard; Samuel Dare; Henry Dowell; Richard Howard; Wm. Smith; Henry Huntt; Richard Alsops; John Griffin Junr; Richard Howard; John King; Robert Peters; James Hemmingway; Philip Huntt; James Smith; Edward Ansell; James Mules; Daniel Ross Junr; Isaac Simmons; Jacob Perkins; William Deale; Samuel Lyles; William Nowell; Helarey Wilson; Edward Griffin; John Galloway; Abraham Ross; Fielder Parker Junr; Wm. Parker son George; Isaac Stallings; Daniel Febbins. [Md. Hist. Soc., MS 1146, Box 1]

1777/Thomas Truman Greenfield, Capt; Micael Tawney, 1 Lieut.; Robert Skinner, 2 ditto; James Mackall, Ensign; Kinsey Freeman; John Norfolk Junr; Joseph Hardacer; Jacob Bowen Junr; Leonard Skinner; James Morsell; Leonard Hows; John Burkhead; John Ralph; Benj. Buckmaster; Abraham Fowler; Francis King; Henry Adderton; Richd. Stanforth; Sam. Hance Junr.; Aron Ogden; John Harrison; Robert Lee; Francis Williams Junr; Benj. Hance; Delah Taylor; Benj. Lee; George Gray; Jeremiah Leach; John Ramsey Junr; Benj. Stennet; John Dotson; James Leach; Benj. Dasheal; Isaac Eadds; Saml. Harrison; Thomas Jones Junr; Moses Ogden; John Miller; Philip Holt; Wm. Harrison of James; Wm. Harrison of Wm.; George Harrison; Benj. Fowler; Benj. King of James; John Lyon; James Ruff; Thomas Freeman; Joshua Leach Junr; Benj. Stallings; James Stanforth; Philip Sullivan; Elias Woolf; John Wiley Junr; Wm. Wood of Leonard; James Ogdin; Richd. Hudson; John Breeze; Robert Freeland; Robert Freeland Junr; John Essex; John Lansdale; David Arnold; Richd. Mayhue; Phenus Stallings; Joseph Matrece(?); Edward Steward; Philip Dossey; Clement Skinner; Elisha Ogden; Wm. Howes; Edward Talbott; Abraham Osque; Joseph Hall; Henry Buckmaster; Aron Williams Junr. [Md. Hist. Soc., MS 1146, Box 1]

1780 July 14/Calvt. County
Sir. I have inclosed you a list of the Military Stores in this County except 2 small Barrells, and a little lead, which were left some time ago at

CALVERT COUNTY

the mouth of Patuxent in the care of Mr. Edmund Clare; the weight of which I cannot ascertain, but will as soon as possible, and transmit it by the Post. I have sent down to St. Leonards Creek, and order'd the musketts &c. stowed there to be brought to Hunting Town to be clean'd and repair'd if necessary. The Number of militia enrolled in this County agreeable to the late Act of Assembly amounts to 734 men in one Battalion -
Capt Woods Company 74; Capt. Cleland 67; Capt. Greenfields 67; Capt. Wilsons 76; Capt. Smiths 74; Capt. Leatch's 55; Capt. Skinners 66; Capt. Graham's 53; Capt. Parrans 86; Capt. Freelands 59; Capt. Williamson's 57 - 734.
  We were obliged to enroll more men in some Company's than the Act of Assembly requires, for their residences was so great from the place where the others exercised, that they could not attend.
I am your Excely's most ... sevt. Benj. Mackall...
[Md. Hist. Soc., MS 1146, Box 1]

CAROLINE COUNTY, 28th Battalion

From the Scharf Collection, held by the State Archives -
A Return of the Twenty Eight Battallion of Militia belonging to Caroline County and State of Maryland Taken and Returned this Thirteenth Day of August Anno Domini 1777 By William Whitely Lieutenant and Commander in Chief of the aforesaid County.

1777 Aug 13/William Hopper, Capt; Henry Casson jun. 1 Lieut; James Seth, 2 Lieut; Solomon Kenting, Ensign; Robert wls; Henry Baker; James Baker; Edward Barwick; James Barwick; William Bell; William Bell jun; Robert Bell; Asa Banning; John Barwick; Ezekiel Cosill; Able Chilton; James Burtice; David Colwell; Edward Colwell; Thomas Casson; Matthew Derochbroom; John Deroachbroom; Aaron Diett; William Dulaney; Dudley Fisher; William Hopkins; William Hardcastle; Walter Jackson; Jacob Jump; Andrew Jump; Thomas Jump; Peter Jump; Allemby Jump; Solomon Jump; Isaac Jump; William Jump; Benjamin Jump; Elijah Jump; Christopher Jump; Thomas Keets; James Mason; John Nelson; James Overstocks; Francis Porter; William Purnall; Thomas Purnall; William Purnall junr; Richard Priest; George Spence; Benjamin Stevins; John Stant; Herrington Sylvester; William Sylvester; Matthew Tilghman; John Tharpe; John Thawley; Edward Thawley; John Wootters; Thomas Wootters; John Williams; Solomon Webber; John Webber; Richard Wootters; James Wootters; Benja. Wooters; Lemuel Wooters; Garey Leverton; James Kenting; Henry Fisher; John Roe. Total 70. [Scharf Coll., State Arch.]

1777 Aug 13/Vincent Price, Capt; John Reynolds, 1 Lieut; James Dwigans, 2 Lieut; David Robertson, Ensign; William Dickinson; Ralph Adams; Nathan Anthony; Morgan Anthony; William Banning; Ebenezer Bright; Thomas Barrow; James Bell; Henry Bellwood; Daniel Baynard; William Burton; Henry Clift; James Clymer; Henry Coltron; Abner Clements; John Cooper; John Cooper junr; Cloudsberry Cooper; Aaron Cooper; John Cooper; Aaron Downes; William Downes; Aaron Downes junr; William Dickinson jun; James Dwiggans junr; John Dwigans; John Diggans; William Eagle; John Fountain; Massey Fountain; John Fountain junr; Aaron Floyd; John Freeman; Mathyas Freeman; Perry Gannon; John Harper; James Hicks junr; Giles Hicks junr; Levin Hicks; James Hambleton; John Hobbs; John Hobbs Junr; Jacob Hobbs; John Jones; Clement Jerborough; Samuel Kinimont;

APPENDIX B: MUSTER ROLLS AND OTHER LISTS

John King; Daniel Lambdon; Richard Loockerman; Jacob Loockerman; Edwin Luneiford(?); Thomas Leverton; Richard Mason; Daniel Martindale; David Morgan; Andrew Price; Vincent Price junr; Philip Pikc; Matthew Paulon; William Robinson junr; Richard Roe; Daniel Skinner; William Summers; William Sevorad; Benjamin Sutton; James Sutton; Henry Sharpe; Athell Stewart; William Stewart; David Vinson; James Willson; Henry Ward; Solomon Yewell. Total Amo. 76. [Scharf Coll., State Arch.]

1777 Aug 13/Henry Downes Capt; William Jackson; Thomas Hardcastle Thomas Burk; Edward Burk; John Bush; Thomas Cooper junr; John Cooper; Emanuel Craynor; William Colscott; Dennis Calahan; Francis Clymor; John Colscott junr; John Chestell(?); Nehemiah Cooper; Abroll(?) Clift; Thomas Curtice; John Dawson; Nathan Dwigans; William Gordon; Hepsebeath Gill; John Hunt; John Hill; Hanson Holson; Thomas Hicks; John Hardcastle; Aaron Hardcastle; William Hill; Henry Jones; James Jones; Robert Jones; James Jones of Jas.; John Jones of do.; Alexander King; Howell Kenting; Solomon Kenting; Benjamin Kinemont; Henry Kemp; Joshua Lucas; Henry Martindale; David Morgan; Samuel Martindale; Stephen Martindale; Peter Oxenham; Oneal Price; Nathaniel Pratt; William Perry; John Ryall; William Robinson; William Roe; Anthony Roe; Thomas Howell; Michael Smith; Nathan Smith; John Sutton; Charles Seth; Thomas Thomas; William Vaulx; Solomon Willson; William Willson; Elisha Willson; Daniel Walker; Nathan Wheatly; James Johnson; Lemuel Martindale; John Brown; McMurdy Jones; Jacob Pratt. Total Amo. 68 [Scharf Coll., State Arch.]

1777 Aug 13/William Haslett, Capt; Christopher Driver, 1 Lieut; William Rich, 2 Lieut; Robert Poslethwaite, Ensign; Peter Rich; John White junr; Robert Willson; Robert Alexander; Levin Baynard; William Baynard; Thomas Bending; Benjamin Blunt; James Bostick; Arnill Blades; John Baynard; Jonah Bradley; Thomas Bostick; Thomas Cox (Cou?); William Coock; Mark Cooper; Abram Cooper; Thomas Chance; Levi Chance; Thomas Cook; Risdon Cook; Ferdnando Casson; David Casson; Samuel Draper; John Draper; Ephraim Draper; Joseph Dixon; William Douglass; Joseph Everitt; Thomas Fountain; Samuel Fountain; James Fountain; John Griffeth; Zachariah Green; Joseph Garnor; Cloudsberry Glanden; Herrington Glandon; John Garrett; Zebulon Green; Daniel Hines; William Herd; Joseph Herd; Daniel Hughes; William Jewell; William Kelly; William Kidd; Charles Lecompte; Nathan Lecompte; Thomas Lecompte; William Long; John Long; Gallient Layne; David Melvill; Isaac Merrick; Lambert Merrick; James Pinfield; Michal McRyon; John Rogers; William Rogers; Benson Stainton; John Skiner; Frederick Skinner; Francis Sherwood; Nixon Sylvester Newnam; Thomas Skinner; Christopher Willson; Richard Willoby; Edward White; Samuel Willoby; James White; Solomon Willoby; Anthony Wise; Clark Warren; Edgar Rumbly; Jacob Rumbly; William Smith (Turk). Total amo. 81 [Scharf Coll., State Arch.]

1777 Aug 13/Thomas Hughlett, Capt.; Robert Hardcastle, 1 Lieut; Peter Harrington, Ensign; Moses Boon; Isaac Boon; William Boon, junr; Benjamin Townstind(?); Jacob Boon; Willson Boon; James Boon; John Boon; John Hand; Benjamin Rouse; Joseph Rouse; Edward Rouse; Solomon Rouse; Samuel Rouse; Bartholomew Jadwin; Nathan Kern; William Brown; Thomas Abbitt; Cooper Kenderdine; William Ewin; Thomas Strawhan; David Davis; Hugh Roberts; John Shadden; Amos Andrews; Rich Chance; Batchelor Chance; William Elliott; Henry

CAROLINE COUNTY

Henrick; William Herrick; Henry Oldfield; George Hutton; William Hutton; William Pamarr; John Hinson; Thomas Pinder; Ezerail Merrick; Jerimiah Montigue; Harrison Montigue; John Chilton; Absolom Chance; Tilghman Chance; Joseph Whitbey; James Boon; Anthony Chilton; Benjamin Whitley; William Richardson; Perry Richardson; Thomas Harrington; William Garnett; Joseph Wood; James Bartlett; William Salsberry; John Clove; Thomas Swan; William Chilton; James Hardcastle; William Parrott; James Boon; John Tolson; Ezekiel Hunter; Isaac Buckinham; John Erwin; Robert Erwin; Solomon Hardcastle; Walter Layne; Philip Richardson; John Erwin; Robert Erwin. Total Amo. 72 [Scharf Coll., State Arch.]

1777 Aug 13/William Chipley; Richard Mason; Thomas Knotts; James Boon; James Lamarr; Richard Mason (Taylor); John Lamarr; Charles Lamarr; Joseph Boon; James Sylvester; Henry Curry; William Curry; Anthony Cox(?); Joseph Matthews; Greenbury Matthews; Joseph White; Matthew Chilton; Thomas Townshend; James Coghill; Solomon Coghill; Peter Chance; Sheverall(?) Garner; Durdin Orrell; James Porter; William Auston; Edward Eubanks; Thomas Swan; Solomon Swan; Lenry(?) Beck; John Smith; Foster Boon; George Smith; Job Smith; John Purnal; Richard Purnal; John Green; Thomas Harvey; Thomas Delany; Nathaniel Knotts; Edward Beck; Aquilla Beck; Henry Eylor(?); James Barns; Phillip Kinimont; Risdon Fisher; James Fisher; Richard Fisher; Nathan Hunter; John Bryann; John Spurry; Thomas Hobbs; James Cannon; William Cannon; Solomon Cannon; Purnall Sylvester; Herrington Sylvester; William Graydock; Nathaniel Saterfield; Peter Countess; John Hancock(?); Cloudsberry Sylvester; William Buley; John Potts; Nathan Whitbey; John Storey; Hinson Glandon; Samuel Bryley; Richard Stout; Thompson Bradley; Alexander Walters (Watters?); Hinson Saterfield; Nathaniel Bradley; Perry Boon; William Knotts; Thomas Reed; James Reed; John Longfellow; Joshua Chilcutt(?); William ...pherd (Shepherd?); Robert Gadd; John Potts; Thomas Dulany. Total Amo. 81 [Scharf Coll., State Arch.]

1777 Aug 13/Samuel Jackson, Capt; Ezekiel Robinson, 1 Lieut; Solomon Mason, 2 Lieut.; William Jackson; William Ewbanks; James Ewbanks; James Swift; James Countiss; Griffith Stradley; James Jackson; James Jackson Junr; James Conner; Daniel MaGuinney; Job Garrett; John Newcomb; John Swift; James Swift; Thomas Swift; James Burt; William Burt; Garland Lamarr; Lemuel Lamarr; Thomas Wheeler; Samuel Swift; Richard Swift; John Brown; Solomon Hobbs; James Hobbs; Thomas Jackson; John Ridgeway; Joshua Ridgeway; Joshua Brown; John Davis; John Powell; Jonas Gland; William Moore; Peter Jackson; Philip Harrington; Nickson Sherwood; George Saterfield; Jadwin Montegue; John Montegue; John Ewbanks; George Ewbanks; James Baggs; John Emory; Solomon Saterfield; Daniel Robertson; Samuel Jackson Junr; Arthur Emmory; James Culbreth; John Gregg; John Culbreth; John Deford; Vincent Williams; John Kopes; Vincent Swift; John Harkings (Huckings, Huchings); Alexander Robinson; William Broadey; William Padgett; John Jackson; Nathan Baughstick; James Powell; George Powell; John Lambdin; John Clements; Thomas Goldsborough. total Amo. 69 [Scharf Coll., State Arch.]

1777 Aug 13/John Fountleroy, Capt.; Young Keen, 2 Lieut; Richard Keen, Ensign
James Williams; Laban Glanden; William Glanden; Henry Mason; William Batchelor; Thomas Mathews; John Mansfield; Isaac Baggs; John Matthews;

APPENDIX B: MUSTER ROLLS AND OTHER LISTS

Thomas Matthews of Jno.; Charles Heath; Henry Griffith; James Black; Jacob Williams; James Banks; Thomas Studham (Steedham?); Henry Poor; Edward Dobson; John Layn; John Layn; William Holding; (name obliterated); Solomon Davis; Gideon Swift; Robert Pippin; William Pippin; Uriah Pipin; William Fouracres; Abram Dyrs; Symon (Lymon?) Dyrs; George McAfee(?); Jacob McCoombs; Sylvinus Prougharve (Proughawe?); Charles Keen; Edward Keen; Thomas Keen; William Harper; William Bryley; Nathan Slaughter; John Slaughter; John Slaughter junr; William Williams; Winchester Mason; Thomas Mason John Legh; William Legh; James Roe; Joseph White; James Townshend; James Merrick; Samuel Booker; William Benney; Cloudsberry Matthews; James Slaughter; John Able; Joseph Crafton; James Milson; Thomas Hopkins; Phillimon Davis; James Gashford; Davis Jadwin; Absolom Taylor; Edward Jones; John Devilish; Nathan Clove. Total amo. 68 [Scharf Coll., State Arch.]

CAROLINE COUNTY, 14th Battalion

A Return of the 14th Battalion of Militia belonging to Caroline County and State of Maryland dated 13 Aug 1777. Submitted by William Whitly Lieutenant. 14th Battalion - Matt. Driver, Senr, Colo.; Nathaniel Potter, Major

1777 Aug 13/Joseph Richardson, Capt; Thomas Loockerman, 1st Lieut; Alexander Waddle, 2nd Lieut; Richard Frampton, Ensign; Thomas Ozmont; Zedok Mears; Bromwell Andrew; Elijah Clark; Moses Alford; Maccobins(?) Alford; Samuel Alcock; Matthyas Alford; Risdon Bozman; John Voss Baker; George Blades; Thomas Blades; Levin Blades; Joseph Billetor; James Billetor; Richard Clark; William Cartwright; Benjamin Caulk; John Cohee; Amos Cohee; John Coleman; Caleb Clark; Joseph Clift; John Cremeen; John Durgan; Manus Dawson; Henry Dickinson; Robert Dean; Benjamin Edgell of John; Walter Edgell; William Edgell; Daniel Edgell; Henry Edgell; Abram Edgell; Edward Eaton; Thomas Eaton; Richard Eaton; Levi Eaton; Anderton Eaton; Stephen Fleharty; Rigby Foster; Nathan Ferriss; William Frampton; Isaac Gamble; John Green; John Gibson; Solomon Hobbs; Henry James; William Kelly; Dennis Kelly; James Lynch; William Munnett; William Minner; Thomas Noell; Joseph Newnam; Henry Austin; Daniel Richardson; William Ryon; John Stevens; John Sharpe; William Sharpe; James Sharpe; James Stradley; Salathiel Stradley; John Turner; Richard Thomas; Jervis Willis; John Willoughby; Moses Walker; William Willoughby; Henry Webster; John Waddle; Robert Waddle; James Waddle; William Webster; Nathaniel Warrington; Owen Connerly. [Militia Lists of Daus. of Founders and Patriots, held by Md. Hist. Soc.]

1777 Aug 13/John Mitchell, Capt; Peter Richardson, 1st Lieut; Richard Collison, 2d Lieut; John Chezum, Ensign; Aaron Alford; Dennis Brooks; Henry Bowdle; William Banning; Thomas Barns; Benjamin Brooks; Anthony Banning; Henry Banning; Emory Collins; Peter Caulk; Samuel Cheezum; William Cheezum; John Crumpton; James Cohee; James Chipley; James Corkrin; Thomas Conner; Mark Clift; William Cook; John Carter; Richard Denny; James Edmondson; Benjamin Edgell of James; Levi Faiston; Charles Frazier; William Gow; Charles Graham; Edward Pinder Galonthon; Zadock Harvey; John Hughs; Thomas Hopkins; John Harris; Nicholas Harris; John Hobbs; Ezekiel Johnson; William Jones; John Jordan; John Killman; Joseph Mullikin; Ambrose Mitchell; Richard Mitchell; John Oram; William Perry; Thomas Prouce; Pearce Spence; Allen

CAROLINE COUNTY

Parker; John Prouce; Thomas Perry; William Rumbold; John Reeves; Thomas Rumbold; William Scowdrick; Joseph Sherwood; David Sisk; Thomas Chilcutt; Henry Turner; Robert Thomas; Thomas Turner; Henry Turner; Ellis Thomas; John Thomas; Henry Willis; John Willis; Joshua Willis; Richard Willis; Robert Willis; Thomas Willis; William Walker; William Walker Junr; John Walker; George Willson; Thomas Valliant; Thomas Vickers; John Valliant; Daniel Valliant. [Militia Lists of Daus. of Founders and Patriots, held by Md. Hist. Soc.]

1777 Aug 13/Shadrack Liden, Capt; John Hooper, 1 Lieut; James White, 2d Lieut; Seth Evitt, Ensign; Boaz Adams; Curtice Andrew; Luke Andrew; William Andrew; Michael Anderson; William Anderson; John Bullock; Anderton Blades; John Beauchamp; John Cremean; Peter Collison; Elijah Cremean; John Craynor; Aaron Craynor; William Collison; Thomas Dukes; Zebelun Dukes; Isaac Dukes; Richard Day; John Dawson; Jonas Dawson; Samuel Fountain; Roger Fountain; William Fountain; Solomon Grace; James Grace; George Grace; Thomas Grace; John Harper; Thomas Hooper; John Harvey; Thomas Harding; Joshua Hobbs; John Ireland; Samuel Ireland; Samuel Ireland Junr; James Johnson; William Johnson; Levin Johnson; Joseph Kelly; Hugh Marshall; Ralph Marshall; Gideon McKimmey; John Melvill; John Morris; John Pert; Henry Rumbly; Shadrack Rumbly; John Rumbly; David Reece; James Rumbly; Richard Sparks; Ralph Smith; John Stanton; Solomon Towers; Elijah Tylor; William Tull; Levin Tull; Jonathan Willson; Bartholomew Vaine; Joshua Smith; William Smith; Southey Smith; James Towers; Elijah Simpson; James Perry; Reubin Connerly; John Dillin; John Morgan; Solomon Morgan; Thomas Smith; Charles McKeel; Betel Stevens. [Militia Lists of Daus. of Founders and Patriots, held by Md. Hist. Soc.]

1777 Aug 13/Nehemiah Andrew, Capt.; Solomon Webster, 1st Lieut.; Aaron Manship, 2nd Lieut; David Woolford; Beauchamp Andrew; Nehemiah Andrew junr; Jeremiah Andrew; Joseph Blades; William Covey; Allin Connerly; John Clymer; Jacob Cremeen; Curtice Cremeen; Salathiel Cremeen; Joshua Dean; Edmond Flowers; Greenbury Faukenor; William Gray; William Gray Junr; James Gray; Tyler Hall; Laban Holland; Levi Holland; Richard Holland; John Morgan; Benjamin Morgan; Nathan Mainship; Elijah Mainship; Philip Ploughman; Francis Rowens; Joseph Rowens; William Rowens; Nicholas Stubbs; James Sullivan; James Sisk; Jesse Weatherly; Jesse Waddell; Samuel Ozmont; Owen Layne; Richard Layne; John Goutee; Abnor Weatherly; Edward Rowe; John Covey; John Caulk; William Weatherly; John Weatherly; Job Weatherly; Isaiah Weatherly; Isaac Weatherly; Caleb Busick; John Lyster; John Shearman; James Tucker; William Cotteral; John Delahay; James Dilling; Florince Sullivane; Fletcher Sullivane; John Sullivane; Darby Sullivane; Daniel Sullivane; William Sullivane; Thomas Towers; Moses Dean; John Webster; Richard Webster; William Jackson; Edward Harding; James Mills; Thomas Fowler; Thomas Jenkins; Richard Jenkins; Jessee Hubbert; Joshua Dilling. [Militia Lists of Daus. of Founders and Patriots, held by Md. Hist. Soc.]

1777 Aug 13/Joseph Douglass, Capt; Thomas Eaton, 1 Lieut; Joseph Nicols, 2 Lieut; John Dawson, Ensign; Shadrack Willis; William Murphy; Charles Twyford; Alexander Griffith; Elijah Dean; William Williams; Jacob Wright; Isaac Nicols; Thomas Clarkson; William Andrews; Iky Nicols; James Summers; James Douglass; Lewis Ross; Eber Jones; William Willis; Samuel Davis;

APPENDIX B: MUSTER ROLLS AND OTHER LISTS

Aquilla Davis; Baptiz Davis; Richard Noble; Levin Noble; Solomon Rigging; Salathiel Faulkenor; Abram Lewis; Asa Faulkener; Jessee Williams; John Nicols; William Camper; James Dopson; Jonathan Eaton; Aaron Lewis; Jacob Faulkenor; Benjamin Faulkenor; James Outerbridge; William Dean; John Layton; Richard Ozmont; Richard Ozmont junr; Henry Means; Elijah Willis; James Wright; Jervis Willis; John Young; Levin Wright; James Wright; Joseph Watkins; Edward Wright; Lenard Outerbridge; William Harrison; James Anderson; John Poole; Levi Brown; Jessee Brown; George Griffith; Henry Pritchard; Jinkins Sulivane; Moses Leverton; Thomas Nicols; William Lyster; Aaron Dunker; Joseph Stark; Warrington Evans; Elijah McKimmey; Owen Sullivan; Hugh McBride; John Sullivan; Daniel Sullivane. [Militia Lists of Daus. of Founders and Patriots, held by Md. Hist. Soc.]

1777 Aug 13/Richard Andrew, Capt; Henry Richards, 1st Lieut; Samuel Andrew, 2nd Lieut; Frederick Causey, Ensign; Edward Minner; Elisha Minner; Francis Carey; Anthony Ross; Edward Ross; William Dawson; Perry Hennecy; John Robinson; Levin Wright; Lamuel Wright; Duke Storey; Isaac Anderson; Thomas Smith; Thomas Morine; Joshua Wright; Levin Smith; Ezekiel Smith; Richard Smith; Isaac Smith; William Ross; Thomas Banning; Isaac Andrew; Thomas Stack; William Andrew; William Snow; Edward Russum; Patrick Spence; Thomas Hubbert; John Walker; James Langrell; Major Middleton; Rowland Waddell; Phillemon Lecompte; John Lecompte; Peter Stant; John Pritchard; Edward Pritchard; Charles Layton; Able Loard; Benjamin Kelly; Thomas Williams; Elijah Dawson; James Barton; William Barton; John Fisher; Abram Collins; Isaac Collins; William Causey; Isaac Causey; Hubbert Cawsey; William Peters; Beachamp Cawsey; Thomas Willis; Ezekiel Willis; John Harris; Michal Todd; Nathan Todd; George Andrew; Richard Pearson; Ezekiel Reed; Brown Twiford; Thomas Covington; Thomas Webster. [Militia Lists of Daus. of Founders and Patriots, held by Md. Hist. Soc.]

1777 Aug 13/John Stafford, Capt.; Solomon Causey, 1 Lieut; Jessee Grayless, 2 Lieut; Preiston Godwin, Ensign; Zebdial Potter; Thomas Cawsey; Nehemiah Cawsey; William Morgan; Abram Stafford; Jervis Stafford; George Kirkman; John Wheatly; Oliver Hackett; Zebelon Cawsey; Levin Caulk; Rubin Ross; Henry Templeman; William Grayless; John Stafford jun; Selathiel Vaulz; Solomon Warring; Abram Evitt; James Stafford; James Ross; Joy Hobbs; William Hobbs; Mathias Hobbs; Richard Chance; James Hambleton; John Hodson; John Richardson; Samuel Carlile; John Curry; Levin Smith; Aaron Mowbrey; William Bishop; Thomas Orrell; William Stevens; Robert Bishop; Benjamin Harris; Olivi Salisberry; Nehemiah Salisberry; James Swiggate; Henry Swiggate junr; Isaac Payne; John Payne; John Salisberry; Edward Willoby; James Willson; William Swiggate; Johnson Swiggate; Harmon Swiggate; James Ewing; James Leverton; Joseph Foster; Thomas Foster; Josiah Ginn; Jethrew Vinson; Nathan Gladson; Solomon Morgan; George Morgan; Zebulon Hobbs; Jeremiah Roads; Daniel Higgnutt; Azell Stevens; Abram Mason; John Walker; James Harris; John Breeding; Nicholas Price; Nathan Hill; William Harris; Solomon Morgan; John Chilcutt; Lawrence Driskell; William Munnett; Abram Munnett; Thomas Wiett; James Barwick post(?); William Stokes; Limuel Stokes; Thomas Rathall. [Militia Lists of Daus. of Founders and Patriots, held by Md. Hist. Soc.]

1777 Aug 13/Andrew Fountain, Capt; John Willson, 1 Lieut; James Chaffinch, 2 Lieut; Benjamin Dixon, Ensign; Bartholomew Feddeman; Hawkins Feddeman; Gary

CAROLINE COUNTY

Hobbs; Peter Hobbs; John Cooper; James Parnarr (?); John Simpson; William Carey; Owin Cooper; Stephen Cooper; Anthony Harper; William Harper; Joshua Lyster; Philip Harney; Joseph Harney; James Salisberry; John Salisberry; John Lucas; Michal Lucas; Samuel White; James Scott; Thomas French; John Fountain; Joseph Bland; Nehemiah Draper; Benjamin Swiggate; William Cahall; Benjamin Shaw; William Dean; Benjamin Whittington; Joseph Whittington; William Sanxten; Joshua Jones; William Lucas; Anthony Layne; James Layne; Edward Pearson; Aaron Wootters; William Tallboy; Robert Tallboy; John James; John Roe; Thomas Roe; Obediah Roe; Richard Kinnard; Tilghman Blades; David Swift; John Wootters; Lawrence Porter; Robert Porter; Reuben Wootters; Jonathan Greenbergh; Joshua Barwick; McCalvey Armswith; James Morgan; George Jackson; William McMahan; James Barwick; Nicholas Bright; Jonas Bright; George Bright; John Cahall; Thomas Stradley Cox; Price Dill; Foster Hooper; William Fountain; John Johnson; William Lecompte; Joseph Merotho; Uriah Merrideth; Andrew Miffin; Thomas Orell; William Owens; William Quinnely; Michal Stewart; Andrew Stapleford; Solomon Wooters; Elijah Wooters; Thomas White. [Militia Lists of Daus. of Founders and Patriots, held by Md. Hist. Soc.]

12 June 1781/To His Excellency Thomas Sim Lee, Esq.
Your Excellency & Honours/Agreeable to your request of the 30th May I have ordered the drafts to March there is five that refuses to March or furnish substitutes in thare rume - if the Assembly have dun aney thing in respect of the 4p Ct. I shall be glad you would inform me that I may proceed in the Collections of it. I am with respect Your Excellency & Honours - Most Obedt. Humbl. Servt. Wm. Whiteley.
NB Inclosed you have the Inrolement of our Light Horse.
The following is the enrolment for a Company of Horse for Caroline County - Henry Dickinson, Captain; Vincent Price, junr. Lieut.; Charles Daffin, Coront.; William Hopper; William Robinson; John Hardcastle; Richard Mason; Timothy Price; Joseph Douglass; Joseph Nicols; John Dawson; James Summers; William Summers; Ambros Mitchell; Joseph Richardson, junr. [Militia Lists of Daus of Founders and Patriots, held by Md. Hist. Soc.]

CECIL COUNTY, 30th Battalion

3 Mar 1776/Petition of [Capt.] Baruch Williams's Company of Militia. To Council of Safety.
Company was formed after December 1774; Jeremiah Baker was chosen captain; on August 1, 1775, the convention ordered another election, but disputes over choice of a second lieutenant caused Baker to refuse captaincy again; [Nathaniel?] Ramsey was next chosen but he joined Provincial troops; Williams was appointed by the Convention; he is "a stranger to most of the company"; he now offers to resign if Council will commission Baker.
Signed: Arthur Alexander, Edward Alexander, John Alexander, Jr., Neal Burley, Daniel Bryson, John Cameron, George Cather, John Carswell, Moses Crabstein, James Dogan, Michael Dougherty (M), James Gaston, William Gettrick [?], James Grantly, William Green, John Hargan, David Henery, Samuel Henry, John Hall, John Hall, Jr., John Johnston, Edward Justice, Nicholas Kelley, Jr., John Kelley, John King, John McCall, Samuel McCollagh, Jr., John McCollaugh, James McCollough, Willliam McCulloch, William McKeown,

APPENDIX B: MUSTER ROLLS AND OTHER LISTS

John McVegh, Sr., Benjamin McVey, Jacob McVey, son of Benjamin, John McVey, John MvVey, son of Benjamin, Hugh Moor, John Nickelson, William Sanders, Thomas Sewell, Thomas Smith, Joseph Stephenson, John Stevenson, Bazel Swann, John Thompson, William Wakefield, John Willson, George Wilson, John Wilson (M). [Calendar of Md. State Papers - The Blue Books]

CHARLES COUNTY

After 6 Mar 1776/Memorial from Pomokey Company, Charles County. To Council of Safety. On first making up company, the memorialists chose John Dent as captain and Samuel Ward as first lieutenant; Ward died and Henelin Truman Stoddart was chosen first lieutenant; Dent became a brigadier general and Stoddart a major; Henry Ward formerly second lieutenant, was selected as captain, George Dent, son of John, first lieutenant and John Grant ensign; Capt. Ward was chosen by a majority of 15; by a majority of two, "a Succeeding Committee" selected Thomas Hanson Marshall captain; this interferes with "the Progress of Justice due to the merit of Inferior Officers that hath behaved themselves well"; commissions would be pleasing to memorialists. Signed: James Adams, William Aytheay [?], Samuel Clements, John Conaway, Richard Dawson, John Delozier, Charles Dement, William Downs, John Grant, Clark Hall, Edward Hust, George Jewell, Elisha King, Samuel Maccattee, Walter McPherson, Ignatius Mahoney, Henry Marbury, Hugh Middletown, John Monnow, Henry Queen, George Roland, Gorden Roland, William Rowe, Bayne Smallwood, Hezekiah Smallwood, Henry Steward, John Turner, Zachariah Wade, Giles Vermillioin, John Ward, William Ward, Joseph Wheeler, Luke Wheeler. One name defaced. [p. 26 of Calendar of Md. State Papers - The Red Books]

19 Mar 1776/Charles Co. We ... whose names are subscribed, do here byt enrol ourselves into a company of militia...
Francis Mastin, Capt; Richd. Speake first Lieutenant; Keabard Smallwood Second Liuetenant; William Jones Ensign;
Sergants: Samuel Luckett; William Taylor; George Dunnington; Walter Winter Corporals: Humphrey Dossy(?); William Elgin; Robt. Talor; Elijah Warden for ...; John Robertson; Lawson Speake; Benjamin Benson; William Stoddert; William Norris; Noah Maddocks; John Bryan; Walter Posey; Pryor Posey; James Scott; Samuell Maddox; Anthony Gray; Edward Skinner; George Speake; William Maddox; John Howard; Seth Lomax; William Hussy; John Clinkscales; Bennet Brawner; Alex. Evens; William Price; John D. Scott; Joseph Dyall; Rhody Posey; Jesse Dyne; David Luckett; Jerard Fowke; Ignatious Luckett; Ignatious Maddox; John Franklin; Richd. Robertson; Thos. Skinner son of Thos.; William Allin; Samuell Allin; James Lee; John Brawner; James Murdock; James Woodward; Jerimiah Addams. [Md. Hist. Soc., MS 1814]

CHARLES COUNTY, 12th Battalion
1777/Capt. Jno. Hanson's Muster roll of Militia, 12th Battn.
Jno. Hanson Capn.; Henry Massey Hanson, 1st Lieut.; James Russell, 2d Lieut.; Jno. Griffin, Ensign; Jessee Boswell, Sergt; Peter Griffin, Sergt; James Griffin, Sergt; Jno. Wathen, Sergt; Benja. Luckett, Corpl; James Latimer, Corpl; Robt. Rogers, Corpl; Josias Boswell, Corpl; Saml. Roby (of Jno.), Drummer; Walter Brooks, Fifer; Privates: Thos. Padget; Dan'l Mcdaniel; Jessee Macrae; Jas. Acton; Elijah Boswell; Edwd. Clements; James

CHARLES COUNTY

Padget; Gust's Boswell; Henry Acton; Thos. Kellon; Wm. Brooks; Joseph Boswell; Thos. Russell; Basil Roby; Wm. Marshall; Wm. Loveless; Wm. Roby (of Wm.); Richd. Boswell; Notley Maddocke; Benja. Roby (of Saml.); Joseph Roby; Thos. Roby; Edwd. Deakins; Edwd. Kerrick; Saml. Roby Ju.; Jno. Williams; Wm. Kellon; Joseph Chrismond; Benja. Roby (of Rd.); Igna's Hamilton; Wm. E. Smithson; Jno. Pickrell; James Philips; James Chattam; Leon'd Roby Ju.; Philip Wedding; Jacob Moreland; Saml. Howell; Edwd. Newman; George Clements; Thomas Latimer; Wm. Dodson; Zach. Roby; Henry Maddocke; Fran's Hill; Philip A. Murray; John Corbet; Marmad. Semmes; Saml. Carrington; Robt. Young; Jno. Tennison; Saml. Williams; Igns. Boswell; Nichs. Wathen; Leond. Martin; Michael Martin; Walter Power; Allan Mcdaniel; Wm. Haroy; Joshua Morris; Wm. Roby (of Bena.); Randolph B. Latimer; Jno. Loveless; Edwd. Boswell; Jno. G. Gardner; Isaac Mcdaniel. [Militia Lists of Daus. of Founders and Patriots]

1777/Capt. Walter Hanson's Muster Roll of Melitia - Walter Hanson, Capt; Thomas Semmes, 1st Lieut.; John Beall Turner, Ensign; Haskins Hanson, Sergt; Gerrerd B. Causeen, Sergt; Wm. Hanson of Wm., Sergt; Alexr. S. W. Hawkins, Corpl; Nicholas H. Sewall, Corpl; Walter Mcpherson, Corpl; Samuel Chandler, Corpl; Samuel Tubman, Clerk; Privates: Notley Luckitt; Elias Clerke; William B. Smoote; Thos. H. Luckitt; William Wathen; John Dodson; Jacob Morris; Charles Mankin; Thomas Hopwell; Thomas Douglass; Cornelius Maddox; Mark Latimer; Isaac Smoot Latimer; Walter Morris; Aaron Chrisman; Samuel Cox; Joseph Matthews; William Cox; Edward S. Ware; Hugh Cox; George Keech; Moab Freeman; Obediah Scrogin; Nathaniel Freeman; John Jamestone; John M. Chrisman; Benjamin Shaw; Jestinion Nott; Thomas Gilpin; James Reaves; John Verdin; Benjamin N. Gilpin; John B. Hamelton; Ignatious Manery; Thomas Hawkins; Charles Goodrick; Thomas Pickrin; Ignatious Wathen; Francis Sewell; James Holding; Lewis Sewell; John Brown; William Tyre Junr; John Chandler; Jacob Miller; Francis Ware of Jacob; Samuil Douglas; Benjamin Maddox; William Mead; Thomas G. Hopewell; John Cox; Joseph Tyre; Raphael Tyre; James Price; Michael Lawson; Thomas Franklin; George Goodrick; John Tyre; Landsdale Godfrey; Benjamin Lomax; Thomas Lomax; Smith Hawkins; Peter H. Robey; Richard Verdin; Francis Cox; Richard Cox; Gustavus Campbell; Michael Howard; John Tranor. [Militia Lists of Daus. of Founders and Patriots]

1777/A List of Capn. Clarkson's Compy. of Militia, 12th Battn. - Henry Clarkson, Capt; Thos. A. Dyson, 1st Lieut.; Jona. Swann, 2d Lt.; Barton Thorn, Ensign; Thos. Swann, Sergt; Chas. Davies, Sergt; Thos. Dent Jur., Sergt; Geo. Dyson, Sergt; Benja. Davies, Corpl; Aquilla Davies, Corpl; Benja. Poston, Corpl; Saml. Murphy, Corpl; privates: Jno. Dement; Gerard Dyson; Igns. Cohoe; Mattw. Stone; Hatch Dent; Jos: Allen; Jno. Poston; Adam Gill; Abm. Murphy; James Lyon; Elias Davies; Henry Dent; Walter Moreland; Zed. Swann; Jno. Berry; Will: Bath; Roswell Good; Philip Davies; Zach. Swan; Leond. Highfield; Wm. Dement; James Johnson; Edwd. Davies; Wm. Allbritton; Walt. Burch; Benet Davies; Per. Thorn; Shad. Hunt; Gideon Dent; Benj. Wetherton; Wm. Poston; Andw. Hilton; Henry Redman; Wm. Dent; Peter Scallion; Thos. Swann, Ju.; Solomon Poston; Zeph. King; Walt. Lyon; Jessee Davies; Walter Dent; Walt. Suit; Wm. Roby; Edwd. Dement; Geo. Davies; Jona. Burch; Saml. Dent; Thos. Gillam; Rand. Davies; Barton Poston; Per. Mitchell; Benja. Sego; Wm. Harrison; Philip Kinniman; Benja. Wood; Wm. Burch; Thos. Hudson; James Matthew; Jno. Kinneman; Jno. Stewart; Rd. Weatherton; Jno. Edwards. [Militia Lists of Daus. of Founders and Patriots]

APPENDIX B: MUSTER ROLLS AND OTHER LISTS

1777/A List of Capt. Benj. Lusby Curry's Compy. - Benj. Lusby Curry, Capt.;
Hezh. Dent, Lieutenant; Francis Posey, Lieutenant; Isaac Smoot, Ensign;
Joseph Dent, Sergant; Thos. Matthews, Sergant; Zach. Dent, Sergant; Wm.
Bently, Corporal; Charles Simpson, Corporal; Gustavus Nally, Corporal;
Privates: Hezh. Cooksey; John Baker Wathen; Bennett Wathen Junr; Abraham
Hancock; Benj. Dent; Mathew Blair; Samuel Cooksey Barron; Henry Simpson;
Zacaih. Williams; Wm. Hancock; Titus Dent; Walter Boarman; John Hancock;
Randolph Hopkins; Elisha Ferrell; Archibald Walker; Isaac Campbell Junr;
Thos Hatch Dent; Igns. Black; Wm. Higdon Junr; Henry Josha. Jamison;
Gustavus Cartright; Igns. Nally; Wm. Williams; Martain Wathen; Dan. Barron;
... S Cooksey; John Baptist Wathen; Henry Duggard; Patk. Ferrell; Thos
Hancock; Bennett Mudd; George Chark; Benj. Posey; Leonard Higdon; John
Semmes; Bennett Wathen Senr; James Ferrell; Joseph Boarman; Benj. Burtles;
Jestn. Williams; Oliver Barron; Shad. Dent; Bennett Hoskins; Richd. Burch;
Igns. Hardman; James Simpson; Garrard Boarman; Jestn. Coosey; Thos. McCann;
Wm. Milone; Wm. Jones; Frans. Higden; Henry Cooksey; Frans. Montgomery;
Igns. Simpson; Frans Simms; Henry Boarman Junr; Birnard Nally; Wm. Higdon of
Benj.; John Hinckin (Henekin?), Drummer(?). [Militia Lists of Daus. of
Founders and Patriots]

1777/A List of Capt. Alexr. McPhersons Compy. - Alexr McPherson, Capt.;
Henry Boarman, Lieut.; Edward Semmes, Lieut.; Igns. Francis Garner, Ensign;
Edward Boarman Junr, Sergant; William Waters, Sergant; William Montgomery,
Sergant; Joseph Townly, Sergant; Basil Smith, Corporal; Raphael Boarman,
Corporal; Joseph Gardiner, Corporal; Elias Oden, Corporal; Privates: Joseph
Sanders; Edward Boarman Senr; Joseph Boarman; Josias OBryan; Barton Wathen;
Thomas Ogdon; John Smith Junr; Jeremiah Dyer; Henry Mudd; Richard Gardner;
William Gibbins; James Edilin; Henry Thos. Mudd; John Johnson; Luke Morran;
Gabril Morran; Samuel Morran; Samuel Bggett(?); John Boling; William Tubb;
James Boarman; Francis Queen; Richard Edelin; Thomas Thomas; Abednego
Dunning; Richard Beaven; James Boon; Cornelius OBryan; Edward Boswell; Henry
Beaven; Raphael Hagon; Isaac Lewis; Richard Blanford; Thos. C. Reeves; Henry
Gardiner; Thos. Osborn Senr; John Wheatly; John C. Waters; Walter Jamison;
Walter Burch; Stephen Gibbins; Edward Beaven; James Dunning; Leonard Nally;
William Turner; Joseph Montgomery; Benjamin Jamison Junr; Stephen Roby;
Benjamin Hagon; John Williams Camron; Henry Camron; Richard Spalding; James
Blanford; Thos. J. Boarman Junr; Thos Camron; James Camron; Randolph Turner;
Leonard Jamison; Igns. Mudd; Nehemiah Gibbins; Mathew Smith; William
Gardiner; Igns. Montgomery; Basil Montgomery; Leonard Icrick (Terich?);
William Boarman; Benjamin Tenisson; John B. Camron; Nicholas Smith.
[Militia Lists of Daus. of Founders and Patriots]

1777/A List of Captn Jno. Barnham's Company of Militia, 12th Battn. -
Commissioned Officers - John Barnham, Capt.; Bennet Dyson, Lieut.; Zach.
Chunn, 2 Lieut; Kendly Smoot, Ensign; Benj. Burk, Sergt; Frans. Hemsley,
Sergt; Walter Ihanietz(?), Sergt; Babt. Brent Junr, Sergt; Wm. B. Smoot,
Corpl; Leonard Wood, Corpl; Gerard Wood, Corpl; John Edilin, Corpl; Thos.
Hambleton Philips, Drummer; Privates: Thos. Ching; Wm. Foster; Garrard
Braydy; James Morriss; Gustavis Davis; Baptist Hamilton; Zach. Dutton; Wm.
Suit; Joseph Gray; Butler Stoonstreet; Leonard Stoonstreet; Robt. Sly; Thos.
Bond; Saml. Turner; Thos. Scott; Jonathan Furguson; James Waseman(?); James
Gray; Charles Allbritan; John Bts. Higdon; Wm. Comton; Robt. Brent Junr;

CHARLES COUNTY

Peter Mugg; Saml. Swann; Zaphh. Swann; Zaphh. Murphy; Townly King; Jonathan Scallion; Henry Chunn; Raphel Boarman Junr; Frans. Edilin; John Braydy; James Scott; John Gill; Thos. Rider; Saml. Leech; Geo. Higgs; Wm. Gray; John Wilson Comton; John Boarmon; Abraham Barrow(?); Hezh. Murphey; Absalom Thorn; Edward Edelin; Wm. Davis; James Simmes; Zachh. Mattingly; Saml. Grayham; Edward Willis (?); Geo. Gray; Elazor(?) Davis; Eleazar Chunn; Charles Montgomery; Jonathan Gill; Charles Love; Saml. Amery; Wm. Anderson; Jerem. Nisfield (?)_; Owen Braydy; Wm. King; Robt. King; Walter Scroggin; John Huntington; Luke Huntington; Jestinian Thos. Benet(?); Saml. Reives; Patrick Mcglew; James Swann. [Militia Lists of Daus. of Founders and Patriots]

1777/A List of Capt. John Thomas's Compy. of Militia - John Thomas, Capt.; John Gardner, Lieut; Henry Lyon, Lieut; Rich'd Eastip(?), Ensign; Zachh. Lyon, Sergant; Wm. Barker, Sergant; John R. Adams, Sergant; John Gibson, Sergant; Hezh. Billingsley, Corpral; Calib Thomas, Corpral; Glaven(?) Hunt, Corpral; Joshua Mudd, Corpral; Privates: Clement Gardner; John Billigsley Junr; Igns. Gardner; John Smith Junr; George Davis; George Walls; Joseph Lyon; Basil Hickey; Richd. Bivings son of Bar.; Jonathan White; Hezh. Ruter; Samuel Adams; John Taylor son of Igns.; Wm. Ladamon; Wm. Richards; Thos. Richards; Philip Thomas; Paul Biving; Whealer Biving; John Taylor son of Staffd.(?); Wm. Thomas son of Wm.; Thos Thomas; Benj. Bivings; Richd. Bivings Junr; Johnthan Cooksey; James Taylor; Allen Thomas; Philip Cooksey; Andrew Cooksey; Nathan Maddox; Zaph. Barrough; Wm. Hunt; Edward Taylor; Wm. Thomas son of John(?); Henry Mayhew; Samuel Right; Thos. Have(?); Eljah Rollings; Joseph Ruter; Joseph(?) Barker; Samuel Perry; John Beaden; Isaac Thomas (?); John Jefferson; Alphonsus Sorat; John McClain; Wm. White; James Bilingslay; John Leach; John Right; Thos. McAtee. [Militia Lists of Daus. of Founders and Patriots]

1777/A Muster roll of Peter Wood's compy. of Militia - Peter Wood, 2d Lieut.; Will. Moran, Sergeant; Benja. Ogdon, Sergeant; Thos. Davis, Sergeant; John Adams, Sergeant; Edwd. Burch, Corpl; Thos. Odan, Corpl; James Wallace, Corpl; Vincent Odan, Corpl; Privates: Leond. Letchworth; Jno. Beavin; Robt Gill Ju.; James Taylor; Jonathan Moran; Benja. Wood; Jno. Moran Ju.; Joseph Johnson; Murrel(?) Morgan; Jno. Estep; Thos Hunt Ju.; Jno. Lyon; Zachariah Johnson; Michael Hazard; George Morton; Joseph Morton; Benjamin Hunt; Peter Carricoe; James Carroll; Jessee Burch; James Canter; Isaac Canter; James Bramhall; Allan Harben; Wm. Harben; Abraham Parker Ju.; Robt Dawson; Jonathan Burroughs; Jona. Bramhall; Charles Gill; Leond. King; Saml. Stallions; Lawrance Venables; Hugh Perrie; Wm. Clark; Jos. Anderson Ju.; Andw. Moran Ju.; Wm. Bramhall; Richd. Wheatly; Frans. Hicky; Theodore Venables Ju.; Zach. Bramhall; Jona. Parker; Charles S. Forbes; Josiah Johnson; Edwd. Anderson; James Forbes; John Forbes; Joseph Anderson; James Smith; Isaac Oden; John Morton; Jno. Wheatly; Richd. Wallace; Thos. Wheatly; Robt Cowley; Willm. Anderson; James Grayer; Saml. Venables; Abraham Wilson; Thomas West; Huet Johnson; Jonathan Johnson; Stephen Penn; Ezekiel Venables; Saml. Bloxham; Charles S. Smith; Joshua Demar; Frans. Demar. [Militia Lists of Daus. of Founders and Patriots]

APPENDIX B: MUSTER ROLLS AND OTHER LISTS

A List of Capt. Yates's comp. of Militia [1777]
Jona. Yates, Capt.; Jno. Lancaster, 1st Lt.; Jno. Neale, 2d Lt.; Raphael Boarman, Ensign; John Vincent, Sergt.; Edwd. Warren, Sergt.; Jos: Shaw, Sergt.; Chandler Ford, Sergt.; Jno. Oakly, Corpl; Phil: Thomas, Corpl; Jno. Shaw, Corpl; Benja. King, Corpl; Privates: Andw. Minitree; Wm. Vincent Senr; Jezrul Penn; Walter Fearson; Jno. Thompson; Robt Oakly; Jno. Bateman; Ninian Burrage; Thos. Dutton; Thos. Smoot; Jas. Wilder; Wm. Simpson; Jos: Fearson; Wm. Shaw; Rand. Brandt; Rd. May; Chas. Bateman; Chas. Doyne; Aaron Goodrick; Walter Goodrick; Wm. F. Neale; Wm. Vincent Ju.; Thos. Evans; James Maddocke; Geo: Steele; Benja. Bateman; Chas. Cutts; Chas. Bradly; Igns. Boarman; Jas. Reeves; Clem. Craycroft; Jas. Neale; Thos. Duly; George James; Wm. Compton; Rd. Boarman; Baker Howard; Jno. Diggs; Levi Chunn; Towny Maddox; Thos. Reeves; Paul Minitree; Rd. Bateman; Aly (Aty?) Kearton; Jno. Smoot; Thos. Rigg; Asa King; Wm. Maddox; Jno. B. Wilder; Wm. Boarman; Moses Guy; Henry Hamsly; Gerd. Norwood; David Ratcliff. [Militia Lists of Daus. of Founders and Patriots]

CHARLES COUNTY, 26th Battalion

1777/A List of Capt Benj. Cawood's Compy of Militia - Benjamin Cawood, Capt.; Benjamin Beaven, Lieut; Elijah Moore, Lieut; Thos. Mcdaniel, Ensign; Joseph Owen, Sergt.; Thos. Thompson, Sergt.; Henry Beane, Sergt.; Thos. Beane, Sergt.; John Wedding of Thos., Corporal; Wm. Wright(?), Corporal; Igns. Biggott, Corporal; Henry Miles of Joseph, Corporal; Edward Jenkins, Clerk; Mathew More Junr, Drummer; Privates: Samuel Berry; Cigger(?) Richards; John V. Logan; John Vayne Junr; James Montgomery; Thos. Harvin Jun.; Willm. Vayne; Wm. Steward; Wm. Baden; Wm. Hays of Wm.; Igns. Loveless; John Loveless; Edward D. Harvin; Jonathan Ogden; Henry Ozburne; Joseph Ozburne; George Moore; Philip Morland; Hezh. Moore; Stephen Morland; Benjamin Garner; Peter Garner; Stephen Miles of Henry; Wm. Miles; James Cohoe; John Smoot; Wm. Warren; John Morland; Hezh. Reeves; Michl. Hines Roby; Joseph Padgett; Joshua Montgomery; Charles Blanford of Thos.; Wm. Blanford; Samuel Darnall; John Glassco(?); Isle Wright (Whight?) Junr; Wm. Mobley; Elextius Hays; Thos. Speake; Leonard Beane; Rhods(?) Vinson; Thos. Smith; Annanias Harvin; James Loveless; Thos Darnall Junr; John Boarman; Peter Montgomery; John Jackson; Richd. Blanford of Charles; Thos. Glassco; Zachh. Morland; Wm. Hughs Junr; Joseph Miles Senr; James Hagon; Wm. Hays Senr; Thos. Weding Junr; Benj. Darnall; Wm. Morland; Jonathan Mcdaniel. [Militia Lists of Daus. of Founders and Patriots]

1777/A List of Capt. Hezh. Garner's Company - Hezk. Garner, Capt.; Frans. B. Franklin, Lieut.; Willm. Milstead, Lieut; Zeph. Franklin, Ensign; Jerimh. Gray, Sergeant; Frans. Clinkscale, Sergeant; Peter Dunnington, Sergeant; Richd. Price, Sergant; John Dunning, Corpl; John Milstead, Corpl; Willm. Franklin, Corpl; John Warder, Corpl; Privates: Hezh. Evans; Anthony C. Gray; Joseph Gray; George Gray; Boly Allden; Edward Gray; Rhody Bowie; James Scott; Bartin Bell; George Skinner; Jeremiah Davis; Willm. Allen of Wm.; James Allin; Zachah. Martin; Thomas Delozier; Igns. Southerland; Samuel Milstead; Edward Milstead; John Delozier; Wm. Delozier; Wm. Steward; James Steward; Adam Clinkscales; Igns. Clinkscales; Wm. Clinkscales; Henry Gray Junr; George Allin; Jesse Davis; John N. Gray; Wm. May; Wm. Dyer; Richd. Clinkscales; James Warder; Joseph Warder; Joseph Dyer; Thos. Thompson; Thos.

CHARLES COUNTY

Nelson; John Clements; John Mankin; James Mankin; Barton Brawner; Wm.
Brawner; Robt. Southerland; Wm. Smoot; John Nally; David Scott; Samuel
Allin; Thos. Davis; Jardin Sanders; David Linsy Ward; Willm. Turney; Wm.
Carpinter; Robt. Scott; Barton Flanigan; John Franklin; Hezh. Franklin;
Robt. Franklin; Robt. Golden; Elijah Chark; Jacob Johnson; Thos. Bullman;
Jesse Allin; Philip Warder; Willm. Price; Richd. Davis; John Russell; Jesse
Warder; John Johnston. [Militia Lists of Daus. of Founders and Patriots]

1777/A List of Capt. Willm. McPhersons compy., 26th Battn. - Wm. McPherson,
Capt.; Peter Green, Lieut.; Thos Green, Lieut.; Leonard Hamilton, Ensign;
Richd. Edelin, Sergt.; Walter Smith, Sergt.; George McAtee, Sergt.; James
Slater, Sergt.; Thos. M. Green, Corpl.; ; Edward Guinn, Corpl.; Thos Beale,
Corpl; Leonard Thompson, Corpl.; Wm. Sone; Privates: Joseph Coomes; George
Thompson; Joseph Green Thompson; Josh. Green; Daniel McPherson; James McAtee;
Wm. Mcatee; Wm. Beale; Thos. H. Hanson; Benj. Harris; Henry Green; Thos.
Smallwood; John B. Wills; Wm. Coomes of Jos.; Charles Ash; Richd. Slater;
Thos. Roland; John Guy; Wm. Atchsion (sic); Basil Clements; Joseph Carries;
Frans. Edelin; Joseph Atchison; Bennet H. Clements; Bennett Hamilton; John
Slater; Igns. Simmes; Nehemh. Slater; Wm. Guy Junr; James Achison; Wm.
Downs; Henry McAtee; Leonard Gates; Samuel Latimer; Walter Burn; John Cox;
John H. Roby; John Mcatee; Nicholas Coomes; John Clements of Wm.; Isaac
Steward; Thos. Griffis; Hezh. Johnson; Saml. Borker(?); Wm. Spalding; Benj.
Adams; Ellis Thomas; Edward Hamilton; Eisha (sic) Athey; Basil Beall;
Ebeazer Athey; Basil Stonestreet; James Calary; Duke Hamilton; Joshua
Atchson; Hezh. Athey; Charles Thomson; Wm. Duxon; Richd. Roby; Edward
Clements; Wm. Cox; Henry Edelin; Wm. Stone. [Militia Lists of Daus. of
Founders and Patriots]

1777/A List of Capt Thos. H. Marshalls compy., 26th Battn. - Thos. H.
Marshall, Capt; Geo. Dent son of John, 1st Lieut.; John Grant, Ensign;
Horatio Middleton, Sergt.; Thos. Craycroft, Sergt.; Igns. Mahaney, Sergt.;
John Delozier, Sergt.; Wm. Padgett, Corpl.; Robt. C. Hall, Corpl.; Richd.
Dawson, Corpl.; Gordan Roland, Corpl.; George Tubman, clerk; Privates: John
Marshall; Thos. Marshall son of Thos.; Mosses Harvey; Hugh Middleton; Wm.
Downes; John Smallwood; Zacha. Murphey; Richd. Brent; James Burk; Jonathan
Long; Zacha. Wade; Geo. Dawson; Charles Dement; Benj. Dawson; John Munroe;
Walter McPherson; Geo. Bland Junr; Wm. Tylor; Elish. King; Benj. Fendall;
Owen Conner; James Parmer; Thos. Munroe; Richd. White; Richd. Cox; Saml.
Crown; John Adams; Peter Dent; Geo. Dent son of Peter; Theodore Dent; Wm.
Hamilton; Geo. Steward; Henry Steward; John Ward; Wm. Ward; Thos. Ward;
Saml. Middleton; Saml. Clements; Edward Husk Jun.; Frans Virmillion; Guy
Virmillion; Edward Virmillion; Giles Virmillion; Pryor Smallwood; Thos.
Smallwood; Hezh. Smallwood; Jno. C. Bennet; John Virmillion; Wm. Hall; Alex.
Mcdonold; Wm. Rowe; John Dent; Anthony Rowe; Benj. Douglass; John Pemy(?);
Wm. Cromill; Pearson Chapman; Bayne Smallwood; Wm. Alexander; Thos. Hooper;
Benj. Elmer(?); John Lambert; Henry Dawson; John Harrold; Edward Curtain;
Wm. Curtain. [Militia Lists of Daus. of Founders and Patriots]

1777/A List of Capt. Francs. Mastin's Compy. of Militia, 26th Battn. -
Frans. Mastin, Capt.; Richd. Speake, Lieut.; Saml. Luckett, Lieut.; Wm. Gray,
Ensign; Privates: Elijah Wardin; Joell(?) Fagg; Simond Greenleaves; Samuel
Elgin; Saml. Madox; Henry Woodword; Lawson Speake(?); Benj. Benson; Benj.

APPENDIX B: MUSTER ROLLS AND OTHER LISTS

Jones; Clement Thomas; Rhody Maddox; John Rhenn; Thos. Skinner of Thos.; Joseph Semmes Junr; Wm. Buchannon; Rhody Posey Junr; Jesse Woodward; George Maddox; James Skinner Senr; Rodey Posey; James Bartlett; Fran: Posey; Jno. Posey of Jno.; Jno. Maddox; Daniel Marr; Geo. Buchananan(sic); Benj. Maddox; Nehmp:(?) Posey; Wm. Edglin; Robt. Tailor; James McDavis; Richd. Posey; John Minner Jur; Leond. Maddox; Jno. Posey; Jno. Bohannon; Wm. Fagg; Wm. Gray; Geo: Posey; Benj. Lattemore; Thos. Lomox; Zach. Wade; Jeremh. Howard; Ewell Owens; James Ratcliff; William Skinner; Gerard Rison; Richd. Robinson; Alex. Evens; James McGachanon(?); Edwd. Skinner; James McDoland; Jest. Ridgley; Jerh. Adams; Williamson Thomson; Richd. Woodward; James Fenisus(?); Samuel Murdock; Josh. Simms Junr; Harrison Elgen; Price(?) Posey; James Mordock; Noah Maddox; James Skinner Senr; Jona. Haislip; ... Lomox; Josh. Evans; Willm. Norris; Wm. Allen Senr(?); Jest. Payne; Jno. Marr. [Militia Lists of Daus. of Founders and Patriots]

1777/A List of Capt. Sinnett's Comp. of Militia, 26th Battn. - Robt. Sinnett, Capt.; Jno. Muschett, 1st Lt.; Wm. Maconchie, 2d Lt.; Saml. Stone, Ensign; Wm. Barnes, Sergt.; Mattw. Rigg, Sergt.; Igns. Simpson, Sergt.; Jno. Briscoe, Sergt.; Jno. Chattam, Corpl; Zach. Allen, Corpl; Henry Simpson, Corpl.; James Simpson, Corpl.; Privates: Thos. Sanders Ju.; Rd. Adams; Jno. Barker; Jno. Barker Ju; Leond. Gilpin; Thos. Goly; Joseph Shirclift; Nichs. Craycroft; Jno. Wallace; Thos. Stone; Wm. B. Stone; Joseph Manning; Clem. Smith; Rd. Marshall; Wm. H. Stone; Thos. Posey; Jno. Timms; James Kerrick; James Simpson; Chas. Muncaster; James Muncaster; J.F.R. Sanders; Edwd. Sanders; Jno. Robertson; Igns. Higdon; Zach. Mcdaniel; Jno. Flurry; Wm. Flurry; Chas. Tims; Joseph Mankin; Thos. Highfield; Geo: Adams; Jessee Douglass; Rd. H. Reeder; Rd. Mankin; Jas. Fitzgerrell; Danl. Norriss; Igns. Quaid; Wm. Morrison; Morris Jas. McDon..; Thos. Owen; Theops. Hanson; Jno. Reardan; Saml. Hanson (of Waltr.); Wm. Hutchison; Jno. Butler; Chas. Tyers; Joseph Simms; Jno. Mankin; Jos. Smith; Chas Davies; Jno. A. Clements; Leonard. Wheeler; Johnson McCoy; Hugh McCoy; Walter Manning; Jno. D. Scott; Oswald Boye; Jessee Doyne; Gerrard Fowke Ju.; Thos. Maddox; Edwd. Flurry Ju.; Benja. Davies (of Rd); Abraham Boye; Wm. Timms. [Militia Lists of Daus. of Founders and Patriots]

1777/A List of Capt. Richd. Bennet Mitchells Compy. - Richd. Bennett Michell, Capt; Peter Fernandies, Lieut; Wm. Barnes, Lieut.; Charles Garner, Ensign; Nathan Nally, Sergant; Henry Brawner, Sergant; Thos. G. Howard, Sergant; Richd. Mitchell, Sergant; Wm. Farmer, Corporal; Labon Haislip, Corporal; John Reeder, Corporal; Thos. Ostro, Corporal; Privates: Walter Johnson; Benedict Wheeler; Smith Mudd Invalid; James Mudd Invalid; John Clements of Jacb Inv.
Walter Clements of Do, Invalid; John Clements of Jos.; Samuel Michell; Jacob Adams; John Hall; Stephen Lomax; Joseph Nelson; John Haislip of Robt.; Wm. Haislip; Luke Lomax; Charles Clements; Benjamin Wheeler; Igns. Wheeler of Richd.; Patk. Duffy; Edward Welch; Shadric Baker; John Haislip of Henry; John Mudd; Mark Norry; John Dorton(?); Wm. Godgrace of Robt.; Joseph Townly, Inval.; Wm. Brown of John; John Nelson of John; Wm. Nelson of Thos.; Wm. Howard; Elijah Green; Joseph Wheeler; Igns. Wheeler of Clems.; Archad. Johnson Junr; Edward Brawner; Richd. Mudd Invalid; Walter West(?) Lomax; Jeremiah Mudd Junr; George Welch; Clement Wheeler; Wm. Wheeler; Benjamin Gray, Inv.; Benjamin Brawner, Inv.; Samuel Haislip; Frans. Clements of

CHARLES COUNTY

Jacob, Inv.; Wm. Davis Inv.; Henry Mcatee Inv.; Henry Marbury; Josias Smoot; Stephin Nottingham Inv.; Ignatious Wood; Wm. Gray; Luke Wheeler; Walter Clements Inv.; Leonard Clements Inv.; Henry Speake; George Ward; John Stone; Walter Page; Heny Queen; John Bowe Jun.; Chist. Layman, Inv.; Richd. Gray of Richd.; John Hurry; Oswell Brooke; Walter Clement, Inv.; Henry Wood; Henry Smith; George Jenkins; Peter Davis; Richd. Thompson; Charles Clement of Walter; Thos. Wheeler, Inv. [Militia Lists of Daus. of Founders and Patriots]

1777/A List of Capt. Samuel Smallwoods Compy. of Militia - Samuel Smallwood, Capt.; Isaac Smallwood Middleton, Lieut.; Frans. Acton, Lieut.; James Boyden Smallwood, Ens.; Benjamin Berry, Sergt.; Prier Berry, Sergt.; Hezh. Berry, Sergt.; Luke Smallwood, Sergt.; George Willitt, Corpl; Joseph Simpson, Corpl; Bennedict Sanders, Corpl; Leonard Burch, Corpl; Richd. Tubman, Clerk; Privates: Wm. Alex Wilson; John Burch; Henry McAtee of Jas.; Joseph Berry; John Berry; Ebenezer Payne; Walter Wilkerson; Mark Richardson; John Clements of John; Joseph Hiton; Frans. Payne; Igns. Payne; Igns. Brimhall; Anthony Oneale; Igns. Steward; Stepan Cawood; Wm. Cawood; Notly Ford; Charles Inness; Shadrick Nally; James Innes; Richd. Marlor; Benj. Padgett of Benj.; Benj Padgitt of Wm.; Hugh Stephens; Thos Berry of Humy.; Benj. Berry of Humy.; Aiton Morlere; James Morlere; James Gales; Thos Hill; Leonard Hill; Nicholas Boone; Igns. Winsor; Joseph Winsor Junr; John Acton of John; John Kidwell; Mathew Kidwell; James Kidwell; Samuel Moreland; James Moreland; Philip Moreland; Dennis Curtain; Aaron Padgitt; Thos. Hicks; Jonathan Cantor; Charles Ferrell; Joseph Hill; Robt. Hicks; Patrick Moreland; Isaac Morland; Charles Maddox; Lyde Stone Smallwood; Walter Steward; James Smallwood; Thos. Berry of Saml.; Alexr. Wilkerson; Elijah Robinson. [Militia Lists of Daus. of Founders and Patriots]

1777/A List of Capt. Willm. Winters Compy. of Militia - Willm. Winter, Capt.; George Dent, Lieutenant; Burd.(?) Hamilton, Lieutenant; John Bush, Ensign; Samuel Carroll, Sergant; Roger Fowke, Sergant; Thos. Perry Junr, Sergant; Igns. Ryon, Sergant; Thos. Reed, Sergant; John Shomatt, Corporal; John L. Wright, Corporal; Robt. Knox, Corporal; Privates: John Ashford; John Carrall; Willm. Dunnington; Elijah Dunnington; Kennedy Ferrell; Chandler Kyson; Rhoday Ratliff; John Smith; Samuel Davis; Richd. Elgin; John Fitzjarrell; Daniel Johnson; Thos. Keibert; Hudson Williams; Wm. Carroll; Thos. Jackson; Edmond McAtee; Thos. Ashford; Zachah. Davis; Wm. Groves(?); Andrew Gray; James McLean; Charles Nevitt; John Pickin; John Perry Junr; Samuel Wright; Butler Ashford; John Carpenter; John Groves; Wm. Maddox; John B. Shomatt; Benjamin Edelin; Josias Adams; John S. Chilton; John Cooper; Richd. Carroll; Hezekiah Dunnington; Charles Luchie(?); Robt. Martain; Phillip Risten(?); Andrew Baillie; George Elgin; Coleb Hudson; Hamidathy Hamilton; Willm. Citchen; Wm. McLean; Wm. Murdock; Uzziah Posey; Samuel Woodward; Reuben Dyer; Joseph English; Joshua Thompson; James Tallmise; Robt. Wright; Frans Perry; Rhody Adams; Burdit Ratliff; Ignatious Ratliff. [Militia Lists of Daus. of Founders and Patriots]

APPENDIX B: MUSTER ROLLS AND OTHER LISTS

DORCHESTER COUNTY

Before 10 Sep 1776/Petition of Castle Haven Company, Dorchester County [19th Battalion]. To Convention of Maryland. They "have laboured under repeated impositions" from Capt. Joseph Byus and request his removeal or an opportunity to prove their accusations; when they were called for duty, Byus purchased a quantity of provisions; because sundry provisions were given to them, they used only part of what he purchased for his own use; it was only by chance they discovered a true account of the provisions and recovered the money due them; Byus has also instructed his non-commissioned officers to knock any man down for the smallest offence; attested by William Thomas. Signed: Martin Abit (M), John Childerston, William Childreston (M), Richard Clarridge, Young Clarridge, Philemon Colvill (M), Andrew Cooke, Henry Cooke, John Cooke, Standly Cooke, Thomas Cooke, James Durgin (M), Isaac Fardwell, William Frazor (M), William Hubbart, John Killmon, Thomas Killmon, Moses Lecompte, Edward Lee, John Lee (M), Andrew Marshall, Eligea Marshall, James Marshall (M), John Marshall (M), John Mitchell (M), Reuben Mitchell (M), Thomas Mitchell, Gilbert North (M), Richard Philips [?], William Procter, Charles Seward, John Seward (M), William Seward, Edward Thomas, James Thomas, John Thomas, John Thomas (M), William Thomas, Charles Wheeler, Nehemiah Whiteley, Job Willoughby, Thomas Wright. [Calendar of Maryland State Papers - The Red Books. Also see Archives of Md., XII, pp. 390-1]

11 Sep 1776/Petition of Capt. John Todd's Company, Dorchester County. Subscribers request that commissions be issued to the following offices who were elected by ballot in the presence of Maj. [Daniel] Fallin; Capt. John Todd, 1st Lt. James Davis, 2nd Lt. John Robinson, Ens. Michael Todd. Signed by Roger Adams, Daniel Andrews, Isaac Andrews (M), John Andrews, Joseph Andrews, Levin Andrews, Reuben Andrews, Stanaway Andrews, Leavin Bramble (M), Lewis Bramble (M), William Cannon, Arthur Hart, Henry Hartt, Jacob Isley, John Insley (M), Levi Johnson (M), Jacob Jones, Samuel Jones, Asa Langrell, Andrew McKinsey, Thomas Moore (M), John Murphy (M), William Murphy, Ambrose Ratton (M), Job Robinson (M), Mansfield [?] Street, Thomas Street [M], Edward Willey, William Willey [M], William Willey, Jr. [M], Phillip Wingate [M], Bryan Woodlan [M]. [p. 57 of Calendar of Md. State Papers - The Blue Books]

FREDERICK COUNTY

9 Mar 1776/We whose names are subscribed to hereby enroll our selves into a company of militia, agreeable to the resolution of the Provincial Convention ...Henery Boteler Capt; Thomas Odle Lieut; John Nicholls Lieut; Bartin Philpot Ensign; Sergts: Daniel Givens; Archibald Nicholls; Henery Edwd. Boteler; William Nicholls; Corporalls: Patrick Norris; Jacob Grim; Nathanl. Dixson; Jeremiah Fulsom
Rank and file: Flayl Pain; Charles Woolvertoon; James Austin; James Allen; Henery Musgrove; Barton Garret; Flayl Nicholls; James Hase; Charles Maglohen; Postumus Clagett; John McCallester; Archbald McCallester; Thomas McColl; Samuel Prater; George Warters; Michal George; John Deboy; Adam Boot; Hugh McCoy; Henery Ault; Henery Bouser; William Blair; Lennard Lodwick; Lennard Carnor; William Ault; Francis Worley; John Ault; Thomas Austin;

FREDERICK COUNTY

Charles Philpot; Jeremiah Nelley; Alexander Grimm; Michal Hany; Thomas Owens; Daniel Malhoney; Abraham Richards; William Sabater; William Booth; John Nervey; Thomas Harrison; John Rinker; George Lewis; William Gladhill; Robt. Booth. [Md. Hist. Soc., MS 1814]

16 Apr 1776/Frederick County - Skipton District
Thomas Waring, Captain; James Prather, 1st Lieutenant; Thomas Humphrey, 2d Lieutenant; John Jeremiah Jacob, Ensign
Serjeants: Joseph Reid; James Zealison; Joshua Sereshfield; Syrus Simpkins
Corporals: John Kimberly; David Swank; Thomas Johnson; Jacob Slaughter
Fifer: Valentine Horn
Privates: Thomas Candry; Dickerson Simpkins; Michael Collier; Charles Clinton; John Baker; Thomas Chenoweth; John Hays; Alexander McLany; Benjamin Gooden; Joseph Gooden; Benjamin Freeland; Moses Gooden; Joshua Davis; Edward Irons; Jonathan Irons; James Guest; Lewis Davison; Edward Wood; Isaac Collier; John Hollit; John Prichard; Elijah Hewitt; Thomas Mellor; James Puttee; Timothy Downing; Jacob Sapps; Arthur Chenoweth; Elsly Power; James Power; Samuel Harris Junr; James Harris; Stephen Harris; George Ffrench; William Gorden; Christopher Waggener; John Purcell; Thomas Purcell; John Scott; Gabriel Jacob; William Postlewait; Philip Trammel; William Keys; David Cysard; James Pearce; John Shephard; Samuel Shephard; Nicholas Trammel; Benjamin Pearcse; Richard Wilson; Charles Prather; Henry Conrod; Mark Lee; Edward Butler; Jeremiah Allen; John Tate; Jonathan Clarke; Barzellia Clarke; Christan Snidiker; John Cockran; John Bowman; James Banfield; William Clouse; Silvester Tipton; John Bell; Caleb Russel; William Cowin; Josept(?) Nichols; George Kelley 68 - Certified by the Committe of Observation Tuesday April 30th 1776. [Md. Hist. Soc., MS 1814]

11 Jan 1781/[Sam'l Duvall; Jno. W. Charlton; Raphael Brook; Sam'l Noland; Philip Mcconey; Edward Hall; Nicholas Dawson; William Jacobs; Richard Sheckles; Thomas Noland; Sam'l Boone; John Johnson; Joseph Swearingen; Sam'l Hanson; Rich'd Richards; Jeremiah Belt 3d; George Schnertzel; William Meng; Peter Grosh; Nathan G. Thomas; Abraham Faw; Jacob Gomber; Sam'l Price; Frederick County, to Gov. Lee] (Pr. Mr. Boone) May it please your Excell'y In consequence of an Act of the General Assembly to encourage the raising of a Voluntier Troop of Light Horse in each County we the subscribers have enrolled for the purpose of forming courselves into a Troop of Light Dragoons on the Terms prescribed by the Law; and we take the Liberty to recommend Doctr. Philip Thomas to be commissioned as Captain, & John Ross Key esr. as Lieut to the Troops by your Excellency and the Honorable Council, we shall use every exertion to equip ourselves with all possible expedition and shall acquaint your Excellency & the Honble Council as soon as we have everything ready.
We have deferred recommending a person for Cornet until the number of subscribers is increased. [Maryland Calendar of State Papers - The Red Books, No. 28, Letter 31. Also Archives of Md., Vol. XLVII, pp. 12-13

25 June 1781/Frederick Troops/Capt. Jno. R. Key; Philip Marony, Cort.; Usher Charlton; Abraham Faw; Nichos. Dawson; Peter Grosh; Thos. Nolan; Joseph Swearengen; Jacob Gumbare; Henry Gross; Henry Mainyard; Saml. Duvall; Richd. Sheckells; James Hook Junr.; Frederick Shull; Will. Simm; Will. Ming; Basil

APPENDIX B: MUSTER ROLLS AND OTHER LISTS

Wood; Philip Morningstar; Benj. Musgrove; Nathl. Thomas; Alexr. Warfield; John Shelman Jr.; George Snatsell; Geo. Michael Hook; Will Jacobs; Ed. Hall. The Above is the Fredk. Troop of Horses Commanded by Jno. Ross Key which was Appraised by us. Bernard O'Neill; Leonard M. Deakins; Thos. Beall of Geo. [Maryland Calendar of State Papers - The Red Books, No. 30, Letter 91. Also see Archives of Md., Vol. XLVII, p. 314.]

2 June 1783/"Have not yielded their service"
[The first two names given are the names of the two men who were drafted; the second is the name of the man who was actually appointed for active service. The remarks, therefore pertain to the reason for the second man not "yielding his service."]
Conrad Shrader, Colo. Baker Johnson - says he furnished a recruit but after repeated applications to him on the subject has never ... appeal.
Benja. Ogle of Benja., John Harbough - Discharged being very poor & having a wife & three children.
Simeon Heo, Capt Philip Rodenpieller - says he is overage and refuses to pay ... he was a commisison ... & is sick.
Peter Leatherman, Samuel Brandenburgh - never appeared.
Leonard Everly, George Miller - never appeared.
Conrad Miller, John Keller Junr - discharged from ... having a subst. on duty & delca... ... last furnished another subst.
Mathias Northsinger, Michael Smith (nailor) - hath not appeared.
Michael Arthur, Jacob Coventry - hath not appeared.
Daniel Hook, Benjamin Rice - appeared ready to march after siege of York.
William Sergeant, Samuel Northsinger - paid 8.5 pounds in lieu(?) of his service.
James Farthing, Archibald Grimes - neither appointed, both discharged on account of poverty & having families.
Eli Peirpoint (dead), Philip Ropp - paid 6 pounds ...
William Laws, Abraham Arnold - hath not appeared, gone to Redstone.
Anthony Deardurf, Samuel Shaws - discharged being very poor & ... & two yg. [young] children)
Andrew Robinson, Thomas Harrison - ordered to pay 6.75 pounds but hath not done it.
Peter Nelson, Michael Carn - Discharged. Hath a family, is poor & had just served his tour in the Mill (?)
Jacob Hinkle Junr, Major Abraham Haff - discharged on acct. of sickness.
Josey Davis, Thomas Schley Junr - has a large family & is poor but ... pay a small sum of money.
George Hardesty, Laben Hicks - gone to Montgomery County.
Nathan Thomas, Chrisr. Stanley - absconded
Barnett Ott, Joseph Cumberidge - will not appear
George Sulgar, William Scaggs - marched with cattle to Fredericksburg.
Christian Waggoner, Thomas Witten - Discharged, being poor & having a large family and was ill 2 mos. after ...
Thomas Major, Stephen Pierce - gone to the ancient ...
Stephen Howell, Harman Upperhour - Discharged having been ... unable to serve by a long fit of sickness.
John Bowden, Robert Miller - Appeared before Majr. Smallwood. Quaker suffered (?) to return him from Annapolis ... paid 9.15 pounds.

FREDERICK COUNTY

Jacob Slick, Jacob Switzer - agreed to join & pay money in lieu of their service. paid 9.5 pounds.
Henry McKinsey, John Warner - Discharged being an invalid, is poor & has a family.
Richard Orputt, John Mikesell - [has] wife, three small children & is poor - discharged.
Nathl. Burkett, Joseph Aller - agreed to pay an equal part of the expence - paid 6 pounds.
William Plane/Robert McMin - called, ses he was engaged as a cooper for the public but it was on wages. ordered to pay L7.10.of which he has paid 2 pounds(?)
Melchor Hubor, John Smith - hath not appeared
George Giger, Thomas Hartwell - Discharged having a wife & eight children & is poor
Robert Hammitt, Casper Rine - never appeared
Joshua Hobbs, Benja. Clary - Discharged ... of the ...... is poor & has a family
Thos. Baldwin, John Hall - Discharged rendered unfit for duty by sickness
Yate Plummer, Henry Roberts - .... appeared before Gl. Smallwood & suffered (?) to return home
John Young Junr, Frederick Shryer - Never appeared
Philip Angleberrg, Wm. Beaven - Discharged is poor & has a wife & three children
John Floore, David Jurer - gone to Virginia
Patrick Cunnan, Earnest Gotshall - hath not appeared
John Welder, Jacob Ott - hath not appeared
(submitted by) P. Thomas Lt. Fr. County, June 2d 1783

HARFORD COUNTY

From History of Harford County by Walter W. Preston, published in 1901. Press of Sun Book Office, Baltimore.

"We whose names are subscribed do hereby enroll ourselves into a company of militia, agreeable to the resolutions of the Provincial Convention held at Annapolis the 26th day of July, 1775, and we do promise and engage that we will respectively march to such places within this province, and at such times, as we shall be commanded by the convention or council of saftey, of this province, or by our officers, in pursuance of the orders of the said convention or council, and there, with our whole power, fight against whomsoever we shall be commanded by such authority as aforesaid."

Josias Carvil Hall's Company - No. 1
Witness our hands this 12th day of Sept., 1775
Josias Carvil Hall, Capt.; William Young, 1st. Lieut.; John Beadle Hall, 2d Lieut.; Thomas Hall, Ensign; James Webster; Freeborn Brown; Michael Gilbert, Jr.; Edward Hall, Edward Carvel Tolley; John Patterson; Thos. Peregrine Frisby; Richard Ruff; Richard Wilmott, Jr.; Garrett Garrettson; George Young; Aquila Paca, Jr.; Francis Holland; Benedict Edward Hall; Thomas Giles; William Smith, Jr.; John Copeland; John Diemer; Bennet Mathews; Josias Hall; James White Hall; Gabriel Christie; John Rumsey; Samuel Gover;

APPENDIX B: MUSTER ROLLS AND OTHER LISTS

James Holmes; William Annin; Arthur McCann; James Mathews; Joseph Butler; John Lee Webster; Aquila Hall, Jr.; William Loney; Joseph Finley; James Osborn, Jr.; Robert Morgan; Phil Henderson; George Presbury; Joshua Browne; Robert Stokes; Daniel Richardson; William Hollis, Jr.; William Hall; Thaddeus Jewett; James Paca; William Bradford, Jr.; Larkin Hammond; Roger Mathews; John Carlisle; Joseph Wheeler; Parker Lee; Bennett Wheeler; Henry Neill; Alex. Lawson Smith; John Matthews; William Hall of Aquila; Josias Wheeler; Thomas Orr; James Perkins; William Young

... a sufficient number being inhabitants of Maryland, in Harford county, adjacent to the Lower Cross Roads, having enrolled themselves, and on the 26th day of December, 1774, met and made choice of their several officers, in which position said company continued mustering once a week until the 16th day of September, 1775, at which time said company having met, subscribed their names to the following enrollment:
John Archer, Captain - No. 2 Lower Cross Roads Militia Company
John Archer, Captain; Edward Prall, 1st Lieut.; James Allison, 2d Lieut.; Samuel Smith, Ensign; John Archer; Edward Prall; James Allison; George Barclay; William Boardsman; John Stevenson; Samuel Smith; Charles Moore; William Grimes; John Tinny; John Welch; John Monahon; John Jebb; Ralph Smith; Peter Laughlin; George Tollenger; Arthur Monahon; John Smith; George McGlaughlan; John Hawthorn; Alexander Jeffrey; Jonathan White; Jacob Slack; Robert Criswell; James Walker; Andrew Harriot; John Perkins; William Martin; Robert Hart; Robert McGloughlan; Edward Thompson; Daniel Clarke; John Mills; Patrick Heany; Robert Smith; Hugh Diver; John Croesen; John Jamison, farmer; Richard Croesen; John Jamison, innkeeper; John Townsley; John Townsley, Jr.; John Blackburn, Jr.; James Lee; Joseph Shaghnassey; James Sheredine; Andrew Wilson; Patrick Cretin; William Harrison; Joseph Jervis; John Curry; Michael Donel; William Hassett; John McCann; George Vandegrift; Archer Hays; William Williams; John Davidson; James Moore; Samuel Doherty; Isac Guyton; Thomas Rowntree; James Hews; George Butler; William McClure; Joseph Brownley; James Cain; James Harris; David Dickson; Talbot Odle; Daniel Price; Ralph Smith; Edward Short; Thomas Hill; Matthew McClintock; James May; Nevin Kerr; Ezekiel Vanhorn

Charles Anderson, Captain - No. 3 Witness our hands this 23rd day of September, 1775:
Charles Anderson, Capt.; Geo. Patterson, 1st Lieut.; Nathan Bayles, 2d Lieut; Michael Gilbert, Ensign; Parker Gilbert; James Pritchard; William Boner; Harmon Pritchard; Ephraim Byard; Benjamin Smith; Daniel Dunahoo; Joseph Harris; Philip Donavin; Daniel Bayles; James Hanna; William Donavin; Eleazer Pritchard; Isaac Johnson; Pat. Fowler; Benjamin Bayles; John Cooley; Samuel Bayles; Joseph McFadden; Daniel Anderson; James Byard; Robert Cluver; Micaja Mitchell; Richard White; Richard Rutter; John Carroll; Thomas Shearer; Samuel Gilbert; John Williams; James Barns; Thomas Gorrell; Samuel Swart; William Jarvice; Aquila Gilbert; John Cummins; Dennis Dunham; Andrew Ferguson; Robert Small; Ichabod Smith; Abraham Robinson; Robert West; Alexander Hanna; Thomas Gallion; Joshua Wood; Ephraim Cole; Abadiah Pritchard; James Cole; Benjamin Silver; William Silver; James Wood; Andrew Ramsay; Robert Nixon; Robert Carswell; William Brannon; Jonas Bayles; John Gallion; Charles Baley; Benjamin Culver; David Smith; James Boner of Barney

HARFORD COUNTY

Aquila Hall, Captain - No. 4
Witness our hands the 9th day of September, 1775:
Aquila Hall, Captain; Samuel Griffith, 1st Lieut.; Jacob Forwood, 2d Lieut;
John Chancey, Ensign; Levin Mathews; Caleb Beck; John Adams; Samuel Hanson;
John Major; George Little; John Clarke; John Brown; John Hall Hughes; Henry
Vansickle; Hollis Hanson; Zebedee Bennett; John Whitacre; Hezekiah Whitacre;
Robert Faulkner; Jesse Manly; Nehemiah Barnes; William Jones; Abraham
Bennett; Thomas Hanson; John Dorrah; John Beck; William Smith; Jonas
Stevenson; Joseph Smith; Thos. Cowley; Benjamin Chancey; Edward Morris;
James Steward; Thos. Barrett; William Mooberry; John Mathews; James Redman;
John Casseldine; William Murphy; Edward Horton Brucebanks; John Cowin;
Thomas Woodward; Joseph Johnson; George Capeland; Archibald Johnson; George
Drew; Jacob Combes; George Chancey; John Ruff; James Chancey; Francis Pitt;
James Oliver; John Johnson; Robert Brown; James Kimble, Jr.; Thomas Sutton;
James McCarty; Peter Lovell; Thomas Brown; Stephen Crouch; William Rice;
John Manly; James Phillips; James Jones; Michael Kennard; Francis Garland;
Amos Hollis; Michael Connoway; Benjamin Osborne; Nathan Gallion; Garrett
Garrettson; William Osborne; William Redding; Edward Ward; James Lenagin;
Samuel Dooley; John Biggs; Thomas Blackiston; Thomas Browning; John Hanson;
Benjamin Bennett; William Johnson; Robert McGaw; James Drew; John McBride

Captain John Rodgers - No. 5
Witness our hands this 15th day of September, 1775.
John Rodgers, Captain; Wm. Godsgrace, 1st Lieut; James Giles, 2d Lieut. and
adjt.; Matthew Alexander, Ensign
Sergeants: Daniel McPhail; Thomas Gash; William Welsh; Archibald Beaty
Corporals: William Williams, Samuel Howell, David Thompson, Alexander Burns
John Orr, Drummer; James Hurley, Fifer
Peter Fort; John Singleton; Jonathan Grant; Jackson Laverty; Robert Hunt;
Philip McDonald; John Marshall; Joseph Montgomery; John Calgrove; William
Wise; Samuel Beach; David Deaver; Belcher Michael; William Mitchell, Jr.;
James Mitchell; William Evitt; Patrick McDonald, James Edwards; Francis
Faust; Richard Watts; Thomas West; Archibald McCurdy; William Vantworth;
John Lovell; James Ward; William Hill; Thomas Walker; John Porter; John
Walker; Walter Taylor; Samuel Fowler; William Murphy; William Perry Fowler;
Hugh Munroe; John Mitchell; William Coen, Jr.; James McKnight; Daniel
Deaver; Stephen Hargrass; John Osborn; Andrew Evitt; George Veach; Ralph
Platt; Thomas Boyle; William Cantler; James Seale, Jr.; Samuel Richardson;
Ozwain Sutton; Michael West; Joseph Steel; Daniel Williams; John Williams;
Jonathan Knight; Samuel Pritchard; William Shy; Thomas Knight; Samuel Durbin
Daniel McPhail, Clk.

Benjamin Rumsey, Captain - No. 6
Witness our hands this 16th day of September, 1775:
Benjamin Rumsey; Alexander Cowan; John Beale Howard; Isaiah Linton; Thomas
Gassaway Howard; Clement Lewis; William Copeland Goldsmith; Jonathan W.
Lewis; John Day, Jr.; George Gouldsmith Presbury; John Hammond Dorsey; Roger
Boyce; Benjamin Wilson; Samuel G. Osborn; John Allender, Jr.; James Bailey;
John Sewell; Joseph Cromwell; Henry Garrett; James Arnold; Otho French;
William Price; James Maxwell, Jr.; William Branan; John Christie; James
Adams; Henry Hays; William Allender; Josias Smith; Edward Day, Sr.; Joseph
Hewett; John Devin; Isaac Hall; John Gray; Richard Holloway; Daniel

APPENDIX B: MUSTER ROLLS AND OTHER LISTS

Tredwell; Benjamin Scarff; William Reed; James Price; Richard Wooden; Zep. Tolley; Thomas Cole; William Osborn; Moses Haslet; John Robert Harrison; Nicholas Eckson; John Wilson, doctor; Joseph Finley; Thomas Taylor; Walter James; John Mitchell; Thomas Stocksdale; Joshua France; Robert Stewart; James Foster; Hugh Stewart; John Thompson; Levin Ingram; John Huston; John Clark; John Phips; John Woolen; Major Woolen; Richard Hackett; John Stewart

Captain John Taylor's Company - No. 7
Witness our hands and seals this 9th day of September 1775:
John Taylor, Captain; Samuel Caldwell, Lieut; Thomas Hutchins, 2d Lt.; Vincent Richardson, Ensign; Jonathan Ady; Greenbury Chaney; John Carson; John Armstrong; Stephen White; John Saunders; William Jenkins; James Cox; Barnard Riely; William Ewing; William Norris of Joshua; James Walker; Aquila Norris of Thomas; David Harry; Hugh Bay; William Sargent, Sr.; John Allen; William Sargent, Jr; George Garrettson; William Marret; Thomas Freeman; Charles Herbert; Nathaniel Shepherd Armstrong; Stephen Fell; Daniel Thomas; William Bayd; John Cooper; Charles Gillaspey; Robert Conn; James Camp; Robert Travis; Samuel Richman; Thomas Hutchins; John Quinn; Samuel Standiford, Jr.; Edward Norris of Joshua; Thomas Richardson, Jr.; James McCurty; Andrew Bay; James Everett of Samuel; William Handersides; John Gillaspey; Robert Wilson; Samuel Brown; Israel Taylor; John Larramore; Peter Bond; Nathaniel Yardley; Moulden Amos; William Robinson; William Ady; Torrance Flannagan; James Moore; John Corbet; David Calwell; William Byfoot; Vincent Richardson; William Richardson; Moses McComas; John Norris of James; Charley Riley; John Wilson; Charles O'Close; Daniel Norris; Thomas Ford; Abel Green; Andreas Hughes; John Brown; Joseph Pearson; Amos Jones; Walter Martin; Thomas Robinson; John Kennedy; Richard Noland; John Conn; Richard McKinley; Daniel Fraley; John Buckley; James Huggins

Captain Greenberry Dorsey's Company - No. 8
Enrolled October 31, 1775
Greenberry Dorsey, Captain; John Wood, 1st Lieut.; William Barnes, 2d Lieut.; Cyrus Osborn, Ensign
Sergeants: Nathaniel Swain; James Deaver, Joseph Everist, John Howell
Corporals: Lloyd Mash, Joseph Fields, Baltus Fie, Thomas Ayres
James Taylor, Jr., Clerk
Privates: James McCracken; Isaac Toulson; Frisby Dorsey; Ashberry Cord; John Kimble; Samuel Pritchard; Obadiah Pritchard; Charles Pritchard; Thomas Pritchard; William Pritchard; George Dougherty; John Gordon; John Everist; Utey Combest; Asa Taylor; John Collins; Israel Combest; Jacob Combest; George Childs; Stephen Taylor; Robert Taylor; Mosey Loney; Thomas Simpers; Stephen Kimble; Isaac Dulany; Richard Berry; Thomas Lancaster; James Ford; Samuel Collins; James Kelly; Samuel Thompson; Samuel Tush; Richard Harrison; Gabriel Swain; Patrick McClain; Josias Kimble; James Fitzgerald; Benjamin Everist; Isaac Collins; Harmon Hill; Edward Evans; John Clark; Alexander Gordon; Amasa Taylor; Roger Sheedy; John Connolly; John Connolly, Jr.; William Collins; John Deaver; Reuben Sutton; William Daugherty; John Lee; Michael Melanhy; Charles Hipkins; Michael Carey; Roland Kimble; Evan Evans; Issac Duzent; John Morris; Horatio Harrison; Thomas Deaver; Micajah Deaver; Benjamin Ford; John Kirk; James Kimble; George Williamson; John Walker; William Wraine; Usher Tracey; Jacob Collins; John Lovatt; John McComas; Samuel Gallion; Moses Collins; Freeborn Garrettson; William Gray Duzan; John

HARFORD COUNTY

Giant; Samuel Jenkins; Charles White; Giles Kimble; Thomas Chrisholm; James Denison; Abraham Taylor; Hugh Orr; John Atkinson, Jr.; William Evans; William Evans, Jr.; John Barnes; Richard Pearce; John Bruce; Daniel Campbell; Jacob Duzart

Captain James Stewart's Company - No. 9
James Stewart, captain; James Talbott, first lieutenant; John Ware, second lieutenant; Jesse Pritchard, ensign; privates, 65.

Captain John Love's Company - No. 10
Witness our hands this 14th day of September, 1775:
John Love, Captain; Grafton Preston, Lieut.; Job Key, 2d Lieut; Nathaniel West, Ensign; James Scott, 1st Sergeant; James Munday, 2d Sergt.; Stephen Hill, 3rd Sergt.; Thos. Sheredin, 4th Sergt.; Corporals - Walter Billingslea, first; Robert Clark, second; James Preston, third; John Thomas, fourth
Privates: William Miles; Matthew Sweany; Thomas Able; Michael Lorden; George Rydon; James Rigdon; Peter Henley; John Callinder; Henry Green; Hugh Pugh; Bernard Johnson; Edmund Bull; James Deale; Alexander Huston; Benjamin Rhoades; Thomas Pennick; Jacob Johnson; Patrick Campbell; Lemuel Howard; Thomas Thurston; David Clark; Robert Taylor; Edward Bussey; Leonard Green; James Whitaker; Thomas Wheeler; John Woodward; Vincent Goldsmith; William Clark; John Wild; Edward Freeman; Philip McGuire; Thomas Rhoades; Thomas Johnston; John Paine; James Thomas; William West; Henry Thomas; Jacob Bull; James Craton; John Craton; Thomas Thompson; David Thomas; Josias Wheeler; William McMullin; Thomas Hill; James Allen; Ralph Pyle; John Welsh; William Cooper; John Ruckman; William Strowd; Leonard Green of Benjamin; William Fulton; William Baggot; Jonathan West; Bartholomew Savage; Martin Preston; John Carr; Barnet Preston; Isaac Pinnick; Barnet Pain; Isaac Arkwright

Captain Jacob Bond's Company - No. 11
Witness our hands this 9th day of December, 1775:
Jacob Bond, Captain; Thos. Johnson, 1st Lieut.; Jas. McComas, 2d Lieut.; Martin Preston, Ensign; William McMath; Aquila Scott of James; Patrick Hughes; Joseph Barns; Samuel McMath; John Barnes; William Anderson; James Curry; William Barnes; James Steel; Benjamin Scott; Elijah Joice; Buckler Bond; Joseph Saunders; Thomas Smith; John Drennen; Roderick McKenzie; Edward Hamilton; Daniel Scott of Aquila; Aquila Scott of Aquila; Thomas Pendegast; James Moriarty; William King; Michael Carr; Samuel Wilmott: William Brown; Christopher Clemens; Thomas Knight; William Smith; James Jarvis; Andrew Warwick; John Norris of Benjamin; William Cuthbert; James Amoss of James; Isaac Rose; Jacob Bull; Edmund Bull; Jacob Bull, Jr.; Nathaniel Smithson; John Pain; Henry Greer; James Deal; John Price; John Ruckman; John Lewis; Patrick Campbell; William Stephens; Moses Ruth, Jr.; William McMillan; Robert Fremble; Samuel Durham; Aquila Durham; Peter Potee; Mordecai Durham; John Durham of Joshua; Samuel McMillan; William Bond of Joshua; James Kelly; Robert Johnson; William Johnson; Benjamin Preston; James Moores, tanner; James Moores of John; Henry Ruff, Jr.; James Hanna; Patrick Reid; Isaac Whitacre; Jacob Bond, Jr.; Thomas Hinks; William Smithson; James Bond; James Bridge; Francis Williams

APPENDIX B: MUSTER ROLLS AND OTHER LISTS

Alexander Rigdon's Company - No. 12
Witness our hands this 2d day of December, 1775:
Alexander Rigdon, Captain; Daniel Carter, 1st Lieut.; Richard Deaver, Jr., 2d. Lt.; William Jones, Ensign
Sergeants: Joseph Wilson, Charles Johnson, Walter Denny, John Flat
Corporals: Christopher Fort, William Rose, Joseph Kerns, Samuel Peacock
Privates: William Smith; William Jenkins; Thomas Burke; Thomas Miles; George Johnston; Jeremiah Hawkins; John Donehay; John Whiteford; John Johnson; William Brakenridge; William Eken; John Brakenridge; John Frost; John Hudson; Jesse Kent; John Bullock; Gregory Hawkins; Samuel Hill; Philip Crail; Robert Hawkins; James Frost; James Queen; Joshua Ward; Luke Peacock; James Ward; John McGaw; Benjamin McCreary; Thomas Jones; Thomas Hudson; John Roberts; William Roberts; Robert Kennedy; John Kearns; William Gibson; Samuel Morgan; William Rigdon; Walter Lewis; Aquila Deaver; Seaborn Tucker; Jacob Jones; James Deaver; Stephen Rigdon; William Clark; John McClain; Benjamin Jones, Jr.; James Delong; Joseph Smith; Thomas Johnson; Robert Clark, Jr.; Isaac Jones; John Watkins; Isaac Jones of William; John Catherwood; James Benson; James Leakin; William Betts; Joseph Gibbons

Capt. William Bradford's Company - No. 13
Witness our hands this 30th day of September, 1775:
William Bradford, Capt.; Joseph Rose, 1st Lieut.; Hugh Kirkpatrick, 2d Lieut.; Edward McComas, Ensign; Samuel Vance; John Jones; Michael Mather; William Gail; William McComas; Benjamin Rickets; Samuel Power; Isaac Wheeler; Thomas Mather; Alexander Crawford; Solomon McComas; Daniel Lynch; David Vance; Robert Braser; William Norris; Joseph Stiles; Richard Bull; James Carroll; John Kitely; Thomas Yeaman; John Power; Samuel Stallins; James Nower; Alexander McComas, Jr.; William Boyer; Edward McKinsey; John Kean; Aaron McComas; John Pool; Alexander McComas; Thomas Cunningham; Edward Hanson; Zachariah Smith; William Yoe; Isaac Fryer; George Cunningham; Abraham Andrew; John Bull; William May; James Kelly; Reuben Ross; John Vance; Basil Smith; William Eadin; Benjamin McComas; William Saunders; John Ellis; Samuel Wiggins; John Brooks; John Morris; John McComas of William; Stephen White; Thomas Mason; James Dobbins; William Goddin; Aaron Goddin; Tayman Byfoot; William Ross

Charles Baker's Company - No. 15
At Josias Hitchcock's, Jr., in Harford county, 27th January, 1776:
Elected by ballot:
Charles Baker, Captain; Moses Johnson, 1st Lieut.; Richard Hutchins, 2d Lieut.; Nicholas Amoss, Ensign; Sergeants for the Jarrettsburg Company of Militia - Timothy Tate; Martin Parker; William Brittain; Mordecai Amoss; Rank and File - James Garrettson; Richard Robinson; William Parker; Bennett Green; Samson Eagon; Henry Scarff; John Rockhold; Michael Rutledge; Edward Gatheridge; Aquila Clark; Charles Rockhold; Andrew Cravan; William Hitchcock; Josias Hitchcock; Henry Hitchcock; John Evans; Edward Robinson; Jas. Scott; William Bosley; Aquila Miles; Richard Shipley; Thomas Rutledge; Jonathan Cunningham; Thomas Thomas; James Everett; Samuel Foster; Morris Baker; James Donnelly; Jacob Davis; Thomas Slade; Richard Perkins; Henry Scharff; Richard Everett; Daniel Pocock; John Warrick; William Warrick; William Barton; James Campbell; Andrew Thompson; Thomas Cunningham; Thomas James, Jr.; James Currey; John Davis; Walter Rice; Joseph Jones; Thomas

HARFORD COUNTY

Conner; James Richardson; George Chalk; John Chalk; James Turk; Nicholas Day; Henry Day: Peter Carroll; Henry Enlows; Matthew Creswell; James Hunt; Abram Rutledge; Robert Clark; John Corbett; Lewis Corbett; Peter Miller; William Baldwin; Underwood Guyton; Morris Lane

Captain William Webb's Company - No. 16
Witness our hands this 14th day of October, 1775:
William Webb, Captain; Ignatius Wheeler, Jr., 1st Lieut.; William Fisher, Jr., 2d Lieut.; John Webb, Jr., Ensign; Richard James; George Rogers; William Whiteford; Robert Gilchrist; Michael Daugherty; William Crooks, Jr.; Hugh Whiteford; Robert McCradey; John Beaver; Gilbert Crockett; Thomas Jones; Samuel Crockett; Andrew Lindsay; Archibald Ingram; James Clark; James Anderson; James Linam; John Beshang; Thomas Brown; Michael Sivers; Stephen Marford; Philip Albert; Patrick Halfpenny; Ralph Ellison; Thomas Duff; Simon Jordon; Charles Beaver; Thomas Beaver; Enclidus Scarborough; Francis Jenkins; James King; Benjamin Thomas; Nathaniel Smith; William Sparks; Baker Rigdon; John Smith; James Lewis; Robert McNear; James Phillips; John Jackson; Stophel Penchieff; William Hart; Francis King; William King; Godfrey Fye; John Morrow; Edmund Callahan; Hugh McGough; Thomas Crooke; John Taylor; John McFaden; James Hutcheson; Joseph Wilson; Robert Griffin; John Beaven; Levi Low; William Thoriman; John Barnhouse; William More; John Smith, Jr.; Thomas Ellett; Samuel Ellett; William Smith; William Lytle; Jonas Gilbert; William Murdock; Daniel More; Thomas Gallion; James Alexander; James Barnett; Robert Williamson; James Garrettson; Daniel Lindsay; John Wright; Archibald Wilson; George Patrick; James McDaniel; James Allen; Sedgwick James; John Scarborough; John Woodward; Richard Trotter; James Trotter; James Jackson

John Patrick, Captain - No. 17
Witness our hands this 1st April, 1776:
John Patrick, Captain; Winston Dallam, First Lieut.; Samuel Baylis, 2d Lieut; Richard Ward, Ensign; Samuel Hopkins; Chas. Worthington; Samuel Worthington; Barnet Daugherty; Joseph Amoss; Joseph McKinney; James Love; Charles Bevard; Jas. Bevard; William Snodgrass; Job Barnes; John West; Thomas Armott; Robert James; William Husband; Ezekiel Barnes; John Hilton; Richard Dallam; Gideon Gover; Jonathan Sterrett; John Dallam; Hugh Deaver; Thomas Stapleton; James Morris; John Scantlin; Thos. Stephenson; William Brannon; David Armstrong; Philip Warnock; Samuel Hawkins; Reuben Jones; William Scarborough; Patrick McMurray; Michael Knight; William Silver; Robert Creswell, Sr.; Robert Creswell, Jr.; Thomas Scarborough; John Flynn; Andrew Scott; Enclidus Scarborough, Sr.; William McLaney; George Carroll; Andrew Ramsay; William Ammott; John Reese; James Murfey; Arthur Macken; Josiah Stapleton; Robert Morgan, Jr.; Michael Norris

HARFORD COUNTY, 8th Battalion
After 29 June 1776/Petition to Council of Safety. Dissatisified that Capt. [Bennett] Bussey and his two lieutenants have received commissions, a majority of the company have elected the following officeres to be commissioned: Capt. James Barton, 1st Lt. Joshua Amos of James, 2nd Lt. Joseph Hartley, Ens. Archibald Robinson.
Signed: James Blaney, William Browne, George Colman, Staford Forisdail, John Hitchcock, Josias Hitchcock, Randel Hitchcock, James Noris, John Noris,

APPENDIX B: MUSTER ROLLS AND OTHER LISTS

Aquilla Parker, Richard Robinson, William Robinson, John Taylor, David Whitford, David Williams. [p. 50 of Calendar of Maryland State Papers - The Blue Books]

16 May 1781/Return of Class's in Harford County which were draughted and have not procured substitutes, 16 May 1781:
No. of Class/Persons draughted
1/Edward Morgan/a poor married man
2/Robert Culver/married & several children
6/Wm. James
9/Samuel Bond
10/Richard Rutter
14/James Maxwell
17/James Hall of Joshua/Mov'd into Baltimore County
[Md. Hist. Soc., MS. 1146]

KENT COUNTY

1776 Apr 16 St. Clair Capt. William, Milita Company enrollment, Kent County. We whose names are ..... Captain William St. Clair; 1st Lieutenant Wm. Mires; 2nd Liet. Samuel Beck; Ensign George Jackson, Thomas Jurey; George Vt. Mann; John Woodland; Thomas Roberts; Peter Danskin; David Wallis; Thomas Yeats; Jacob Kisner; George Lyon; John Haive; John E. Englert; John Smith; John Bradshaw; Luke Miars Jr.; Christopher Carter; Thomas Pratt; Joseph Parsons; Ebenezer Blackiston; James Webb; George Perry; John Hocksworth; William Walls; Thomas Hocksworth; George Saunders; Thomas Heath; Gabriel Vineman; Gabriel Wineman Jr.; Meshack Massy; Abednigo Massy; Robert Marley; Isaac Stanley; Joseph Stanley; Ebenezer Stanley; John Stanley; John Deale; John Beck; John Scaggs Jr.; John Tucker; Jr.; George Gullet; William Clarke; Samuel Cosden; Andrew Brown; Thomas Lewis; Benjamin Farrow; William McDaniel; James Breward; William Blaney; William Perres (Penes?); John Tucker; Corns. Comegys; Robert Reddock; Richard Shepperd. [Md. Hist. Soc., MS 1814]

KENT COUNTY, 27th Battalion

"Copy of 26th Batalion of Malitia under the command of Col. Donaldson Yeates, Kent County." [This roll is erroneously marked "26th" Battalion although it is in fact the 27th Battalion.]
William Henry, Lt. Col.; Jonathan Worth, Major

1st Company - William Maxwell, Capt.; John Rasin, 1st Lieut.; Thos. Smith 2d Lieut; Wm. Merritt, Ensign; James McClure, 1 Sergt.; Nathl. Toulson, 2d Sergt.; Joseh.(?) Greenwood 3d Sergt.; John Woodal, 4th Sergt.; James Stavely, 1st Corpl.; James Morris, 2nd Corpl.; David Newel, 3d Corpl.; Will. Dickson, 4th Corpol.
1st Class: Francis Knock Junior; Edward Freeman; John Stavely; James Sullivan; Pere Thrift; Robert Stewart; Willm. Fann; Willm. Gay; John Howard
2d Class: Willm. Baldwin; Joseph Stavely; John Giant; John Reed; Richd. Skeggs; Richd. Hart; Christopher Hall; Daniel Smith; George Basin; Aquilla

KENT COUNTY

Page; Daniel Donowin; James McBride; John Curry; Nathl. Knock; Peregrine Sullivan; Wm. Folks; John March Junr.; John Parsons
4th Class: John Dixon Taylor; Isaac Strawhan; John Thrift; James Jones; Samuel Strawhan; Thomas Rasin; Wm. Merrit Junior; Walter Harris
5th Class: John Reading; James Usilton; Morris Marah; Michael Bonner; Wm. Blay Tilden; Wm. Knock junior; William James; William Stewart Farmer
6th Class: Henry Brice; Hynson Wright; John Sullivan Junior; Isaac Smith; Richd. Sewel; Robt. Gay junior; Willm. Slipper; John Gale; George Grant
7th Class: John Dugan(?) Junr; James Chapple; Moses Ford; Moses Price; Thomas Strawhan; Thos. Hynson; Willm. Quillen; James Howard; Andrew Kelly
8th Class: John Beazley; John Stewart; Isaac Freeman; John Chesterman; Stephen Giant; Samuel Dulce (Dulee?); William Duyer; William Hynis; Joseph Underlin. [Militia Lists of Daus. of Founders and Patriots]

2d Company - Wm. Woodal, Captain; Thos. Boyer, 1st Lieut.; Richd. Peacock, 2 Lt.; Simd. Hackett, Ensign; Isaac Cornelius, 1 Sergt.; Richd. Moffett, 2 Sergt.; Wm. Newcom, 3 Sergt.; George Moffett, 4 Sergt.; Andrew Parks, 1st Corpl.; Matthew Smith 2 Corpl.; Chls.(?) Deford, 3 Corporal; Thos. Armstrong, 4 Corporal
1st Class: Joshua Vansant; Jacob Moffett; Benjamin Arnors(?); Francis Rutter; Thomas Woodal; George Hall; Edward Woodal; Francis Hanes; John Coleman; Wm. St. Clair; Benjamin Burchinal
2d Class: Haley Moffett; George Smith; John Simpson Junr; John Kearton; Will. Smith junior; Charles Hanes; William Laurance
3d Class: Ebenezier Castaloe(?); Enock Massey; Hynson Hall; James Rain; John Woodall Junr; John Miers(?); Josiah Massey; James Redgrave; Joseph Boots
4th Class: Joseph Redgrave; Elijah Daily; James Woodal; John Conor; Willm. Smith Senior; John Smith; Samul. Comiges; John Palmer
5th Class: Willm. Hales; Moses Moffett; John Howard; John Simpson Jr.; Isaac Boyer; James Smith (son William); Jacob Riley; James Hanes; George Tillard; Wm. Boots
6th Class: Cambel St.Clair; George Cornelius; Oliver Smith; John Turner; Wm. Woodal; Jesse Moffett; Christopher Williams; Joseph Burchinal; Carty Ellis; John Wallis; Alphonso Boots
7th Class: Bartly Palmer; Jeremiah Arno; William Smith; Joseph Burch; George Vansant; Richard Hooper(?); Vincent Hatchison; William Herring; Edward Wm. Johnson; John Broxton
8th Class: William Graham; Nathl. Massey; Joshua Browning; Isaac Riley; John Woodal son Jas; James Farow; Isaac Spencer; Thomas Hanes; John Comeges; William Moffett. [Militia Lists of Daus. of Founders and Patriots]

3d Company - Jeremiah Ford, Capt.; Thomas Smith, 1 Lieut.; Marmaduke Medford, 2 Lt.; Benjamin Ferry, Ensign; Patrick Ferrell, 1st Sergt.; Benjn. Briscoe, 2d Sergt.; Alexander Briscoe, 3d Sergt.; John Newell, 4th Sergt.; Jacob Briscoe, 1st Corpl.; Daniel Groome, 2d Corpl.; Thomas Lamb, 3d Corpl.; Daniel Greenwood, 4th Corpl.
1st Class: Joseph Rasin; Charles Jones; Michael Corse senior; Francis Cann; John Fatom; Francis Lamb junior; James Cann
2d Class: John Lassals; James Jones; Edward Crew; Cornelius Howard; John Howard Junior; John Gale; William Briscoe; Willm. Delihunty

177

APPENDIX B: MUSTER ROLLS AND OTHER LISTS

3d Class: Philip Durgan; William Redding; George Moore; Joseph Hart; Joseph Middleton; Robert Midleton; Thomas Parks; George Greenwood; St. Leagar Everitt
4th Class: Jacob Course; John Parks; John Pa..er(?); Benjn. Howard; Michl. Course junior; Griffith Jones junior; James Lamb; Thos. Howard; Thos. Drugan
5th Class: John Heckman; George Ford; James Hart; James Kelly; Leonard Howard; John Dinning; Joseph Greenwood; Thomas Mason; McCale Medford
6th Class: William Howel; William Ustleton; Zacarih. Dill (Ditt?); William Gale; Wm. Redgrave senior; Isaac Briscoe; Edward Ford; Hezekh. Massy; John Angur
7th Class: John Eunock; Francis Lamb Senr; David Davis; Moses Briscoe; Jams. Miller; Robt Buchannan; Willm. Collins; Francis Uselton
8th Class: Benjn. Collins; John Sullivan; Ths. Hebron Junr.; Michl. Jobson; John Iffield(?); George Hedinger; Jas. Greenwood; Charles Ford; Josh. Howard. [Militia Lists of Daus. of Founders and Patriots]

Fourth Company - George Little, Captain; John Massy, 1 Lieut.; William Knock, 2 Lt.; William Little, Ensign; James Spear, 1st Sergt.; Danl. Tose Massy, 2 Sergt.; Samuel Cosden, 3 Sergt.; Azariah Bostick, 4 Sergt.; Joseph Turner 1st Corpl.; Staphen Massy, 2 Corpl.; Thos. Reed, 3d Corpl.; Robert Little, 4 Corpl.
1st Class: Lambert Simmons (Simmes?); Michael Burns; John Skaggs; Danl. Rochester; Isaac Clayton; Holland Webb; William Burris; Robert Geddis; Benjamin Bezly
2d Class: Lewis Davis; John Gray; John Giant; Robert Reynold; Abram. Cartwright; Joel Newnam; James Berry; William Spearman; Jas. Hynson; David McKimmy
3d Class: Gilbert Simmons; John Deal; Thomas Boyer; John Blackiston; William Coombs; Joseph Reynald; Jacob Boots; Rigebel Simmons
4th Class: James Russel; Isaac Stanly; William Pryor; George Little; Jacob Clyton; Abraham Allin; Willm. Francis; Benjn. Chairs; John Harper; Thomas Boyer Senr
5th Class: Thoms. Gallilee; Thos. Nicholson; John Stanly; Robert Marly; James Susee(?); Ephraim Vansant; Nathan Chairs; Nichl. Rennals; Andrew McMullin
6th Class: John Bryon; John Pryor; Benjn. Richardson; Willm. Turner; Joseph Massy; John Spearman Jr.; Eben Massy; Joseph Stanly; Willm. Geddis; Eben Stanly
7th Class: Lambert Smith; Willm. Brown; John Webb; Willm. Harper; Zorabl. French; John Sewel; Thos. Hawksworth; Mingo McKinly; Christopher Fields
8th Class: Wm. Simmons; Isaac Middlebrook; Wm. Nevel(?); Abram Reynols; Jeremiah Simmons; Thomas Simmons; Abraham Boyer; John Crouch. [Militia Lists of Daus. of Founders and Patriots]

Fifth Company - Gilbert Falconer, Capt.; John Whittington, 1 Lieut.; Wm. Mires, 2d Lieut.; Stepn. Mires, Ensign; Abednego Massy, 1st Sergt.; Jonathan Jobson, 2 Sergt.; David Wallis, 3d Sergt.; Thomas Jones, 4th Sergt.; Benjn. Farrow, 1st Corpl.; John Greenwood, 2 Sergt. (Corpl.); John Walls, 3d Corporal; William Walls, 4th Corpl.
1st Class: Masheck Massey; George Lyons; Ebenezor Blackston; John Colgin; Joseph Williamson; Walter Dunn; John Tucker; James Baley; Jesse Norris; Wm. Mires, son Stephen

KENT COUNTY

2d Class: John Shepard; James Hynson; Luke Mires junior; John Bradshaw; John Arano; Peter Burch; George Gullet; David Webb; Morgan James; John McDowell; James Boyer
3d Class: John Belford; Nathan Keach; James Brewer; John Whaly; John Spearman; George Fountain; Jacob Comeges; James Mires; Thomas Jury; Salathieal Freeland; John Richardson
4th Class: Joseph Boushell; Robt. Canniford; Samuel Beck; Wm. Mott; Pearce Bowers; John Sealy; Robt. Webb Junr; John Daley; Willm. Britton; Stephen Howard; John Thomas
5th Class: John Hayes; Joseph Porter(?); Lewis Welch; John Burnsides; John Mires; Thomas Nicholson; Spear Piper; Thomas Roberts; Elies Boyer; Robert Hall
6th Class: Abram Whittington; George Maran(?); Stephen Mires; Willm. Harris; Daniel Haly; John Curry; Nathan Keach; Abram Marly; Willm. King
7th Class: Wm. Greenwood; John Englet; Isaac Hurlock; Jos. Parsons; Wm. Comegys; John Reynolds; George Saunders; John Boulton; Nicholas Stoops; Jeremiah Sullivan
8th Class: James Whittington; David Lewis; George Smith; Dennis Earl; Jacob Umberson; John Mett; John Cox; Gambriel Vincemor; Willm. Hunter; Richard Pratt. [Militia Lists of Daus. of Founders and Patriots]

Peregrine Brown, Capt.; John Day, 1st Lieut.; Isaac Freeman; James Woodland; Wm. Wilson, Sergt.; Edward Freeman, 2 St.; John Vansant, 3 Sergt.; James W... (Wilcock?), 4 Sérgt.; John Wilson, 1st Corpl.; Benjn. Vansant, 2d Corpl.; Christr. Vansant, 3d Corpl.; Francis Lennon, 4th C.
1st Class: John Miller; Benjamin Riley; James OBryon; Henry Taylor; Michael Parsons; John Hurt; Barny Thompson; William Grant; Thomas Pearce; Stephen Anderson; William Jackson
2d Class: William Clarke; James Hants(?); William Smith; Thomas Burns; Lambert Smith; Conrad Whiteman; John Bolton; Robt. Maxwell Junr.; Jacob Vansant; George Browning; Govants (Genl. Vanst.?) Newcomb
3d Class: Daniel Forgusson; John Forman; John White; Samuel Beedle; Allen Woodal; James Wise; William Haley; George Wilson S Richd. (son Richard?); Isaac Redgrave; John Cayton; Spencer Beedle
4th Class: James Pearce; Charles McClain; Archabald Wright; James Beedle; James McCay; Willm. Forrester; John Maxwell
5th Class: Jonathan Devonpert; Thomas Taylor; Danl. McGillegus; John Harris; Peter Jones; Joshua Carearl(?); Willm. Riley; James Wilson
6th Class: John Dillis; Daniel Hull; John Bone(?); Harmon Beedle; Jacb. Reynols; John Smith Sn Nat. (son of Nat?); Henry Knock; Wm. Richardson; Matt. Richardson Jr.; John Winter; Wm. Dollis
7th Class: Willm. Rogers; Richd. Stork; Robt. Latham; John Bivins; Willm. Stephens; Danl. Cornelius; Robt. Maxwell; Garret Vansant; Wm. Brown; John Woodland
8th Class: James Greedy; James Dollis; George Mason; Joseph Lary; Joseph (blank); George Perry; John Tolson; John Mitchel; Richd. Caulk. [Militia Lists of Daus. of Founders and Patriots]

Seventh Company - Nathl. Comegys, Capt.; Jams. Wilmer, 1st Lieut.; Frans. Wallis, 2d Lieut.; Corn. Comegys, Ensign; John Cray, 1st Sergt.; Charles Rolliston, 2d S.; Thomas Sappin, 3 St.; John Cosden, 4th St.; Lambert

APPENDIX B: MUSTER ROLLS AND OTHER LISTS

Flowers, 1st C.; Robert Young, 2d Corp.; Dnl. Wm. Parker, 3d C.; John Dugan, 4th Corpl.
1st Class: James Tulley; Samuel Tiller; Hugh Pearce; Henry Wiatt; James Wilson; Josiah Stimal(?); James Baly
2d Class: James Hynson; John Haley; Jonas Denning; William Hull; James Stell(?); Stephen Denning; Samuel Wiatt; Asa Stewart; James Butcher; John Wallis
3d Class: Phillip Warner; William Worth; James Hicks(?); Henry Pinnington; Frederick Armington; Reuben Harding; Willm Wilmer; Fragget Tillard
4th Class: Christopher Billican; Henry Wallis; George Denning; Eusau Brooks; Nathl. McClannan; Willm. Keating; Willm. Kelly; James Durity; Malaciah Ambrose
5th Class: Hugh Wallis; Joshua Vansant Jr.; Jess(?) Cosden Senr.; Robert Mansfield; Willn. Wiatt; Nathl. Herring; Danl. Herring; Wm. Keene; Thomas Dowling; Robert Maxwell
6th Class: Johnson Brooks; Edward Tiller; John Wallis Doctor; George Burris; James Porter; John Clk Vansant; Nick. Riley; John Sappington; Francis Sherrard
7th Class: Richard Green; Isaac Walters; Samuel Wallis; William Berry; Jas. Sappington; John Greenwood; John Findley
8th Class: John Brooks; John Hanvey(?); John Woodland; Sam Mansfield; Abraham Freeman; George Black; Nich. Denning; Richd. Hurt. [Militia Lists of Daus. of Founders and Patriots]

```
                           1332
Capt Jno. Wilmer's Comp     80
                           1412
```

John Lambert Wilmer, Capt.; John Wilson, Lieutenant; Robert Moody, Lieutenant; George Medford, Insign; Sergants: Thos. Sanders; John Browning; Samuel Wilson; Samson Redgrave; Corprels: John Williams; Eli Bostick; John Stevenson; Elisha Massey
1st Class: Wm. Boyer son of John; Wm. French; Thos. Stevens; Thos. Price; John Moffett; Benjn. Webb; Benjm. Price; Augt. Boyer; Wm. Manfeild; Samuel Freeman
2nd Class: Henry Ferrell; Wm. Ellis; Thos. Ferrell; Nath. Glann; Abr. Jeneys; Thos. McHenry; Robert Money; Peter Meekings; Thos. Ellis
3rd Class: Elijah McKey; John Manfeild; Philip Morow; Henry Bantham Senr(?); Elijah Massey; Richard Penington; Peter Severe; Jeremiah Simons; John Sanders
4th Class: John Brown; James Boyer; Richd. Bevens; Henry Bantham Junr; Joshua Burgan; John Burgas; Absolam Chrisfield; Gidion Clarke; Isaac Dawson; Mathew Elbern
5th Class: Thos. Welsh; John Weaver; John Wilson son of Tho(?); Nicholas Haney; Enoch Johns; Wm. Hanson; Wm. Grindage; Isaac Newland; James Bentlay
6th Class: Thos. Boyer; Lambert Scott; John Scott; Wm. Boyer Senr; Peter Watson; John Crouch; Thos. Boyer son of Nt.(?); Wm. Gibson; Wm. Francis; Samuel Comegys
7th Class: John Williamson; Wm. McDowell; Js. McDowell; Edw. Comgys; Andrew McMulin; Js. Rusell; Lewis Bantham; Wm. Vansant; Richd. Redgrave
8th Class: Abr. Sanders; Edw. Strong; Peter Turdey (?); James Vansant; Charles Watts; James Welch; John Wilson Junr; Nicholas Smith; John White; David Williams. [Militia Lists of Daus. of Founders and Patriots

KENT COUNTY

"Viz. Within is A Return of Captn. John Wilmores Company. Doctr. Bordly has the Returns of the other Seven Companys of the 27th Battalion it was said there was more Companys for this - Battalion but I can't find either privates or officers for such Company or the Ground they stand on you will find in the other Returns many classes with only Eight privates so that I think you find on averdgeing the whole but about Seventy privates to a company which makes 560 privates to this Battalion 4 commissioned and 6 non Commissioned officers to a Company makes 96 (+) 560 (+) - 656. This includes all sectaries (secretaries) to John Maxwell Esqr.
/s/ Donaldson Yeates"

KENT COUNTY, 13th Battalion

13th Batt. of Militia under Command of Col. Richard Graves, June 1775
Benj. Chalmers, Lt. Col.; Isaac Perkins, Major; Willm. Frisby, Major

1st Co - Robert Cruikshank, Capt.; Anthony Banning, 1st Lieut.; Thomas Masling, Lieut.; George Gilbert, Ensign
1st Class: Nathaniel Dyer; John Jones; William Mathews; Edward Smith; James Dunn Jnr.; Edward Davis; Joseph Hopkins; James Ringgold Jr.; William Shield
2nd Class: Britain Masling; William Dowling; Wm. Strong; John Burk; Richard Lennox; Major Stewart
3rd Class: Thomas Granger; James Hurt; John Lowman; Francis Skervin; Richard Smyth; James Ringgold; George Duncan; James Masling; John Wales; Arthur Bordley
4th Class: John Burk Junr; Thomas Delahunty; Edward Cannon; John Lynch; John Eads; Henry Eads; William Glenn; John Gird; Valentine Warum
5th Class: Edward Alford; William Fray Junr; John Simmonds; John Gray Parish; William Money; James Griffith; Hamor Masling; Joseph Blackiston
6th Class: James Grant; Thomas Hadley; James Eads; Wm. Kendoll; John Magnor Jr.; Wm. Buckingham; Henry Bashwell
7th Class: John Frazier; George Clark; Aquilla Jones; Nathan Atkins; Thomas Lord; John Ringgold Junr; Mordeca Delahunty; William Mason Junr
8th Class: Wm. Greenfield; John Dew; William Shaw; William Boddy; Richard Lane; Jonathan Eads; James Frazier; James Kendoll; Joseph Score. [Militia Lists of Daus. of Founders and Patriots]

2nd Company - Morgan Brown, Capt; John Rolph, 1st Lieut.; Levin (Sovrin?) Merritt, 2nd Lieut.; Charles Neil, Ensign
1st Class: John Grimes (Games?); Aaron Trencher; William Solway; George Wilson; Joseph Hopkins; Joseph Eldridge; William Trew; Edward Beck
2nd Class: Wm. Harwood; Joseph Byram; James Byram; Patrick Ahern; James Casemark; Wm. Mansfield; Wm. Pearce Junr; James Smith
3rd Class: Jeremiah Nicols; Peregrine Glenn; Elisha Clark; Wm. Dennison; John Sutton; Jesse Clark; James Cork; Joseph George
4th Class: John Stewart; Alexander Giddis(?); Henry Troth; Morris Megonagil; John Clarke Junr; Wm. Byram; Nicholas Brown; Charles Baker
5th Class: William Mason; James Blackiston; William Smith; William Clark; Charles Pearce; Nathan Byran; Henry Curry; John Ashley
6th Class: Henry Price; Elias Ringold; Robert George; Abraham Boots; Jesse Comegys; Elijah Clark; John Byram; Abraham Milton

APPENDIX B: MUSTER ROLLS AND OTHER LISTS

7th Class: Stephen Byram; Thomas Sudler; John Boddy; William Baker; Richard Milton; Edward Comegys; Thomas Punney; Thomas Stapleford
8th Class: Richard Wilson; James Harrison; John Barratt; Francis Masling; James Lovegrove; Wm. Burchinal; Samuel Thomas. [Militia Lists of Daus. of Founders and Patriots]

3rd Company - Alexander Anderson, Captain; George Hartshorn, 1st Lieut.; Philip Davis, 2nd Lieut.; William Worrell, Ensign; Saml. Smith, 2nd Lieut.; John Sturgis, Ensign
1st Class: Barney Corse; John Beverlin; Coro. (?) Connway; Thomas Woodal; John Shaves; John Apsley; Philip Fray; Samuel Hammond; Simon Moore
2nd Class: Samuel Wallis; Henry Price; James Wilson; Thomas Chipchase; Barthm. Forman; Jere McHaffey; Thomas Humphry; James Brewer; Benjamin Wroth; Robert Davis
3rd Class: Thomas Weaver; George Waller (Wallis?); Wm. Roberts; James Covington; Thomas Huff; Samuel Forman; John Moore; William Sluby; Charles Copper
4th Class: John Wethered; Robert Anderson; William Pearce; Joseph Exel Thomas; Simon Halbert; James Smith; Daniel Holyoak; Thomas Ireland; Matthew Dean
5th Class: John Lorain; James Riedderford (Rudderford?); John Scott; Kinvin Wroth; Thomas Woodard; John Sullivan; William Trew; Josias Ringgold; John Frisby
6th Class: Solomon Dawson; John Deighton; Samuel Crouch; James Wilmer; William Hall; James Hamilton; John Smith; Moses Berry
7th Class: Thomas Thomas; Isaac Hackett; George Moore; Charles Whealer; Shem Hadley; Benja. Benney; Thoms Covington; Joseph Conden(?); Thoms Ringgold; John T. Ricketts
8th Class: Thomas McCoppin; Samuel Sinnet; Tobias Ashmore; Thomas Caton; Thomas Kent; John Gleaves; Charles Miller; Simon Worrell; James Blake.
[Militia Lists of Daus. of Founders and Patriots]

4th Company - John Moore, Capt.; Simon Wickes, 1st Lieut.; Thomas Crow, 2nd Lieut.; Samuel Beck, Ensign; Comm'd 2nd Lieut. June 1778
John Ricketts, 1st Sergt.; Benjamin Andrews, 2nd Sergt.; William Copper, 3rd Sergt.; William Grant, 4th Sergt.; Henry Prosser, 1st Corp.; Wm. Glanvill, 2nd Corp.; Vincent Hatchison, 3rd Corp.; James Crouch, 4th Corp.
1st Class: Samuel Grant; John Costley; James Frisby Junr; Lewis Atkinson; Samuel Hutson; Jonathan Grant; Richard Fillingham; Richard Mungar; John Carvill Hynson; John Tiller; Charles Hynson Junr; Morgan Hurt
2nd Class: Henry Lynch; James Saunders; John Hartley; Richard Brice; John Martin; Thomas Mansfield; Peter Arnold; Patrick Carr; John Young; Samuel Hammond; James Dolvin; John Dickey
3rd Class: Hezekiah Dunn; Wm. Drummond; Andrew Childs; Thomas Quick; James Massy; Wm. Shaw; John Carradine; Nathan Hatcheson; John Taylor; Kelly McCarty; James Ross; Richard Brummel
4th Class: William Ivey; John Hatchison; Joseph Reed; Samuel Wickes; Samuel Button (Butters, Buttew?); Robert Wharton; Thomas Wharton; Stephen Boddy; Benajah Tullingham; John Brice; Thomas Griffith; James Evans
5th Class: Elisha Nab; John Pearce; Thomas Reardon; John Elliott; Benjamin Forster; James Wilson; Richard Kirkwood; Philip Holmes; John Curry; Darius Dunn; Samuel Mungar; Joseph Wickes Jr.

KENT COUNTY

6th Class: Joseph Rumney; James Tharp; Benja. Hatchison; Charles Morgan; William Hall; William Griffith; John Clark; James Dunn; John Burk Junr; Wm. Hynson Crabbin; Elisha Winters; Edward Gibbs
7th Class: James Brummel; James Darrington; John Fitzgerald; Stephen Kendoll; Wm. Robertson; Benja. Clever; James Mansfield; Edward Whaland; William Dunn; William Caulk; George Tucker; John Boddy
8th Class: Ephraim Stoker; Richard Spencer; John McGregory; William Merchant; Thomas Crosley; John Housroof; Richard Kirkwood Junr; Robert Dunn; William Wilson; Norris Copper; William Watson; Thomas Whaland. [Militia Lists of Daus. of Founders and Patriots]

5th Company - Marmaduke Tilden, Capt.; Samuel Reed, 1st Lieut.; Andrew Pearce, 2nd Lieut.; Charles Tilden, Ensign; Alexander Beck, 1st Sergt.; Joshua Beck, 2nd Sergt.; John Reed, 3rd Sergt.; John Whaland, 4th Sergt.; Daniel Beck, 1st Corpl.; John Patten, 2nd Corpl.; Jonathan Comegys, 3rd Corpl.; Aquilla Attix Jr., 4th Corpl
1st Class: Daniel Davis; John Merry; Philip Jones; Samuel Whitehouse; John Hill; John Devor; John Roberts; Isaac Redgrave; William Riley; (blank) Randol
2nd Class: James Thompson; St. Leger Meeks; Hales Everitt; John Beck; Daniel Spencer; George Watts; Robert Meeks; Edward Beck Junr; Nehemiah Crouch
3rd Class: Theophilas Meeks; Alexander Apsley; James Chalmers; James Beck; Thomas Jones; Joshua Willis; Wm. Herring; James Benton; Wm. Braffett; Samuel Beck
4th Class: John Kennard Jr.; Stephen Kennard; Wm. Kerney; Wm. Kennard Jr.; William Hurst; Nathan Beswick; John Jones; James Wroth; George Shakes
5th Class: James Pullet; Daniel Kennard; Hugh Spencer; Arthur Dillen; Dennis Kennard; Jacob Foreman; Edward Apsley; John Griffith; Wm. Meeks; Robert Randal
6th Class: John Timms; Richard Spencer; Moses Alford; Moses Berry; Pere Spencer; Kinvin Wroth Jr.; Aqua. Attix; John Blanchford; Stephen Causey
7th Class: Christr. Knight; Richard Peacock; John Randal; Thomas Horny; Bartus Punney; Wm. Hamar; Jonathan Spencer; Wm. Forster (Foster?); John Cowarden
8th Class: Kinvin Wroth; Samuel Tishe; James Wroth Junr; John Nusom; Edward Pearce; John Gidley; Wm. Pearce; James Steen (Stun?); Thomas Trew; John Kennard. [Militia Lists of Daus. of Founders and Patriots]

6th Company - Richard Gresham, Capt.; David Crane, 1st Lieut.; Saml. Bullock, 2nd Lieut.; John Rollingson, Ensign; Edmond Lynch, 1st Segt.; Daniel Turner, 2nd Sergt.; John Williams, 3rd Sergt.; Abrham Haynes, 4th Sergt.; Robert Taylor, 1st Corpl.; James Laurence, 2nd Corpl.; James Greenwood, 3rd Corpl.; Abednego Jackson, 4th Corpl.
1st Class: John Strahan; Philip Trulock; James Groom; William Smith; Charles Milward; George Ferguson; John Hudson; Jacob Falconer; Isaack Maccay; William Mears
2nd Class: John Hix; Daniel King; John Turner; Thomas Corse; William Taylor; John Blackiston; Alexander Glems; William Dougherty
3rd Class: John Rausell(?); James Cannon; Noble Simmonds; Peregrine Cooper; John Daily; James Ware; Dennis Hurley; Thomas Jones; Pearce Lamb; Wm. Tennant

APPENDIX B: MUSTER ROLLS AND OTHER LISTS

4th Class: Benjamin Jones; Thomas Costley; Charles Groome; Samuel Tillard; Edward Engram; Thomas Trew; Isaac Cammell; Jacob Trulock; Pearce Lamb Jr.; John Matthews
5th Class: Edward Stewart; Joseph Numbers; John Ustleton; Thomas Broadaway; Michael Flaharty; John Sullivan; Abrham Taylor Junr; Froget Tillard; Henry Brooks; James Dunkin
6th Class: John Corse; Abner Vickers; Thomas Blackiston; Aquilla Meeks; John Lynch; Samuel Bennett; Nicholas Lynch; John Willis
7th Class: James Wells; Matthew Brooking; Richard Redding; Richard Carpenter; Wm. Dugan; John Watson; Joseph Sill; Lambert Cavender
8th Class: William Greenwood; Richard Hynson; Andrew Scott; George Reed; John Burgin; James Woodal; Benjamin Oston; John Numbers. [Militia Lists of Daus. of Founders and Patriots]

7th Company - John Page, Captain (resigned)
1st Class: Wm. Elburn Jr.; Geo. Frazier; Michael Miller; Alexander Beck Jr.; Isaac Redue; James Williamson; William Hynson; Joseph Copper; John Jones Hillpoint; Wm. Ayres; John Rogers
2nd Class: William Crabbin; John Enloes; Charles Coleman; Edward Bird; Walter Miller; William Frazier; Francis Benton; Nathan Brooks
3rd Class: James Score; Joseph Wikers; William Parker; Thomas Smith; Nathan Shaw; John Berry; William Davis; William Smith; Alexander Beck
4th Class: Benjamin Joiner; Wm. Fry Junr; Benjamin Dedman; Richard Knight; George Merchant; James Bradshaw; Stephen Blackiston; John Hinds; William Brice
5th Class: Wm. Hurst; John Yearly; James Miller; Thomas Miller; Thomas (son of Thomas); Edward Shaw; Thomas Collins; Michael Atkinson; Robert Summers
6th Class: Richard Jones; Joseph Brown; Peregrine McFall; David Ashly; John Holder; John Stinson; John Frazier; Wm. Stevens; Andrew Martin
7th Class: Sabret Huxter; John Jones; Benjamin Benton; James Hague; Richard Miller; Samuel Miller; Nathl. Miller; Samuel Crouch; George Gibbs
8th Class: Nathaniel Rogers; John Gordon; Nathl. Hynson; James Hodges; Samuel Taylor; John Hurt; Wm. Browny; William Ringgold; Robert Butler.
[Militia Lists of Daus. of Founders and Patriots]

William Frisby, Capt., 4 May 1778; James Lloyd, 1st Lieut., resigned; Willm. Wilmer, 2nd Lieut.; Richard Willis, Ensign; Jas. Rolinson, 1st Sergt.; Simon Smith, 2nd Sergt.; Philip Taylor, 3rd Sergt.; Joel Willis, 4th Sergt.; Richard Smith, 1 Corporal; Joel Higinbottom, 2nd Corporal; John Jones, 3rd Corporal; Thos. Gamble, 4th Corporal
1st Class: Samuel Smith; Thos. Edwards; Blackiston Wilmer; George Burk; James Niel; John Griffith; Jas. Lynch; John Swift; John Dinson
2nd Class: Joseph Frisby; John Davis; Wm. Ashly; Wm. Dial; John Hiag; Thomas Mansfield; Richard Lowman; Anthony Bannon; Thos. Bowers Jr.
3rd Class: Thomas James; James Plimton; John Tharp; John Smith Junr; Joseph Brischo; Thomas Bowers; James Ashly; Edward Ashly; John Ashly Jr.
4th Class: John Jones; Joseph Harris; Stephen Smith; Hyth Taylor; John Ashley Junr; William Yeates; Edward Carrol; Owen Whaland; James Smith
5th Class: James Clark; Sutton Smith; Richd. Kennard; William Shurvin; Olivr. Higenbottom; Sol. Bennet; Mich. Underhill; Thomas Cartor; Richd. Frisby

KENT COUNTY

6th Class: Charles Tilden; Abram Ashly; Wm. Brown; John Culbert; Darius Jones; Sterling Thomas; George Higinbottom; Benjamin Conaway; Absalom McCay
7th Class: Benjamin Higinbottom; Saml. Bennet; William Dawson; Darius Gramble; James Copper; Robt. Greenfield; Thos. Dunk; Hynson Smyth; George Smith
8th Class: Gustavs. Hanson; David Brown; Thos. Dew; Henry Hosier; Patrick Flinn; John Caton; Wm. Kennard. [Militia Lists of Daus. of Founders and Patriots, held by Md. Hist. Soc.]

9th Company - Pere Letherbury, Capt.; John Watkins, 1st Lieut.; James Claypoole, 2nd Lieut.; James Piper, Ensign
1st Class: Thomas Whaland; Wm. Pattin; John Hartley; John Palmer; Samuel Chaplin; John Offley; Richard Thomas Junr; Lazarus Tittle; John Hanagan
2nd Class: James Simpson; Walter Anderson; William Rowell; Owen Kennard; William Yardsley; William Ramsey; James Hendley; Richard Thomas S; John Elbert; Donald McQuin
3rd Class: Charles Baker Jr.; John Kenady; William Wallis; Thomas Kemp; John Ringgold; Joseph Lusby; Wm. Russel; William Bowers; William Collins
4th Class: John McKim; Wm. Perkins; Cuthbert Hall; Ezekiel Forman; David Metzler; Joshua Clarke; Alexander Danskin; William Vickers; Barrot Boddy; Dean Reed
5th Class: James Vickers; John Wright; William Kenedy; William Woolaston; Samuel Roberts; Dennis McNamara; Jacobus Hinds; Robert Reed; Daniel Fisher; Hugh McKinley
6th Class: James Corse; Blackston Chandler; Philip Brooks; Thomas Anderson; James Anderson Jr.; Robert Roberts; Wm. Robertson; C.(?)_ Joshua Guttery; Thomas Thornton; William Forbes(?)
7th Class: Wm. Barrat; John Blakeway; William Jones; Philemon Tilghman; John Tittle; Edward Hopkins; Charles Hakett; John Green; Timothy Mara; William McKim
8th Class: David Boyd; John Watkins; Wm. Dunkan; James Kelly; Jacob Shaffer; Jeremiah Banon; Samuel Perkins; Richard Morris. [Militia Lists of Daus. of Founders and Patriots, held by Md. Hist. Soc.]

KENT COUNTY, 27th Battalion

27th Batt. of Maryland Militia Commanded by Colo. Donaldson Yeates
1st Company - Capt. Wm. Maxwell; Jno. Reason, 1st Lt.; Thos. Sewall, 2nd Lt.; Wm. Merritt, Ensign
Serjants: James McCluer; Natn. Toulson; Joseph Greenwood; John Woodall
Corporals: James Staple; James Norris; David Newell; Wm. Dixson
James Sullivan; Pere Thrift; William Gay; Jno. Howard Senr.; Francis Knock Jr.; Saml. Jones; Edward Murphey; Isaac Hynes; Joseph Briscoe; Richard Hartt; Joseph Stavely; Jno. Joyant; Jno. Read; Richard Scaggs; George Reason; Asa Stewart; Jno. Mires; Geo. Newcomb; Wm. Comegys; Jno. Burgin; Aquila Page; Wm. Folkes; Jno. March Junr; John Parsons; Jesse Morris; John Cahoon; Isaac Shawhorn; James Jones; Thomas Rasin; Walter Harris; Benj. Johnston; James Uslington; Wm. Knock Jr.; Wm. Stuart Farn.; James Pennington; Thomas Shawhorn Junr; Robert Redgrave; Amos Reed; John Greenwood; Henry Breese; Richard Sewell; John Dixson; Joseph Duyer; Alphonso Comegys; James Myres; Blackston Chandlee; John Hartt; John Duyer Junr; James

MUSTER ROLLS AND OTHER LISTS

Chappell; Moses Foard; Moses Price; Thos. Shawhorn Senr.; William Quillen; James Howard; Andrew Kelley; John Briscoe; James Taylor; John Bolton; Samuel Norris; James Woodall; John Stewart; Stephen Joyant; Samuel Dulce; Joseph Underlin; Wm. Redgrave Junr; George Lamb; William Turner; Michael Jobson; William Maxwell. [Militia Lists of Daus. of Founders and Patriots, held by Md. Hist. Soc.]

2nd Company - Jesse Cosden, Capt.; Saml. Comegys, 1st Lt.; Cuthbert Hall, 2nd Lt.; John Haley, Ensign
Sergeants: George Hall; Thomas Armstrong; Edward Wm. Johnston; Haley Moffett
Corporals: Joshua Browning; John Woodall; John Kerton(?); George Cornelius
Jacob Moffett; Benjamin Arno; Francis Rutter; Thomas Woodall; Edward Woodall; William Woodall; Isaac McCay; George Smith; John Smith; William Smith Junr; William Laurence; Simon Hackett; Lambert Vansant; Ebenzer Casleton; Isaac Redgrave; Daniel Forguson; Hynson Hall; John Woodall; Josiah Massey; James Redgrave; Jonas Tiller; James States; Joseph Williams; Elisha Dayley; James Woodall; John Palmer; David Stoops; Richard Peacock; William Graham; Joseph Reynolds; Francis Spry; John Rollinson; John Burgin; William Hales; Moses Moffett; James Smith; George Titter(?); Wm. Boots; Thomas Boyer; Wm. Smith (son John); Lambert Smith; John Weaver; Robert Moffett; George Moffett; James Broxton; John Turner; Jesse Moffett; Christopher Williams; Alfonso Boots; Francis Sherrard; Matthew Smith; Bartley Palmer; Jeremiah Arno; Wm. Smith Senr; George Vansant; Vincent Hatchinson; John Broxton; Nicholas Stoops; William Graham Senr; Isaac Spencer; John Comegys; William Hunter; Richard Moffett; Nicholas Smith. [Militia Lists of Daus. of Founders and Patriots, held by Md. Hist. Soc.]

3rd Company - Capt. Jeremiah Ford; Thomas Smith, Lt.; Marmaduke Medford, Lt.; Benj. Torry, Ensign
Sergts.: John Newell; Jacob Briscoe; Daniel Groome; Thomas Lamb
Corpls.: Daniel Greenwood; Alexander Briscoe; Griffith Jones; James Jones
Charles Jones; Michael Corse Sen.; Francis Cann; John Tatom; Francis Lamb Junr; James Cann; Thomas Chandlee; James Berywalls; Richard Trusby (Truths?); John Lassells; Edward Crew; Cornelius Howard; John Howard Junr; John Gale; William Briscoe; Wm. Dilehuntey; Richard Coby; Thomas Jones; Phillip Drugan; Wm. Reding; George Moore; Joseph Hart; Joseph Midleton; Robert Usselton; Thomas Parks; George Greenwood; St. Legar Everitt; James Corse; John Ellorne; John Pavin; Benjamin Howard; Michael Corse Junr; James Lamb; Thomas Howard; Thomas Drugan; Nathaniel Howell; Isaac Copper; George Corse; John Anger; William Lamb; John Hickman; James Hartt; James Kelley; Linard Howard; McCall Medfeord; Robert Hartt; Anthony Pushpin; William Dugan; John Crew; William Howell; William Usselton; William Gale; William Redgrave Sen.; Isaac Briscoe; John Anger Senr; Robert Daugherty; James Strong; Robert Rasin; Ebenezer Turner; Rasin Gale; John Eunocks; Francis Lamb Senr; David Davis; Moses Briscoe; James Miller; John Lamb; William Collins; Francis Usselton; Robert Buchhanan; Jacob Jackson; Daniel Cunningham; John Sullivan; Thoms Mebber(?); John Effield Junr; Charles Ford; Joseph Howard; James Butler; Benjamin Gilbert; Jno. Wetherhead; Lambert Phillips. [Militia Lists of Daus. of Founders and Patriots, held by Md. Hist. Soc.]

KENT COUNTY

4th Company - Capt. William Knock; Lts.: Wm. Little; Danl. Massey; Stephen Massey, Ensign
Sergeants: Joseph Massey; Azariah Bostick; Thomas Fowler; Joseph Turner; Corpls: Robert Little; William Turner; William Harper; John Spearman Lambert Simmons; Patrick Fowler; John Wd. Pennington; John Scaggs; James Smen (Simon?); Joel Newman; James Hynson; Elias Deal; John Jobson; John Dixson; Gilbert Simmons; John Deal; John Blackston; Archibald Simmons; Isaac Stanley; Benjamin Cleaves; Robert Reynolds; Jeremiah McDonald; James Bryon; Thomas Galalee; John Stanley; Robert Marby; Nathan Cleaves; Andrew McMullin; James Waters; Benjamin Kithison; William Turner; Ebenezer Massey; Ebenezer Stanley; William Ward; John Smith; William Hogans; John Taylor; John Reynolds; John Webb; Zarababel French; Christopher Fields; Ruben Neal; John Zelifso; James Bostick; James Black; James Spencer; Zorobabel French Junr; David Wells; James Conner; William Simmons Junr; Isaac Middlebrook; William Pell; Joseph Burch. [Militia Lists of Daus. of Founders and Patriots, held by Md. Hist. Soc.]

5th Company - Gilbert Falconar, Capt.; John Whittington, 1st Lt.; Wm. Mires, 2nd Lt.; Stephen Mires, Ensign
Sergts.: Abednego Massey; Jonathon Jobson; Andrew Parkes; Joseph Parsons Corpls.: Garrett Vansant; Archb. Hannah; John Arno; John Watts (Walls?) George Lyons; Eben Blackston; John Colgan; Joseph Wilkison; Wm. Mires (son Stephen); Joseph Rawlins; Abram. Comegys; John Blackiston; John White; Peter Covington; James Hynson; Luke Mires; John Bradshaw; James Boyer; Lewis Turey; Wm. Dawson; Natl. Knock; Jas. Bruer; Geo. Fountain; Jacob Comegys; Stephen Mires; Jas. Mires; Jas. Harrison; Thos. Corse; Thos. Rowlins; Isaac Weaver; Jonathon Jester; Jos. Burchanell; Saml. Beck; Wm. Molt; Pearce Bowers; Robert Webb; Stephen Howard; Jno. Thomas; Danl. Shawhorn; Terey Gandley; Jno. Mires; Spiar Piper; Charles Realy; Stephen Phillips; Abram. Whittington; Stephen Mires; Wm. King; Joshua Covington; Geo. Barcus; Geo. Sanders; Wm. Watts (Walls?); Jas. Readis; Jno. Rowlins; David Wellden; Wm. Jones; Denis Earle; Jacob Humborson; Richd. Pratt; Benjamin Sill; Jno. Thomas Doctr. [Militia Lists of Daus. of Founders and Patriots, held by Md. Hist. Soc.]

6th Company - Capt. John Day; Isaac Freeman, Lt.; James Woodland, Lt.; Wm. Wilson, Ensign
Sergts.: Edward Freeman; Jas. Wilson (son of Jas.)
Corpls.: Robert Maxwell Junr; Jas. Wilson; Geo. Wilson; Wm. Dolles Benj. Riley; John Hurt; Barnett Thompson; Wm. Grant; Thos. Pearce; Geo. Wilson; Geo. Wilson (son Jno.); Wm. Wise; Ben. Cole; Wm. Smith; Lambt. Smith; Wm. Clark; Jacob Vansant; Geo. Browning; Geo. Vansant; Henry Knock; Joseph Redgrave; Spencer Boodle; Jas. Henry; Wm. Williams; Jno. Harris Junr; Wm. Armstrong; Geo. Mason; Jas. Pearce; Archd. Wright; Wm. Forrester; Ben Everitt; Charles Irons; Nathl. Browne; Chrisr. Vansant; Jonathan Davenport; John Dollis; Thomas Taylor; Francis Lennard; John Wright; Abram. Redgrave; Abram. Woodland; Wm. Richardson; Smith Bagwell; Wm. Hirrin; Cornel. Comegys; Jas. Pennington; Jas. Pennington; Wm. Rogers; Robert Laythem; Jno. Bevans; Daniel Cornelius; Robert Maxwell Senr; Josh. (Joseph?) Rasin; Isaac Toney(?); Edward Comegys; Jas. Greedy; Josh.(?) Lary; Josh. (Joseph?) Davenport; Jno. Mitchel; Wm. Rasin; Jas. Lawrence; Nathl. Knock; Alexr.

MUSTER ROLLS AND OTHER LISTS

Stewart. [Militia Lists of Daus. of Founders and Patriots, held by Md. Hist. Soc.]

7th Company - Nathaniel Comegys, Capt.; James Willmer, Lieut.; Francis Wallis, Lieut.; John Woodland, Ensign
Sergts.: John Gray (Cray?); John Cosden; Charles Rolison; Doctr. Wm. Parker
Corpls.: Samuel Mansfield; Geo. Dennen; Jonas (?) Denning; Isaac Dawson
Henry Wyatt; Wm. Jackson; Jas. Baley; Jas. Miney; Hartley Sapington; Geo. Bell; Jas. Hynson; Jas. Steel; Stephen Denning; Wm. Hull; Jas. Butcher; Jno. Wallace senr; Levering Alley; Jas. Willson; Jas. Tenant; Michael Parsons; John Jones; Samuel Wyatt; Mordecai Dilahunte; Andrew Kerr; James Martin; Isaac Elbert; Wm. Worth; Jas. Hicks; Henry Pennington; Frederick Armington; Thomas Smith; John Murphy; Wm. Burgin; Wm. Taylor; Isaac Cork; Christopher Bellican; Henry Wallis; Wm. Keyton; Malichi Ambrose; Wm. Kelly; Jas. Durity; Wm. Riley; Nathan Hartt; Thos. Corse; John Gibbs; Hugh Wallis; Robert Mansfield; Wm. Wyatt; Natl. Herrin; Robert Maxwell Junr; Jas. Hatchison; Edward Stewart (?); Natl. Piner; Jacob Riley; Geo. Williamson; Saml. Lynch; Wm. Eccleston; Edw. Tiller; John Wallis (Doctor); John Vansant; Nicholas Riley; Jno. Sappington; Wm. Ireland; John Wallis Senr neck; John Wallis Junr; Edward Beck; Abraham Taylor; Simon Lovemoney(?); Richd. Green; Jno. Smith; Jas. Sappington; Edward Sutton; Simon Irons; Benjamin Busly(?); Peregrine Reed; Geo. Cole; Cuff Gibs; John (Hauvey, Harvey ?); Geo. Black; Nichs. Denning; Richard Hurtt; James Smith; John Eccleston Junr; William Herrin; James Farrow; Wm. Mann; John May; Samuel Wallis; Prince Buckskin.
[Militia Lists of Daus. of Founders and Patriots, held by Md. Hist. Soc.]

8th Company - John Lambert Willmor, Capt.; John Wilson, 1st Lieut.; Robert Moodey, 2nd Lieut.; George Medford, Ensign
Sergts.: Thomas Sanders; Jno. Writson Browning; Saml. Wilson; Samson Redgrave
Corpls.: John Williams; Elisha Massey; Wm. Boyer (son of Jno.); Wm. French
Thos. Stevens; Thos. Price; Benjamin Webb; Benjamin Price; Wm. Mansfield; Saml. Freeman; Wm. Boyer; Jesse Heath; Cornelius Hartt; William Ellitt; Jonas Blackskin; Thos. Elliss; Wm. Elliss; Thomas Ferrell; Nathaniel Glann; Robert Money; Joseph Deford; Elijah McKey; Elijah Massey; Richd. Pennington; Richd. Bantham; Eli Williams; James Greenwood; Nathl. Clark; Peter Carr; Jno. Brown; Jas. Boyer; Henry Bantham Junr; Absolom Chrisfield; Gideon Clarke; Hiram Wilson; Eli White; John Wilson; Enoch Johns; Wm. Hanson; Wm. Grindage; Isaac Newland; James Bentley; James Fessler (Fisster?); Lambert Scott; Wm. Boyer Senr; Peter Watson; Thos. Boyer; Wm. Gibson; Robert Hucheson (Hachison?); Joseph Carroll; Saml. McDowell; Jno. Williamson; Wm. McDowell; Jas. McDowell; Jas. Russell; Wm. Vansant; Richd. Redgrave; Wm. McDowell; Richard Simons; John Teleforth (Telefroth?); John Nowland; Abraham Sanders; James Vansant; Charles Watts; John Wilson Jr.; John White; Thomas Emison; Charles Brown; Charles Deford; David Simmons. [Militia Lists of Daus. of Founders and Patriots, held by Md. Hist. Soc.]

KENT COUNTY

Kent County, 13th Battalion under the command of Col. Richard Graves

1st Company - Thomas Maslin, 1st Lieut.; Thomas Grainger; Brittain Maslin; Nathaniel Dyer; James Hustt; Wm. Fry, Jnr; Wm. Greenfield; Wm. Dowland; John Burk, Jr.; Aquilla Jones; Geo. Gilbert; John Simmonds; Thos. Delehunty; William Matthews; Nathaniel Atkins; Francis Skirvin; Richard Lain; William Strong; Edward Smith; James Dunn, Jr.; James Eades; Henry Eades; Jonathan Eades; James Frazier; William Glenn; James Griffith; William Kindall; James Maslin; Hamor Maslin; James Ringgold, Jr.; William Shield; Valentine Wareham; John Wales; John Magnor Junr; Wm. Mason, Sen.; Wm. Mason, Jr.; Joseph Blackiston; Matthew Richardson, Jr.; Daniel Perkins; John Shield; Edward Hadley; James Caulk; John Lynch; William Smyth; Stephen Byram; James Vickers; Wm. Fraizer; Samuel Beck; James Clark; Lewis Atkinson, Samuel Maslin; David Ashly; Thomas Fraizer; William Salway; David Ashley; Thomas Frazier; Wm. Salway. [Militia Lists of Daus. of Founders and Patriots, held by Md. Hist. Soc.]

Quaker Neck, 2nd Company - Capt. Morgan Brown; John Ralph, 1st Lieut.; Charles Neal, Ensign; Thomas Blake, Sergt.; John Gordon, Sergt.; Robert Simmonds, Sergt.
1st Class: Aaron Trencher; Geo. Willson; Joseph Eldridge; Wm. Trew; Edward Beck; George Forguson; Wm. Fairfield; Joel Higginbottom; David Sullivan; David Pearce
2nd Class: Patrick Ahern; Wm. Mansfield; James Smyth; Saml. Shearman; Richard Lennox; Samuel Pearce; Joseph Clark
3rd Class: Jeremiah Nichols; Pere: Glenn; Elisha Clark; Wm. Dennison; John Sutton; Joseph George; James Byram; George Duncan; Marma: Tilden; Charles Tilden, Jr.; Frederick Glenn
4th Class: John Stewart; Nicholas Brown; Edward Sutton; Edward Cannon; Samuel Troth; Alexander Glenn; Henry Troth; Bartus Wilkins, Jr.
5th Class: Wm. Mason; Wm. Clark; Charles Pearce; Nathan Bryam; Henry Curney; Henry Brooks; Wm. Covington; Charles Triesses(?); Gideon Comegys
6th Class: Robert George; Jesse Comegys; Elijah Clark; John Byram; Abraham Milton; John Kendall; James Birchinial; Thomas Garnett
7th Class: Wm. Baker; Edw. Comegys; Thomas Punney; Thomas Stapleford; Joseph Comegys; Daniel Beck; Samuel Thomas Junr; Thomas Lord; Nathaniel Kennard
8th Class: James Harrison; John Barrott; Francis Maslin; Wm. Burchinial; Samuel Thomas; Andrew Scott; James Lennox; James Kindall; George Brown; Thos. Wilkins. [Militia Lists of Daus. of Founders and Patriots, held by Md. Hist. Soc.]

Chester - 3rd Company - Philip Davis, Captain; Saml. Sinnott, 2nd Lieut.; John Sturgis, Ensign; Thomas Woodall, 1st Sergt.
1st Class: Barney Corse; John Shears; John Apsley; Philip Fray; Samuel Hammond; Samuel Chaplin; Daniel Hull; John Chesterman
2nd Class: Thomas Chipchase; Benjamin Wroth; Thomas Huff Sen.; James Hague; Joseph Garnett; George Waller
3rd Class: Wm. Roberts; John Cherington; Thomas Huff, Jr.; Wm. Slubey; John Forman; David Hull; Daniel Herring
4th Class: Robert Anderson; William Pearce; Joseph Exel. Thomas; Simeon Halbert; Gideon Haines; James Smyth; Thomas Ireland; Daniel Hollioake; Valentine Bendor; Thomas Warren; William Forman

MUSTER ROLLS AND OTHER LISTS

5th Class: John Lorain; Kinsman Wroth; John Frisbey; Alex. Calder; Samuel Wilkins; Edward Harris; Thomas Smyth
6th Class: James Hamilton; John Smyth; Benjamin Andrews; Richard Weathered; John Tharp; Simon Moore, 4th Sergt.
7th Class: George Moore; Charles Wheeler; Shem Hadley; Thomas Covington; Thomas Ringgold; Samuel Bennett; Edward Worrell; John Body; Wm. Dixson
8th Class: Tobias Ashman; James Covington; John Gleaves; James Blake; Philip Bishop; Wm. Worrell; John Roatch; Wm. Brown. [Militia Lists of Daus. of Founders and Patriots, held by Md. Hist. Soc.]

Lowr Langford Bay, 4th Company - Simeon Wickes, Capt.; Thomas Crow, 1st Lieut.; Samuel Beck, 1st Lieut.
1st Class: John Elliott; Henry Prosser; James Crouch; Saml. Hutson; Richard Mungar; Jno. Carvill Hynson; John Tiller; Charles Hynson; John Jones; Martin Wheat; Ebenezer McGregory
2nd Class: Richard Brice; Peter Arnold; John Young; Edward Bird
3rd Class: Andrew Childs; Alexander Beck Sen.; Nathan Hatchison; John Taylor; Kelly McCarty; James Ross; Charles Copper
4th Class: Wm. Jory; John Hatchison; Samuel Wickes; Robert Worton; Thomas Worton; Benajah Fillingame; John Brice; Thomas Griffith; James Evans; John Eades; Wm. Perkins; James Strong; Richard Berrey
5th Class: Elisha Nabb; Thomas Reardon; Benjm. Foster; James Wilson; Darius Dunn; Saml. Mungar; Joseph Wickes; James Lloyd
6th Class: Benjm. Hatchison; Charles Morgan; William Hall; Wm. Griffith; John Clark; Edwd. Gibs; James Bowen; Peter Stokes
7th Class: James Darrington; James Brumel; Stephen Kindall; Wm. Caulk; Saml. Grant; Joseph Wickes Jr.
8th Class: Ephraim Stokes; Richard Kirkwood; Wm. Watson; Thos. Whaland; David Griffith; Richard Hynson; Wm. Shaw; James Kenley; John Adkinson; James Brice. [Militia Lists of Daus. of Founders and Patriots, held by Md. Hist. Soc.]

Worton, 5th Company - Saml. Reed, 1st Lieut.; Charles Tilden, 2nd Lieut.; Robert Meeks, Ensign
Sergts.: Joshua Beck; John Whaland; Moses Alfred; Jonathan Comegys
1st Class: John Hill; John Roberts; Charles Jones; Wm. Cowarding; James Lynch; Wm. Dunn
2nd Class: Hales Everitt; John Beck; George Watts; Nehemiah Crouch; Owen Kennard; William Deal; Richard Hosier Jr.; Dunkin McDonald
3rd Class: Theophilus Meeks; Alexander Apsley; James Beck; Joshua Willis; Wm. Herring; Thomas Webb; John Ashley Jr.; Wm. Drumer; James Benton; William Bruffit; John Flatman; William Steen
4th Class: John Kennard; Wm. Kennard; James Wroth; Geo. Shakes(?); Joseph Reed; John Ashley Senr
5th Class: Hugh Spencer; Dennis Kennard; Jacob Forman; Edw. Apsley; Robert Randall; Thos. Woodard; Thos. Calvert; Wm. Dunken (sawer); Geo. Gyant
6th Class: Oliver Higginbottom; John Timms; Kinvin Wroth Jr.; John Blanchford; Stephen Causey; Moses Berrey; Wm. Atkinson
7th Class: Richard Peacock; Bartus Punney; William Hamer; John Cowarding; Edw. Whaland; Saml. Hosier; Thomas Dunken
8th Class: James Wroth Junr; John Newsom; Edward Pearce; James Steen (Stun?); Wm. Dunkin (Saylor); John Attix; Wm. Middleton; Samuel Tush;

KENT COUNTY

Richard Hosier; Henry Hosier. [Militia Lists of Daus. of Founders and Patriots, held by Md. Hist. Soc.]

6th Company - David Crane, Captain; Saml. Bullock, 1st Lt.; Henry Trulock, 2nd Lt.; John Williams, Ensign
Sergts.: Daniel Turner; Abednigo Jackson; Richard Rodney
Corpls.: James Greenwood; Dennis Hurley
1st Class: Charles Millward; Philip Trulock; John Hayne; James Groom; Henry Taylor; James Lewis; John Ashbury; John Hudson; Jacob Lamb; John Cooper
2nd Class: John Forguson; Daniel King; John Turner; William Taylor; John Taylor; St. Leger Meeks; Robert Davis
3rd Class: Pergrine Cooper; Wm. Tennant; James Ware; Saml. Trulock; Pearce Lamb Senr; John Dennis; John Looman; Benj. Greenwood
4th Class: Benjamin Jones; Charles Groome; Isaac Cannell; Jacob Trulock; John Matthews; Pearce Lamb Junr; Edw. Ingram; Saml. Toulson; John Kingham
5th Class: Michael Fluharty; Benj. Kelley Junr; Abraham Taylor Junr; Wm. Meeks Senr; Solomon Bennett; James Forguson; Peter Isselow
6th Class: Aquilla Meeks; John Lynch; John Willis; Edmond Lynch; Richd. Adams
7th Class: James Wells; Joseph Sils; Saml. Cavendar; Jacob Jones Junr; John Tittle Junr; Richard Willson; George Greenwood Junior
8th Class: John Burgan; Benj. Auston; John Martin; Wm. Clark Harkness; Benjamin Greenwood. [Militia Lists of Daus. of Founders and Patriots, held by Md. Hist. Soc.]

Eastern Neck, 7th Compy - James Williamson, Capt.; Morgan Hurt, 1st Lieut.; James Dunn (son of Hezekiah), 2nd Lieut.
1st Class: William Elburn Junr; John Jones (S.C.); Michael Miller; Alexander Beck; William Ayres; Vincent Hatchison; James Mansfield
2nd Class: Charles Coleman; Walter Miller; Nathan Brooks; Wm. Crabin; Benj. Worrell; John Stattet (Stallet?); James Dolvin; John Glenn
3rd Class: Joseph Wickes; Wm. Parker; John Berry; Wm. Davis; Wm. Smyth; James Brown; Benj. Higginbottom; Wm. Glanvill; Hezekiah Dunn; Thomas Quick
4th Class: Mathew Dean; Benj. Joyner; Benj. Dedman; George Merchant; James Bradshaw; Stephen Blackiston; Wm. Brice; John Hinds; Joshua Cockey
5th Class: James Mansfield; Wm. Hurst; James Miller; Thomas Miller son of Thomas; Robert Summers; Edwd. Shaw; Michael Atkinson; John Yardsley; Wm. Yearly
6th Class: Joseph Brown; Wm. Stevens; Peregrine McFall; Andrew Martin; Henry Basset; Walter Miller; Elias Ringgold; Samuel Dunn
7th Class: Samuel Miller; Samuel Crouch; George Gibbs; John Jones (E.N.); John Fitzgerald; David Jones; Wm. Dugan; Wm. Foster
8th Class: James Hodges; Samuel Taylor; John Hurt; Nathanl. Hynson; William Brown; Robert Butler; William Merchant; Benjm. Higginbottom; David Brown. [Militia Lists of Daus. of Founders and Patriots, held by Md. Hist. Soc.]

8th Company - Geo. Harshorn, Capt.; James Rollison, 1st Lieut.; Simon Smyth, 2nd Lieut ; Joel Willis, Ensign
Sergts.: Owen Whaland; Thomas Gamble; Samuel Smyth; Thomas Edwards
1st Class: John Swift; John Duetson; Geo. Burk; Moses Alfred; George Hanson Junr; James Neal; John Brown

MUSTER ROLLS AND OTHER LISTS

2nd Class: Thos. Mansfield; Darius Jones; Richard Looman; Darius Copper; Alexander Glenn Junr; Joseph Byram
3rd Class: John Tharp; John Smyth Junr; James Ashley; Thomas James; Edward Ashley; James Plymton; Saml. Kennaday; Abraham Rolison; Edwd. Scanlan; Darius Beck
4th Class: John Caton Senr; James Smyth; Stephen Smyth; Height Taylor; Edward Carroll; Archibald Surrell
5th Class: Oliver Higginbottom; Michael Underlin
Thos. Caton; Wm. Skervin; David Willson; Joseph Harris Junr
6th Class: William Brown; James Harris; Abraham Ashley; Mo: Greenfield; George Hanson Senr; Absolom McCoy; Benj. Higginbottom; William Dawson; Darius Gamble
7th Class: Richard Smyth; James Copper; Hynson Smyth; George Smyth; Michael Smyth; William Copper; John Caton Junr; Christopr. Knight; Henry Thomas
8th Class: Gustavus Hanson Junr; Thomas Bowen; William Copper Junr; Patrick Flynn; Saml. Looman; John McGregory; John Fraizer; James Higginbottom; Wm. Kennard. [Militia Lists of Daus. of Founders and Patriots, held by Md. Hist. Soc.]

Chestertown, 9th Company - Pere Letherbury, Capt.; John Watkins, 1st Lieut.; James Claypoole, 2nd Lieut.; James Piper, Ensign; John Wickes, 1st Sergt.; Robert Blake, 2nd Sergt.; Robt. Constable, 3rd Sergt.; John Fenell, 4th Sergt.; David Boyd, 1st Corporal; Edw. Hopkins, 2nd Corporal; Lazarus Tittle, 4th Corporal
1st Class: John Hartley; John Palmer; John Harrigan; William McKinney; Robert Burns; Joseph Bostridge; Peter Bradgurg; Wm. Kennaday; Matthew Simpson
2nd Class: Walter Anderson; Richard Thomas; Donald McQuin; Thomas Barton; Thomas Lorain; Thomas Lynch; Philip Chaplin; Thomas Patton
3rd Class: Wm. Wallis; Thos. Kemp; Wm. Russle; Wm. Colins; John Fenwll son of John; Wm. Meeks; John Sapington; Richard Geddis; Benj. Chambers
4th Class: Joshua Clark; Alexander Danskins; William Vickers; Bartus Body; Dean Read; John Matsler; Andrew Myars; William Tilghman; Thomas Smyth Junr
5th Class: Robert Reid; John Hutson; David Halbert; Thomas Sudler; Thomas Jinate; Joseph Score
6th Class: Philip Brooks; Thomas Anderson; William Robertson; Joshua Guttry; Wm. Forbes; Joseph Rumney; Thos. Perkins; John Maxwell; Thomas Harris; John Bryan
7th Class: John Blackway; Charles Hackett; John Green; George Tucker; Wm. McDaniel; Peter Vance; Edwd. Wright; Wm. Prune; John Ringgold Junr; Jacob Shaffer; Jere. Banon Jnr.; Richd. Morris; Thomas Du; Thomas Jones; Benj. Vickers; James Barnes. [Militia Lists of Daus. of Founders and Patriots, held by Md. Hist. Soc.]

MONTGOMERY COUNTY, Upper Battalion

An Exact list of all the Free male Inhabitants of Montgomery County from the age of sixteen to fifty years as allso the Distribution of said Inhabitants into Company and Batallions as Directed by an Act of assembly passed last session, for the Better Reglation of the militia. [Militia Lists of Daus. of Founders and Patriots]

MONTGOMERY COUNTY

Officers & Privates for the Upper Battallion
Zadock Magruder 1st Colonell; Frans. Deakins, Lieut ditto

1st Company: Sollamon Simpson; Zachh. Ellis;
Thos. Veitch; Jno. Harwood, Sollamon Ellis; Geo. Hauskins/30 Aug 1777
Michl. Dowden; John Dowden; Zeph. Ellis; Hugh Tomlinson; Mathew Willson;
Geo: Hardy; Geo: Hoskinson; Thos. Dowden; Walter Harden; Zephh. Swann; Grove
Tomlinson; Willm. Collier; Shadrick Ellis; Joseph Jones; John Warring; Thos.
Warring; John Young; Saml. Douglas; Joshua Harbin; Andrew Hutts; Wm.
McDaniel Jur.; Henry McDaniel; Hazel Williams; Abijah Fife; Joseph Fife;
Jonathan Fife; John Fife; Geo: Gentle; Willm. Hawkes; Stephen Gentle;
Joseps. Arnold; Chas. Lucas; Elisha Williams;John Robeson; Shadrick Locker;
Notley Talbott; Barton Dyson; Zephh. Wood; William Draper; Willm. Arnold;
Chas. Allison; Isaac Johnson; Ninian Clagett; Joseph Poole; Chas. Hoskenson;
Thos. Allison; Griffith Willitt; Phillip Green; Saml. Blackmore; Terrance
Rigney; William Jewell; Jas. Soaper; Geo. Willson; Wm. Tomlinson; Joshua
Ellis; Edwd. Jones; Hezekiah Roberts; Chas. Hungerford; Jas. Fyfe Jur.;
Benjn. Ward; Geo: Graft; Jonathan Tucker; Basil Roberts. [Militia Lists of
Daus. of Founders and Patriots, held by Md. Hist. Soc.]

2 Co.: Richd. Smith; Thos. Hays; John Summers; Willm. Summers Junr; Simon
Reeder; Jas. Magruder; John Clagett; Bennett Hagon; Leonard Hagan; Thos.
Newton; Thos. Knott; Moses Mattingly; Henry Clagett; Jerre: Hays; Aristarcus
Wood; Chas. Hays; Levy Hays; Walter White; Haz: Veitch; Geo: Hays; Humphy.
B. Tomlinson; Geo: Hardisty; Henry Star; Geo: Collins; Richd. Owen; Thos.
Wayman; Geo: Lashley; John Stephens; Henry Hunter; William Jerrard; William
Walker; Robt. Walker; John Bennett (?); Leven Hays; John Partrick; Seth
Gaither: Basil Hays; Chas. Scott; Thos. Miller; Saml. Hays; Thos. Hays Junr;
Leonard   Hays; Notley Hays; Wm. Ray; Saml. Love; Michl. Standlers(?);
Zachh. Jacobs; Edwd. Jacobs; Benjn. Lovelace; Elkonah Lovelace; Bennet
Jackson; Thos. Whiting Riggs; Phillip Jones; Martin Kyser; Edwd. Stephens;
Richd. Collins; Richd. Hoggins; Leonard Wayman; Lawrance Owen; Joseph
Stallings; Joseph Renegar; Stephen Caton; William Summers Sr. [Militia
Lists of Daus. of Founders and Patriots, held by Md. Hist. Soc.]

3rd Co.: Wm. Vears; Ben: Darby; Ben: Summers; Saml. Dyson; John Belt; Jacob
Howard; Thos. Howard; Geo. Howard; William Howard; Thos. Summers senr; Thos.
Summers Jur.; Geo: Summers; John Summers; Thos. Summers; Fras. Murphey;
Isaac Darnal; John Wellman; James Taylor; Caleb Summers; John Johnson;
Jonathn. Johnson; Chas. Caton; Jas. Willson; Greeny. Riggs; Ben: Lewis;
Isaac Lewis; John Vears; James Leitch; Horatio Roberts; Henry Willcoxen;
Robt. Den. Dawson; Nichos. Dawson; (name impossible to read); Josias Darby;
Philip Dyson; Stephen Laton (Caton?); Basil Dyson; Arther Tall; John
Dougherty; Wm. Dougherty; Danl. McDade; Leond. Williams; Andrew Burtle;
Bernard Nisbett; Edwd. Clark; Stephen Cawood; Stearman Chilton; Thos. Jones;
Laurance Allnutt; Jas. Allnutt; Wm. Allnutt; John Allnutt; Maddox Dyson;
Zeph. Dyson; Nathan Smith; Archd. Smith; Elijah Vears; Leonard. Love; John
Purdam; John Mullikin; Bennet Wellman; John Edwards; John Richards; Wm.
Atchison; Henry Atchison; Chas. Gassaway; Henry Russell; Saml. Johnson; John
Caton. [Militia Lists of Daus. of Founders and Patriots, held by Md. Hist.
Soc.]

MUSTER ROLLS AND OTHER LISTS

4th Co.: John Walter; Geo: Walter; Saml. Watson; David Walter; Levy Walter; Joseph Neill; John Gatton; Richd. Gatton; Benjn. Riggs; David Davis; Jas. Aldridge; Leond. Jones; Chas. Burkley; Martin Thomas; Fras. Kitely; John Howard; Jas. Sears; John Roby; Barthw. Johnson; Patrick Robey; Joseph Fergusson; Isaac Green; Hez: Gatton; Soll: Hickman; Wm. Hickman; Ben: Gatton; Thos. Beeding; Edwd. Beeding; Jos. Beeding; Hy. Beeding; Zach. Barlowe; Thos. Fletchall; John Gillam; Thos. Gillam; Jas. Henley; Gabl. Baxter; Peter Smith; Jas. Waters; Alex: McKintosh; Wm. Denns; Wm. Evans; Hy. McLockland; Mark Elliott; Ben: Elliott; Jo: Elliott; Jas. Steall; Van Swearingin; Danl. Kersy; Wm. Douglas; Abra: Fletcher; Geo: Fletcher; Elkahan Watson; Jas. Feilds; Joseph Feilds; Mathew Fields; John Furgusson; Danl. Furgusson; Basil Fargusson; Elias Furgusson; Neill Maginniss; Robt. Webber; Leonard Watkins; Joseph Jones; John Dickson; William Hickman; Clemt. Walter; Willm. Dixon. [Militia Lists of Daus. of Founders and Patriots, held by Md. Hist. Soc.]

5th Co.: Frederick Sprigg; Thos. Kirk; Chas. Busey; Wm. Chapman; John Higgins; Thos. Hinton; John Hinton; Richd. Hinton; Phillip Hinton; Thos. Hinton Jur.; Joseph Lewis; Richd. Andrews; Edwd. Andrews; Chas. Andrews; Michl. Hinton; Edwd. Cheyney; Thos. Kirk Junr; Saml. Carnstable; Wm. Lee; Stephen Warman; Zeph. Harris; Ben: Johnson; Nathan Burdet; Joseph Mattingly; Bernd. Mattingly; John Vinson; John Yates; Thos. Hurley; Josiah Leitch; Wm. Leitch; Benjn. Leitch; Joseph Burton; Jacob Rhoads; Elisha Rhoads; Edwd. Ward; Uriah Layton; Willm. Scissill; Archd. Scissill; Thos. Scissill; Caileb Cash; Ben: Busey; John Nicholson; Nehemiah Holland; John Hinton Jur.; John Kimboll; Paul Busey; Clem: Fitzjerrald; Wm. Holland Jr.; Richd. Berry; Saml. Hobbs; Wm. Holland Sr.; Joshua Jordon; Isaac Luten; Ashwood Layton; Basil Soaper; Joseph Waters; Joseph West; Hugh McSherry; Wm. Burdet; Edwd. Busey; Nichos. Rhodes; Archd. Chapple; Geo: Kirk; Henry Busey; John Rhoads. [Militia Lists of Daus. of Founders and Patriots, held by Md. Hist. Soc.]

6th Co.: Thos. Sprigg; William Norris; Geo. Norris; John Harris; Jesse Harris; John Reed; Maths. Hemstone; Jerre: Plummer; Ben: Gaither; Jo: Jacobs; Nathn. Harris; Jas. McDade; David Carlile; Norris Harris; Danl. McDade; Richd. ODanel; Chisr. Hamstone; Robt. McDade; Basil Knott; Wm. Knott; Joshua Green; Geo: Blessatt; Willm. Williams; Geo: Carter; John Riggs; Nathan More; Saml. More; Zephh. McCray; Danl. Henry; Isarel Case; Sam'l Lewis (?); Willm. Lewis; Jesse Alnutt; Asa Darby; Stephen Wood; Robt. Spates; John Meloy; Will: Briggs; Richd. Purdie; Reph Green; Zachh. Knott; Joseph Chew; Edwd. Wyvell; Joshua Perry; Nin: Nicholls; Archd. Nicholls; John Cash; John Ennis; Babtis Thompson; Edmd. Wayman; John Willson; Thos. Philpott; Thos. Talbott; Robt. Lashley; Thos. Halfpenny; Saml. Simmons; Igns. Warthin; Hez: Wheat; Jo: Chiswell; Jonan. Madding; Jno. Madding; Richd. Madding; Wm. Cash. [Militia Lists of Daus. of Founders and Patriots, held by Md. Hist. Soc.]

7th Co.: Jno. Cartwright; Thos. Chilton; Jno. Hardy; Barton O Neill; Jas. Robeson; Josias Davis; Wm. McDaniel; John Poole; Jonathn. Madden; Zachh. Askey; Wm. Young; Rosewell Dyson; Danl. Whaling; Wm. Lucas; Geo: Gentle; Benley Davis; Notley Thomas; Thos. Edelin; Geo: Warring; John Willson; Geo: Windham; Geo: Bowen; John Burke; Barton Lovelace; Jas. Selby; Jas. Willson; Chas. Nisbett; David Lowe; Jesse Adams; Thos. Lazenby; Phill: Shekleworth;

MONTGOMERY COUNTY

Henry ...(too faint); Humphry Godman; Ralph Neall; Bartan Edelin; Wm. Thomas; Jas. Thomas; Joshua Caton; Nin: Veatch; Nin: Veatch Jur; Soll: Veatch; Jas. Sears; Thos. Warner; Hugh Ogdon; Will: Davis; Saml. Davis; John Higdon; Jno. Higdon Ju.; Joseph Higdon; Geo: Campbell; Wm. Wallace; Aaron Clark; John Ellis; Wm. Ellis; David Ogdon; Hugh Ogdon; Saml. Riggs; Robt. Lazenby; Ben: Newman; Jacob: Newman; Wm. Wilkinson; John Bowen; Saml. Lintrige; Saml. Cartwright; Wm. Thomas; Alexr. Barruck. [Militia Lists of Daus. of Founders and Patriots, held by Md. Hist. Soc.]

8th Co.: John Harwood; Wm. Blackmore; John Moxley; Alexr. Whitaker; Trewman White; Wm. Woodyard; Chas. Sanders; Ingns. Yates; Thos. Yates; Wm. Ridgeway; Geo: Beall; Joshua Hunter; Thos. Cartwright; Arther Steall; Lews. Stephens; Jese Grace; Leond. Wheler; Wm. Moxley; Jas. Campbell; John Taylor; Mark Chilton; Thos. Green; Jno. Williams; Abra: Jones; Andrew Williams; Richd. Avery; Ereas Campbell; Hanson Whelor; Jas. Harben; Elias Harbin; Thos. Owen; Jno. Williams; Basil Tolbert; Jas. Gatton; (impossible to read); Jno. Veitch; Jo: Locker; Jno. Miles; Jno. McLeary; Thos. Walker; Will: Sears; Wm. Dowell; Thos. Talbert; Duncan Sinclear; Ephrm. Davis; Geo: Talbott; Wm. Catoe; Bennet. Green; Maths. Burn; Elihu Hickman; Richd. Dowell; Laurence Craige; John Gibson; Zadock Hardy; Peter ONeil; John Dowell; Philip Dowell; Richd. Veatch; Silas Veatch; Carlton Belt; Josiah Willson; Nichos. Peddicoat; Archd. Allin; Adam Burn; Saml. Shearbutt; Peter Dowell; John Seaburn; Notley Coats; Conrod Myers; Will: Burn. [Militia Lists of Daus. of Founders and Patriots, held by Md. Hist. Soc.]

MONTGOMERY COUNTY, Middle Battalion

Officers and Privates for the Middle Battalion -
1st Co.: Gerrard Briscoe,; Basil Gaither - 30 Augt 1777; Wm. Burton; Chas. Davis; Len: Richards; Ben: Williams; Nathl. Harris; Ben: Higdon; John Hilleary; Zadoc Jarvis; Elisha Jarvis; William Bateson; Wm. Park (Pack?) Senr; Wm. Park (Pack?) Junr; Thos. Leitch; Nichos. Seybert; Isaac Tuple; Saml. Hardesty; Colbert Pelly; John Rollins; Thos. Rollins; Patrick Ouchterlony; Nichos. Speaks; Jacob Barnet; Joseph West Senr; Archd. Trail; Lodowick Yost; Geo: Heater(?); John Gordon; Wm. Saffle; Jas. Saffle; Basil Adamson; John Adamson; Willm. Williams Junr; Kensey Adamson; Chas. Bause(?); Alexr. Willson; Saml. Gouldy; Chas. Williams; John Beckwith; Amos Williams; Michl. Haws; Jas. Wiett; Alexr. Wiett; Thos. West; Thos. Selby of Jo.; Jno. Anderson; Jas. Anderson Char. ONeall; Richd. Walker; John Willson; Stephen Tucker; Willm. Sansbury; Thos. Chattle; Jas. Cary; Griffith Davis; Richd. Davis; Lodowick Davis; Richd. Selby; Thos. Selby; Zachariah Selby; Danl. Candler; Erasmus West; John Kelly; John House; Alexr. House; John Curd; John Davis; Willm. House; Gregory Page Tucker; Hezekiah Gray; Fryday Cross; Thos. Kelly; Thos. Pack; Richd. Pack; Henry Hilleary; David Trail Junr; Basil Trail; Jas. Leitch; Chas. Saffle. [Militia Lists of Daus. of Founders and Patriots, held by Md. Hist. Soc.]

2nd Co.: Amon Riggs, 4 Sep 1777; Geo: Cullom, 4 Sep 1777; Brock Mockbee; Nathan Linthcum; Saml. Hocker; Benoni Dawson; Isaac Waters; John Jones; Blanford Davis; Vachel Davis; Thos. Nicholls; Saml. Green; John Jenkins; Partrick Durham; Thos. Lord; John Wheat; Philip Hocker; Partrick McDermet;

MUSTER ROLLS AND OTHER LISTS

Brock Case; Thos. Case; Jas. Case; Archd. Mullikin; Lewis Mullikin; Jas. Simpson; Philip Dougherty; Neill Dougherty; John McDade; Jesse Mills; Zachh. Linthicum; Chas. Stewart; Nathl. Linthicum; Jas. Trott; Henry Trott; Jacob Williams; Thos. Broadhead; Ninn. Mockbee; Allin Mockbee; William Benson; Thos. Benton; John ...; Geo: Heathman; Jas. Trail; Wm. Trail; John Mullikin; Richd. Fryer; Zachh. Riley; Jas. Riley; Jerre: Riley; Wm. Waters; Richd. Northcraft; Edwd. Northcraft; Joel Holland; Willm. Burton(?); John Burton(?); John Watts; Edmond Collins; Henry Seybert; Bennedick Groseman; Walter Fryer; Archd. Holland; Joseph Penny; Ben: Burdett; Jno. Pinchback; Archd. Mobberly; Wm. Vinson; Fras. Cullom; John Farmer; Greeny. Griffith; Caleb Griffith; Howard Griffith; Thos. Sheppard; William Olliver; Basil Smith; Hez: Griffith; John Willing; John Hughes; Jonathan Heathman; Thos. Prather; Geo: Seybert; Thos. Waters. [Militia Lists of Daus. of Founders and Patriots, held by Md. Hist. Soc.]

3 Co.: Archd. Orme; Thos. Beall; Alexr. Clagett; Zephh. Beall; Eanock Kerby; Levin Beall; Zachh. Dowden; Willm. Leach; Wm. Smallwood; John Nicholls; Jas. Chambers; John Chambers; Thos. Nicholls Senr; Chas. Tracey; Martin Houser; Benjn Ray; Nathan Offutt; John Dougherty; John Tucker of Edwd.; Jas. More; Robt. Drake; Peter Noe (Roe?); Ben: Stephens; Alexr. Tray; Edwd. Metcalf; John Buckland; Darby Murphy; Ben: Vincent; John Hopkins Junr; Saml. Offutt; Richd. Clark; Clemt. Clark; Adin Pencoast; Wm. Sparrow; Ben: Dove; Thos. Sparrowe; John Thompson; Bennet Greenwell; John Barrs; Richd. Cooke; ... ; Geo: Griffith; Henry Counce; Thos. Dowden Junr; Francis Downing; Saml. Smith; Isaac Windsor; Joseph Bains (Barns?); Saml. Martin; Wm. Rennalls; Harrison Pelly; Zepheniah Berch; Brooke Beall; Tobias Butler; Thos. Nicholls Junr; Thos. Shearbutt; Richd. Collins; Basil Magruder; Annenias Barker; Harman Renegar; Geo: Renegar; Saml. Gilkey(?); John Tucker; Zephh. Dowden; Jas. Pelly; John Clagett; Abraham Feilds; Edwd. Allphin; Phillip Houser; Joseph Braddock; Jas. Perry; Chas. Perry; Fras. Harper Jur.; John Thomas; Wm. Idaire; Bennett Weltman(?); John Doran. [Militia Lists of Daus. of Founders and Patriots, held by Md. Hist. Soc.]

4th Co.: Nathl. Pagman; Ben: Gaither; Saml. Riggs; William Gaither; John Dickerson; Robt. Redman; Geo: Bowman; Ephrm. Gaither; John W. More; Wm. Nicholson; Geo: Gew; Wm. Coy; Zadock Dickerson; John Holland; John Windsor; Fras. Redman; Ben: Redman; Richd. Stephens; Otho Holland; Wm. Redman; Josias Chambers; Stephen Holland; John Holland Jur.; Jerre Willman; Henry Gue; Joseph Holland; Thos. Collins; Jas. Collins; Jacob Bowman; Henry Ball; David Macklefish; David Gee; Elisha Griffith; Edwd. Chambers; John Macklefish; Thos. Johnson(?); Joseph (portion of page missing); Basil Mullikin; Joshua Cutmore; Aaron Gartrill; John Vennables; Benja. Blowers; Basil Darby; John Penn; James Boswell; Danl. Day; John Chambers; John Baker; Jas. Thompson; James Paradice; Thos. Wright; Saml. Darby; Henry Burriss; Wm. Leach; Joseph Johnson; Thos. Smith; Benjn. Griffith; Joseph Gew; Johnsey Morgan; Richd. Morgan Junr; Saml. Selby; Nichos. Boswell; Hugh Hyland; Danl. Leary; Edwd. Feild; John Everly; George Ham; John Johnson; Nathan Musgrove; Christopher Coy; Mark Riley; Cornelius Sullivan. [Militia Lists of Daus. of Founders and Patriots, held by Md. Hist. Soc.]

5th Co.: Saml. West; John Ray; Nathl. Crawford; Hy. ONeall; Richd Hopkins; Ben: West; Richd. West; Jacob Rhentzell; John Brown; Nichos. Bailey; Basil

MONTGOMERY COUNTY

West; Jas. Ball; Alexr. Adams; Osburn West; William West; Ben: West; Joseph West; John S. Crawford; John Crabb; Ben: Peak; Thos. Peak; Lewis Peak; Zachh. Offutt; Wm. M: Offutt; Nathl. Offutt; Saml. Offutt; Elias Pritchet; Chas. Pritchet; Mordecai Stewart; Jacob Stoner; Wm. Ray; John Nicholls; Thos. Nicholls; Evin Jones Junr; Nathan Jones; Ben: ...; Natt: Hughes; Nichols. Smith; Will: Tracy; John ONeall; John Austin; Wm. ONeall; John Ball; Zachh. Thompson; Wm. Thompson; Nathan Thompson; Thos. Sansbury; Jno. Bailey Junr; Richd. Allison Senr; Richd. Allison Junr; Henry Alison; Zacdock Willson; Richd. Wootten; Jonathn.; Allison; Wm. Newton; Philip Kersey; Saml. Peak; William Pritchett; Jas. Burnsides; Josiah Boone; Arnold Boone; Laurance Holt; Ben: Allison; Bennet Clements; Oswell Clements; Willm. McGrath; Joshua Allison; David Harry; Edwd. West; Abra: Benjamin; Richd. Crabb; Alexr. E. Beall; Thos. E. Beall; Leonard Davis; Martin Fisher; Doctr. T. S. Wootton; John White. [Militia Lists of Daus. of Founders and Patriots, held by Md. Hist. Soc.]

6th Co.: Robert Owen; Edwd. Crow; Nichos. Ray; John ... 3 Aug 1777; Thos. Conner; Thos. Appleby; Thos. Aldridge; Jonathn. Browning Junr; Archd. Browning; Nathn. Browning; Nathn. Browning Junr; Ben: Browning; Sam: Barber; Jno. Barber; Thos. Baldwin; John Beale; Thos. Burgee; Richd. Conner; Saml. Dowles; Lewis Duvall; John Ellis; Richd. Lanham; Nathan Harrison; Greeny. Harrison; Joshua Harrison; Allin Harvey; Wm. Harvey; Jo: Hall; Greeny. Hobbs; Chas. Hobbs; John Hopwood; James Butler; Willm. Inman; Stephn. Jury; Richd. Johnson; Edwd. Jones; Hugh Kennedy; Jonathn. Lewis; Hy Lazear; Wm. Sudeley(?); Henry Nelson; (name obliterated); Wm. Owen; Jesse Page; Ben: Penn; John Perry; Will: Stamps; Jno. Quardon; Abra: Shekell; Henry Story; Joshua Scissill; Joseph Penn; Lloyd Ward; Jno. Owen Junr; Thos. Windsor; Chas. Penn; Caileb Penn; Edwd. Penn; Ben: Davis Penn; Thos. Smith; John Cox; Geo: Haymon; William Farmer; John Byer; Luke Davis; Saml. Musgrove of Anthy.; Saml. Musgrove of Saml.; Aquilla Duvall; Saml. Crow; Joshua Crow; Wm. Byall; Forrest Davis; Levy Duvall; Joseph Lambeth; Jas. Warrin; Jas. Toole. [Militia Lists of Daus. of Founders and Patriots, held by Md. Hist. Soc.]

7th Co.: John Bruce; John Sutor; Greeny. Gaither; John Kennedy; Nichols Gaither; Nacy Waters; Burgess Gaither; Johnsey Gaither; Saml. Carter; John Edwards; Will: Knox; Mordecai M: Mitchell; Willm. Schligo; Levin Casey; Robt. Edmn. Beall; John Easton; Basil Robertson; James Jurden; John Turner; John Gee; Jno. McDonald; Michl. Colgan; Ben: Gray; John Phillips; Will: Ryan; John Hughes; Ignas. Green; Clemt. Green; Robert Allcock; Thos. Hoult; Mathew Aves; Thos. Longdon; Richd. Leach; John Rennals; Jas. Peak; Robert Crawford; Wm. Lowery; Thos. Holland; John Leach; ... ; Jacob Rickets; Richd. Rickets; Benjn. Rickets; Robt Rickets; Ben: Sedwick; John Cooke; Zadock Ford; Jas. Groome; Jacob Elliott; Anthony Rickets Junr; Dennis Cahill; Nathan Owden; Josias Owden; Gerard Owden; Wm. Gray; Jerre: Gray; Adin Gray; Michl. Mummart; William Mummart; Wm. Jane; Jasper Peddicoart; Wm. Wright senr; Wm. Wright Jur.; Saml. Phillips; William Stewart; Nacy Pigman; Wm Cahoe; Robt. Ridgeway; Andrew Rhentzell; Alexr. Sutes (Lutes?). [Militia Lists of Daus. of Founders and Patriots, held by Md. Hist. Soc.]

8th Co.: Richd. Brooke; Hy. Griffith Junr; Paul Hoy; Basil Brooke; Benjn. Holland; Willm. Pegg; Edwd. Penn of Edward; Philamon Plummer; John Plummer;

MUSTER ROLLS AND OTHER LISTS

Richd. Macklefish; Ben: Griffith of Jas.; Silvanus Mare; Christopher Buzby; Jacob Hines; John Pencoast; Willm. Pencoast; Doctr. Jas. Shasto; Thos. Brooke; Basil Windsor; Aaron Rollings; Chas. Burriss; Roger Brooke; John Griffith; Geo: Roberson; John S. Windsor; John Ferrill; Willm. Ireland; John Davis; Saml. Koy; Thos. Shaw; David Beggarly; Saml. Lazenby; John Connolly; Michl. Connelly; Edwd. Owen Williams; William Howard; Abra: Boyd; Edwd. Clark; Thos. Miles; Chas. Griffith; Saml. (?) Brooke; Hance Lannam; Azel Butt; Wm. N: Williams; Jo: Simms; Elexious Simms; Basil Giddins; Josiah Bean; Christopher Bean; Josiah Trundle; Ben: Nicholls; Aaron Freeman; Josias Hoskinson; Zachh. Butt; Jas. Kein; Peter Maguier; Thos. Connolly; Richd. Callehan; Jas. Burgess; Thos. Giddins; Robt. Taylor; John Biggs; John Ward; Greeny Belt. [Militia Lists of Daus. of Founders and Patriots, held by Md. Hist. Soc.]

MONTGOMERY COUNTY, Lower Battalion
Officers and Privates for the 29th (Lower) Battalion - Coll. John Murdock; Lieut. Wm. Deakins; Maj. George Beall -

1 Co.: John Gaither; Jerre. Ducker; Zeph. Beall; John Shekell; Chas. Gartrill; John Williams; Felter Myers; Weaver Waters; Robt. Alexr. Beall; Weaver Barns; Jere: Beall; Nichos. Hawker; Walter Mitchell; Josephus Waters; Thos. Waters; Danl. Lewis; Alexr. Lazenby; Geo: Fightmaster; Fras. Gartrell; Saml. J. Godman; Edwd. Browning; Clemt. Williams; Saml. Moore; Zephh. Jones; John Beall; Shadrick Case; Jere: Berry; Archd. Moson; Zachh. Downs; John Aldridge; Henry Lazenby; William Jackson; Wm. Fitzjerrald; Saml.(?) Wells(?); Richd. (?) W... Johns(?); Jo... Lazenby; John Tucker; Jo: Estep; Sam: Thomas; John Thomas; Richd. Thomas Junr; Richd. Cowman(?); Felter Pock(?); Geo: Snell; Thos. ...; Saml. McDougle; Alexr. McDougle; Jo: Gartrell; Ben: Penn; Elias Lazenby; Joseph Lazear; John Lazear; Basil Burton; Josias Holmes; John Barnes; Thos. Mitchell; Nathan Mitchell; Zephh. Browning; Jerre. Browning; John Ballott; Capril Holland; Jonathan Mason; Thos. Barnes; Thos. Rickets; John King; John Gartrill; Richd. William; Thos. Boram; Nathan Rozan; John Dennis; Thos. Cross; March Rickets; Edwd. Burgess; Zadock Conner; Joseph Browning; Robert Orme. [Militia Lists of Daus. of Founders and Patriots, held by Md. Hist. Soc.]

2 Co.: Elias Harden; Allen Bowie; Jas. Lackland; Saml. Swearingin; Jere. Lewis; Saml. Beall; Edwd. Gates; Ignas. Roby; John Boyd; David Lewis; Edwd. Beall; John Willcoxen Senr; John Baker; Aaron Prather; Zadock Lackland; Wm. Tucker; Jere: Beall; Zeph. Beall; John Fitzgerrald; Berry Roby; Geo. Cashall; Basil Harden; Thos. Owen; John Willcoxen Junr; Wm. Duke; Nathan Glaze; Anthy. Willcoxen; Wm. Harden; Sollaman Holland; Erasmus Perry; Ben: Beggarly; Wm. Boyd; Isaac Duckett; Wm. P. Williams; Walter Prather; Hugh Smith Dunn; Wm. Beckwith; Thos. Cramphin; Joseph Benton; ...; Wm. Lanham; Basil Wheat; Jas. Ferrell; Zachh.(?) ...ther; Rignal (?) ...; Thos. B...; ...; John ...; Thos. Swearingen Senr; Thos. Swearingin Junr; Barrack Prather; Wm. Roberson; Danl. Smith Junr; Nathan Holland; Richd. Butt; Jno. B. Magruder; Isaac Magruder; Thos. Clark; Swearingin Butt; Aseriah Prather; Danl. Beall; Mussum Ridgeway; Joseph Ricketts; Michl. Lytton; Basil Glaze; Nin: Edmn. Beall; John Harden; Natt: Glaze; Henry Ferrell; Wm. Henly; Saml. White Junr; Allin Garrott; Jonathan Glaze; Edwd. Garrott; Edwd. Harden;

MONTGOMERY COUNTY

Josiah Harden; Doctr. Jo: Hall; Josephus Beall; Nichos. Berry; Wm. Harden;
Elias Harden Jur. [Militia Lists of Daus. of Founders and Patriots, held by
Md. Hist. Soc.]

3rd Co.: Alexr. McFaddon; John Peter; Peter Kirtz; Wm. Carter; John
Threlkield; Nichos. Limbery; Ben: Becraft; Theodorous Croutz; Thos. Brannum;
Vallentine Boseham (Boreham?); Jacob Trisler; John Randols; John Soyl; Paul
Gaunor; Frederick Wetzill; Willm. Veal Steuart; Nichos Paull; Anthy.
Gastler; Tobias Yost; Jacob Risener; Robt. Moses; John Mountz; Alexr. White;
Nichos. Kirtz; Simon Bowshave; Ben: Notley Pearce; Danl. Rhentzill; John
Dayley; Frederick Cochantopher; Robt. Peter Junr; Wm. Dixon; Thos. Ingram;
Philip Kyber; Michl. Casner; Felter Borase; John Hill; N...(?) Tucker(?);
Robert Collins; Robt. Craig; Wm. Willson; Jas. Maw; Richd. Tyler(?); ...;
Thos. Brandis; John Anthman (Aukman?); Hugh Gibney; Robt. Bignal; Thos.
Fletcher; Elisha Fowler; Michl. Mountz; Alexr. Contee; Butler Stonestreet;
Thos. Cavin; Geo: Winbugar; Henry Clavely; Seybert Beale; John Sutton;
Walter Smith; Thos. Richardson; Nichos. Lingham; Doct. W. Baker; Richd.
Coats; Richd. Thompson; Wm. Schofeild; Robt. Sutton; Robert Peter Senr;
Danl. Carroll Junr; Joseph Schofield. [Militia Lists of Daus. of Founders
and Patriots, held by Md. Hist. Soc.]

4th Co.: 29 Aug 1777 - William Bailey; Hez: Magruder; Stophel Kysor; Josiah
Magruder; Isaac Brooke; Richd. Magruder; John Busey; Norman B. Magruder;
Richd. K. Clagett; Thos. Mattax; Thos. Maccubbin; Alexr. Beall; Christphr.
Cochantofer Junr; John Kyser; Jacob Kyser; Adam Myers; John Hawkins; Nichos.
Pearce; Geo: Reed; Perry Groves; Nathl. Robertson; Hez: Speaks; Peter Young;
Ben: Early(?); Clem: Beall; Wm. Steall; Zadock Soper; Jo: Sprigg Belt; Sam:
Busey; Aaron Lannam; Jno. Chapple; Thos. Clark; Bennedick Clark; Burgess
White; Geo: Harris; Edwd. Magruder; Ezekiel Magruder; Robt. Thomas; Joshua
... maker (Shumaker?); John Nicholls; ...; Zephh. ...; Chas. Mack...;
Lanslott ...; Saml. ...; Jas. ...; Wm. W...; Peter Becraft; Thos. Reg...on;
Thos. Chapple; Paul Summers; John Smith; John Williams; Wm. Thawing; Hez:
Tucker; Wm. Tucker; Walter Tucker; Joseph Tucker; Edwd. King; Jo: B. Beall;
Jacob Hess; Henry Jones; Thos. Graves; Archd. Magruder; Sam: B. Magruder;
Leond. Cochantofer(?); Thos. Hugh; Thos. Higdon; Michl. Cochantofer; John
Graves; Joshua Collins; Thos. Austin; Thos. Johns; Wm. Aberry; William B.
Magruder. [Militia Lists of Daus. of Founders and Patriots, held by Md.
Hist. Soc.]

5th Co.: John Johnson; Jesse Willcoxen; Abra: Young; Saml. B. Magruder; Ben:
Harris; Wm. Talbott; Richd. Blacklock; Berch(?) Cheshire; Nin: B. Magruder;
Wm. Clements; Wm. O. Magruder; John Clagett; Mordicai Offutt; Ben: Giddins;
Walter Magruder; Barruck Odle; Nathan Clagett; Wm. Nichols; Enoch Magruder;
Levin Magruder; Zachh. Gatton; David ONeill; Jas. Wallace Jur.; Natt.
Wallace; Wm. Willitt; Saml. Dyson; Leo: Green; Bennet Woodard; Thos. Flint;
William Benton; William Collier; Thos. Lucas; Jonathan Sparrow; David
Shehon; Nin: Magruder; Wm. Lodge; Geo: Tucker; Thos. Janes; Elisha Williams;
(several names obliterated); Jas. ...; John N. Cheshire; Ben: S. Benton;
Zachh. Maccubbin; Isaac Ridgeway; Saml. Ducket; Edwd. Addams; Absolum
Farlowe; John Herron; Edwd. Hughes; Zeph. Wallace; John Jackson; John Laman;
Hugh Elder; Alexr. Tucker; Harbert A. Wallace; Will: Wallace; Will: Moses;
Jas. Nevitt; Nin: Willitt; Joseph Gill; Joshua Gragg; John Bell; Chas.

MUSTER ROLLS AND OTHER LISTS

Greenfield; Chas. Magruder; Alexr. Austin; Josias Willcoxen; William Albery; Sam: Wade Magruder; John Cheshire; Barny Muffett; Benjn. Sparrow. [Militia Lists of Daus. of Founders and Patriots, held by Md. Hist. Soc.]

6th Co.: Joseph Magruder; Jos. White; John Morris; Thos. Scott; Geo: Offutt; Rezin Offutt; Saml. Clagett; Geo: Cooke; Edwd. Eades; Jo: Clagett; John Douly; Thos. Edmonston; Laurance Hurdle; Andrew Maguire; Hy: Offutt; Ignatius Speak; Barton Douly; Henry Child; Thos. Shields; Jas. Haislip; Will: Grant; Jas. Flemming; Wm. Davis; John Flemming; Zachh. Offutt; Will: Jones; Richd. Roberts; Jas. Offutt; Wm. Murphey; Jas. Douly; Wm. Offutt; Thos. Offutt; Mac: Edmonston; John Murphy; Thos. Crawford; Thos. Clark; William Gatton; John McCormack; ... Beall; John W...; Geo. ...; John Remin...(?); Alexr. Offutt; Chas. ...; Jacob ...; ...; Geo: ...; Stephen ...; Will: Hays (?); Thos. Duley; Thos. Offutt Junr; Elijah Contee(?); John Feiler(?); Martin Speak; Zephh. Offutt; Philip Harp; Jos. Jones; Zachh. Clagett; Willm. Offutt the 3rd; Chas. Coventry; John Trevere(?); Cornelius Morris; Natt. Offutt of Edwd.; John Hitch; John Dent; Elisha Harrison; Chas. Jones; Wm. Middleton; Hez: Hurdly; Joseph Atkins; Thos. Drane; Richd. Speak. [Militia Lists of Daus. of Founders and Patriots, held by Md. Hist. Soc.]

7th Co.: Thadeus Beall; Thos. Edmonston; Edwd. Wheler; Richd. Beall; John Young; Henry Davis; Thos. Wood; Edwd. Fitzjerrald; Thos. Willmot; Chas. Chainey; Jonathan Nixon; Jas. Nixon; Chas. Rennals Jur; Ralph Knott; Hugh Nixon; Osburn Dunn; John McDonald; Jere: Orme; Edwd. Janes; William Dun; Saml. Williams; Humpy. Westly; Wm. Wheler; Chas. Orme; John Bateman; Lasarus Isaac; Archd. Linthicum; Lauson Beall; John Bates; Geo: Short; Absolum Beddo; Chas. Case; John Willson; John Short; Tison Beall; Jno.(?) Beall of Lawson; David Beall; ... Beall; Fras. Ratleaf; Wm. Knighters; Geo: Letman(?); Robt. Willmot; Joshua Nixon; Basil Lucas; Elisha Hoskinsson; Thos. La...; Stehn. Lannam; Stepn. Willson; Thos. Trundle; John Smith; Robt. Wright; Lewis Lannam; Jere: Knott; Henry Pearce; Babtis Pearce; Thos. Tucker; Aaron Orme; Wm. Culver; Thos. Tucker; John Selby; Jas. Keith; Wm. Walker; Hez: Short; Basil Shaw; Morris Brashears; Ely Orme; David Tucker; Sam. J. Orme. [Militia Lists of Daus. of Founders and Patriots, held by Md. Hist. Soc.]

8th Co. - Robert Beall; Aaron Harris; Zadock Harris; Chas. Phillips; Fras. Woodard; Wm. Clark; John Trundle; John Lee; Danl. Lee; John Sassell; Will: Willson; David Blois; Leod. Day; Saml. Scissill; John Madding; Danl. Williams; Jos: Tucker; Martin ..fman; Nin: Barrott; John Williams; John Collins; Nimrod Parish; Griffith Stallings; John Bennet; Zachh. Mockbee; Joseph Alby; Wm. Lashey; Thos. Woodard; Thos. Willson; Joseph Francis; Jas. Willson; Thos. James; Jos. Madding; Ben: More; Henry Beggarly; Saml. Lambeth; Hez: Woodard; Wm. Pollard; Jas. White; Philip Tracy; Thos. Beall; Jas. Castree(?); Saml. Day; Josiah Burgess; Wm. Hall; Basil White; Chas.(?) Blois; Ben: ...; John Beton; John Willson; Jas. Scissill; Thos. Lashley; Robt. Housley; Wil: Tannehill; Jas. Marshall; Roger Cahoe; John Watson; Hy. Gittings; Dudley Green; Zachh. Beall; Edmond Trout; John Abbington; Boules Abbington; Danl. Carroll; Jas. Lee; John Lee Senr; Zadock Willson; John Lashley; Jas. Macketee(?); Hy. Tucker; Ben: Gedilin(?). [Militia Lists of Daus. of Founders and Patriots, held by Md. Hist. Soc.]

[Submitted by] Chas. Gr. Griffith Lieut of Montgomery County

MONTGOMERY COUNTY

Middle Battalion

A List of different companies in the middle Battn of Montgomery County with the different classes as returned by Coll. Archibald Orme the 15th of July 1780.

1st Compy: John Ray, Capt.; Henry Oneal 1st Lieut; Richd. West, Ensign; Basil West, 1st Sergt.; Nichos. West, 2nd do; John Brown, 3rd do; Lewis Peak, 4th do; Jonathan Allison, 1st Corp.; Alexr. Adams, 2nd do; Philip Casey, 3rd; John H.(A?) Nichols, 4th
Class No. 1: William Newton; Charles Preechet(?); Nathl. Offutt; Willm. Howard; Wm. McNear; Wm. Nichols of Saml.; Robert Crawford;
Class No. 2: Benj. Peak; Gerrard Smith; George Ray; Francis Payne; Burch Allison; John Randell; Jas. Johnson; George Campbell
Class No. 3: Andrew McGuire; Jesse Mills; Nathan Jones; Benj. West; Wm. McGreath; Evan Jones Junr; John Bailey Junr; Nathl. Hughes; Abraham Stoner; Elisha Allison
Class No. 4: Elias Preechet; Philip Hopkins; Thomas West; James Suter; Giles Easton; Richd. Thompson; Wm. Hoult; Wm. Medly; Basil Bailey
Class No. 5: Martin Fisher; Wm. Ray; Wm. Thompson; John Oneal; Richard Hurdle; Oliver Stevens; Wm. Priest; John Sutton
Class No. 6: Benjn. Willett; Wm. Tracy; John Crawford; Wm. West; Joseph Ford; Richd. Harry; Rezin Fields; Jeremiah Crall; Alexr. Crawford
Class No. 7: Thos. E. Beall; Thos. Peak; Wm. Preechet; Thos. Nichols; James Burnsides; Willm. Nichols of Lin...(?); James Chapple; Wm. Wallace Clements; Caleb Summers
Class No. 8: Josiah Bean; Wm. Oneal; Nathan Harris; Abijah Fife; James Day; John Baptist Chesshire; John(?) Paine; George Wilson; ... Priest

2nd Company: Benjamin Ray, Capt; Saml. Offutt, 1st Lieut.; Bennit Greenwell, 2nd do; Joseph Barnes, Ensign
Class No. 1: James Allison; Wm. Sparrow; Benj. Vincent; Saml. Guilkey; Edward Medcalf; Ananias Barker; Jacob Tisue; Wm. Hall; Joseph Ogden; Osburn Piles
Class No. 2: Benjn. Dove; Harmon Renigar; Benjamin Ward; Zechah. Dowden; Tobias Butler; James Hadley; Henry Chambers; Basil Callico; Wm. Devenport; John Ogden; Wm. Stewart; Leaven Beall
Class No. 3: John Thompson; Zephah. Dowden; James Moore; Francis Harper; Peter Noe; Cornelius Barker; Leonard Green; John Barnes
Class No. 4: Philip Houser; Thomas Dowden; Thomas Malone; Thomas Roberts; Wm. Williams; John Thompson; Benjn. Burtle; Wm. Harp
Class No. 5: John Chambers of Hy.; Friday Cross; John Chambers of Wm.; Thomas Fields; Benn. Sparrow; Jonathan Sparrow; Rezin Ferguson; James Dodsworth; Richd. Johns; George Beall Junr
Class No. 6: Archd. Holland; Clement Dowden; Wm. Brown; Daniel Quary; Danl. McCartee; Joseph Woodard; Danl. Casey; Henry Frederick
Class No. 7: Charles Tracey; Nathan Offutt; Darby Murphy; James Harbin; John Mackbee; Ignatius Callico; John Roberts
Class No. 8: Thos. Sherbott; Isaac Winsor; George Rennager; Harrisson Pella; Wm. Reynolds; Wm. Leach; Alexr. Campbell; John Wood; Wm. Roberts; Wm. Harper; Alexr. Beall

APPENDIX B: MUSTER ROLLS AND OTHER LISTS

3d Company: Brock Mockbee, Capt; Nathan Linthacum, 1st Lt.; Thos. Nichols, 2nd Lt.; Benoni Dorsin, Ensign; Isaac Waters, 1 Sergt; John Hethman, 2 do; John Mcdade 3 do; Wm. Benson, 4 do; Walter Fryer, 1 Corpl; Saml. Hawken, 2 do; Wm. Buxton, 3 do; Lodowick Davis, 4 do
Class No. 1: Zechah. Linthacum; Ninn. Mockbee; Thos. Buxton; Zachah. Riley; Howard Griffith; Jas. Robertson; Wm. Wornell
Class No. 2: John Watts; Basil Smith; Israel Case; John Wheat; Philip Hawker; Greeny. Griffith; Elijah Riley
Class No. 3: Lewis Mullikin; Philip Doherty; John Mcdade; Henry Trott; Thos. Lawd (Laws?); Neil Doherty; Zechah. Wheat;
Class No. 4: Wm. Smith; Joseph Penna; Benjn. Burdit; Archd. Mobley; John Farmer; Josiah W. Coxen; Joseph Wheat
Class No. 5: John Jones; Nathan Aldridge; Nathan Linthacum Junr; Partrick McDurmet; Brock Case; James Case; Francis Cullem
Class No. 6: Nathl. Ducker; Thos. Case; John Smith; Archd. Trail; Nichl. Doherty; George Thompson; John Buxton
Class No. 7: Thos. Broadhead; George Hethman; Jas. Trail; Alexr. Catlett; James Riley; Jereh. Riley; John McDaniel
Class No. 8: Richd. Northcraft; Edwd. Northcraft; Joel Holland; Francis Woodard; Nichos. Enniss; Edwd. House; John Huston

4th Company: John Wm. Moore, Capt; Stephen Holland, 1st Lieut.; Zadok Dickason, 2nd do; Joseph Leek, Ensign; Henry Burriss, 1st Sergt; Richd. Stevens, 2nd do; Saml. Darby, 3rd do; John Vennables, 4th do; Gerrard Gaither, 1st Corp.; Basil Waters, 2nd do; Caleb Darby, 3 do; George Bowman, 4 do
Class No. 1: George Gue; Wm. Redman; John Holland Senr; Mark Riley
Class No. 2: Nichs. Boswell; Charles Redman; John Maginniss; Abner Macklefish; John Shearwood; Wm. Paradise; Thos. Collins; David Gee; Jas. Boswell
Class No. 3: John Griffith; Richd. Price; Charles Burráce(?); Joseph Johnson; Joseph Gue; Thomas Brooke; Henry Ball; Thomas Johnson; Thomas G...(?);
Class No. 4: John Byer; Nichos Pigno(?); Ezekiel Cadwell; Basil Brooke; George Ham; Otho Holland; James Paradice
Class No. 5: Henry Macklefish; Joseph Redman; Wm. Burriss; Benjn. Redman; John Holland Junr; Jeremiah Wellman; Jacob Bowman; John Baker; Jesse Lewis
Class No. 6: John Pancoast; John Winsor; Basil Mullikin; John Penn; Jas. Thompson; Thos. Wright; James Collins
Class No. 7: Richd. Macklefish; Joseph Wright; Wm. Pancoast; John Gartrell; Thos. Smith; Francis Redman; Joshua Cutmore
Class No. 8: John Plummer; Dennis Morgan; Benjn. Blowers; Danl. Day; John Chambers; Benjn. Griffith; Hugh Island

A List of the different companies in the middle Battn. of Montgomery County with the classes as returned by Coll. Archibald Orme the 15th of July 1780 - 5th Company: Lodowick Yost, Capt; Griffith Davis, 1st Lieut; Wm. Williams, 2 do.; John Adamson, Ensign; John Kelly, 1st Sergt.; Orsban Trail, 2nd do.; James Anderson 3rd do.; Thos. Rawlings, 4th do.; Thomas Holland, 1st Corpl.; Chas. Williams, 2nd do; Wm. Coy, 3rd do; Wm. Davis, 4th do; Class No. 1: Wm. Peck Senr; Zadok Jarvis; Elisha Jarvis; John Williams; Shadrack Harrison; Benj. Turley; David Trail (of Jas.); Moses Harrison

MONTGOMERY COUNTY

Class No. 2: Charles Saffle; Wm. Fulks; Thomas Leech; Jas. Cary; Thomas
Legg; Zadok. Spece(?); Benjn. Holland; Jas. Candler; Saml. Golden; Richard
Selby; John Hillery; Benjn. Williams; Calvert Pelly; Joseph Joseph; Aaron
Freeman; Rezin Holland
Class No. 4: James Saffle; Michael Haws; Jas. Wright; Leonard Skinner; Wm.
Batson; George Rose; Thomas Magill
Class No. 5: Alexr. Wilson; Basil Trail; John Shaw; John Murphy; Matthew
Wilson; John Legg; Josias Moore; George Hardisty
Class No. 6: John Anderson; Wm. Patterson; Jacob Barnett; Alexr. Wright;
John Beckwith; George Heater; John Golden
Class No. 7: Thos. Chattle; Henry Hillery; Wm. Saffle; Amos Williams; Wm.
Montgomery; Kensey Adamson; Wm. Tracey; Shadrach Case
Class No. 8: Thos. Selby Junr; Benjn. Higdon; Wm. Burton; Leonard Richards;
Joshua Saffle; Thos. Culey; John Richards; Saml. Peak; Hezeh. Peak

6th Company: Thomas Conner, Capt; Saml. Crow, 1st Lt.; Thos. Owen, 2nd do.;
Henry Nelson, Ensign;
Class No. 1: Edward Penn; Benjn. Davis Penn; Richd. Connner; Wm. Stamp;
Allan Harry; Charles Penn; James Tool; Levi Duvall
Class No. 2: Joshua Crow; James Warrin; Caleb Penn; Thos. Hillard; John
Beall; Wm. Harry; Jonathan Browning
Class No. 3: Archibald Browning; Nathan Browning Senr; Nathan Browning Junr;
Dennis Brian; Thos. Winsor; Thos. Appleby; Thos. Smith
Class No. 4: John Cox; Alexr. Beall; Edwd. Jones; Jonathan Lewis; Henry
Lazier; James Norwood; Wm. Owen
Class No. 5: Richd. Shekels; John Perry; Joseph Hall; John Hopwood; James
Butler; Stephen Jewry(?); Richd. Johnson
Class No. 6: Zadok Duvall; Saml. Barber; Nathan Harrisson; Charles Harry;
Thos. Wilson; George Walker; Greeny. Harrisson
Class No. 7: Richd. Weedon; Benj. Penn; John Quardon(?); Abraham Shekels;
Joshua Scicell; Joseph Penn; Lloyd Ward; John Owen
Class No. 8: Jon Pormer(?); Edward Hallon; David Macklefish; Nichos. Ray;
Stephen Norwood; John Harden; Charles Hobbs

7th Company: Benj. Rickets, Capt; Benj. Gray, 1st Lieut; Jacob Elliott, 2nd
do; Joseph Rickets, Ensign; Anthony Rickets, 1st Lieut; Alexr. Mcdough, 2nd
do; Wm. Lowerry, 3rd do; Clement Green, 4th do; Josiah Perden(?), 1st Corpl;
Kinsey Hughes, 2nd do; Jas. Jordan, 3rd do; Adin Gray, 4th do
Class No. 1: Robert Rickets; Nacey Pigman; James Shafts; Mathias Gray; Henry
Lodget; Elias Adgate; Ignatius Green; John Green
Class No. 2: Michael Colgin; Benjn. Sedgewick; Joseph Rickets; Thomas
Clarke; Robert Housley; John Boyd; Wm. Boyd; Kinsey Harriss
Class No. 3: Saml. Carter; Jonathan Palmer; Jereh. Gray; Richd. Waters;
Thos. Ogdan; Greeny. Belt; Thos. Burch; Wm. Clarke
Wm. Sayvert; Thos. Holland; Richard Rickets; Wm. Caho; Robert Ridgeway; Wm.
Ireland; Solomon Holland
Class No. 5: John Leach; Jacob Rickett; Wm. Gray; Gerrard Owden; Jasper
Peddicoat; Mark Rickets; John B. Magruder
Class No. 6: Nathan Owden; Wm. Rickets Junr; Nacey Green; Silvanus Moore;
Aaron Cobeth; Philip Dorus(?); Richard Davis
Class No. 7: James Groom; John Edwards; Abraham Boyd; Roger Brooke; Chas.
Burgess; Danl. Smith Junr; Timothy Brenan

APPENDIX B: MUSTER ROLLS AND OTHER LISTS

Class No. 8: Thoms. Holt; Wm. Pegg; Clement Summers; Basil Winsor; John Killehock(?); Jeffrey Magruder; Nacey Waters

A List of the different companies in the lower Battn. of Montgomery county with the different Classes as returned by Coll. John Murdock the 15th of July 1780 -
1st Company: Wm. Bailey, Capt; Hezh. Magruder, 1st Lieut; Stophel Kiser, 2nd do; Josiah Magruder, Ensign
John Busey, 1st Sergt; Isaac Brooke, 2nd do; Richard Magruder, 3; James Slicer 4th Sergt.; Thos. Chapple, 1st Corpl; Hezh. Speak, 2nd do; Saml. King, 3d do Zepah. Burch, 4th
Class No. 1: Wm. Stiles; Hy. Jeans; Robert Thomas; Charles Coats Jones; Zechah. Robertson; Daniel Magruder; George Chapple; Baptist Joy
Class No. 2: Richard C. Clagett; Peter Becraft; Zeckah. Evans; George Harriss; Benjn. Goodrick; Paul Summers; Hezekh. Summers; Philip Kiser
Class No. 3: Thos. McCubbin; Christopher Cochentoffer; John Chapple; Wm. Tucker; John Nichols; Joseph Adkins; Thomas Miles; Aaron Lanham
Class No. 4: George Read; Thomas Clarke; Henry Priest; Baptist Tuttle; Hanson Vermillion; Thos. Greenfield; Saml. Mackettee
Class No. 5: Edward Magruder; Edwd. King; Walter Tucker; Joseph Sprigg Belt; Henry Jones; John Barber; Zepah. Mockbee; Kid: Marcus
Class No. 6: Wm. B. Magruder; Archd. Magruder; Samuel Busey; Saml. Beall Magruder; Benedict Clarke; Zechah. Mockbee; John Graves; Michael Cochentaffer
Class No. 7: Normand B. Magruder; Wm. Steal; Nathan Robertson; John Hawkins; Joshua Shoemaker; Wm. Windham; Robt. Robertson; Benjn. Early; John Madding
Class No. 8: Clement Beall; Charles McHettee(?); Lancelot Crown; Jas. Collins; Nathan Collins; Walter Clagett; Peter Young; Benjn. Madding
2nd Company: Jesse Wilcoxen, Capt; Saml. B. Magruder, 1st Lieut.; Wm. Talbert, 2 do; Richard Blacklock, Ensign; Wm. Clements; 1st Sergt; Alexr. Tucker, 2d do; Ninian Magruder, 3d do; Burch Cheshire, 4th; Daniel Nichols, 1st Corpl.; Benjn Smith Benton, 2d do; Alexr. Wallace, 3rd do; Isaac Ridgeway, 4th do
Class No. 1: Mordecai Boffutt; David Shepone; Wm. T. Chambers; Wm. Moore; Barney Maffatt; Joseph Mitchell; Zechah. Austin
Class No. 2: John Johnson; Wm. Sedgewick; John Sedgewick; Hugh Elder; Nathan Benton; Wm. Wallace; Wm. Collier
Class No. 3: John Clagett; David Oneal; Elisha Williams; Charles Greenfield; Jas. Ball; Edwd. Hughes; John Ferrill
Class No. 4: Leaven Magruder; Benedict Woodard; Richd. Gatton; Jas. Higgins; John Len...(?); Lewis Wilcoxen; Ninn. Riley Junr; Thos. Austin
Class No. 5: Benjn. Gittings; Walter Magruder; Saml. Dyar; Wm. Benton; Chas. Magruder; George Gingle; Richd. Price; Wm. McNear
Class No. 6: Thomas Flint; Thoms. Lewis; Saml. Duckett; John Herring; Moses DeSelm; Ninian Willett; James Riley
Class No. 7: Ninian B. Magruder; Baruch Odle; Nathan Clagett; Wm. Lodge; Wm. Willett; Wm. Allnutt; Wm. Tucker
Class No. 8: William Offutt Magruder; Zechah. McCubbin; Edward Adams; James Shearlock; Barton Moore; John Gill; Enoch Magruder

3rd Company: Joseph Magruder, Capt; Joseph White, 1st Lieut; John Marcus; 2nd do; Thos. Scott; Ensign; George H. Offutt, 1st Sergt; Rezin Offutt, 2nd

MONTGOMERY COUNTY

do; Saml. Clagett, 3rd do; Joseph Clagett, 4 do; Basil Beall, 1st Corpl.;
George Viley (?), 2nd do; Zechah. Clagett, 3rd do; Nathan Offutt, 4th do
Class No. 1: Zadok Offutt; Charles Coventry; Henry Childs; Barton Duley;
Charles Eeds; James Offutt of Wm.; Henry Downes; John Childs; Henry Vernall
Class No. 2: Hezekiah Offutt; John McCornack; Thos. Clarke; James Flemming;
John Barker; Walter Draine; Elias Magruder; Jesse Offutt; Ezekl. Offutt;
Leonard Clarke
Class No. 3: John Hetch; John Bogler; David Lowe; George Umble; Wm. L.
Davis; Chas. Cradock; Benjn. Bean; Walter Evans; Francis Downing; Nathl.
Offutt
Class No. 4: Wm. Jones; Ignatius Speaks; Charles Murphy; Jas. Duley; Wm.
Moland; John Offutt; Josiah Harp; John Clarke
Class No. 5: Maccalon Edmonston; Alexr. Offutt; Jacob Tucker; Robert
Ridgeway; Hezekh. Clagett; Alexr. Southern; John Hawkins; James Edward
Smith; Aaron Rowlen; Alexr. Allen
Class No. 6: Thomas Shields; John Rimington; Wm. Offutt; Thomas Drain; Saml.
Elliott; Thos. Flint Junr; Philip Murphy; Wm. Harriss
Class No. 7: Richard Roberts; Thos. Offutt Senr; Wm. Gatton; John White;
King(?) English; Saml. Jones; Hezekh. Jones; George Culph Junr
Class No. 8: Thomas Offutt Junr; Stephen Jarbo; Charles Jones Millright;
Philip Harp; Wm. Davis; Kinsey Beall

4th Company: Thomas Edmonston, Capt.; Edward Wheelor, 1st Lieut; Richard
Jones, 2nd do; Jereh. Orme, Ensign; Eli Orme, 1st Sergt; Jonathan Nixon, 2nd
do; Morris Brashears, 3rd do; Auguston Dunn, 4th do; Tyson Beall, 1st Corpl;
James Nixon, 2nd Corpl; Wm. Culver, 3rd Corpl; Ninn. Hoskinson, 4th do;
Class No. 1: Robert Willmore; Daniel Lloyd Senr; Charles Chaney; Stephen
Lanham; John Selby
Class No. 2: Hugh Nixon; Aaron Orme; Thos. Beall (of Allen); John Cross;
Thomas Benson; John Benson
Class No. 3: Thos. Tucker; Richd. Nixon; John Wilmore; Thos. Reynolds
Class No. 4: Lawson Beall; Wm. Kneighton; Francis Ratliff; Philip Orme;
Daniel Lloyd; Elisha Hoskinson
Class No. 5: Wm. Ryan; George Wilson (of Wm.); Matthew Fitzgerrald; Jereh.
Berry; Henry Clarke; Thomas Trundle
Class No. 6: Wm. Wheelor; Stephen Wilson; Joseph Campbell; Jas. Robinson;
Thos. Perry; John Wilson (of Hy.); Chas. Case; Saml. Lloyd
Class No. 7: Saml. Jones; Gabriel Cross; Edward Holland; Thos. Keer; Nathl.
Mitchell
Class No. 8: Absalom Bedds; Thos. Willmott; John Beall; George Letman;
Joshua Nixon; Richard O Brian; Elias Browning

The List of the different companies in the lower Battn. of Montgomery
County. with the different Classes as returned by Coll. John Murdock 15th of
July 1780 -
5th Company: Saml. Swearingon, Capt; Saml. Beall, 1st Lieut.; Anthony
Wilcoxen, 2nd do; George Wilcoxen, Ensign; Baruch Prather, 1st Sergt;
Azariah Prather, 2d do; Henry Ferrill, 3rd do; John Wilcoxen, 4th do; Obed.
Swearingon, 1st Corpl; Azel Butt, 2nd do; Basil Harding, 3rd do; Basil
Prather, 4 do
Class No. 1: Edward Beall; Erasmus Perry; Michael Connoly; John Connoly;
Basil Gittings; Wm. Richards

205

APPENDIX B: MUSTER ROLLS AND OTHER LISTS

Class No. 2: Jonathan Glaze; Walter Prather; Zechah. Prather; Thos. Burriss; Richard Nicholson; Vachel Harding
Class No. 3: Basil Glaze; Wm. Duke; Wm. Hendley; Josephus Beall; John Fitzgerrald
Class No. 4: Richd. Butt; Thos. Belt; Jereh. Beall; Azell Butt; John Doran; Jas. Shaw; Saml. Lazenby
Class No. 5: Swearingon Butt; Michl. Litton; Benjn. Beggarly; Edward Owen; John Biggs; Richd. Callahan; Rignal Butt; David Beggarly
Class No. 6: George Cashill; John Ferrill; Aaron Prather; Masham Ridgeway; Stephen Tall; George Suter
Class No. 7: Edwd. Harding; Berry Roby; Richd. Lanham; Saml. Beall White; Wm. Lanham; Edwd. Garrett; Malcham Tawneyhill; James McDonack; Wm. Seayer
Class No. 8: Wm. Prather; Ambrose Hawker; Henry Chapple; Ninn. E. Beall; Zephah. Beall (of Jas.); Hauzy Lanham; Saml. Bonnifield; Edwd. Gatts (Gates?)
6th Company: Aaron Harriss, Capt; Zadok Harriss, 1st Lieut.; John Trundle, 2nd do; Thos. Beall, Ensign; Philip Tracy, 1st Sergt; Daniel Williams, 2nd do; Josiah Hoskinson, 3rd do; Wm. Harriss Tawneyhill, 4th; Wilson Wilson, 1st Corpl; John Ceicill, 2nd do; Thos. Brooke Beall, 3rd do; Daniel Lee, 4th do
Class No. 1: Jas. Burgess; John Lee Junr; John Bates; Basil Alley; Benjn. Greentree; Jas. Burnes; Jas. Lee; Charles Phillips; James Maddox; Christopher Bean
Class No. 2: Hezekh. Woodard; Zechah. Beall; Roger Caho; Jas. Ceicill; David Bloice; Milborn Cambron; Walter Clarke; Benjn. Cary; Andrew Maginniss
Class No. 3: Henry Beggarly; Charles Bloyce; Caleb Cash; Zechah. White Junr; Roger Hogan; Samuel Purnell; John Duley; ...; Thos. Stallions
Class No. 4: John Beaden; Alexr. Barrett; Leonard Williams; Thos. Gittings; Elias Burgess; Daniel Lee; Thos. Collins; Mark Whalen; Wm. Browen
Class No. 5: John Collins; Joshua Collins; Hillery Lanham; Thos. Wilson (of Hy.); Henry Cambron; Wm. Maddox; John Summers; Jonathan Lucas; James Dowlen
Class No. 6: Joseph Francis; Thos. James; Leonard Combs; Richard Barrett; Robert Edwards; Archd. Osbin; Fredk. Kisener; Henry Pierce; Josiah Bean
Class No. 7: Matthew Whaland; Benjn. Moore; Notley Mitchell; Zechah. Woodard; John Barrett; Alexr. Roberts; John Maddox Wilson - 4; Martin Speaks; Elixus Sims
Class No. 8: Joseph Tucker; Jas. Castor; Jas. Marshall; Zadok Wilson; Joseph Mcketee; Nathan Lanham; Jonathan Wilson; John Lashley; Josiah Trundle; Thos. Connoly

7th Company: Edward Burgess, Capt; Alexr. Estep, 1st Lieut; John Shekells, 2nd do.; Nicholas Hauker, Ensign; John Williams, 1st Sergt.; Samuel Hobbs, 2nd do; Joseph Estep, 3rd do; Saml. Moore, 4th; Felter Myers, 4th Corpl; Richd Williams, 2nd do; Edward Browning, 3rd; Archd. Mason, 4th do
Class No. 1: Robt. Asa Beall; Jeremiah Beall; George Fightmaster; Zechah. Downes; Volentine Pock; George Snell; Thomas Barnes; John Lazier
Class No. 2: Walter Mitchell; Henry Lazinby; Wm. Fitzgerrald; Richard W. Johns; Jeremiah Lewis; John Thomas; Richard Thomas Junr
Class No. 3: John King; John Gartrell; ..immer Waters; Wm. Cyrpuss; Partrick Moran
Class No. 4: Joseph(?) Browning; Robert(?) Orme; Alexander Mason; ..ngley Mason; Joshua Lazier; Solomon Miers; Joshua Lazinby; John Jones; Wm. Newcomb

MONTGOMERY COUNTY

Class No. 5: Charles Gartrell; Weaver Waters; Josephus Waters; Alexr.
Lasinby; Wm. King; Saml. Alley; Thos. Waters
Class No. 6: Isaac Moore; Saml. J. Godman; Clement Williams; Zechah. Jeans;
John Beall; John Aldridge; Philip Barnes; Thos. Wright
Class No. 7: Jacob Burton; Thos. Mitchell; Jereh. Browning; Capil Holland;
Jonathan Mason; Joshua Swain; Thos. Dawson
Class No. 8: Thomas Cross; Saml. Mcdougal; Joseph Gartrell; Basil Burton;
Josiah Holmes; Zephah. Beall; Humphrey Westley; Wm. Rugless

8th Company: Daniel Rintzell, Capt; Tobias Yost, 1st Lieut; Anthony
Rintzell, 2nd do; John Peter Lange, Ensign
Class No. 1: Jacob Trisler; Valentine Rintzell; Thomas Rigdon; John Gant;
Thos. Clarke; Philip Hass; John Orr; Thos. Pierce Junr; Jacob Rintzell; John
Gebhart Junr
Class No. 2: Jacob Risener; Hezekiah Chaney; John Hill; Andrew Witman; Saml.
Nothey; James McDougal; Richard Roaden (Negro); Walter Smith (doctr.);
Thomas Beall (of George)
Class No. 3: David Hurry; Benjn. Contee - 5; Thomas Beatty (of Thos.); Wm.
Green; Saml. McFlowers; Partrick Mcguire; Andrew Rintzell; John Thompson;
Philip Obrian; Charles Reynolds
Class No. 4; Fredk. Cochentoffer; Joseph Garlick; Wm. V. Stewart; Robert
Sutton; Michael Donback; Daniel Bulger; Benjn. Selman Junr; John Beatty;
John Orme
Class No. 5; Wm. Scoolfield; Fouquhart McGree; Anthony Rhintzell; Lott
Darling; James Keene; Anthy. Gusler; Christian Kirtz; Jos: Smith, Doctr.;
John Walter
Class No. 6: Joseph Yates; Thomas Crawford; Alexr. White; John Pringle;
Philip Craver; John Peter Lange; Wm. Rogers; John Bradish; Benjn. Lacey; Wm.
Roustridge
Class No. 7: Fredk. Wetzell; Benjn. Becraft; Robert Rignall; Wm. Murphy;
Thos. Carman; Benjn. Cox; Robert Moses; Fredk. Miley; Benjn. Boyd; James
Anderson
Class No. 8: John Mounts; Leonard Cochentoffer; Thos. Igram; Noah Wilson;
Benjn. Selman Senr; Geo. Winebeiger; Thos. Taylor; Middleton Belt; John
Gebhart Senr; Joseph Thompson

PRINCE GEORGE'S COUNTY, 25th Battalion

10 Apr 1776/Petition of Prince George's County Militia Company. To Council
of Safety. Since 30 out of 50 votes - amoung four candidates for the
captaincy - were for Alexander Beall, Jr., petitioners trust William
Hamilton will not be appointed; postscript suggests Sgt. Peter Brown of
Capt. [Barton] Lucas's company be asked about William Hamilton.
Signed: Thomas Adams, Jr., John Beall, Thomas Beall, Thomas Bean, George
Sel[?] Bence, John Bozwell, Samuel Brashears, Jr., Thomas Brown, William
Brown, Jr., Philip Cissil, William Conn, John Cook, Joseph Cook, Alexander
Crawford, Basil Crawford, Thomas Crawford, James Furguson, Jr., John
Furguson, Josiah Gordon, Theophilus Hughes, Isaiah Hurley, Philip James,
Patrick Law, Jonathan Manley, William Marthis, William Mathews, John Mayhew,
Jr., James Mockbe, Jeremiah Moore, William Mullikin, Henry Purdy, James Ray,
Josias Ray, Henry Scott, Josias Shaw, Nathaniel Suit, John Tilley, Thomas

MONTGOMERY COUNTY

Tilley, Jr., Henry Tuell [?], Abednego White, Clement Wilson, David Wilson, Ignatius Wilson, James Wilson, Josias S[ollers] Wilson, Thomas Wright. Calendar of Maryland State Papers - The Red Books. Also see Archives of Maryland, XI, 324-325.

10 Sep - 25 Oct 1776/Petition of Caleb Hayley, Prince George's County. To Council of Safety. The petitioner is a member of a militia battalion; while in Annapolis, he fell and has been sick seven weeks since then; he desires payment for his time; his statement is endorsed by his commander, Capt. Joshua Robert Selby; also by Marsh M[aree'n] Duvall, John Macgill, Thomas Williams and Richard Wootton. p. 87 of Calendar of Maryland State Papers - The Red Books. Also see Archives of Maryland, XII, pp. 402-3.

17 April 1781/[Josa. Beall, Lieut. Ps. Gs. Cty Bladensburgh to His Excely. Thos. Simm Lee, Esqr.]
Agreeable to order I have sent the Prisoners Under Guard committed to the Care of Capn. William Patterson now a resident of this Town a person who has formerly been in the regular Service & has shewn a good deal of Spirit in Turning out on the present occasion. It is with Pleasure I can asshure Your Excellency & Honors that the Militia of this county Turned out with Spirit & alacraty nothing but arms were wanting to have embodied a Considerable force on the river, inclosed you have a list of thos Brave men who Attacked the Enemies boats under the Muzzalls of the Cannon of their shiping, & secured one of their Boats & Crew out of three that landed, and there is reason to belive that another of their boats crews suffered very mutch as I could perceive but very few hands in her, on her return, to their shiping, who sent another boat off to assist her in geting along side. Wee have only to regret the want of some field Peices & persons who could have managed them well, had that been the case I think it would have been in our powers last friday to have destroyed all their shiping excepting one that fell down Earley in the morning, the rest had all got under way but from the winds springing up very hard from the North West about sun rise they were all obliged to come to in a Cluster within about half a mile of Mr. Diggses Point where they were obliged to remain that and the Next day, on Sunday morning they got under way earley in the morning I sent an Express to Coll'l. Lyles desiring he would observe their motion and Act with the men under his command Accordingly, and to let me know if they Attempted a landing below, and went myself to broad creek to meet the prisoners, ...
[P.S.] Just before closing this John Turnbull Quarter Master of the Upper Battalion who I had ordered to press men and horses to Guard the prisoners to Annapolis informs me that many persons who he pressed for that purpose absolutely refuesed to go themselves or let him have their horses, if some Steps are not taken with those people it will be impossible for me to forward any busness whatever

List of the Officers & men who captured the Boat Crew.
Lieut. Osborn Williams; J. Queen, Ensign; John Oakley appointed to Act on this occasion as Brigadge major; Henry Lyles, Guide. Joseph Cross (of Thomas) highly worthy of the Esteem of every brave man. Privates: Isaac Duckett, Samuel Wheeler, Rd. Burgess (volunteer), Zachariah Moore, Walter Williams, Thomas Sansbury, Henry Hilleary, Richard Hill, Thomas Holly, James Pedrry Jun., James Buckham, Benjamin Sansbury, William Shaw, Benjamin Oden,

PRINCE GEORGE'S COUNTY

Henry Onions, Aaron Beall, James Wood, Waring Belt, William Turner, John Sansbury, James Wilson, John Magill, John Tyler, James Tate, Robert Lanham, Benjamin Fowler, Thomas Bennett, Joseph Gordon.

QUEEN ANNE'S COUNTY

After 20 Sep 1776/Petition of a Militia in Queen Anne's County. To Convention of Maryland. Their captain, James O'Bryan, is about to be promoted to a field officer to the Lower Battalion of Queen Anne's County; they recommend that the following officers be commissioned: Capt. John Register Emory, 1st Lt. William Ringgold, 2nd Lt. Charles Cook, Ens. James Stinson.
Signed: James Austin, Thomas Baker, James Baley (M), Michael Blackiston, William Brigs, James Brown, John Brown, John Carmon, William Carmon, Charles Cattelen, Benjamin Coppag, Eiga. [?] Coventon, Joseph Crouch, John Davis (M), Nathan Davis, Charles Devons, John Downing, John Duncan, Robert Emmory [?], William Faulcom, Edward Floyd, Solomon Green, Solomon Hadley [?], Peter Hand, Thomas Hand, Thomas Harris, Thomas Hollingsworth, James Honey, Lambeth Kent, John Killen [?], Robert Love, Matthew Mason, Thomas McCosh, William McCosh, John Meradith, Thomas Meradith, William Meradith, Thomas Potts, Earnautt Register, James Seney, John Smith (M), William Stenson, Daniel Suthrland, John Tarr, William Tarring, John Trockam [?], Nathaniel Tucker, Thomas Vanderford, John Watson, William Whight; two names illegible. p. 59, Calendar of Maryland State Papers (Blue Books)

ST. MARY'S COUNTY

Return of St. Mary's County Militia by Col. J. Jordan
An Account of the able bodied male white persons from 16 to 50 years of age in St. Marys Coty as returned to me by the men appointed for that purpose -
Upper Battn. of Militia 770 men
Lower Battn. of do.   777
Total   1547
On examination I find the above return to be very erronious, many men above fifty and some not sixteen, others not able bodyed. On the hole I do not believe that we have more than twelve hundred effective, it has not been in my power to assertain the number certainly. Richd. Barnes.

William Killgour; John Edward of Jn//Leonard Wood; Jonathan Edwards; Benjamin Edwards; Jno. Johnson Sothoron; Benjamin Suit; Jno. Edwards (Senr); Thomas Edwards; John Bladen True; James Seager; James Billinsley; Alexander Graham; Samuel Suit; William Hill; Samuel Sothoran; Leven Sothoran; Richard Sothoron (Sr.); Hezekiah Burroughs; Jno. Burroughs (junr); William Burroughs; Samuel Burroughs; Hezekiah Edwards; Benson Card; Jonathan Anderson; James Burroughs Senr; Benjamin Burroughs Jr; Joshua Eastop; Nathl. Truman Greenfield; John Woodburn; Daniel Woodburn; Jonathan Woodburn; Joseph Moran; Barton King; Cornelius King; Richard Lyon; Philip Davis; Nehemiah Leach; Henry Gilpin; Robert Ribbon; Jno. Wood Senr; Thomas Suit; Dent Suit; William Hammilton; James Broady; George Davis; Lawson Davis; Richd. Sothoran (junr); Richd. Burroughs; William Tysor; George Burroughs; William

APPENDIX B: MUSTER ROLLS AND OTHER LISTS

Cartwright; Thomas Greenfield; James Truman Greenfield; Elias Chapelair; Leonard Lyon; Jno. Dent Suit; Henry Burroughs; Thomas Seagar; William Card; Clement Bittlingsley; George Dent; George Moore; John Wood Junr; Basil Hunt; Joseph Bramhall; Normand Burroughs; Nathan Wood; John Lyon; James Chapelair; James Witherington; Briscoe Davis; Barton Drury; John Garby; John Monroe; Leonard Drury; Jonathan Fowler; William Glover; John Witherington; Misael Wood; James Lattimore; John Harrison; Nathan Harrison; Jonathan Highfield; Leonard Highfield; Gerrard Davis; Leonard Hilton; William Scott; George Harrison; Joseph Harrison; Robert Harrison (junr); Vernon St. Clair; Jacob Hopkins; Matthew Burroughs; William Young; Owen Davis; Henry Clarke; Edwd. Burrage junr; John Bowles; William Diar; William Sumerhill; James Branson; John Breadey junr; William Mattingly; Thomas Riney (of Jno.); Bennit Toon; John Morgan; Notley Tippit (scratched through); Justinian Cartwright; Richard Wathen; James Harbert; Basil Patterson; James Thompson; Leonard Howard; John Vowles; Jno B. Cissill (junr); Henry Norris; Robert Peake; James Payne; Charles Russell; Benjamin Clarke; Ignatius Bowles; Leonard Booth; Peter Howard (Neck); Justinian Wheeler; Stephen French; Austin Howard; Ignatius Clarke; Edmond Barton Cissill; William Wimsatt; Augustin Peake; Ignatius Griffin; John Budd; John Mugg; McGolds Curry; Bennit Hopewell; Ignatius French; Notley Bradburn; Basil Thompson; James Booth; James Thompson (of Mark); Peregrine Howard; Charles Howard; Raphael Thompson (of Arthur); John Tompkins; Raphael Thompson (Sr.); Cyrus Vowles; Philip Briscoe (Junr); James Davis; Thomas Sampson; Henry Bradey; Marcus Hatton Penn; Thomas Harris; John Moore; Edward Smith; James Morris; Clement Briscoe; Leonard Clarke; John Compton; James Sumerhill; James Biscoe; Joseph Alvey; Josias Grindall; Jno. Rawlins; Joseph Owens; Hezekiah Barber; Gerrard Hayden; Samuel Blithin; Joseph Mort; Thomas Bond; Jno. Wattson (junr); Azariah Wattson

Edmond Plowden; William Spink; Joseph Stone; Wilford Reshwick; Elias Smith; John Tennison; Thomas Reshwick; Gerrard Cissill; Vincent Payne; William Hayden; Philip Norris; Joseph Reshwick; Bennit Cissill; Philip Ford; James Bradburn; Martin Henry; Basil Booth; Thomas Clarke; Thomas Anderson; Ignatius Daft; Richard Booth; Arthur Thompson; Robert Mattingly; Henry Yates; Leonard Payne; George Howard; Jno. B. Thompson (junr); Francis Wheeler; Jno. B. Thompson (sr.); Zacharia Mareman; Jno. Thompson (of Thos.); Philip Rourke; Ignatius Taylor; Raphael Payne; Walter Mugg; James Taylor; Jno. Bowles; Jno. B. Cissill; James Bowles; Jno. Cissill; Bennit French; Joshua Mareman; Joseph Mareman; William Mareman; Henry Taylor; Raphael French; Thomas Howard; John Daft; Charles Clarke; Peter Carberry; Daniel Friend; Francis Cissill; William Bowles; Francis Payne; Joshua Clarke; Joseph Carberry; Basil Thompson; Richard Hopewell; William Carpenter; Stephen Wimsatt; Athanasius Thompson; Bernard Cissill; John Mills; William Walter; Thomas Nichols; Henry Swann
Robert Briscoe; Stephen Cawood; Henry Wingate; Elias Barber; John Brookbank Senr; Baptist Barber; John Brookn (sic) (junr); Elkanah Swann; James Andrew Mills; Charles Mills; Barnet White(?) Barber; Thomas Fowler; Zacharia Thomas; Benjamin Cawood; James Hayden; Samuel Higges; James Carter; James Smith; Edward Gardiner; Joseph Turner; James Brookbank; Ignatius Mattingley; Joseph Barber; Luke Barber (junior); Thomas Dutton Nettle; James Bradey; Jonathan Shamwell; Henry Fowler; Michael Cusack; Basil Smith; William Smith; Benjamin Harrison; Thomas Noe; James Wattson (jun); John Tarr; John Myvert

ST. MARY'S COUNTY

Barber; Basil Hayden; Joseph Love; Charles Hayden; Philip Sumerhill; John
Hazeltine; Ignatius Simons; Jesse Swann; Joseph Shamwell; William Shamwell;
Richard Wainwright; John Gardiner; Joshua Hutchinson; John Hendley; Zephania
Pratt; John Pratt; Benjamin Cheshire; Robert Slye Wood; Basil Bradey;
Matthew Compton; Leonard Branson(junr)
Ignatius Abell; Enoch Abell; Barton Abell; Jno. Mills
Roger Clarke (scratched through); Joseph R...(scratched through); Robert
Wa...(scratched through); William Redman (scratched through); Aquila
H...(scratched through); Edmond Abell; Thomas Thompson; Robert Hagar;
Ignatius French; Leonard Moore; Barton Greenwell; ...(scratched through);
Elisha Wise (scratched through); William McClain(?) (scratched through);
Edward Howard (scratched through); Enoch Stone; John Booth Abell; Cuthbert
Abell; Cuthbert Clarke; John Wimsatt; Joshua Abell; James Wimsatt; Basil
Brown; George Abell; John Moore; Henry Ford; William Walker; Ignatius Heard;
Thomas Aud; Joseph Davis; Jno. Harper; Mark Norris (junr); Benedict
Spalding; Joshua Jarboe; Joseph Greenwell (of Thos.); Robert Wimsatt; Thomas
Greenwell; William Norris (of Thos.); Hugh Williams; Roger Walker; Jno.
Basil Nottinghame; Thomas Fenwick; Geo. McCaul Clarke; Francis Plowden;
Clark Abell; Cuthb. Abell (junr); Joseph Stone; Jno. Michael Raley; George
Clarke; Richard Clarke; Gabriel Williams; John Sener; Bennit Hutchins;
Philip Read; Phineas Hurst; Jeremiah Hazle; John B. Thompson; Peter Joyh;
Henry Medley; Henry Spalding; Philip Spalding; Francis Swaits; Robert
Swaits; William Dean; Basil Raily; John Stone; Philip Fenwick; Arthur
McGill; Cuthbert Fenwick; Samuel Harris; Stephen French; Edmond Barton
Greenwell; Robert Greenwell; Henry Greenwell; Sylvester Gatton; John Find(?)
(junr); Martin Yates; John Cissill; Ignatius Greenwell
Basil Mahoney, Athananas Joy, Michael Drury/on the written(?) list/are also
returned on/Capt Roachs List/in the upper Battn.
James Brewer has not returned on any list & ought be on this one/also
Elezius Spalding to be on this list

John Hatton Read; William Stone; Haton Stone; Joseph Hall; Ignatius Peacock;
Zacharia Abell; Charles Jarboe; Anthony Simms; Isaac Clarke; Peter Jarboe;
Henry Raley jr; Ignatius Stone; Ignatius Goddard; Jno. Robinson; Basil
Bright; Robert Abell; Richard Jarboe; Robt. Jarboe; Arthur Hall; Ignatius
Reynolds; Arthur Abell; Thomas Abell; Henry Abell; Richard Wimsatt; Jno.
Basil Norriss; Edmund Norriss; James Norriss; Edmund Heard; Jno. Heard
Norriss; Gabriel Newton; Francis Wheatley(?); James Norriss of Norrh(?);
Stephen Norriss; Jno. Greenwell of James; William Heard; Justinian Mills;
Jno. Basil Thompson; Robt. Goldsberry; Arnold Greenwell

John Smith; Zacharia Forrest; Zephania Forrest; John Smith (junr)
Cornelius Wildman; John Wildman; Raphael Taney;
//"To be struck out" - Basil Mahaney; Athanasius Joy;
James Parsons; Zacharia Barnes; Thomas Spalding junr; Francis Brookes;
William Leach; William King; James Moore; John Hazell junr; Michael Drury -
"to be struck out;" John Raily; John Greenwell; William Fenwick; Philip
Evans; John Deane; Philip Drury; Richard Pithington; Jesse Floyd; Thomas
Brewer; Ignatius Joy junr; John Hutchins; Bennit Spalding; Clarke Spalding;
William Wilkerson; James Deane; Ignatius Russell; Enoch Joy; Enoch Campbell;
Samuel Benfield; Ambrose Carr; Francis Fenwick (Senr); Henry Lucas; James
Heard; Barton Goddard; Jno. Raily (of Jno); John King; George Fenwick;

APPENDIX B: MUSTER ROLLS AND OTHER LISTS

Charles Taney; Edward Spalding; Michael Spalding Junr; Zacharia Brewer;
Enoch Fenwick (junr); John Fenwick; Francis Fenwick (junr); Richard Fenwick;
Joseph Dorsey; Ignatius Goddard; William Clarke; Edward Barton Smith; Basil
Smith; John Raily (of Henry); Archibald Pike; Enoch Drury junr
Edward Abell (scratched through); Samuel Jenifer; John Abell Young
George Rogers; Jno. Rogers; Richd. Rogers; Edward Swann; John Vowls; Moses
Farthing; Aaron Farthing; Robert Shirley; Stephen Hilton; Baptist Wimsatt;
Jno Silance; Cuthbert Fenwick; John Heard (scratched through); Richard Heard
(scratched through); W... (scratched through); Kenelin Clark; George
Barnhouse; William Lee Massey; Joseph Edwards; Jno. Cole; John Edwards;
Francis Cole; Robt. Clarke; Jno. Cissill; James Atkinson; McKelvie Hammitt;
Vincent Thornton; Thomas Wise; Caleb Wise; Adam Wise R
Adam Wise A
Matthew Wise; William Hagar; Francis Bryan; William Wise; Kenelon B. Watts;
Cartwright Hammitt; John Bohanon; Thomas Wooton; George Bohanon; Moses
Bohanon; Robert Young; Ignatius Hall; Joshua Connoly; John Ford; Bennit
Raley; Richard Hammitt; John Bartlet; Caleb Hammitt; Samuel Copeland;
Jeremh. Cole; Richard Smart; James Harber; William Newton; Ignatius Newton;
Noah Greenwell; Richard Noakes(?); Thomas Dillon; Gerrard Bond; John Shanks;
Clement Garner; Stephen Tarlton; Samuel Tennison; Joseph Nevit; William
Cheseldine; William Mills; Gerrard Cheseldine; Ignatius Heard; James
Chittam; Mark Bowen; Barton Mattingly; Baptist Harden; John Geanes; Philip
Liu(?); Bennit Parsons(?); Aaron Thompson; Jeremiah Gibson; Thomas Bolt;
Bennit Cox; John Coode; John Avery; William Bowling; James Leak; William
Woodward; James Brown; William Jordan; Herbert Blackston; Benjamin
Horskins(?); John Goldsmith; Jesse Ord; James Bullock; William Tennison;
Joshua Turner; Kenelin Cheseldine; John Carpenter; John Heard; John Turner;
Alexander Anderson; Baptist Lowe; Bennit Gough; Basil Howard; John Pain;
William Evans; Isachar Mason; Rob King; Peter Joy; John Hilton; Thomas
Pojtwine; Samuel Jordan; John Boyd (junr); Richard Gardner; William Bullock;
William Mollohone; James Thompson; William Thompson; Francis Hilton;
Gustavus Brown

James Roach; Richard Rapier; William Rapier; Joseph Woodward
John Graves (junr); Joseph Thompson; Joshua Graves; John Fenwick; Edward
Campbell; Thomas Forrest; Ignatius Brown; Jeremiah Graves; James Gates;
William Brewer; Ignatius Drury; George Mitts; Michael Drury; Joshua Millard;
Delbert Newton; William Payne; Thomas Joy; Philip Milton; Philip Ford;
Joseph Howard; Peter Drury; M...(?) Da...(?); John Roberts; Ignatius
Mattingly; James Fenwick; Bennit Yates; John Horskins; William Carroll;
Sennit Duvall; Richard Thompson; Joshua Merrill; Raphael Ford; Basil
Mahoney; Athanasis Joy; Peter Ford; William Shaw; James Vessels; William
Hayden; Jesse Alvey; James Wathen; James Russell; James Howard; John Edley;
Cornelius Brothers; Patrick Carberry; Robert Ford; Thomas Mattingly; Philip
Johnson; Willoughby Watts; Joseph Alvey; Joseph Wimsatt; Thomas Hall; James
Knott; Kenelin Peak; Zacharia Newton; John Carpenter

Thomas Attoway Reeder; Jno. Hooper Brome; Jno. Cartwright; Zacharia Hammitt
Richard Miles; Joseph Crook; Thomas Dixon; Ignatius Hill; Jesse Joseph;
Absolom Dixon; Leonard Wathen; Charles Neale; Charles Sumerhill; Zacharia
Hill (junr); Joseph Hill; Bennit Hutchinson; Walter Billinsley; Thomas
Bigges; Sergt James Burroughs (of Jno.); Robert Clarke Tysor; Peter Dixon;

ST. MARY'S COUNTY

Sergt Philip Bryan; Jno. Jones; Hooper Brome; Jesse Greenwell; James Leach; Thomas Goldsmith; Edward Hill; Jno. Davis; Peregrine Cahill; Francis Cole; Sergt. Basil Hall; Thomas Wakelin; James Booker; Joseph Booker; Thomas Gryar; Nicholas Drury; Jno. Hardesty; Edward Wathen; Jno. Bapts. Toon; Luke Mattingly; William Baker; Thomas Daft; Jno. Virmier; Richd. Spalding; Enoch Spalding; James Murray; William McGee; Bennit Hazle; Jno. Bapts. Goddard; James Walker; Henry Philips; Justinian Crook; Wm. Bryan; Samuel Keymer; Joseph Johnson; Jno. Wakelin; Jno. Knott; Jno. Baptist Brewer; William Burn; Zacharia Hills Jun.

Zephania Haskins; John Medcalf; Jesse Tennison; Peter Brown (jun); Nicholas Brown; John Drury; Henry Booth; Jesse Bullock; Kenelin Medcalf; Jeremiah Evans; Charles Hazeldine; Nathan Rollins; John Seale; John Alvey; James Milton; John Field; Jesse Ford; John Wathen; James Mills; Peter Howard; Raphael Greenwell; Matthew Daft; Luke Graves; Jeremiah Lancaster; Charles Joy; J... W...; Ignatius Campbell; Andrew McLoney; George Spalding; John Brodoc

Clement Parsons; Robert Hammitt; Benj. Buckler; Robert Clarke; Thomas Bridget; Charles Bridget; Joseph Thompson; James Knott; Jno. Hill; Oswel Thompson; James Waren Wathen; Joseph Wathen; Joseph Howard (of Ben); Basil Thompson; George McKinock; Leonard Johnson (of David); Joseph Walker; Edwards Hazle; William Hancock; Stephen Walker; Jno. Smith Mahoney; Jesse Crook; Jas. Stevens (scratched through); Nathl. Knott; Benjamin Darley

James Barnes; Joseph Mudd; Jesse Edwards; John James; Jonathan Wood; Zacharia Billinsley; Joseph Hammitt; Jesse Lock; Clement Joseph; Joseph Joseph; James Williams; James Keech; Jonathan Tippit; Michael Lyon; John Cole; John Keech; Joseph Waters; Jeremiah Robertson; William Wakelin; Ignatius Cusack; William Wheatley; James Suit; Stouston(?) Edwards; John Seager; Joseph Noe; Allen Billinsley

Peter Richie; Thomas Burrage; James Compton; Joseph Stevens; George Milton; Elisha Harbert; Ephraim Vessells; Jonathan Moran; William Fowler; Samuel Burroughs Sr.; Charles Fowler; Charles Scott; James Stevens; John Harbert; Hezekiah Moran; Rhode French; William Harbert; John Riney (junior)

Joseph Fish; James Fish; Richard King; George Biscoe; Enoch Breeden; Philip Abell; Stephen Stiles; Richard Evans; Bennit Fenwick; Aaron Abell; Jno.King (of Chs. Junr); George Aisquith; William Fitzjoek; James Hopewell; Roger Clarke; Joseph Ramsdin; Rhode Wilman; William Redman; Acquilla Hall; Myre(?) Wise; Elijah Wise; William McLean; Edmond Howard; Jno. Hall; Joseph Newton; Jessea(?) Thornton; Thomas Silences; John Martindale (scratched through); Gustavus Horner; William Bond (scratched through); Henry Neale; John Blackistone; John Lamb; Joseph Shanks; William Gardner; James Heard; Basil Brooke; James Lowe; Rhodolph Gibson (scratched through); William Oard(?); Jno. Gibson (of Wm.); Joseph Woens; Joseph Fluld (Flield?); John Bayley; William Goodin; Kenelin McWilliams; Thomas Auston; Jeremiah Long; Rob Long; Joseph Hargiss (scratched through); Jonathan Howard; Samuel Pherson; Jeremiah Flower; John Blair; Thomas Shanks (scratched through); Jeremiah Neale; Ralph Lancaster; Roswell Gibson; Peregrine Long

APPENDIX B: MUSTER ROLLS AND OTHER LISTS

Philip ...; Bennet Combs; James Williams; James Gough; Robt. Ford; Jno.
Heard of Ml.(?); Robt. Matting; Rhode Beverley; Jno. Aud; Igns. Gough; Josh.
Booth; Thos. Greenwell; Philip Nottingham; William Greenwell; Enoch Medley;
Joseph Aud; Jno. Medley; Nics. Greenwell; Jno. Ford; Igns. Norris; Wm.
Fenwick; Bartn. Norris; Jeremh. Millburn; Geo. Medley; Nichs. Mills; Henry
Wimsatt; Igns. Peake; Mattw. Heard; Ralph Spalding; Richd. Heard; Bennr(?)
Norris; Petr. Peak; Robt. Cole; Richd. Clarke; Clemt. Greenwell; Philip
Norris (of Thos.?); Bernd. Mills; Wm. Greenwell of Wm.; Joseph Greenwell;
Ralph Heard; Igns. Shirley; Rode Norris; Jams. Greenwell; Bennt. Brewer;
Edmd. Norris; Jas. Greenwell; John Wheatley

Jno. Greenwell; Archd. Greenweld; Jno. Railey; Jos. Greenwell; Tim. Bowes;
Saml. Abell; Jno. Bapts. Payne; Henry Reader; Bennet Riley; Vinct. Norris;
Jams. Peake; Jas. Mills; Php. Combs; Edmd. Cole; Steph. Goldsburry; Wm. Aud;
Robt. Aud; Archd. Taylor; Edwd. Greenwell; Jno. Masson; Steph. Gough; Jno.
Manning; Ralph Sissill; Clemt. Norris; Step. Greenwell; Ralph. Combs; Igns.
Greenwell; Robt. Thomas; Bernd. Newton; Silvtr. Strange; Bent. Nottingham;
Jas. Bould; ; Richd. Booth; Php. Norris; Jesse Greenwell; William Medley;
Henry Pike(?); Stepn. Greenwell; Josep. Medley; Igns. Wimsatt; Rhode Hacket;
Thos. Jarboe; Thos. Norris; Robt. Fenwick; Gerrd. Norris

Thos. Grain(?); Igns. Swan; Thos. Shadnick; James Crance; Joseph Cox; Igns.
Wooten; Thos. Watts; John Moore; Abram Dennis; Moses Flower; John Booth;
Jacob Duvall; Clem Howard; John Ross; John Wooten; James Haith; George
Brewer; Zach. Kendrick; Robt. Bean; Mark Penn; John Cox Junr; Thos. Howard;
Henry Watts; John Norris; John Sutton; Thos. Hebb; Jams. Waughop; Bennet
Lane (Lone?); James Tarlton; Joseph Hebb; John Shadrick; George Cole; Caleb
Glebb

Alexander Watts; Igns. Combs; Geo. H. Leigh; John Taylor Junr; Bapt. Newell;
Geo. Armsworthy; Stephen Lynch; Arthur Dillihay; James Taylor; John Bean of
Ben; John Ends; William Warren; Henry Rich; William Fish; John Thomson Junr;
William Thomas; John Reeder; Joshua Redman; Benjn. Bean Senr; Thos. Green
Abby; Vincen Ends Junr; John Truman; John Coloson; James Dyer; Edwd..
Warren; Marshak Cain; Stephen Addams; Geo. Bean; Henry King Junr; John
Taylor Senr; Geo. Taylor; Stephen Henning; Henry Nowell; John Cole of Val;
John McClayland; John Armsworthy; Igns. Lowe; Edwd. Jenkins; James Lowry;
John Bean of Robt.; Jeremiah King; Thos. Hilton; Jeremiah Jenkins; George
Combs

Wm. B. Smart; Geo. Guyther; Josias Langley; Joshua Tarlon; James Fenwick;
Thos. Chilton; John McColey; Wm. Norris; Williby Nuigent; Joseph Baxter;
Abner Wherritt; Robt. Nugent; Thos. Bean; Henry Allison; Wm. Hebb Junr;
Richd. Fenwick; Francis Gibbions; Thos. Wherrett; Nicholas More; Richd.
McKay; Henry Chilton; Bennet Moore; John Hendley; Jesse Chiverall; George
Jenkins; John Chilton; William Hammett; John Wherritt; Ben Redman; John
Morris; Rubin McKenny; Simpson Williams; James Goldsberry; Phil Leigh; John
Tarlton; Nichs. Goldsberry; James Leigh; David Johns; Jere Nugent; John
Allison; Alexander Bean; John Goings; John M Duall; Anthony Baxter

Jeremiah Nowell; John Armstrong; William Martin Junr; Luke Crisman; Solomon
Adams; William Lowerwell; Abraham Armsworthy; Thos. Cook Senr; Thos.

ST. MARY'S COUNTY

Calloson; James Cox; Thos. Files; George Cox; Henry King Senr; William Atkinson; John Goldsberry; Thos. Ridgely; Thos. Marten; Benj. Thompson; Stephen Bennet; William Goldsbury; William Taylor Junr; Bent. Armsworthy; John Bats; Henry Goldsbury; Bent. Henning; William Reeder; William Combs; John Gibbins; Joseph Taylor; Thos. Lynch; Robt. Grieves; Joseph Fenwick; William Martin

John Horn Abell; R. Armstrong; Wm. Bennet; B Williams; Wm. Holton; John Dunbars; John Fenwick; James White; Edmd. Basey; Lanford Dossey; Igns. Briscoe Junr; James Smith; Charles Wriderwood; Josep Jeffery; Jno. Dossey; Mordicai Jones; James Richardson; Joseph Riork; Robt. Bennett; Robt. Dunkinson; Thos. Timmon; Thos. Egerton; Michl. Byrn; Richd. Barnhouse; Richd. Fitzgeffery; Wm. Smith; Thos. Richardson; McHay Briscoe; Thos. Kain; Stephen Briscoe; Joseph Bennett; John Smith senr; Bennet Briscoe; James Egerton; James Biscoe; Joseph Biscoe; Henry Coffey; James Crawley; James Langley; Josph Briscoe; Nathl. Hickman; Wm. Smoot; Cutht. Smoot; Jno. Egerton; Jonathan Biscoe; Joseph Abell; James Payne; Thos. Smoot; ... Fitzjeffery; ....; Hugh Hopewell; John Asquith; John Chesley; Robt. Jarboe; Thos. Scofield; Henry Sewell; Joseph Dent; Wm. Leatherland; Hopewell Kerby; Francis Kerby; Charles Dantt; Mchl. Beaverly; James Allison; Nathan Adams; Abm.(?) Addams; Bent. Price; Arch. Price; John Newton; Bent. Mcflaland; Jereh. Rhodes; James Price; Jonathn Redman; Abintl.(?) Shermantine; Edwd. Watson; Robt. Wise; Senica(?) Chezaldine; James Taylor; Henry Taylor; Wm. Taylor; Barton King; Roger Welch; Wm. Kerbey; Geo. Shirley; Richd. Wiseman; Acquilla Davis; Jonathan Duke; Jno. Bapt. Hill; Wm. Hilton; Tobosia Liman; John H. Milburn; Nichs. Fielder; John Allison; Wm. Kerbey; Eliger Vessells; Ephim Hollady; Thos. Adams; Robt. Taylor; Matts. Breeden; Adam Beverly; ......;

Matths. Jones; Elias Henny; John Smoot; Leven Thomas; Wm. A. Thomas; Isaac Richardson; Thos. Briscoe Junr; Richd. Bennet; Henry Gill; John Thomas; Bennet Tarlton; Saml. Collwel; Joseph Johnson; Wm. Stones; Philip Spalding; Matts. Artis; Edwd. Hopwood; Richd. Barnhouse; Wm. Dossey; Wm. Thomas; Saml. Higgins(?); Thos. Hall; Wm. Richardson; John Sanner Junr; John Smith Senr; Basil Hoplins; Austin Taylor; John Coad; Tylor Thomas; Richd. Taylor; Nichs. Byrn; Jno. Reece; Wm. Crane; James Dossey; Parker Jenifer; Moses Daress(?); Gabriel Bean; Igns. Green; Stephen Gough; Igns. Biscoe Senr

Vernon Smith; John Smith; Charles Kerbey; Nichs. Sewall; Wm. Belwad(?); Mattw. Wise; Wm. Daffin; Lewis Oliver; Josep Price; Wm. Baker; Robt. Daffin; Tilgh (Ilgh, Hgh?) Davis; George Hopewell

SOMERSET COUNTY, Salisbury Battalion

[No date given] A list or Muster Roll of the Company of Officers and Soldiers under the Command of Capt. Sampson Wheatly
John Horsey, Lieut; Wm. Wheatly, Ensign; Thos. White, Wm. Jewel (?), ..., John White, Sergts; Cornelius Ward, Aaron Sterling, Thos Lord, Corps.

APPENDIX B: MUSTER ROLLS AND OTHER LISTS

Solds. - Jacob Moor, Nathaniel Daugherty, Daniel Dies, John Sterling, Joseph Sterling, Isaac Moor, Wm. Williams, James Graham, Jacob Ward, David Summers, Richard Summers, Lazarus Summers, Jonathan Summers, George Summers, Thos. Summers, Saml. Summers, Solomon Benson, John Ward, Thos. Megummery, John Bigger, Stephen Bigger, Jonathan Bigger, Henry Lord, Peter Lord, Stephen Daugherty, Phillip Dyes, Patrick McKinedey(?), Robt. Dukes, James Holly, Jonathan Whealer, Saml. Ward, Peter Daugherty, Jonathan Roach, Thos. Moor, John Daugherty, Henry Miles, Thos. Bird, Stephen Moor, John Caton, Thos. Culling, John Bellsworth (Bedsworth?), James Ward, Solomon Bird, Isaac Daughty, Revell Horsey, John Gunby, Wm. Taylo, Wm. Whaly, James Stern, Coalbourn Taylor, Joseph Ward, Arthur Williams, Bratshe Moor, Planner Roach

Rt. of Militia in Somerset County by George Dashiell 1780 Salisbury Battalion. Copies of the Several Rolls of Militia in Somerset County.

1780/Viz. Nanticoke Point Compy.
Jno. Span Conway, Capt; John McClester, 1st Liut.; Jno. Evans (of Nichs.), 2nd Ditto; Wm. Stewart, Ensign; Will Waller; John Dashiell, Sergt.; Joseph Dashiell, Sergt.; John Sibbey (Libbey, etc.?), Sergt.; Levin Walter, Corpl.; Jno. Dashiell (of Winder), Corpl.; Danl. Walter, Corpl.; George Willin, Corpl.; George Willin, Corpl.; Robert Hopkins; Robt. Walter; James Windsor; John North; James Mezeck; George Purbush; Clemt. Willen; Solo. Winright; David Hickman; Isaac Dickerson; Evans Winright; Henry Barkley; George Mezack; John Hughs; Saml. Ballard; Levin Willin; George Collier Hopkins; John Jones; George Ballard; Wm. Francis Dashiell; George Evan(?); Saml. Laramour; James Willin; Daniel Mcintire; Stephen Hopkins; Elijah Willin; John Holbrook; Ben. Selby; Joshua Evans More; Will Bounds; John Rencher; Wm. Jackson; Wm. Hopkins; Wm. Douglas; Richd. Elensworth; Daniel Frasher; Cannon Winright; James Evans; Jonah Phillips; Abednego Green; Thos. Laramore; Saml. Covington; Charles Wilten(?); David Hopkins; Joseph Barkley; Elijah Laramore; Robt. Wilson; Joshua Atkinson; Levi Hopkins; John C...; Roger ...; Elihu ...; Thos. J...; James ...; Saml. ...; John ...; Gilbert Dunn; Nichs. Swanston(?); Saml. Willin; James Dashiell; Jesse Phillips; Wm. Jenkins; Henry Selby; John Phillips; Levin Willen Junr; John Nucomb; James Walter; James Owens; Thos. Laramore; John Willen Junr; John Robertson; John Evans; Abraham Bartlet; James Smith; James Porter; Charles Hopkins; Isaac Barkley; Wm. Stevens; Henry Cordary(?); Saml. Fluellin(?); Willen(?) McIntire; Thos. Willen; Thos. Smith; Wm. Porter Junr; Dickerson Dority; Douty Bounds.
[Militia Lists of Daus. of Founders and Patriots, held by Md. Hist. Soc.]

1780/Quantico Copy. Henry Gale, Capt; James Polk, 1st Lt.; Jno. Leatherbury 2nd Do; Joseph Wails; Wm. Moore Junr, Sergt.; Wm. Stanford, Sergt.; Wm. Venables, Sergt.; Pierce (Price, Priest?) Russell, Sergt.; Thos. Stanford, Sergt.; Richd. Ackworth, Corpl.; Obediah Stanford; Jacob Mezeck; John Hopkins; George Bennet; Wm. Moore; Geo. Gale; George Saunders; Arthur Denwood; Wm. Donoho Senr; Lill(?) Bennet; Wm. Hall; Joseph Nutter; Ben Nelson; John Smith; Nichs. Surman; Elisha Green; George Robertson; Charles Rider; Henry Nicholson; Richardson Donoho; Robt. Dashiell; John Askelley(?); Dowty Collier; George Tull; Will Harris; Stephin Hickman; Charles Gates; John ... portion obliterated); Joseph Humphris; Charles Surman; James Beard; Thos. Cannon; Nichs. Evans(?) Collier; Wm. Collier; Levin Moore; Michael

SOMERSET COUNTY

Green; Hugh Floyd; Natt. Kemp; John Nelson Junr; James Robertson; John Waters Junr. [Militia Lists of Daus. of Founders and Patriots, held by Md. Hist. Soc.]

1780/Rewastico Compy. William Turpin, Capt; Edwd. Kellum, 2nd Lt.; Joseph Piper, Ens; James Phillips; Nichs. Cantwell, Sergt.; Constant Weatherly, Sergt.; Henry Ackworth, Sergt.; Levin Follin, Corpl.; John Lankford, Corpl.; Eph. Ackworth, Corpl.; Benjn. Baker; Wm. Taylor; Wm. Gosle; James Grear; James Weatherly; George Twilley; John Horsy(?); Thos. Russel; Levin Carmichael; John Ackworth; Roger Nicholson; Thos. Goslee; Ben Mezick; Wm. Davis; Levin Loyd; John Grumble; Richd. Tulley; John Carmichael; Richd. Tebrew(?); Wm. Harris; John Bennet; Wm. Taylor Sen; John Tulley; John Smith; Archd. Stevens; Joshua Alphe(?); James Bennet; Robt. Dorman; James Train; Wm. Langsdale; John Anderson; James Anderson; James West; Wm. Lowe; Charles Henderson; John Langsdale; Elisha Rhoads; Ben. Tulley; Wm. Nutter Senr; Wm. Gupton(?); Ezekiel Taylor; John Walls(?); George Phillip; Joseph Wrigh (Weigk?); Wm. Alphe(?); Stephen Stevens; John Rencher; Jacob Gibson; Wm. Bowland; James Loyd; Saml. Paramore; Everton Kenerly; Wm. Dorman; Joshua Merril; Thos. Bedsworth; Levin Wright; George Anderson; John Hobbs; Fisher Roberts; Charles Phillips; James Paramore; Wm. Loyd; Joseph(?) Twilley; Stephen Twilley; Edward Bennett. [Militia Lists of Daus. of Founders and Patriots, held by Md. Hist. Soc.]

1780/Barron Creek Compy. Joseph Venables, Capt; Benj. Venables, 1st Lt.; John Weatherly, 2nd do; Mckimmey Porter; Thos. Cooper; Joseph Gilliss; Danl. Da..ey; James H...; Joshua Taylor; Ben Davis (?); Jacob Quinton; Drummond Simpson; Wm. James; Eph. Wilson; Levi(?) Dashiell; Levin Handy; Stephen Wright; John Wilson; Isaac Wright; James Robertson; Solomon Wright; George Dashiell; Beauchamp Hull(?); John Robertson; Cornelius Ready; James Trader; Joseph Collins; Saml. Davis; Benjn. Graham; John Cooper; Patrick McLally(?); Charles Culver; Isaac Robertson; Daniel James; Wm. Stewart; Jacob Taylor; Wm. Gilliss; Richd. Williams; Joshua Huffington; Abraham Cooper; Isaac Taylor; James Dean; Angelo Huffington; John Day; Train Ackworth; Jacob Robertson; Daniel Condry; Jonathan Huffington; Barkley Taylor; Wm. McDaniel; James Wilson; John Glastin; James Smith; John Huffington; William Lankford; Thos. Condary; Charles Weatherly; Charles Badley; Edwd. McDaniel; John Taylor; James Badley; Aaron Sterling(?); Thos. Venables; Ezekiel Graham; Joseph Melvin; Joshua Wright; Isaac Giles; Daniel Irins(?); Levi Harrison; Michael Holland; Saml. Venables; Saml. Cooper; Jesse Weatherly; Moses ...rsey; Wm. Robertson; James McDaniel; James Tully; Joseph Gillis Junr; Handy Wright; John Robertson (of Jno.). [Militia Lists of Daus. of Founders and Patriots, held by Md. Hist. Soc.]

1780/Black Water Co. Levin Irving, Capt; Gilliss Polk, 1st Lieut.; James Hainey, 2nd do; Isaac Henry Ensn.; Robt. Swiggrt(?), Sergt.; Thos. Hitch, Sergt.; John Scroggin, Sergt.; John Bird, Sergt.; Benjn. McClenmen, Corpl.; John Leonard, Corpl.; Wm. Mills, Corpl.; Joseph Scrogin, Corpl.; Charles Wails; Archibald Smith; Elijah Moore; Ben. Bird; Isaac Dashiel; Ezekiel Bell; Thos. Waller(?); Will Gusston(?); Clarkson Cox; Rob Anderson; Isaac Maddux; Wm. Row; John Darby(?); John Leatherberry; Joseph Leonard; Richd. Hainey; Geo. Hitch; Ezekiel Hitch; Ben Lankford; Thos. McClennen; Ben Dashiell; Elisha Laurance; Mitchel Jackson; Joseph Nichols; Charles Nichols;

APPENDIX B: MUSTER ROLLS AND OTHER LISTS

... Hitch; Eben. Waller; Thos. Waller; Mathias Aliphant; Thos. Cox; Isaac Vincent; John Maddux; Richd. Trader(?); Alexr. Maddux; Levin Culver; Elijah Hitch; Joshua Maddux; Hutson Lowe; Wm. McBride; Joshua Nichols; Isaac Handy; Wm. Wails; Will Daily; Elias Hitch; Geo. Fletcher; Saml. Fletcher; Wm. Martin; John Smith; Martin Luther Handy; John Noble; Wm. Oram; Thos. Bird; Levin Fletcher; John Johnson; George Layfield; Isaac Giles. [Militia Lists of Daus. of Founders and Patriots, held by Md. Hist. Soc.]

1780/Salisbury Co. - James Bennet, Capt; Wm. Byng, Ensign; Archelius Ricords; Elijah Humphris; Ezekiel Green; James Anderson; Edward Dickerson; John Fowler; Gillis Howard; Handy Turpin; Thos. Fletcher; Joseph Anderson; James Booth; George Moses(?); Henry Trader(?); Carman(?) L...k; George Stevens; Hamilton Austin; Ben Carmichael; Wm. Dymock; John Luca(?); Ben Nutter; Isaac Wilkins; Robt. Layfield; John Austin; Elijah Austin; Stephen Christopher; James McKey; Abraham Gullet; Wm. Godderd; George Wilson; Eph. Wilson; Saml. Williams; Thos. Lowe; Stephen Toadvine; John Baker(?); Benj. Riley; John Cooksey; Benjn. Stevens; Levi Stevens; George Sackwell(?); ...len Layfield; Zibble(?) Jenkins; Ezekiel Jenkins; Frans. Jones; Jacob Lurton(?); John Maddux; John Jenkins; Joseph Jenkins; Levi Brown; David Jenkins; Jonathan Jenkins; Richd. ...; Charles Lucas Hails; Geo. James; Ruben Washbourn. [Militia Lists of Daus. of Founders and Patriots, held by Md. Hist. Soc.]

1780/Mi: Creek Co. - Josiah Dashiell, Capt; Epp. Stevens, 1st Lt.; Joseph Gilliss, 2nd do; Thos. Fountain, Ens.; John Chetam, Sergt.; David Stanford, Sergt.; Joshua Hilman, Sergt.; Walker Chetam, Sergt.; James Anderson, Corpl.; Jacob Morris, Corpl.; Isaac White, Corpl.; Geo. Surman, Corpl.; Matt Dashiells; Danl. Sharp; Ben Jones; John Hilman; Henry Banks; Joshua Fullirton(?); Thos. Beard; John Redish; Joshua Humphris; Jonathan Knight; Joshua Knight; James Knight; Josiah Knight; Robt. Mallone; John Goslee; John Morriss; Jones Bounds; Thos. Whallen; Levi Collins; Joseph Goslee; Jas. Fairfax(?) Dashiell; John Christopher; Wm. Jones; James Adams; Stephen Taylor; Solo. Taylor; Mills Baily; Geo. Baily Senr; Isaac Hayman; Joshua Hayman; Jno. Harris Hayman; Ben. Hitch; Joshua Stanford; Francis Disharoon; George Sharpe; Joshua Disharoon; James Disharoon; Nutor Disharoon; Stephen Disharoon; Ezekiel Hilman (?); Thos. Collins Junr; Levin Gunby; John Redish Junr; Zadock Taylor; Levin Gilliss; David P..or(??); Thos. Martin; John Gore; Alexr. McLaughlin; Wm. Beard; Joseph Morris Junr; Wm. Collins; Wm. Johnson; Aaron Donaly; Thos. Redish; Wm. Christopher; Thos. Gilliss; Wm. Mallone; Geo. Goslee; Wm. Owens; Will. Davis Allen; Danl Burgin; Revel Hayman. [Militia Lists of Daus. of Founders and Patriots, held by Md. Hist. Soc.]

1780/White Haven Copy. - Joseph Cotman, 1st Lieut.; Lambert Hyland; Isaac(?) Bowman, Sergt.; Charles Jones, Sergt.; Arnold Ballard, Sergt.; Saml. McClammy, Sergt.; Matthias Hobbs, Corpl.; Levin Jones, Corpl.; Ben. Bayly, Corpl.; James Jones; Matthew Mungan; Thos. Numan; Abraham Covington; Thos. Mitchel; Stephen Bayly; Phillip Covington; Levin Covington; Thos. Waters; Arthur McGrath; James Fitzarrold; Planner Williams; Stephen Horsey; Will. Hilman; Thos. Burgin; Wm. Jones; David Revel; Wm. Roberts; Michael Dorman; Jesse Dorman; Saml. Adams; John Adams; Willm. Cotman; George Bayly; Elias Bayly; John Leatherbury; Wm. Gale; Phillip Jones; Wm. Harris; John

SOMERSET COUNTY

Fitzjarrald; Peter Turburt(?); Joseph Tulley; Thos. Hains; Wm. Heath; John Rencher; Robt. Elzey; Moses Green; Joseph Gladden; John Ritchey; Isaac Daugherty; Thos. Warbleton; Thos. Covington; Alexr. Pracice(?); Thos. Rencher; Ben Ballard; Smith Sims; Jolley Leatherbury; Andw. Adams; Will Adams Junr; Presley Brereton; John Brereton; David Dalf(?); Lill Bayly; Joseph Brereton; James Polk; John Polk; Henry Lowe; Thos. Holbrook; John Holbrook; Henry Holbrook; Wm. Dockery; Edward Fowler; John Done. [Militia Lists of Daus. of Founders and Patriots, held by Md. Hist. Soc.]

SOMERSET COUNTY, Princess Ann Battalion

1780/Monie Company: Thos. Irving, Capt; Jno. Dashiell, 1st Lt.; Jno. Jones, 2nd Lt.; Gowon Wright Ensn.
Robt. Jones, Sergt.; Wm. Sassen(?), Sergt.; Wm. Laws, Sergt.; Wm. Jones, Sergt.; Wm. Phebus, Corpl.; John Woolford, Corpl.; Jno. Wright, Corpl.; Wm. McDorman, Corpl.; Joseph Austin; Henry Wingate; Wm. Martin; Frans. White; Wm. Webb; Thos. Moor; John Sassen; Thos. Noble; Mesheck Webster; John Phebus Junr; James Kelley; James Wallace; Henry Wingate; Thos. White; Wm. Shelton; Henry Walston Miles; Wm. King; Jas. Jones (DQ); Edwd. Roberts; Wm. Ballard; Thos. Martin; Phil Wingate; Jno. Laws (DQ); Oliver Coston; Jno. Windsor Junr; James Lecount; James Muir; George Phebus Junr; James Martin; George Jones; Geo. Jones (DQ); Wm. Stewart; Levin Shone(?); Barkley Roberts; John Handy; Richd. Roe; James Galloway; Jno. Martin; Thos. Jones; George Dorman; George Abbet; Wm. Webster; Richd. Wallace; Ezekiel Foskey; Loyd Abbet; John Phebus; John Laws (Monie); Wm. Windsor; Henry Walston (DQ); Wm. Horner; Joseph Cantwell; John Webster; James Ballard; John Cavender; Ballard Reed; Thos. Bozman; Isaac Gibson; Jabez Webster; Edmond Price; Lill. Timmons; George Austin; John Jones; Underwood Roberts; Michl. Timmons; Wm. Ballard (of Arnold); John Evans; Thos. Martin Junr; John Abbet; James Reed; Wm. Smith; John White Junr; John Hopkins; Ben. Sasser Junr; Joseph Walston; Jno. Roberts; David Wallace; Levi Johnson; John Horner; Benj. Horner. [Militia Lists of Daus. of Founders and Patriots, held by Md. Hist. Soc.]

1780/Princess Ann Copy. - John Jones, Capt; Jno. Denwood, 1st Lt.; Thos. Maddux, 2nd do; Alexr. Adams, Ens.; Heber(?) Whittingham, Sergt.; Isaiah Dorman, Sergt.; John Bloodsworth, Sergt.; Jesse King, Corpl.; Saml. Taylor, Corpl.; Wm. Ballard, Corpl.; Joseph Ward; Stephen Heath; John Smulling(?); John Dorman; Wm. Denston; Wm. Stewart; John Howard; Wm. Pollitt; John Wilkins; Planner King; Joshua Pollitt; Chane(?) Dorman; Wm. Pollitt (of Thos.); George Pollitt; Samuel Miles (of Wm.); Joshua Davis; Abraham Taylor; Joseph McVeigh; Stephen Pollitt; Ezekiel Savage; Jesse Ward; Ben. Pusey; John Mungar; Solomon Ward; Thos. Pollitt of Wm.; Solo. Long; Joshua Polk; John Gray; John Collins; John Law; Jonathan Pollitt Junr; David Prior; Fredk. Dignen; Upshur King; James Hammond; John Elliot; Beauchamp Hull; Wm. King; Saml. Pollitt; Thos. Pollitt; Charles Vaughn; Levi Lankford; Lill Pollitt; Edwd Smith; Levi Ward; Acquilla Snelling; Wilson Heath; Lill Harris; Willm. Christopher; Matthew Ward; Thomas Davis; John Hayman Junr; Henry Coston; Spencer Luk...(?); Benton Riggen; Jesse Walston; Ezekiel Layfield; Levin Dorman; Will Hill; Joshua Taylor; Ben Polk Junr; Levin Ballard; John Pollitt; Wm. Benston; John Mitchel; Levin King; James Ballard;

APPENDIX B: MUSTER ROLLS AND OTHER LISTS

Arthur King; James Robertson; Nehemiah Pollitt. [Militia Lists of Daus. of Founders and Patriots, held by Md. Hist. Soc.]

1780/Pocomoke Company - George Waters(?); Wm. Stevens, 1st Lt.; Robt. Jenkins King, Ens.; John Howard, Sergt.; Francis Lane(?), Sergt.; John Marshall, Sergt.; Josiah Braughton, Corpl.; Levin Pollitt, Corpl.; John Schoolfield, Corpl.; Lill Dreddon, Corpl.; Brittain Powell; Jonathan Cluff; Josiah Warrick; Wm. Bell White; Joshua Mitchel; Willm. Dear; Nehemiah Tindal; Levi Powel; Wm. Bloyce; John Braughton Junr; Charles Braughton; Saml. Adams; John Purkins; Phil Adams (of Hope); Saml. Collins; Thos. Adams; Michl. Cluff Junr; John Blades; Stephen Mills; Eph. Dredden; Elias Benston; Jacob Adams; Levi Beauchamp; Will Ward; Wm. Hutchins; Robt. Jenkins Henry; Gilbert Ford; Aaron Tilghman; Saml. Taylor; James Holland; Zadock Dorman; Henry Schoolfield; Will Camneron; Wm. Waddey(?); John Taylor; Thos. Dreaden; Phill Adam; Kellum Braughton; Elijah Braughton; George Adams; James Nuton; Phill Collens Adams; Robt. Merril; Wm. Cotman; Jesse Powell; Thos. Beauchamp; Fountain Beauchamp; George Schoolfield; Wm. Adams; Stephen Schoolfield; James Harper; John Bload; Joseph Handy; Wm. Summers; Wm. Mills; Thos. Williamson Benston; Jonathan Dreaden; John Spencer; James Bruff; Wm. Powell; James Atkinson; Elzey Maddux; Levin Powel; Jesse Ward; John Paden; James Dreaden; Wm. Cluff; Jonathan Tull; James Dickerson; Wm. Hall. [Militia Lists of Daus. of Founders and Patriots, held by Md. Hist. Soc.]

1780/Capt. James Elzey's Co.- John Irving, 1st Lt.; Will. Jones, 2nd Lt.; Jno. Flemming(?), Ens.; Joseph Tilghman, Sergt.; John Riggen, Sergt.; Joshua Boston, Sergt.; Willm. Matthews, Sergt.; Jabez Tilghman, Sergt.; Joshua Boston, Corpl.; Elijah Hall, Corpl.; Charles Banister, Corpl.; Jesse Matthews, Corpl.; John Revel; Eph. Lankford; Wm. Matthews; Robt. Matthews; Phillip Ba...us(?); John Layfield; Teague Riggen; John Bolen(?); Robert Dukes; Levi Matthew; Isaac Munrow; Boar (Boaz?) Walston; Lill Landen; Charles Redden; Saml. Miles; Bartholomew Hunt; James Haddock; Henry Davis; Wm. Warrick; George Mitchel; John Price; John Wilson; Arnold Elzey; James Riggen; Whittey Gray; Denwood Matthews; James C. Vessels; Arthur Warrick; Thos. Fisher; Edmond Smullen(?); Neho.(?) Turpin; Wm. Carrol; John Rounds; Saml. Sanders; George Miles; Levin Revel; Wm. Gibbons Senr; Wm. Gibbons Junr; Samuel Smith; James Wilson; John Loca(?); Wm. Strawbridge; Peter Walston; Thomas Hariss; Joshua Smith Junr; George Shipham; Will Dreaden; Esau Boston; Joseph Allen; Wm. McGrath; James Irving; Thos. Fitchett; Thos. Collins; Wm. Smullin; Wm. Miles (of James); George Thomas; James Gibbens; John Malcom; Ezekiel Gibbins; Henry Potter; John Tull; Eph. Collins; Josiah Gibbens; John Harris (Haines?); Thos. Gibbbens of Thos.; Thos. Gibbins Junr; James Matthews; John Phillips; John Durham; James Irving; Wm. Elzey. [Militia Lists of Daus. of Founders and Patriots, held by Md. Hist. Soc.]

1780/St. Asaphs Copy. - Benj. Schoolfield, 1st Lt.; Robt. Bayly, 2nd do; Isaac Curtis, Ensn.; Wm. Bozman, Sergt.; James Hill, Sergt.; Hope Adams, Sergt.; Ambrose Dixon, Sergt.; Stephen White, Corpl.; Willm. Cox, Corpl.; Isaac Beauchamp; Risdon Bozman; Wm. Moor; Isaac Dixon; Wm. Wood; Ephm. Marshall; Elijah Moore; Joseph Barret; Richd. Boston; Joshua Lankford; Andrew McCreddy; Levin Riggen; Jesse Lankford; Ezekiel Lankford; John Merchant; Wm. Porter; John Campbell; Thos. Moor; Joseph Beal(?); Zadock Wheeler; Wm. Braughton; Potter Karsley; Randolph Lord; Ben. Holland

SOMERSET COUNTY

Matthews; Wm. Lankford; Elias Summers; Baily Matthews; Wm. Adams; Neal Calvert; Stephen Riggen; Robt. Marshall; Isaac Adams; Isaac Marshall; Thos. Jones; Saml. Carsley; David Matthews; Benjn. Connaway; David Collingham; Wm. Carman (Carnan?); John Riggen; Thos. Johnson; Jacob Mathews; Risdon Marshall; Levin Taylor; David Matthews; Isaac McCreddy; Lodowick Milbourn; Jesse Johnson; Danl. Beauchamp; Jno. Beauchamp; Saml. Curtis; Edw. Beauchamp; Jesse Dakus(?); Saml. Bedsworth; Jacob Lankford; Danl. Boston; Wm. Catlin; Levin Williams; Stephen Coulbourn; John Milbourn. [Militia Lists of Daus. of Founders and Patriots, held by Md. Hist. Soc.]

1780/Great Annemessix Copy - Isaac Handy, Capt.; Ballard Bozman, 1st Lt.; Lazarous Maddux, 2nd do.; James Curtis Ensn.; Danl. Maddux, Sergt.; James Waters, Sergt.; Wm. Turpin, Sergt.; Levin Miles, Sergt.; Charles Hall; Wm. Lister; James Hall; John Beauchamp; Wm. Miles; Wm. Levy (Long?); Jno. Haile(?); Robt. Haile(?); Tubman Waters; Stoughton Maddux; Elzey Maddux; Isaac Miligan; John Miligan; Levin Tull; John Fountain; Wm. Cullen; Danl. Haycock; John Turpin; Isaac Calbert; Thos. Williams; Obed. Outen; Beauchamp Davis; Joshua Beaucham; Thos. Lister; Levin Boston; Charles Avery; Thos. Ford; Joseph Dawson; Obediah Walston; Thos. Walston; Charles Walston; Joseph Landen; Levin Walston; David McDaniel; Thos. Tull; James Killum; Thos. Hall; Thos. Maddux; Thos. Mills; Saml. Handy; Saml. Kellum; Thos. Davis; Wm. Hammond; Wm. Tilghman; John Wilson Junr; Thos. Evans; Jesse Dory(?); Joseph Sims(?); John Wilson Senr; Joshua Turpin; John Jones; John Gibson; James Layfield; John Williams; Joseph Rouse(?); Thos. Sadler; Litt(?) Williams; James Willis; Wilson Hammond; John Reddin; Isaac Beauchamp; George Hall; George Tull; Nehemiah Ford; Owen Evans; Wm. Tull; John White Roach; Barnaby Harris. [Militia Lists of Daus. of Founders and Patriots, held by Md. Hist. Soc.]

1780/Little Annemessex Co. - Henry Miles, Capt.; John Horsey, 1st Lt.; Nathl. ...tty(?), 2nd do; Wm. Dixon, Ensn.; Levi Holland, Sergt.; John Summers, Sergt.; Aaron Sterling, Sergt.; John Horsey; Thos. Summers, Corpl.; Aaron Sterling (of Henry), Corpl.; Saml Lawson, Corpl.; Stephen Parramore, Corpl.; Lill Sterling; Robt. Dies; Levi Miles; James Ward Junr; Eli Riggen; James Boston; John Roach; Josiah Sterling; Traves Sterling; George Croswell; Lawson Croswell; Ephm. Sterling; Geo. Croswell Junr; Isaac Moore Junr; Marmaduke Mister; Richd. Evans; John Sterling; Henry Sterling; Stephen Summers; Cornelius Ward; Stephen Ward; Ben. Williams; Wm. Miles; Jno. Riggen; Hance Lawson; Joseph Ward; James ...; Dennis Mongomery; Ezekiel Ward; Dukies(?) Riggen; James Summers; Jacob Summers; Elijah Linton; Richd. Bratcher; Stephen Horsey; Spencer Tyler; Benj. Hopkins; Stephen Hopkins; Joshua Salisbury; Wm. Coulbourn; Danl. Dies; Jno. Taws; Jesse Daugherty; Thos. Lord (of Henry); Thos. Lord; James Bloyth; Thos. Moor; Thos. Ward; John Numan; John Knips(?); James Ward; Willm. Wilson; John Ward; Stephen Ward; Wm. Ward; John Dies(?); John Parkes; Arthur Parkes; Job Parkes; Thos. Evans; Wm. Mister Evans; Jesse Evans; Levin Evans; David Tylor; Smith Horsey Junr. [Militia Lists of Daus. of Founders and Patriots, held by Md. Hist. Soc.]

1780/Watkinses Point Copy. - John Williams, Capt.; John Turpin, 1st Lt.; Thos. Dixon, 2nd do; Thos. Handy, Ens; Saml. Hall, Sergt.; Joseph Bird, Sergt.; Michael Holland, Sergt.; John Tull, Sergt.; Wm. Coulbourn, Corpl.;

APPENDIX B: MUSTER ROLLS AND OTHER LISTS

Wm. Whittington Senr, Corpl.; James Whittington, Corpl.; Wm. Whittington, Corpl.; John Conway; Edw. Wyatt; Stephen Riggen; George Summers; Wm. Wilson; Joseph Lankford; David Lindsey; Isaac Kellum; Nathan Cohoon; Henry Cohoon; Killum Lankford; Michael Wheatley; John Moor; Cyrus Trehearn; Ben: Lankford; Wm. Wheatley; Thos. Lankford; Nathaniel Bell(?); John Bell; Saml. Cullins; Jacob Milbourn; Dennis Taylor; Saml. Trehearn; Obed. Trehearn; George Wilson; Saml. Tomerlson(?); Isaac Outen; Zoro. Maddux; Sampson Wheatly; Stephen Ward; Will Roach; Isaac Ward; Wm. Darcus; Dickerson Douty; Joshua Merril; Thos. Cox; Solo. Coulbourn; John Wilson (of Jno); Jesse M. Lankford; ... Long; Robt. Riggen; Kirk Gunby; Benj. Gunby; Isaac Gunby; Levi Adams; Thos. Tull; Levin Tull; Henry Potter; Joseph Caton; Wm. Kellum; Lodowick Milbourn; Bartholomew Twiford; Thos. Mitchel; Robt. Coulbourn; John Johnson; Elijah Johnson; John Cox; James Trehearn; Levi Ward; Wm. Riggen; Wm. Cottingham; Michael Benston; John Coulbourn; Lill Johnson; Nehemiah Riggen; Hope Hull. [Militia Lists of Daus. of Founders and Patriots, held by Md. Hist. Soc.]

I Certify that the above is true copy of the Several militias roll of Somerset County made the 24th of July 1st in virtue of an Act Entitled an Act for the Speedy enrolments of .. Militia Given under my hand this 19th of August 1780 - George Dashiell Coty Lieut.

TALBOT COUNTY, 4th Battalion

An Exact list of all the white male Inhabitants of Talbot County from the age of sixteen to fifty years, as also the Distribution of said Inhabitants into Battalions, Companies and Classes, as directed by an Act of Asssembly of the State of Maryland - August 23d 1777

Fourth Battalion -
Wye Compy 1st Class: Alimby Millington; George Beswicks; John Corkrel; Jona. Gary; Thomas Porter; Wm. Lane; Solomon Levick; John Gibson; Nathan Beswicks; Thomas Plummer;
2d Class: Edward Roberts; Thomas Silvester; James Croney; David Silvester; Levin Stacy; Joseph Callighan; John Sancton; Robt. Gilhust; Brooks Thornton; John Carslick;
3d Class: Griffin Shields; Robt. Warner; John Jones; Richd. George; James Hawkins; James Lane; Wm. Edmondson; Ebenezr. Kinnard; John Chevous; James Lane
4th Class: John Ratliff; Wm. Webb; James Benny; Robt. Peckern; David Parsonnett; Danl. Nicholson; Saml. Nichols; Wm. Middleton; James Carridine; George Hall
5th Class: Moses Butler; Wm. Harrington; Edwd. Swett; Wm. Bordly; Isaac Pamer; Robt. Griffin; Josua Kinnard; Solo. Harriss; Henry Baker; Edwd Griffin;
6th Class: Woolman Gibson 3rd; Levi Plummer; John Roberts; Thomas Cadner; Edwd. Millis; Robt. Cole; Thomas Gannon; Wm. Porter; George Plummer; Christr. Hart
7th Class: Jacob Garron; Abner Miller; James Stant; Mark Rux; Nicholson Millington; Joseph Bewly; Francis Baker; Charles Miller; John Ferry; Jno. Vickers Thornton

TALBOT COUNTY

8th Class: Aquilla Follin; Woolman Warner; Wm. German; John Jenkenson; John Chambers; James Gallahan; Nathn. Thornton; Griffin Callighan; James Wrench. [Militia Lists of Daus. of Founders and Patriots, held by Md. Hist. Soc.]

Union Compy. 1st Class: Thomas Dawson; Richd. Barrow; Perry Priestly; Wm. Whittocks; Wm. Trippe; Saml. Neighbours; Thomas Turner; Stevin Durdan; James Robson; John Bowdle; John Hopkins; James Holladay; John Berry
2d Class: Robt. Baxter; John Tibbles; James Barron; Peter Barnett; Henry Tibbles; Wm. Bullin; Edwd. Parkerson; Robt. Neal; Lambeth Booker; James Anthony; Thomas Catrop; John Barrow; John Reader; Rizden Harwood
3d Class: Jas. Lloyd Chamberlain; Phil Pronce; Edwd. Needles; Sharp Harwood; Wm. Loveday; Jacob Handy; Wm. Catrop; Thos. Akin; Chrisr. Bruff; James Bowman; Gary Warner; Andrew Barrow
4th Class: John Catrop; Mattw. Shaw; Peter Edmondson; Thos. King; Leml.(?) Jno. Catrop; Peter Denny; Michl. Caile; John Webb; Wm. Weaver; David Fleming; Thomas Jordan; Greenwd. Leg; John Bozman; John Nikels
5 Class: John Cosley; Phil. Ferril; James Merchant; John Kersey; Giles Meads; Elbert Downs; David Davis Barrow; James Gause; James Seth; Joseph Neal; James Wainwright;
6 Class: Wm. Burgess; James Bullen; Aaron Atkinson jur; Saml. Mullikin; John Jones; Thomas Love; Richd. Harwood; Saml. Neal; Wm. Rose; Tristm. Needles; Nichs. Loveday; Wm. Price; Wm. Dawson Thomas; Alexr. McCallum
7th Class: John Chapman; Joseph Parrott; John Jackson; John Heron; James Barnwell; John Fleming; James Millis; John Dickinson; John Clark; Richd. Bruff; Wm. Levill (Sewill?); Denny Lary; Nathan Walker; Aaron Atkinson
8th Class: John Vining; Greenby. Goldsborough; Saml. Edmondson junr; Jacob Gibson; Wm. Thomas; Archd. Smith; Joseph Parsons; Thomas Morgan junr; Robt. Bond; Edwd Carslake; Richd. Tilghman; Saml. Sharp; Thomas Harper; Thomas Wickersham. [Militia Lists of Daus. of Founders and Patriots, held by Md. Hist. Soc.]

Volunteer Compny. 1st Class: Thomas Buckley; Lambert Coburn; Anthony Sewel; Dennis Cairy; John Armstrong; Wm. Madrid; Henry Buckley; John Price
2d Class: John Start; Wm. Anderson; John Alexander; Francis Chapline; George Jenkins; Thomas Welch; Wm. Akers jun.; Thomas Buckley; John Parrott jun; Danl. Berry; James Priestly
3d Class: John Prichard; Wm. Prichard; Wm. Chaplain; John Chaplain; Richd. Hickson; Thos. Martin 3d; Richd. Martin; Henry Martin; John Eldrick; Wm. Cummins; Richd. Dardan
4 Class: Saml. Prichard; Peter Webb junr; Wm. Gore; John Armstrong; John Johnson; Saml. White; John Berry; Ruebin Allin; Saml. Buckley; Noble Barnett; Danl. Walker; Thomas Pharris
5 Class: John Handcock; Wm. Allin; John Newnam; Joseph Durdan; Foster Armstrong; John Love; Thomas Barnett; Howell Powell; Wm. Bent; Joseph Foster; Danl. Landman
6 Class: Saml Dickinson; Richd. Barnett; Michl. Rogers; John Duncan; James Chaplin; James Mullikin; James Miers; Thomas Price; Henry Martin; Philn. Philips; Alexr. McKinsey
7 Class: Maths. Merrick; Owen Troy; Joseph Rogers; Saml. Mullikin; James Buckley; Wm. Rakes; Solo. Martin; James Alexander; James Hopkins
8th Class: Wm. Giddis; Jesse Mullikin; John Parrott; Wm. Tucker; Thos. Chaplin; Thos. Martin jun.; John Armstrong; Thos. Robinson; Henry Bowdle;

APPENDIX B: MUSTER ROLLS AND OTHER LISTS

Peter Foster. [Militia Lists of Daus. of Founders and Patriots, held by Md. Hist. Soc.]

Bullin Brook Compy. 1st Class: Robt. Brown; Isaiah McGuire; Solo. Brinsfield; Moses Brinsfield; Nathl. Hull; Moses Carr; James Standley; Wm. Foster; George Troth; John Nowls
2d Class: John Johnson junr; Henry Higgins; James Parott; Wm. Arington; James Small; John Hull; James Hardin; Thomas Higgins; Thos. Cuthcart; John Patterson
3d Class: Wm. Mackey; John Hurley; Findly McCl...(see original); James Tobin; James Dickinson; Francis Walker; James Arrington; Joseph Frantom; Joseph Hardin Junr; Thomas Barnett
4th Class: Philip Mackey; James Cliff; John Fleming; Walter Prichard; Theofilus Small; Tristm. Bowdle; Thomas Napp; Wm. Higgins; Danl. Russel
5 Class: Arnold Buckley; John Frantim; Allin Burgess; Thomas Elsby; Abner Parrott; Solo. McGaina; Charles Lee; Sales Cannon; Saml. Abbott Junr;
6 Class: Evin Jones; Mark Delahay; Joseph Carr; Wm. Conner; Henry Harriss; Wm. Harriss; David Jones; John Ardry; Thomas Cloyd; Soln. Birckhead
7 Class: John Lee junr; Henry West; Solo. Jones; Thos. Fleming; James Corney; Wm. Clark junr; John Clemmons; Joseph Foster; Saml. Eason
8 Class: John Higgins; John Brown; Thomas Bullin; Jeffery Miller; John Skinner; Arthur Holland; Michl. Callahan; James Satchel; John Rathel.
[Militia Lists of Daus. of Founders and Patriots, held by Md. Hist. Soc.]

Sword in Hand Compy. 1st Class: Cloudsberry Austin; James Price; Charles Nabb; Andw. Price; Joseph Rathel; Danl. Chapman; Thomas Roach; John Dawson; Chrisr. Cooper
2d Class: Thos. Larimore; John Cockrain; Nathan Price; Joseph Berry; Nathl. Hopkins; Wm. Taylor; Wm. Porter; Jarman Cade; Henry Johnson; John Fearn
3d Class: Joseph Bowman; ...man (Truman?) Aurundal; Wm. Matthews; Saml. Bowman; John Crowder; John Barwick; Abraham Sherwin; Elijah Dewling; Nathan Kirby
4 Class: John Merchant; Chrisn. Hews; Perry Anderson; John Nash; Wm. Dewling; Thos. Aukin; John Kirby junr; Jonan. Floyd; George Stevens
5 Class: Wm. Noley; James Thomas; Andrew Green; Thomas Turner; James Berry junr; James Austin; Robt. Broadway; Francis Armstron
6 Class: Wm. Rathel; John Nabb; Michl. Kerby junr; Saml. Register; John Register; Perry Parrott; Charles Allen; Benjn. Kirby; Isaac Chambers;
7th Class: Vachal Sweer; Thomas Stewart; Lambert Kerby; Wm. Morgan; Edwd. Henrix; James Dawson; Robt. Lowther; Richd. Jones; John Dewling; James Price
8 Class: Danl. Newnam; Andrew Matthews; Thos. Matthews; James Gregory; Cloudsberry Kirby; Wm. Gregory; George Hunt; Edwd. Turner; John Gore.
[Militia Lists of Daus. of Founders and Patriots, held by Md. Hist. Soc.]

Volunteer Company 2d - 1st Class: James Foresain; George Foresain; Wm. Humes; John Berkhorn(?); Thomas Kirby; James Condon; John Gilon; Thos. Brasscup; John Crump; Robt. Fowler; Thomas Parker; John Bandy
2d Class: John Liddle; Abel Grace; James Jackson; Robt. Dixon; Patrick Dunn; Nathan Porter; John Kirby; Griffin Chambers; John Blake; Wm. Warring; Jona. Cheesley; James Kindrick

TALBOT COUNTY

3 Class: Henry Davis; Adam Eubanks; Wm. Parrish; John Campbell; Thomas Robinson; Parot Kerby; Morris Kerby; James Willson; Emanuel Allin; Richd. Greenhawk; Saml. Neighbours; James Willson junr; John Warring
4 Class: James Gilon; Henry Lowe; James Kennady; John Maggs; Vincent Pinkine; Danl. Kirby; John Gilon junr; Mark Foster; Levi Faulkner; Walter Gore; Wm. Pearson; Wm. Srakan(?); John Porter junr
5 Class: Abraham Bowen; Michl. Pinkins; John Austin; David Lucus; Richd. Thornton; Charles Pickering; James Dewling; James Cheesley; Wm. Shields
6 Class: Vincent Price; Wm. Horney; Joseph Hobs; Andrew Stewart; Nichs. Sherwood; John Hull; Levi Pearson; Thoms. Cornon; Jona. Hewey; Richd. Norton; Wm. Tizzard; Richd. Beswicks; John Bandy
7 Class: Robt. Harwood; Wm. Dixon; Thos. Fitzgerald; Philip Norris; Nathan Foster; Isaac Falkner; Hynson Falkner; Saml. Gore; Wm. Snelling
8 Class: Wm. Burgess; James Stewart; Wm. Bowdle; Thos. Pearson; Thos. Harwood; Wm. Hamilton 3d; Peter Cole; David Kerby; Roger McColister; Aaron Kerby. [Militia Lists of Daus. of Founders and Patriots, held by Md. Hist. Soc.]

Third haven Compy. 1st Class: Nathan Walker; Joseph Quinton; Benja. Pearsons; Allin Merrick; Henry Delahay; Wm. Potts; Thos. Coleburn; James Norris; Joshu Stoker
2 Class: Wm. Marshall; David McGinny; Solo. Corner junr; Wm. Walker junr; John Atton Sanxton; James Hopkins; James Higgins; James Sanxton; James Berry; Josephus Bell
3d Class: John Edwards; Robt. Waits; Wm. Maynadier(?); Edwd Bromwell; Henry Troth; Thos. Willson; James White; Andw. Calender; Edwd. Stevens; Solo. Homes junr
4 Class: Thos. Delahay; Henry Parrott; John Willson; Moses Adams; Wm. Long Helsby; John Nicols; James Berry junr; Solo. Holmes; John McGinny
5 Class: Bartho. Gully; Isaac Sanxton; Wm. Walker 3d; Wm. Lamax; Richd. Hays; James Akers; Francis Neal; Thos. Sewel; Quinton Kemp; Nathan Sewel; Thos. Mcclayland
6 Class: Peter Richardson; Eusebeus Adams; Wm. Stack (Slack?); Thos. White; Joseph Cox; James McGinney; Joseph Kemp; Wm. Goody
7 Class: John Ridgway; Thos. Sherwin; John Cooper; James Walker junr; Saml. Jenkins; John Macmahan; Richd. Street; Foster Price Junr; Andrew Merrick
8 Class: Joseph Davis; Joseph Jones; Charles Gully; John Brin; John Cain; Thos. Austin; Wm. Baley; John Liddleton; Wm. Brinn; Joseph Price. [Militia Lists of Daus. of Founders and Patriots, held by Md. Hist. Soc.]

Hand & Hand Co. 1 Class: Wm. Price; John Fairfield; John Morris; Saml. Hutchings; James Parrott jun; Wm. Ceacil; Lodman Aurandle; George Willson; John Boe(?); Traverse Garland; Jacob Falkner; Wm. Love; Wm. Millington
2d Class: Thos. Whitely; Moses Kirby; John Canahan; Jacob Faulkner jun; Wolman Gibson; Jona. Ausman; Aaron Parrott; Danl. Willson; Benjn. Kirby; Cornelious Taylor; John Ceacil; Park Webb; Robt. Kerby junr
3 Class: Joshua Clark; Jona. Shanahan; John Price; Hugh Price; Jere. Lee; Richd. Vickers; Wm. Frampton; James Parrott; George Nix; Wm. Barwick; Thos. Ausman; John Frampton
4 Class: John Aurundle; Elijer Dee; James Fairbanks; Richd. Oxenham; Isaac Millington; John Webb; Robt. Gardin; Henry Covy; Thomas Parrott; Danl. Croney; Southy Willson; Joseph Anthony

APPENDIX B: MUSTER ROLLS AND OTHER LISTS

5 Class: John Mackimmy; Benona Watron; Edwd. Williams; John Frampton; John Silvester; James Kemp jun; Saila Parrot; Richd. Millington; Robt. Jefferson (Hefferson?); Richd. Frampton; John McCulluck; Wm. Anthony
6 Class: Thos. Jackson; Chas. Manship; Robt. Frampton; Thos. Comerford; Thos. Loveday; Thos. Frampton; Abner Nunam; Benja. Huggins; Thos. Dudley; James Andrews; Wm. Whitby; John Kemp
7 Class: Abner Kerby; James Register; Wm. Harriss; James Hutchings; John Wheatly; Wm. Aurundle; Edwd. Turner; David Robinson; Thomas Nutrell; John Bridges; Nathl. Cooper jun; Joseph Frampton
8 Class: Richd. Milington; George Dudly; Henry Manship; Joseph Turner; Richd. Dudly; Bradbury Sylvester; Saml. Williams; Danl. Cristian; Wm. Gary; Howell Powell; John Parrott; James Webb. [Militia Lists of Daus. of Founders and Patriots, held by Md. Hist. Soc.]

TALBOT COUNTY, 38th Battalion

Hearts of Oak Compy - 1st Class: Jonatn. Porter; Saml. Sewel; John Seamore; Henry Watts; Robt. Newcomb; Andrew Orem; Wm. Barney; John Purse; James Wiles; James Marshall
2d Class: John Hopkins 3d; Thos. Leonard junr; Wm. Leonard; John Stoker; John Ridgway; John Marshal; Arthur Marshal; Robt. Sheaves; Jonan. Leonard; Wm. Watts
3 Class: John Mather; Wm. Morris; John Robson; Thos. Barnett Sewel; Wm. Sewel; Richd. Tarr; Richd. Valient; Solo. Cockburn; Benja. Hopkins
4 Class: Antho. Kerby; Emory Kerby; George Pickering; Joseph Seamore; Joseph Marshall; Foster Maynard; Wm. Norwood junr; Wm. Valient; John Bartlett; Richd. Bartlett
5 Class: James Keathly; Alex: Gordon; John Leonard; Henry Robson; Elijah Smith; Abraham Bromwell; Jona. Cockburn; Saml. Short; Robt. Tuffey(?); Wm. Oram
6 Class: Thomas Kemp; John Caulk; James Hopkin Leonard; Robt. Robson; James Erl Denny; John Spry; John Sewell; Wm. Matthews; Nichs. Oram; John Murphy
7 Class: Edwd Eaton; Meredith Marshall; John Cockey; Jona. Harriss; Joseph Sewel; Thos. Applegarth; Henry Seamour; John Norwood; Joshua Hopkins; James Ridway
8 Class: Moses Stains; John Dawson; Benjn. Denny; John Eaton; Richd. Eaton; James Leonard; John Rolison 3d; Denny Hopkins; Joseph Hopkins; John Vandike. [Militia Lists of Daus. of Founders and Patriots, held by Md. Hist. Soc.]

Broad Creek Compy. 1 Class: Robt. Haddoway; Thomas Jepherson; John Lowry; Wm. Dawson; John Camper; Alex: Singclare; Danl. Caulk; Edmond Waymon; Alexa: Larimore
2d Class: Joseph Dawson; James Jones; Saml. Hunt; Alexr: Larimore; Joseph Denny; Thos. Richardson; John Caulk junr; James Lowry junr; Ralph Dawson
3d Class: John Cooper; Edwd Ladnaham; John Winterbottom; Robt. Winterbottom; Thos. Winterbottom; Joshua Richardson; James Fairbanks; John Singclare; Richd. Gordon
4 Class: Richd. Cooper; Hugh Dawson; Peter Hunt; Wm. Harrison; Wm. Camper; Robt. Jones; James Basil (Baul?); Wm. Mason; Wm. Jones
5 Class: Rolen Haddaway; Wm. Barnes; James Hunt; Wm. Haddaway; James Larimore; Robt. Larimore; Wm. Grace; James Haddaway; Robt. Harrison

TALBOT COUNTY

6 Class: Robt. Lowry; Joseph Lowry; Joseph Harrison; Thos. Groves; Nathl. Applegarth; Jacob Keathly; Jona. Larimore; John McConikin; Joseph Caulk
7 Class: Richd. Mansfield; John Haddaway; Thomas Camper; Mark Sewel; George Cox; Peter Richardson; Joseph Larimore; Nathl. Leddenham; Peter Haddaway
8 Class; Peter Haddaway; Saml. Auld; Wm. Jones; Danl. Fairbanks; Patrick McQuay; Adam Camper; Lambert Rimmer; Nathan Porter; Philan: Auld. [Militia Lists of Daus. of Founders and Patriots, held by Md. Hist. Soc.]

Miles River Compy 1 Class: Wm. Sherwood; Woolman Gibson; James Swan; Henry Winstandly; Robt. Boyd; Wm. Hart; Thomas Auld; Lamboth Condon
2d Class: James Craig; Robt. Davis; John Swan; John Skinner; Solo. Kinnernet; Epheram McWay; Wm. Biscoe; Holiday Dulin
3d Class: Wm. Holland; John Ray; Lewis Latterman; Wm. Warner; Edmond Blades; Thos. Mansfield; Wm. Shield; Philip Potts
4 Class: Wm. Clayland; Arthur Bryan; James McCarter; Solo. Kinnemont; John Colvert; Thos. Keys; Richd. Standfield; Wm. Haseldine
5 Class: John McWay; Charles Vickers; Wm. Rice; Sikes Blake; Wm. Blake; John Nuttall; Richd. Harrington; James Haseldine
6 Class: John Hewey; John Gibson junr; Robt. Hopkins; Edmond Blades Junr; Woolman Hewey; Philip Nuttell; James Sewell
7 Class: Wm. Blades; Hopkins Kennement; Charles Sherwood; Benja. Roberts; James Ayrs; Richd. Skinner; Wm. Lundergan
8 Class: Moses Ringrose; Charles Gardener; John Osmond; Wm. Winstandly; Denton Carroll; Benja. Sheald; Wm. Porter. [Militia Lists of Daus. of Founders and Patriots, held by Md. Hist. Soc.]

United Compy. 1st Class: Thos. Ashcraft; John Auld; James Love; Phill Hambleton; Henry Connerly; Jonan. Winters
2d Class: Wm. Hambleton; Robt. Gossage; Thos. Sherwood; Jona. Harrison junr; John Grace; Wm. Hopkins
3d Class: John Hambleton 3d; Jona. Leonard; Thos. Townsend; Marma: Spencer; Wm. Harrison junr; Danl. Gossage
4th Class: Wm. Hambleton; Charles Gossage; Wm. West; Saml. Vinton; J. J. Hopkins; Charles Daffin; Hall Hennon
5 Class: Gorge Gleve; James Hews; James Ryall; Solo. Vinton; Thomas Nash; James Jefferson
6 Class: Benja. Blades; Dunken Cambell; Wm. Harrison; Thos. Townsend jr(?); Lijah Marshall; Joseph Hopkins
7 Class: Danl. Richardson; John Bruff; James Braddock; Hugh Sherwood; Hugh Porter; Phill Skinner; Danl. Haddaway
8 Class: Thos. Wales; John Thompson; Thos. Harrison; Eph: Chick Toop; James Grace; Nathl. Grace; Wm. Davis. [Militia Lists of Daus. of Founders and Patriots, held by Md. Hist. Soc.]

Oxford Compy. 1 Class: Standley Robinson; James Hopkins; Moses Hopkins; James Patterson; Alexr. Troup; Michl. Cork; Robt. Sherwood; Woolmn. Woolcut
2d Class: John Harrison; Jona. Domokoy; Wm. Bridges; Francis Holmes; James Coleston; Peter Hopkins; Dennis Hopkins; Hugh Sherwood
3d Class: Noah Corner; Edwd. Markland; Wm. Coleston; Thos. Baker; David Robinson 3d; Nichs. Goldsborough; Jacob Brumwell; Edwd. Oram
4 Class: Richd. Easley; James Thomas; John Bradsha; John Singleton; Joseph Bowdle; John Emihall; Moses Rigby; Hugh Oram

APPENDIX B: MUSTER ROLLS AND OTHER LISTS

5 Class: Joseph Skinner; Charles Cruikshanks; Edwd. Smith; Wm. Tutle; Charles Pickering; John Biggs; Danl. Sherwood
6 Class: James Cray; Alexr. Cray; Saml. Willis; Jams. Parsons; John Higby; David Kerr; John Hopkins; Alexr. James
7 Class: Edwd. Brumwell; Henry Smith; Saml. Chamberlaine; Thomas Watts; Edwd. Man Sherwood; John Valient; Saml. Sherwood; Alexa. McKinsey
8 Class: Nichs. Thomas; Wm. Coward; John Coleston; Joseph Allingham; Danl. Bartlett; Geo: Cook; Joseph Norwood; Thos. Blanch; Thos. Keer. [Militia Lists of Daus. of Founders and Patriots, held by Md. Hist. Soc.]

Bayside Compy. 1st Class: Solo. Harrison; John Lowe; John Larimore; Danl. Lambden; John Reough; Robt. Role; Wm. Willaby; John Hall; John Ball
2d Class: John Caulk; Benja. Harrison; Robt. Harrison; John Plummer; Richd. Covey; James Sears; Ths. Smith; Richd. Badsy; Allen Brerely
3 Class: John Haddaway; Thos. Sands; Joseph Kemp; John Porter; John Cryer; James Collison; Aaron Ringrose; Geo: Applegarth jr(?)
4 Class: Robt. Lamden junr; Haddaway Cooper; James Trippe; Nichs. Cumings; Lloyd Tilghman; Wm. Sears; Chas. McCarty; Thos. Haddaway; John Haddaway
5 Class: John Harrison; Joseph Porter; James Jones; James Barrow; Robt. Richardson; Wm. Lowe; Wrightson Lamden; Wm. Cummins; Richd. Dawson
6 Class: Thos. Lamn. Haddaway; Joshua Wrightson; Joseph Kemp; Adam Edgar; Solo. Horney; Thos. Cummings; David Morris; Nichs. Dawson; Nichs. Sherwood
7 Class: Robt. Applegarth; John Jones; Chrisr. Spry; Benja. Kemp; John Cummings; Nichs. Brice; Thos. Horney; Joseph Porter; Henry Doret
8 Class: Geo: Collison; James Wrightson; Phil: Plummer; Wm. Cooper; Risdon Harriss; Joseph Edgar; John Horney jun; Wm. Haddaway; John McNulty.
[Militia Lists of Daus. of Founders and Patriots, held by Md. Hist. Soc.]
total in 38th Battn. 399
Total of the Militia class'd 1082 Privates
Chrisr: Birckhead, Lieut. of Talbot County

A List of the Militia of Talbot County July 3d 1780 - 4th Battalion

Wye Company:
Woolman Gibson 3d, Capt; Robert Hall, 1st Lieut.; Jereh. Garland, 2d Do; William Alloway, Ensn.; Thos. Roberts, Sergt.;
Thos. Roberts junr, Corpl.; George Williams Do
1st Class: Alemby Millington; George Beswicks; John Corkrill; Thomas Porter; Wm. Lane; John Philips; Samuel Sewel; John Fontleray; Jacob Gibson; James Jones
2d Class: Edward Roberts; Levin Stacy; Joseph Callighan; John Sangston; Brooks Thornton; James Willson junr; John Park; Solomon Plummer; Nathan Beswick; Wm. Taylor
3d Class: Griffin Shields; Richard George; James Lane; William Edmondson; John Chevous; Gewil(?) Plummer; Phill Nuttle; John Buller; Samuel Foreman; Samuel Fountain
4th Class: Robert Pickering; David Parsonnett; George Hall; Hopkins Kinnimont Plummer (of James); Dennis McCormack - Sub; Richard Kinnard; John Gibson 3d; William Sweat; Richard Beswicks

TALBOT COUNTY

5th Class: Edward Sweat; Robert Griffin; Joshua Kennard Sub; Henry Baker; Isaac Palmer; Robert Dwiggins; James Kinnard; William Jackson; Aaron Sweat; James Bracknell
6 Class: John Roberts; Thomas Cotner; William Porter; George Plummer; Christr Heart; John Hall; William Hardcastle; Nathaniel Pratt; Joshua Elbert; Joseph Sewel
7th Class: Jacob Garren; James Stant; Joseph Buly; Francis Baker; John Tarring; Charles Camper; John Smith; Francis Armstrong; John Gardner
8th Class: Aquilla Falling; John Cotner; William German; John Chambers; James Gallaghane; Griffin Gallighane; Richard Norton; Wiliam Kemp; Samuel Baker. [Militia Lists of Daus. of Founders and Patriots, held by Md. Hist. Soc.]

Volunteer Company: John Daugherty, Capt.; Able Grace, 1st Lieut.; James Stewart, 2d Do; Vincent Price, Ensign; Traverse Garland, Sergt.; Carter Cockayne, Sergt.; James Gilon, Sergt.; Levi Pearson, Sergt.;
1st Class: James Condan; John Blake (of Wm.); George Foresain; Thomas Brascup; Edward Eubanks; Lambert Kirby; Quinton Wallen; John Greenhawk; James Faulkner; Henry Snelling; Nathan Allin; Isaac Dobson
2d Class: Robert Dixon; Nathan Porter; John Kirby; William Warren; Jonathan Chusly; James Hendrick; John Hobbs; John Pinkind; Peter Harwood; Joseph Atkinson; Fisher Rakes; George Stevens
3d Class: Henry Davis; William Parish; John Cambell; Morris Kirby; John Warring; Joseph Bush; John Allin; Alexr., Anderson; Thos. Hurry; Aaron Merrick; Greenbury Faulkner; Isaac Faulkner junr
4th Class: James Kennedy Sub; Daniel Kerby; Levi Faulkner; Walker Gore; Wm. Pearson; Hugh McCullock; John Sherwood; William Shaw; Sampson Warren; Thomas Benny; Henry Covey; Edward Jackson
5th Class: John Austin; David Lucas; Benjamin Benny; Joshua Faulkner; Morgan Lucas; James Duling; Michl. Pinkind; James Cheesly; Wm. Shields; John Turner; Thomas Eubanks; Philip Norris
6th Class: Joseph Hobbs; Richard Norton; Wm. Tizzard; Woolman Hussay; Thomas Sherwood; John Hunt; William Chapman; John Dobson; Jonan. Lary; Robert Cheesely; John Dixon junr
7th Class: William Dixon; Isaac Faulkner; Hinson Faulkner, Sub; Samuel Gore; Ebenezer Kinnard; Valiant Turner; John Fleming; Richd. Kirby; Nathan Foster; James Foster; Richd. Haseldine; Perry Anderson
8th Class: William Bowdle; Thomas Harwood; Wm. Hamilton 3d; Peter Cole; David Kirby (son of Bill); Aaron Kirby; Robert Floyd; Jona. Cockayne; Philp. Kinnemont; James Haseldine; Rubin Gray. [Militia Lists of Daus. of Founders and Patriots, held by Md. Hist. Soc.]

Union Company: Richard Bruff, Capt; Willm. Milward, 1st Lt.; Saml. Barrow, Ensign; William Rose, Sergt.; John Fleming; Henry Tibbles, Sergt.; John Barrow, Sergt.
1st Class: Perry Priestly; Wm. Whittocks; Wm. Trippe; Richard Barrow; James Holliday; John Berry; Wm. Glin Callum; Saml. Neighbours jr; James Robinson; Stephen Darden, Sub; James Crouch; Wm. Needles; Wm. McCallum sub; James Dawson; Nicholas Cox
2d Class: Samuel Woods; John Tibbles; Robert Neal; Lambeth Booker; Wm. Marsh Catrop; Wm. Bullen; Isaac Gilpin; George Cook; Henry Richardson; Thomas Catrop; Thomas Skinner; Wm. Troth junr; Isaac Sylvester; James Love

APPENDIX B: MUSTER ROLLS AND OTHER LISTS

3d Class: James Lloyd Chamberlaine, Sub; Edward Needles; Wm. Catrop; Christr. Bruff; James Bowman; Andrew Barrow; John Love; Sharp Harwood; Nicholas Barrott; Lambert Hopkins; Wm. Skinner; James Flemming; Charles Gully
4th Class: John Catrop; Peter Edmondson; Peter Denny; Wm. Weaver; Wm. Warton; Joseph Denny; Mathew Shaw; Thomas King; Lemon John Catrop; George Pickering; Levin Jacobs; John Mags; Thomas Cooper
5th Class: John Cosly; John Kersy; David Davis Barrow; Joseph Neal; James Seth; James Wainright; James Barrow; Wm. Smith; Henry Dickinson; Robert Burch; James Merchant; George Poney; Edward Draper
6th Class: James Bullen; Aaron Atkinson junr; Soln. Atkinson; Thomas Love; Richd. Harwood, Sub; Daniel Merrick; Tristram Needles; Wm. Dawson Thomas; Alexr. McCallum, Sub; John Chapman; Thomas Yates; Stephen Catrop; Edward Cox
7th Class: Nathan Walker; John Heron; Aron Atkinson senr; Wm. Lavil, Sub; John Dickinson; James Neighbours; John Jackson; John Clark; Andrew Williams; John Roberts - Saml. Coffin (Coffree?); John Thomas; John Crisp
8th Class: Jacob Gibson junr; William Thomas; Archibald Smith; Joseph Pearsons; Thomas Morgan junr; Robert Bond; Saml. Sharp - sub; Thomas Wickersham; John Jenkins; Andrew Matthews; George Moore; Emory Kerby; James Barnwell. [Militia Lists of Daus. of Founders and Patriots, held by Md. Hist. Soc.]

Volunteer Company - 1st Class: Thomas Gordon; Thomas Buckley; Lambert Coburn; Anthony Sowel; Dennis Cairy; John Armstrong; Wm. Madrid; Henry Buckley; John Price; Wm. Stevens, sub; James Chaplaine
2d Class: William Anderson; Francis Chaplaine; George Jenkins; Thomas Welch; Robert Martin; John Parrott junr; Daniel Berry; James Priestly; Thomas Anderson; John Winson; John Barnaby
3d Class: John Prichard; Wm. Prichard; Wm. Chaplaine; John Chaplaine; Richard Hickson; Thos. Martin junr, sub; Pierce Jones; Samuel Buckley; Richard Martin; Henry Martin junr, sub; John Eldrick; Wm. Cummins
4th Class: Saml. Prichard; Peter Webb junr; William Gore; John Johnson; Samuel White; Samuel Buckley; Noble Barnett; Daniel Walker; Thomas Pharis; John Harriss; John Holmes junr
5th Class: John Handcock; Wm. Allin; John Nunam; Joseph Dardan, sub; Foster Armstrong; John Love; Thomas Barnett; Howel Powel; William Bent (Bond?); Daniel Landman; Woolman Hickson
6th Class: Saml. Dickinson; Richard Barnett; Michael Rogers; James Chaplaine; James Mullikin; Thomas Price; Henry Martin, sub; James Alexander; Wm. Helsby junr; Edward Trippe junr; Wm. Alexander
7th Class: Mathias Merrick; Owen Troy; Joseph Rogers; Samuel Mullikin; James Buckley; William Rakes; Solomon Martin; James Alexander; William Stevens junr; Thomas Summers; James Holt
8th Class: Jesse Mullikin; John Parrott; Wm. Tucker; Thomas Chaplaine; Thomas Robinson; Henry Bowdle; James Mullikin junr; Wm. Mullikin; Peter Browning; Henry Daren. [Militia List of Daus. of Founders and Patriots, held by Md. Hist. Soc.]

Sword in Hand Company - John Thomas Capt; Samuel Thomas, 1st Lt.; Wm. Goldsborough junr; Wm. Benny

TALBOT COUNTY

1st Class: Chas. Walker Benny; Cloudsbury Austin; James Price senr; Andrew Price; Joseph Rathel; Daniel Chapman; Thomas Roach; John Dawson; Christopher Cooper; John Murphy junr
2d Class: Richard Austin junr; Thomas Larymore; John Cockrain; Nathan Price; Joseph Berry; Nathaniel Hopkins; Wm. Taylor; Wm. Porter; Jarman Cade; John Fearns; Aaron Fitzjifferas
3d Class: Daniel Cheezum; Lodman Arundal; Wm. Matthews; Samuel Bowman; John Crouder; John Barwick; Christr. Hughs; Abraham Sherwin; Elijah Duling; Nathan Kerby; William Loveday; Henry Johnson junr
4th Class: John Gregory; John Merchant junr; Christopher Hews; Wm. Duling; John Kerby junr; Jonathan Floyd; George Stevens; Charles Nabb junr; Thomas Ogdin Townsend
5th Class: Elisha Stewart; William Knowly; James Thomas; Andrew Green; Thomas Turner; James Berry junr; James Austin; Francis Armstrong; Samuel Turbott; James Townsend
6th Class: Wm. Rathel; John Nabb; Michl. Kerby junr; Samuel Register; John Register; Perry Parrott; Charles Allin; Benjamin Kerby; Isaac Chambers; Nicholas Loveday
7th Class: Charles Stewart; Vachel Severe; Thomas Stewart; Lambert Kerby junr; Wm. Morgan; Edward Henrix; James Dawson; Robert Louther; Richard Jones; John Duling
8th Class: Slyter Parrott; Danl. Nunam; Andrew Matthews; James Gregory senr; Cloudsbury Kerby; Wm. Gregory; George Hunt; Edward Turner; John Gore; Benjamin Johns. [Militia List of Daus. of Founders and Patriots, held by Md. Hist. Soc.]

Bullinbrook Company - Randolph Johnson Capt; Wm. Clark, 1st Lieut.; Solon. Robinson, 2d Do; Walter Jenkins, Ensign; James Jones, Sergt.; Matthew Hardikin, Sergt.; John Roberts, Sergt.; John Lee, Corpl.; Wm. Stevens junr, Corpl.; Walter Prichard, Corpl.; Wm. Berridge, Drummer; Jams. Mackmahan, Fifer
1st Class: Solomon Brinsfield; Moses Brinsfield; Nathaniel Hull; Moses Carr; James Standley; Wm. Foster; George Troth; John Knowles; Oliver Lee
2d Class: James Parrott; Wm. Harrington; John Hull; James Harding; Thomas Higgins; John Patterson; Elexr. McClayland; Levin Ball; Thomas Bullin; Stephen Drummond
3d Class: Wm. Mackey; James Tobin, sub; Jas. Dickinson jr, sub; Francis Walker; James Harrington; Thomas Barnett 3d; Thomas Helsby (of Wm.); Nathan Duling; George Price; Perry Brinsfield
4th Class: Philip Mackey; John Fleming; Theophilus Small; Tristram Bowdle; Thos. Napp; John Merrick; James Fairbrothers; Wm. Nicols; James Hopkins
5th Class: Arnold Buckley; Allin Burgess; Thomas Helsby; Abner Parrott; Sales Cannon; Smuel Abbott junr; John Brown; George Thompson; Solomon Harriss
6th Class: Evin Jones; Mark Delahay; Joseph Carr; Wm. Carney; Henry Harriss; Wm. Harriss; David Jones; John Ardery; Samuel Abbott senr
7th Class: Henry West; Thos. Fleming; James Horney; Wm. Clark junr; John Clemmonse; Samuel Eason; Richard Moore; John Akers; Richard Hopkins
8th Class: John Higgins; Thomas Bullen; Jeffery Miller; John Skinner; John Rathel; John Higgins junr; James Akers; Samuel Farrow; John McMahan.
[Militia List of Daus. of Founders and Patriots, held by Md. Hist. Soc.]

APPENDIX B: MUSTER ROLLS AND OTHER LISTS

Third Haven Company - Levin Spedding, Capt; Edward Stevens, 1st Lieut.; John Brown, 2nd do; Wm. Berry, Ensign; Wm. Walker, Sergt.; Benjn. Kemp, Sergt.; John Brinn, Sergt.; Joseph Price
1st Class: Joseph Bunton; Benjamin Parsons; Henry Delahay; Thomas Coburn; Joshua Stoker; Solomon Jones; John Connolly; Nicholas Sherwood; Benjn. Stoker; Robert Spedding; Wm. Street; James Lloyd
2d Class: Wm. Marshall; Danl. McGuinia; Wm. Walker junr; Thomas Hopkins; James Sangston; James Berry senr; Solomon Carney junr; John Mullikin; Richard Walker; Isaac Cox junr; Wm. Sherwood
3d Class: John Edwards; Edward Bromwell, sub; Henry Troth (son of Henry); Thomas Willson; James White; Andrew Callender; Thomas Holmes junr; John Bowdle; Francis Armstron; Richard Oxenham; John Knowles
4th Class: Thomas Delahay; Henry Parrott; John Willson junr; Moses Adams; Wm. Lang Helsbey; John Nicols; James Berry junr; Solomon Holmes senr; John McGuinea; Daniel Berry; Joseph Ridgway
5th Class: Wm. Walker 3d; Wm. Lomacks; Richard Hays; Francis Neal; Thomas Sewel; Quinton Kemp; Nathan Sewel; Thomas McClayland; Elisha Spencer; Henry Higgins; Edward Pattison
6th Class: Peter Richardson; Joseph Kemp; Wm. Gooddey; Wm. Delahay; Nichs. Pampilion; Abraham Farrington; Thomas Jones; Thomas Turner; Robert Lloyd; Robert Wailes; John Duncan
7th Class: John Ridgway; Thomas Sherwin; John Cooper; James Walker junr; Samuel Jenkins; John McMahan; Richard Street; Foster Price junr; Roger Kelly; Samuel Short; Wm. Callender
8th Class: Joseph Davis; Charles Gully; John Cane; Thomas Austin; Wm. Baily; John Littleton; Wm. Brinn; Perry Watts; Peter Barnett; John Walker; Abraham Severe. [Militia List of Daus. of Founders and Patriots, held by Md. Hist. Soc.]

Hand in Hand Company - Nathl. Cooper, Capt.; Richard Johns, 1st Lieut.; Timothy Lane Price, 2d Do; John Hardcastle, Ensign
1st Class: Wm. Price: John Morriss; James Parrott junr; Wm. Cecill; Lodman Aurendal; George Willson; Wm. Love; Thos. Cecill junr; Francis Hopkins; Thomas Kendall; John Ridgway; James Morriss
2d Class: Thomas Whitby; Moses Kerby; Jonathan Osmond; Aaron Parrott; Daniel Willson; Cornelius Taylor; John Cecil; Park Webb; James Williams; James Dudley; Thomas Jadvin; David Kerby
3d Class: Joshua Clark; Jonathan Shanahan; John Rice; John Frampton; Wm. Frampton; Thomas Osmond; Gilbert Price; Charles Suters; John Burgess; Charles Ridgway; Wm. Tomlinson; Peter Parrott
4th Class: Isaac Millington; Robert Jadvin; Thomas Parrott; John Hobbs; Robert Griffin; James Meeds; Samuel Dudley; Parrott Clark; Ase Gill; Richard Kerby; James Hardcastle; George Brown
5th Class: Edward Williams; James Kemp junr; Saila Parott; Richard Frampton; Richard Millington; Joseph Bell; Edward Parkerson; Hugh Works; James Ridgway; Thomas Meeds; George Burgess; James Russel
6th Class: Charles Manship; Robert Frampton; Thomas Commerford; Thomas Loveday; Thomas Frampton; Abner Nunam; Thomas Dudley; Wm. Whitby; John Kemp; Rigby Foster; Banoni Watson; Richd. Grainger
7th Class: Abner Kerby; James Register; Wm. Aurundle; Edward Turner; John Bridges; Joseph Frampton; James Matthews; Gary Warner; Moses Gill; Samuel Price; Wm. Vickers; Peter Oxenham

TALBOT COUNTY

8th Class: Richard Millington; George Dudley; Henry Manship; Richard Dudley; Daniel Christian; Wm. Gary; Howel Powel; John Parrott; Daniel Lambdon junr; Wm. Ridgway (of Charles); Wm. Dudley; Greenwood Leg. [Militia List of Daus. of Founders and Patriots, held by Md. Hist. Soc.]

Bayside Company: George Impy Dawson, Capt.; Robert Haddaway, 1st Lt.; Basil Sewel, 2nd Do; Francis Porter, Ensign; John Lowe, Sergt.; Thomas Auld, Sergt.; John Kersey, Sergt.; John Hall, Sergt.; James Cummins, Corpl.; John McKnoulty jr Do.; Solomon Harrison, Do; Peregrine Singclaire, Do
1st Class: John Larimore; Daniel Lamdin jr; Robert Rolle; John Ball; Henry Dorsett; Robert Reddish; Wm. Wales; Wm. Williby; Danl. Lamden; James Hariss
2d Class: John Caulk (son of Jas.); John Plummer; Richd. Badsay; Allin Brerely(?); Richard Covey; Robt. Applegarth junr; John Hughs; Edward Harrison; Daniel Lambden; Robert Sands
3d Class: Joseph Kemp; John Porter; John Cryer; James Collison; Aaron Ringrose; George Applegarth; Thomas Sands; John Cook; Oakley Haddaway
4th Class: Robert Lambdin junr; Haddaway Cooper; Nicholas Cummins; John Wilkinson; John McDonald; John Bootman; John Bryan; Wm. Cardiff; Thos. Lurty Haddaway
5th Class: John Harrison; Joseph Porter (son of Joseph); James Jones; James Barrow; Wrightson Lambdin; Wm. Cummins; Noah Harriss; Henry Elliott; Jona. Sinclaire
6th Class: Thos. Lambden Haddaway; Joshua Wrightson; Soloman Horney; David Morriss; Nicholas Dawson; Nicholas Sherwood; Thomas Cooper; Christopher Spry; Thos. McKnoutly
7th Class: John Jones; Benjamin Kemp junr; John Cummins; Thomas Harney; John Plummer junr; Charles Smith; Thomas McQuay; Edward Collison; Robt. Harrison
8th Class: George Collison; Risden Harris; Joseph Edgar; John Horney junr; Wm. Haddaway; James Wrightson jr.; Wm. Lambden; Solomon Cummins; John Harrison. [Militia List of Daus. of Founders and Patriots, held by Md. Hist. Soc.]

United Company: Thos. Hopkins, Capt; Hugh Auld, 1st Lieut; John Hambleton 2d Do; Thos. Harrison, Ensign; Thos. Harrison junr, Sergt.; Joseph Graham, Sergt.; Robert Gossage, Sergt.; Thos. Dodson, Sergt.; Hugh Hopkins, Corpl; John Blades, Corpl; Edmond Blades
1st Class: Thomas Ashcraft; Philimon Hambleton; Henry Connolly; Jona. Winters; Thomas Blades; Levi Blades; Samuel Tennant; Robert Harrison
2d Class: Jonathan Harrison junr; John Grace; Wm. Hopkins; Wm. Harrison; Abraham Bromwell; Thomas Royal; Robert Dodson; George Townsend
3d Class: Jonathan Leonard; Marmaduke Spencer; Wm. Harrison junr; Daniel Gossage; Ezekiel Blades; Isaiah Blades; Wm. Windstandley; Benjn. Blades junr
4th Class: Charles Gossage; Samuel Vinton; John Kinnemont; Thomas Groves; Nathaniel Harrison; John Kerby; Joshua Richardson
5th Class: James Hughs; James Royall; Thomas Nash; Solomon Vinton; Robert Richardson; Thomas Purnal; Danl. Hopkins
6th Class: Duncan Cambell; Wm. Harrison senr; Thomas Townsend junr; Elijah Marshall; Joseph Norwood; Joseph Harrison (of Thos.); John Durgan
7th Class: Danl. Richardson; John Bruff; Hughs Porter; Danl. Haddaway; Joseph Harrison 3d; Nathaniel Grace; Joseph Dawson

APPENDIX B: MUSTER ROLLS AND OTHER LISTS

8th Class: Thomas Wales; Ephraim Chick Toop; Nathaniel Grace; Wm. Davis; James Grace; Jona. Spencer; Zebulon Skinner; John Hopkins junr. [Militia List of Daus. of Founders and Patriots, held by Md. Hist. Soc.]

Broad Creek Company: Wm. Hambleton, Capt.; John Caulk, 1st Lt.; James Lowry 2d Do; James Barns, Ensign; David Fairbanks, Sergt.; Daniel Bridges, Sergt.; John Hunt, Sergt.; Robert Dawson, Corpl.; Wm. Higgins, Corpl.; Robt. Dawson junr, Corpl.; Thomas Ball, Corpl.; Richd. Linthicum, Drummr.; Hugh Sherwood, Fifer
1st Class: Thomas Jefferson; Wm. Dawson; John Camper; Alexr. Sinclaire; Edward Wayman; Alexr. Larymore junr; Richd. Larymore; Thomas Jefferson; Benjamin Harrison
2d Class: James Jones; Samuel Hunt; Thomas Richardson; Ralph Dawson; Henry Weeden; Peter Fairbanks; John Lowry; John Carter; John Dawson; James Jefferson
3d Class: John Cooper; Edward Leadenham; John Winterbottom; Robert Winterbottom; James Fairbank; John Sinclaire; George Jefferson; Thomas Cooper; Thos. Winterbottom
4th Class: Richard Cooper; Hugh Dawson; Wm. Harrison; Wm. Camper; James Ball; Wm. Mason; Wm. Jones; Daniel Auld junr; Robert Jones junr
5th Class: Wm. Haddaway; James Larimore; Robert Larimore; William Grace; James Haddaway; Robert Harrison; Rubin Jones; Wm. Applegerth
6th Class: Robert Lowry; Joseph Lowry; Joseph Harrison; Nathl. Applegerth; Jona. Larimore; Joseph Caulk; Danl. Winterbottom; Peter Caulk; Peter Fairbanks; Wm. Sinclaire
7th Class: Richard Mansfield; John Haddaway; Thomas Camper; Mark Sewel; Nathl. Leadenham; Joseph Hunt; John Larimore; Thomas Fairbanks
8th Class: Peter Haddaway; Samuel Auld; Wm. Jones junr; Danl. Fairbanks; Patrick McQuay; Abraham Camper; Lambert Rimer; Nathan Porter; Philemon Auld; John Leadenham; John McQuay. [Militia List of Daus. of Founders and Patriots, held by Md. Hist. Soc.]

Hearts of Oak Company: Henry Banning, Capt.; Mordica Skinner, 1st Lt.; Henry Coliston, 2d Do; Perry Benson, Ensign; John Robson, Sergt.; Andrew Robson, Sergt.; Thomas Robson, Sergt.; Andrew Orim, Sergt.; John Stoker, Corpl.; John Cook Leonard, Corpl.; John Cockey, Corpl.; Danl. Richardson, Corpl.; Wm. Matthews, Drumr.; Francis Spry, Fifer
1st Class: Jonathan Porter; John Seamore; John Purse; Wm. Barney; James Marshall; James Bartlett; James Wailes; Joseph Benson; Henry Seamore; Francis Hopkins junr; Elliott Shanahan
2d Class: John Hopkins 3d; Thomas Leonard; Wm. Leonard; Robert Cheaves; Arthur Marshall; Jonathan Leonard; Thos. Robinson; Benjamin West; Wm. Marshall; Hugh Watts; Nicholas Oram; Thomas Kees
3d Class: John Robinson; Thos. B. Sewel; George Cox; Jonathan Tarr; Richard Tarr; Richard Valient; John Dawson; Thomas Richardson jr; Henry Coburn; Thomas Jones; Joseph Valient
4th Class: Anthony Kerby; Joseph Seamore; Joseph Marshall; Foster Maynard; Wm. Norwood junr; Wm. Valient; John Bartlett; Richard Bartlett; Cloudsbury Kerby; Elijah Stoker; Samuel Kerby
5th Class: James Keithly; John Leonard; Henry Robson; Elisha Smith; Jonathan Coburn; Wm. Orim; John Shanahan; Richd. Spencer; John Skinner; Wm. Marshall junr; Wm. Watts

TALBOT COUNTY

6th Class: Thos. Kemp; Henry Bulling; James K. Leonard; James E. Denny; John Sewel; John Spry; Richard Denny; James Hopkins; Jeremh. Coleston; Perry Spencer; Nicholas Orem; John Murphy
7th Class: Edward Eaton; Marydeth Marshall; Jonan. Harriss; Joseph Sewel; Thos. Applegerth; James Benson; Joseph Leonard; Benjn. Kerby; John Norwood; Hashua Hopkins
8th Class: Joseph Denny; Benjn. Denny; John Dawson; John Eaton; Richd. Eaton; John Robinson 3d; Denny Hopkins; Joseph Hopkins; James Eubank; Thos. Robinson; Edward Norwood. [Militia List of Daus. of Founders and Patriots, held by Md. Hist. Soc.]

Oxford Company: Edward Man Sherwood, Capt; David Robinson junr, 1st Lt.; James Delahay, 2d Do; Thos. Robinson, Ensign
1st Class: James Hopkins; Moses Hopkins; James Sherwood; John Brown; Richd. Coward
2d Class: John Harrison junr; Wm. Bridges; Francis Holmes; James Coleston; Thos. Coward; Chars. Markland
3d Class: Noah Carner; Edward Markland; Wm. Coleston; Thomas Baker; Nichs. Goldsborough; Jacob Bromwell; Edward Orem; John Stevens junr
4th Class: James Thomas; John Singleton; Moses Rigby; John Bozman; Chs. Pickering junr; Spedden Orem
5th Class: Edward Smith; Wm. Tuttle; Charles Pickering; Henry Delahay; Dennis Hopkins; Saml. Coliston
6th Class: James Cray; Alexr. Cray; Samuel Willis; Alexr. James; Nicholas Martin
7th Class: Edward Bromwell; Henry Smith; Saml. Chamberlaine, Sub; John Valient; Alexr. McKinsey; Patrick Mullikin
8th Class: John Coliston; Danl. Bartlett; George Cook; Joseph Norwood; Thos. Blanch; Greenbury Goldsbury. [Militia List of Daus. of Founders and Patriots, held by Md. Hist. Soc.]

Miles River Company: Charles Gardiner, Capt.; Richard Harrington, 1st Lt.; Richard Start, 2d Do; Robert Farquston, Ensign; James Welch, Sergt.; John Ray, Sergt.; John Swan, Sergt.; Woolman Hewey, Sergt; John Osmant, Corpl; Perry Robert; Andrew Skinner, Corpl; Wooln. Gibson junr, Corpl
1st Class: James Swan; Wm. Heart; Lambert Condon; Henry Winstandly; James Price; Thos. Hewey; Philimon Sherwood
2d Class: Robert Davis; Wm. Biscoe; John Warner; Solomon Nuttle; John Vandike; John Blake (of Peter); John Martin
3d Class: Wm. Holland; Dr. C. Lewis Lotterman; Jereh. McQuay junr; Jacob Keethly; John Blake; James Turner; Robt. Robertson
4th Class: Arthur Bryan; James McCarter; John Colbert senr; Richd. Standfield; Jereh. McSweeny; Levin Mansfield; Jonathan Biscoe
5th Class: John McQuay; Sikes Blake; John Nuttle junr; Charles Vickers; Jonathan Sherwood; James Farquson; Nathan Knotts
6th Class: John Hewey; Robert Hopkins; Edmond Blades junr; James McGuina; Jona. Hopkins; Robert Cross
7th Class: Wm. Blades; Charls. Sherwood; Benjn. Roberts junr; James Ayres; Richd. Skinner; Wm. Ferguson
8th Class: Moses Ringrose; Benjn. Shields; Wm. Porter; John Vining; James Benson; James Bracco. [Militia List of Daus. of Founders and Patriots, held by Md. Hist. Soc.]

APPENDIX B: MUSTER ROLLS AND OTHER LISTS

Talbot County Aug. 14th 1781
Sir/ Inclosed you have a list of the Men draughted on the 30th July; there are several of them will come under the exemption of your Letter of the 3d inst. There are also some Quakers draughted, who are principled agt. bearing Arms. I should be glad to receive your Excellancies directions in respect to them.
    I now send by Capt. Daugherty, several of the Draughts & Substitutes from this County a list of whom he will deliver; and should have sent them sooner but the Gentleman appointed to provide quarters and necessaries for the Recruits (nor myself) had either provisions or Money to forward them, nor could we procure it 'till a meeting of the special Council.
    I also inclose you a List of the Select Militia of this County with a Certificate of Officers recommended for sd. Company, Commissions for whom you'll please to send me by the bearer. also Commissions for some Militia Officers I left a minute of with yr. Clark. I am yr. Excelliencies most obedt. Hble. Servt. Christr. Birckhead
    N.B. I also send two prisoners from the Brittish. C.B.
    What Draughts remain I shall have collected as soon as possible. C.B.
[Militia List of Daus. of Patriots, held by Md. Hist. Soc.]

WASHINGTON COUNTY
A List of Capt. Daniel Clapsadle Compy. as now Classd.
First Battalion, No. 1

Capt. Clapsadle; 1 Lietn. Frederick Nichodemus; 2 do. Christian Lance; Ensign Peter Baker; 1 Sergent. William Scott; 2 do. Anthony Bell; 3 do. Jacob Lighter; 4 do. Abraham Lighter
1 Corprel Andrew Fogler; 2 do. John Gabbey; 3 do. Michael Harckell; 4 do. Conrod Nichodemus
1st Class: Bolcher Shomaker; Christian Sides; Christopher Brandenbugh; Peter Fleger; Michael Powett; John Flake; William Shanefin; Thomas Cross; Samuel Bachtell Junr
2d Class: Peter Shew son of Peter; Davoll Cow; David Scott; Isaac Nicewonder; William Downey son of William; John Brumboch; John Wagoner; Frederick Harkell; Peter Witzell
3d Class: Henry Clapper Junr; George Stuart; Melchar Sallady; George Hudson; Henry Shriver; Elias Reeter; Ruben Tudero; George Carter; Peter Lighter
4th Class: George Headler; Mathias Lizer; William Gormon; Bryan Munrow; Frederick Cow; John Thompson; Peter Simon; Osborn Sprigg; Henry Smith
5th Class: Henry Snyder; Jacob Wisner; Christopher Fogler; Conrod Reyler; Martin Jacob; Abraham Terush; William Baird; Martin Lowman; Christian Metts
6th Class: Daniel Mowing; John Hands; John Dilts; William Dilts; Ezekiah Downey; William Downey Junr; Henry Funk (at Bachtells); Martin Wagoner; George Baker
7th Class: Christopher Lighter; Peter Stuckey; Baptist Heafner; Samuel Downey; David Downey; Isaac Bachtell; Christian Lance Junr; Ludwick Hart; Ludwick Mowing; Christopher Pence
8th Class: James Downey Junr; Phillip Rimely; James Scott; Joseph Downey; William Downey; John Downey; John Heafner; Jacob Brumbock; Adam Lighter (at Jacob Lighter). [Md.Hist. Society, MS 1146]

WASHINGTON COUNTY

A List of Officers & Men in Capt. Henry Botelers Compy.
1 Lietn. Thomas Odel; 2 do. John Nicholls; Ensign (blank)
1 Sergt. Daniel Giveings; 2 do. Henry Edward Boteler; 3 do. William Nicholls;
4 do. Trail Nicholls
1 Corpl. Jacob Grim; 2 do. Frederick Rorer; 3 do. Nicholas Shifler; 4 do.
John Doll
1st Class: Jacob Long; William Gilson; Adam Caplinger; Peter Yosty; Youst
Garner; Jacob Mariaty; Michael Henry; John Linsley; William Conner
2d Class: Jacob Nave; William Patrick; Stophel Ransbarger; James Dean; John
Hill; Hugh McMeme; Michael George; Henry Musgrove; William Eastern
3d Class: Phillip Booker; Henry Hufman; John Harns; Jacob Roser; Samuel
Roser Junr; Felty Hill; Patrick Norris; Jeremiah Risley; John Rinker
4th Class: Stophel Corts(?); Conrod Damm; John Tanner; George Boot; John
Iginter; Henry Bouser; John Rodrick; William Gladhill; Adam Boot
5th Class: Jacob Titer; Ludwick Mocoman; John Lore (Lord?); Massam Dean;
James Ray; Daniel Risley; Francis Worley; James Allen; Thomas Jacob
6th Class: George Corman; Michael Corts; George Lewis; Marten Grims; John
Walter; Casper Peck; Henry Ault; Leonard Carnon; James Hayes
7th Class: Peter Putman; Joseph Morehead; John Houser; Rudolph Brown; Jacob
Picklehimer; Tiller Younger; John Austain; Jacob Rodrick
8th Class: John Putman; Jacob Lance; John Rorer; George Toice; William
Lewis; John Huffer; James(?) Turner(?). Capt. Butler hav(in)g resigned.
Thomas Odel will be Capt. John Nichols. 1st. Lieut. [Md. Hist. Soc., MS
1146]

A List of Capt. Nichodemus's Compy. as now Classd. Second Battn., No. 6
1 Lietn. Michael Glasser; 2 do. Martain Bilmire; Ensign Leonard Bilmire
1 Sergent. Peter Shank; 2 do. Frederick Barkman; 3 do. Michael Tobe; 4 do.
Henry Hufman
1 Corperel Peter Treslen; 2 do. Henry Powless; 3 do. Goddard Hoof; 4 do.
Nicholas Shifler
1st Class: Phillip Morgon; John Hendderick; Daniel Stonesifer; John Ringer;
Nicholas Sallott; Frederick Rod; John Thomas; William Foltz; Christian
Thomas
2d Class: Jacob Line; George Stosser (Stofser?); Michael Tom; Henry Sotsser;
Joseph Hess; Benjn. Non; Henry Godey; Michael Thomas Junr
3d Class: Conrod Woolfhill; Jacob Fastnaught; Mathias Staufer; Wendle
Shegten; Leonard Bell; James Hurdell; Peter Powers; Henry Baker
4th Class: Peter Baker; Stale (Stab?) John; Adam Shally; Peter Thomas;
George Lin; Peter Bill(?); Jacob Hess; Adam Doll
5th Class: Michael Belmire; Adam Fasnight; Jacob Hein; Leonard Cretzen;
Valentine Wise; Thomas Mehaney; Adam Gornd; Peter Burkman
6th Class: Peter Barken; Andrew Barken; John Shae (Shad?); John Cou(?);
Christian Hess; Samuel Baker; John Bronds; Jacob Browner
7th Class: John Bambergen; Michael Gerber; William Morgon; Moses Morgon;
Samuel Hofsteth; Conrod Ringer
8th Class: John Paules; Phillip Grond; Jacob Thomas; Benjn. Boill; George
Kneebell; Adam Snider; Christian Miller. [Md. Hist. Soc., MS 1146]

A List of Capt. Samuel Hughes Compy as now Class.
1 Lietn. David Gillespie; 2 do. Robert Douglass; Ensign (blank)

APPENDIX B: MUSTER ROLLS AND OTHER LISTS

1 Sergt. John Sibert; 2 do. Adam Mong Senr; 3 do. George Stiffer (Stiffee?);
4 do. Daniel Hogmire
1 Corpl. Adam Mong Junr; 2 do. George Colleyflour; 3 do. Charles Gorden; 4
do. Daniel Booker
1st Class: George McWilliams; John Douglass; John Curren; Thomas Cunstable;
Jacob Shaver; Adam Hoover Senr; Jacob Howard; David Shaver
2d Class: John Day; Joseph Williams; John Carr; Samuel Hogmire; Michael
Steer; John Hilderbrand; Benedict Bowman; Martin Hackler; Adam Tom
3d Class: Mathew Williams; William Allen; Phillip Odleberger; Abraham
Deeder; John Augusteen Junr; Jacob Rover; Michael Ray; Peter Sibert; Michael
Specer
4th Class: James Williams; Stophel Hughett; George Augusteen; David Shaw;
Jacob Mong; Thomas Dun; Ludwick Hugett; Frederick Stair; Casper Stair
5th Class: John McWilliams; Nicholas Hughett; Michael Shackley; Peter
Hoover; Andrew Heminder; Martin Rorer; Frederick Shrinehart; Jacob Shank
6th Class: Phillip Odleburger Junr; Andrew Beard; John Young; George Hammon;
Adam Hoover; Tempest Tucker; John Woolf; Joseph Williams
7th Class: Robert Allison; Samuel Landers; Christian Bare; Mathias Tom;
Michael Colleyflour; Henry Gathor; Jacob Shaver; Jacob Woolf
8th Class: Hugh McGlocklan; Martin Hartell; John Roser; Martin Snider;
Andrew Stiffer; Frederick Stair; George Winters. [Md. Hist. Soc., MS 1146]

Return of Capt. Adam Ott's Company of Select Militia in Washington County
Capt. Adam Ott; Lieutt. Nicholas Shockey; Ensign John Simkins
Sargts: Andrew Clinesmith (Clieresmith); Hezekiah Clagett; Daniel Nied
Corps.: John Barkman; Jonathan Hagar; Jacob Craver
Drum. John Everly
Fife - Conrod Cofferath
Privates: Robert Douglass; William Boyd(?) Junr; John Blackburn; Peter
Swoop; John Fisher; John Sheimer; Jacob Aue; Daniel Miller; James Williams;
John Righter; Michael Collyflower; Henry Schnebely; Daniel Carneira; William
Baird Junr; George Kershner; Lawrence Mishlar; Henry Queer; George Tangler;
Jacob Wolfkill John Stack; Jacob Boom; John Schnebly; Adam Stertzman;
Leonard Adleman; Nicholas Huet; Isaac McFaddin; David Whetstone; Jacob
Heflybower; John Snider; Henry Scyster; Jacob Cruiz; Jacob Bowman; Jacob
Wyory; John Easter; Christian Hockey; Peter Conn; George Overacre; George
Simkins; Benjamin Pennybaker; John Cline; William Pulling; Martin Divelly;
Adam Bower; Martin Pifer; Jeremiah Hoss. [Md. Hist. Soc., MS 1146]

A List of Capt. James Wallings Company as now Class. No. 5, Second Battn.
Capt. James Walling; 1 Lietn. James Patterson; 2 Lietn. John Rutter; Ensign
John Simkins; 1 Sergt. Perry McCoy; 2d do. Joseph Drake; 3 do. Thomas
Winders; 4 do. William Rutter
1 Corperel Henry Lourie; 2 do. George Lefler; 3 do. Daniel Conrod; 4 do.
Michael Shekly
1 Class: James Dunwoody; Joseph McCoy; Jacob Tudewiler; Mark Beaty; Jacob
Warner; (blank) Woulf; John Gearhart; Robert Forker; Christian Dailing
2d Class: John McCoy son Daniel; George Bond Junr; Joseph Fitch; Charles
McGill; John Hany; Jacob Stover; Samuel Trantle; George Whitemire; John
Direling
3d Class: Samuel Funk; Charles Mungomery; Henry Sullems; Henry Snyder; John
Winders; John Oair; Abraham House Junr; Henry Kenister; Francis Garner

WASHINGTON COUNTY

4th Class: John Bouman; Archibald McCoy; Daniel Speace; David Bear; Lowdick Keidy; Gasper Loughman; Peter Witzell
5 Class: Daniel Booker; Lott Darling; James McCoy; John Ingham; George Kessinger; Edmond Rutter Junr; Jacob Tridle; John Knave; Valentine Messersmith
6th Class: Jacob Rice; William Baird; Jacob Martain; Henry Knave; Alexander Rutter; Aron Donaldson; Jacob Avery; Daniel Haller
7th Class: Charles Bell; William Cummings; John Avey; Christopher Newcommer; George Hyman; David Glister; Benjn. Bowman; John Bond
8th Class: Daniel McCoy; Henry Funk; John McCoy son Archild.; Daniel Windless; Henry Newcommer; Joseph Perrin; Delashmett Walling; Isaac Houser; Walter Bond. [Md. Hist. Soc., MS 1146]

A List of Capt. Jeremiah Spires's Compy. as now Classd. No. 8, Second Battn.
Capt. Jeremiah Spires N.B. First Lieut. advanced to Capt.   John is ...other. officers... ???
1 Lietn. Amos Davis; 2 Lietn. John Fowler; Ensign Laven Dorsey
1 Sergent. James Luckett; 2 do. Jeremiah Jacobs; 3 do. Aron Lacklan; 4 do. Dennis Davis
1 Corperel Samuel Luckett; 2 do. Edward Shahan; 3 do. Joshua Fowler; 4 do. John Wade
1st Class: Henry Mahoney; Henry Barns Junr; Thomas Hudgin; Edward Dyall; Gabriel Baker; Phillinor Farmer; Zachariah Roads; John McClane
2 Class: Michael Stonebraker; David Barns; Meshack Baker; Samuel Kelly; James Talbert; Henry Farmer; John Garhart; Silvanus Barns
3d Class: John Mance; Bartholomew Carrico; John Knode Junr; Simon Doyle; Daniel Cally; William Roby; William Silby; Joseph Evy
4th Class: Michael Miller; Michael Cap; Green Gilpin; Zebediah Baker; Nathan Barnes; Michael Walmore; Hezekiah Barnes; Richard James
5th Class: Peter Palmore; Henry Wade; William Willson; Michael Hains Ruby; Nathan Edmonson; Thomas Hez. Luckett; William Coefer
6th Class: George Gantz; Morris Baker; Joseph Hains; Isaac Ridgley; William Roads; Archibald McKinley; Joseph Waters
7th Class: Jacob Knave; Nathan Petticord Senr; Nathan Petticord Junr; Joshua Barns Junr; Thomas Owens; Samuel Fletcher
8th Class: John Carrico; William Kendell; Phillip Hains; Joshua Barns; Ezekiel Barns; Basil Carrico. [Md. Hist. Soc., MS 1146]

A List of Capt James Smiths Compy as now Class.   Second Battn. No. 4
1 Liet. Robert Smith; 2 do. Christian Ekell; Ensign Peter Mellott (not fit)
1 Sergt. Benjn. South; 2 do. Thomas Melott (fit for a officer)
1 Corpl. John Cross
1st Class: John Lowman; Jacob Knode (Knoe?); George Benhard; Christr. Sidner; John Cofield; Jacob Witrick; William Chiney; Andrew Beontrer; David Funk; Ephaim Shiles Junr
2d Class: William Crossley; John Lieter; George Lower; Ignatious Simms; Ignatious Knott; Leonard Woolf; Ezekiel Chiney; James Kirkpatrick; George Kishman; Aron Bowman
3d Class: Thomas Powell; Christian Avey; George Mies; James Urvin; Benjn. Melott; John Chiney; Jacob Brown; Peter Palmour; John Neldie; Jacob Neldie

APPENDIX B: MUSTER ROLLS AND OTHER LISTS

4th Class: Peter Slouser; Henry Hoofman; Peter Evie; George Spurringer; John Moore; George Davis; Ludwick Comgrome; William Skeles; James Crossley
5th Class: Adam Migsove; John Lovens; Valentine Stonebraker; Conrod Seavner; George Powell; Theodotious Melatt; John White; Joseph Funk; Daniel Bowman
6th Class: John Shaver; John Bennit; Joseph Huskings; William Adams; Jeremiah Chiney; William Kirkpatrick; Nicholas Rese(?)
7th Class: Valentine Paphenbarger; Christian Neldie; Mathias Knode; Jacob Petay; Francis Gaven; Michael Caye; Frederick Sidner; Martin Kishman
8th Class: William Shellers; Arthur Ohara; John Putman; Jacob George; Thomas Lazier; Jacob Saulgiber; Jacob Woolf; Nathan Chiney. [Md. Hist. Soc., MS 1146]

First Battn. Capt. Bells Compy. No. 2
A List of Capt. Peter Bells Compy. as now Classd.
Capt. Peter Beall; 1 Lieut. Jacob Ott; 2 do. Michael Ott; Ensign William Conrod; 1 Sergeant Frederick Roser; 2. do John Stonecyfer; 3. do Martin Fifer; 4. do Peter Sailer; 1 Corporal Simon Househalter; 2. do Peter Hout, 3 do. John Conn; 4. do Jacob Fisher Junr
1st Class: Adam Dile; Nathaniel Morgan; Jonas Emerick; William Bishop; Martin Funk; Peter Smith; Peter Hess; Francis Cryley
2d Class: Rudolph Pligh(?); Dewalt Celhoffer; Jost. Wyant; William Muffett (Mussett?); Henry Wykell; Thomas Leveings(?); Peter Hoak; Peter Croft
3d Class: Abraham Bower; John Oster; Phillip Hornish; Martin Harry; Jacob Craver; Andrew Miller; Peter Hefley; Frederick Croft
4th Class: Jacob Harry; Michael Fesler; Jonathan Harry; Jonathan Hayer; Balzer Gull; George Arnold; John Sailer; Henry Mull
5th Class: Peter Woltz; Joseph Cline; Henry Bowert; Phillip Reefnaugh; Martin Stake; Harmon Criley; Isaac Cnady; John Funk
6th Class: Melchar Bellhover; Francis Wagoner; David Harry; Jacob Nicholl; Thomas Rinehart; John Snyder; Phillip Oster; John Howard
7th Class: Jacob Rozer; William Scott; Henry Tootwiler; John Rage; Earnst Ditz; Adam Ott; John Parks; Phillip Creeybam(?)
8th Class: Joseph Hindman; Thomas Shoeman; John Onsell; George Dill; George Rinehart; Jacob Wirey; John Wise. [Militia Lists of Daus. of Founders and Patriots, held by Md. Hist. Soc.]

Second Battn. Capt John Renolds Compy No. 2
A List of Capt. John Renolds Compy. as now Classd.
Capt. John Renolds; 1 Liet. Abraham Baker; 2. do Christopher Orendorff; Ensign William Walker; 1 Sergent Frederick Knisterick; 2. do Leonard Hinkle; 3. do David Grove; 4. do Thomas Stuart; 1 Corporal George Hick(?); 2. do Peter Ekle; 3. do James Melon; 4. do Jacob Russell junr
1st Class: Francis Renold; Jacob Piper (Farmer); John Hoffman; Jeremiah Foster; John Bark; Robert Crummy; Michael Carnes; David Meek; John Banks
2d Class: Jacob Schoff; Joseph Reynolds (son John); George Fleck; George Shuman; Thomas Smith; Thomas Wiles; John O. Doniel; William Stockwell
3d Class: George Wukle (Wickle?); Phillip Thaman; John Melone Junr; James Black; Tiller Younger; Henry Smith; John Middcalf(?) Junr
4th Class: Conrod Hinkle; Jacob Bimson (Brinson?); William Nowell Junr; Joseph Nowell; John Black; Henry Smith; James Graham; Ludwick Michael
5th Class: Samuel Donelson; Richard Moore; William Easten; Henry Sook

WASHINGTON COUNTY

6th Class: Peter Graybill; Joseph Reynolds son Willm.; Moses Hobins; Michael Hoffman; Clement Pearce; Jacob Clam; Joseph James
7th Class: Thomas Newell; Jacob Hoofman; Andrew Thomas; George Painter; Samuel Wolgamot Junr; Adam Pashanbarger; Henry Pashanbarger; Michael Clainle(?)
8th Class: John Shuman Junr; James Melone; Nicholas Walker; William Codd; George Russell; George Gerick; Andrew Flack; Peter Jolly. [Militia Lists of Daus. of Founders and Patriots, held by Md. Hist. Soc.]

Capt. Daniel Cresap; 1 Liet. Samuel Hubbs; 2 do John Hench; Ensign Joseph Inlow; 1 Sergt John Coy Senr; 2 do John Kennady; 3 do John Rubart; 4 do Aaron Huffman; 1 Corpl. John Eatherington; 2 do Reynon Bowman; 3 do Peter Duwitt; 4 do Benjn. Quick
1st Class: Joshua Eatherington; William Caster; Samuel Fergeston; Edward Dawson Junr; William Lee
2d Class: John Marshall; James Tomlinson; Thomas Quick; Samuel Lee; Moses Munrow; John Bacorn; William Ray; Jeremiah Anderson
3d Class: Gaspert. Dust; Benjn. Eatherington; Elijah Keykindell; Samuel Clifton; Abraham Blew; William Dawson Senr; Thomas Dawson; Benjn. James
4th Class: William Dawson Junr; Timothy Trasey; Joseph Collard; Edward Dawson; James Dawson Junr; Samuel Right; Richard Ruth; Samuel Hannah
5th Class: Zephaniah Beall; Moses Hufman; Evan James; Joseph Mounce; Barton Lovett; Joseph Davis; Allom Dawson; David Smith
6th Class: Reynon Bowman; John Coy Junr; Aaron Eatherington; Thomas Fields; Cornelious Ward; Moses Ayres Junr; Michael Heater; Nehemiah Martin
7th Class: Henry Cuntryman; Henry Dewitt; John Baken; Joseph Creysop; William Ogle; Josiah Lee Junr; Ebenezer Davis; Josiah Anderson
8th Class: James Dawson Senr; Jonathan Culver; Terrence Dial; James Williams; George Saport(?); William Markwell; Isaac Titsword(?); Peter Countryman; Robert Munrow. [Militia Lists of Daus. of Founders and Patriots, held by Md. Hist. Soc.]

A List of the Officers & Men in Capt. Joseph Chapline's Compy.
1 Lieut. James Chapline; 2 do Thomas Crampton; Ensign James Stewart
1st Class: John Norris; George Linganfelder; Lewis Wilson; John Hymes; Peter Wagoner; Peter Hill; Peter Myres; Thomas McKoy; Thomas Jackson; Daniel Beall
2d Class: Robert Cammel; William Whitemire; Frederick Cairns; Andrew Hymes; George Deale; James McNutt; James Fitch; William Roberts; William McNutt; William Patterson
3d Class: Jacob Tussy; John Duncan; George Bower; Edward Power; William Bradford; Barnard McNutt; Robert Huflman; David Jackson; Thomas Jones
4th Class: Benedict Igonder; Frederick Fox; David Miller; Peter Wise; Jacob Walter; Robert McNutt; Bennona Swearengan; William Reed; Frederick Mirs (Moss?);
5th Class: Henry Igonder; Michael Fox; Jacob Sulf; William Renwick; Jacob Saintaman; Alexr. McNutt; James McKoy Junr; John Ferguson Junr; Raymon Shanton
6th Class: Phillip Smith; Philip Deale; William Strider; Conrod Highburger; Frederick Myres; Joseph Morrison; Robert Renwick; Ozias Crampton; Henry Boyer

APPENDIX B: MUSTER ROLLS AND OTHER LISTS

7th Class: Michael Marker; Ludwick Crotzinger; John Mahaman; Abraham Highbarger; John Wilkins; Thomas Sheapheard; James Norman; Ignatious Thompson; George Myre
8th Class: Varner Hatnick; Teter Wise; Leonard Spong; Daniel Branch; Jacob Bruner; George Fredk. Waterbager; John McKoy; John Burroughs; Moses Chapline. [Militia Lists of Daus. of Founders and Patriots, held by Md. Hist. Soc.]

Capt. Barnett Johnston; 1 Lietn. Phillip Pindell; 2 do Thomas Hines; Ensign Robert Ford; 1 Sergt. Jacob Jones; 2 do Dugal Campbell; 3 do Abraham Cox; 4 do Richard Acton; 1 Corpl. John Flint; 2 do Jeremiah Silwell; 3 do William Sewell; 4 do John Powell
1st Class: Simon Saradeham; Samuel Mount; David Mackmans; John Ham; William Yates; Thomas Pindell; William Welsh; John Gallagough; Samuel Putts; William Wiggins
2d Class: Thomas Muggs; Isaac Cox; Charles Anderson; Phillip Howard; Evan Gines; William Johnson; George Sterronton; Uriah Wiggins; George Barringhart; John Burgess
3d Class: Morress Burnitt; Daniel Anderson; Michael Gillsat(?); Jacob Stein(?); Joel John; John Norriss; James King; Thomas Phelps; James Mills; Benja. Johnson
4th Class: John Sugart; John Powell; John Wiggins; Thomas Norriss; John King; Jacob Cox; Robert Smith; Leonard Beans; John Longnaker; William Sewell
5th Class: William Martin; Joseph Martin; Nathaniel Tarter; John Gillipis; Joseph Hust; Robert Clarke; Samuel Jones; John Flint; Thomas Lamster; William Harrison Junr
6th Class: John Mount; Even Mires; Daniel Dunisin; John Meloney; William Adams; Samuel Sayes; William Martin; Richard Flora Junr; Mainyard Rockwell; Henry Right
7th Class: William Skinner; Thomas Righdout; John Wegg; Joseph Valganote(?); James Malcomb; Thomas Jacques; William Stockwell; John Dunnisin; George James; Francis Wareman
8th Class: James Tinsley; Thomas Bean; Mathias Otto; Peter Snider; Robert Tawch(?); John Sinn; William Mathews; John Snider; Jacob Lover; Henry Bean; Archibald Brison. [Militia Lists of Daus. of Founders and Patriots, held by Md. Hist. Soc.]

Capt. James Prather; 1 Lietn. Thomas Humphrys; 2 do. Joseph Reed; Ensign Charles Prather; 1 Sergt. Thomas Punsell; 2 do John Clarke; 3 do Samuel Posselwaite; 4 do John Bowman; 1 Corpl John Kinnely; 2 do Benjn. Pierce; 3 do. Christian Snidwar; 4 do Richard Chinsoth; Drumr. Elisha Clarke; Fifer Valentine Horne
1st Class: Isaac Colliar; John Baker; Benja. Poore; Thomas Hollett; John Hartley; James Stotherd; Richard Matinlee; Thomas Wiggins; Joseph Groves
2d Class: John Beall; Timothy Downing; John Hollett; William Clowse; Barzilla Clarke; Robert Shephard; Peter Parker; William Grimes; John Constable
3d Class: John Faits; William Ray(?); John Scott; Michael Collier; James Poore; William Posselwait; William Chinoath(?); James Hill; Jonathan Irons
4th Class: James Prather; David Cossart; James Cragg; Samuel Shephard; John Commings; Thomas Johnson; John Jones

WASHINGTON COUNTY

5th Class: William Gorden; George French; Phillip Tramill; George Miller; John Grimes; Thomas Constable; (space) Graverod; Thomas Parvin
6th Class: John Shephard; John Punsell; Caleb Russell; Senica Murakin; Isaac Lamaster; Daniel Pierce; Joseph Nicholls
7th Class: Jeramiah Allan; Ersley Poore; William Cowen; George Callay; Stephen Constable; (blank) Fisher
8th Class: Henry Conrod; James Pierce; Gabriel Jacobs; Joshua Stratford; William Beall; James Shepheard; Thomas Giztey (Girtey?); James Gesott.
[Militia Lists of Daus. of Founders and Patriots, held by Md. Hist. Soc.]

Capt. Griffith Johnston; 1 Lietn. Jeremiah Willison; 2 do Andrew Dew; Ensign William Moore; 1 Sergt. Jessey Barkshire; 2 do Thomas Hullock; 3 do Samuel Robonitt; 4 do Thomas Allen; 1 Corpl Richard Barkshire; 2 do Jacob Flaker; 3 do George Moore; 4 do Moses Robonitt
1 Class: Obediah Jushey; John Moore; William House; Elisha Robinitt; Edward Willison; Joseph Lasher; Phillip Pindergrass; Peter Snider
2d Class: Moses Robinett; Cornelious Willison; Jacob Flake; Joseph Robinett; Henry Bean; Henry Warman; Laurance Pendergrass; William Pury
3d Class: Moses Robinett; Basil Purill(?); William Davinslary(?); James Shugans; George Moore Junr; Thomas Bean; George Hollaway; Michael Sniveley
4th Class: John Evans; Henry Berkshire; Patrick Cavanner; Hezekiah Hyatt; Robert Twigg; Robert Pendergrass; Samuel Hayes
5th Class: Robert Faulker; Thomas Allen; John Burkshire; John Lasher; Joseph Lasher Junr; Francis Twigg; Francis Worman; Thomas Shaws
6th Class: Richard Burkshire; George Miller; William Crabtree; Michael Stockwell; William Swales; Richard Reed; James Cambell; Robert Wells
7th Class: George Moore; Samuel Robinett; Ezekiel Robinett; John Willison Junr; Richard Willison Junr; Truman Jarrett (Jarvett?); John Twigg; Ezekiel Beavis
8th Class: Mathew Rice (Rue?); John Grimes; Richard Willison Senr; John Willison Senr. [Militia Lists of Daus. of Founders and Patriots, held by Md. Hist. Soc.]

We whose names are thereunto Subscribd do Inrole ourselves into a Company of Militia agreable to the Resolves of the Provincial Convention held at the City of Annapolis this 26th Day of July 1775. We do hereby promise and Engage that we will Respectfully March to such places within this province and at such times as we shall be commanded by the Convention or Council of this Province or by our officers in pursuance of the said orders of the Convention or Cousill of Safety and there with our whole might fight against whomesoever we shall be Commanded by such Authority as aforesaid -- Witness our hands this 28th Day of Augt. 1776...

Charles Coulson, Capt.; George Richardson, Lieut; Edward Grimes, Lieut.; Peter Williams, Insign; Edward Derbin, Sergt; John Derbin, Sergt.; Aaron Parker, Sergt.; Jacob Quick, Sergt.; William Derbin, Corpl; Dennis Quick, Corpl; Gasper Banager, Corpl; Henry Porter, Corpl; Jacob Froman; Tean Friend; John Friend; William Ashby; Martin Miller; Jessy Tomlinson; James Smith; James Tomlinson; Peter Wampole; Zeb. Hogg; Jacob Ruple; James Noseland (Hogeland?); Stephen Workman; Isaac Workman; Jacob Workman; John Workman; Benjamin Murdock; Thos. Cancannon; Joseph Workman; Andrew Workman;

APPENDIX B: MUSTER ROLLS AND OTHER LISTS

John Glassner; Richard Trotter; Dennis Carter; Thomas Jones; Philip Crow; Godfrey Richards; Joseph Logston; William Logston; Thomas Logston; Timothy Conner; Leonard Reed; George Otter; Henry Matley; John Sap; Andrew Quick; Thomas Quick; Britten Lovett; Joseph Collard; Jacob Crow; Robert Gregg Junr; Robt Gregg Senr; James Tittle; Henry Wheeler; John Lindsey; Robart Parker; George Glassner; John Crow; Sampson Winn; Goodfree Wolfhart; Isaac Richards; Pall(?) Welker; Andrew Welker   [Md. Hist Soc MS 1146]

A List of Capt Basil Williams Compy as now Classd
Capt Williams; 1 Lieutn Joshua Barnes; 2 do Zapheniah Spires; Ensign Zadock Williams; 1 Sergent Elisha Hiatt; 2 do Peter Barnes; 3 do Elisha Lackland; 4 do. Jonathan Simmons; 1 Corporal William Hays; 2 do. Able Barnes; 3 do. Rignal Prather; 4 do Basil Williams
Tarott Williams; Joseph Clark Junr; Phillip Salladay; John Brown; Basil Roads; Peter Tuter Junr; John Grant; Christian Answinger
2d Class: Frederick Bower; Abraham Miller; Vachel Gaither; Thomas Bateman; John Bateman Senr; Jacob Tuter; Richard Jams; John Tuter
3d Class: Phillip Hester; Clement Howard; Jacob Walker; Ezekiel Roads; Phillip Tarr; Martin Hoover; John Downing Senr; Alian Miller
4th Class: John Phelps; George Fogle; Peter Plecher; George Styer; Henry Spangle; Francis Tuter; Henry Hoover; William Clark
5 Class: Edward Shawness; Francis Akord; Michael Hargil; John Pottenger; Henry Nave; Jeremiah Wells; John Downing Junr
6th Class: John Baptist Kendle; Jost Plecher; John Saladay; Frederick Savety; Phillip Fectar; James Quinton; Hugh Lamaster
7th Class: Balsar Passenback; John Gaither; Christian Fye; Ludwick Myers; John Bateman Junr; David Woodhouse
8th Class: Lawrance Williams; Eleven Williams; William Smith; Adam Myer; Richard Simmons; Levy Simmons   [Md Hist. Soc MS 1146]

A List of Capt. Hogmires Compy as now Classd
Capt Hogmire; 1 Lietn. John Charlton; 2 Lietn Martin Ridenour; Ensign Mathias Hickman; 1 Sergent. Richard Allender; 2 do George Ridnour; 3 do Daniel Perry; 4 do William Webb; 1 Corperel Peter Shaver; 2 do John Webb Junr; 3 do Ludwick Riple; 4 do John Coaler
1st Class: Peter Kaiser; Phillip Baird; James Dunwoody; Christopher Hyple; Peter Lighter; Phillip Stamburgh; Joshua Hixs; David Elliott; John Good
2d Class: Adam Woolheader; Michael Kaiser; Thomas Estler; George Gontz; Jacob Gontz Junr; Adam Hahn
2d Class: George Lambert Junr; Peter Newcomer
3d Class: Jacob Fose; Goodheart Fausett; Christian Kingreigh(?); John Nicewonger; William Stone; James Flack; Nicholas Honsaker; George May
4th Class: Christopher Good; George Tom; Henry Hoover; William Mock; Michael Mencer; Valentine Shockey; Peter Winling
5th Class: Phillip Burkett; Henry Darby; John Hoover Junr; Allen McDonneld; Casper Booker; Frederick Howard; Jacob Shaver
6th Class: Jacob Bumgarner; Joseph Gontz; John Darby; Abraham Good; George Coaler Junr; Richard Anderson; Andrew Branstreter; Thomas Charlton
7th Class: Samuel Sanders; John Fegate; George Burkett; Morris Baker; Henry Bronce; Christian Lantz; Christopher Stover
8th Class: Andrew Baugh; Henry Fose; Jacob Houk; Davolt Mong; John Sides; Michael Fose; George Hardweigh.   [Md. Hist. Soc., MS 1146]

WASHINGTON COUNTY

Capt Charles Clinton; 1 Lietn. Dickinson Simpkins; 2 do John House; Ensign David Swank
1 Sergt. Joshua Switchfield; 2 do. Silas Simpkins; 3 do. Stephen Workman; 4 do. Jacob Quick
1 Corpl. Thomas Thairman; 2 do. Thomas Cordry; 3 do. Peter Bonhan; 4 do. George Glasener
1st Class: Peter Williamms; Aaron Parker; John Landrey Junr; Dennis Quick; Robert Parker; Edward Dubin; John Delang; Bartin Laman
2d Class: Godfrey Richards; Nicholas Dubin; John Workman; Lowden Trotter; Thomas Kincannon; Moses Gooding; John Lowman; Frederick Valentine; Samuel McKinsey
3d Class: John Crow; James Winters; Timothy Conner; Henry Potter; Joshua Davis; Thomas Plummer; Godfrey Woolford; Benjn. Stanton
4th Class: Thomas Thairman; Leonard Reed; Henry Matley; Gabriel McKinsey; Thomas Logston; Jacob Warkman; John Laisher; Michael Stanton; Aaron Freeland
5th Class: George Glasner; Alexander Meloney; Cornelius Devour; Edward Grimes; William Longston; Isaac Workman; William Workman; Dennis Carter; Calip Luman; William Ruggles
6th Class: Andrew Quick; Jacob Shouth; George Young; Edward Jecons; Benjn. Gooding; Joseph Gooding; Benjn. Nicholls; Thomas Johnston; Gilbreath Willson; Lewis Davis; Robert Gregg Senr; Robert Gregg Junr; Charles Colson; Jacob Crow; Daniel McKinsey; George Richardson; Andrew Workman; Aaron McKinsey
8th Class: Thomas Cordry; Peter Banham; Isaac Laycock; Jacob Mossley; John Durbin; John Glassner; William Durbin; Joshua Luman. [Md. Hist. Soc., MS 1146]

A List of Capt. Facklers Compy. as now Class.
Capt. Fackler; 1 Lietn. John Shryock; 2. do Leonard Shryock; Ensign Michael Domer; 1 Sergent. Nicholas Hockey; 2 do. Michael Divle; 3 do. Andrew Baggs; 4 do. Benjn. Campbell
1 Corperel John Leydia; 2 do Jacob Woolslayer; 3 do. Adam Wiry; 4 do. Frederick Hiskell
1st Class: Francis Burgiss; Conroad Sheets; John Winkencome; John Hinds; John Simon; William Pullin; Thomas Long; Edward Woods
2d Class: Phillip Dusinger; Samuel Young; Jacob Wisner; Peter Wagoner; Adam Smith; Daniel Nead; John Barnes
3d Class: Christian Shock; John Ragan; John Robinson; Jacob Earhart; William Conner; David Furney; Peter Con; Hugh Mackardell
4th Class: Noah Hart; Manuel Piper; Nicholas Upp; Frederick Ware; Michael Ernest; George Wise; Joseph Sprigg; Peter Eversole
5th Class: Casper Potterff; William Brown; Christopher Trupp; Isaac Reu; John Harry; Luke Fister; Henry Monninger; Christian Rorer
6th Class: Leonard Nave; William Pope; Jacob Lowrey; Daniel Beall; John Harman; Michael Frentle; Bostian Power; Hugh Hagan; Harmon Claper
7th Class: George Smith; Phelix Moyer; John Woodcock; Peter Linn; Michael Lowrey Junr; John Blackburn; John Smith; Adam Stasman; Henry Miller
8th Class: Michael Nave; George Linn; John Fackler; Peter Hose; Thomas Sprigg; John White; Paul Chistman; (blank) Caller; (blank) Riley. [Md. Hist. Soc., MS 1146]

APPENDIX B: MUSTER ROLLS AND OTHER LISTS

A List of Capt. John Bennets Compy. as now Class.
1 Lietn. William Hill; 2 do. David Jones; Ensign Peter Brough; 1 Sergent.
Mordica Madden; 2 do. Henry Ash; 3 do. Jeremiah Jack; 4 do. Balser Mondy
1 Corperel John Shnider; 2 do. George Gull; 3 do. George Kisinger; 4 do.
John Bonnett
1st Class: Frederick Raimer; William Paul; Henry Claycomb; Thomas Charlton;
Mathias Smisar; James Prather; Joseph More; Peter Wilan; George Rough
2d Class: William Blackburn; Hugh Gillaland; Joseph Boyd; Jacob Oster; Peter
Wart; Adam Fisher; Leonard Trumpour; Casper Hoofman; David Conner
3d Class: Casper Snider; Richard Hallett; Richard Menson; Peter Oster;
Thomas McCollum; Nicholas Nisbitt; Jacob Snider; Mathias Wellbarger; Peter
Rough
4th Class: John Jack; George Miller; Christophel Erret; Abraham Tonner;
Andrew Sparling; Phillip Potturff; Nicholas Rufe; John King
5th Class: Phillip Fetfer; John Mondy; Joseph Smith; John Gilbert; John
Oster; Godfree Painter; Henry Stutts; Joseph Firey
6th Class: John Sollomon Miller; Thomas McMacken; Michael Fivicoat; Thomas
Prather; Joseph Brough; Mathias Rufe; John Anthony; Jacob Haines
7th Class: William Black; Jacob Heston; Joseph Thompson; David Pattorf;
William Jones; James McClane; John Magee; Thomas Gillispie
8th Class: Phillip Reaplogle (Reaylogle?); John Pry; Phillip More; James
Strong; George Young; Felix Leer(?). [Md. Hist. Soc., MS 1146]

A List of Capt. John Collars Compy. as now Classd.
1 Lietn. John McLaughlan; 2d do. Ludwick Young; Ensign George Callar
1 Sergent Luke Sholey; 2 do. John Gillespie; 3 do. Henry Miller; 4 do.
George Dunn
1 Corperel Jacob Barnt; 2 do. Adam Cammen; 3 do. Neel Dougherty; 4 do. Jacob
Crisse(?)
1st Class: Henry Ridenour; Daniel Miller; Phillip Renner; John Mowing; Peter
Rentch; John Rentch (son Joseph); John Miller (son Hance); Simon Kesinger;
John Miller (son Conrod)
2d Class: John Adams; Michael Shank; Abraham Gansinger; William Berryhill;
Jacob Studebaker; Henry Miller (son Hance); Charles Heffle; Abraham Miller;
Thomas Ruten
3d Class: Henry Foard; Peter Adams; Abraham Lidey; John Grabral; Henry
Stoneking; Daniel Cammer; Adam Coon; Stephen Mowing; John Frike; George
Tenglen
4th Class: George Derr; Christian Shank Jnr.; Henry Shnebley Junr; Ludwick
Cameron; Conrod Brandlinger; David Miller; Stephen Miller; John Clapper
(Stiller); James Foard; James Watson - in margin: Joseph Piper
5th Class: Henry Shnebley; Jacob Miller (son of Conrod); Daniel Cossert;
Daniel Muffett; Jacob Young; Rudoph Roof; Henry John Snyder; John Miller
Dunken; Abraham Prifhen; George Boughman
6th Class: Martin Bachley; John Miller (son Jacob); Jacob Brumbough Junr;
John Clapper; George Charles; John Rentch; Phillip Kessaken; Michael
Prushelbaugh
7th Class: Henry Culp; Christian Alder; John Jilanard; Henry Houser; James
Pints; Teaten Barnes; John Hagan; Nicholas Caw - added in margin: Michael
Householder
8th Class: John Class; Rudolph Jilanard; John Shnebley; Christian Shank
Senr; Jacob Miller (son Jacob); Jacob Adams; Nicholas Smith; John Henry

WASHINGTON COUNTY

Clapper; Adam Hooraw; David Conner; Robert Foard - [added in margin]; William Sprouts; John Pickelman. [Md. Hist. Soc., MS 1146]

A List of Capt. Bakers Compy. as now Classd.
Capt. Isaac Baker; 1 Lietn. (blank); 2 Lietn. (blank); Ensign. (blank)
1 Sergent. Josiah Price; 2 do. Andrew Potterf; 3 do. John Millhouse; 4 do. Thomas Worley
1 Corperel Jno. Mcfall; 2 do. Jacob Syvert; 3 do. Fras. Campbell; 4 do. David Kennedy
1st Class: Patrick Malarry; Samuel Wallace; John Becklehimer; David Statsman; James Maze; Peter Bruner; Christr. Whetstone; John Rowland; Walter Beatty; Martin Pottarff; Daniel Statsman
2d Class: William Baker; John Burk; William Morrison; James Dixon; Paul Huston; Robert Campbell; Phillip Dile; William Jones; Henry Cow; David Harbison
3d Class: Frederick Devarn; George Cruthers; David Hilderbrand; Daniel Miller; Frederick Shackler; Balser Young; Michael Carnan; Phillip Davis; Phillip Creag; Stephen Wobrey Junr
4th Class: Peter Albright; David Bread; Samuel Reed; James McGlanglen; Nicholas Fitzgerald; Isaac Teeter; John Hippenliser; John Huston; John Campbell
5th Class: Boston Davis; Daniel Campbell; Christopher Thomas; Felix Leer; James Adair; John Snyder; John Harmuell; Shaderick Williams; John Baker; Peter Shaver; Jacob Snyder
6th Class: Paul Shaver; Adam Troup; John Heatherington; Phillip Hilderbrand; Godfree Helson; Michael Mullen; Ossias Welch; Thomas Blackburn; Thomas Essix
7th Class: Thomas Mugg; William Worley; John Kephart; Jacob Stockey; Maths. Crow; James Maxwell; James Blair; Joseph Cughs; Frederick Reever; Henry Augle
8th Class: Mathias Willberger; Francis Killough; William Mackey; George Kswable (Kevable?); Henry Butterbaugh; Peter Carnan; Jacob Teeter; Simon Pottarff; Jacob Cow; John Jacob Syvert; Henry Ornest. [Md. Hist. Soc., MS 1146]

A List of Capt. Martin Kershners Compy.
1 Lietn. John Kershner; 2 do. David Kershner; Ensign Jacob Hix
1 Sergent. David Ridenour; 2 do. Jacob Kibler; 3 do. Adam Miller; 4 do. David Wolgamaot
1 Corperel Nicholas Ridenour; 2 do. David Coone; 3 do. Alexander McClanahan; 4 do. Jacob Tisher; Bearnhard Tant (Phifer)
1st Class: David Miller; Nicholas Boone; Martin Etenire; John McTarden; Daniel Tisher; John Nicewonder; Thomas Meek; Angle Gansburger
2nd Class: Michael Bowe; Christian Cose(?); Joseph Stup; Conrod Oster; Phillip Kershner; Martin Ridenour; John Washerbaugh; Walter Boyd
3d Class: Michael Akcringbarger; Henry Tice; Adam Lidy; Jacob Bincklar; Abraham Troxell Junr; Henry Ridenour; Balser Peter; Adam Hartman; Henry Calklazer
4th Class: George Troxell; John Rush; Nicholas Martin; Jacob Hoghanour; Jacob Asby; David Conner; John Wirtman; Mathias Snoak; Henry Wisoger
5th Class: John Miller; John Bowman; Martin Rigenbough; Thomas Jones; George Oblenoner; Frederick Basel; Jacob Shup; Frederick Shanefin; George Friend

APPENDIX B: MUSTER ROLLS AND OTHER LISTS

6th Class: Nicholas Long; Jonathan Jones; John Long Junr; Conrod Brown; Henry Cuntryman; Even Lowis; Andrew Postater; Phillip Friend Junr; Stophel Friend
7th Class: George McClane; Michael Young; Jacob Jones; Henry Fairman; Jacob Hur; David Meek; John Tisher; John Gutry Junr; Lodwick Ridenour
8th Class: Jacob Tiller; Leonarhart Phifer; Jacob Ridenour; Phillip Alanger; Peter Gensberger; Christopher Fox; Henry Statsman Junr; Peter Bragoner; Joseph Hixon. [Md. Hist. Soc., MS 1146]

A List of Capt. Jacob Sarers Compy. as now Classd.
Capt Jacob Sarer; 1 Lietn. George Sarer; 2 Lietn. John Funk; Ensign John Bowlen; 1 Sergnt. Joseph Price; 2. do. Isaac Sharer; 3 do. Baustin Baker; ; 4 do. Edmond Rutter Jnr; 1 Corperel Christopher Tilhart; 2 do. Jacob Pence; 3 do. John Monninger; 4 do. Thomas Brooke Junr
1 Class: Thomas Brooke Senr; Peter Creger; John Foster; Frederick Flaker; Frederick Keger Junr; Jacob Rockenbaugh; Peter Smith; Phillip Shilling; William Jennings
2 Class: Phillip Brigh; Thomas Meckelfish; Robert Martin; David Smith; James Winders; Daniel Whetstone; Daniel Cyster; Abraham Eversole; Jacob Hoover Junr
3 Class: Henry Youst; Martin Clabback; Martin Shultz; John Troutman; John Lee; Jacob Hoofman; William Ax(?); John Wagoner; John Westerbarger
4 Class: Jacob Cowman; John Fague; George Fague; Henry Plumb; Andrew Potts; Henry Cyster; George Smith; Henry Roland
5th Class: George Barnhart; Peter Mock; Adam Shoop; William Lee; George Custer; Valentine Woltzlager; Jacob Swank; Jacob Hoover Senr
6th Class: George Bower; Phillip Gable; Richard Mackelfish; Jacob Root; Gerrett Stonebraker; John Swank; Jacob Zacharias; James Craton
7th Class: John Direworth; William Kinets; Peter Sarer; Martin Shackley; John Wageley; Christopher Walker; William Foye; John Hoover
8th Class: Phillip Earhart; Jacob Smith; Mathias Harshman; Abraham Earleywine; Richard Laurance; Jacob Cyster; Mathias Rye. [Md. Hist. Soc., MS 1146]

A List of Capt. Peter Swingles Compy. (No. 3, Second Balttn.) as now Classd.
1 Lietn. John Householder; 2 do. Nicholas Mourer; Ensign John Horne; 1 Sergt. John Shell; 2 do. Thomas Carter; 3 do. Michael Stover; 4 do. Daniel Creamer
1 Corpl. Godfrey Creamer; 2 do. Henry Mahorney; 3 do. Nicholas Andrews; 4 do. George Graver
1st Class: John Wagoner; Michael Miller; John Bean; Christian Swatzel; Zachariah Spires; Charles Headricks; Michael Airkolt; Laurance Robey
2d Class: Syar Bowman; Adam Bamgardner; Adam Householder Junr; Joseph Melott; Henry Haaz(?); Richard Carter Junr; John Hoss; Joseph Byerley
3d Class: Peter Riechart; John Deal; Peter Reed; Leonard Swingle; John Miller (Cooper); John Stock; Jacob Lezin; Owen Robey
4th Class: George Noy; Casper Riechart; David Rowland; Abraham Rowland; Morris Deal; James Brand Junr; Elie Williams; Jonathan Adams
5th Class: Jacob Grove; Lodwick Beaner; George Conrod; Nicholas Swingley; William Thompson; Francis Blackwell; Stephen Stillwell; Abraham Nave;
6th Class: Christian Crugle; Christian Rowland; John Andrews; Adam Grave; John Cugle; George Swingle Junr; Thomas Stuart; Casper Kotchmiller

WASHINGTON COUNTY

7th Class: George Davis; Eustatious Elinger; Henry Rowland; John Hoover; John Miller (weaver); Jacob Rowland Junr; Melcher Shat; George Stuart; Arthur John Roby
8th Class: Daniel Gorman; John Riechart; Jacob Miller; John Swatzell; John Brandbun; Jeremiah Bany; Michael Swingly; John Yates; Samuel Swereingen Junr; George Swingley Junr Recomd. for Captn of this Compy. Household put into the ranks other officers to now. [Md. Hist. Soc., MS 1146]

WORCESTER COUNTY

9 Apr 1776/We whose names are here subs..... 9 Apr 1776
Ebenezer Handy, Captn; George Parsons, Lieut.; James Perdue, Lieut.; Boaz Walston, Esn.; Jonathan Parsons, Sergt.; George Smith, Sergt.; Nathaniel Dixon Sergt.; Peter Gordy, Corpor.; Mathias ..tin, Corpl.; Elisha Davis, Corpl.; Saml. Parsons, Corpl.
John Bruington; Jacob Parker; Shadrick Crouch; John Hearn; George Vance; Joshua Freoney; Isaiah Smith; Elijah Smith; John Davis; John Perdue; Levin Disharoon; Thomas Elzey; George Perdue; Elisha Parker, Senr; Elisha Parker Junr; Benjamin Willis; Ignasius Anderson; Levin Smith; Solomon Harting; Charles Harris; Joseph Waller; Spencer Davis; Isaac Phillips; Hezekiah Maddux; Saml. Smith; Wm. Parsons; Henry Bruington; Saml. Bruington; Charles Roach; Smith Christopher; Levin Turner; George Davis; Saul Shockly; Fredk. Hill; Jinkins Parker; John Braugton; Solomon Layfield; Outerbrige Dixon; Wm. Oliphant; Revil Wharton; Smith Lingo; Wm. Holland; Wm. Gordy; Wm. Beauchamp; Wm. Bigland; Wm. Layfield; Elijah Hearn; Benjamin Smith; Micajah Hancock; Thomas Crouch; John Bigland; James Bruington; Levin Hobbs; George Lowe; Thos. Taylor; Levin Smith; Edmund N. Nelms; Wm. Bruington; John(?) Smith; Benjamin Parker; Isaiah Wright; Littleton Beauchamp; John Flint; George Perdue Junr; Archabald Smith; James Perdue Senr; Thomas Hanley. [Md. Hist. Soc., MS 1814]

Snowhill November 15th 1777
Sir/In Consequence of an order I received two days ago from the House of Delegates, I have sent your inclosed the List of all the able Bodied Male white Persons in this County. and the Rolls of all the Companys and the Battalions as they stand offic'd - you remember that I attended your Excellency and Counsil as soon as I recd. the Act. & could have a list with the Roll of each Company, and you Commissioned the proper Officers, and Indulgd. me with the lists and rolls to Class the Companys. and to make what Alterations might be found necessary. As soon as I had done that I requested my clerk to copy them fare and Inclose them to your Excellency, which he did, But being cald to the Western Shorre of Virginia on Necessary Businiss he gave them to a friend of his to deliver to me, which he never did, by which means this delay has happened Contrary, to my Expectation or Knowledge - I would most gladly alttend with the papers to know if there is any thing Else that the Assembly may want me to comply with, but am prevented by Indisposition. I have done everything in my power to furnish Arms for this County but have not been able to get any as yet; I am in great hopes the Assembly will do something with those Insurgents that are out in these two lower Countys as they are in our present state a very grate Hurt to the Common Cause. one of them met my servant on the road as I sent him to Snowhill the day before Yesterday for the Lists and rolls of the

APPENDIX B: MUSTER ROLLS AND OTHER LISTS

Companys and asked him for his letters. the Negro denied he had any he then asked him what he was going for if he had no letters. the Boy told him he was going for the Doctr. for me & Immediately put whip to his horse and made his Escape. Altho the Other followed him a Considerable distance under lash.
I have Inclosed you the Depositions that is against the Prisinors that was sent from this county to Cambridge. Capt. Mitchell's Lieut and Ensign have never received their Commissions since they were appointed, We hope to receive them by the first Oppertunity except the Assembly should choose to Recommend any other Persons.
   I have wrote you twice relative to A. Mr. McGarment to which I have not yet recd. any Answers,
   I am with Grate Regard & Esteem your very Humbl. Servt. Joseph Dashiell, Lieut. of Worcester County. [Militia Lists of Daus. of Founders and Patriots, held by Md. Hist. Soc.]

A Roll of Captn. John Parramores company
John Parramore, Capt; Henry Ayres 1 Lieut; John Selby, 2 Do; Levin Hill, Ensign; Moses Hudson; Charles Bennett; Willm. Benett; Jessy Bennett; Richard Taylor; Jacob Taylor; John Johnson; Curtis Clouds; Saml. Brittingham; Thomas Brittingham; Elijah Brittingham; Levin Newton; Kiah Massey; Joshua Stirgiss; Stephen Sturgiss; Hinman Cowley; Mickail Tarr Junr; Israel Tarr; James Selby; Philip Selby; Daniel Selby; Eli Tarr; Ebenezer Hancock; John Hancock; Parker Watson; Glenn Kilpin; Robert Slocam; William Slocam; Thomas Slocam; Littleton Reed; Sothey Veasey; Willm. Tarr; Levin Reed; Saml. Hudson; Jessey Dickerson; James Linny; Henry Willit; John Dory(?); John Tarr (Junr); John Blair; Ezekiel Coston; James Bennett; Willm. Bennett; Levin Sturgiss; Saml. Tarr (Sen); Michl. Tarr (of Saml.); Nehemiah Tarr; Arthur McFaddin; Levin Watson; Bartley Cambell; John Johnson; Willm. Crafford; Brittingham Henderson; Obed Taylor; Joshua Taylor; Willm. Price; James Johnson; John Tindall; John Veasey; Arthur Roley(?); Saml. Pain. [Militia Lists of Daus. of Founders and Patriots, held by Md. Hist. Soc.]

A roll of Capt. William Richardson's Company Vizt. (Date of 30 Aug 1777 next to the names of the commissioned officers); Samuel Smyley, Capt; William Richardson, 1 Lieut.; John Outton Sturgis, 2 Lieut; John Ayres, Ensign; Jesse Ennis (scratched through); William Allen; Eli Adams; William Allen; Benjamin Aydolett; Joshua Beachborad; Morgain Braishier; John Benson; James Collins; Ephraim Collins; Jeremiah Carey; James Conner; Bartholomew Conner; Parker Dukes; William Dukes; John Dukes; Eliakim Duberly(?); Shalmanzar Dennis; Joseph Davis; William Floyd; David Groomes; James Gutthery (Gutthuy ?); Levin Hopkins; Laban Hudson; John Harper; Elisha Hill; Elisha Jones; Wm. Harrison; Hezekiah Johnson; Southy Jester; John Nearn; Spencer Pepper; Levin Pain; Esau Pilchard; Jabez Pilchard; Thomas Parradice; Arthur Price; Thomas Robbins; Outton Sturgis; Richard Sturgis (scratched through); Kendall Simpson; John Savage; Zadok Selby; William Selby; John Satchell; John Townsend; Alexr. Townsend; Elijah Tarr; John Tarr (of Michael); Elisha Tarr; William Turner; Eli Tarr (of Michael); Nathan Watson; William Sturgis; William Dreadon; Robt. Richardson (of John); Lazarous Townsend; Samuel Teague; Elisha Taylor; John Ball (scratched through); Hudson (blank) (of Truitt) (sic); Parker Selby of Parker. [Militia Lists of Daus. of Founders and Patriots, held by Md. Hist. Soc.]

WORCESTER COUNTY

(Sinepuxent Batt., Worcester Co. about 1780)
A Role of Capt. Postly Compy.
1st Class: Isaac Evans; Matthias Davis; Hillery Pitt; William Roans; William Round; Prisgrave Kennitt; Benjamin Betherds; James Tingle; William Banum
2nd Class: Daniel Coe Betherds; Gershom Clark; Archibald Johnson; Joshua Hickman; Sam Johnson; Elijah Holloway; Robert Mitchell; William Truitt; William(?) Hall(?)
3 Class: Esau Williams; Elihu Powell; John Watson; Belitha Collins; Levin Mitchell; Elisha Collins; Luke Pennewill; Jesse Holloway; Truit Jarman
4 Class: Thomas Dale; Zadok Powell (of Wm.); John Pope Mitchell; Levi Fall; Warran Hadder; Solomon Cary; John Quillen; Powell Smock; William Campbell
5th Class: John Postly; William Powell; Matthew Roan; Isaac Bratton; Nehemiah Truitt; Jesse Williams; Jno. Powell (of Sam); Abisha(?) Davis
6 Class: Isaac Warran; Joshua Morss(sic); Adam Bratten; William White; John Lindal; Chas. N. Williams; Annanias Warran; George Burk
7th Class: Hampton Hopkins; William Hickman; Jesse Cropper; David Williams; Gamage Evans; Robert Johnson; Ismeal Williams; Belitha Powell
8th Class: James Dale; John Hadder; William Covington; James Daws; Zadock Powell (of Thos.); Sam. Logwood; William Kennitt; William Brattin. [Militia Lists of Daus. of Founders and Patriots, held by Md. Hist. Soc.]

A Role of Captn. Rackliff Copy.
1 Class: Sam: H. Round; John Massey; Joseph Waters; Isaac Hill; Joshua Massey; Thomas Hudson; William Holloway; William Caudry; John Tubbs; Joshua Stevens
2 Class: Jesse Dunkin; Isaac Taylor; William Collins; David Fassitt; George Tayler; Thomas Purnell (of Wat.); Brittingham Smock; Benjamin Quillin; Ebenezer Evans
3d Class: William Stevenson; Solomon Campbell; Alexander Tayler; Isaac Williams; Robert Betts; William Fassitt; Joshua Ennis; Kendle Patty; Joseph Tubbs; William Bowen
4th Class: Thomas Selby; John Hudson Junr; Wm. Purnell (of Eupa?); Rouse Fassett; Sam Tayler Junr; Levi Cropper; Powell Patty Junr; David Taylor; Annanias Hudson; Thomas Tittel
5th Class: Richard Hall; Thomas Rowlen; James Purnell; Levi Mills; Noble Cropper; Jno. Fassitt; Henry Sneed; Edward Demmick; Stephen Hill; William Townsend
6th Class: John Taylor; Sam Mills; Powell Penewell; Solomon Hamblin; Kendle Collier; Stephen Smock; Wm. Evans; Peter Purnell; Jno. Schoolfield; Levi Pepper
7th Class: Rubin Cropper; McKemmy Hudson; Ebenezer Jones; John Stevens; Dunkin Murray; Gilbert Bedle; Isaac Ayres; James Mitchell; Peter Collier
8th Class: William Purnell (Quipco(?)); Jno. Benston; John Kerby; Jesse Cropper; Jno. Curren; James Watters; Valentine Ryon; Henry Brumbly; Alexander Massey. [Militia Lists of Daus. of Founders and Patriots, held by Md. Hist. Soc.]

A Role of Capn. Jno. Coe's Compy.
1st Class: John Coe; Seth Hudson; James Godfrey; Jno. H. Latchamp; David Hudson; Thomas Latchamp; Nathaniel Richards; Sackor Mumford; Gamage Evans
2d Class: Joseph Bratten(?); Isaac Dunkin; Beletha Brazer; Isaac Lynch; John Johnson; Beletha Townsend; Charles Tayler; Levin Baker; Godfrey Baker

APPENDIX B: MUSTER ROLLS AND OTHER LISTS

3d Class: James Laws; Chs. Godfrey; Elisha Webb; William Townsend; Waitman Cannon; Philip White; Jacob Lynch; George McGee; William Ake
4th Class: John Miller; Belitha Godfrey; Luke Ellison; William Chandler; Nehemiah Lachamp; Eliphas Dazey; Nehemiah Luer(?); Benjamin Clark; Thomas Purkins
5th Class: Zadok Cropper; William Bowen; Stephen Mumford; John Aydolitt; Annanias Hudson Junr; Levin Coffen; Levin Cropper; James Conner; Armwell Vigerous
6th Class: David Lynch; Wm. Allison; David Tubbs; Solomon Purkins; John Beachamp; John Falkner; Lott Hudson; John Showell; Zadok Selby
7th Class: Asa Coe; Israel Townsend Jr; Dennis Hudson; John Evans; Thomas McNeill; Obed Aydolett; Bethewell Showell; Job Hudson
8th Class: John Tull; William Hayward; John B. Hayward; Eli Showell; Jesse Smith; William Webb; Scarborough Webb. [Militia Lists of Daus. of Founders and Patriots, held by Md. Hist. Soc.]

A Role of Militia of Sinepuxen Battalion Class'd this 25th day July 1780 -
Class 1st: Captn. Matthew Purnell; John Smith; William Jones; Thomas Pointer; Elias Burbage; John Burbage; Ephraim Calhoon; William Powell Truett
2d Class: Joshua Hodge; Hezekiah Beavens; Elias Webb; Annanias Bradford; Milby Smith; Zadok Powell; William Hozer; Elijah Powell
3d Class: John Jones; Elisha Hill; James Lewis; Bilitha Griffen; John Seers; William Henderson; John Smith Junr; John Williams
4th Class: Thomas Smith; Benjamin Timmons; Edward Bishop; Isaac Bradford; Levin Bradford; Elijah Timmons; John Jarman; Solomon Bradford
5th Class: Stephen Timmons; John Schoolfield; Sam Timmons; Patty Truitt; William Holland; Rives Townsend; Thomas Townsend
6th Class: William Richards; Elisha Wheeler; Joseph Taylor; Avery Bradford; Isaac Hill; Stephen Tayler; John Warren
7th Class: Jeptha Webb; Joseph Timmons; Wm. Franklin; Zepheniah Webb; Elisha Bradford; Nehemiah Hadder; John Jones Junr
8th Class: John Webb; William Bassitt; John Henderson; John Richards; Jeremiah Townsend; Isaac Richards; Levi Smith. [Militia Lists of Daus. of Founders and Patriots, held by Md. Hist. Soc.]

A Role Captn Wm. Purnells Compy -
1 Class: William Truitt Junr; Jesse Henderson; Isaac Savage; James Mumford; Dunnock Dennis; Jesse Mumford; Elias Peniwell
2d Class: William Brittingham (of Natn); Thomas Hogstler(?); William Bradford (of Sam); Eli Truitt; John Patrick; Thomas Gladson; Sam Dredon
3d Class: Joseph Ennis; John Gornwell; Jeremiah Hales; John Johnson; Levin Holland; Sam Nicholes; Rodger Hook
4th Class: Littleton Robins; James Givens; Curtis Henderson; Jesse Waters; John Deverix; Levin Riggin; Absolom Pittel
5th Class: Belitha Brittingham; Sacker Paker; Matthew Davis; Archibald Hudson; William Hook; Stephen Ward; Sam Brittingham
6th Class: William Truitt Senr; Cornelius Ennis; Edward Hammond; John Selby Purnell; Sam Bradford; Benjamin Truitt; Thomas Brittingham; Levi Hudson
7th Class: Rounds Truitt; Jacob Teage; John Wheeler; John Greer; Major Mumford; George Mumford; Joseph Porter
8th Class: William Purnell; John McCauley; Robert Schoolfield; Isaac Killiam; Zadok Sturges; Ralph Houston; William Brittingham; Joshua

WORCESTER COUNTY

Brittingham. [Militia Lists of Daus. of Founders and Patriots, held by Md. Hist. Soc.]

A Role of Captn. E. Purnells Compy. -
1 Class: John Pridix; John Bowen; John Duberly; John Smock; Edward Morris; Laben Ennis; Edward Burbage; William Waite
2d Class: James Stevenson Senr; James Bradford; John Morris; Samuel Bowles; Jesse Bowen; Levin Purnell; Levin Bowen; William Burbage
3 Class: Outton Truitt; Henry Brumbly; Cornelius Morris; James Morris; Peter Parker; Ephraim Heather; Chambers Collins; Whittington Richardson
4th Class: Elisha Purnell; Edward Hammond; William Griffen; Belitha Hook; William Morris; Rackliff Bowen; Jethrew Morris; James Stevenson Jr.
5th Class: Ezekiel Knox; Hammond Ranolds; Benjamin Davis; Elijah Bowen; Matthias Mumford; Thomas Burbage; Wm. Richardson; Jno. Jackson
6th Class: Jesse Jones; Edward Hammond; Michael Holland; George Ennis; Jesse Cropper; George Jones; Jno. Hancock; Jeptha Bowen; John Jones
7th Class: Benjamin Purnell; Elijah Jarman; Mathew Purnell; Levi Cropper; John Outton; David Bowen; Selathell Burbage; Isaac Morris; William Greer
8 Class: Thomas Jones; Whittington Hancock; John Collins; Philip Morris; Elisha Bowen; Sam. Merchment; Zedakiah Hammond; William Greer. [Militia Lists of Daus. of Founders and Patriots, held by Md. Hist. Soc.]

A Role of Captn. Thos. Purnells Compy -
1st Class: Captn. Thomas Purnell; Coulborn Long; Parker Selby; James Wilson; Shadrick Hadder; David Willis; Peal Franklin; John Smith; George Wainright; Sam Long
2d Class: Wm. Gault; Charles Rackliff Jun.; John McCray; Henry White; McKemmy Smock; Isaac Hammond; John Franklin; Isaac Williams; Bishop Henderson; Moses Dredon
3d Class: James Quinton; Philip Marsh; John Walker; David Fitzgerrald; John Hudson; James Cropper; Charles Merchment; Edward Davis; Purnell Parker; John Willis
4th Class: Jno. Davis; Wm. Gray; Wm. Hudson; Nehemiah Davis; Elisha Long; Sam Long of Wm.; Wm. Merrill; Labin Cropper; Jno. Smith Junr; Richard Smith
5 Class: Jno. White; Lemuel Franklin; Zadok Mumford; Major Cropper; Purnell Smith; Jno. Marshall Jr.; Thos. Lamberson; Jno. Hudson (of Wm.); James Smashey; Wm. Watts; Isaac Hammond
6th Class: Isaac Morss; Eli Davis; Jesse Selby; Ebenezer Franklin; George Tayler; Henry Franklin; Jno. Rackliff; Jno. Parris; Robert Hudson; Edmond Cropper; Isaac Gray
7th Class: Levin Ryly; Henry Hudson; Jesse Long; Dennis Hudson; Wm. Lister; Wm. Handly; Elias Penewill; Levin Davis; Wm. Penewill; Evans Pepper; Jno. Franklin
8 Class: Nathanial Rackliff; Rackliff Penewill; William Long; Thomas Greer; William Cropper Jr; Stephen White of Jno.; Daniel Long; Hampton Burbage; Isaac Marshall; William Campbell; Jno. Bradford. [Militia Lists of Daus. of Founders and Patriots, held by Md. Hist. Soc.]

A Role of Captn. Dales Compy - 1 Class: Richard Hudson; Jno. Wedger; Jesse Gray; Eramus Harrison; Jno. Hamblin; Wm. Collier; David Gray; Annanias Powell; ... Baker

APPENDIX B: MUSTER ROLLS AND OTHER LISTS

2d Class: Josiah Dale; Annanias Hudson; Jno. Dale; Sam: Holland; Rouse Harrison; Seth Wally; Joseph Gray; Annanias Davis; Jonathan Cary
3d Class: Jno. Brevard; Sam Quillen; Jesse Davis; Dale Evans; Charles Walley; Jno. Dennis Junr; Jesse Dale; Lemuel Showell; Jerrediah Gray
4th Class: Jno. Holland; Archibald Baker; James Dale; George Baker; Jno. Justice; Caleb Wayatt; John Hudson; James Halloway; Alexander Warrington
5th Class: James Fassitt; Benjamin Gray; Levi Hollaway; Belitha Bratten; John Powell; Jesse Powell; Ebenezer Holloway; Elias Mason Clark; Templin Hancock
6th Class: Sam Bratten; Johnson Gray; Thomas Powell; Elihu Hazard; Elisha Holloway; Ebenezer Dale(?); Jersey Mumford; James Mumford; Thomas Gray
7th Class: Campbell Dale; Aaron Holloway; Solomon Cary; Elisha Showell; Levin Baker; Smith Lingo; Isaac Brittingham; Mordica Powell; Jno. Walter
8 Class: Elisha Larrance; Levi Davis; Levi Powell; Thomas Wally; Henry Hancock; Geo: Hayward Aydolett; Jacob Hollaway; Selathel Baker; Zadok Baker; Benjamin Gray Senr. [Militia Lists of Daus. of Founders and Patriots, held by Md. Hist. Soc.]

Wicomico Battalion Classed the 15th July 1780 As follows (to wit)

Captn. Handy's Compy: 1st Class: Archabald Smith, Ensign; William Bigland; Elisha Jones; Levin Smith; Spencer Davis; Solomon Smith; Jehu Smith; John Giles
2d Class: Edmd. Wm. Nelms 2 Liet.; Chas. Harris; John Caldwell; Thos. Handly; Geo: Perdue Junr; Geo: Perdue Senr; Stephen Dikes; Jas. Townsend
3d Class: Jno. Dashiell, 1st Lieut.; Saml. Parsons; Joshua Freoney; Jno. Oliphant; Jas. Perdue; Isaiah Wright; Peter Gordy; Geo: Parker Junr
4th Class: William Bruington; Saml. Bruington; Jacob Parker; Shadk. Crouch; Peter Johnson; Benja. Parker; Jno. Flintt; Saml. Bruington
5th Class: Jas. Bruington; Job Buly; Thos. Crouch; Geo: Smith BP(BS?); Elisha Parker Senr; William Parsons; Geo: Parsons; Elijah Hearn
6th Class: Jonathan Parsons; Phillip Busey(?); Jno. Perdue Jun; Elisha Parker Junr; William Willis; Geo: Price; Benja. F.A.C. Dashiell; Levin Turner
7th Class: Jno. Bigland; Jordan Parsons; Wm. Gordy; Jno. Perdue; Frank Gurly; Saml. Brooks; Saml. Smith
8th Class: Robt. Handy Captn; Levin Disharoon; Jno. Bruington; Levin Parsons; Titus Buly; Jno. Hall; Thos. Taylor; Saul Shockly. [Militia Lists of Daus. of Founders and Patriots, held by Md. Hist. Soc.]

Captn. Davis's Compy. - 1st Class: Wm. Dennis; Jno. Campbell; Saml. Truitt of G.; Caleb Rain; Jno. Hosier; Wm. Timons; Jas. Davis; Wm. Rain
2d Class: Rounds Givens; Jas. Lewis; Jno. Adkins; Shadk. Davis; John Bassett; John Reed; Wm. Brittingham; Eben. Truitt
3d Class: Battw. Slatter; Elisha Timons; Geo: Penniwell; Jno. Brittingham; Thos. Lewis; Wm. Powell; Jesse Smith; Henry Dennis
4th Class: Jno. Davis Captn.; Jno. Rane; Stanten Atkins; Jno. German; Jno. Parsons Junr; Benja. Davis; Richd. Peniwell; Jno. Duncan
5th Class: Gavily Woodley; Phillip Davis; Wm. Layfield; Nehemiah Timmons; Jno. Scott; Geo: Truitt; Truitt Brittingham
6th Class: Robt. Davis; Wm. Brittingham; Elisha Penewill; Mathias Dennis; Jno. Dennis; Wm. Atkins; Zephaniah Parsons; Wm. Smith;

WORCESTER COUNTY

7th Class: George Givins; Stephen Atkins; Porter Parsons; Zachariah Parsons; Jno. Gray; Jedediah Truitt; Wm. Turner
8th Class: Joshua Dennis; Jacob Hath; Wm. Bethard; Nimrond Atkins; Midleton Adkins; Fassat Brumbly; Arthur Lewis. [Militia Lists of Daus. of Founders and Patriots, held by Md. Hist. Soc.]
Capt. Shockley Compy. - 1st: Elijah Shockly; Elisha Penewell; Christopher Glass; Wm. Taylor; Nathl. Dixon; Stephen Fountain; Micajah Hancock; Milby Dorman
2d Class: Sampson Shockly; Joshua Holloway; Thos. Cathell; Nathl. Whaly; Jno. Bratten; Elijah Hancock; Stephen Stanford; Moses Hollaway
3d Class: Jno. Richardson; Wm. Willis; Thos. Powell; Benja. Birdwell; Saml. McGee; Jonathan Givins; Daniel McGee; Wm. Dikes
4th Class: Jonathn. Cathell; Saml. Pope; Abel Willis; Joshua Owens; Saul Davis; Jonathan Shockly; Ben Cohoon; Geo: Lowe
5th Class: Wm. Beacham; Edwd. McGlamery; Outerbridge Dixon; Joshua Hancock; Daniel Dikis; Wm. Hannan; Smith Hath; Zorabable Savage
6th Class: Jas. Thomson; Benja. Lowe; David Bridell; Wm. Twigg; Steven Dean; Ben Leonard; Mathias Austin; Jno. Driskell
7th Class: Steven Christopher; Ben. Willis; Joshua McGee; Steven Beacham; Hezekiah Carey; Fredk. Barnicastle; Adam Driskill; Elijah Christopher
8th Class: Daniel Cathiel; Jesse Stanford; John McGee; Jno. Bridell; Jonathan Noble; Levin Cary; Jona. Noble of Joseph. [Militia Lists of Daus. of Founders and Patriots, held by Md. Hist. Soc.]

Capt. Bennett Compy - Joshua Selby; Major Dorman; Wm. Townsend; Levin Owens; Ephraim Townsend; Spencer Owens; Jonathan Stanford; David Pusey
2d Class: Nathan Anderson; David Layfeild; Mathew Dorman; Darby Riggen; Henry Atkinson; Absolom Townsend of Joshua; Thos. Loca; Benett Cooper
3d Class: Thos. Atkinson; Jno. Dreaden; Wm. Townsend; Job Newton; Elget Ruark; Wm. Townsend (of Dickson); Hugh Vestry; Solomon Townsend
4th Class: Charles Bennett Captn; Jno. Riggen; Thos. Layfield; Smith Johnson; Littleton Riggin; Jesse Watson; Eliacam(?) Johnson; Ohly (Okly?) Owens
5th Class: Joseph Richards; Cannon Wainright; Merrell(?) Maddux; Lazarus(?) Madux; Jas. Bussell; Elijah Collins; Henry Johnson; Levin Dentson
6th Class: Rowland Beavans; Wm. Smullen; John Dukes; Elias Benston; Jas. Wonnell; Major Cluff; Levin Owens; Hezekiah Ruark
7th Class: Saml. Tilghman; Thomas Cluff; Bur..ll Drumman; Saml.(?) Smullen; George Puzey; Peter Owens; Jno. Powell
8th Class: Angelo Atkinson; Wm. Johnson; Thos. Mungar; Isaac Puzey; Frdk. Britt; James Townsend; Abraham Denston; John Wells. [Militia Lists of Daus. of Founders and Patriots, held by Md. Hist. Soc.]

Captn. Dennis's compy. - Thomas Victor; Saml. Dreaden; Jonathan Eshom; James Ward; Richd. Shockly; Milby Christopher; Saml. Stevenson
2d Class: Jno. Townsand; Robt. Dukes; Joshua Buttler; George Adkinson; Steven White; Jackson Turner; Jno. Shockley
3d Class: Jno. Caudry; Wm. White; Wm. Dredden; Joseph Eshom; Sewell Dredden; Solomon Eshom; Levi Lamberson
4th Class: Barclay White; Ezar (Isac?) Bridell; Jno. Ruark; Isaac Dreden; Jno. Killam; Edmund Crapper; Levi Robbins

APPENDIX B: MUSTER ROLLS AND OTHER LISTS

5th Class: Benja. Dennis Captn.; Isaac Nicholson; Wm. Noble; Wm. McDaniell; James Victor; Jno. Mumford
6th Class: John Victor; Elie Adams; Daniel Esom; Wm. Dickerson; Thos. Cottingham; Elijah Cottingham
7th Class: Levi Outten; Josiah Robins; Wm. Shockly; Levin Townsend; Jno. Nicholson; Solomon Shockly; Joshua White
8th Class: Joseph Gray; George Turner; James McDaniel; Daniel Ruark; Major Selby; David Adams; John McDaniel. [Militia Lists of Daus. of Founders and Patriots, held by Md. Hist. Soc.]

Captn. Perdue's Compy. - Wm. Farlow; Jno. Baker; Eljah Fox Junr; Major Wilkins; Hezekiah Maddux; Thos. McClish; Jacob Evans; George Davis
2d Class: Wm. Speer; Geo: Truitt; Thos. Donaway; Wm. Oliphan; Geo: Truitt (of Jacb.); Ben Farlow; James Hath; Henry Cockurll (Corkurll?)
3d Class: Jno. Shockly; Ratcliff Blizard; Wm. Twilly; Jno. Dennis; Isaac Phillips; Jesse Gray; Ben. Shockly; Elijah Wales
4th Class: James Perdue; Joseph Richardson; Gabriel Powell; Wm. German; Jno. Parsons; Thos. Truitt; Boaz Walston; Joab Jerman
5th Class: Samuel Bethards; John Hearn; John Cole; Belitha Bratten; Joseph Dennis; Elijah Smith; Matthew Richardson
6th: Joseph Brittingham; Henry Turner; Thomas White; Zadock Turner; Alaner (Claner?) Shore; Jno. Farlow; Jas. Dennis
7th Class: Jesse Bratten; Saul Baker; Maddux Hamlin; Ignatius Anderson; Wm. Lewis; Danl. Fooks; Geo: Farlow
8th Class: Wm. Bethards; Elisha Vinson; Saul Layfeild; Jacob Elliott; Joshua Mitchell; George Smith; Littleton Becham. [Militia Lists of Daus. of Founders and Patriots, held by Md. Hist. Soc.]

Captn. Quinton's Compy. - 1st Class: Jas. Townsend; Ezekiel Selby; Jas. Tarr; Wm. Handy; Jno. Gibbs; Wm. Willis
2d Class: Phillip Quinton; Elijah Powell; Andw. Brown; Zadock Townsend; Cornelius Dickerson; Daniel Selby
3d Class: Wm. McCauley; Saml. Dorman; Wm. Bowen; Wm. Ball; Levi Holland; Wm. Selby Junr; Wm. Powell
4th Class: Wm. Atkinson; Thos Barnes Junr; Major White; Wilson Brown; Mercey Maddux; Peirce Reed; Wm. Bevans
5th: Jno. Kellam(?); Thomas Bevans; James Williams; Jabez Willis; Elias Townsend; John Allexander
6th Class: Jno. Scott; Levin Blake; Jno. Flemin; Jonathan Caudry; Jno. Dorman; Jno. Bevans
7th: Wm. Cottingham; Danford(?) Townsend; Saml. Pane; Wm. Brown; Josiah Ward; Solomon Townsend; Wm. Atkinson Selby
8th Class: Wm. Bevans; Jno. Cottingham; Jno. Selby; Abraham Gibbs; James Selby; Joshua Dredden; Charles Townsend. [Militia Lists of Daus. of Founders and Patriots, held by Md. Hist. Soc.]

Captn. Horsey's Compy - Isaac Dixon; Geo: Disharoon; Jesse Fooks; Jno. Taylor; Wm. Fooks; Thos. Fooks; Saul Causey
2d Class: Sothy Tignol; Wm. Butler; Jno. Brown; Joseph Rigs; David Cathell; Wm. Vance; Wm. Toadvine
3d Class: Wm. Stirgis; Adkins Dennis; James Roach; John Harrison; Levi Cathell; Ezekiell Ruark; Levin Cacey; Jno. Cathell

WORCESTER COUNTY

4th Class: John Stirgis; Chas. Phillips hill (liett?); David Brown; Joshua Stirgiss;; Chas. Roach; Saml. White; Jonathan Shockly; Todd Levingston
5th Class: Jonathan Riggen; Arnold Toadvine; Wm. Riggen; Moses Driskell; James Hayman; Bennett Cooper; Alexr. Porter
6th Class: Richd. Mills; Ruben McGee; Geo: Brown; Wm. Smullen; Jno. Toadvine; Zadock Ennis; Henry Toadvine; Patrick Causey
7th Class: Saml. Horsey; Joshua Hayman; Wm. Wilson; Joshua Morris; Geo: Levingston; Geo: Driskell; Elisha ODear; Jacob Tull
8th Class: Bela Crapper; Shadk. Driskell; Adam Christopher; Ben. Johnson; Isaac Hayman; Elgett Driskell; Moses Driskell Senr; Chas. Hayman. [Militia Lists of Daus. of Founders and Patriots, held by Md. Hist. Soc.]

Capt. Layfields Company - 1st Class: John Trehorn Henderson (Sergt.); Ezekiel Young; Abraham Newton; Naboth Boston; Esau Boston; Levin Oakey; Israel Peakock; Handy Tull; David Long
2 Class: Joseph Houston (Sergt.); James Henderson; Solomon Johnson; James Houston; John Melvin; Wm. Merrill; Stephen Roach; Daniel Young; Thomas Lambden (Junr)
3 Class: Thomas Marshall (1 Lieut.); Isaac Henderson; Southey Sterling; James Dickerson; George Melvin; James Selby; Thomas Layfield; Purnell Brittingham; John Sterling
4 Class: Joseph Henderson (Sergt.); George Layfield; Milby Young; Daniel Kelly; Littleton Taylor; James Townsend; James Campbell; William Melvin; John Young
5 Class: Littleton Long (Ensign); Wm. Marshall; John Kelly(?); Levin Blades; John Cain; Jesse Long; Smart Henderson; Thomas Tyler; Zepheniah Benson
6 Class: Isaac Layfield, Captn; Levi Carey; Ephraim Young; Thomas Henderson; Alexander McCready; Jenckins Henderson; Wm. Holland Henderson; Levi Henderson; Robert Melvin
7 Class: George Marshall (Sergt.); Levi Houston; Riley Slocomb; William Spires; John Gunby; Levin Merrill; Levi Peacok; Solomon Webb; Esau Merrell Dickerson
8 Class: Henry Dennis (2 Lieut.); Wm. Taylor; Josiah Merrill; Wm. Blake; Joseph Schoolfield; John Peacock; Jacob Henderson; Thomas Merrill; Wm. Merrill Henderson; Isaac Boston. [Militia Lists of Daus. of Founders and Patriots, held by Md. Hist. Soc.]

Capt Handys company - 1 Class: Capt. William Handy; Geo. Downs; Matthias Outten; Francis Randall; James Bennett; Joseph Kellam; Alexander McAllen
2 Class: Wm. Stevens Hill; Levin Long; Sterling Hudson; Jesse Nelson; James Selby; John Ball; Jonathan Hutchinson
3 Class: Joshua Townsend; Joseph Bishop; William Tarr; James R.(?) Morris; George Dennis; Cornelius Patrick; Andrew Catherwood
4 Class: James Stevenson; Holland Smock; Jesse Hughs; Moses Nelson; John Evans; Jonathan Nelson; Moses Chaille
5 Class: William Wise; James Ruark; Major Gornwell; Arthur McFadden; John Chambers; Thomas Lane; John Hall
6 Class: Nehemiah Dorman; John Murray; Gilbert Laws; George Martin Junr; James Duer; Henry Truitt; Joshua Pepper
7 Class: Patrick Glasgow; Patrick Waters; Elias Taylor; Samuel Cox; Hugh Stevenson; Thomas Sturgis; Isaac Dreadon; John Townsend

APPENDIX B: MUSTER ROLLS AND OTHER LISTS

8 Class: John Gunn; William Done; Richard Sturgis; Matthias Handy; McKimmy Porter; Yelverton P. Probart; James McFadden; Peter Chaille. [Militia Lists of Daus. of Founders and Patriots, held by Md. Hist. Soc.]

Capt Waltons Company - 1 Class: Eliakim Johnson (1 Lieut.); Aaron Blake; Ambrose Willett; Robt. Purnell; John Brittingham; Elisha Jones; John Snead; Morgan Bradshaw
2 Class: Stephen Allen (Sergt.); William Ellis; John Chaille; Urias(?) McHenry; Nathaniel Brittingham; Henry Ballard; Wm. Selby; Walter Pruitt
3 Class: William Aydelott Sergt.; Richard Roley; Levi Roberson; Daniel Ballard; James Blake; Selby Newton; David Dixon; John Winters; Daniel Hancock
4 Class: Fisher Walton Capt.; George Blake; Charles Veazy; Solomon Cary; Joshua Beachboard; Robert Lamberson; William Hancock; William Brittingham; Saml. Tarr
5 Class: John Jones (sergt.); Benja. Tull; William Ballard; Benja. Holland; Israel Webb; John Purnell; George Selby; Abraham Sturgis; William Newton
6 Class: George Layfield (2d Liut.); Selby Benson; John Floyd; Josiah Roberson; Hezekiah Johnson; John Parnell (of John); Joshua Sturgis (of Outten); James Aydelot; John Watson
7 Class: Giles Jones (Sergt.); Leml. Johnson; James Cheswicks(?); Benja. Pruitt; George Furnis; Eli Tarr (of Eli); Robert Gibbs; Nathaniel Davis; Justice Carey
8 Class: Joshua Duer; Jacob Merrill; Smith Carey; Joshua Riggen; John Redden; Benja. Bonnewell; Azdok Ordis(?); Staten Trader; John Allen. [Militia Lists of Daus. of Founders and Patriots, held by Md. Hist. Soc.]

Capt Pattersons Compy. - 1 Class: James Tull, Sergt.; William Gillett; William Mills; John Conner; James Phillips; George Stevenson; John Pain; Smith Melvin
2 Class: Jonathan Stevenson (2d Lieut.); Silas Chapman; Robert Mills; Anderson Patterson; Levi Ball; James McCready; Aaron Hudson; Samuel Smith
3 Class: Noble Dreadon (Sergt.); Elijah Burnett; Smith Lamberson; Esau Pilchard; Wm. Conner; Littleton Melvin; John Roberson; Levin Pain
4 Class: William Smith (Sergt.); Samuel Blades; Major Jones; Daniel Jones; John Brumbly; John Davis; James Burnett; Jabez Pilchard; Ayres Smith Millor
5 Class: James Stevenson (1 Lieut.); William Allen (of Aaron); William Dubberly; Zorababel Hill; Eliakim Dubberly; Levi Ellis; Levin Anderson; Zephaniah Davis; Elijah Brittingham
6 Class: James Patterson (Capt.); Ayres Gillett; Wm. Young; Jonathan Melvin; Major Watson; Jesse Chenicks(?); Nehemiah Bratten; Saml. Lamberson; Jehu Taylor
7 Class: Benja. Stevenson (Ensign); James Virden; Elijah Townsend; James Davis (of Ben); Daniel Mason; William Allen; Nehemiah Redden; Saml. Mills; Major Davis
8 Class: Joseph Stevenson (Sergt.); Holland Price; Levi Pilchard; Broadwater Hill; James Smith; John Mills; James Jones; William Waters; Jesse Elliss. [Militia Lists of Daus. of Founders and Patriots, held by Md. Hist. Soc.]

Capt. Smyly's Company - 1 Class: Samuel Smyley, Captn; Parker Selby; Outton Sturges; Bartholomew Campbell; Spencer Pepper; Hezekiah Massey; Archibald Hudson

WORCESTER COUNTY

2 Class: John Ayres (Ensign); John Townsend; Thomas Parradice; Caleb Guttery; Curtis Henderson; Levin Watson; Parker Dukes
3d Class: Zadok Selby (Sergt.); Ephraim Collins; James Collins; Daniel Sturgis; Samuel Brittingham; Thomas Brittingham; Jeremiah Carey
4th Class: John Outten Sturgis (2 Lieut.); Edward Blake; Jesse Armstrong; Kendal Simpson; John Dukes; Levin Newton; William Dukes
5 Class: William Richardson (1 Lieut); Middleton Harmon; Abel Harmon; Elijah Tarr; Henry Willett; Elijah Brittingham
6 Class: Nehemiah Holland (Sergt.); William Dryden; Southey Jester; William Crafford; John Savage; John Benson
7 Class: Ezekiel Cartor(?) (Sergt.); Littleton Reed; John Harper; Levin Roberts; Arthur Price; Levin Reed
8 Class: William Sturgis (Sergt.); David Grooms; John Holiston; John Travers; Bartholomew Conner; Eli Adams. [Militia Lists of Daus. of Founders and Patriots, held by Md. Hist. Soc.]

Capt. Parramor's Compy. - 1 Class: Levin Hill (Ensign); Samuel Hopkins; John Tarr Junr; James Lindsay; Nehemiah Tarr; George Blake (of Sarah); Ebenezer Hancock; William Bennett
2 Class: John Parramore; John Hancock; Jesse Bennett; Samuel Bratten; Laban Hudson; Saml. Henderson; Daniel Selby; William Sturgis
3 Class: Moses Hudson (Sergt.); Michael Tarr (of Michl.); Alexander Richardson; John Blake; James Johnson; Danl. Stevens; Thomas Slocumb; John Veazy
4 Class: Thomas Taylor (Sergt.); Joshua Sturgis; Glyn Relper (Relsen?); Michael Tarr (of Saml.); Thomas Milbourn; Ayres Greer; Oliver Blake; Charles Bennett
5 Class: Henry Ayres (Lieut); John Johnson; John Blair; Obed Taylor; Hinnan(?) Cowly; Wm. Waltom; Joshua Tarr; Thomas Richardson
6 Class: Philip Selby (Sergt.); Joshua Taylor; William Slocomb; Brittingham Henderson; Arthur Rowley; Wm. Cowley; Jeremiah Harmon; Charles Walls
7 Class: Levin Sturgis (Sergt.); Eli Tarr; John Tarr (of Saml.); Israel Tarr; James Ballard; Ephraim Henderson; Elijah Justice; Wm. Bennett
8 Class: John Selby (Lieut.); Elijah Brittingham; Daniel Johnson; Saml. Hudson; George Burch; Jesse Dickerson; Azariah Tarr; William Henderson; Saml. Harper. [Militia Lists of Daus. of Founders and Patriots, held by Md. Hist. Soc.]

INDEX TO APPENDIX B

This is an index to Appendix B only. Ranks and titles are not included in the index except when the given name is not available. Parentheses are used to show the number of times that name appears on the indicated page.

... Benjamin 197, 200
... Charles 200
... Elihu 216
... George 200(2)
... Henry 195
... Jacob 200
... James 199(2), 216, 221
... John 196, 197, 198 216(2)
... Joseph 179, 196
... Lanslott 199
... Philip 214
... Ribnal 198
... Richard 218
... Roger 216
... Samuel 199, 216
... Stephen 200
... Thomas 198
... Zephaniah 199
...FMAN Martin 200
...MAKER Joshua 199
...PHERD William 153
...RSEY Moses 217
...THER Zachariah 198
...TIN Mathias 249
...TTY Nathaniel 221

ABBET George 219; John 219; Loyd 219
ABBINGTON Boules 200; John 200
ABBITT Thomas 152
ABBOTT Samuel 224, 231(2)
ABBY Thomas Green 214
ABELL Aaron 213; Arthur 211; Barton 211; Clark 211; Cuthbert 211(2); Edmond 211; Edward 212; Enoch 211; George 211; Henry 211; Ignatius 211; John Booth 211; John Horn 215; Joseph 215; Joshua 211; Philip 213; Robert 211; Samuel 214; Thomas 211; Zacharia 211
ABERRY William 199
ABIT Martin 166
ABLE John 154; Thomas 173
ACHISON James 163
ACKWORTH Ephraim 217; Henry 217; John 217; Richard 216; Train 217
ACTON Francis 165; Henry 159; James 158; John 165; Richard 242
ADAIR James 247
ADAM Phill 220

ADAMS Alexander 197, 201, 219; Andrew 219; Benjamin 163; Boaz 155; David 256; Edward 204; Eli (Elie) 250, 256, 259; Eusebeus 225; George 164, 220; Hope 220(2); Isaac 221; Jacob 164, 220, 246; James 158, 171, 218; Jeremiah 164; Jesse 194; John 161, 163, 171, 218, 246; John R. 161; Jonathan 248; Josias 165; Levi 222; Moses 225, 232; Nathan 215; Peter 246; Phil 220; Phill Collens 220; Ralph 151; Rhody 165; Richard 164, 191; Roger 166; Samuel 161, 218, 220; Solomon 214; Thomas 207, 215, 220; Will 219; William 145, 220, 221, 240, 242
ADAMSON Basil 195; John 195, 202; Kensey 195, 203
ADDAMS Abm. 215; Edward 199; Jerimiah 158; Stephen 214
ADDERTON Henry 150
ADGATE Elias 203
ADKINS John 254; Joseph 204; Midleton 255
ADKINSON George 255; John 190
ADLEMAN Leonard 238
ADY Jonathan 172; William 172
AHERN Patrick 181, 189
AIRKOLT Michael 248
AISQUITH George 213
AKCRINGBARGER Michael 247
AKE William 252
AKERS James 225, 231; John 231; William 223
AKIN Thomas 223
AKORD Francis 244
ALANGER Phillip 248
ALBERRY William 200
ALBERT Philip 175
ALBRIGHT Peter 247
ALBY Joseph 200
ALCOCK Samuel 154
ALDER Christian 246
ALDRIDGE James 194; John 198, 207; Nathan 202; Thomas 197
ALEXANDER Arthur 157; Edward 157; James 175, 223, 230(2); John 157, 223; Matthew 171; Robert 152; William 163, 230

INDEX TO APPENDIX B

ALFORD Aaron 154; Edward 181;
  Maccobins 154; Matthyas 154; Moses
  154, 183, 190, 191
ALIPHANT Mathias 218
ALISON Henry 197; Thomas 193
ALLAN Jeramiah 243
ALLBRITAN Charles 160
ALLBRITTON William 159
ALLCOCK Robert 197
ALLDEN Boly 162
ALLEN Aaron 258; Adam 143; Alexander
  205; Charles 149, 224; Edward 145;
  James 166, 173, 175, 237; Jeremiah
  167; John 144, 149, 172, 258;
  Joseph 159, 220; Richard 149;
  Staphen 258; Thomas 243(2);
  William 149, 162, 164, 238,
  250(2), 258(2); William Davis 218;
  Zachariah 164
ALLENDER John 171; Richard 244;
  William 171
ALLENGHAM Joseph 143(2)
ALLER Joseph 169
ALLEXANDER John 256
ALLEY Basil 206; Levering 188; Samuel
  207
ALLIEN William 150
ALLIN Abraham 178; Archibald 195;
  Charles 231; Emanuel 225; George
  162; James 162, 163; John 229;
  Nathan 229; Ruebin 223; Samuel
  158, 163; William 158, 223, 230
ALLINGHAM Joseph 228; Stephen 148
ALLISON Benjamin 197; Burch 201;
  Charles 193; Elisha 201; Henry
  214; James 170(2), 201, 215; John
  214, 215; Jonathan 197, 201;
  Joshua 197; Richard 197(2); Robert
  238; William 252
ALLNUTT James 193; John 193; Laurance
  193; William 147, 193, 204;
  Zacheus 148
ALLOWAY William 228
ALLPHIN Edward 196
ALNUTT Jesse 194
ALPHE Joshua 217; William 217
ALSOPS Richard 150
ALVEY Jesse 212; John 213; Joseph
  210, 212
ALZEY Arnold 220
AMBROSE Malaciah 180; Malichi 188
AMERY Samuel 161

AMMOTT William 175
AMOS James 175; Joshua 175; Moulden
  172
AMOSS James 173; Joseph 175; Mordecai
  174; Nicholas 174
ANDERSON Alexander 182, 212, 229;
  Charles 170, 242; Daniel 170, 242;
  Edward 161; George 217; Ignatius
  (Ignasius) 249, 256; Isaac 156;
  James 156, 175, 185, 195, 202,
  207, 217, 218(2); Jeremiah 241;
  John 195, 203, 217; Jonathan 209;
  Joseph 161(2), 218; Josiah 241;
  Levin 258; Michael 155; Nathan
  255; Perry 224, 229; Richard 244;
  Rob 217; Robert 182, 189; Stephen
  179; Thomas 185, 192, 210, 230;
  Walter 185, 192; William 155,
  161(2), 173, 223, 230
ANDREW Abraham 174; Beauchamp 155;
  Bromwell 154; Curtice 155; Daniel
  166; George 156; Isaac 156;
  Jeremiah 155; Luke 155; Nehemiah
  155(2); Richard 156; Samuel 156;
  William 155, 156
ANDREWS Amos 152; Benjamin 182, 190;
  Charles 194; Edward 194; Isaac
  166; James 226; John 166, 248;
  Joseph 166; Levin 166; Nicholas
  248; Reuben 166; Richard 194;
  Stanaway 166; William 155
ANGER John 186(2)
ANGLEBERRG Philip 169
ANNIN William 170
ANSELL Edward 150
ANSWINGER Christian 244
ANTHMAN John 199
ANTHONY James 223; John 246; Joseph
  225; Morgan 151; Nathan 151;
  William 226
APPLEBY Thomas 197, 203
APPLEGARTH George 228, 233; Nathaniel
  227; Robert 228, 233; Thomas 226
APPLEGERTH Nathaniel 234; Thomas 235;
  William 234
APSLEY Alexander 183, 190; Edward
  183, 190; John 182, 189
ARANO John 179
ARCHER John 170(2), 231
ARDRY John 224
ARINGTON William 224
ARKWRIGHT Isaac 173

INDEX TO APPENDIX B

ARMINGTON Frederick 180, 188
ARMOTT Thomas 175
ARMSTRON Francis 232
ARMSTRONG David 175; Foster 223, 230;
 Francis 224, 229, 231; Jesse 259;
 John 172, 214, 223(3), 230;
 Nathaniel Shepherd 172; R. 215;
 Thomas 177, 186; William 187
ARMSWITH McCalvey 157
ARMSWORTHY Abraham 214; Bennet 215;
 George 214; John 214
ARNO Benjamin 186; Jeremiah 177, 186;
 John 187
ARNOLD Abraham 168; David 150; George
 240; James 171; Joseph 193; Peter
 182, 190; William 143, 193
ARNORS Benjamin 177
ARRINGTON James 224
ARTHUR Michael 168
ARTIS Matthias 215
ARUNDAL Lodman 231
ASBY Jacob 247
ASGRUE John 149
ASH Charles 163; Henry 246
ASHBURY John 191
ASHBY William 243
ASHCRAFT Thomas 227, 233
ASHFORD Butler 165; John 165; Thomas
 165
ASHLEY Abraham 192
Ashley David 189; Edward 192; James
 192; John 181, 184, 190(2)
ASHLY Abram 185; David 184, 189;
 Edward 184; James 184; John 184;
 William 184
ASHMAN Tobias 190
ASHMORE Tobias 182
ASKELLEY John 216
ASKEW Benjamin 146
ASKEY Henry 146; Zachariah 194
ASQUE Benjamin 150
ASQUITH John 215
ATCHISON Henry 193; Joseph 163;
 Joshua 163; William 163, 193
ATHEY Ebeazer 163; Eisha 163;
 Hezekiah 163
ATKINS Joseph 200; Nathan 181;
 Nathaniel 189; Nimrod 255; Stanten
 254; Stephen 255; William 254
ATKINSON Aaron 223(2), 230; Angelo
 255; Aron 230; Henry 255; James
 212, 220; John 173; Joseph 229;
 Joshua 216; Lewis 182, 189;
 Michael 184, 191; Solomon 230;
 Thomas 255; William 190, 215, 256
ATTIX Aquilla (Aqua.) 183(2); John
 190
ATTWELL Benjamin 143
ATWELL Robert 143; Samuel 143
AUD John 214; Joseph 214; Robert 214;
 Thomas 211; William 214
AUE Jacob 238
AUGLE Henry 247
AUGUR John 178
AUGUSTEEN George 238; John 238
AUKIN Thomas 224
AUKMAN John 199
AULD Daniel 234; Hugh 233; John 227;
 Philan: 227; Philemon 234; Samuel
 227, 234; Thomas 227, 233
AULNUTT James 148
AULT Henery (Henry) 166, 237; John
 166; William 166
AURANDLE Lodman 225
AURENDAL Lodman 232; ...man 224
AURUNDLE John 225; William 226, 232
AUSMAN Jonathan 225; Thomas 225
AUSTAIN John 237
AUSTIN Alexander 200; Cloudsberry
 (Cloudsbury) 224, 231; Elijah 218;
 George 219; Hamilton 218; Henry
 154; James 148, 166, 209, 224,
 231; John 197, 218, 225, 229;
 Joseph 219; Mathias 255; Richard
 231; Sam. 148; Thomas 166, 199,
 204, 225, 232; William 148;
 Zechariah 204
AUSTON Benjamin 191; Thomas 213;
 William 153
AVERY Charles 221; Jacob 239; John
 212; Richard 195
AVES Mathew 197
AVEY Christian 239; John 239
AVIS David 149; Jervis 149; John
 149(2)
AX William 248
AYDELOT James 258
AYDELOTT William 258
AYDOLETT Benjamin 250; George Hayward
 254; Obed 252
AYDOLITT John 252
AYRES Henry 250, 259; Isaac 251;
 James 235; John 250, 259; Moses
 241; Thomas 172; William 184, 191

INDEX TO APPENDIX B

AYRS James 227
AYTHEAY William 158

B... Thomas 198
BA...US Phillip 220
BACHLEY Martin 246
BACHTELL Isaac 236; Samuel 236
BACORN John 241
BADEN William 162
BADLEY Charles 217; James 217
BADSAY Richard 233
BADSY Richard 228
BAGGOT (See Bggett, Biggott) William 173
BAGGS Andrew 245; Isaac 153; James 153
BAGNALL Thomas 144
BAGWELL Smith 187
BAILEY Basil 201; James 171; John 197, 201; Nicholas 196; William 199, 204
BAILLIE Andrew 165
BAILY George 218; Mills 218; William 232
BAINE Bartholomew 155
BAINS Joseph 196
BAIRD Phillip 244; William 236, 238, 239
BAKEN John 241
BAKER ... 253; Abraham 240; Archibald 254; Baustin 248; Benjamin 217; Charles 174, 181, 185; Doct. W. 199; Francis 222, 229; Gabriel 239; George 236, 254; Godfrey 251; Henry 151, 222, 229, 237; Isaac 149(2), 247; Isaac Oystin 149; James 151; Jeremiah 157; John 149, 167, 196, 198, 202, 218, 242, 247, 256; John Voss 154; Levin 251, 254; Meshack 239; Morris 174, 239, 244; Nathan 149(2); Peter 236, 237; Samuel 229, 237; Saul 256; Selathel 254; Shadric 164; Thomas 209, 227, 235; William 149, 182, 189, 213, 215, 247; Zadok 254; Zebediah 239
BALCH Stephen B. 147
BALDWIN Thomas 169, 197; William 175, 176
BALEY Charles 170; James 178, 188, 209; William 225

BALL Henry 196, 202; James 197, 204, 234; John 144, 197, 228, 233, 250, 257; Levi 258; Levin 231; Thomas 234; William 256
BALLARD Arnold 218, 219; Ben 219; Daniel 258; George 216; Henry 258; James 219(2), 259; Levin 149, 219; Samuel 216; William 219(3), 258
BALLMAN Henry 144
BALLOTT John 198
BALY James 180
BAMBERGEN John 237
BAMGARDNER Adam 248
BANAGER Gasper 243
BANDY John 224, 225
BANFIELD James 167
BANHAM Peter 245
BANISTER Charles 220
BANKS Henry 218; James 154; John 240
BANNING Anthony 154, 181; Asa 151; Henry 154, 234; Thomas 156; William 151, 154
BANNON Anthony 184
BANON Jeremiah 185, 192
BANTHAM Henry 180(2), 188; Lewis 180; Richard 188
BANUM William 251
BANY Jeremiah 249
BARBER Baptist 210; Barnet White 210; Elias 210; George 146; Hezekiah 210; John 197, 204; John Myvert 210, Joseph 210; Luke 210; Samuel 197, 203; William 146, 148
BARBOR Cha' 144
BARCLAY George 170
BARCUS George 187
BARE Christian 238
BAREFOOT William 148
BARK John 240
BARKEN Andrew 237; Peter 237
BARKER Ananias (Annenias) 196, 201; Cornelius 201; John 164(2), 205; Joseph 161; William 161
BARKLEY Henry 216; Isaac 216; Joseph 216
BARKMAN Frederick 237; John 238
BARKSHIRE Jessey 243; Richard 243
BARLOW Zachariah 194
BARNABY John 230
BARNES Able 244; Ezekiel 175; Hezekiah 239; James 192, 213; Job 175; John 173(2), 198, 201, 245;

263

INDEX TO APPENDIX B

Joseph 201; Joshua 244; Nathan 239; Nehemiah 171; Peter 244; Philip 207; Richard 209; Teaten 246; Thomas 198, 206, 256; William 164(2), 172, 173, 226; Zacharia 211
BARNET Jacob 195
BARNETT Jacob 203; James 175; Noble 223, 230; Peter 223, 232; Richard 223, 230; Thomas 223, 224, 230, 231
BARNEY William 226, 234
BARNHAM John 160
BARNHART George 248
BARNHOUSE George 212; John 175; Richard 215(2)
BARNICASTLE Frederick 255
BARNS David 239; Ezekiel 239; Henry 239; James 153, 170, 234; John 148; Joseph 173, 196; Joshua 239(2); Leonard 147; Silvanus 239; Thomas 154; Weaver 198
BARNT Henry 246
BARNWELL James 223, 230
BARRAT William 185
BARRATT John 182
BARRET Joseph 220
BARRETT Alexander 206; John 206; Richard 206; Thomas 171
BARRINGHART George 242
BARRON Dan. 160; James 223; Oliver 160; Samuel Cooksey 160
BARROTT John 189; Nicholas 230; Ninian 200
BARROUGH Zaph. 161
BARROW Abraham 161; Andrew 223, 230; David Davis 223, 230; James 228, 230, 233; John 223, 229; Richard 223, 229; Samuel 229; Thomas 151
BARRS John 196; Joseph 147
BARRUCK Alexander 195
BARTLET Abraham 216; John 212
BARTLETT Daniel 228, 235; James 153, 164, 234; John 226, 234; Richard 226, 234
BARTON Isaac 144; James 156, 175; Thomas 192; William 156, 174
BARWICK Edward 151; James 151, 156, 157; John 151, 224, 231; Joshua 157; William 225
BASEL Frederick 247
BASEY Edmond 215

BASHWELL Henry 181
BASIL James 226
BASIN George 176
BASITT William 252
BASSETT John 254
BATCHELOR William 153
BATEMAN Benjamin 162; Charles 162; John 162, 200, 244(2); Richard 162; Thomas 244
BATES John 200, 206
BATH William 159
BATS John 215
BATSON William 203
BATTEE Fardenando 143(3); John 143
BATTESON William 195
BAUGH Andrew 244
BAUGHSTICK Nathan 153
BAUL James 226
BAUSE Charles 195
BAXTER Anthony 214; Joseph 214; Robert 223
BAY Andrew 172; Hugh 172
BAYD William 172
BAYFIELD George 150
BAYLES Benjamin 170; Daniel 170; Jonas 170; Nathan 170; Samuel 170
BAYLEY John 213
BAYLIS Samuel 175
BAYLY Benjamin 218; Elias 218; George 218; Lill 219; Robert 220; Stephen 218
BAYNARD Daniel 151; John 152; Levin 152; William 152
BEACH Samuel 171
BEACHAM Steven 255; William 255
BEACHAMP John 252
BEACHBOARD Joshua 250, 258
BEADEN John 161, 206
BEAL Joseph 220
BEALE John 197; Seybert 199; Thomas 163; William 163
BEALL ... 200(2); Aaron 209; Alexander 199, 201, 203, 207; Alexander E. 197; Allen 205; Basil 163, 205; Brooke 196; Clement 199, 204; Daniel 198, 241, 245; David 200; Edward 198, 205; George 146, 168, 195, 198, 201, 207; James 206; Jeremiah 198(2), 206(2); Jo: B. 199; John 198, 200, 203, 205, 207(2), 242; Josa. 208; Josephus 199, 206; Kinsey 205; Lawson

INDEX TO APPENDIX B

(Lauson) 200(2), 205; Levin
(Leaven) 196, 201; Ninian E. 206;
Ninian Ednond 198; Peter 240;
Richard 200; Robert 200; Robert
Alexander 198; Robert Asa 206;
Robert Edmond 197; Samuel (Smuel)
198, 205; Thadeus 200; Thomas 168,
146, 196, 200, 205, 206, 207(2);
Thomas Brooke 206; Thomas E. 197,
201; Tyson (Tison) 200, 205;
William 243; Zachariah (Zechariah)
200, 206; Zephaniah 196, 198(2),
206, 207, 241
BEAN Alexander 214; Ben 214; Benjamin
205, 214; Christopher 198, 206;
Gabriel 215; George 214; Henry
242, 243; John 214(2), 248; Josiah
198, 201, 206; Robert 214(2);
Thomas 207, 214, 242, 243
BEANE Henry 162; Leonard 162; Thomas
162
BEANER Lodwick 248
BEANS Leonard 242
BEAR David 239
BEARD Andrew 238; James 216; Thomas
218; William 144, 218
BEATTY John 207; Thomas 207; Walter
247
BEATY Archibald 171; Mark 238
BEAUCHAM Joshua 221
BEAUCHAMP Daniel 221; Edward 221;
Fountain 220; Isaac 220, 221; John
155, 221(2); Levi 220; Littleton
249; Thomas 220; William 249
BEAUSEY Charles 150' William 150
BEAVANS Rowland 255
BEAVEN Benjamin 162; Edward 160;
Henry 160; John 175; Richard 160;
William 169
BEAVENS Hezekiah 252
BEAVER Charles 175; John 175; Thomas
175
BEAVERLY Michael 215
BEAVIN John 161
BEAVIS Ezekiel 243
BEAZLEY John 177
BECHAM Littleton 256
BECK Alexander 183, 184(2), 190, 191;
Aquilla 153; Caleb 171; Daniel
183, 189; Darius 192; Edward 153,
181, 183, 188, 189; James 183,
190; John 171, 176, 183, 190;
Joshua 183, 190; Lenry 153; Samuel
176, 179, 182, 183, 187, 189, 190
BECKLEHIMER John 247
BECKWITH John 195, 203; William 198
BECRAFT Benjamin 199, 207; Peter 199,
204
BEDDO Absolum 200
BEDDS Absalom 205
BEDLE Gilbert 251
BEDSWORTH John 216; Samuel 221;
Thomas 217
BEEDING Edward 194; Henry 194; Joseph
194; Thomas 194
BEEDLE Harmon 179; James 179; Samuel
179; Spencer 179
BEGGARLY Benjamin 198, 206; David
198, 206; Henry 200, 206
BELFORD John 179
BELL Anthony 236; Bartin 162; Charles
239; Ezekiel 217; George 188;
James 151; John 167, 199, 222;
Joseph 232; Josephus 225; Leonard
237; Nathaniel 222; Robert 151;
William 151(2)
BELLHOVER Melchar 240
BELLICAN Christopher 188
BELLSWORTH John 216
BELLWOOD Henry 151
BELMIRE Michael 237
BELT Carlton 195; Greenbury 198, 203;
Jeremiah 167; John 193; Joseph
Sprigg (Jo: Sprigg) 199, 204;
Middleton 207; Thomas 206; Waring
209
BELWAD William 215
BENCE George Sel 207
BENDING Thomas 152
BENDOR Valentine 189
BENET Jestinian Thomas 161
BENFIELD Samuel 211
BENHARD George 239
BENJAMIN Abraham 197
BENNET George 216; James 217, 218;
John 200, 217, 246; John C. 163;
Lill 216; Richard 215; Samuel 185;
Solomon 184; Stephen 215; William
215
BENNETT Abraham 171; Benjamin 171;
Capt 255; Charles 250, 255, 259;
Edward 217; James 250, 257; Jesse
(Jessy) 250, 259; John 193; Joseph
215; Robert 215; Samuel 184, 190;

INDEX TO APPENDIX B

Solomon 191; Thomas 209; William 250(2), 259(2); Zebedee 171
BENNEY Benjamin 182; William 154
BENNIT John 240
BENNY Benjamin 229; Charles Walker 231; James 222; Thomas 229; William 230
BENSON Benjamin 158, 163; James 174, 235(2); John 205, 250, 259; Joseph 234; Perry 234; Selby 258; Solomon 216; Thomas 205; William 196, 202; Zepheniah 257
BENSTON Elias 220, 255; John 251; Michael 222; Thomas Williamson 220; William 219
BENT William 230
BENTLAY James 180, 188
BENTLY William 160
BENTON Benjamin 184; Benjamin S. 199; Benjamin Smith 204; Francis 184; Jacob 146; James 183; Joseph 198; Nathan 204; Thomas 196; William 199, 204
BENYON Benjamin 149; Thomas 149
BEONTRER Andrew 239
BERCH Zepheniah 196
BERKHORN John 224
BERKSHIRE Henry 243
BERREY Moses 190; Richard 190
BERRIDGE William 231
BERRY Benjamin 165(2); Daniel 223, 230, 232; Hezekiah 165; Humphry 165; James 178, 224, 225(2), 231, 232(2); Jeremiah 198, 205; John 159, 165, 184, 191, 223(2), 229; Joseph 165, 224, 231; Moses 182, 183; Nicholas 199; Prier 165; Richard 172, 194; Robert 144; Samuel 162, 165; Thomas 165(2); William 180, 232
BERRYHILL William 246
BERYWALLS James 186
BESHANG John 175
BESWICK Nathan 183, 228
BESWICKS George 222, 228; Nathan 222; Richard 225, 228
BETHARD William 255
BETHARDS Samuel 256; William 256
BETHERDS Benjamin 251; Daniel Coe 251
BETON John 200
BETTS Robert 251; William 174

BEVANS John 187, 256; Thomas 256; William 256(2)
BEVARD Charles 175; James 175
BEVENS Richard 180
BEVERLEY Rhode 214
BEVERLIN John 182
BEVERLY Adam 215
BEWLY Joseph 222
BEZLY Benjamin 178
BGGETT Samuel 160
BIGGER John 216; Jonathan 216; Stephen 216
BIGGES Thomas 212
BIGGOTT Ignatius 162
BIGGS John 171, 198, 206, 228
BIGLAND John 249, 254; William 249, 254
BIGNAL Robert 199
BILINGSLAY James 161
BILL Peter 237
BILLETOR James 154; Joseph 154
BILLICAN Christopher 180
BILLIGSLEY John 161
BILLINGSLEA Walter 173
BILLINGSLEY Hezekiah 161; James 209
BILLINSLEY Allen 213; Walter 212; Zacharia 213
BILMIRE Leonard 237; Martain 237
BIMSON Jacob 240
BINCKLAR Jacob 247
BIRCHINIAL James 189
BIRCKHEAD Christopher 236; Francis 143(2); John 143(2); Joseph 143; Matthew 143; Nehemiah 143(2); Samuel 143; Solomon 224
BIRD Benjamin 217; Edward 184, 190; John 217; Joseph 221; Solomon 216; Thomas 216, 218
BIRDWELL Benjamin 255
BIRKHEAD Nemiah 148
BISCOE George 213; Ignatius 215; James 210, 215; Jonathan 215, 235; Joseph 215; William 227, 235
BISHOP Edward 252; Henderson 253; Joseph 257; Philip 190; Robert 156; William 156, 240
BITTLINGSLEY Clement 210
BIVING Paul 161; Whealer 161
BIVINGS Bar. 161; Benjamin 161; Richard 161(2)
BIVINS John 179

INDEX TO APPENDIX B

BLACK George 180, 188; Ignatius 160; James 154, 187, 240; Jon 240; William 246
BLACKBURN Benjamin 148; Charles 148; David 148; Edward 147; John 170, 238, 245; Nathan 148; Thomas 148, 247; William 246; Zach. 148
BLACKISTON Ebenezer 176; James 181; John 178, 183, 187; Joseph 181, 189; Michael 209; Stephen 184, 191; Thomas 171, 184
BLACKISTONE John 213
BLACKLOCK Richard 199, 204
BLACKMORE Samuel 193; William 195
BLACKSKIN Jonas 188
BLACKSTON Eben 187; Ebenezor 178; Herbert 212; John 187
BLACKWAY John 192
BLACKWELL Francis 248
BLADES Anderton 155; Arnill 152; Benjamin 227, 233; Edmond 227(2), 233, 235; Ezekiel 233; George 154; Isaiah 233; John 220, 233; Joseph 155; Levi 233; Levin 154, 257; Samuel 258; Thomas 154, 233; Tilghman 157; William 227, 235
BLAIR James 247; John 213, 250, 259; Mathew 160; William 166
BLAKE Aaron 258; Edward 259; George 258, 159; James 182, 190, 258; John 224, 229, 235(2), 259; Joseph 146, 150(2); Levin 256; Oliver 259; Peter 235; Robert 192; Sarah 259; Sikes 227, 235; Thomas 150, 189; William 227, 229, 257
BLAKEWAY John 185
BLANCH Thomas 228, 235
BLANCHFORD John 183, 190
BLAND George 163; Joseph 157
BLANEY James 175; William 176
BLANFORD Charles 162(2); James 160; Richard 160, 162; Thomas 162; William 162
BLESSATT George 194
BLEW Abraham 241
BLITHIN Samuel 210
BLIZARD Ratcliff 256
BLOAD John 220
BLOICE David 206
BLOIS Charles 200; David 200
BLOODSWORTH John 219
BLOWERS Benjamin 196, 202

BLOXHAM Samuel 161
BLOYCE Charles 206; William 220
BLOYTH James 221
BLUNT Benjamin 152
BOARDSMAN William 170
BOARMAN Edward 160(2); Garrard 160; Henry 160(2); Ignatius 162; James 160; John 162; Joseph 160(2); Raphael (Raphel) 160, 161, 162; Richard 162; Thomas J. 160; Walter 160; William 160, 162
BOARMON John 161
BODDEN John 145
BODDY Barrot 185; John 182, 183; Stephen 182; William 181
BODY Bartus 192; John 190
BOE John 225
BOFFUTT Mordecai 204
BOGLER John 205
BOHANNON John 164
BOHANON George 212; John 212; Moses 212
BOILL Benjamin 237
BOKER Casper 244
BOLEN John 220
BOLING John 160
BOLT Thomas 212
BOLTON John 179, 186
BOND Benjamin 145, 149; Buckler 173; George 238; Gerrard 212; Jacob 173(2); James 173; John 148, 239; Joshua 173; Peter 172; Robert 223, 230; Samuel 176; Thomas 160, 210; Walter 239; William 173, 213, 230
BONE John 179
BONER Barney 170; James 170; William 170
BONHAN Peter 245
BONNER Michael 177
BONNETT John 246
BONNEWELL Benjamin 258
BONNIFIELD Samuel 206
BOODLE Spencer 187
BOOKER Daniel 238, 239; James 213; Joseph 213; Lambeth 223, 229; Phillip 237; Samuel 154
BOOM Jacob 238
BOON Foster 153; Isaac 152; Jacob 152; James 152, 153(3), 160; John 152; Joseph 153; Moses 152; Perry 153; William 152; Willson 152

INDEX TO APPENDIX B

BOONE Arnold 197; John 144; Josiah 197; Nicholas 165, 247; Samuel 167
BOOT Adam 166, 237; George 237
BOOTH Basil 210; Henry 213; James 210, 218; John 214; Joshua 214; Leonard 210; Richard 214; Robert 167; William 167
BOOTMAN John 233
BOOTS Abraham 181; Alfonso (Alphonso) 177, 186; Jacob 178; Joseph 177; William 177, 186
BORAM Thomas 198
BORASE Felter 199
BORDLEY Arthur 181
BORDLY Doctr. 181; William 222
BOREHAM Vallentine 199
BORKER Samuel 163
BOSEHAM Vallentine 199
BOSLEY Walter 145; William 174
BOSTICK Azariah 178, 187; Eli 180; James 152, 187; Thomas 152
BOSTON Daniel 221; Esau 220, 257; Isaac 257; James 221; Joshua 220(2); Levin 221; Naboth 257; Richard 220
BOSTRIDGE Joseph 192
BOSWELL Edward 159, 160; Elijah 158; Gustavus 159; Ignatius 159; James 196, 202; Jessee 158; Joseph 159; Josias 158; Nicholas 196, 202; Richard 159
BOTELER Henry (Henery) 166, 237; Henry (Henery) Edward 166, 237
BOTH Richard 210
BOUGHMAN George 246
BOULD James 214
BOULTON John 179
BOUMAN John 239
BOUNDS Douty 216; Jones 218; Will 216
BOURN Thmas 147
BOURNE Jesse 149; Jesse Jacob 149
BOUSER Henry (Henery) 166, 237
BOUSHELL Joseph 179
BOWDEN John 168
BOWDLE Henry 154, 223, 230; John 223, 232; Joseph 227; Tristram 224, 231; William 225, 229
BOWE John 165; Michael 247
BOWEN Abraham 147, 225; Bazil 147(3); Charles 147; David 253; Elijah 253; Elisha 253; George 194; Isaac 147(2); Jacob 150; James 147, 190; Jeptha 253; Jesse 253; John 147(2), 195, 253; Levin 253; Mark 212; Parker 147; Rackliff 253; Thomas 192; Walter 147; William 251, 252, 256; Young 147
BOWER Abraham 240; Adam 238; Frederick 244; George 241, 248
BOWERS Pearce 179, 187; Thomas 184(2); William 185
BOWERT Henry 240
BOWES Tim. 214
BOWIE Allen 198; Rhody 162
BOWIN David 147
BOWLAND William 217
BOWLEN John 248
BOWLES Ignatius 210; James 210; John 210(2); Samuel 253; William 210
BOWLING William 212
BOWMAN Aron 239; Benedict 238; Benjamin 239; Daniel 240; George 196, 202; Isaac 218; Jacob 196, 202, 238; James 223, 230; John 167, 242, 247; Joseph 224; Reynon 241(2); Samuel 224, 231; Syar 248
BOWSHAVE Simon 199
BOYCE Roger 145, 171
BOYD Abraham 198, 203; Benjamin 207; David 185, 192; John 198, 203, 212; Joseph 246; Robert 227; Walter 247; William 203, 238
BOYE Abraham 164; Oswald 164
BOYER Abraham 178; Augustus 180; Elies 179; Henry 241; Isaac 177; James 179, 180, 187, 188; John 180, 188; Nt. 180; Thomas 177, 178(2), 180(2), 186, 188; William 174, 180(2), 188(3)
BOYLE Thomas 171
BOZMAN Ballard 221; John 223, 235; Risdon 154, 220; Thomas 219; William 220
BOZWELL John 207
BRACCO James 235
BRACKNELL James 229
BRADBURN James 210; Notley 210
BRADDOCK James 227; Joseph 196
BRADEY Basil 211; Henry 210; James 210
BRADFORD Annanias 252; Avery 252; Elisha 252; Isaac 252; James 253; John 253; Levin 252; Sam 252(2);

INDEX TO APPENDIX B

Solomon 252; William 170, 174, 241, 252
BRADGURG Peter 192
BRADIE Edward 149
BRADISH John 207
BRADLEY Jonah 152; Nathaniel 153; Thompson 153
BRADLY Charles 162
BRADSHA John 227
BRADSHAW James 184, 191; John 176, 179, 187; Morgan 258
BRAFFETT William 183
BRAGONER Peter 248
BRAISHIER Morgain 250
BRAKENRIDGE John 174; William 174
BRAMBLE Leavin 166; Lewis 166
BRAMHALL James 161; Jonathan 161; Joseph 210; William 161; Zachariah 161
BRANAN William 171
BRANCH Daniel 242
BRAND James 248
BRANDBUN John 249
BRANDENBUGH Christopher 236
BRANDENBURGH Samuel 168
BRANDIS Thomas 199
BRANDLINGER Conrod 246
BRANDT Rand. 162
BRANNON William 170, 175
BRANNUM Thomas 199
BRANSON James 210; Leonard 211
BRANSTRETER Andrew 244
BRAWNER William 163
BRASCUP Thomas 229
BRASER Robert 174
BRASHEARS Morris 200, 205; Samuel 207
BRASSAR John 147
BRASSCUP Thomas 224
BRATCHER Richard 221
BRATTEN Adam 251; Belitha 254, 256; Jesse 256; John 255; Joseph 251; Nehemiah 258; Sam 254; Samuel 259
BRATTIN William 251
BRATTON Isaac 251
BRAUGHTON Charles 220; Elijah 220; John 220; Josiah 220; Kellum 220; William 220
BRAUGTON John 249
BRAWNER Barton 163; Benjamin 164; Bennet 158; Edward 164; Henry 164; John 158

BRAYDY Garrard 160; John 161; Owen 161
BRAZER Beletha 251
BREAD David 247
BREADEY John 210
BREDEN Joseph 149
BREEDEN Enoch 213; Matts. 215
BREEDING John 156
BREESE Henry 185
BREEZE John 150
BRENAN Timothy 203
BRENT Baptist 160; Richard 163; Robert 160
BRERELY Allen (Allin) 228, 233
BRERETON John 219; Joseph 219; Presley 219
BREVARD John 254
BREWARD James 176
BREWER Bennet 214; George 214; James 179, 182, 211; John 144; John Baptist 213; Nicholas 144; Thomas 211; William 212; Zacharia 212
BRIAN Dennis 145, 203
BRICE Henry 177; James 190; John 182, 190; Nicholas 228; Richard 182, 190; William 184, 191
BRIDELL David 255; Ezar 255; Isac 255; John 255
BRIDGE James 173
BRIDGES Daniel 234; John 226, 232; William 227, 235
BRIDGET Charles 213; Thomas 213
BRIGGS William 194
BRIGH Phillip 248
BRIGHT Basil 211; Ebenezer 151; George 157; Jonas 157; Nicholas 157
BRIGS William 209
BRIMHALL Ignatius 165
BRIN John 225
BRINKLEY James 147; William 149
BRINN John 232; William 225, 232
BRINSFIELD Moses 224, 231; Perry 231; Solomon 224, 231
BRINSON Jacob 240
BRISCHO Joseph 184
BRISCOE Alexander 177, 186; Benjamin 177; Bennet 215; Clement 210; Gerrard 195; Ignatius 215; Isaac 178, 186; Jacob 177, 186; John 164, 186; Joseph 185, 215; McHay 215; Moses 178, 186; Philip 210;

INDEX TO APPENDIX B

Robert 210; Stephen 215; Thomas 215; William 177, 186
BRISON Archibald 242
BRITAIN Slater 148
BRITT Frederick 255
BRITTAIN William 174
BRITTINGHAM Belitha 252; Elijah 250, 258, 259(2); Isaac 254; John 254, 258; Joseph 256; Joshua 253; Nathan 252; Nathaniel 258; Purnell 257; Sam 252; Samuel 250, 259; Thomas 250, 252, 259; Truitt 254; William 252(2), 254(2), 258
BRITTON Richard 145; William 179
BROADAWAY Thomas 184
BROADEY William 153
BROADHEAD Thomas 196, 202
BROADWAY Robert 224
BROADY James 209
BRODOC John 213
BORGDAN Samuel 144
BROME Hooper 213; John Hooper 212
BROMWELL Abraham 226, 233; Edward 225, 232, 235; Jacob 235
BRONCE Henry 244
BRONDS John 237
BROOK Raphael 167
BROOKBANK James 210; John 210
BROOKE Basil (Bazil) 149, 197, 202, 213; Isaac 199, 204; Oswell 165; Richard 197; Roger 198, 203; Samuel 198; Thomas 198, 202, 248(2)
BROOKES Francis 211
BROOKING Matthew 184
BROOKN John 210
BROOKS Benjamin 154; Dennis 154; Eusau 180; Henry 184, 189; John 174, 180; Johnson 180; Nathan 184, 191; Philip 185, 192; Samuel 254; Walter 158; William 159
BROOM John 148
BROOME Thomas 148; William D. 148
BROSEMAN Bennedick 196
BROTHERS Cornelius 212
BROUGH Joseph 246; Peter 246
BROWEN William 206
BROWN Andrew 176, 256; Basil 211; Charles 188; Conrod 248; David 185, 191, 257; Freeborn 169; George 189, 232, 257; Gustavus 212; Ignatius 212; Jacob 239;
James 146, 149, 191, 209, 212; Jessee 156; John 145, 152, 153, 159, 164, 171, 172, 180, 188, 191, 196, 201, 209, 224, 231, 232, 235 244, 256; Joseph 184, 191; Joshua 153; Levi 156, 218; Morgan 181, 189; Nicholas 181, 189, 213; Peregrine 179; Peter 207, 213; Robert 145, 171, 224; Rudolph 237; Samuel 172; Thomas 171, 175, 207; William 152, 164, 173, 178, 179, 185, 190, 191, 192, 201, 207, 245, 256; Wilson 256
BROWNE Joshua 170; Nathaniel 187; William 175
BROWNER Jacob 237
BROWNING Archibald 197, 203; Benjamin 197; Edward 198, 206; Elias 205; George 179, 187; Jeremiah 198, 207; John 180; John Writson 188; Jonathan 197, 203; Joseph 198, 206; Joshua 177, 186; Nathan 197(2), 203(2); Peter 230; Thomas 171; Zephaniah 198
BROWNLEY Joseph 170
BROWNY William 184
BROXTON James 186; John 177, 186
BRUCE John 173, 197
BRUCEBANKS Edward Horton 171
BRUER James 187
BRUFF Christopher 223, 230; James 220; John 227, 233; Richard 223, 229
BRUFFIT William 190
BRUINGTON Henry 249; James 249, 254; John 249, 254; Samuel 249, 254(2); William 249, 254
BRUMBLY Fassat 255; Henry 251, 253; John 258
BRUMBOCH John 236
BRUMBOCK Jacob 236
BRUMBOUGH Jacob 246
BRUMEL James 190
BRUMMEL James 183; Richard 182
BRUMWELL Edward 228; Jacob 227
BRUNER Jacob 242; Peter 247
BRYAM Nathan 189
BRYAN Arthur 227, 235; Francis 212; John 158, 192, 233; Philip 213; William 213
BRYANN John 153
BRYLEY Samuel 153; William 154

INDEX TO APPENDIX B

BRYON James 187; John 178
BRYSON Daniel 157; John 145
BUCHANAN Robert 145, 178; Will 146
BUCHANANAN George 164
BUCHANNON William 164
BUCHHANAN Robert 186
BUCKHAM James 208
BUCKINGHAM John 147; William 181
BUCHINHAM Isaac 153
BUCKLAND John 196
BUCKLER Benjamin 213
BUCKLEY Arnold 224, 231; Henry 223, 230; James 223, 230; John 172; Samuel 223, 230(2); Thomas 223(2), 230
BUCKMASTER Benjamin 150; Henry 150
BUCKSKIN Prince 188
BUDD John 210
BULEY William 153
BULGER Daniel 207
BULL Edmund 173(2); Jacob 173(3); John 174; Richard 174
BULLEN James 223, 230; Thomas 231; William 229
BULLER John 228
BULLIN Thomas 224, 231; William 223
BULLING Henry 235
BULLMAN Thomas 163
BULLOCK James 212; Jesse 213; John 155, 174; Samuel 183, 191; William 212
BULY Job 254; Joseph 229; Titus 254
BUMGARNER Jacob 244
BUNTON Joseph 232
BURBAGE Edward 253; Elias 252; Hampton 253; John 252; Selathell 253; Thomas 253; William 253
BURCH Edward 161; George 259; Jessee 161; John 165; Jonathan 159; Joseph 177, 187; Leonard 165; Peter 179; Richard 160; Robert 230; Thomas 203; Walter 159, 160; William 159; Zephaniah 204
BURCHANELL Joseph 187
BURCHINAL Benjamin 177; Joseph 177; William 182
BURCHINIAL William 189
BURDET Nathan 194; William 194
BURDETT Benjamin 196
BURDIT Benjamin 202
BURGAN John 191; Joshua 180
BURGAS John 180

BURGEE Thomas 197
BURGESS Allin 224, 231; Charles 203; Edward 198, 206; Elias 206; George 232; James 198, 206; John 232, 242; Josiah 200; Richard 208; William 223, 225
BURGIN Daniel 218; John 184, 185, 186; Thomas 218; William 188
BURGISS Francis 245
BURK Benjamin 160; Edward 152; George 184, 191, 251; James 163; John 181(2), 183, 189, 247; Thomas 152
BURKE John 194; Thomas 174
BURKETT Edward 147; George 244; Nathaniel 169; Phillip 244
BURKHEAD Abraham 143; John 150
BURKLEY Charles 194
BURKMAN Peter 237
BURKSHIRE John 243; Richard 243
BURLEY Neal 157
BURN Adam 195; James Kent 147; Mathias 195; Walter 163; William 195, 213
BURNES James 206
BURNETT Elijah 258; James 258
BURNITT Morress 242
BURNS Alexander 171; Michael 178; Robert 192; Thomas 179
BURNSIDES James 197, 201; John 179
BURRACE Charles 202
BURRAGE Edward 210; Ninian 162; Thomas 213
BURRIS George 180; William 178
BURRISS Charles 198; Henry 196, 202; Thomas 206; William 202
BURROUGHS Benjamin 209; George 209; Henry 210; Hezekiah 209; James 209, 212; John 209, 212, 242; Jonathan 161; Matthew 210; Normand 210; Richard 209; Samuel 209, 213; William 209
BURT James 153; William 153
BURTICE James 151
BURTIS Samuel 145
BURTLE Andrew 193; Benjamin 201
BURTLES Benjamin 160
BURTON Basil 198, 207; Jacob 207; John 196; Joseph 194; Thomas 144; William 151, 195, 196, 203
BUSEY Ben: 194; Charles 194; Daniel 149; Edward 194; Henry 194; John

INDEX TO APPENDIX B

199, 204; Paul 194; Phillip 254; Samuel 199, 204
BUSH John 152, 165; Joseph 229
BUSICK Caleb 155
BUSLY Benjamin 188
BUSSELL James 255
BUSSEY Bennett 175; Edward 173
BUTCHER James 180, 188
BUTLER Capt. 237; Edward 167; George 170; James 186, 197, 203; John 164; Joseph 145, 170; Moses 222; Robert 184, 191; Tobias 196, 201; Vacey 144; William 256
BUTT Azel(1) 198, 205, 206; Richard 198, 206; Rignal 206; Swearingin (Swearingon) 198, 206; Zachariah 198
BUTTERBAUGH Henry 247
BUTTERS Samuel 182
BUTTLER Joshua 255
BUTTON Samuel 182
BUXTON John 202; Thomas 202; William 202
BUZBY Christopher 198
BYALL William 197
BYARD Ephraim 170; James 170
BYER John 197, 202
BYERLEY Joseph 248
BYFOOT Tayman 174; William 172
BYNG William 218
BYOD William 198
BYRAM James 181, 189; John 181, 189; Joseph 181, 192; Stephen 182, 189; William 181
BYRAN Nathan 181
BYRN Michael 215; Nicholas 215
BYUS Joseph 166

C... John 216
CACEY Levin 256
CADE Jarman 224, 231
CADNER Thomas 222
CADWELL Ezekiel 202
CAHALL John 157; William 157
CAHILL Dennis 197; Peregrine 213
CAHO William 203
CAHOE Roger 200; William 197
CAHOON John 185
CAILE Michael 223
CAIN James 170; John 225, 257; Marshak 214
CAIRNS Frederick 241

CAIRY Dennis 223, 230
CALAHAN Dennis 152
CALARY James 163
CALBERT Isaac 221
CALDER Alexander 190
CALDWELL John 254; Samuel 172; William 144
CALENDER Andrew 225
CALGROVE John 171
CALHOON Ephraim 252
CALKLAZER Henry 247
CALLAHAN Edmund 175; John 144; Michael 224; Richard 206
CALLAR George 246
CALLAY George 243
CALLEHAN Richard 198
CALLENDER Andrew 232; William 232
CALLER (blank) 245
CALLICO Basil 201; Ignatius 201
CALLIGHAN Griffin 223; Joseph 222, 228
CALLINDER John 173
CALLOSON Thomas 215
CALLUM William Glin 229
CALLY Daniel 239
CALVERT Neal 221; Thomas 190
CALWELL David 172
CAMBELL Bartley 250; Duncan (Dunken) 227, 233; James 243; John 229
CAMBRON Henry 206; Milborn 206
CAMDEN Joseph 149
CAMERON John 157; Ludwick 246
CAMMEL Robert 241
CAMMELL Isaac 184
CAMMEN Adam 246
CAMMER Daniel 246
CAMNERON Will 220
CAMP James 172
CAMPBELL Alexander 201; Bartholomew 258; Benjamin 245; Daniel 173, 247; Dugal 242; Edward 212; Enoch 211; Ereas 195; Francis 247; George 195, 201; Gustavus 159; Ignatius 213; Isaac 160; James 174, 195, 257; John 220, 225, 247, 254; Joseph 205; Patrick 173(2); Robert 247; Solomon 251; William 251, 253
CAMPER Abraham 234; Adam 227; Charles 229; John 226, 234; Thomas 227, 234; William 156, 226, 234

INDEX TO APPENDIX B

CAMRON James 160; John B. 160; John Williams 160; Thomas 160; Henry 160
CANAHAN John 225
CANCANNON Thomas 243
CANDLER Daniel 195; James 203
CANDRY Thomas 167
CANE John 232
CANN Francis 177, 186; James 177, 186
CANNELL Isaac 191
CANNIFORD Robert 179
CANNON Edward 181, 189; James 153, 183; John 145; Sales 224, 231; Solomon 153; Thomas 216; Waitman 252; William 153, 166
CANTER Isaac 161; James 161
CANTLER William 171
CANTOR Jonathan 165
CANTWELL Joseph 219; Nicholas 217
CAP Michael 239
CAPELAND George 171
CAPLINGER Adam 237
CARBERRY Joseph 210; Patrick 212; Peter 210
CARD Benson 209; Sabrett 148; William 149, 210
CARDIFF William 233
CAREARL Joshua 179
CAREY Francis 156; Hezekiah 255; Jeremiah 250, 259; Justice 258; Levi 257; Michael 172; Smith 258; William 157
CARLILE David 194; Samuel 156
CARLISLE John 170
CARMAN Thomas 207; William 221
CARMICHAEL Ben 218; John 217; Levin 217
CARMON John 209; William 209
CARN Michael 168
CARNAN Charles 145; Michael 247; Peter 247; Robert 145; William 221
CARNEIRA Daniel 238
CARNER Noah 235
CARNES Michael 240
CARNEY Solomon 232; William 231
CARNON Leonard 237
CARNOR Lennard 166
CARPENTER John 165, 212(2); Richard 184; William 210
CARPINTER 3illiam 163
CARR Ambrose 211; Jacob 149; John 173, 238; Joseph 224, 231; Michael 173; Moses 224, 231; Patrick 182; Peter 188; Samuel 150; Seaborn 149
CARRADINE John 182
CARRALL John 165
CARRICO Bartholomew 239; Basil 239; John 239
CARRICOE Peter 161
CARRIDINE James 222
CARRIES Joseph 163
CARRINGTON Samuel 159
CARROL Edward 184; William 220
CARROLL Daniel 146, 199, 200; Denton 227; Edward 192; George 175; James 161, 174; John 170; Joseph 188; Peter 175; Richard 165; Samuel 165; William 165, 212
CARSLAKE Edward 223
CARSLEY Samuel 221
CARSLICK John 222
CARSON John 172
CARSTABLE Samuel 194
CARSWELL John 157; Robert 170
CARTER Christopher 176; Daniel 174; Dennis 244, 245; George 194, 236; James 210; John 148, 154, 234; Richard 248; Samuel 197, 203; Thomas 248; William 199
CARTOR Ezekiel 259; Thomas 184
CARTRIGHT Gustavus 160
CARTWRIGHT Abram. 178; John 194, 212; Justinian 210; Samuel 195; Thomas 195; William 154, 210
CARY Benjamin 206; James 195, 203; Jonathan 254; Levin 255; Richard 144; Solomon 251, 254, 258
CASE Brock 196, 202; Charles 200, 205; Isarel 194, 202; James 196, 202; Shadrach (Shadrick) 198, 203; Thomas 196, 202
CASEMARK James 181
CASEY Daniel 201; Levin 197; Philip 201
CASH Caleb (Caileb) 194, 206; John 194; William 194
CASHALL George 198
CASHILL George 206
CASLETON Ebenzer 186
CASNER Michael 199
CASSELDINE John 171
CASSON David 152; Ferdnando 152; Henry 151; Thomas 151
CASTALOE Ebenezier 177

INDEX TO APPENDIX B

CASTER William 241
CASTOR James 206
CASTREE James 200
CATHELL David 256; John 256; Jonathan 255; Levi 256; Thomas 255
CATHER George 157
CATHERWOOD Andrew 257; John 174
CATHIEL Daniel 255
CATLETT Alexander 202
CATLIN William 221
CATOE William 195
CATON Charles 193; John 185, 192(2), 193, 216; Joseph 222; Joshua 195; Stephen 193(2); Thomas 182, 192
CATROP John 223, 230; Lemon John 230; Lemuel John 223; Stephen 230; Thomas 223, 229; William 223, 230; William Marsh 229
CATTELEN Charles 209
CATTERTON Michal 150
CAUDRY John 255; Jonathan 256; William 251
CAULK Benjamin 154; Daniel 226; James 189, 233; John 155, 226(2), 228, 233, 234; Joseph 227, 234; Levin 156; Peter 154, 234; Richard 179; William 183, 190
CAUSEEN Gerrerd B. 159
CAUSEY Frederick 156; Isaac 156; Patrick 257; Saul 256; Solomon 156; Stephen 183, 190; William 156
CAVANNER Patrick 243
CAVENDAR Samuel 191
CAVENDER John 219; Lambert 184
CAVIN Thomas 199
CAW Nicholas 246
CAWOOD Benjamin 162, 210; Stephen 165, 193, 210; William 165
CAWSEY Beachamp 156; Hubbert 156; Nehemiah 156; Thomas 156; Zebelon 156
CAYE Michael 240
CAYTON John 179
CEACIL John 225; William 225
CECIL John 232
CECILL Thomas 232; William 232
CEICILL James 206; John 206
CELHOFFER Dewalt 240
CHAFFEY John 143
CHAFFINCH James 156
CHAILLE John 258; Moses 257; Peter 258

CHAINEY Charles 200
CHAIRS Benjamin 178; Nathan 178
CHALK George 175; John 175
CHALMBNERS John 144
CHALMERS Benjamin 181; James 183
CHAMBERLAIN James Lloyd 223
CHAMBERLAINE James Lloyd 230; Samuel 228, 235
CHAMBERS Benjamin 192; Edward 196; Griffin 224; Henry 201(2); Isaac 224, 231; James 196; John 196(2), 201(2), 202, 223, 229, 257; Josias 196; Orton 146; William 201; William T. 204
CHANCE Absolom 153; Batchelor 152; Levi 152; Peter 153; Rich 152; Richard 156; Thomas 152
CHANCER Tilghman 153
CHANCEY Benjamin 171; George 171; James 171; John 171
CHANDLEE Blackston 185; Thomas 186
CHANDLER Blackston 185; John 159; Samuel 159; William 252
CHANEY Charles 205; Greenbury 172; Hezekiah 207
CHAPELAIR Elias 210; James 210
CHAPLAIN John 223; William 223
CHAPLAINE Francis 230; James 230; John 230; Thomas 230; William 230
CHAPLIN Hugh 144; James 223; Philip 192; Samuel 185, 189; Thomas 223
CHAPLINE Francis 223; James 230, 241; Moses 242
CHAPMAN Daniel 224, 231; John 223, 230; Pearson 163; Silas 258; William 194, 229
CHAPPELL James 186
CHAPPLE Archibald 194; George 204; Henry 206; James 177, 201; John 199, 204; Thomas 199, 204
CHARK Elijah 163; George 160
CHARLES George 246; King 213
CHARLTON Edward 147; James 147; John 244; John W. 167; Thomas 148, 244, 246; Usher 167
CHATTAM James 159; John 164
CHATTLE Thomas 195, 203
CHEAVES Robert 234
CHEESELY Robert 229; James 225; Jonathan 224
CHEESLY James 229

INDEX TO APPENDIX B

CHEEZUM Daniel 231; Samuel 154;
  William 154
CHENEY Lewis 147; Thomas 147
CHENICKS Jesse 258
CHENOWETH Arthur 167; Thomas 167
CHERINGTON John 189
CHESELDINE Gerrard 212; Kenelin 212;
  William 212
CHESHIRE Benjamin 211; Berch(?) 199;
  Burch 204; John 200; John N. 199
CHESLEY John 215
CHESSHIRE John Baptist 201
CHESTELL John 152
CHESTERMAN John 177, 189
CHESWICKS James 258
CHETAM John 218; Walker 218
CHEVOUS John 222, 228
CHEW John 143(2); Joseph 194;
  Nathaniel 143(2); Richard 143
CHEYNEY Edward 194
CHEZALDINE Senica 215
CHEZUM John 154
CHILCUTT John 156; Joshua 153; Thomas
  155
CHILD Henry 200
CHILDERSTON John 166
CHILDRESTON William 166
CHILDS Andrew 182, 190; Gabriel 147;
  George 172; Henry 205; John 205
CHILTON Able 151; Anthony 153; Henry
  214; John 153, 214; John S. 165;
  Littleton 147; Mark 195; Matthew
  153; Stearman 193; Thomas 194,
  214; William 153
CHINEY Ezekiel 239; Jeremiah 240;
  John 239; Nathan 240; William 239
CHING Thomas 160
CHINOATH William 242
CHINSOTH Richard 242
CHIPCHASE Thomas 182, 189
CHIPLEY James 154; William 153
CHISHOLME Archibald 144
CHISWELL Jo: 194
CHITTAM James 212
CHIVERALL Jesse 214
CHRISFIELD Absolam (Absolom) 180, 188
CHRISHOLM Thomas 173
CHRISMAN Aaron 159; John M. 159
CHRISMOND Joseph 159
CHRISTIAN Daniel 233
CHRISTIE Gabriel 169; John 171
CHRISTMAN Paul 245

CHRISTOPHER Adam 257; Elijah 255;
  John 218; Milby 255; Smith 249;
  Stephen 218; Steven 255; William
  218, 219
CHUNN Eleazar 161; Henry 161; Levi
  162; Zach. 160
CHUSLY Jonathan 229
CISSIL Philip 207
CISSILL Bennit 210; Bernard 210;
  Edmond Barton 210; Francis 210;
  Gerrard 210; John 210, 211, 212;
  John B. 210(2)
CITCHEN William 165
CLABBACK Martin 248
CLAGETT Alexander 196; Henry 193;
  Hezekiah 205, 238; Jo: 200; John
  193, 196, 199, 204; Joseph 205;
  Nathan 199; Ninian 193; Postumus
  166; Richard C. 204; Richard K.
  199; Samuel 200, 205; Walter 204;
  Zachariah (Zechariah) 200, 205
CLAINLE Michael 241
CLAM Jacob 241
CLAPER Harmon 245
CLAPPER Henry 236; John 246(2); John
  Henry 247
CLAPSADLE Daniel 236
CLARA John 148, 149
CLARE Edmund 149, 151
CLARK Aaron 195; Aquila 174; Benjamin
  252; Bennedick 199; Caleb 154;
  Clement 196; David 173; Edward
  193, 198; Elias Mason 254; Elijah
  154; Elijah 181, 189; Elisha 181,
  189; George 181; Gershom 251;
  James 175, 184, 189; Jesse 181;
  John 172(2), 183, 190, 223, 230;
  Joseph 189, 244; Joshua 192, 225,
  232; Kenelin 212; Nathaniel 188;
  Parrott 232; Richard 154, 196;
  Robert 173, 174, 175; Thomas 198,
  199, 200; William 161, 173, 174,
  181, 187, 189, 200, 224, 231(2),
  244
CLARKE Barzellia 167; Barzilla 242;
  Benedict 204; Benjamin 210;
  Charles 210; Cuthbert 211; Daniel
  170; Elisha 242; George 211;
  George McCaul 211; Gideon (Gidion)
  180, 188; Henry 205, 210; Ignatius
  210; Isaac 211; James 144; John
  171, 181, 205, 242; Jonathan 167;

INDEX TO APPENDIX B

Joshua 185, 210; Leonard 205, 210;
Richard 211, 214; Robert 144, 212,
213, 242; Roger 211, 213; Thomas
203, 204, 205, 207, 210; Walter
206; William 176, 179, 203, 212
CLARKSON Henry 159; Thomas 155
CLARRIDGE Richard 166; Young 166
CLARY Benjamin 169
CLASS John 246
CLAVELY Henry 199
CLAYCOMB Henry 246
CLAYLAND William 227
CLAYPOOLE James 185, 192
CLAYTON Isaac 178
CLEAVES Benjamin 187; Nathan 187, 204
CLELAND Capt 151; Thomas 147
CLEMENS Christopher 173
CLEMENT Charles 165; Walter 165(2)
CLEMENTS Abner 151; Basil 163; Bennet
197; Bennet H. 163; Charles 164;
Edward 158, 163; George 159; Jacob
164, 165; John 153, 163(2),
164(2), 165; John A. 164; Joseph
164; Leonard 165; Oswell 197;
Samuel 158, 163; Walter 164, 165;
William 163, 199, 204; William
Wallace 201
CLEMMONS John 224
CLEMMONSE John 231
CLERKE Elias 159
CLEVER Benjamin 183
CLIERESMITH Andrew 238
CLIFEY Isaac 144
CLIFF James 224
CLIFT Abroll 152; Henry 151; Joseph
154; Mark 154
CLIFTON Samuel 241
CLINE John 238; Joseph 240
CLINESMITH Andrew 238
CLINKSCALE Francis 162
CLINKSCALES Adam 162; Ignatius 162;
John 158; Richard 162; William 162
CLINTON Charles 167, 245
CLMYER James 151
CLOUDS Curtis 250
CLOUSE William 167
CLOVE John 153; Nathan 154
CLOWER William 145
CLOWSE William 242
CLOYD Thomas 224
CLUFF Jonathan 220; Major 255;
Michael 220; Thomas 255; William
220
CLUVER Robert 170
CLYMER John 155
CLYMOR Francis 152
CLYTON Jacob 178
CNADY Isaac 240
COAD John 215
COALE John 143
COALER George 244; John 244
COALTER Niel 144
COATS Notley 195; Richard 199
COBETH Aaron 203
COBURN Henry 234; Jonathan 234;
Lambert 223, 230; Thomas 232
COBY Richard 186
COCHANTOFER Christopher 199; Leonard
199; Michael 199
COCHANTOPHER Frederick 199
COCHENTAFFER Michael 204
COCHENTOFFER Christopher 204; Leonard
207
COCKAYNE Carter 229; Jonathan 229
COCKBURN Jonathan 226; Solomon 226
COCKENTOFFER Frederick 207
COCKEY John 145, 226, 234; Joshua
145, 191
COCKRAIN John 224, 231
COCKRAN John 167
COCKURLL Henry 256
CODD William 241
COE Asa 252; John 251
COEFER William 239
COEN William 171
COFFEN Levin 252
COFFERATH Conrod 238
COFFEY Henry 215
COFFIN Samuel 230
COFFREE Samuel 230
COFIELD John 239
COGHILL James 153; Solomon 153
COHEE Amos 154; James 154; John 154
COHO Roger 206
COHOE Ignatius 159; James 162
COHON Nathan 222
COHOON Ben 255; Henry 222
COLBERT John 235
COLE Ben. 187; Edmond 214; Ephraim
170; Francis 212, 213; George 188,
214; James 170; Jeremiah 212; John
212, 213, 214, 256; Peter 225,

INDEX TO APPENDIX B

229; Robert 214, 222; Thomas 172; Val 214
COLEBURN Thomas 225
COLEGATE John 145; Richard 145
COLEMAN Charles 184, 191; John 154, 177
COLESTON James 227, 235; Jeremiah 235; John 228; William 227, 235
COLGAN John 187; Michael 197
COLGIN John 178; Michael 203
COLISTON Henry 234; John 235; Samuel 235
COLLAR John 246
COLLARD Joseph 241, 244
COLLEYFLOUR George 238; Michael 238
COLLIAR Isaac 242
COLLIER Dowty 216; Isaac 167; Kendle 251; Michael 167, 242; Nicholas Evans 216; Peter 251; William 193, 199, 204, 216, 253
COLLINGHAM David 221
COLLINS Abram 156; Belitha 251; Benjamin 178; Chambers 253; Edmond 196; Elijah 255; Elisha 251; Emory 154; Ephraim 220, 250, 259; George 193; Isaac 156, 172; Jacob 172; James 196, 202, 204, 250, 259; John 172, 200, 206, 219, 253; Joseph 217; Joshua 199, 206; Levi 218; Moses 172; Nathan 204; Richard 193, 196; Robert 199; Samuel 172, 220; Thomas 184, 196, 202, 206, 218, 220; William 172, 178, 185, 186, 192, 218, 251
COLLISON (See also Coloson) Edward 233; George 228, 233; James 228, 233; Peter 155; Richard 154; William 155
COLLWEL Samuel 215
COLLYFLOWER Michael 238
COLMAN George 175
COLOSON John 214
COLSCOTT John 152; William 152
COLSON Charles 245
COLTRON Henry 151
COLVERT John 227
COLVILL Philemon 166
COLWELL David 151; Edward 151
COMBES Jacob 171
COMBEST Israel 172; Jacob 172; Utey 172

COMBS Bennet 214; George 214; Ignatius 214; Leonard 206; Philip 214; Ralph 214; William 215
COMEGES Jacob 179; John 177
COMEGYS Abram. 187; Alphonso 185; Cornelius 176, 179, 187; Edward 180, 182, 187, 189; Gideon 189; Jacob 187; Jesse 181, 189; John 186; Jonathan 183, 190; Joseph 189; Nathaniel 179, 188; Samuel 180, 186; William 179, 185
COMERFORD Thomas 226
COMGROME Ludwick 240
COMIGES Samuel 177
COMMERFORD Thomas 232
COMMINGS John 242
COMPTON James 213; John 210; Matthew 211; William 162
COMTON John Wilson 161; William 160
CON Peter 245
CONAWAY Benjamin 185; John 158
CONDAN James 229
CONDARY Thomas 217
CONDEN Joseph 182
CONDON James 224; Lambert 235; Lamboth 227
CONDRY Daniel 217
CONN John 172, 240; Peter 238; Robert 172; William 207
CONNAWAY Benjamin 221
CONNELLY Michael 198
CONNER Bartholomew 250, 259; David 246, 247(2); Dennis 250; James 153, 187, 252; John 147, 258; Owen 163; Richard 197, 203; Thomas 154, 175, 197, 203; Timothy 244, 245; William 224, 237, 245, 258; Zadock 198
CONNLY Allin 155; Henry 227; Owen 154; Reubin 155
CONNOLLY Henry 233; John 172(2), 198, 232; Thomas 198
CONNOLY John 205; Joshua 212; Michael 205; Thomas 206
CONNOWAY Michael 171
CONNWAY Coro. 182
CONOR John 177
CONROD Daniel 238; George 248; Henry 167. 243; William 240
CONSTABLE John 242; Robert 192; Stephen 243; Thomas 243

277

INDEX TO APPENDIX B

CONTEE Alexander 199; Benjamin 207; Elijah 200
CONWAY John 222; John Span 216
CONWELL Richard 149; William 149
CONWILL Arthur 148; John 148
COOCK William 152
COODE John 212
COOK Charles 209; George 228, 229, 235; Henry 144; John 207, 233; Joseph 207; Risdon 152; Thomas 152, 214; William 154
COOKE Andrew 166; George 200; Henry 166; John 166, 197; Richard 196; Standly 166; Thomas 166
COOKSEY ... S. 160; Andrew 161; Henry 160; Hezekiah 160; John 218; Johnthan 161; Philip 161
COOLEY John 170
COOMBS William 178
COOMES Joseph 163(2); Nicholas 163; William 163
COON Adam 246
COONE David 247
COOPER Aaron 151; Abraham 217; Abram 152; Ark 152; Bennett 255, 257; Christopher 224, 231; Cloudsberry 151; Haddaway 228, 233; John 151(2), 152, 157, 165, 172, 191, 217, 225, 226, 232, 234; Nathaniel 226, 232; Nehemiah 152; Owin 157; Peregrine 183, 191; Richard 226, 234; Samuel 217; Stephen 157; Thomas 152, 217, 230, 233, 234; William 173, 228
COOSEY Jestinian 160
COPELAND John 169; Samuel 212
COPPAG Benjamin 209
COPPER Charles 182, 190; Darius 192; Isaac 186; James 185, 192; Joseph 184; Norris 183; William 182, 192(2)
CORBET John 159, 172
CORBETT John 175; Lewis 175
CORD Ashberry 172
CORDARY Henry 216
CORDRY Thomas 245(2)
CORK Isaac 188; James 181; Michael 227
CORKREL John 222
CORKRILL John 228
CORKRIN James 154
CORKURLL Henry 256

CORMAN George 237
CORNELIUS Daniel 179, 187; George 177, 186; Isaac 177
CORNER Noah 227; Solomon 225
CORNEY James 224
CORNON Thomas 225
CORSE Barney 182, 189; George 186; James 185, 186; John 184; Michael 177, 186(2); Thomas 183, 187, 188
CORTS Michael 237; Stophel 237
COSDEN Jess 180; Jesse 186; John 179, 188; Samuel 176, 178
COSE Christian 247
COSILL Ezekiel 151
COSLEY John 223
COSLY John 230
COSSART David 242
COSSERT Daniel 246
COSTLEY John 182; Thomas 184
COSTON Ezekiel 250; Henry 219; Oliver 219
COTERAL William 155
COTMAN Joseph 218; William 218, 220
COTNER John 229; Thomas 229
COTTINGHAM Elijah 256; John 256; Thomas 256; William 222, 256
COTTON Jeremiah 149; John 148
COU John 237; Thomas 152
COULBOURN John 222; Robert 222; Solomon 222; Stephen 221; William 221(2)
COULSON Charles 243
COUNCE Henry 196
COUNSELMAN Frederick 145
COUNTESS Peter 153
COUNTISS James 153
COUNTRYMAN Peter 241
COURSE Jacob 178; Michael 178
COVENTON Eiga. 209
COVENTRY Charles 200, 205; Jacob 168
COVEY Henry 229; John 155; Richard 228, 233; William 155
COVINGTON Abraham 218; James 182, 190; Joshua 187; Levin 218; Peter 187; Phillip 218; Samuel 216; Thomas 156, 182, 190, 219; William 189, 251
COVY Henry 225
COW Davoll 236; Frederick 236; Henry 247; Jacob 247
COWAN Alexander 171

INDEX TO APPENDIX B

COWARD Richard 235; Thomas 235; William 228
COWARDEN John 183
COWARDING John 190; William 190
COWEN William 243
COWIN John 171; William 167
COWLEY Hinman 250; Robert 161; Thomas 171; William 259
COWLY Hinnan 259
COWMAN Jacob 248; Joseph 148; Richard 198
COX Abraham 242; Anthony 153; Benjamin 207; Bennit 212; Clarkson 217; Edward 230; Francis 159; George 215, 227, 234; Hugh 159; Isaac 232, 242; Jacob 242; James 172, 215; Jeremiah 147; John 148, 159, 163, 179, 197, 203, 214, 222; Joseph 214, 225; Nicholas 229; Richard 159, 163; Samuel 159, 257; Thomas 152, 218, 222; Thomas Stradley 157; William 159, 163, 220; Young 148
COXEN Josiah W. 202
COY Christopher 196; John 241(2); William 196, 202
CRABB John 197; Richard 197
CRABBIN William 184; William Hynson 183
CRABIN William 191
CRABSTEIN Moses 157
CRABTREE William 243
CRADOCK Charles 205; Thomas 145
CRAFFORD William 250
CRAFORD William 259
CRAFTON Joseph 154
CRAGG James 242
CRAIG James 227; Robert 199
CRAIGE Laurence 195
CRAIL Philip 174
CRALL Jeremiah 201
CRAMPHER Danmund 148
CRAMPHIN Thomas 198
CRAMPTON Ozias 241; Thomas 241
CRANCE James 214
CRANDALL John 143
CRANE David 183, 191; Sampson 148; William 149, 215
CRANFORD James 147; Lemuel 147; Nathan 147; William 147
CRAPPER Bela 257; Edmund 255
CRATON James 173, 248; John 173

CRAVAN Andrew 174
CRAVER Jacob 238, 240; Philip 207
CRAWFORD Alexander 174, 201, 207; Basil 207; John 201; John S. 197; Nathaniel 196; Robert 197, 201; Thomas 200, 207(2)
CRAWLEY James 215
CRAY Alexander 228, 235; James 228, 235; John 179, 188
CRAYCROFT Clem. 162; Nicholas 164; Thomas 163
CRAYNOR Aaron 155; Emanuel 152; John 155
CREAG Phillip 247
CREAMER Daniel 248; Godfrey 248
CREEDDY Peter 148
CREEYBAM Phillip 240
CREGER Peter 248
CREMEAN Elijah 155; John 155
CREMEEN Curtice 155; Jacob 155; John 154; Salathiel 155
CRESAP Daniel 241
CRESWELL Matthew 175; Robert 175(2)
CRETIN Patrick 170
CRETZEN Leonard 237
CREW Edward 177, 186; John 186; Philip 244
CREYSOP Joseph 241
CRILEY Harmon 240
CRISMAN Luke 214
CRISP John 230
CRISSE Jacob 246
CRISTIAN Daniel 226
CRISWELL Robert 170
CROCKETT Gilbert 175; Samuel 175
CROESEN John 170; Richard 170
CROFT Frederick 240; Peter 240
CROMILL William 163
CROMWELL Joseph 171; Thomas 145
CRONEY Daniel 225; James 222
CROOK Jesse 213; Joseph 212; Justinian 213
CROOKE Thomas 175
CROOKS William 175
CROPPER Edmond 253; James 253; Jesse 251(2), 253; Labin 253; Levi 251, 253; Levin 252; Major 253; Noble 251; Rubin 251; William 253; Zadok 252
CROSBEY John 150; Joseph 150
CROSBY Burdin 149
CROSLEY Thomas 183

INDEX TO APPENDIX B

CROSS Cabriel 205; Friday (Fryday) 195, 201; John 144, 205, 239; Joseph 208; Robert 235; Thomas 198, 207, 208, 236
CROSSLEY James 240; William 239
CROSWELL George 221(2); Lawson 221
CROTZINGER Ludwick 242
CROUCH James 182, 190, 229; John 178, 180; Joseph 209; Nehemiah 183, 190; Samuel 182, 184, 191; Shadrack (Shadrick) 249, 254; Stephen 171; Thomas 249, 254
CROUDER John 231
CROUTZ Theodorous 199
CROW Edward 197; Jacob 244, 245; John 244, 245; Joshua 197, 203; Mathias 247; Samuel 197, 203; Thomas 182, 190
CROWDER John 224
CROWE Sam. 144
CROWN Lancelot 204; Samuel 163
CRUGLE Christian 248
CRUIKSHANK Robert 181
CRUIKSHANKS Charles 228
CRUIZ Jacob 238
CRUMMY Robert 240
CRUMP John 224
CRUMPTON John 154
CRUTCHLEY Thomas 143
CRUTHERS George 247
CRYER John 228, 233
CRYLEY Francis 240
CUGHS Joseph 247
CUGLE John 248
CULBERT John 185
CULBRETH James 153; John 153
CULEY Thomas 203
CULLEM Francis 202
CULLEMBER Jeremiah 148
CULLEN William 221
CULLING Thomas 216
CULLINS Samuel 222
CULLOM Francis 196; George 195
CULLUMBER Benjamin 149; Jesse 149; John 147, 148; Nathaniel 149; Richard 149; William 147
CULLUMBRE Charles 149
CULP Henry 246
CULPEPPER Michael 148
CULPH George 205

CULVER Benjamin 170; Charles 217; Jonathan 241; Levin 218; Robert 176; William 200, 205
CUMBERIDGE Joseph 168
CUMINGS Nicholas 228
CUMMINGS John 228; Thomas 228; William 239
CUMMINS James 233; John 170, 233; Nicholas 233; Solomon 233; William 223, 228, 230, 233
CUNNAN Patrick 169
CUNNINGHAM Daniel 186; George 174; Jonathan 174; Thomas 174(2)
CUNSTABLE Thomas 238
CUNTRYMAN Henry 241, 248
CURD John 195
CURNEY Henry 189
CURREN John 238, 251
CURRENT Matthew 149
CURREY James 174
CURRY Benjamin Lusby 160; Henry 153, 181; James 173; John 156, 170, 177, 179, 182; McGolds 210; William 153
CURTAIN Dennis 165; Edward 163; William 163
CURTICE Thomas 152
CURTIS Isaac 220; James 221; Samuel 221
CUSACK Ignatius 213; Michael 210
CUSTER George 248
CUTHBERT William 173
CUTHCART Thomas 224
CUTMORE Joshua 196, 202
CUTTS Charles 162
CYRPUSS William 206
CYSARED David 167
CYSTER Daniel 248; Henry 248; Jacob 248

D'SHIELD Lewis 145
DA... M... 212
DA..EY Daniel 217
DAFFIN Charles 157, 227; Robert 215; William 215
DAFT Ignatius 210; John 210; Matthew 213; Thomas 213
DAILING Christian 238
DAILY Elijah 177; John 183; Will 218
DAKUS Jesse 221

INDEX TO APPENDIX B

DALE Campbell 254; Ebenezer 254; James 251, 254; Jesse 254; John 254; Josiah 254; Thomas 251
DALEY John 179
DALF David 219
DALLAM John 175; Richard 175; Winston 175
DAMM Conroad 237
DANSKIN Alexander 185; Peter 176
DANSKINS Alexander 192
DANTT Charles 215
DARBY Asa 194; Basil 196; Ben: 193; Caleb 202; Henry 244; John 217, 244; Josias 193; Samuel 196, 202
DARCUS William 222
DARDAN Joseph 230; Richard 223
DARDEN Stephen 229
DARE Gideon (Gedeon, Guideon) 143(2), 148, 149; John 149; Nathaniel 148; Samuel 146, 150; William 146
DAREN Henry 230
DARESS Moses 215
DARLEY Benjamin 213; Moses 145
DARLING Lott 207, 239
DARNAL Isaac 193
DARNALL Benjamin 162; Samuel 162; Thomas 162
DARRINGTON James 183, 190
DASHEAL Benjamin 150
DASHIEL Isaac 217
DASHIELL Ben 217; Benjamin F. A. C. 254; George 216, 217, 222; James 216; James Fairfax 218; John 216(2), 219, 254; Joseph 216, 250; Josiah 218; Levi 217; Robert 216; William Francis 216; Winder 216
DASHIELLS Matt 218
DAUGHERTY Barnet 175; Capt. 236; Isaac 219; Jesse 221; John 216, 229; Michael 175; Nathaniel 216; Peter 216; Robert 186; Stephen 216; William 172
DAUGHTY Isaac 216
DAVENPORT Jonathan 187; Joseph 187; Josh. 187
DAVEY William 145
DAVID Joseph 147
DAVIDGE Robert 144
DAVIDSON John 170
DAVIES Aquilla 159; Benet 159; Benjamin 159, 164; Charles 159, 164; Edward 159; Elias 159; George 159; Jessee 159; Philip 159; Rand. 159; Richard 164
DAVINSLARY William 243
DAVIS Abisha 251; Acquilla 215; Amos 239; Annanias 254; Aquilla 156; Baptiz 156; Beauchamp 221; Ben 217, 258; Benjamin 253, 254; Benley 194; Blanford 195; Boston 247; Briscoe 210; Capt. 254; Charles 195; Daniel 183; David 152, 178, 186, 194; Dennis 239; Ebenezer 241; Edward 181, 253; Elazor 161; Eli 253; Elisha 249; Ephraim 195; Forrest 197; George 161, 209, 240, 249(2), 256; Gerrard 210; Griffith 195, 202; Gustavis 160; Henry 200, 220, 225, 229; Hgh 215; Ilgh 215; Jacob 174; James 149, 166, 210, 254, 258; Jeremiah 162; Jesse 162, 254; John 153, 174, 184, 195, 198, 209, 213, 249, 253, 254, 258; Joseph 211, 225, 232, 241, 250; Josey 168; Joshua 167, 219, 245; Josias 194; Lawson 209; Leonard 197; Levi 254; Levin 253; Lewis 178, 245; Lodowick (Ludowick) 195, 202; Luke 197; Major 258; Matthew 252; Matthias 251; Nathan 209; Nathaniel 258; Nehemiah 253; Owen 210; Peter 165; Philip (Phillip) 149, 182, 189, 209, 247, 254; Phillimon 154; Richard 163, 195, 203; Robert 182, 191, 227, 235, 254; Samuel 155, 165, 195, 217; Saul 255; Shadrack 254; Solomon 154; Spencer 249, 254; Thomas 161, 163, 219, 221; Tilgh 215; Vachel 195; William 144, 161, 165, 184, 191, 195, 200, 202, 205, 217, 227, 234; William L. 205; Zachariah 165; Zephaniah 258
DAVISON Lewis 167
DAWKINS Alexander 148; Charles 148, 149; James 149; Jesse 148; Joseph 148; William 148(2)
DAWS James 251
DAWSON Allom 241; Benjamin 163; Benoni 195; Edward 241(2); Elijah 156; George 163; George Impy 233; Henry 144, 163; Hugh 226, 234; Isaac 180, 188; James 224, 229,

INDEX TO APPENDIX B

231, 241(2); John 152, 155(2), 157, 224, 226, 231, 234(2), 235; Jonas 155; Joseph 221, 226, 233; Manus 154; Nicholas 167(2), 193, 228, 233; Ralph 226, 234; Richard 158, 163, 228; Robert 161, 234(2); Robert Den. 193; Solomon 182; Thomas 207, 223, 241; William 156, 185, 187, 192, 226, 234, 241(2)
DAY Daniel 149, 196, 202; Edward 171; Henry 175; James 201; Jesse 149; John 171, 179, 187, 217, 238; Leonard 200; Nathan 149; Nicholas 175; Richard 148, 155; Robert 149(2); Samuel 200
DAYLEY Elisha 186; John 199
DAZEY Eliphas 252
DEAKINS Edward 159; Francis 193; Leonard M. 146, 168; William 198
DEAL Elias 187; James 173; John 178, 187, 248; Morris 248; William 190
DEALE George 241; Henry 149; Jacob 147; James 149, 173; John 176; Joseph 143; Philip 241; Richard 148; Samuel 146, 150; Thomas 143; William 146(2), 150
DEAN Elijah 155; James 217, 237; Joshua 155; Massam 237; Mathew (Matthew) 182, 191; Moses 155; Robert 154; Steven 255; William 156, 157, 211
DEANE James 211; John 211
DEAR William 220
DEARDURF Anthony 168
DEAVER Aquila 174; Daniel 171; David 171; Hugh 175; James 172, 174; John 172; Micajah 172; Thomas 172
DEBOY John 166
DEDMAN Benjamin 184, 191
DEE Elijer 225
DEEDER Abraham 238
DEFORD Charles 177, 188; John 153; Joseph 188
DEIGHTON John 182
DEITCH John 145
DELAHAY Henry 225, 232, 235; James 235; John 155; Mark 224, 231; Thomas 225, 232; William 232
DELAHUNTY Mordeca 181; Thomas 181
DELANG John 245
DELANY Thomas 153
DELEHUNTY Thomas 189

DELIHUNTY William 177
DELONG James 174
DELOZIER John 158, 162, 163; Thomas 162; William 162
DEMAR Francis 161; Joshua 161
DEMENT Charles 158, 163; Edward 159; John 159; William 159
DEMMICK Edward 251
DENISON James 173
DENNEN George 188
DENNING George 180; Jonas 180; Nicholas 180, 188; Stephen 180, 188
DENNINS Jonas 188
DENNIS Abram 214; Adkins 256; Benjamin 256; Dunnock 252; George 257; Henry 254, 257; James 256; John 191, 198, 254(2), 256; Joseph 256; Joshua 255; Mathias 254; Shalmanzar 250; William 254
DENNISON William 181, 189
DENNY Benjamin 226, 235; James E. 235; James Erl 226; Joseph 226, 230, 235; Peter 223, 230; Richard 154, 235; Walter 174
DENSTON Abraham 255; William 219
DENT Benjamin 160; George 158, 163(2), 165, 210; Gideon 159; Hatch 159; Henry 159; Hezekiah 160; John 158, 163(2), 200; Joseph 160, 215; Peter 163(2); Samuel 159; Shadrach 160; Theodore 163; Thomas 159; Thomas Hatch 160; Titus 160; Walter 159; William 159; Zachariah 160
DENTON Edward 149; George 148; John 147, 148; Thomas 147, 149
DENTSON Levin 255
DENWOOD Arthur 216; John 219
DERBIN Edward 243; John 243; William 243
DEROACHBROOM John 151
DEROCHBROOM Matthew 151
DERR George 246
DERRIMPLE --- 149
DESELM Moses 204
DEVARN Frederick 247
DEVENPORT William 201
DEVER Richard 174
DEVERIX John 252
DEVILISH John 154
DEVIN John 171

282

INDEX TO APPENDIX B

DEVONPERT Jonathan 179
DEVONS Charles 209
DEVOR John 183
DEVOUR Cornelius 245
DEW Andrew 243; John 181; Thomas 185
DEWITT Henry 241
DEWLING Elijah 224; James 225; John 224; William 224
DIAL Terrence 241; William 184
DIAR William 210
DICKASON Zadok 202
DICKERSON Cornelius 256; Edward 218; Esau Merrell 257; Isaac 216; James 220, 257; Jesse (Jessey) 250, 259; John 196; William 256; Zadock 196
DICKESON Brittingham 145
DICKEY John 182; Henry 154, 157, 230; James 224, 231; John 223, 230; Samuel 223, 230; William 151(2)
DICKS John 149
DICKSON David 170; John 194; William 176
DIEMER John 169
DIES Daniel 216, 221; John 221; Robert 221
DIETT Aaron 151
DIGGANS John 151
DIGGS John 162
DIGNEN Frederick 219
DIKES Stephen 254; William 255
DIKIS Daniel 255
DILAHUNTE Mordecai 188
DILE Adam 240; Phillip 247
DILEHUNTEY William 186
DILL George 240; Price 157; Zacariah 178
DILLEN Arthur 183
DILLIHAY Arthur 214
DILLIN John 155
DILLING James 155; Joshua 155
DILLIS John 179
DILLON Thomas 212
DILTS John 236; William 236
DINNING John 178
DINSON John 184
DIRELING John 238
DIREWORTH John 248
DISHAROON Francis 218; George 256; James 218; Joshua 218; Levin 249, 254; Nutor 218; Stephen 218
DISNEY --- 146; William 146(2), 150
DITT Zacariah 178

DITZ Earnst 240
DIVELLY Martin 238
DIVER Hugh 170
DIVLE Michael 245
DIXON Absolom 212; Ambrose 220; Benjamin 148, 156; David 258; Isaac 220, 256; James 149, 247; Jesse 149; John 229; Joseph 152; Nathaniel 249, 255; Obid 149; Outerbridge 249, 255; Peter 212; Robert 224, 229; Thomas 212, 221; William 194, 199, 221, 225, 229
DIXSON John 185, 187; Nathaniel 166; William 185, 190
DOBBINS James 174
DOBSON Edward 154; Isaac 229; John 229
DOCKERY William 219
DOCKETT John 148
DODD John 145
DODSON John 159; Robert 233; Thomas 233; William 159
DODSWORTH James 201
DOGAN James 157
DOHERTY Neil 202; Nicholas 202; Philip 202; Samuel 170
DOLL Adam 237; John 237
DOLLES William 187
DOLLIS James 179; John 187; William 179
DOLVIN James 182, 191
DOMER Michael 245
DOMOKOY Jonathan 227
DONALDSON Alex. 144; Aron 239; George 148
DONALY Aaron 218
DONAVIN Philip 170; William 170
DONAWAY Thomas 256
DONBACK Michael 207
DONE John 219; William 258
DONEHAY John 174
DONEL Michael 170
DONELSON Samuel 240
DONIEL John O. 240
DONNELLY James 174
DONOHO Richardson 216; William 216
DONOWIN Daniel 177
DOOLEY Samuel 171
DOPSON James 156
DORAN John 196, 206
DORET Henry 228
DORITY Dickerson 216

283

INDEX TO APPENDIX B

DORMAN Chane 219; George 219; Isaiah 219; Jesse 218; John 219, 256; Levin 219; Major 255; Mathew 255; Michael 218; Milby 255; Nehamiah 257; Robert 217; Samuel 256; William 217; Zadock 220
DORRAH John 171
DORREMPLE Jesse 148; William 148
DORSETT Henry 146, 233
DORSEY Aquila 144; Benjamin 147; Daniel 147; Francis 147; Frisby 172; Gilbert 144; Greenberry 172; James 147; John 147, 148; John Hammond 171; Joseph 147, 212; Laven 239; Philip 147; Philip 148; Samuel 147
DORSIN Benoni 202
DORTON John 164
DORUS Philip 203
DORY Jesse 221; John 250
DOSSEY James 215; John 215; Lanford 215; Philip 150; William 215
DOSSY Humphrey 158
DOTSON Benjamin 147; James 147; John 150
DOUGHERTY George 172; John 193, 196; Michael 157; Neill (Neel) 196, 246; Philip 196; William 183, 193
DOUGLAS Samuel (Samuil) 159, 193; William 194, 216
DOUGLASS Benjamin 163; James 155; Jessee 164; John 238; Joseph 155, 157; Robert 237, 238; Thomas 159; William 152
DOULY Barton 200; James 200; John 200
DOUTY Dickerson 222
DOVE Benjamin 196, 201; Marmaduke 149
DOWDEN Clement 201; John 193; Michael 193; Thomas 193, 196, 201; Zachariah (Zecharia) 196, 201; Zephaniah 196, 201
DOWELL Henry 146, 150; John 143(2), 147, 195; Peter 195; Philip 195; Richard 195; Thomas 147; William 195
DOWLAND William 189
DOWLEN James 206
DOWLES Samuel 197
DOWLING Thomas 180; William 181
DOWNES Aaron 151(2); Henry 152, 205; William 151, 163; Zechariah 206

DOWNEY David 236; Ezekiah 236; James 236; John 236; Joseph 236; Samuel 236; William 236(3)
DOWNING Charles 148; Francis 196, 205; John 209, 244(2); Richard 148; Timothy 167, 242
DOWNS Elbert 223; George 257; William 158, 163; Zachariah 198
DOYLE Simon 239
DOYNE Charles 162; Jessee 164
DRAIN Thmas 205
DRAINE Walter 205
DRAKE Joseph 238; Robert 196
DRANE Thomas 200
DRAPER Edward 230; Ephraim 152; John 152; Nehemiah 157; Samuel 152; William 193
DREADEN James 220; John 255; Jonathan 220; Samuel 255; Thomas 220; Will 220
DREADON Isaac 257; Noble 258; William 250
DREDDEN Ephraim 220; Joshua 256; Sewell 255; William 255
DREDDON Lill 220
DREDEN Isaac 255
DREDON Moses 253; Sam 252
DRENNEN John 173
DREW George 171; James 171
DRISKELL Elgett 257; George 257; John 255; Lawrence 156; Moses 257(2); Shadrack 257
DRISKILL Adam 255
DRIVER Christopher 152; Matthew 154
DRUGAN Phillip 186; Thomas 178, 186
DRUMER William 190
DRUMMAN Bur...ll 255
DRUMMOND Stephen 231; William 182
DRURY Barton 210; Enoch 212; Ignatius 212; John 213; Leonard 210; Michael 211(2), 212; Nicholas 213; Peter 212; Philip 211
DRYDEN William 259
DU Thomas 192
DUBBERLY Eliakim 258; William 258
DUBERLY Eliakim 250; John 253
DUBIN Edward 245; Nicholas 245
DUCKER Jerremiah 198; Nathaniel 202
DUCKET Samuel 199
DUCKETT Isaac 198, 208; Samuel 204

INDEX TO APPENDIX B

DUDLEY George 233; James 232; Richard 233; Samuel 232; Thomas 226, 232; William 233
DUDLY George 226; Richard 226
DUE John 149
DUER James 257; Joshua 258
DUETSON John 191
DUFF Thomas 175
DUFFY Patrick 164
DUGAN John 177, 180; William 184, 186, 191
DUGGARD Henry 160
DUKE Andrew 149; Jonathan 215; Moses P. 148; William 198, 206
DUKES Isaac 155; John 250, 255, 259; Parker 250, 259; Robert 216, 220, 255; Thomas 155; William 250, 259; Zebelun 155
DULANEY William 151
DULANY Isaac 172; Thomas 153
DULCE Samuel 177, 186
DULEE Samuel 177
DULEY Barton 205; James 205; John 206; Thomas 200
DULIN HoliDay 227
DULING Elijah 231; James 229; John 231; Nathan 231; William 231
DULY Thomas 162
DUN Thomas 238; William 200
DUNAHOO Daniel 170
DUNBARS John 215
DUNCAN George 181, 189; John 209, 223, 232, 241, 254; John Miller 246
DUNHAM Dennis 170
DUNISIN Daniel 242
DUNK Thomas 185
DUNKAN William 185
DUNKEN Thomas 190; William 190
DUNKER Aaron 156
DUNKIN Isaac 251; James 184; Jesse 251; William 190
DUNKINSON Robert 215
DUNN Auguston 205; Darius (Darrius) 182, 190; George 246; Gilbert 216; Hezekiah 182, 191, 191; Hugh Smith 198; James 181, 183, 189, 191; Osburn 200; Patrick 224; Robert 183; Samuel 191; Walter 178; William 183, 190
DUNNING Abednego 160; James 160; John 162

DUNNINGTON Elijah 165; George 158; Hezekiah 165; Peter 162; William 165
DUNNISIN John 242
DUNWOODY James 238, 244
DURBIN John 245; Samuel 171; William 245
DURDAN Joseph 223; Stevin 223
DURGAN John 154, 233; Philip 178
DURGIN James 166
DURHAM Aquila 173; John 173, 220; Joshua 173; Mordecai 173; Partrick 195; Samuel 173
DURITY James 180, 188
DURUMPLE John 148
DUSINGER Phillip 245
DUST Gaspert. 241
DUTTON Thomas 162; Zach. 160
DUVALL Aquilla 197; Gabriel 144; Jacob 214; Levi (Levy) 197, 203; Lewis 197; Marsh M. 208; Samuel 167(2); Sennit 212; Zadok 203
DUWITT Peter 241
DUXON William 163
DUYER John 185; Joseph 185; William 177
DUZAN William Gray 172
DUZART Jacob 173
DUZENT Issac 172
DWIGANS James 151; John 151; Nathan 152
DWIGGANS James 151
DWIGGINS Robert 229
DYALL Edward 239; Joseph 158
DYAR Samuel 204
DYCUS Isaac 144
DYER James 214; Jeremiah 160; Joseph 162; Nathaniel 181, 189; Reuben 165; William 162
DYES Phillip 216
DYMOCK William 218
DYNE Jesse 158
DYRS Abam 154; Lymon 154; Symon 154
DYSON Barton 193; Basil 193; Bennet 160; George 159; Gerard 159; Maddox 193; Philip 193; Rosewell 194; Samuel 193, 199; Thomas A. 159; Zepheniah 193

INDEX TO APPENDIX B

EADDS Isaac 150
EADES Edward 200; Henry 189; Jacob 147, 148; James 189; John 190; Jonathan 189; Thomas 147
EADIN William 174
EADS Henry 181; James 181; John 181; Jonathan 181
EAGAN John R. 149
EAGLE William 151
EAGON Samson 174
EARHART Jacob 245; Phillip 248
EARL Dennis 179
EARLE Denis 187
EARLEYWINE Abraham 248
EARLY Benjamin 199, 204
EASLEY Richard 227
EASON Samuel 224, 231
EASTEN William 240
EASTER John 238
EASTERN William 237
EASTIP Richard 161
EASTON Giles 201; John 197
EASTOP Joshua 209
EATHERINGTON Aaron 241; Benjamin 241; John 241; Joshua 241
EATON Anderton 154; Edward 154, 226, 235; John 226, 235; Jonathan 156; Levi 154; Richard 154; Richard 226, 235; Thomas 154, 155; William 143
ECCLESTON John 188; William 188
ECKSON Nicholas 172
EDELIN Bartan 195; Benjamin 165; Edward 161; Francis 163; Henry 163; Richard 160, 163; Thomas 194
EDES Joseph 146
EDGAR Adam 228; Joseph 228, 233
EDGELL Abram 154; Benjamin 154(2); Daniel 154; Henry 154; James 154; John 154; Walter 154; William 154, 164
EDILIN Francis 161; James 160; John 160
EDLEY John 212
EDMONDS William 148
EDMONDSON James 154; Peter 223, 230; Samuel 223; William 148, 222, 228
EDMONS Easom 149
EDMONSON Nathan 239
EDMONSTON Mac: 200; Maccalon 205; Thomas 200(2), 205

EDWARDS Benjamin 209; Hezekiah 209; James 171; Jesse 213; John 159, 193, 197, 203, 209(2), 212, 225, 232; Jonathan 209; Joseph 212; Robert 206; Stouston 213; Thomas 184, 191, 209
EEDS Charles 205
EFFIELD John 186
EGERTON James 215; John 215; Thomas 215
EICHELBURGER Barnet 144
EKELL Christian 239
EKEN William 174
EKLE Peter 240
ELBERN Mathew 180
ELBERT Isaac 188; John 185; Joshua 229
ELBURN William 184, 191
ELDER Hugh 199, 204
ELDRICK John 223, 230
ELDRIDGE Joseph 181, 189
ELENSWORTH Richard 216
ELGEN Harrision 164
ELGIN George 165; Richard 165; Samuel 163; William 158
ELINGER Eustatious 249
ELIOT Mark 194
ELISHA John 149
ELLETT Samuel 175; Thomas 175
ELLIOT John 148, 219
ELLIOTT Ben: 194; David 244; Henry 233; Jacob 197, 203, 256; Jo: 194; John 182, 190; Mathew 144; Samuel 205; William 152
ELLIS Carty 177; John 174, 195, 197; Joshua 193; Levi 258; Shadrick 193; Sollamon 193; Thomas 180; William 180, 195, 258; Zachariah 193; Zephaniah 193
ELLISON Luke 252; Ralph 175
ELLISS Jesse 258; Thomas 188; William 188(2)
ELLORNE John 186
ELLT Benjamin 149
ELMER Benjamin 163
ELSBY Thomas 224
ELZEY James 220; Robert 219; Thomas 249; William 220
EMERICK Jonas 240
EMIHALL John 227
EMISON Thomas 188
EMMORY Arthur 153; Robert 209

INDEX TO APPENDIX B

EMORY John 153; John Register 209
ENDS John 214; Vincen 214
ENGLERT John E. 176
ENGLET John 179
ENGLISH Joseph 165; King 205
ENGRAM Edward 184
ENLOES John 184
ENLOWS Henry 175
ENNIS Cornelius 252; George 253; Jesse 250; John 194; Joseph 252; Joshua 251; Laben 253; Zadock 257
ENNISS Nicholas 202
ENT William 223
ENTLE George 193
ENTON James 190
ERNEST Michael 245
ERRET Christophel 246
ERWIN John 153(2); Robert 153(2)
ESHOM Jonathan 255; Joseph 255; Solomon 255
ESOM Daniel 256
ESSEX Isaac 148; John 150; Joseph 148
ESSIX Thomas 247
ESTEP Alexander 206; Jo: 198; John 161; Joseph 206
ESTLER Thomas 244
ETENIRE Martin 247
EUBANK James 235
EUBANKS Adam 225; Edward 153, 229; Thomas 229
EUNOCK John 178
EUNOCKS John 186
EVAN George 216
EVANS Dale 254; David 145; Ebenezer 251; Edward 172; Evan 172; Gamage 251(2); Henry 145; Hezekiah 162; Isaac 251; Jacob 256; James 182, 190, 216; Jeremiah 213; Jesse 221; John 174, 216(2), 219, 243, 252, 257; Joshua 164; Levin 221; Nicholas 216; Owen 221; Philip 211; Richard 148, 213, 221; Thomas 221(2); Walter 205; Warrington 156; William 173(2), 212, 251; William Mister 221; Zeckariah 204
EVENS Alexander 158, 164; Thomas 162
EVERETT James 172, 174; Richard 149, 174; Samuel 172
EVERIST Benjamin 172; John 172; Joseph 172

EVERITT Ben 187; Hales 183, 190; Joseph 152; Richard 147; St. Legar (Leager) 179, 186; Thomas 149
EVERLY John 196, 238; Leonard 168
EVERSOLE Abraham 248; Peter 245
EVIE Peter 240
EVITT Abram 156; Andrew 171; Seth 155; William 171
EVY Joseph 239; George 153; James 153; John 153; William 153
EWIN William 152
EWING James 156; Thomas 145; William 172
EYLOR Henry 153

FACKLER Capt. 245; John 245
FAGG Joell 163; William 164
FAGUE George 248; John 248
FAIRBANK James 234
FAIRBANKS Daniel 227, 234; David 234; James 225, 226; Peter 234(2); Thomas 234
FAIRBROTHERS James 231
FAIRFIELD John 225; William 189
FAIRMAN Henry 248
FAISTON Levi 154
FAITS John 242
FALCONAR Gilbert 187
FALCONER Gilbert 178; Jacob 183
FALKKNER Jacob 225
FALKNER Hynson 225; Isaac 225; John 252
FALL Levi 251
FALLIN Daniel 166
FALLING Aquilla 229
FANN William 176
FARDWELL Isaac 166
FARGUSON William 235
FARGUSSON Basil 194
FARLOW Ben 256; George 256; John 256; William 256
FARLOWE Absolum 199
FARMER Henry 239; John 196, 202; Philinor 239; William 164, 197
FAROW James 177
FARQUSON James 235
FARQUSTON Robert 235
FARRINGTON Abraham 232
FARROW Benjamin 176, 178; James 188; Samuel 231
FARTHING Aaron 212; James 168; Moses 212

INDEX TO APPENDIX B

FASNIGHT Adam 237
FASSETT Rouse 251
FASSITT David 251; James 254; John 251; William 251
FASTNAUGHT Jacob 237
FATOM John 177
FAUKENOR Greenbury 155
FAULCOM William 209
FAULKENER Asa 156
FAULKENOR Benjamin 156; Jacob 156; Salathiel 156
FAULKER Robert 243
FAULKNER Greenbury 229; Hinson 229; Isaac 229(2); Jacob 225; James 229; Joshua 229; Levi 225, 229; Robert 171
FAUSETT Goodheart 244
FAUST Francis 171
FAW Abraham 167(2)
FEARN John 224
FEARNS John 231
FEARSON Joseph 162; Walter 162
FEBBINS Daniel 149, 150
FECTAR Phillip 244
FEDDEMAN Bartholomew 156; Hawkins 156
FEGATE John 244
FEILD Edward 196
FEILDS Abraham 196; James 194; Joseph 194
FEILER John 200
FELL Stephen 172
FENDALL Benjamin 163
FENELL John 192(3)
FENISUS James 164
FENWICK Bennit 213; Cuthbert 211, 212; Enoch 212; Francis 211, 212; George 211; James 212, 214; John 212(2), 215; Joseph 215; Philip 211; Richard 212, 214; Robert 214; Thomas 211; William 211, 214
FERGESTON Samuel 241
FERGUSON Andrew 170; George 183; Rezin 201
FERGUSSON Joseph 194
FERGUSTON John 241
FERNANDIES Peter 164
FERRELL Charles 165; Elisha 160; Henry 180, 198; James 160, 198; Kennedy 165; Patrick 160, 177; Thomas 180, 188
FERRIL Phil. 223
FERRILL Henry 205; John 198, 204, 206

FERRIS Nathan 154
FERRY Benjamin 177; John 222
FESLER Michael 240
FETFER Phillip 246
FIE Baltus 172
FIELD John 213
FIELDER Nicholas 215
FIELDS Christopher 178, 187; Joseph 172; Mathew 194; Rezin 201; Thomas 201, 241
FIFE Abijah 193, 201; John 193; Jonathan 193; Joseph 193
FIFER Martin 240
FIGHTMASTER George 198, 206
FILES Thomas 215
FILLINGAM Richard 182
FILLINGHAME Benajah 190
FIND John 211
FINGLEY John 180
FINLATTER Alexander 145
FINLEY Joseph 170, 172
FIREY Joseph 246
FISH Benjamin 144; James 213; Joseph 213; William 214
FISHER (blank) 243; Adam 246; Daniel 185; Dudley 151; Henry 151; Jacob 240; James 153; John 156, 238; Martin 197, 201; Richard 153; Risdon 153; Thomas 220; William 143, 175
FISSTER James 188
FISTER Luke 245
FITCH James 241; Joseph 238
FITCHETT Thomas 220
FITZARROLD James 218
FITZGEFFERY Richard 215
FITZGERALD James 172; John 183, 191; Nicholas 247; Thomas 225
FITZGERRALD David 253; John 198, 206; Matthew 205; William 206
FITZGERRELL James 164
FITZHUGH Peregreine 148
FITZJARRALD John 219
FITZJARRELL John 165
FITZJEFFERY ... 215
FITZJERRALD Clem: 194; Edward 200; William 198
FITZJIFFERAS Aaron 231
FITZJOEK William 213
FIVICOAT Michael 246
FLACK Andrew 241; James 244
FLAHARTY Michael 184

INDEX TO APPENDIX B

FLAKE Jacob 243; John 236
FLAKER Frederick 248; Jacob 243
FLANIGAN Barton 163
FLANNAGAN Torrance 172
FLASSNER John 244
FLAT John 174
FLATMAN John 190
FLECK George 240
FLEGER Peter 236
FLEHARTY Stephen 154
FLEMIN John 256
FLEMING David 223; John 223, 224, 229(2), 231; Thomas 224, 231
FLEMMING James 200, 205, 230; John 200, 220
FLETCHALL Thomas 194
FLETCHER Abraham 194; George 194, 218; Levin 218; Samuel 218, 239; Thomas 199, 218
FLIELD Joseph 213
FLINN Patrick 185
FLINT John 242(2), 249; Thomas 199, 204, 205
FLINTT John 254
FLOORE John 169
FLORA Richard 242
FLOWER Jeremiah 213; Moses 214
FLOWERS Charles 148; Edmond 155; Lambert 180
FLOYD Aaron 151; Edward 209; Hugh 217; Jesse 211; John 258; Jonathan 224, 231; Robert 229; William 250
FLUELLIN Samuel 216
FLUHARTY Michael 191
FLULD Joseph 213
FLURRY Edward 164; John 164; William 164
FLYNN John 175; Patrick 192
FOARD Henry 246; James 246; Moses 186; Robert 247
FOGLE George 244
FOGLER Andrew 236; Christopher 236
FOLKES William 185
FOLKS William 177
FOLLIN Aquilla 223; Levin 217
FOLTZ William 237
FONTLERAY John 228
FOOKS Daniel 256; Jesse 256; Thomas 256; William 256
FORBES Charles S. 161; James 161; John 161; William 185, 192

FORD Benjamin 172; Chandler 162; Charles 178, 186; Edward 145, 178; George 178; Gilbert 220; Henry 211; James 172; Jeremiah 177, 186; Jesse 213; John 212, 214; Joseph 201; Moses 177; Nehemiah 221; Notly 165; Peter 212; Philip 210, 212; Raphael 212; Robert 212, 214, 242; Thomas 172, 221; Zadock 197
FOREMAN Jacob 183; Samuel 228
FORESAIN George 224, 229; James 224
FORGUSON Daniel 186; George 189; James 191; John 191
FORGUSSON Daniel 179
FORISDAIL Staford 175
FORKER Robert 238
FORMAN Barthm. 182; Ezekiel 185; Jacob 190; John 179 189; Samuel 182; William 189
FORREST Thomas 212; Zacharia 211; Zephania 211
FORRESTER William 179, 187
FORSTER Benjamin 182; William 183
FORT Christopher 174; Peter 171
FORWOOD Jacob 171
FOSE Henry 244; Jacob 244; Michael 244
FOSKEY Ezekiel 219
FOSTER Benjamin 190; James 172, 229; Jeremiah 240; John 248; Joseph 146, 156, 223, 224; Mark 225; Nathan 225, 229; Peter 224; Rigby 154, 232; Samuel 174; Thomas 156; William 160, 191, 224, 231
FOUNTAIN Andrew 156; George 179, 187; James 152; John 151(2), 157, 221; Massey 151; Roger 155; Samuel 152, 155, 228; Stephen 255; Thomas 152, 218; William 155, 157
FOUNTLEROY John 153
FOURACRES William 154
FOWKE Gerrard 164; Jerard 158; Roger 165
FOWLER Abraham 150; Benjamin 150, 209; Charles 213; Daniel 144; Edward 219; Elisha 199; Henry 210; Jesse 148; John 218, 239; Jonathan 210; Joshua 239; Jubb 144; Pat. 170; Patrick 187; Robert 224; Samuel 171; Thomas 155, 187, 210; William 144, 149, 213; William Perry 171

INDEX TO APPENDIX B

FOX Christopher 248; Edward 143(2); Eljah 256; Frederick 241; Michael 241
FOYE William 248
FRAIZER Alexander 147; John 192; Thomas 189; William 189
FRALEY Daniel 172
FRAMCOS Joseph 200, 206
FRAMPTON John 225, 226, 232; Joseph 226, 232; Richard 154, 226, 232; Robert 226, 232; Thomas 226, 232; William 154, 225, 232
FRANCE Joshua 172
FRANCIS William 178, 180
FRANKLIN Ebenezer 253; Francis B. 162; Henry 253; Hezekiah 163; Jacob 143(2); John 143(2), 158, 163, 253(2); Lemuel 253; Peal 253; Robert 163; Thomas 144, 159; William 162, 252; Zephaniah 162
FRANTIM John 224
FRANTOM Joseph 224
FRANY John Baptis Deli 150
FRASHER Daniel 216
FRAY Philip 182, 189; William 181
FRAZIER Charles 154; George 184; James 181, 189; John 181, 184; Thomas 189; William 184
FRAZOR William 166
FREDERICK Henry 201
FREELAND Aaron 245; Benjamin 167; Capt 151; Frisby 148; Jacob 148; James 144; Peregrin 148; Robert 150(2); Salathieal 179
FREEMAN Aaron 198, 203; Abraham 180; Edward 173, 176, 179, 187; Isaac 177, 179, 187; Israel 147; John 148, 151; Kinsey 150; Mathyas 151; Moab 159; Nathaniel 159; Patison 149; Samual 146, 148, 180, 188; Thomas 148, 150, 172
FREMBLE Robert 173
FRENCH Benjamin 143; Bennit 210; George 167, 243; Ignatius 210, 211; Otho 171; Raphael 210; Rhode 213; Stephen 210, 211; Thomas 157; William 180, 188; Zarababel (Zorababel, Zorobabel) 178(2), 187
FRENTLE Michael 245
FREONEY Joshua 249, 254
FRICK Peter 145

FRIEND Daniel 210; George 247; John 243; Phillip 248; Stophel 248; Tean 243
FRIKE John 246
FRISBEY John 190
FRISBY James 182; John 182; Joseph 184; Richard 184; Thomas Peregrine 169; William 181, 184
FROMAN Jacob 243
FROST James 174; John 174
FRY William 184, 189
FRYER Isaac 174; Richard 196; Walter 202; William 147
FULKS William 203
FULLIRTON Joshua 218
FULSOM Jeremiah 166
FULTON William 173
FUNK David 239; Henry 236, 239; John 240, 248; Joseph 240; Martin 240; Samuel 238
FURGUSON James 207; John 207; Jonathan 160
FURGUSSON Daniel 194; Elias 194; John 194
FURNEY David 245
FURNIS George 258
FYE Christian 244; Godfrey 175
FYFE James 193

G... Thomas 202
GABBEY John 236
GABLE Phillip 248
GADD Robert 153
GAIL William 174
GAITHER Basil 195; Beal 144; Ben: 194; Benjamin 196; Burgess 197; Ephraim 196; Gerrard 202; Greenbury 197; John 198, 244; Johnsey 197; Nichols 197; Seth 193; Vachel 244; William 196
GALALEE Thomas 187
GALE Edward 144; George 216; Henry 216; John 177(2), 186; Rasin 186; William 178, 186, 218
GALES James 165
GALLAGHANE James 229
GALLAGOUGH John 242
GALLAHAN James 223
GALLERWAY John 146
GALLIGHANE Griffin 229
GALLILEE Thomas 178

290

INDEX TO APPENDIX B

GALLION John 170; Nathan 171; Samuel 172; Thomas 170, 175
GALLOWAY James 219; John 150; Samuel 147
GALONTHON Edward Pinder 154
GAMBLE Darius 192; Isaac 154; Thomas 184, 191
GAMES Absolem 149; Howerton 149; John 181; Robert 149
GANDLEY Terey 187
GANNON Perry 151; Thomas 222
GANSBURGER Angle 247
GANSINGER Abraham 246
GANT John 207
GANTT Edward 147; Thomas 149
GANTZ George 239
GARBY John 210
GARDENER Charles 227; Isaac 149; John 149; Kinsey 149; Robert 148; William 149(2)
GARDIN Robert 225
GARDINER Charles 235; Edward 210; Henry 160; John 211; Joseph 148, 160; William 160
GARDNER Clement 161; Ignatius 161; John 161, 229; John G. 159; Richard 160, 212; William 213
GARHART John 239
GARLAND Francis 171; Jeremiah 228; Traverse 225, 229
GARLICK Joseph 207
GARNER Benjamin 162; Charles 164; Clement 212; Francis 238; Hezekiah 162; Ignatius Francis 160; Peter 162; Sheverall 153; Youst 237
GARNETT Joseph 189; Thomas 189; William 153
GARNOR Joseph 152
GARREN Jacob 229
GARRET Barton 166
GARRETT Edward 206; Henry 171; Job 153; John 152
GARRETTSON Freeborn 172; Garrettson 169, 171; George 172; James 174, 175
GARRON Jacob 222
GARROTT Allin 198; Edward 198
GARTRELL Charles 207; Francis 198; Jo: 198; John 202, 206; Joseph 207
GARTRILL Aaron 196; Charles 198; John 198

GARY Gedion 144; Jonathan 222; William 226, 233
GASH Thomas 171
GASHFORD James 154
GASSAWAY Charles 193
GASTLER Anthony 199
GASTON James 157
GATES Charles 216; Edward 198, 206; James 212; Leonard 163
GATHERIDGE Edward 174
GATHOR Henry 238
GATTON Ben: 194; Hezekiah 194; James 195; John 194; Richard 194, 204; Sylvester 211; William 200, 205; Zachariah 199
GATTS Edward 206
GAULT William 253
GAUNOR Paul 199
GAUSE James 223
GAVEN Francis 240
GAY Robert 177; William 176, 185
GEANES John 212
GEARHART John 238
GEATON William 145
GEBHART John 207(2)
GEDDIS Richard 192; Robert 178; William 178
GEDILIN Benjamin 200
GEE David 196, 202; John 197
GENSBERGER Peter 248
GENTLE George 194; Stephen 193
GEORGE Jacob 240; Joseph 181, 189; Michael (Michal) 166, 237; Richard 222, 228; Robert 181, 189
GERBER Michael 237
GERICK George 241
GERMAN John 254; William 223, 229, 256
GESOTT James 243
GETTRICK William 157
GEW George 196; Joseph 196
GIANT John 173, 176, 178; Stephen 177
GIBBENS James 220; Josiah 220; Thomas 220; William 220
GIBBINS Ezekiel 220; John 215; Nehemiah 160; Stephen 160; Thomas 220; William 160
GIBBIONS Francis 214
GIBBONS John 145; Joseph 174; William 220

INDEX TO APPENDIX B

GIBBS Abraham 256; Edward 183; George 184, 191; John 188, 256; Robert 258
GIBNEY Hugh 199
GIBS Cuff 188; Edward 190
GIBSON Bartholomew 146, 150; Isaac 219; Jacob 217, 223, 228, 230; Jeremiah 212; John 148(2), 149, 154, 161, 195, 213, 221, 222, 227, 228; Peter 148; Rhodolph 213; Richard 148; Roswell 213; William 174, 180, 188, 213; Woolman 222, 225, 227, 228, 235
GIDDINS Basil 198; Benjamin 199; Thomas 198
GIDDIS Alexander 181; William 223
GIDLEY John 183
GIGER George 169
GILBERT Aquila 170; Benjamin 186; George 181, 189; John 246; Jonas 175; Michael 169, 170; Parker 170; Samuel 170
GILCHRIST Robert 175
GILES Isaac 217, 218; James 171; John 254; Thomas 169
GILHUST Robert 222
GILKEY Samuel 196
GILL Adam 159; Ase 232; Charles 161; Henry 215; Hepsebeath 152; John 161, 204; Jonathan 161; Joseph 199; Moses 232; Robert 161
GILLALAND Hugh 246
GILLAM John 194; Thomas 159, 194
GILLASPEY Charles 172; John 172
GILLESPIE David 237; John 246
GILLETT Ayres 258; William 258
GILLIPIS John 242
GILLIS Joseph 217; William 217
GILLISPIE Thomas 246
GILLISS Joseph 217, 218; Levin 218; Thomas 218
GILLSAT Michael 242
GILON James 225, 229; John 224, 225
GILPIN Benjamin N. 159; Green 239; Henry 209; Isaac 229; Leonard 164; Thomas 159
GILSON William 237
GINES Evan 242
GINGLE George 204
GINN Josiah 156
GIPSON Alby 146
GIRD John 181

GIRTEY Thomas 243
GIST John 145; Joshua 145; Mordecai 144
GITTINGS Basil 205; Benjamin 204; Henry 200; Thomas 206
GIVEINGS Daniel 237
GIVENS Daniel 166; James 252; Rounds 254
GIVINS George 255; Jonathan 255
GIZTEY Thomas 243
GLADDEN Joseph 219
GLADHILL William 167, 237
GLADSON Nathan 156; Thomas 252
GLAND Jonas 153
GLANDEN Cloudsberry 152; Laban 153; William 153
GLANDON Herrington 152; Hinson 153
GLANN Nath. 180; Nathaniel 188
GLANVILL William 182, 191
GLASENER George 245
GLASGOW Patrick 257
GLASNER George 245
GLASS Christopher 255
GLASSCO John 162; Thomas 162
GLASSER Michael 237
GLASSNER George 244; John 245
GLASTIN John 217
GLAZE Basil 198, 206; Jonathan 198, 206; Nathan 198; Natt: 198
GLEAVES John 182, 190
GLEBB Caleb 214
GLEMS Alexander 183
GLENN Alexander 189, 192; Frederick 189; John 191; Peregrine 181, 189; William 181, 189
GLEVE Gorge 227
GLISTER David 239
GLOVER William 210
GODDARD Barton 211; Ignatius 211, 212; John Baptist 213
GODDERD William 218
GODDEY William 232
GODDIN Aaron 174; William 174
GODEY Henry 237
GODFREY Belitha 252; Charles 252; James 251; Landsdale 159
GODGRACE Robert 164; William 164
GODING Moses 245
GODMAN Humphry 195; Samuel J. 198, 207
GODSGRACE William 171
GODWIN Preiston 156

INDEX TO APPENDIX B

GOINGS John 214
GOLDEN John 203; Robert 163; Samuel 203
GOLDSBERRY James 214; John 215; Nicholas 214; Robert 211
GOLDSBOROUGH Greenbury 223; Nicholas 227, 235; Thomas 153; William 230
GOLDSBURRY Stephen 214
GOLDSBURY Greenbury 235; Henry 215; William 215
GOLDSMITH John 212; Thomas 213; Vincent 173; William 144; William Copeland 171
GOLY Thomas 164
GOMBER Jacob 167
GONTZ George 244; Jacob 244; Joseph 244
GOOD Abraham 244; Christopher 244; John 244; Roswell 159
GOODEN Benjamin 167; Joseph 167; Moses 167
GOODIN William 213
GOODING Benjamin 245; Doctr. 146; Joseph 245
GOODRICK Aaron 162; Benjamin 204; Charles 159; George 159; Walter 162
GOODY William 225
GORDEN Charles 238; William 167, 243
GORDON Alexander 172, 226; John (Jon) 145, 172, 184, 189, 195; Joseph 209; Josiah 207; Richard 226; Thomas 230; William 152
GORDY Peter 249, 254; William 249, 254
GORE Christian 145; John 218, 224, 231; Samuel 225, 229; Walker 229; Walter 225; William 223, 230
GORMAN Daniel 249
GORMON William 236
GORND Adam 237
GORNWELL John 252; Major 257
GORRELL Thomas 170
GORWOOD William 144
GOSLE William 217
GOSLEE George 218; John 218; Joseph 218; Thomas 217
GOSSAGE Charles 227 233; Daniel 227, 233; Robert 227, 233
GOTSHALL Earnest 169
GOTT Ezekiel 143; Joseph 143

GOUGH Bennit 212; Ignatius 214; James 214; Stephen 214, 215
GOULDY Samuel 195
GOUTEE John 155
GOVANE J. 144
GOVER Gideon 175; Samuel 169; William 149
GOW William 154
GRABRAL John 246
GRACE Abel (Able) 224, 229; George 155; James 155, 227, 234; Jese 195; John 227, 233; Nathaniel 227, 233, 234; Solomon 155; Thomas 155; William 226, 234
GRAFT George 193
GRAGG Joshua 199
GRAHAM Alexander 209; Benjamin 217; Capt 151; Charles 154; Ezekiel 217; James 216, 240; Joseph 233; Thomas 144; William 177, 186(2)
GRAHAME James 148; John 147
GRAIN Thomas 214
GRAINGER Richard 232; Thomas 189
GRAMBLE Darius 185
GRANGER Andrew 145; Thomas 181
GRANT Francis 146; George 177; James 181; John 158(2), 163, 244; Jonathan 171, 182; Samuel 182, 190; William 179, 182, 187, 200
GRANTLY James 157
GRAVE Adam 248
GRAVEL Benjamin 144
GRAVER George 248
GRAVEROD (blank) 243
GRAVES Jeremiah 212; John 199, 204, 212; Joshua 212; Luke 213; Richard 181; Thomas 199
GRAY Adin 197, 203; Andrew 165; Anthony 158; Anthony C. 162; Benjamin 164, 197, 203, 254(2); David 253; Edward 162; George 150, 161, 162; Henry 147, 162; Hezekiah 195; Isaac 253; James 148, 155, 160; Jeremiah (Jerimiah, Jerremiah) 162, 197, 203; Jerrediah 254; Jesse 253, 256; John 144, 148, 171, 178, 188, 219, 255; John N. 162; Johnson 254; Joseph 160, 162, 254, 256; Joshua 144; Mathias 203; Richard 149, 165; Rubin 229; Thomas 147(2), 254; Whittey 220; William 147(2),

INDEX TO APPENDIX B

155(2), 161, 163, 164, 165, 197, 203, 253
GRAYAM Samuel 161
GRAYBELL Philip 145
GRAYBILL Peter 241
GRAYBLE Andrew 145
GRAYDOCK William 153
GRAYER James 161
GRAYLESS Jessee 156; William 156
GREAR James 217
GREEDY James 179, 187
GREEN Abednego 216; Abel 172; Andrew 224, 231; Benjamin 173; Bennet (Bennett) 174, 195; Clement 197, 203; Dudley 200; Elijah 164; Elisha 216; Ezekiel 218; Henry 163, 173; Ignatius 197, 203, 215; Isaac 194; John 144, 153, 154, 185, 192, 203; Joshua (Josh.) 163, 194; Leonard 173(2), 199, 201; Michael 144, 217; Moses 219; Nacey 203; Peter 163; Phillip 193; Reph 194; Richard 180, 188; Samuel 195; Solomon 209; Thomas 163, 195; Thomas M. 163; William 157, 207; Zachariah 152; Zebulon 152
GREENBERGH Jonathan 157
GREENFIELD Capt 151; Charles 200, 204; James Truman 210; Mo: 192; Nathaniel Truman 209; Robert 185; Thomas 204, 210; Thomas Truman 150; William 181, 189
GREENHAWK John 229; Richard 225
GREENLEAVES Simond 163
GREENTREE Benjamin 206
GREENWELD Archibald 214
GREENWELL Arnold 211; Barton 211; Bennet (Bennit) 196, 201; Clement 214; Edmond Barton 211; Edward 214; Henry 211; Ignatius 211, 214; James 211, 214(2); Jesse 213, 214; John 211(2), 214; Joseph 211, 214; Noah 212; Raphael 213; Robert 211; Stephen 214(2); Thomas 211(2), 214; William 214(2)
GREENWOOD Benjamin 191(2); Daniel 177, 186; George 178, 186, 191; James 178, 183, 188, 191; John 178, 180, 185; Joseph 176, 178, 185; William 179, 184
GREER Ayres 259; Henry 173; John 252; Thomas 253; William 253(2)

GREGG John 153; Robert 244(2), 245(2)
GREGORY James 224, 231; John 231; William 224, 231
GRENWELL Joseph 214; Nicholas 214
GRESHAM Richard 183
GREVE Dower 149
GREVES Robert 149
GRIEVES Robert 215
GRIFFEN Bilitha 252; Edward 146; John 146, 150; William 253
GRIFFETH John 152
GRIFFIN Edward 150, 222; Ignatius 210; James 158; John 150, 158; Peter 158; Robert 175, 222, 229, 232; Samuel 149
GRIFFIS Thomas 163
GRIFFITH Alexander 155; Benjamin 196, 198, 202; Caleb 196; Charles 198; Charles Gr. 200; David 190; Elisha 196; George 156, 196; Greenbury 196, 202; Henry 154, 197; Hezekiah 196; Howard 196, 202; James 181, 189, 198; John 150, 183, 184, 198, 202; Lewis 150; Marshal 150; Samuel 171; Thomas 182, 190; William 183, 190
GRIM Jacob 166, 237
GRIMES Archibald 168; Edward 243, 245; John 181, 243(2); William 170, 242
GRIMM Alexander 167
GRIMS Marten 237
GRINDAGE William 180, 188
GRINDALL Josias 210
GRISLER Christopher 145
GROND Phillip 237
GROOM James 183, 191, 203
GROOME Charles 184, 191; Daniel 177, 186; James 197
GROOMES David 250
GROOMS David 259
GROSH Peter 167(2)
GROSS Henry 167
GROUTMAN John 248
GROVE David 240; Jacob 248
GROVER John 149
GROVES John 165; Joseph 242; Perry 199; Thomas 227, 233; William 165
GRUMBLE John 217
GRUNDLE Thomas 205
GRYAR Thomas 213
GRYER Walter 196

INDEX TO APPENDIX B

GUE George 202; Henry 196; Joseph 202
GUEST James 167
GUILKEY Samuel 201
GUINN Edward 163
GULL Balzer 240; George 246
GULLET Abraham 218; George 176, 179
GULLY Barthomew 225; Charles 225, 230, 232
GUMBARE Jacob 167
GUNBY Benjamin 222; Isaac 222; John 216, 257; Kirk 222; Levin 218
GUNN John 258
GUPTON William 217
GURLY Frank 254
GUSLER Anthony 207
GUSSTON Will 217
GUTRY John 248
GUTTERY C. Joshua 185; Caleb 259
GUTTHERY James 250
GUTTHUY James 250
GUTTRY Joshua 192
GUY John 163; Moses 162; William 163
GUYTHER George 214
GUYTON Isac 170; Underwood 175
GYANT George 190

H... Aquila 211
H... James 217
HAAZ Henry 248
HACHISON Robert 188
HACKET Rhode 214
HACKETT Charles 192; Isaac 182; Oliver 156; Richard 172; Simd. 177; Simon 186
HACKLER Martin 238
HADDAWAY Daniel 227, 233; James 226, 234; John 227, 228(2), 234; Oakley 233; Peter 227(2), 234; Robert 233; Rolen 226; Thomas 228; Thomas Lambden (Lamn.) 228, 233; Thomas Lurty 233; William 226, 228, 233, 234
HADDER John 251; Nehemiah 252; Shadrick 253; Warran 251
HADDOCK James 220
HADDOWAY Robert 226
HADLEY Edward 189; James 201; Shem 182, 190; Solomon 209; Thomas 181
HAFF Abraham 168
HAGAN Hugh 245; John 246; Leonard 193
HAGAR Robert 211; William 212
HAGER Jonathan 238

HAGON Benjamin 160; Bennett 193; James 162; Raphael 160
HAGUE James 184, 189
HAHN Adam 244
HAILE John 221; Robert 221
HAILS Charles Lucas 218
HAINES Gideon 189; Jacob 246; John 220
HAINEY James 217; Richard 217
HAINS Joseph 239; Phillip 239; Thomas 219
HAISLIP Henry 164; James 200; John 164(2); Jonathan 164; Labon 164; Robert 164; Samuel 164; William 164
HAITH James 214
HAIVE John 176
HAKETT Charles 185
HALANHEAD Richard 146
HALBERT David 192; Simeon 189; Simon 182
HALES Jeremiah 252; William 177, 186
HALEY John 180, 186; William 179
HALFPENNY Patrick 175; Thomas 194
HALL Aquila (Acquilla) 170(2), 171, 213; Arthur 211; Basil 213; Benedict Edward 169; Caleb 145; Charles 221; Christopher 176; Clark 158; Cuthbert 185, 186; Edward (Ed.) 144, 167, 168, 169; Elijah 220; Elisha 144, 147(2); George 177, 186, 221, 222, 228; Hynson 177, 186; Ignatius 212; Isaac 171; James 176, 221; James White 169; Jo: 197, 199; John 157(2), 164, 169, 213, 228, 229, 233, 254, 257; John Beadle 169; Joseph 203, 211; Joshua 176; Josias 169; Josias Carvil 169; Jospeh 150; Richard 144, 251; Robert 179, 228; Robert C. 163; Samuel 221; Thomas 169, 212, 215, 221; Tyler 155; William 148, 163, 170(2), 182, 183, 190, 200, 201, 216, 220, 251
HALLER Daniel 239
HALLETT Richard 246
HALLON Edward 203
HALLOWAY James 254
HALY Daniel 179
HAM George 196, 202; John 242
HAMAR William 183

295

INDEX TO APPENDIX B

HAMBLETON James 151, 156; John 227,
  233; Philimon 233; Phill 227;
  William 227(2), 234
HAMBLIN John 253; Solomon 251
HAMELTON John B. 159
HAMER William 190
HAMILTON Baptist 160; Bennett 163;
  Burd. 165; Duke 163; Edward 163,
  173; Hamidathy 165; Ignatius 159;
  James 182, 190; Leonard 163;
  William 163, 207(2), 225, 229
HAMLIN Maddux 256
HAMMETT William 214
HAMMILTON William 209
HAMMITT Caleb 212; Cartwright 212;
  Joseph 213; McKelvie 212; Richard
  212; Robert 169, 213; Zacharia 212
HAMMON George 238
HAMMOND Acquilla 150; Edward 252,
  253(2); Isaac 253(2); James 219;
  Larkin 170; Samuel 182(2), 189;
  Thomas 144; William 145, 149, 221;
  Wilson 221; Zedakiah 253
HAMOND George 146
HAMSLY Henry 162
HAMSTONE Christopher 194
HANAGAN John 185
HANCE Benjamin 147, 148, 150; John
  148; Joseph 148; Kinsey 148;
  Richard 147; Samuel (Sam.) 148,
  150
HANCOCK Abraham 160; Daniel 258;
  Ebenezer 250, 259; Elijah 255;
  Henry 254; John 153, 160, 250,
  253, 259; Joshua 255; Micajah 249,
  255; Templin 254; Thomas 160;
  Whittington 253; William 160, 213,
  258
HAND John 152; Peter 209; Thomas 209
HANDCOCK John 223, 230
HANDERSIDES William 172
HANDLEY James 185
HANDLY Thomas 254; William 253
HANDS John 236
HANDY Capt. 254; Ebenezer 249; Isaac
  218, 221; Jacob 223; John 219;
  Joseph 220; Levin 217; Martin
  Luther 218; Matthias 258; Robert
  254; Samuel 221; Thomas 221;
  William 256, 257
HANER Elisha 147

HANES Charles 177; Francis 177; James
  177; Thomas 177
HANEY Nicholas 180
HANLEY Thomas 249
HANNA Alexander 170; James 170, 173
HANNAH Archb. 187; Nicholas 144;
  Samuel 241
HANNAN William 255
HANNON Patrick 145
HANSON Edward 174; George 191, 192;
  Gustavus 185, 192; Haskins 159;
  Henry Massey 158; Hollis 171; John
  158, 171; Samuel 164, 167, 171;
  Theops. 164; Thomas 171; Thomas H.
  163; Walter 159, 164; William 159,
  180, 188
HANTS James 179
HANVEY John 180
HANY John 238; Michal 167
HARBE James 195
HARBEN Allan 161; William 161
HARBER James 212
HARBERT Elisha 213; James 210; John
  213; William 213
HARBIN Elias 195; James 201; Joshua
  193
HARBISON David 247
HARBOUGH John 168
HARCKELL Michael 236
HARDACER Joseph 150
HARDCASTLE Aaron 152; James 153, 232;
  John 152, 157, 232; Robert 152;
  Solomon 153; Thomas 152; William
  151, 229
HARDEN Baptist 212; Basil 198; Edward
  198; Elias 198, 199; John 198,
  203; Josiah 199; Walter 193;
  William 198, 199
HARDESTY Edward Hansin 146; Elisha
  148; Elisha Hansin 146; George
  150, 168; Henry 148; John 146,
  213; Jorge 146; Joseph 146, 148,
  150(2); Richard 148; Samuel 195;
  Thomas 146(4), 147, 148, 149, 150;
  William 150
HARDIKIN Matthew 231
HARDIN James 224; Joseph 224
HARDING Basil 205; Edward 155, 206;
  James 231; Reuben 180; Thomas 155;
  Vachel 206
HARDISTY George 193, 203
HARDMAN Ignatius 160

INDEX TO APPENDIX B

HARDWEIGH George 244
HARDY George 193; John 194; Zadock 195
HARGAN John 157
HARGIL Michael 244
HARGISS Joseph 213
HARGNEY James 146
HARGRASS Stephen 171
HARIS John 194
HARISS James 233; Thomas 220
HARKELL Frederick 236
HARKINS John 153
HARKNESS William Clark 191
HARLEY Jon. 144
HARMAN John 245
HARMON Abel 259; Jeremiah 259; Middleton 259
HARMUELL John 247
HARNEY Joseph 157; Philip 157; Thomas 233
HARNS John 237
HAROY William 159
HARP Josiah 205; Philip 200, 205; William 201
HARPER Anthony 157; Francis 196, 201; James 220; John 151, 155, 178, 211, 250, 259; Samuel 259; Thomas 223; William 154, 157, 178, 187, 201
HARRIGAN John 192
HARRINGTON James 231; Peter 152; Philip 153; Richard 227, 235; Thomas 153; William 222, 231
HARRIOT Andrew 170
HARRIS Aaron 200; Barnaby 221; Benjamin 147, 148(2), 156, 163, 199; Charles 249, 254; Edward 190; George 199; James 156, 167, 170, 192; Jesse 194; John 154, 156, 179, 187, 220; Joseph 147, 170, 184, 192; Lill 219; Nathan 194, 201; Nathaniel 195; Nicholas 154; Norris 194; Richard 147; Risden 233; Robert 144, 146; Samuel 211; Stephen 167; Thomas 192, 209, 210; Walter 177, 185; Will 216; William 147(3), 156, 179, 217, 218; Zadock 200; Zephaniah 194
HARRISON Benjamin 143(2), 147, 210, 228, 234; Edward 233; Elisha 147, 200; Eramus 253; George 150, 210; Greenbury 197; Henry 146, 147(2), 150; Horatio 143, 172; James 150, 182, 187, 189; John 150, 210, 227, 228, 233(2), 235, 256; John Robert 172; Jonathan 227, 233; Joseph 210, 227, 233(2), 234; Joshua 197; Levi 217; Moses 202; Nathan 197, 210; Nathaniel 233; Richard 146, 150, 172; Robert 147, 210, 226, 228, 233(2), 234; Rouse 254; Samuel 150; Shadrack 202; Solomon 228, 233; Thomas 167, 168, 227, 233(3); William 147, 150(2), 156, 159, 170, 226, 227(2), 233(3), 234, 242, 250
HARRISS Aaron 206; George 204; Henry 224, 231; John 230; Jonathan 226, 235; Kinsey 203; Noah 233; Risdon 228; Samuel 167; Solomon 222, 231; William 205, 224, 226, 231; Zadok 206
HARRISSON Greenbury 203; Nathan 203
HARROLD John 163
HARRY Allan 203; Charles 203; David 172, 197, 240; Jacob 240; John 245; Jonathan 240; Martin 240; Richard 201; William 203
HARSHMAN Mathias 248
HARSHORN George 191
HART Arthur 166; Christopher 222; James 178; Joseph 178, 186; Ludwick 236; Noah 245; Richard 176; Robert 170; William 175, 227
HARTELL Martin 238
HARTING Solomon 249
HARTLEY John 182, 185, 192, 242; Joseph 175
HARTMAN Adam 247
HARTSHORN George 182
HARTT Cornelius 188; Henry 166; James 186; John 185; Nathan 188; Richard 185; Robert 186
HARTTWELL Thomas 169
HARVEY Allin 197; John 155, 188; Mosses 163; Thomas 153; William 197; Zadock 154
HARVIN Annanias 162; Edward D. 162; Thomas 162
HARWOOD John 193, 195; Peter 229; Richard 223, 230; Rizden 223; Robert 225; Sharp 223, 230; Thomas 225, 229; William 181
HASE James 166

INDEX TO APPENDIX B

HASELDINE James 227, 229; Richard 229; William 227
HASKINS Zephania 213
HASLET Moses 172
HASLETT William 152
HASS Philip 207
HASSETT William 170
HATCHESON Nathan 182
HATCHINSON Vincent 186
HATCHISON Benjamin 183, 190; James 188; John 182, 190; Nathan 190; Vincent 177, 182, 191
HATH Jacob 255; James 256; Smith 255
HATNICK Varner 242
HAUKER Nicholas 206
HAUSKINS George 193
HAUVEY John 188
HAVE Thomas 161
HAWK Machl. 144
HAWKEN Samuel 202
HAWKER Ambrose 206; Nicholas 198; Philip 202
HAWKES Robert 144; William 193
HAWKINS Alexander S. W. 159; Gregory 174; James 222; Jeremiah 174; John 199, 204, 205; Robert 174; Samuel 175; Smith 159; Thomas 159
HAWKSWORTH Thomas 178
HAWS Michael 195, 203
HAWTHORN John 170
HAYCOCK Daniel 221; Basil 211; Charles 211; Gerrard 210; James 210; William 210, 212
HAYER Jonathan 240
HAYES James 237; John 179; Samuel 243
HAYLEY Caleb 208
HAYMAN Charles 257; Isaac 218, 257; James 257; John 219; John Harris 218; Joshua 218, 257; Revel 218
HAYMON George 197
HAYNE John 191
HAYNES Abraham 183
HAYS Archer 170; Basil 193; Charles 193; Elextius 162; George 193; Henry 171; Jerremiah 193; John 167; Leonard 193; Leven 193; Levy 193; Notley 193; Richard 225, 232; Samuel 193; Thomas 193(2); William 145, 162(2), 200, 244
HAYWARD John B. 252; William 252
HAZARD Elihu 254; Michael 161
HAZELDINE Charles 213

HAZELL John 211
HAZELTINE John 211
HAZLE Bennit 213; Edwards 213; Jeremiah 211
HEADLER George 236
HEADRICKS Charles 248
HEAFNER Baptist 236; John 236
HEANY Patrick 170
HEARD Edmund 211; Ignatius 211, 212; James 211, 213; John 212(2), 214; Matthew 214; Ml. 214; Ralph 214; Richard 212, 214; William 211
HEARN Elijah 249, 254; John 249, 256
HEART Christopher 229; William 235
HEATER George 195, 203; Michael 241
HEATH Charles 154; Jesse 188; Stephen 219; Thomas 176; William 219; Wilson 219
HEATHER Ephraim 253
HEATHERINGTON John 247
HEATHMAN George 196; Jonathan 196
HEBB Joseph 214; Thomas 214; William 214
HEBRON Thomas 178
HECKMAN John 178
HEDINGER George 178
HEFFERSON Robert 226
HEFFLE Charles 246
HEFLEY Peter 240
HEFLYBOWER Jacob 238
HEIN Jacob 237
HELEN Dawkins 148
HELLEN Benjamin 149; Edmund 148; Jacob 148; James 149; Peter 148; Scarth 149; William A. 148
HELSBEY William Lang 232
HELSBY Thomas 231(2); William 230, 231; William Long 225
HELSON Godfree 247
HEMINDER Andrew 238
HEMMINGWAY James 150
HEMSLEY Francis 160
HEMSTONE Mathias 194
HEMSWORTH Hugh 146
HENCH John 241
HENDDERICK John 237
HENDERSON Brittingham 250, 259; Charles 217; Curtis 252, 259; Ephraim 259; Isaac 257; Jacob 257; James 257; Jenckins 257; Jesse 252; John 252; John Trehorn 257; Joseph 257; Levi 257; Phil 170;

INDEX TO APPENDIX B

Samuel 259; Smart 257; Thomas 257;
William 252, 259; William Holland
257; William Merrill 257
HENDLEY John 211, 214; William 206
HENDLY James 149
HENDRICK James 229
HENEKIN John 160
HENERY David 157
HENLEY James 194; Peter 173
HENLY William 198
HENNECY Perry 156
HENNING Bennet 215; Stephen 214
HENNON Hall 227
HENNY Elias 215
HENRICK Henry 153
HENRIX Edward 224, 231
HENRY Daniel 194; Isaac 217; James 187; Martin 210; Michael 237; Robert Jenkins 220; Samuel 157; William 176
HENSLEY Edward 144
HENSWORTH Hugh 150
HENTON Thomas 147
HEO Simeon 168
HERBERT Charles 172
HERD Joseph 152; William 152
HERN Charles 144
HERON John 223, 230
HERRICK William 153
HERRIN Nathaniel 188; William 188
HERRING Daniel 180, 189; John 204; Nathaniel 180; William 177, 183, 190
HERRON John 199
HESS Christian 237; Jacob 199, 237; Joseph 237; Peter 240
HESTER Phillip 244
HESTON Jacob 246
HETCH John 205
HETHMAN George 202; John 202
HEWETT Joseph 171
HEWEY John 227, 235; Jonathan 225; Thomas 235; Woolman 227, 235
HEWITT Elijah 167
HEWS Christian 224; Christopher 231; James 170, 227
HIAG John 184
HIATT Elisha 244
HICK George 240
HICKEY Basil 161
HICKMAN David 216; Elihu 195; John 186; Joshua 251; Mathias 244;

Nathaniel 215; Sollomon 194;
Stephin 216; William 194(2), 251
HICKS Giles 151; James 151, 180, 188;
Laben 168; Levin 151; Robert 165;
Thomas 152, 165
HICKSON Richard 223, 230; Woolman 230
HICKY Francis 161
HIGBY John 228
HIGDEN Francis 160
HIGDON Benjamin 160, 195, 203;
Ignatius 164; John 195(2); John
Baptist 160; Joseph 195; Leonard
160; Thomas 199; William 160(2)
HIGENBOTTOM Oliver 184
HIGGES Samuel 210
HIGGINBOTTOM Benjamin 191(2), 192;
James 192; Joel 189; Oliver 190, 192
HIGGINS Henry 224, 232; James 204, 225; John 194, 224, 231(2); Samuel 215; Thomas 224, 231; William 224, 234
HIGGNUTT Daniel 156
HIGGS George 161
HIGHBARGER Abraham 242
HIGHBURGER Conrod 241
HIGHFIELD Jonathan 210; Leonard 159, 210; Thomas 164
HIGINBOTTOM Benjamin 185; George 185; Joel 184
HILDERBRAND David 247; John 238; Phillip 247
HILL Broadwater 258; Charles Phillips 257; Edward 213; Elisha 250, 252; Felty 237; Francis 159; Frederick 249; Harmon 172; Ignatius 212; Isaac 251 252; James 220, 242; John 152, 183, 190, 199, 207, 213, 237; John Baptis 215; Joseph 143(2), 165, 212; Leonard 165; Levin 250, 259; Nathan 156; Peter 241; Richard 208; Samuel 174; Stephen 173, 251; Thomas 165, 170, 173; Will 219; William 152, 171, 209, 246; William Stevens 257; Zacharia 212; Zorababel 258
HILLARD Thomas 203
HILLEARY Henry 195, 208; John 195
HILLERY Henry 203; John 203
HILLPOINT John Jones 184
HILLS Zacharia 213

INDEX TO APPENDIX B

HILMAN Ezekiel 218; John 218; Joshua 218; William 218
HILTON Andrew 159; Francis 212; John 175, 212; Leonard 210; Stephen 212; Thomas 214; William 215
HINATE Thomas 192
HINCKIN John 160
HINDMAN Joseph 240
HINDS Jacobus 185; John 184, 191, 245
HINES Daniel 152; Jacob 198; Thomas 242
HINKLE Conrod 240; Jacob 168; Leonard 240
HINKS Thomas 173
HINSON John 153
HINTON John 194(2); Michael 194; Phillip 194; Richard 148, 149, 194; Thomas 147, 194(2)
HIPKINS Charles 172
HIPPENLISER John 247
HIRRIN William 187
HISKELL Frederick 245
HITCH ... 218; Benjamin 218; Elias 218; Elijah 218; Ezekiel 217; George 217; John 200; Thomas 217
HITCHCOCK Henry 174; John 175; Josias 174(2), 175; Randel 175; William 174
HITON Joseph 165
HIX Jacob 247; John 183
HIXON Joseph 248
HIXS Joshua 244
HOAK Peter 240
HOBBS Charles 197, 203; Gary 157; Greenbury 197; Jacob 151; James 153; John 151(2), 154, 217, 229, 232; Joseph 229; Joshua 155, 169; Joy 156; Levin 249; Mathias (Matthias) 156, 218; Peter 157; Samuel 194, 206; Solomon 153, 154; Thomas 153; William 145, 156; Zebulon 156
HOBINS Moses 241
HOBS Joseph 225
HOCKER Philip 195; Samuel 195
HOCKEY Christian 238; Nicholas 245
HOCKSWORTH John 176; Thomas 176
HODGE Joshua 252
HODGES James 184, 191
HODSON John 156
HOFFMAN John 240; Michael 241
HOFSTETH Samuel 237

HOGAN Roger 206
HOGANS William 187
HOGELAND James 243
HOGG Zeb. 243
HOGGINS Richard 193
HOGHANOUR Jacob 247
HOGMIRE Capt. 244; Daniel 238; Samuel 238
HOGSTLER Thomas 252
HOLBROOK Henry 219; John 216, 219; Thomas 219
HOLDER John 184
HOLDING James 159; William 154
HOLISTON John 259
HOLLADAY James 223
HOLLADY Ephim 215
HOLLAND Archibald 196, 201; Arthor 224; Benjamin 197, 203, 258; Capil 207; Capril 198; Edward 205; Francis 169; James 220; Joel 196, 202; John 196(2), 202(2), 254; Joseph 196; Laban 155; Levi 155, 221, 256; Levin 252; Michael 217, 221, 253; Nathan 198; Nehemiah 194, 259; Otho 196, 202; Rezin 203; Richard 155; Samuel 254; Solomon (Sollaman) 198, 203; Stephen 196, 202; Thomas 197, 202, 203; William 194(2), 227, 235, 249, 252
HOLLANDSHEAD Francis 147; John H. 147; William 147
HOLLAWAY George 243; Jacob 254; Levi 254; Moses 255
HOLLENDSHEAD Richard 146
HOLLETT John 242; Thomas 242
HOLLIDAY James 229
HOLLINGSWORTH Samuel 146; Thomas 146, 209
HOLLIOAKE Daniel 189
HOLLIS Amos 171; William 170
HOLLIT John 167
HOLLOWAY Aaron 254; Ebenezer 254; Elijah 251; Elisha 254; Jesse 251; Joshua 255; Richard 171; William 251
HOLLY James 216; Thomas 208
HOLMES Francis 227, 235; James 170; John 230; Josiah 207; Josias 198; Philip 182; Solomon 225, 232; Thomas 232
HOLSON Hanson 152

INDEX TO APPENDIX B

HOLT Benjamin 148; Francis 147; James 230; Laurance 197; Philip 150; Thomas 204
HOLTON William 215
HOLYOAK Daniel 182
HOMES Solomon 225
HONEY James 209
HONSAKER Nicholas 244
HOOF Goddard 237
HOOFMAN Casper 246; Henry 240; Jacob 241, 248
HOOK Belitha 253; Daniel 168; George Michael 168; James 167; Rodger 252; William 252
HOOKE Andrew 145
HOOPER Abraham 148; Foster 157; Isaac 148; John 155; Richard 177; Roger 147; Thomas 155, 163
HOOVER Adam 238(2), 247; Henry 244(2); Jacob 248(2); John 244, 248, 249; Martin 244; Peter 238
HOPEWELL Bennit 210; George 215; Hugh 215; James 213; Richard 210; Thomas G. 159
HOPKINS Benjamin 221, 226; Charles 216; Daniel 146, 233; David 145, 216; Dennis 227, 235; Denny 226, 235; Edward 185, 192; Francis 232, 234; George Collier 216; Hampton 251; Hashua 235; Hugh 233; J. J. 227; Jacob 210; James 223, 225, 227, 231, 235(2); John 196, 216, 219, 223, 226, 228, 234(2); Jonathan 235; Joseph 181(2), 226, 227, 235; Joshua 226; Lambert 230; Levi 216; Levin 250; Moses 227, 235; Nathaniel 224, 231; Peter 227; Philip 201; Randolph 160; Richard 196, 231; Robert 216, 227, 235; Samuel 175, 259; Stephen 216, 221; Thomas 154(2), 232, 233; William 151, 216, 227, 233
HOPLINS Basil 215
HOPPER William 151, 157
HOPWELL Thomas 159
HOPWOOD Edward 215; John 197; John 203
HORN Valentine 167
HORNBY William 147
HORNE John 248; Valentine 242
HORNER Benjamin 219; Gustavus 213; John 219; William 219

HORNEY James 231; John 228, 233; Solomon (Soloman) 228, 233; Thomas 228; William 225
HORNISH Phillip 240
HORNY Thomas 183
HORSEY Capt. 256; John 215, 221(2); Revell 216; Samuel 257; Smith 221; Stephen 218, 221
HORSKINS Benjamin 212; John 212
HORSY John 217
HOSE Peter 245
HOSIER Henry 185, 191; John 254; Richard 190, 191; Samuel 190
HOSKENSON Charles 193
HOSKINS Bennett 160
HOSKINSON Elisha 205; George 193; Josiah 206; Josias 198; Ninian 205
HOSKINSSON Elisha 200
HOSS Jeremiah 238; John 248
HOUK Jacob 244
HOULT Thomas 197; William 201
HOUSE Abraham 238; Alexander 195; Edward 202; John 195, 245; William 195, 243
HOUSEHALTER Simon 240
HOUSEHOLD John 248
HOUSEHOLDER Adam 248; Michael 246
HOUSER Henry 246; Isaac 239; John 237; Martin 196; Philip (Phillip) 196, 201
HOUSLEY Robert 200, 203
HOUSROOF John 183
HOUSTON James 257; Joseph 257; Levi 257; Ralph 252
HOUT Peter 240
HOWARD Austin 210; Baker 162; Basil 212; Ben 213; Benjamin 178, 186; Charles 210; Clem 214; Clemen. 244; Cornelius 177, 186; Edmond 213; Edward 211; Frederick 244; George 193, 210; Gillis 218; Jacob 193, 238; James 145, 177, 186, 212; Jeremiah 164; John 144, 146(2), 150, 176, 177(2), 185, 186, 158, 194, 219, 220, 240; John Beale 171; Jonathan 213; Joseph 186, 212, 213; Joshua 178; Lemuel 173; Leonard (Linard) 178, 186, 210; Michael 159; Peregrine 210; Peter 210, 213; Phillip 242; Richard 150(2); Stephen (Staphen) 179, 187; Thomas 178, 186, 193,

INDEX TO APPENDIX B

210, 214; Thomas G. 164; Thomas Gassaway 171; William 144, 164, 193, 198, 201
HOWEL William 178
HOWELL John 172; Nathaniel 186; Samuel 159, 171; Stephen 168; Thomas 152; William 186
HOWES William 150
HOWS Leonard 150
HOY Paul 197
HOZER William 252
HUBBART William 166
HUBBERT Jessee 155; Thomas 156
HUBBS Samuel 241
HUBOR Melchor 169
HUCHESON Robert 188
HUCHINGS John 153
HUCKINGS John 153
HUDGIN Thomas 239
HUDSON (blank) 250; Aaron 258; Annanias 251, 252, 254; Archibald 252, 258; Coleb 165; David 251; Dennis 252, 253; George 236; Henry 253; J. 144; Job 252; John 147, 174, 183, 191, 251, 253(2), 254; Laban 250, 259; Levi 252; Lott 252; McKemmy 251; Moses 250, 259; Richard 150, 253; Robert 253; Samuel 250, 259; Seth 251; Sterling 257; Thomas 159, 174, 251; William 253(2)
HUET Nicholas 238
HUFF Thomas 182, 189(2)
HUFFER John 237
HUFFINGTON Angelo 217; John 217; Jonathan 217; Joshua 217
HUFFMAN Aaron 241
HUFLMAN Robert 241
HUFMAN Henry 237(2); Moses 241
HUGETT Ludwick 238
HUGGINS Benjamin 226; James 172
HUGH Thomas 199
HUGHES Andreas 172; Christopher 144; Daniel 152; Edward 199, 204; John 196, 197; John Hall 171; Kinsey 203; Nathaniel 201; Natt: 197; Patrick 173; Samuel 237; Theophilus 207
HUGHETT Nicholas 238; Stophel 238
HUGHLETT Thomas 152

HUGHS Christopher 231; James 148, 233; Jesse 257; John 154, 216, 233; Michael 144; William 162
HULL Beauchamp 217, 219; Daniel 179, 189; David 189; Hope 222; John 224, 225, 231; Nathaniel 224, 231; William 180, 188
HULLOCK Thomas 243
HUMBORSON Jacob 187
HUMES William 224
HUMPHREY Thomas 167
HUMPHRIS Elijah 218; Joseph 216; Joshua 218
HUMPHRY Thomas 182
HUMPHRYS Thomas 242
HUNGERFORD Charles 193; John 149
HUNT Bartholomew 220; Basil 210; Benjamin 161; George 224, 231; Glaven 161; Henry 146; James 175, 226; John 152, 229, 234; Joseph 234; Peter 226; Philip 146; Robert 171; Samuel 226, 234; Shad. 159; Thomas 161; William 161
HUNTER David 149; Ezekiel 153; Henry 193; Joshua 195; Nathan 153; William 148, 149, 179, 186
HUNTINGTON John 161; Luke 161
HUNTT Henry 150; John Wilkinson 150; Ortor 149; Philip 150; William 147
HUR Jacob 248
HURDELL James 237
HURDLE Laurance 200; Richard 201
HURDLY Hezekiah 200
HURLEY Dennis 183, 191; Isaiah 207; James 171; John 224; Thomas 194
HURLOCK Isaac 179
HURRY David 207; John 165; Thomas 229
HURST Phineas 211; William 183, 184, 191
HURT James 181; John 179, 184, 187, 191; Morgan 182, 191; Richard 180
HURTT Richard 188
HUSBAND William 175
HUSK Edward 163
HUSKINGS Joseph 240
HUSSAY Woolman 229
HUSSY William 158
HUST Edward 158; Joseph 242
HUSTER Sabret 184
HUSTON Alexander 173; John 172, 202, 247; Paul 247
HUSTT James 189

INDEX TO APPENDIX B

HUTCHESON James 175
HUTCHINGS Clement 147; Francis 147, 148; Ignatious 147; James 226; John 147; Joseph 147; Samuel 225; Stephen 147; Thomas 147
HUTCHINS Bennit 211; John 211; Richard 174; Thomas 172(2); William 220
HUTCHINSON Bennit 212; Jonathan 257; Joshua 211
HUTCHISON William 164
HUTSON John 192; Samuel 182, 190
HUTTON George 153; James 143; William 153
HUTTS Andrew 193
HYATT Hezekiah 243
HYLAND Hugh 196; Lambert 218
HYMAN George 239
HYMES Andrew 241; John 241
HYNES Isaac 185
HYNIS William 177
HYNSON Charles 182, 190; James 178, 179, 180, 187(2), 188; John Carvill 182, 190; Nathaniel 184, 191; Richard 184, 190; Thomas 177; William 184
HYPLE Christopher 244

ICRICK Leonard 160
IDAIRE William 196
IFFIELD John 178
IGINTER John 237
IGONDER Benadict 241; Henry 241
IGRAM Thomas 207
IHANIETZ Walter 160
IJAMS Vachal 144
INGHAM John 239
INGRAM Archibald 175; Edward 191; Levin 172; Thomas 199
INLOW Joseph 241
INMAN William 197
INNES James 165
INNESS Charles 165
INSLEY Jacob 166; John 166
IRELAND Gideon 149; Gilbert 149; John 148, 155; Joseph 147; Samuel 155(2); Thomas 149, 182, 189; William 148, 188, 198, 203
IRINS Daniel 217
IRONS Charles 187; Edward 167; Jonathan 167, 242; Simon 188

IRVING James 220(2); John 220; Levin 217; Thomas 219
ISAAC Lasarus 200; Thomas 150
ISAACKS Richard 147
ISACKE Thomas 146
ISLAND Hugh 202
ISSELOW Peter 191
IVEY James 149; John 149; William 182

J... Thomas 216
JACK Jeremiah 246; John 246
JACKSON Abednego (Abednigo) 183, 191; Abraham 145; Bennet 193; David 241; Edward 229; George 157, 176; Jacob 186; James 153(2), 175, 224; John 153, 162, 175, 199, 223, 230, 253; Mitchel 217; Peter 153; Samuel 153(2); Thomas 153, 165, 226, 241; Walter 151; William 152, 153, 155, 179, 188, 198, 216, 229
JACOB Gabariel 167; John Jeremiah 167; Martin 236; Thomas 237
JACOBS Edward 193; Gabriel 243; Jeremiah 239; Jo: 194; Levin 230; Will 168; William 145, 167; Zachariah 144, 193
JACQUES Thomas 242
JADVIN Robert 232; Thomas 232
JADWIN Bartholomew 152; Davis 154
JAFFREY James 146
JAMES Alexander 228, 235; Benjamin 241; Daniel 217; Evan 241; Fessler 188; George 162, 218, 242; Henry 154; John 157, 213; Joseph 241; Morgan 179; Philip 207; Richard 175, 239, 244; Robert 175; Sedgwick 175; Thomas 174, 200, 206, 184, 192; Walter 172; William 176, 177, 217
JAMESTONE John 159
JAMISON Benjamin 160; Henry Joshua 160; John 170(2); Leonard 160; Walter 160
JANE William 197
JANES Edward 200; Thomas 199
JANQUARY Abraham 143
JARBO Stephen 205
JARBOE Charles 211; Joshua 211; Peter 211; Richard 211; Robert 21, 215; Thomas 214
JARMAN Elijah 253; John 252; Truit 251

INDEX TO APPENDIX B

JARRETT Truman 243(2)
JARVIC William 170
JARVIS Elisha 195, 202; James 173; Zadoc (Zadok) 195, 202
JEANS Henry 204; Zechariah 207
JEBB John 170
JECONS Edward 245
JEFFERS John 146
JEFFERSON Bazil 147; Benjamin 147(2); George 234; Henry 147; James 227, 234; John 161; Robert 226; Thomas 234(2)
JEFFERY Josep 215
JEFFREY Alexander 170
JENEYS Abr. 180
JENIFER Parker 215; Samuel 212
JENKENSON John 223
JENKINS David 218; Edward 162, 214; Ezekiel 218; Francis 175; George 165, 214, 223, 230; Jeremiah 214; John 195, 218, 230; Jonathan 218; Joseph 218; Richard 155; Samuel 173, 225, 232; Thomas 155; Walter 231; William 172, 174, 216; Zibble 218
JENNINGS William 248
JEPHERSON Thomas 226
JERBOROUGH Clement 151
JERMAN Joab 256
JERRARD William 193
JERVIS John 144; Joseph 170
JESTER Jonathon 187; Southey (Southy) 250, 259
JEWEL William 215
JEWELL George 158; William 152, 193
JEWETT Thaddeus 170
JEWRY Stephen 203
JILANARD John 246; Rudolph 246
JOBSON John 187; Jonathan 178, 187; Michael 178, 186
JOHN Joel 242; Stab 237; Stale 237
JOHNS Benjamin 147, 231; David 214; Enoch 180, 188; Kinsey 143; Richard 145, 201, 232; Richard W. 206; Richard W... 198; Thomas 199
JOHNSON Archibald (Archabald) 164, 171, 251; Baker 168; Barthomew 194; Ben: 194; Benjamin 242, 257; Bernard 173; Charles 174; Daniel 165, 259; David 213; Edward William 177; Eliakim (Eliacam) 255, 258; Elijah 222; Ezekiel 154;
Henry 150, 224, 231, 255; Hezekiah 163, 250, 258; Huet 161; Isaac 170, 193; Jacob 163, 173; James 152, 155, 159, 201, 250, 259; Jeremiah 149; Jesse 221; John 150, 157, 160, 167, 171, 174, 193, 196, 199, 204, 218, 222, 223, 224, 230, 250(2), 251, 252, 259; Jonathan 161, 193; Joseph 149(2), 161, 171, 196, 202, 213, 215; Josiah 161; Lemuel 258; Leonard 213; Levi 166, 219; Levin 155; Lill 222; Moses 174; Peter 254; Philip 212; Randolph 231; Richard 147, 197, 203; Robert 144, 173, 251; Sam 251; Samuel 148, 193; Smith 255; Solomon 257; Thomas 148, 167, 173, 174, 196, 202, 221, 242; Walter 164; William 145, 147, 149(2), 155, 171, 173, 218, 242, 255; William Sergant 148; Zachariah 161
JOHNSTON Barnett 242; Benjamin 185; Christopher 145; Edward William 186; George 174; Griffith 243; John 157, 163; Thomas 173, 245
JOICE Elijah 173; Richard 143(2)
JOINER Benjamin 184
JOLLY Peter 241
JONES Abraham 195; Amos 172; Aquilla 181, 189; Ben 218; Benjamin 148, 164, 174, 184, 191; Charles 177, 186, 190, 200, 218; Charles Coats 204; Daniel 258; Darius 185, 192; David 191, 224, 231, 246; Ebenezer 251; Eber 155; Edward 154, 193, 197, 203; Elisha 250, 254, 258; Evan (Evin) 197, 201, 224, 231; Francis 218; George 219(2), 253; Giles 258; Griffith 178, 186; Henry 152, 199, 204; Hezekiah 205; Isaac 174(2); Jacob 166, 174, 191, 242, 248; James 148, 152(2), 171, 177, 185, 186, 218, 219, 226, 228(2), 231, 233, 234, 258; Jesse 253; John 147, 151, 152, 174, 181, 183, 184(3), 188, 190, 191(2), 195, 202, 206, 213, 216, 219(3), 221, 222, 223, 228, 233, 242, 252(2), 253, 258; Jonathan 143(2), 248; Joseph 174, 193, 194, 200, 225; Joshua 157; Leonard 194; Levin 218; Lewis 149; Major 258;

INDEX TO APPENDIX B

Matthias 215; McMurdy 152;
Mordicai 215; Morgan 143(2); Moses
148; Nathan 197, 201; Peter 179;
Philip (Phillip) 183, 193, 218;
Pierce 230; Reuben 175; Richard
184, 205, 224, 231; Robert 152,
219, 226, 234; Rubin 234; Samuel
166, 185, 205(2), 242; Solomon
224, 232; Thomas 145, 148, 150,
174, 175, 178, 183(2), 186, 192,
193, 219, 221, 232, 234, 241, 244,
247, 253; William 154, 158, 160,
171, 174(2), 185, 187, 200, 205,
218(2), 219, 220, 226, 227,
234(2), 246, 247, 252; Zephaniah
198
JORDAN Col. J. 209; James 203; John
154; Samuel 212; Thomas 223;
William 212
JORDON Joshua 194; Simon 175
JORY William 190
JOSEPH Clement 213; Jesse 212; Joseph
203, 213
JOY Athananas 211; Athanasis 212;
Athanasius 211; Baptist 204;
Charles 213; Enoch 211; Ignatius
211; Peter 212; Thomas 212
JOYANT John 185; Stephen 186
JOYH Peter 211
JOYNER Benjamin 191
JUMP Allemby 151; Andrew 151;
Benjamin 151; Christopher 151;
Elijah 151; Isaac 151; Jacob 151;
Peter 151; Solomon 151; Thomas
151; William 151
JURDEN James 197
JURER David 169
JUREY Thomas 176
JURY Stephen 197; Thomas 179
JUSHEY Obediah 243
JUSTICE Edward 157; Elijah 259; John
254

KAIN Thomas 215
KAISER Michael 244; Peter 244
KARSLEY Potter 220
KEACH Nathan 179(2)
KEAN John 174
KEARNS John 174
KEARTON Aly 162; Aty 162; John 177
KEATHLY Jacob 227; James 226
KEATING William 180

KEECH George 159; James 213; John 213
KEEN Charles 154; Edward 154; Richard
153; Thomas 154; Young 153
KEENE James 207; William 180
KEEPORTS George Peter 145
KEER Thomas 205, 228, 234
KEETHLY Jacob 235
KEETS Thomas 151
KEGER Frederick 248
KEIBERT Thomas 165
KEIDY Lowdick 239
KEIN James 198
KEITH James 200
KEITHLY James 234
KELLAM John 256; Joseph 257
KELLER John 168
KELLEY Andrew 186; Benjamin 191;
George 167; James 186, 219;
Nicholas 157
KELLON Thomas 159; William 159
KELLUM Edward 217; Isaac 222; Samuel
221; William 222
KELLY Andrew 177; Benjamin 156;
Daniel 257; Dennis 154; James 172,
173, 174, 178, 185; John 157, 195,
202, 257; Joseph 155; Roger 232;
Samuel 239; Thomas 195; William
152, 154, 180, 188
KELUM Isaac 222
KEMP Benjamin 228, 232, 233; Henry
152; James 226, 232; John 226,
232; Joseph 225, 228(2), 232,
233; Natt. 217; Quinton 225, 232;
Thomas 185, 192, 226, 235; William
229
KENADY John 185
KENDALL John 189; Thomas 232
KENDELL William 239
KENDERDINE Cooper 152
KENDLE John Baptist 244
KENDOLL James 181; Stephen 183;
William 181
KENDRICK Zachariah 214
KENEDY William 185
KENERLY Everton 217
KENISTER Henry 238
KENLEY James 190
KENNADAY Samuel 192
KENNADY James 225; John 241
KENNARD Daniel 183; Dennis 183, 190;
John 183(2), 190; Joshua 229;
Michael 171; Nathaniel 189; Owen

305

INDEX TO APPENDIX B

185, 190; Richard 184; Stephen
   183; William 183, 185, 190, 192
KENNEDAY William 192
KENNEDY David 247; Hugh 197; J. 144;
   James 229; John 172, 197; Robert
   174
KENNEMENT Hopkins 227
KENNITT Prisgrave 251; William 251
KENT Daniel 147; Isaac 149; Jesse
   174; Lembeth 209; Thomas 182
KENTING Howell 152; James 151;
   Solomon 151, 152
KEPHART John 247
KERBEY Charles 215; William 215(2)
KERBY Aaron 225; Abner 226, 232;
   Anthony 226, 234; Benjamin 231,
   235; Cloudsbury 231, 234; Daniel
   229; David 225, 232; Eanock 196;
   Emory 226, 230; Francis 215;
   Hopewell 215; John 231, 233, 251;
   Lambert 224, 231; Michael 224,
   231; Morris 225; Moses 232; Nathan
   231; Parot 225; Richard 232;
   Robert 225; Samuel 234
KERN Nathan 152
KERNEY William 183
KERNS Joseph 174
KERR Andrew 188; David 228; Nevin 170
KERRICK Edward 159; James 164
KERSEY John 223, 233; Phliip 197
KERSHNER David 247; George 238; John
   247; Martin 247; Phillip 247
KERSY Daniel 194; John 230
KERTON John 186
KESINGER Simon 246
KESSAKEN Phillip 246
KESSINGER George 239
KEVABLE George 247
KEY Job 173; John R. 167; John Ross
   167, 168
KEYKINDELL Elijah 241
KEYMER Samuel 213
KEYS Thomas 227; William 167
KEYTON William 188
KIDD William 152
KIDWELL James 165; John 165; Mathew
   165
KILBER Jacob 247
KILLAM John 255
KILLEHOCK John 204
KILLEN John 209
KILLGOUR William 209

KILLIAM Isaac 252
KILLMAN John 154
KILLMON John 166; Thomas 166
KILLOUGH Francis 247
KILLUM James 221
KILPIN Glenn 250
KIMBERLY John 167
KIMBLE Giles 173; James 171, 172;
   John 172; Josias 172; Roland 172;
   Stephen 172
KIMBOLL John 194
KINCANNON Thomas 245
KINDALL James 189; Stephen 190;
   William 189
KINDRICK James 224
KINEMONT Benjamin 152
KINETS William 248
KING Alexander 152; Arthur 220; Asa
   162; Barton 209, 215; Benjamin
   150, 162; Cornelius 209; Daniel
   183, 191; Edward 199, 204; Elisha
   158, 163; Francis 150, 175; Henry
   146, 149, 214, 215; James 148,
   150, 175, 242; Jeremiah 214; Jesse
   219; John 146, 149, 150(2), 152,
   157, 198, 206, 211, 213, 242, 246;
   Leonard 161; Levin 219; Planner
   219; Richard 213; Rob 212; Robert
   161; Robert Jenkins 220; Samuel
   204; Thomas 223, 230; Townly 161;
   Upshur 219; William 146, 149, 161,
   173, 175, 179, 187, 207, 211,
   219(2); Zeph. 159
KINGHAM John 191
KINGREIGH Christian 244
KINIMONT Phillip 153; Samuel 151
KINNARD Ebenezer 222, 229; James 229;
   Josua 222; Richard 157, 228
KINNELY John 242
KINNEMAN John 159
KINNEMONT John 233; Philip 229;
   Solomon 227
KINNERNET Solomon 227
KINNIMAN Philip 159
KIRBY Aaron 229; Benjamin 224, 225;
   Bill 229; Cloudsberry 224; Daniel
   225; David 229; John 224(2), 229;
   Lambert 229; Morris 229; Moses
   225; Nathan 224; Richard 229;
   Thomas 224
KIRK George 194; John 172; Thomas
   194(2)

INDEX TO APPENDIX B

KIRKMAN George 156
KIRKPATRICK Hugh 174; James 239;
  William 240
KIRKWOOD Richard 182, 183, 190
KIRSHAW James 149
KIRTZ Christian 207; Nicholas 199;
  Peter 199
KIRWIN John 146
KISENER Frederick 206
KISER Philip 204; Stophel 204
KISHMAN George 239; Martin 240
KISINGER George 246
KISNER Jacob 176
KITELY Francis 194; John 174
KITHISON Benjamin 187
KNAVE Henry 239; Jacob 239; John 239
KNEEBELL George 237
KNEIGHTON William 205
KNIGHT Christopher 183, 192; James 218; Jonathan 171, 218; Joshua 218; Josiah 218; Michael 175; Richard 184; Thomas 171, 173
KNIGHTERS William 200
KNIGHTON Nicholas 144
KNIPS John 221
KNISTERICK Frederick 240
KNOCK Francis 176, 185; Henry 179, 187; Nathaniel 177, 187(2); William 177, 178, 185, 187
KNODE Jacob 239; John 239; Mathias 240
KNOE Jacob 239
KNOTT Basil 194; Ignatious 239; James 212, 213; Jeremiah 200; John 213; Nathaniel 213; Ralph 200; Thomas 193; William 194; Zachariah 194
KNOTTS Nathan 235; Nathaniel 153; Thomas 153; William 153
KNOWLES John 231, 232
KNOWLY William 231
KNOX Ezekiel 253; Robert 165; William 197
KOPES John 153
KOTCHMILLER Casper 248
KOY Samuel 198
KRIPPS Michael 145
KSWABLE George 247
KYBER Philip 199
KYSER Jacob 199; John 199; Martin 193
KYSON Chandler 165
KYSOR Stophel 199

L...K Carman 218
LA... Thomas 200
LACEY Benjamin 207
LACHAMP Nehemiah 252
LACKLAN Aron 239
LACKLAND Elisha 244; James 198;
  Zadock 198
LADAMON William 161
LADNAHAM Edward 226
LAIN Richard 189
LAISHER John 245
LAMAN Bartin 245; John 199
LAMARR Charles 153; Garland 153;
  James 153; John 153; Lemuel 153
LAMASTER Hugh 244; Isaac 243
LAMAX William 225
LAMB Francis 177, 178, 186(2); George 186; Jacob 191; James 178, 186; John 186, 213; Pearce 184, 191(2); Thomas 177, 186; William 186
LAMBATH William 149
LAMBDEN Daniel 228, 233; Thomas 257; William 233
LAMBDIN John 153; Robert 233; Wrightson 233
LAMBDON Daniel 152, 233
LAMBE Pearce 183
LAMBERSON Levi 255; Robert 258; Samuel 258; Smith 258; Thomas 253
LAMBERT George 244; John 163
LAMBETH Joseph 197; Samuel 200
LAMDEN Daniel 233; Robert 228; Wrightson 228
LAMDIN Daniel 233
LAMSTER Thomas 242
LANAGIN James 171
LANAVAN John 145
LANCASTER Jeremiah 213; John 162; Ralph 213; Thomas 172
LANCE Christian 236(2); Jacob 237
LANDEN Joseph 221; Lill 220
LANDERS Samuel 238
LANDMAN Daniel 230; Daniel 223
LANDREY John 245
LANDSDALE Thomas 144
LANE Benjamin 150; Bennet 214; Francis 220; James 222(2), 228; Morris 175; Richard 149, 150, 181; Thomas 143(3), 257; William 222, 228
LANGE John Peter 207(2)
LANGLEY James 215; Josias 214

INDEX TO APPENDIX B

LANGREL Asa 166
LANGRELL James 156
LANGSDALE John 217; William 217
LANHAM Aaron 204; Chard 206; Hauzy 206; Hillery 206; Nathan 206; Richard 197; Robert 209; Stephen 205; William 198, 206
LANKFORD Ben 217; Benjamin 222; Ephraim 220; Ezekiel 220; Jacob 221; Jesse 220; Jesse M. 222; John 217; Joseph 222; Joshua 220; Killum 222; Levi 219; Thomas 222; William 217, 221
LANNAM Aaron 199; Hance 198; Lewis 200; Stephen 200
LANSDALE John 150
LANTZ Christian 244
LAPPE John 144
LARAMORE Thomas 216(2)
LARAMOUR Samuel 216
LARIMORE Alexander 226(2); James 226, 234; John 228, 233, 234; Jonathan 227, 234; Joseph 227; Robert 226 234; Thomas 224
LARKIN Thomas 143
LARKINS William 143(2)
LARRAMORE John 172
LARRANCE Elisha 254
LARSON Thomas Copper 144
LARY Denny 223; Jonathan 229; Joseph 179; Josh. 187
LARYMORE Alexander 234; Richard 234; Thomas 231
LASHER John 243; Joseph 243(2)
LASHEY William 200
LASHLEY George 193; John 200, 206; Robert 194; Thomas 200
LASINBY Alexander 207
LASSALS John 177
LASSELLS John 186
LATCHAMP John H. 251; Thomas 251
LATHAM Robert 179
LATIMER Isaac Smoot 159; James 158; Mark 159; Randolph B. 159; Samuel 163; Thomas 159
LATON Stephen 193
LATTEMORE Benjamin 164
LATTERMAN Lewis 227
LATTIMORE James 210
LAUGHLIN Peter 170; Thomas 143
LAURANCE Elisha 217; Richard 248; William 177

LAURENCE James 183; William 186
LAVERTY Jackson 171
LAVIELLE Abraham 148; Daniel 148; John 148
LAVIL William 230
LAW John 219; Patrick 207
LAWD Thomas 202
LAWRANCE John 148
LAWRENCE James 149, 187; Lorrewell 147
LAWS Gilbert 257; James 252; John 219(2); Thomas 202; William 168, 219
LAWSON Hance 221; Michael 159; Samuel 221
LAYCOCK Isaac 245
LAYFEILD David 255; Saul 256
LAYFIELD ...len 218; Capt. 257; Ezekiel 219; George 218, 257, 258; Isaac 257; James 221; John 220; Robert 218; Solomon 249; Thomas 255, 257; William 249, 254
LAYMAN Christ. 165
LAYN John 154(2)
LAYNE Anthony 157; Gallient 152; James 157; Owen 155; Richard 155; Walter 153
LAYTHEM Robert 187
LAYTON Ashwood 194; Charles 156; John 156; Uriah 194
LAZEAR Henry 197; John 198; Joseph 198
LAZENBY Alexander 198; Elias 198; Henry 198; Jo. 198; Robert 195; Samuel 198, 206; Thomas 194
LAZIER Henry 203; John 206; Joshua 206; Thomas 240
LAZINBY Henry 206; Joshua 206
LEACH Asahel 148; Benjamin 149; James 149, 150, 213; Jeremiah 150; John 161, 197, 203; Joshua 148, 150; Nehemiah 209; Richard 197; William 196(2), 201, 211
LEADENHAM Edward 234; John 234; Nathaniel 234
LEAK James 212
LEAKIN James 174
LEARY Daniel 196
LEATCH Capt 151
LEATHERBERRY John 217
LEATHERBURY John 216, 218; Jolley 219
LEATHERLAND William 215

INDEX TO APPENDIX B

LEATHERMAN Peter 168
LECH Thomas 147
LECOMPTE Charles 152; John 156; Moses 166; Nathan 152; Phillemon 156; Thomas 152; William 157
LECOUNT James 219
LEDDENHAM Nathaniel 227
LEE Benjamin 150; Charles 224; Daniel 200, 206(2); Edward 166; James 158, 170, 200, 206; Jeremiah 225; John 144, 166, 172, 200(2), 206, 224, 231, 248; Josiah 241; Mark 167; Oliver 231; Parker 170; Robert 150; Samuel 241; William 194, 241, 248
LEECH Samuel 161; Thomas 203
LEEK Joseph 202
LEER Felix 246, 247
LEFLER George 238
LEG Greenwood 223, 233
LEGG John 203; Thomas 203
LEGH John 154; William 154
LEIGH George H. 214; James 214; Phil 214
LEITCH Benjamin 194; James 193, 195; Josiah 194; Thomas 195; William 194
LEMON Joseph 146
LEN... John 204
LENNARD Francis 187
LENNON Francis 179
LENNOX James 189; Richard 181, 189
LEON Christopher 145
LEONARD Ben 255; James 226; James Hopkin 226; James K. 235; John 217, 226, 234; John Cook 234; Jonathan 226, 227, 233, 234; Joseph 217, 235; Thomas 226, 234; William 226, 234
LETCHWORTH Leonard 161
LETHERBURY Pere 185, 192
LETMAN George 200, 205
LEVEINGS Thomas 240
LEVERTON Garey 151; James 156; Moses 156; Thomas 152
LEVICK Solomon 222
LEVIE Nathan 146
LEVILL William 223
LEVINGSTON George 257; Todd 257
LEVY William 221
LEWIN Samuel 143

LEWIS Aaron 156; Abram 156; Arthur 255; Ben: 193; Clement 171; Daniel 198; David 179, 198; George 167, 237; Isaac 160, 193; James 175, 191, 252, 254; Jeremiah 198, 206; Jesse 202; John 173; Jonathan 197, 203; Jonathan W. 171; Joseph 194; Samuel 194; Thomas 144, 176, 204, 254; Walter 174; William 194, 237, 256
LEYDIA John 245
LEZIN Jacob 248
LIBBEY John 216
LIDDLE John 224
LIDDLETON John 225
LIDEN Shadrack 155
LIDEY Abraham 246
LIDY Adam 247
LIETER John 239
LIGHTER Abraham 236; Adam 236; Christopher 236; Jacob 236(2); Peter 236, 244
LIMAN Tobosia 215
LIMBERY Nicholas 199
LIN George 237
LINAM James 175
LINDAL John 251
LINDSAY Andrew 175; Daniel 175; James 259
LINDSEY David 222; John 244
LINE Jacob 237
LINGANFELDER George 241
LINGHAM Nicholas 199
LINGO Smith 249, 254
LINN George 245; Peter 245
LINNY James 250
LINSLEY John 237
LINTHACUM Nathan 202(2); Zechariah 202
LINTHCUM Nathan 195
LINTHICUM Archibald 200; Nathaniel 196; Richard 234; Zachariah 196
LINTON Elijah 221; Isaiah 171
LINTRIGE Samuel 195
LISBEY James 146
LISTER Thomas 221; William 221, 253
LITTIG Philip 145; Yost 145
LITTLE George 171, 178(3), 187; William 178, 187
LITTLETON John 232
LITTON Michael 206
LITZINGER George 145

INDEX TO APPENDIX B

LIU Philip 212
LIZER Mathias 236
LLOYD Daniel 205(2); James 184, 190, 232; Robert 232; Samuel 205
LOARD Able 156
LOCA John 220; Thomas 255
LOCK Jesse 213
LOCKER Jo: 195; Shadrick 193
LODGE William 199, 204
LODGET Henry 203
LODWICK Lennard 166
LOGAN John V. 162
LOGSTON Joseph 244; Thomas 244, 245; William 244
LOGWOOD Samuel 251
LOMACKS William 232
LOMAX Benjamin 159; Luke 164; Seth 158; Stephen 164; Thomas 159; Walter West 164
LOMOX ... 164; Thomas 164
LONE Bennet 214
LONEY Mosey 172; William 170
LONG ... 222; Coulborn 253; Daniel 253; David 257; Elisha 253; Jacob 237; Jeremiah 213; Jesse 253, 257; John 152, 248; Jonathan 163; Levin 257; Littleton 257; Nicholas 248; Peregrine 213; Rob 213; Robert 145; Sam 253(2); Solomon 219; Thomas 245; William 152, 221, 253(2)
LONGDON Thomas 197
LONGFELLOW John 153
LONGNAKER John 242
LONGSTON William 245
LOOCKERMAN Jacob 152; Richard 152; Thomas 154
LOOMAN John 191; Richard 192; Samuel 192
LORAIN John 182, 190; Thomas 192
LORD Henry 216, 221; John 237; Peter 216; Randolph 220; Thomas 181, 189, 195, 215, 221(2)
LORDEN Michael 173
LORE John 237
LOTTERMAN C. Lewis 235
LOUGHMAN Gasper 239
LOURIE Henry 238
LOUTHER Robert 231
LOVATT John 172
LOVE Charles 161; James 175, 227, 229; John 173, 223, 230(2); Joseph 211; Leonard 193; Robert 209; Samuel 193; Thomas 223, 230; William 225, 232
LOVEDAY Nicholas 223, 231; Thomas 226, 232; William 223, 231
LOVEGROVE James 182
LOVELACE Barton 194; Benjamin 193; Elkonah 193
LOVELESS Ignatius 162; James 162; John 159, 162; William 159
LOVELL John 171; Peter 171
LOVEMONEY Simon 188
LOVENS John 240
LOVER Jacob 242
LOVETT Barton 241; Britten 244
LOW Abraham 149; Levi 175
LOWE Baptist 212; Benjamin 255; David 194, 205; George 249, 255; Henry 219, 225; Hutson 218; Ignatius 214; James 213; John 228, 233; Thomas 218; William 217, 228
LOWER George 239
LOWERRY William 203
LOWERWELL William 214
LOWERY Charles 144; William 197
LOWIS Even 248
LOWMAN John 181, 239, 245; Martin 236; Richard 184
LOWREY Jacob 245; Michael 245
LOWRY James 214, 226, 234; John 226, 234; Joseph 227, 234; Robert 227, 234
LOWTHER Robert 224
LOYD James 217; Levin 217; Thomas 147; William 217
LUCA John 218
LUCAS Basil 200; Charles 193; David 229; Henry 211; John 157; Jonathan 206; Joshua 152; Michal 157; Morgan 229; Thomas 199; William 157, 194
LUCIE Charles 165
LUCKETT Benjamin 158; David 158; Ignatious 158; James 239; Samuel 158, 163, 239; Thomas Hezekiah 239
LUCKITT Notley 159; Thomas H. 159
LUCUS David 225
LUER Nehemiah 252
LUK.. Spencer 219
LUMAN Calip 245; Joshua 245
LUNDERGAN William 227
LUNEIFORD Edwin 152

INDEX TO APPENDIX B

LURTON Jacob 218
LUSBY John 149; Joseph 185; Robert 144
LUTEN Isaac 194
LUTES Alexander 197
LUX George 145
LYBRANT Christian 144
LYLES Col. 208; Henry 147, 208; Samuel (Sam.) 146(2), 150(2); Thomas 146(2), 150(2); William 146, 149, 150
LYNCH Daniel 174; David 252; Edmond 183, 191; Henry 182; Isaac 251; Jacob 252; James 154, 184, 190; John 181, 184, 189, 191; Nicholas 184; Samuel 188; Stephen 214; Thomas 192, 215
LYON George 176; Henry 161; James 147, 159; John 150, 161, 210; Joseph 161; Leonard 210; Michael 213; Richard 209; Robert 145; Thomas 148; Walt. 159; Zachariah 161
LYONS George 178, 187
LYSTER John 155; Joshua 157; William 156
LYTLE William 175
LYTTON Michael 198

MACCATTEE Samuel 158
MACCAY Isaack 183
MACCUBBIN Charles 144; Thomas 199; Zachariah 199
MACE Thomas 143
MACGILL John 208
MACK... Charles 199
MACKALL Benjamin 148, 151; James 148, 150; John 146, 148(2); Leven 147; Thomas 149
MACKARDELL Hugh 245
MACKBEE John 201
MACKELFISH Richard 248
MACKEN Arthur 175
MACKETEE James 200
MACKETTEE Samuel 204
MACKEY George 150; Philip 224, 231; William 224, 231, 247
MACKFARLAND George 148
MACKIMMY John 226
MACKLEFISH Abner 202; David 196, 203; Henry 202; John 196; Richard 198, 202

MACKMAHAN James 231
MACKMANS David 242
MACKON George 146
MACMAHAN John 225
MACMANI Nathaniel 144
MACONCHIE William 164
MACRAE Jessee 158
MADDEN Jonathan 194; Mordica 246
MADDING Benjamin 204; John 194, 200, 204; Joseph 200; Richard 194
MADDOCKE Henry 159; James 162; Notley 159
MADDOCKS Noah 158
MADDOX Benjamin 159, 164; Charles 165; Cornelius 159; George 164; Ignatious 158; James 206; John 164; Leonard 164; Nathan 161; Noah 164; Rhody 164; Samuell 158; Thomas 164; Townly 162; William 158, 162, 165, 206
MADDUX Alexander 218; Daniel 221; Elzey 220, 221; Hezekiah 249, 256; Isaac 217; John 218(2); Joshua 218; Lazarous 221; Mercey 256; Merrell 255; Stoughton 221; Thomas 219, 221; Zoro. 222
MADING Jonan. 194
MADOX Samuel 163
MADRID William 223, 230
MADUX Lararus 255
MAFFATT Barney 204
MAGEE John 246
MAGGS John 225
MAGILL John 2091 Thomas 203
MAGINNISS Andrew 206; John 202; Neill 194
MAGLOHEN Charles 166
MAGNOR John 181, 189
MAGOFFIN Joseph 145
MAGRUDER Alexander Wilson 150; Archibald 199, 204; Basil 196; Charles 200, 204; Daniel 204; Edward 199, 204; Elias 205; Enoch 199, 204; Ezekiel 199; Hezekiah 199, 204; Isaac 198; James 193; Jeffrey 204; John B. 198, 203; Joseph 200, 204; Josiah 199, 204; Levin (Leaven) 199, 204; Ninian 199, 204; Ninian B. 199, 204; Norman (Normand) B. 199, 204; Richard 199, 204; Samuel B. 199(2), 204; Samuel Beall 204;

INDEX TO APPENDIX B

Samuel Wade 200; Walter 199, 204;
William B. 199, 204; William O.
199; William Offutt 204; Zadock
193
MAGS John 230
MAGUIER Peter 198
MAGUIRE Andrew 200
MAHAMAN John 242
MAHANEY Basil 211; Ignatius 163
MAHONEY Basil 211, 212; Henry 239;
Ignatius 158; John Smith 213
MAHORNEY Henry 248
MAINSHIP Elijah 155; Nathan 155
MAINYARD Henry 167
MAJOR John 171; Thomas 168
MALARRY Patrick 247
MALCOM John 220
MALCOMB James 242
MALHONEY Daniel 167
MALLER Michael 144
MALLONE Robert 218; William 218
MALONE Thomas 201
MANCE John 239
MANERY Ignatious 159
MANFEILD John 180; William 180
MANKIN Charles 159; James 163; John
163, 164; Joseph 164; Richard 164
MANLEY Jonathan 207
MANLY Jesse 171; John 171
MANN George Vt. 176; William 188
MANNING John 148, 214; Joseph 164;
Walter 164
MANSFIELD James 183, 191(2); John
153; Levin 235; Richard 227, 234;
Robert 180, 188; Sam 180; Samuel
188; Thomas 182, 184, 192, 227;
William 181, 188, 189
MANSHIP Aaron 155; Charles 226, 232;
Henry 226, 233
MARA Timothy 185
MARAH Morris 177
MARAN George 179
MARBURY Henry 158, 165
MARBY Robert 187
MARCH John 177, 185
MARCUS John 204; Kid: 204
MARE Silvanus 198
MAREMAN Joseph 210; Joshua 210;
William 210; Zacharia 210
MARFORD Stephen 175
MARIATY Jacob 237
MARKER Michael 242

MARKLAND Charles 235; Edward 227, 235
MARKWELL William 241
MARLEY Robert 176
MARLOR Richard 165
MARLY Abram 179; Robert 178
MARONY Philip 167
MARQUESS James 146
MARQUIS James 150
MARR Daniel 164; John 144, 164;
Thomas 147
MARRET William 172
MARRIOTT John 144
MARSH Philip 253
MARSHAL Arthur 226; John 226
MARSHALL Andrew 166; Arthur 234;
Eligea 166; Elijah 233; Ephraim
220; George 257; Henry 148; Hugh
155; Isaac 221, 253; James 166,
200, 206, 226, 234; John 163, 166,
171, 220, 241, 253; Joseph 226,
234; Lijah 227; Mardeth 235; Mark
146; Martin 148; Meredith 226;
Ralph 155; Richard 146, 147, 164;
Risdon 221; Robert 221; Thomas
146(2) 150, 163, 257; Thomas H.
163; Thomas Hanson 158; William
148, 159, 225, 232, 234(2), 257
MARTAIN Jacob 239; Robert 165
MARTEN Thomas 215
MARTHIS William 207
MARTIN Andrew 184, 191; George 257;
Henry 223(2), 230(2); James 188,
219; John 182, 191, 219, 235;
Joseph 242; Leonard 159; Luther
146; Michael 159; Nehemiah 241;
Nicholas 235, 247; Richard 223,
230; Robert 230, 248; Samuel 196;
Solomon 223, 230; Thomas 219(2),
223(2), 230; Walter 172; William
170, 214, 215, 218, 219, 242(2);
Zachariah 162
MARTINDALE Daniel 152; Henry 152;
John 213; Lemuel 152; Samuel 152;
Stephen 152
MASH Lloyd 172
MASLIN Brittain 189; Francis 189;
Hamor 189; James 189; Samuel 189;
Thomas 189
MASLING Britain 181; Francis 182;
Hamor 181; James 181; Thomas 181
MASON ..ngley 206; Abram 156;
Alexander 206; Archibald 206;

INDEX TO APPENDIX B

Daniel 258; George 179, 187; Henry 153; Isachar 212; James 151; Jonathan 198, 207; Matthew 209; Richard 152, 153(2), 157; Solomon 153; Thomas 154, 174, 178; William 181(2), 189(3), 226, 234; Winchester 154
MASSEY Abednego 187; Alexander 251; Daniel 187; Ebenezer 187; Elijah 180, 188; Elisha 180, 188; Enock 177; Hezekiah 258; John 251; Joseph 187; Joshua 251; Josiah 186; Kiah 250; Masheck 178; Nathaniel 177; Stephen 187; William Lee 212
MASSON John 214
MASSY Abednego (Abednigo) 176, 178; Daniel Tose 178; Eben 178; Hezekiah 178; James 182; John 178; Joseph 178; Josiah 177; Meshack 176; Staphen 178
MASTIN Francis 158, 163
MATHER John 226; Thomas 174
MATHEW Michael 174
MATHEWS Bennet 169; George 145; Jacob 221; James 170; John 171; Levin 171; Roger 170; Thomas 153; William 181, 207, 242
MATINLEE Richard 242
MATLEY Henry 244, 245
MATRECE Joseph 150
MATSLER John 192
MATTAX Thomas 199
MATTHEW Levi 220
MATTHEWS Andrew 224, 230, 231; Baily 221; Benjamin Holland 221; Cloudsberry 154; David 221(2); Denwood 220; Greenbury 153; James 159, 220, 232; Jesse 220; John 153, 154, 170, 184, 191; Joseph 153, 159; Robert 220; Thomas 154, 160, 224; William 189, 220(2), 224, 226, 231, 234
MATTING Robert 214
MATTINGLEY Ignatius 210; Barton 212
MATTINGLY Bernard 194; Ignatiuus 212; Joseph 194; Luke 213; Moses 193; Robert 210; Thomas 212; William 210; Zachariah 161
MAULDING Jeremiah 148
MAW Edward 144; James 199; William 144

MAXWELL James 171, 176, 247; John 179, 181, 192; Robert 179(2), 180, 187(2), 188; William 176, 185, 186
MAY George 144, 244; James 170; John 188; Richard 162; William 162, 174
MAYHEW Henry 161; John 207
MAYHUE Richard 150
MAYNADIER William 225
MAYNARD Foster 226, 234
MAZE James 247
McAFEE George 154
McALLEN Alexander 257
McATEE Edmond 165; George 163; Henry 163, 165(2); James 163, 165; John 163; Thomas 161; William 163
McBRIDE Hugh 156; James 177; John 171; William 218
McCALL G. 144; John 157
McCALLESTER Archbald 166; John 166
McCALLUM Alexander 223, 230; William 229
McCANN Arthur 170; John 170; Thomas 160
McCARTEE Daniel 201
McCARTER Arthur 145; James 227, 235
McCARTY Charles 228; James 171; Kelly 182, 190
McCAULEY John 252; William 256
McCAY Absalom 185; Isaac 186; James 179
McCIM Alexander 146
McCL... ndly 224
McCLAIN Charles 179; John 161, 174; Patrick 172; William 211
McCLAMMY Samuel 218
McCLANAHAN Alexander 247
McCLANE George 248; James 246; John 239
McCLANNAN Nathaniel 180
McCLAYLAND Elexander 231; John 214; Thomas 225, 232
McCLENMEN Benjamin 217
McCLENNEN Thomas 217
McCLESTER John 216
McCLINTOCK Matthew 170
McCLISH Thomas 256
McCLUER James 185
McCLURE James 176; William 170
McCOLESTER John 146
McCOLEY John 214
McCOLISTER Roger 225
McCOLL Thomas 166

INDEX TO APPENDIX B

McCOLLAGH Samuel 157
McCOLLAUGH James 157; John 157
McCOLLUM Thomas 246
McCOMAS Aaron 174; Alexander 174(2);
   Benjamin 174; Edward 174; James
   173; John 174; Moses 172; Solomon
   174; William 174(2)
McCOMMAS John 172
McCONEY Philip 167
McCONIKIN John 227
McCONNELL Charles 145
McCOOMBS Jacob 154
McCOPPIN Thomas 182
McCORMACK Dennis 228; John 200, 205
McCOSH Thomas 209; William 209
McCOY Absolom 192; Archibald 239(2);
   Daniel 238, 239; Hugh 164, 166;
   James 239; John 238, 239; Johnson
   164; Joseph 238; Perry 238
McCRACKEN James 172
McCRADEY Robert 175
McCRAY John 253; Zephaniah 194
McCREADY Alexander 257; James 258
McCREARY Benjamin 174
McCREDDY Andrew 220; Isaac 221
McCREERY William 144
McCUBBIN Mechariah 204; Thomas 204
McCULLOCH William 157
McCULLOCK Hugh 229
McCULLUCK John 226
McCURDY Archibald 171
McCURTY James 172
McDADE Daniel 193, 194; James 194;
   John 196, 202(2); Robert 194
McDANIEL Allan 159; Daniel 158; David
   221; Edward 148, 217; Henry 193;
   Isaac 159; James 175, 217, 256;
   John 202, 256; Jonathan 162;
   Thomas 162; William 148, 176, 192,
   193, 194, 217, 256; Zachariah 164
McDAVIS James 164
McDERMET Partrick 195
McDOLAND James 164
McDON... Morris James 164
McDONACK James 206
McDONALD Dunkin 190; Jeremiah 187;
   John 197, 200, 233; Patrick 171;
   Philip 171
McDONNELD Allen 244
McDONOLD Alexander 163
McDORMAN William 219
McDOUGAL James 207; Samuel 207

McDOUGH Alexander 203
McDOUGLE Alexander 198; Samuel 198
McDOWELL James 180, 188; John 148,
   179; Samuel 188; William 180,
   188(2)
McDUALL John 214
McDURMET Partrick 202
McFADDEN Arthur 257; James 258;
   Joseph 170
McFADDIN Arthur 250; Isaac 238
McFADDON Alexander 199
McFADEN John 175
McFALL John 247; Peregrine 184, 191
McFLALAND Bennet 215
McFLOWERS Samuel 207
McGACHANON James 164
McGARMENT Mr. 250
McGAW John 174;D Robert 171
McGEE Daniel 255; George 252; John
   255; Joshua 255; Ruben 257; Samuel
   255; William 213
McGILL Arthur 211; Charles 238
McGILLEGUS Daniel 179
McGINNEY James 225
McGINNY David 225; John 225
McGLAMERY Edward 255
McGLANGLEN James 247
McGLAUGHLAN George 170
McGLEW Patrick 161
McGLOCKLAN Hugh 238
McGLOUGHLAN Robert 170
McGOUGH Hugh 175
McGRATH Arthur 218; William 197, 220
McGREATH William 201
McGREE Fouquhart 207
McGREGORY Ebenezer 190; John 183, 192
McGRILL Edward 144
McGUINEA John 232
McGUINIA Daniel 232
McGUINNEY Daniel 153
McGUIRE Andrew 201; Isaiah 224;
   Partrick 207
McGUIRER Philip 173
McHAFFEY Jere 182
McHENRY Thomas 180; Urias 258
McHETTEE Charles 204
McINTIRE Daniel 216; Willen 216
McKAY Richard 214; Robert 148
McKEEL Charles 155
McKENNY Rubin 214
McKENZIE Roderick 173
McKEOWN William 157

INDEX TO APPENDIX B

McKETEE Joseph 206
McKEY Elijah 180, 188; James 218
McKIM A. 145; John 185; Robert 144;
   William 185
McKIMMEY Elijah 156; Gideon 155
McKIMMMY David 178
McKINEDEY Patrick 216
McKINLEY Archibald 239; Hugh 185;
   Richard 172
McKINLY Mingo 178
McKINNEY James 149; John 149; Joseph
   175; William 192
McKINOCK George 213
McKINSEY Aaron 245; Alexander 223,
   228, 235; Andrew 166; Daniel 245;
   Edward 174; Gabriel 245; Henry
   169; Samuel 245
McKNIGHT James 171
McKNOULTY John 233
McKNOUTLY Thomas 233
McKOY James 241; John 242; Thomas 241
McLALLY Patrick 217
McLANEY William 175
McLANY Alexander 167
McLAUGHLAN John 246
McLAUGHLIN Alexander 218
McLEAN James 165; William 165, 213
McLEARY John 195
McLOCKLAND Henry 194
McLONEY Andrew 213
McLURE A. 144; John 144
McMACKEN Thomas 246
McMAHAN John 231, 232; William 157
McMATH Samuel 173; William 173
McMECHON David 145
McMEME Hugh 237
McMILLAN Samuel 173; William 173
McMIN Robert 169
McMULIN Andrew 180
McMULLIN Andrew 178, 187; William 173
McMURRAY Patrick 175
McNAMARA Dennis 185
McNEAR Robert 175; William 201, 204
McNEILL Thomas 252
McNULTY John 228
McNUTT Alelxander 241; Barnard 241;
   James 241; Robert 241; William 241
McPHAIL Daniel 171(2)
McPHERSON Alexander 160; Walter 158,
   159, 163; William 163
McQUAY Jeremiah 235; John 234, 235;
   Patrick 227, 234; Thomas 233

McQUILLAN Rowland 145
McQUIN Donald 185, 192
McQUINA James 235
McRYON Michal 152
McSHERRY Hugh 194
McSWEENY Jeremiah 235
McTARDEN John 247
McVEGH John 158
McVEIGH Joseph 219
McVEY Benjamin 158(2); Jacob 158
McWAY Epheram 227; John 227
McWILLIAMS George 238; John 238;
   Kenelin 213
MEAD William 159
MEADS Giles 223
MEANS Henry 156
MEARS William 183; Zedok 154
MEBBER Thomas 186
MECKELFISH Thomas 248
MEDCALF Edward 201; James 143; John
   213; Kenelin 213; William 143
MEDFORD George 180, 188; Marmaduke
   177, 186; McCale 178; McCall 186
MEDLEY Enoch 214; George 214; Henry
   211; John 214; Joseph 214; William
   214
MEDLY William 201
MEEDS James 232; Thomas 232
MEEK David 240, 248; Thomas 247
MEEKINGS Peter 180
MEEKS Aquilla 184, 191; Robert 183,
   190; St. Leger 183, 191;
   Theophilas 183, 190; William 183,
   191, 192
MEGONAGIL Morris 181
MEGUMMERY Thomas 216
MEHANEY Thomas 237
MELANHY Michael 172
MELATT Theodotious 240
MELLOR Thomas 167
MELLOTT Peter 239
MELLY James 149; John 149
MELON James 240
MELONE James 241; John 240
MELONEY Alexander 245; John 242
MELOTT Benjamin 239; Joseph 248;
   Thomas 239
MELOY John 194
MELVILL David 152; John 155
MELVIN George 257; John 257; Jonathan
   258; Joseph 217; Littleton 258;
   Robert 257; Smith 258; William 257

INDEX TO APPENDIX B

MENCER Michael 244
MENG William 167
MENSON Richard 246
MERADITH John 209; Thomas 209; William 209
MERCHANT George 184, 191; James 223, 230; John 220, 224, 231; William 183, 191
MERCHMENT Charles 253; Samuel 253
MEROTHO Joseph 157
MERRICK Aaron 229; Allin 225; Andrew 225; Daniel 230; Ezerail 153; Isaac 152; James 154; John 231; Lembert 152; Mathias 223, 230
MERRIDETH Uriah 157
MERRIKEN Joshua 144
MERRIL Joshua 217, 222; Robert 220
MERRILL Jacob 258; Joshua 212; Josiah 257; Levin 257; Thomas 257; William 253, 257
MERRIT William 177
MERRITT Levin 181; Sovrin 181; William 176, 185
MERRY John 183
MESSERSMITH Valentin 239
METCALF Edward 196
METT John 179
METTS Christian 236
METZLER David 185
MEZACK George 216
MEZECK Jacob 216; James 216
MEZICK Ben 217
MgGAINA Solomon 224
MIARS Luke 176
MICHAEL Belcher 171; Ludwick 240
MICHELL Samuel 164
MIDDCALF John 240
MIDDLEBROOK Isaac 178, 187
MIDDLETON Gilbert 144; Horatio 163; Hugh 163; Isaac Smallwood 165; Joseph 144, 178; Major 156; Samuel 163; William 144, 190, 200, 222
MIDDLETOWN Hugh 158
MIDLETON Joseph 186; Robert 178
MIERS James 223; John 177; Solomon 206
MIES George 239
MIFFIN Andrew 157
MIGSOVE Adam 240
MIKESELL John 169
MILBOURN Jacob 222; John 221; Lodowick 221, 222; Thomas 259

MILBURN John H. 215
MILES Aquila 174; George 220; Henry 162(2), 216, 221; Henry Walston 219; James 220; John 195; Joseph 162(2); Levi 221; Levin 221; Richard 212; Samuel 219, 220; Stephen 162; Thomas 174, 198, 204; William 162, 173, 219, 220, 221(2)
MILEY Frederick 207
MILIGAN Isaac 221; John 221
MILINGTON Richard 226
MILLARD Joshua 212
MILLBURN Jeremiah 214
MILLER Abner 222; Abraham 244, 246; Adam 247; Alian 244; Andrew 240; Charles 182, 222; Christian 237; Conrad 168; Conrod 246(2); Daniel 238, 246, 247; David 241, 246, 247; George 168, 243(2), 246; Hance 246(2); Henry 245, 246(2); Isaac 148; Jacob 159, 246(3), 249; James 178, 184, 186, 191; Jeffery 224, 231; John 148, 150, 179, 246(3), 247, 248, 249, 252; John Sollomon 246; Martin 243; Michael 184, 191, 239, 248; Nathaniel 184; Peter 175; Richard 184; Robert 168; Samuel 184, 191; Stephen 246; Thomas 184(2), 191, 193; Walter 184, 191(2); William 149
MILLEY Moses 148
MILLHOUSE John 247
MILLINGTON Alemby (Alimby) 222, 228; Isaac 225, 232; Nicholson 222; Richard 226, 232, 233; William 225
MILLIS Edward 222; James 223
MILLOR Ayres Smith 258
MILLRIGHT Charles Jones 205
MILLS Bernard 214; Charles 210; Cor's 144; James 148, 155, 213, 214, 242; James Andrew 210; Jesse 196, 201; John 149, 170, 210, 211, 258; Justinian 211; Leonard 149; Levi 251; Nicholas 214; Richard 257; Robert 258; Sam 251; Samuel 258; Stephen 220; Thomas 221; William 212, 217, 220, 258
MILLWARD Charles 191
MILONE William 160
MILSON James 154
MILSTEAD Edward 162; John 162; Samuel 162; William 162

INDEX TO APPENDIX B

MILTON Abraham 181, 189; George 213; James 213; Philip 212; Richard 182
MILWARD Charles 183; William 229
MINEY James 188
MING William 167
MINITREE Andrew 162; Paul 162
MINNER Edward 156; Elisha 156; John 164; William 154
MIRES Even 242; James 179, 187; John 179, 185, 187; Luke 179, 187; Stephen 178(2), 179, 187(4); William 176, 178(2), 187(2)
MIRS Frederick 241
MISHLAR Lawrence 238
MISTER Marmaduke 221
MITCHEL George 220; John 179, 187, 219; Joshua 220; Thomas 218, 222
MITCHELL Ambrose 154, 157; James 171, 251; John 154, 166, 171, 172; John Pope 251; Joseph 204, 256; Levin 251; Micaja 170; Mordecai M. 197; Nathan 198; Nathaniel 205; Notley 206; Per. 159; Reuben 166; Richard 154, 164; Richard Bennett 164; Robert 251; Thomas 166, 198, 207; Walter 198, 206; William 171
MITTS George 212
MOBBERLY Archibald 196
MOBLEY Archibald 202; William 162
MOCK Peter 248; William 244
MOCKBE James 207; Allin 196; Brock 195, 202; Ninian 196, 202; Zachariah (Zechariah) 200, 204; Zephaniah 204
MOCOMAN Ludwick 237
MOFFETT George 177, 186; Haley 177, 186; Jacob 177, 186; Jesse 177, 186; John 180; Moses 177, 186; Richard 177, 186; Robert 186; William 177
MOLAND William 205
MOLLOHONE William 212
MOLT William 187
MONAHON Arthur 170; John 170
MONDY Balser 246; John 246
MONEY Robert 180, 188; William 181
MONG Adam 238(2); Davolt 244; Jacob 238
MONGOMERY Dennis 221
MONNETT Isaac 148
MONNINGER Henry 245; John 248
MONNOW John 158

MONROE John 210
MONTEGUE Jadwin 153; John 153
MONTGOMERY Basil 160; Charles 161; Francis 160; Ignatius 160; James 162; Joseph 160, 171; Joshua 162; Peter 162; William 160, 203
MONTIGUE Harrison 153; Jerimah 153
MOOBERRY William 171
MOODEY Robert 188
MOODY Robert 180
MOOR Bratshe 216; Hugh 158; Isaac 216; Jacob 216; John 222; Stephen 216; Thomas 216, 219, 220, 221; William 220
MOORE Barton 204; Benjamin 206; Bennet 214; Charles 170; Elijah 162, 217, 220; George 149, 162, 178, 182, 186, 190, 230, 243(3); Hezekiah 162; Isaac 207, 221; James 170, 172, 201, 211; Jeremiah 207; John 182(2), 210, 211, 214, 240, 243; John William 202; Josias 203; Leonard 211; Levin 216; N. Ruston 145; Richard 231, 240; Robert 145; Samuel 198, 206; Silvanus 203; Simon 182, 190; Thomas 166; William 153, 204, 216(2), 243; Zachariah 208
MOORES James 173(2); John 173
MORAN Andrew 161; Hezekiah 213; John 161; Jonathan 161, 213; Joseph 209; Partrick 206; William 161
MORDOCK James 164
MORE Benjamin 200; Daniel 175; George 210; James 196; John W. 196; Joseph 246; Joshua Evans 216; Mathew 162; Nathan 194; Nicholas 214; Nicholas R. 146; Phillip 246; Samuel 194; William 175
MOREHEAD Joseph 237
MORELAND Jacob 159; James 165; Patrick 165; Philip 165; Samuel 165; Walter 159
MORGAN Benjamin 155; Charles 183, 190; David 152(2); Dennis 202; Edward 176; George 156; James 157; John 155(2), 210; Johnsey 196; Murrel 161; Nathaniel 240; Richard 196; Robert 170, 175; Samuel 174; Solomon 155, 156(2); Thomas 223, 230; William 156, 224, 231

INDEX TO APPENDIX B

MORGON Moses 237; Phillip 237; William 237
MORIARTY James 173
MORINE Thomas 156
MORLAND Isaac 165; John 162; Philip 162; Stephen 162; William 162; Zachariah 162
MORLERE Aiton 165; James 165
MORNINGSTAR Philip 168
MOROW Philip 180
MORRAN Gabril 160; Luke 160; Samuel 160
MORRIS Cornelius 200, 253; David 228; Edward 171, 253; Isaac 253; Jacob 159, 218; James 175, 176, 210, 253, 257; James R. 257; Jesse 185; Jethrew 253; John 155, 172, 174, 200, 214, 225, 253; Joseph 218; Joshua 159, 257; Philip 253; Richard 185, 192; Walter 159; William 226, 253
MOORISON George 143; Joseph 241; William 164, 247
MORRISS David 233; James 160, 232; John 218, 232
MORROW John 175
MORSELL James 150
MORSS Isaac 253; Joshua 251
MORT Joseph 210
MORTON George 161; John 161; Joseph 161
MOSES George 218; Robert 199, 207; William 199
MOSLEY William 195
MOSON Archibald 198
MOSS Frederick 241
MOSSLEY Jacob 245
MOTT William 179
MOUNCE Joseph 241
MOUNT John 242; Samuel 242
MOUNTS John 207
MOUNTZ John 199; Michael 199
MOURER Nicholas 248
MOWBREY Aaron 156
MOWING Daniel 236; John 246; Ludwick 236; Stephen 246
MOXLEY John 195
MOYER Phelix 245
MUDD Bennett 160; Henry 160; Henry Thomas 160; Ignatius 160; James 164; Jeremiah 164; John 164; Joseph 213; Joshua 161; Richard 164; Smith 164
MUFFETT Barny 200; Daniel 246; William 240
MUGG John 210; Peter 161; Thomas 247; Walter 210
MUGGS Thomas 242
MUIR James 219
MULES James 146, 150
MULL Henry 240
MULLEN Michael 247
MULLIKIN Archibald 196; Basil 196, 202; James 223, 230(2); Jesse 223, 230; John 193, 196, 232; Joseph 154; Lewis 196, 202; Patrick 235; Samuel 223(2), 230; William 207, 230
MUMFORD George 252; James 252, 254; Jersey 254; Jesse 252; John 256; Major 252; Matthias 253; Sackor 251; Stephen 252; Zadok 253
MUMMART Michael 197; William 197
MUNCASTER Charles 164; James 164
MUNDAY James 173
MUNGAN Matthew 218
MUNGAR John 219; Richard 182, 190; Samuel 182, 190; Thomas 255
MUNGOMERY Charles 238
MUNNETT Abram 156; William 154, 156
MUNRO Alexander 145
MUNROE Hugh 171; John 163; Thomas 163
MUNROW Bryan 236; Isaac 220; Moses 241; Robert 241
MURAKIN Senica 243
MURDOCK Benjamin 243; James 158; John 198, 204, 205; Samuel 164; William 165, 175
MURFEY James 175
MURPHEY Edward 185; Francis 193; Hezekiah 161; William 200; Zachariah 163
MURPHY Abm. 159; Charles 205; Darby 196, 201; John 166, 188, 200, 203, 226, 231, 235; Philip 205; Samuel 159; William 155, 166, 171(2), 207; Zaphh. 161
MURRAY Dunkin 251; James 213; John 257; Philip A. 159
MUSCHETT John 164
MUSGROVE Anthony 197; Benjamin 168; Henry (Henery) 166, 237; Nathan 196; Samuel 197(2)

INDEX TO APPENDIX B

MYARS Andrew 192
MYER Adam 244
MYERS Adam 199; Charles 146; Conrod 195; Felter 198, 206; Ludwick 244
MYRE George 242
MYRES Frederick 241; James 185; Peter 241

NAB Elisha 182
NABB Charles 224, 231; Elisha 190; John 224, 231
NALLY Birnard 160; Gustavus 160; Ignatius 160; John 163; Leonard 160; Nathan 164; Shadrick 165
NAPP Thomas 224, 231
NASH John 224; Thomas 227, 233
NAVE Abraham 248; Henry 244; Jacob 237; Leonard 245; Michael 245
NEAD Daniel 245
NEAL Charles 189; Francis 225, 232; James 191; Joseph 223, 230; Robert 223, 229; Ruben 187; Samuel 223
NEALE Charles 212; Henry 213; James 162; Jeremiah 213; John 162; Thomas 143; William F. 162
NEALL Ralph 195
NEARN John 250
NEEDLES Edward 223, 230; Tristram 223, 230; William 229
NEIGHBOURS James 230; Samuel 223, 225, 229
NEIL Charles 181
NEILL Henry 170; Joseph 194
NELDIE Christian 240; Jacob 239; John 239
NELLEY Jeremiah 167
NELMS Edmond William 254; Edmund N. 249
NELSON Ben 216; Henry 197, 203; Jesse 257; John 151, 164, 217; Jonathan 257; Joseph 164; Moses 257; Peter 168; Thomas 163, 164; William 164
NERVEY John 167
NETTLE Thomas Dutton 210
NEVEL William 178
NEVIT Joseph 212
NEVITT Charles 165; James 199
NEWCOM William 177
NEWCOMB George 185; John 153; Robert 226; William 206
NEWCOMER Peter 244
NEWCOMMER Christopher 239; Henry 239

NEWEL David 176
NEWELL Baptis 214; David 185; John 177, 186; Thomas 241
NEWLAND Isaac 180, 188
NEWMAN Benjamin 195; Edward 159; Jacob 195; Joel 187
NEWNAM Daniel 224; Joel 178; John 223; Joseph 154
NEWSOM John 190
NEWTON Abraham 257; Bernard 214; Delbert 212; Gabriel 211; Ignatius 212; Job 255; John 215; Joseph 213; Levin 250, 259; Selby 258; Thomas 193; William 197, 201, 212, 258; Zacharia 212
NICEWONDER Isaac 236; John 247
NICEWONGER John 244
NICHODEMUS Capt. 237; Conrod 236; Frederick 236
NICHOLES Sam 252
NICHOLL Jacob 240
NICHOLLS Archibald 166, 194; Benjamin 198, 245; Flayl 166; John 166, 196, 197, 237; Joseph 243; Ninian 194; Thomas 195, 196(2), 197; William 166, 237
NICHOLS Charles 217; Daniel 204; Jeremiah 189; John 199, 204, 237; John A. 201; John H. 201; Joseph 167, 217; Joshua 218; Lin... 201; Samuel 201, 222; Thomas 201, 202, 210; Trail 237; William 199, 201(2)
NICHOLSON Benjamin 145; Daniel 222; Henry 216; Isaac 256; John 194, 256; Richard 206; Roger 217; Stephen 144; Thomas 145, 178, 179; William 196
NICKELSON John 158
NICOLS Iky 155; Isaac 155; Jeremiah 181; John 156, 225, 232; Joseph 155, 157; Thomas 156; William 231
NIED Daniel 238
NIEL James 184
NIKELS John 223
NISBETT Bernard 193; Charles 194; Nicholas 246
NISFIELD Jeremiah 161
NIX George 225
NIXON Hugh 200, 205; James 200, 205; Jonathan 200, 205; Joshua 200, 205; Richard 205; Robert 170

INDEX TO APPENDIX B

NOAKES Richard 212
NOBLE John 218; Jonathan 255(2); Joseph 255; Levin 156; Richard 156; Thomas 219; William 256
NOE Joseph 213; Peter 196; Thomas 210
NOELL Thomas 154, 167
NOLAND Richard 172; Samuel 167; Thomas 167
NOLEY William 224
NON Benjamin 237
NORFOLK James 147, 148(2); John 147(2), 148, 150; Thomas 147; William 147
NORIS James 175; John 175
NORMAN James 242
NORRIS Aquila 172; Barton 214; Benjamin 173; Bennr 214; Clement 214; Daniel 172; Edmond 214; Edward 172; George 194; Gerrard 214; Henry 210; Ignatius 214; James 172, 185, 225; Jesse 178; John 146(2), 150, 172, 173, 214, 241; Joshua 172(2); Mark 211; Martin 149; Michael 175; Patrick 166, 237; Philip 210, 214(2), 225, 229; Rode 214; Samuel 186; Thomas 172, 211, 214(2), 242; Vincent 214; William 158, 164, 172, 174, 194, 211, 214; Zachariah 144
NORRISS Daniel 164; Edmund 211; James 211(2); John 242; John Basil 211; John Heard 211; Stephen 211
NORRY Mark 164
NORTH Gilbert 166; John 216; Thomas 144
NORTHCRAFT Edward 196, 202; Richard 196, 202
NORTHEY Samuel 150
NORTHSINGER Mathias 168; Samuel 168
NORTON Richard 225, 229(2)
NORWOOD Edward 235; Gerd. 162; James 203; John 226, 235; Joseph 228, 233, 235; Stephen 203; William 226, 234
NOSELAND James 243
NOTHEY Samuel 207
NOTT Jestinion 159
NOTTINGHAM Bennet 214; Philip 214; Stephin 165
NOTTINGHAME John Basil 211
NOWEL James 146

NOWELL Gilbert 148; Henry 214; Jeremiah 214; John 147; Joseph 240; William 148, 150, 240
NOWER James 174
NOWLAND John 188
NOWLS John 224
NOWRIE William 146
NOY George 248
NUCOMB John 216
NUGENT Jere 214; Robert 214; Williby 214
NUMAN John 221; Thomas 218
NUMBERS John 184; Joseph 184
NUNAM Abner 226, 232; Daniel 231; John 230
NUSOM John 183
NUTALL John 227
NUTON James 220; Ward 149
NUTRELL Thomas 226
NUTTELL Philip 227
NUTTER Ben 218; Joseph 216; William 217
NUTTLE John 235 Phill 228; Solomon 235

O'BRYAN James 209
O'CLOSE Charles 172
O'NEILL Barton 194; Bernard 168
O'NIELL Bernard 146
OAIR John 238
OAKEY Levin 257
OAKLEY John 208
OAKLY John 162; Robert 162
OARD William 213
OBLENONER George 247
OBRIAN Philip 207; Richard 205
OBRYAN Cornelius 160; Josias 160
OBRYON James 179
ODAN Thomas 161; Vincent 161
ODANEL Richard 194
ODEAR Elisha 257
ODEL Thomas 237(2)
ODEN Benjamin 208; Elias 160; Isaac 161
ODLE Barruck 199; Baruch 204; Talbot 170; Thomas 166
ODLEBERGER Phillip 238
ODLEBURGER Phillip 238
ODONALY Cornialus 144
OFFLEY John 185
OFFUT Mordicai 199; Nathaniel 197; William M. 197

INDEX TO APPENDIX B

OFFUTT (See also Boffutt) Alexander 200, 205; Edward 200; Ezekiel 205; George 200; George H. 204; Henry 200; Hezkekiah 205; James 200, 205; Jesse 205; John 205; Nathan 196, 201, 205; Nathaniel 201, 205; Natt. 200; Rezin 200, 204; Samuel 196, 197, 201; Thomas 200(2), 205(2); William 200(2), 205(2); Zachariah 197, 200; Zadok 205; Zepheniah 200
OGDAN Thomas 203
OGDEN Aron 150; Elisha 150; Hugh 195; John 201; Jonathan 162; Joseph 201; Moses 150
OGDIN James 150
OGDON Benjamin 161; David 195; Hugh 195; Thomas 160
OGG Alexander 148
OGLE Benjamin 168; William 241
OHARA Arthur 240
OHAY William 145
OLDFIELD Henry 153
OLIPHAN William 256
OLIPHANT John 254; William 249
OLIVER James 171; Lewis 215
OLLIVER William 196
ONEAL David 204; Henry 201; John 201; William 201
ONEALE Anthony 165
ONEALL Charles 195; Henry 196; John 197; William 197
ONEIL Peter 195
ONEILL David 199
ONION John 144
ONIONS Henry 209
ONSELL John 240
ORAM Edward 227; Hugh 227; John 154; Nicholas 226, 234; William 218, 226
ORD Jesse 212
ORDIS Zadok 258
ORELL Thomas 157
OREM Andrew 226; Edward 235; Nicholas 235; Spedden 235
ORENDORFF Christopher 240
ORIM Andrew 234; William 234
ORME Aaron 200, 205; Archibald 196, 202; Charles 200; Eli 205; Ely 200; Jeremiah 200, 205; John 207; Philip 205; Robert 198, 206; Sam. J. 200

ORNEST Henry 247
ORPUTT Richard 169
ORR Hugh 173; John 171, 207; Thomas 170
ORRELL Durdin 153; Thomas 156
OSBIN Archibald 206
OSBORN Cyrus 172; James 170; John 171; Samuel G. 171; Thomas 160; William 172
OSBORNE Benjamin 171; William 171
OSMANT John 235
OSMOND John 227; Jonathan 232; Thomas 232
OSQUE Abraham 150
OSTER Conrod 247; Jacob 246; John 240, 246; Peter 246; Phillip 240
OSTON Benjamin 184
OSTRO Thomas 164
OTT Adam 238, 240; Barnett 168; Jacob 169, 240; Michael 240
OTTER George 244
OTTO Mathias 242
OUCHTERLONY Patrick 195
OUTEN Isaac 222; Obednigo 221
OUTERBRIDGE James 156; Lenard 156
OUTTEN Levi 256; Matthias 257
OUTTON John 253
OVERACRE George 238
OVERSTOCKS James 151
OWDEN Gerard (Gerrard) 197, 203; Josias 197; Nathan 197, 203
OWEN Edward 206; John 197, 203; Joseph 162; Lawrance 193; Richard 193; Robert 197; Thomas 164, 195, 198, 203; William 197, 203
OWENS Charles 148; Ewell 164; James 148, 216; Joseph 210; Joshua 255; Levin 255(2); Ohly 255; Okly 255; Peter 255; Samuel 147; Spencer 255; Thomas 167, 239; William 157, 218
OWINGS Caleb 144; Ephriam 145
OXENHAM Peter 152, 232; Richard 225, 232
OZBURNE Henry 162; Joseph 162
OZMONT Richard 156(2); Samuel 155; Thomas 154

P..OR David 218
PA..ER John 178
PACA James 170
PACE Aquila 169

INDEX TO APPENDIX B

PACK Richard 195; Thomas 195; William 195(2)
PADEN John 220
PADGET James 159; Thomas 158
PADGETT Benjamin 165; Joseph 162; William 153, 163
PADGITT Aaron 165; Benjamin 165; William 165
PAGE Aquila (Aquilla) 177, 185; Jesse 197; John 184; Walter 165
PAGMAN (See Pigman) Nathaniel 196
PAIN Barnet 173; Flayl 166; John 173, 212, 258; Levin 250, 258; Samuel 250
PAINE John 173, 201
PAINTER George 241; Godfree 246
PAKER Sacker 252
PALMER Bartly (Bartley) 177, 186; Isaac 229; John 177, 185, 186, 192; Jonathan 203
PALMORE Peter 239
PALMORNE Benjamin 144
PALMOUR Peter 239
PAMARR William 153
PAMER Isaac 222
PAMPILION Nicholas 232
PANCOAST John 202; William 202
PANE Samuel 256
PANTER Christian 148; Francis 149
PANTRY John 149
PAPHENBARGER Valentine 240
PARADICE James 196, 202
PARADISE William 202
PARAMORE Elijah 216; James 217; Samuel 217
PARDO John 149
PARISH John Gray 181; Nimrod 200; William 229
PARK John 228; William 195(2)
PARKER Aaron 243, 245; Abraham 161; Allen 155; Aquilla 176; Benjamin 249, 254; Daniel William 180; Elisha 249(2), 254(2); Fielder (Fealder) 146, 149, 150; George 147, 150, 254; Jacob 249, 254; Jinkins 249; Jonathan 144, 161; Martin 174; Peter 147, 242, 253; Purnell 253; Robert (Robart) 244, 245; Thomas 224; William 146, 150(2), 174, 184(2), 188, 191
PARKERSON Edward 223, 232

PARKES Andrew 187; Arthur 221; Job 221; John 221
PARKS Andrew 177; John 178, 240; Thomas 178, 186
PARMER James 163
PARNARR James 157
PARNELL John 258
PAROTT James 224; Saila 232
PARRADICE Thomas 250, 259
PARRAMORE Capt. 259; John 250, 259; Stephen 221
PARRAN Benjamin 149; Capt 151; Charles Som. 149; Charles Somers. 149; Elexander 149; John 149(2); Richard 149; Thomas 149
PARRIS John 253
PARRISH William 225
PARROT Saila 226
PARROTT Aaron 225, 232; Abner 224, 231; Henry 225, 232; James 225(2), 231, 232; John 223(2), 226, 230(2), 233; Joseph 223; Perry 224, 231; Peter 232; Slyter 231; Thomas 225, 232; William 153
PARSONNETT David 222, 228
PARSONS Benjamin 232; Bennit 212; Clement 213; George 249, 254; James 211, 228; John 177, 185, 254, 256; Jonathan 249, 254; Jordan 254; Joseph 176, 179, 187, 223; Levin 254; Michael 179, 188; Porter 255; Samuel 249, 254; William 249, 254; Zachariah 255; Zephaniah 254
PARTRICK John 193
PARVIN Thomas 243
PASHANBARGER Adam 241; Henry 241
PASSENBACK Balsar 244
PATRICK Cornelius 257; George 175; John 175, 252; William 237
PATTEN John 183; Mathew 146
PATTERSON Andereson 258; Basil 210; Capt. 258; George 170; James 146, 227, 238, 258; John 149, 169, 224, 231; William 203, 208, 241
PATTIN William 185
PATTISON Edward 232; James 150; Jeremiah 149; Richard 149; Thomas 149; William 148
PATTON Mathew 145; Thomas 192
PATTORF David 246
PATTY Kendle 251; Powell 251

322

INDEX TO APPENDIX B

PAUL William 246
PAULES John 237
PAULL Nicholas 199
PAULON Matthew 152
PAVIN John 186
PAYNE Ebenezer 165; Francis 165, 201, 210; Ignatius 165; Isaac 156; James 210, 215; Jestinian 164; John 156; John Baptist 214; Leonard 210; Raphael 210; Vincent 210; William 212
PEABODDY John 144
PEACE William 148, 150
PEACOCK Ignatius 211; John 257; Luke 174; Richard 177, 183, 186, 190; Samuel 174; William 147
PEACOCKE William 146
PEACOK Levi 257
PEAK Benjamin 197, 201; Hezekiah 203; James 197; Kenelin 212; Lewis 197, 201; Peter 214; Samuel 197, 203; Thomas 197, 201
PEAKE Augustin 210; Ignatius 214; James 214; Robert 210
PEAKOCK Israel 257
PEARCE Andrew 183; Baptis 200; Benjamin Notley 199; Charles 181, 189; Clement 241; David 189; Edward 183, 190; Henry 200; Hugh 180; James 167, 179, 187; John 182; Nicholas 199; Richard 173; Samuel 189; Thomas 179, 187; William 181, 182, 183, 189
PEARCSE Benjamin 167
PEARSON Edward 157; Joseph 172; Levi 225, 229; Richard 156; Thomas 225; William 225, 229
PEARSONS Benjamin 225; Joseph 230
PECK Casper 237; William 202
PECKERN Robert 222
PEDDICOART Jasper 197
PEDDICOAT Jasper 203; Nicholas 195
PEDRRY James 208
PEGG William 197, 204
PEIGN Mickal 150
PEIRPOINT Eli 168
PELL William 187
PELLA Harrisson 201
PELLY Calvert 203; Colbert 195; Harrison 196; James 196
PEMY John 163
PENCE Christopher 236; Jacob 248

PENCHIEFF Stophel 175
PENCOAST Adin 196; John 198; William 198
PENDEGAST Thomas 173
PENDERGRASS Laurance 243; Robert 243
PENES William 176
PENEWELL Elisha 255; Powell 251
PENEWILL Elias 253; Elisha 254; Rackliff 253; William 253
PENINGTON Richard 180
PENIWELL Elias 252; Richard 254
PENN Benjamin 197, 198, 203; Benjamin Davis 197, 203; Caileb 197; Caleb 203; Charles 197, 203; Edward 197(2), 203; Jezrul 162; John 196, 202; Joseph 197, 203; Marcus Hatton 210; Mark 214; Stephen 161
PENNA Joseph 202
PENNEWILL Luke 251
PENNICK Thomas 173
PENNINGTON Henry 188; James 185, 187(2); John Wd. 187; Richard 188
PENNIWELL George 254
PENNY Joseph 196
PENNYBAKER Benjamin 238
PEPPER Evans 253; Joshua 257; Levi 251; Spencer 250,258
PERDEN Josiah 203
PERDUE Capt. 256; George 249(2), 254(2); James 249(2), 254, 256; John 249, 254(2)
PERKINS Daniel 189; Isaac 181; Jacob 150; James 170; John 170; Richard 174; Samuel 185; Thomas 192; William 185, 190
PERKINSON John 144
PERRES William 176
PERRIE Hugh 161
PERRIN Joseph 239
PERRY Charles 196; Daniel 244; Erasmus 198, 205; Francis 165; George 176, 179; James 155, 196; John 165, 197, 203; Joshua 194; Samuel 161; Thomas 155, 165, 205; William 152, 154
PERT John 155
PETAY Jacob 240
PETER Balser 247; John 199; Robert 199(2)
PETERS Robert 146, 150; William 156
PETTICORD Nathan 239(2)
PHARIS Thomas 230

323

INDEX TO APPENDIX B

PHARRIS Thomas 223
PHEBUS George 219; John 219(2); William 219
PHELPS John 244; Thomas 242
PHERSON Samuel 213
PHIFER Leonarhart 248
PHILIPS Henry 145, 213; James 159; John 228; Philemon 223; Richard 166; Thomas Hambleton 160
PHILLIP George 217
PHILLIPS Charles 200, 206, 217; Isaac 249, 256; James 171, 175, 217, 258; Jesse 216; John 197, 216, 220; Jonah 216; Lambert 186; Samuel 197; Stephen 187
PHILPOT Bartin 166; Brian 145; Charles 167; Tayman 146
PHILPOTT Bryan 146; Tayman 146, 150; Thomas 144, 194
PHIPS John 172
PIBUS John 143
PICKELMAN John 247
PICKERING Charles 225, 228, 235(2); George 226, 230; Robert 228
PICKIN John 165
PICKLEHIMER Jacob 237
PICKRELL John 159
PICKRIN Thomas 159
PIERCE Benjamin 242; Daniel 243; Henry 206; James 243; Stephen 168; Thomas 207
PIFER Martin 238
PIGMAN Nacey (Nacy) 197, 203
PIGNO Nicholas 202
PIKE Archibald 212; Henry 214
PILCHARD Esau 250, 258; Jabez 250, 258; Levi 258
PILES Leonard 149; Osburn 201
PINCHBACK John 196
PINDELL Nicholas 144; Phillip 242; Thomas 242
PINDER Thomas 153
PINDERGRASS Phillip 243
PINER Nathaniel 188
PINFIELD James 152
PINKIND John 229; Michael 229
PINKINE Vincent 225
PINKINS Michael 225
PINNICK Isaac 173
PINNINGTON Henry 180
PINTS James 246

PIPER Jacob 240; James 185, 192; Joseph 217, 246; Manuel 245; Spear 179; Spiar 187
PIPIN Uriah 154
PIPPIN Robert 154; William 154
PITHINGTON Richard 211
PITT Francis 171; Hillery 251
PITTEL Absolom 252
PLANE William 169
PLATFORD David 149
PLATT Ralph 171
PLECHER Jost. 244; Peter 244
PLIGH Rudolph 240
PLIMTON James 184
PLOUGHMAN Philip 155
PLOWDEN Edmond 210; Francis 211
PLUMB Henry 248
PLUMMER George 222, 229; Gewil 228; Hopkins Kinnimont 228; James 228; Jerremiah 194; John 197, 202, 228, 233(2); Levi 222; Phil: 228; Philamon 197; Solomon 228; Thomas 222, 245; Yate 169
PLUNKET David 145
PLYMTON James 192
POCK Felter 198; Volentine 206
POCOCK Daniel 174
POINTER Thomas 252
POJTWINE Thomas 212
POLC Philip 152
POLK Ben 219; Gilliss 217; James 216, 219; John 219; Joshua 219
POLLARD Willia: 200
POLLITT George 219; John 219; Jonathan 219; Joshua 219; Levin 220; Lill 219; Nehemiah 220; Samuel 219; Stephen 219; Thomas 219(3); William 219(3)
PONEY George 230
POOL John 174
POOLE James 149; John 156, 194; Joseph 193; Richard 149
POOR Henry 154
POORE Benjamin 242; Ersley 243; James 242
POPE Samuel 255; William 245
PORMER Jon 203
PORTER Alexander 257; Francis 151, 233; Henry 243; Hugh 227; Hughs 233; James 153, 180, 216; John 171, 225, 228, 233; Jonathan 226, 234; Joseph 179, 228(2), 233, 252;

INDEX TO APPENDIX B

Lawrence 157; McKimmey (McKimmy) 217, 258; Nathan 224, 227, 229, 234; Robert 157; Thomas 222, 228; William 216, 220, 222, 224, 227, 229, 231, 235
PORTTEOUS Robert 145
POSEY Benjamin 160; Francis 160, 164; George 164; John 164(2); Nehmp: 164; Price 164; Pryor 158; Rhody (Rodey) 158, 164(2); Richard 164; Thomas 164; Uzziah 165; Walter 158
POSLETHWAITE Robert 152
POSSELWAIT William 242
POSSELWAITE Samuel 242
POSTATER Andrew 248
POSTLEWAIT William 167
POSTLY Capt. 251; John 251
POSTON Barton 159; Benjamin 159; John 159; Solomon 159; William 159
POTEE Peter 173; Silvanus 144
POTER Henry 245
POTERFF Casper 245
POTTARFF Martin 247; Simon 247
POTTENGER John 244
POTTER Henry 220, 222; Nathaniel 154; Zebdial 156
POTTERF Andrew 247
POTTS Andrew 248; John 153(2); Philip 227; Thomas 209; William 225
POTTURFF Phillip 246
POWEL Howel 230, 233; Levi 220; Levin 220
POWELL Annanias 253; Belitha 251; Brittain 220; Edward 144; Elihu 251; Elijah 252, 256; Gabriel 256; George 153, 240; Howell 223, 226; James 153; Jesse 220, 254; John 153, 242(2), 251, 254, 255; Levi 254; Mordica 254; Sam 251; Thomas 239, 251, 254, 255; William 149, 220, 251(2), 254, 256; Zadock (Zadok) 251(2), 252
POWER Bostian 245; Edward 241; Elsly 167; James 167; John 174; Samuel 174; Walter 159
POWERS Peter 237
POWETT Michael 236
POWLESS Henry 237
PRACICE Alexander 219
PRALL Edward 170(2)
PRATER Samuel 166

PRATHER Aaron 198, 206; Aseriah (Azariah) 198, 205; Barrack 198; Baruch 205; Basil 205; Charles 167, 242; James 167, 242(2), 246; Rignal 244; Thomas 196, 246; Walter 198, 206; William 206; Zechariah 206
PRATT Jacob 152; John 211; Nathaniel 152, 229; Richard 179, 187; Thomas 176; Zephania 211
PREECHET Charles 201; Elias 201; William 201
PRESBURY George 170; George Gouldsmith 171
PRESTMAN George 145
PRESTON Barnet 173; Benjamin 173; Grafton 173; James 173; Martin 173(2)
PRICE Andrew 152, 224, 231; Archibald 215; Arthur 250, 259; Benjamin 180, 188; Bennet 215; Daniel 170; Edmond 219; Foster 225, 232; George 231, 254; Gilbert 232; Henry 181, 182; Holland 258; Hugh 225; James 159, 172, 215, 215, 224(2), 231, 235; John 173, 220, 223, 225, 230; Josep 215; Joseph 225, 232; Josiah 247; Moses 177, 186; Nathan 224, 231; Nicholas 156; Oneal 152; Richard 162, 202, 204; Samuel 167, 232; Thomas 180, 188, 223, 230; Timothy 157; Timothy Lane 232; Vincent 151, 152, 157, 225, 229; William 158, 163, 171, 223, 225, 232, 250
PRICHARD John 167, 223, 230; Samuel 223, 230; Walter 224, 231; William 223, 230
PRIDIX John 253
PRIEST .. 201; Henry 204; Richard 151; William 201
PRIESTLY James 223, 230; Perry 223, 229
PRIFHEN Abraham 246
PRINGLE John 207; Mark 146
PRIOR David 219
PRITCHARD Abadiah 170; Charles 172; Edward 156; Eleazer 170; Harmon 170; Henry 156; James 170; Jesse 173; John 156; Obadiah 172; Samuel 171, 172; Thomas 172; William 172
PRITCHET Charles 197; Elias 197

INDEX TO APPENDIX B

PRITCHETT William 197
PROBART Yelverton P. 258
PROCTER William 166
PROCTOR John 145
PRONCE Phil 223
PROSSER Henry 182, 190
PROUCE John 155; Thomas 154
PROUGHARVE Sylvinus 154
PROUGHAWE Sylvinus 154
PROUT Arther 147; Daniel 150
PRUCE Joseph 248
PRUITT Benjamin 258; Walter 258
PRUNE William 192
PRUSHELBAUGH Michael 246
PRY John 246
PRYOR John 178; William 178
PUGH Hugh 173
PULLET James 183
PULLIN William 245
PULLING William 238
PUNNEY Bartus 183, 190; Thomas 182, 189
PUNSELL John 243; Thomas 242
PURBUSH George 216
PURCELL John 167; Thomas 167
PURDAM John 193
PURDIE Richard 194
PURDY Henry 207
PURILL Basil 243
PURKINS John 220; Solomon 252; Thomas 252
PURNAL John 153; Richard 153; Thomas 233
PURNALL Thomas 151; William 151(2)
PURNELL Benjamin 253; E. 253; Elisha 253; Eupa(?) 251; James 251; John 258; John Selby 252; Levin 253; Mathew (Matthew) 252, 253; Peter 251; Robert 258; Samuel 206; Thomas 251, 253; Wat. 251; William 251(2), 252(2)
PURSE John 226, 234
PURY William 243
PUSEY Benjamin 219; David 255
PUSHPIN Anthony 186
PUSKIM James 146
PUTMAN John 237, 240; Peter 237
PUTTEE James 167
PUTTS Samuel 242
PUZEY George 255; Isaac 255
PYBUS James 150
PYLE Ralph 173

QUAID Ignatius 164
QUARDON John 197, 203
QUARY Daniel 201
QUEEN Francis 160; Henry 158, 165; J. 208; James 174
QUEER Henry 238
QUICK Andrew 244, 245; Benjamin 241; Dennis 243, 245; Jacob 243, 245; Thomas 182, 191, 241, 244
QUILLEN John 251; Sam 254; William 177, 186
QUILLIN Benjamin 251
QUINN John 172
QUINNELY William 157
QUINTON Capt. 256; Jacob 217; James 244, 253; Joseph 225; Phillip 256

R... Joseph 211
RACKLIFF Charles 253; John 253; Nathanial 253
RAGAN John 245
RAGE John 240
RAILEY John 214
RAILY Basil 211; Henry 212; John 211(2), 212
RAIMER Frederick 246
RAIN Caleb 254; James 177; William 254
RAKES Fisher 229; William 223, 230
RALEY Bennit 212; Henry 211; John Michael 211
RALPH John 150, 189
RAMSAY Andrew 170, 175
RAMSDIN Joseph 213
RAMSEY John 150; Nathaniel 157; William 147, 185; Winmar 147
RANDAL John 183; Robert 183
RANDALL Francis 257; Richard 143; Robert 190
RANDELL John 201
RANDLE Edward 147
RANDOL --- 183
RANDOLS John 199
RANE John 254
RANOLDS Hammond 253
RANSBARGER Stophel 237
RAPIER Richard 212; William 212
RASIN John 176; Joseph 177, 187; Josh. 187; Robert 186; Thomas 177, 185; William 187
RATCLIFF David 162; James 164
RATCLIFT Charles 144

INDEX TO APPENDIX B

RATHALL Thomas 156
RATHEL John 224, 231; Joseph 224, 231; William 224, 231
RATLEAF Francis 200
RATLIFF Burdit 165; Francis 205; Ignatious 165; John 222; Rhoday 165
RATTON Ambrose 166
RAUSELL John 183
RAWLINGS Daniel 149(2); John 149; Thomas 202
RAWLINS John 210; Joseph 187
RAY Benjamin 196, 201; George 201; James 207, 237; John 196, 201, 227, 235; Josias 207; Michael 238; Nicholas 197, 203; William 193, 197, 201, 241, 242
READ Dean 192; George 204; John 185; John Hatton 211; Philip 211
READAN John 164
READER Henry 214; John 223
READING John 177
READIS James 187
READY Cornelius 217
REALY Charles 187
REAPLOGLE Phillip 246
REARDON Thomas 182, 190
REASON George 185; John 185
REAVES James 159
REAYLOGLE Phillip 246
REDDEN Charles 220; John 258; Nehemiah 258
REDDIN John 221
REDDING Richaard 184; William 171, 178
REDDISH Robert 233
REDDOCK Robert 176
REDGRAVE Abram. 187; Isaac 179, 183, 186; James 177, 186; Joseph 177, 187; Richard 180, 188; Robert 185; Samson 180, 188; William 178, 186(2)
REDING William 186
REDISH John 218(2); Thomas 218
REDMAN Ben 214; Benjamin 196, 202; Charles 202; Francis 196, 202; Henry 159; James 171; Jonathan 215; Joseph 202; Joshua 214; Robert 196; William 196, 202, 211, 213
REDUE Isaac 184
REECE David 155; John 215

REED Amos 185; Ballard 219; Dean 185; Ezekiel 156; George 184, 199; James 144, 153, 219; John 176, 183, 194, 254; Joseph 182, 190, 242; Leonard 244, 245; Levin 250, 259; Littleton 250, 259; Peirce 256; Peregrine 188; Peter 248; Richard 243; Robert 185; Samuel 183, 190, 247; Thomas 153, 165, 178; William 172, 241
REEDER John 164, 214; Richard H. 164; Simon 193; Thomas Attoway 212; William 215
REEFNAUGH Phillip 240
REES Christian 145
REESE David 146; John 175
REETER Elias 236
REEVER Frederick 247
REEVES Hezekiah 162; James 162; John 155; Thomas 162; Thomas C. 160
REG...ON Thomas 199
REGISTER Earnautt 209; James 226, 232; John 224, 231; Samuel 224, 231
REID Joseph 167; Patrick 173; Robert 192
REIVES Samuel 161
RELPER Glyn 259
RELSEN Glyn 259
REMIN... John 200
RENCHER John 216, 217, 219; Thomas 219
RENEGAR George 196; Harman 196; Joseph 193
RENIGAR Harmon 201
RENNAGER George 201
RENNALLS William 196
RENNALS Charles 200; John 197; Nicholas 178
RENNER Phillip 246
RENOLD Francis 240
RENOLDS John 240
RENTCH John 246(2); Joseph 246; Peter 246
RENWICK Robert 241; William 241
REOUGH John 228
RESE Nicholas 240
RESHWICK Joseph 210; Thomas 210; Wilford 210
REU Isaac 245
REVEL David 218; John 220; Levin 220
REYLER Conrod 236

INDEX TO APPENDIX B

REYNALD Joseph 178
REYNOLD Robert 178
REYNOLDS Charles 207; Edward 148; Ignatius 211; John 151, 179, 187, 240; Joseph 186, 240, 241; Robert 144, 187; Thomas 205; William 201, 241
REYNOLS Abram 178; Jacob 179
RHENN John 164
RHENTZELL Andrew 197; Jacob 196
RHENTZILL Daniel 199
RHINTZELL Anthony 207
RHOADES Benjamin 173; Thomas 173
RHOADS Elisha 194, 217; Jacob 194; John 194
RHODES Abraham 148; Jeremiah 215; John 144; Nicholas 194
RIBBON Robert 209
RICE Benjamin 168; Jacob 239; John 232; Mathew 243; Walter 174; William 171, 227
RICH Henry 214; Peter 152; William 152
RICHARDS Abraham 167; Cigger 162; Godfrey 244, 245; Hammond 145; Henry 156; Isaac 244, 252; John 193, 203, 252; Joseph 255; Leonard 195, 203; Nathaniel 251; Richard 167; Thomas 161; William 161, 205, 252
RICHARDSON Adam 144; Alexander 259; Benjamin 178; Daniel 154, 170, 227, 233, 234; George 243, 245; Henry 229; Isaac 215; James 175, 215; John 156, 179, 250, 255; Joseph 144, 154, 157, 256; Joshua 226, 233; Mark 165; Matt. 179; Matthew 189, 256; Perry 153; Peter 154, 225, 227, 232; Philip 153; Robert 228, 233, 250; Samuel 171; Thomas 172, 199, 215, 226, 234(2), 259; Vincent 172(2); Whittington 253; William 153, 172, 179, 187, 215, 250(2), 253, 259
RICHIE Peter 213
RICHMAN Samuel 172
RICKETS Anthony 197, 203; Benjamin 174, 197, 203; Jacob 197; Joseph 203; March 198; Mark 203; Richard 197, 203; Robert 197, 203; Thomas 198; William 203
RICKETT Jacob 203

RICKETTS John 182; John T. 182; Joseph 198, 203
RICORDS Archelius 218
RIDDLE J. 145
RIDENOUR David 247; Henry 246, 247; Jacob 248; Lodwick 248; Martin 244, 247; Nicholas 247
RIDER Charles 216; Thomas 161
RIDGELY Thomas 215
RIDGEWAY Isaac 199, 204; John 153; Joshua 153; Masham 206; Mussum 198; Robert 197, 203, 205; William 195
RIDGLEY Absalom 144; Isaac 239
RIDGWAY Charles 232, 233; James 232; John 225, 226, 232(2); Joseph 232; William 233
RIDLEY Jestinian 164; Matthew 146
RIDNOUR George 244
RIDWAY James 226
RIECHART Casper 248; John 249; Peter 248
RIEDDERFORD James 182
RIELY Barnard 172
RIGBY James 148; John 149; Moses 227, 235
RIGDON Alexander 174; Baker 175; James 173; Stephen 174; Thomas 207; William 174
RIGENBOUGH Martin 247
RIGG Matthew 164; Thomas 162
RIGGEN Benton 219; Darby 255; Dukies 221; Eli 221; James 220; John 220, 221(2), 255; Jonathan 257; Joshua 258; Levin 220; Nehemiah 222; Robert 222; Stephen 221, 222; Teague 220; William 222, 257
RIGGIN Levin 252; Littleton 255
RIGGING Solomon 156
RIGGS Amon 195; Benjamin 194; Greenbury 193; John 194; Samuel 195, 196; Thomas Whiting 193
RIGHDOUT Thomas 242
RIGHT Henry 242; John 161; Samuel 161, 241
RIGHTER John 238
RIGNEY Terrance 193
RIGS Joseph 256
RILEY (blank) 245; Benjamin 179, 187, 218; Bennet 214; Charley 172; Elijah 202; Isaac 177; Jacob 177, 188; James 196, 202, 204; Jeremiah

328

INDEX TO APPENDIX B

(Jerremiah) 196, 202; Mark 196, 202; Nicholas 188; Nick. 180; Ninian 204; William 179, 183, 188; Zachariah 196, 202
RIMELY Phillip 236
RIMER Lambert 234
RIMINGTON John 205
RIMMER Lambert 227
RINE Casper 169
RINEHART George 240; Thomas 240
RINEY John 210, 213; Thomas 210
RINGER Conrod 237; John 237
RINGGOLD Elias 191; James 181(2), 189; John 181, 185, 192; Josias 182; Thomas 182. 190; William 184, 209
RINGNALL Robert 207
RINGOLD Elias 181
RINGROSE Aaron 228, 233; Moses 227, 235
RINKER John 167, 237
RINTZELL Andrew 207; Anthony 207; Daniel 207; Jacob 207; Valentine 207
RIORK Joseph 215
RIPLE Ludwick 244
RISENER Jacob 199, 207
RISLEY Daniel 237; Jeremiah 237
RISON Gerard 164
RISTEAU Abraham 145; Thomas 145
RISTEN Phillip 165
RISTON Henry 144
RITCHEY John 219
ROACH Capt 211; Charles 249, 257; James 212, 256; John 221; John White 221; Jonathan 216; Planner 216; Stephen 257; Thomas 224, 231; Will 222
ROADEN Richard (negro) 207
ROADS Basil 244; Ezekiel 244; Jeremiah 156; William 239; Zachariah 239
ROAN Matthew 251
ROANS William 251
ROATCH John 190
ROBBINS Levi 255; Thomas 350
ROBERSON George 198; John 258; Josiah 258; Levi 258; William 198
ROBERT Perry 235
ROBERTS Alexander 206; Allien 149; Barkley 219; Basil 193; Benjamin 227, 235; Edward 219, 222, 228;
Fisher 217; Henry 169; Hezekiah 193; Horatio 193; Hugh 152; John 174, 183, 190, 201, 212, 219, 222, 229, 230, 231; Levin 259; Richard 200, 205; Robert 185; Samuel 185; Thomas 176, 179, 201, 228(2); Underwood 219; William 174, 182, 189, 201, 218, 241
ROBERTSON Basil 197; Daniel 153; David 151; George 216; Isaac 217(2); James 202, 217(2), 220; Jeremiah 213; John 158, 164, 216, 217(2); Nathan 204; Nathaniel 199; Richard 158; Robert 204, 235; William 183, 185, 192, 217; Zechariah 204
ROBESON James 194; John 193
ROBEY Laurance 248; Owen 248; Patrick 194; Peter H. 159
ROBINETT Ezekiel 243; Joseph 243; Moses 243(2); Samuel 243
ROBINITT Elisha 243
ROBINS Josiah 256; Littleton 252
ROBINSON Abraham 170; Alexander 153; Andrew 168; Archibald 175; David 226, 227, 235; Edward 174; Elijah 165; Ezekiel 153; James 205, 229; Job 166; John 147, 148, 156, 166, 211, 234, 235, 245; Richard 164, 174, 176; Solomon 231; Standley 227; Thomas 172, 223, 225, 230, 234, 235(2); William 152(2), 157, 172, 176
ROBONITT Moses 243; Samuel 243
ROBSON Andrew 234; Henry 226, 234; James 223; John 226, 234; Robert 226; Thomas 234
ROBUCK William 144
ROBY Arthur John 249; Basil 15; Benjamin 159(3); Berry 198, 206; Ignatius 198; John 158, 194; John H. 163; Joseph 159; Leonard 159; Michael Hines 162; Richard 159, 163; Samuel 158, 159(2); Stephen 160; Thomas 159; William 159(3), 239; Zach. 159
ROCHESTER Daniel 178
ROCKENBAUGH Jacob 248
ROCKHOLD Charles 174; John 174
ROCKWELL Mainyard 242
ROD Frederick 237
RODE John 149

INDEX TO APPENDIX B

RODENPIELLER Philip 168
RODGERS John 171
RODNEY Richard 191
RODRICK Jacob 237; John 237
ROE Anthony 152; James 154; John 151, 157; Obediah 157; Peter 196; Richard 152, 219; Thomas 157; Walter 144; William 152
ROFF Daniel 146
ROGERS George 175, 212; John 152, 184, 212; Joseph 223, 230; Michael 223, 230; Nathaniel 184; Richard 212; Robert 158; William 152, 179, 187, 207
ROLAND George 158; Gordan (Gorden) 158 163; Henry 248; Thomas 163
ROLE Robert 228
ROLEY Arthur 250; Richard 258
ROLINSON James 184
ROLISON Abraham 192; Charles 188; John 226
ROLLE Robert 233
ROLLINGS Elijah 161
ROLLINGSON John 183
ROLLINS Aaron 198; John 195; Nathan 213; Thomas 195
ROLLINSON John 186
ROLLISON James 191
ROLLISTON Charles 179
ROLPH John 181
ROOF Rudoph 246
ROOT Jacob 248
ROPP Philip 168
RORER Christian 245; Frederick 237; John 237; Martin 238
ROSE George 203; Isaac 173; Joseph 174; William 174, 223, 229
ROSER Frederick 240; Jacob 237; John 238; Samuel 237
ROSS Abraham 150; Anthony 156; Daniel 150; Edward 156; James 156, 182, 190; John 214; Lewis 155; Reuben 174; Rubin 156; William 156, 174
ROUGH George 246; Peter 246
ROUGHTTEN Jobe 146
ROUND Samuel H. 251; William 251
ROUNDS John 220
ROURKE Philip 210
ROUSE Benjamin 152; Edward 152; Joseph 152, 221; Samuel 152; Solomon 152
ROUSTRIDGE William 207

ROVER Jacob 238
ROW William 217
ROWE Anthony 163; Edward 155; William 158, 163
ROWELL William 185
ROWENS Francis 155; Joseph 155; William 155
ROWLAND Abraham 248; Christian 248; David 248; Henry 249; Jacob 249; John 247
ROWLEN Aaron 205; Thomas 251
ROWLEY Arthur 259
ROWLINS John 187; Thomas 187
ROWNTREE Thomas 170
ROYAL Thomas 233
ROYALL James 233
ROZAN Nathan 198
ROZER Jacob 240
RUARK Daniel 256; Elget 255; Ezekiell 256; Hezekiah 255; James 257; John 255
RUBART John 241
RUBY Michael Hains 239
RUCKMAN John 173(2)
RUDDERFORD James 182
RUE Mathew 243
RUFE Mathias 246; Nicholas 246
RUFF Henry 173; James 150; John 171; Richard 169; Sabrett 147
RUGGLES William 245
RUGLESS William 207
RUMBLY Edgar 152; Henry 155; Jacob 152; James 155; John 155; Shadrack 155
RUMBOLD Thomas 155; William 155
RUMNEY Joseph 183, 192
RUMSEY Benjamin 171; John 169
RUPLE Jacob 243
RUSELL James 180
RUSH John 247
RUSSEL Caleb 167; Daniel 224; James 178, 232; Thomas 146; William 185
RUSSELL Caleb 243; Charles 210; George 241; Henry 193; Ignatius 211; Jacob 240; James 158, 188, 212; John 163; Pierce 216; Price 216; Priest 216; Thomas 145, 159, 217
RUSSLE William 192
RUSSUM Edward 156
RUTEN Thomas 246
RUTER Hezekiah 161; Joseph 161

INDEX TO APPENDIX B

RUTH Moses 173; Richard 241
RUTLEDGE Abram 175; Michael 174; Thomas 174
RUTTER Alexander 239; Edmond 239, 248; Francis 177, 186; John 238; Richard 170, 176; William 238
RUX Mark 222
RYALL James 227; John 152
RYAN Hugh 148; James 146; William 197, 205
RYDON George 173
RYE Mathias 248
RYLY Levin 253; Mark 144
RYON Ignatius 165; Valentine 251; William 154

SABATER William 167
SACKWELL George 218
SADLER Thomas 221
SAFFLE Charles 195, 203; James 195, 203; Joshua 203; William 195, 203
SAILER John 240; Peter 240
SAINTAMAN Jacob 241
SALADAY John 244
SALISBERRY James 157; John 156, 157; Nehemiah 156; Olivi 156
SALISBURY Joshua 221
SALLADAY Phillip 244
SALLADY Melchar 236
SALLOTT Nicholas 237
SALSBERRY William 153
SALWAY Willia.. 189(2)
SAMPSON Thomas 210
SANCTON John 222
SANDERS Abr. 180; Abraham 188; Bennedict 165; Charles 195; Edward 164; George 187; J.F. R 164; Jardin 163; John 180; Joseph 160; Samuel 220, 244; Thomas 164, 180, 188; William 158
SANDS Robert 233; Thomas 144, 228, 233; William 144
SANDSBERY Abraham 150
SANGSTON James 232; John 228
SANNER John 215
SANSBURY Benjamin 208; John 209; Thomas 197, 208; William 195
SANXTEN William 157
SANXTON Isaac 225; James 225; John Atton 225
SAP John 244
SAPINGTON Hartley 188; John 192

SAPORT George 241
SAPPIN Thomas 179
SAPPINGTON James 180, 188; John 180, 188
SAPPS Jacob 167
SARADEHAM Simon 242
SARER George 248; Jacob 248; Peter 248
SARGENT William 172(2)
SASSELL John 200
SASSEN John 219; William 219
SASSER Benjamin 219
SATCHEL James 224
SATCHELL John 250
SATERFIELD George 153; Hinson 153; Nathaniel 153; Solomon 153
SAULGIBER Jacob 240
SAUNDERS George 176, 179, 216; James 182; John 172; Joseph 173; William 174
SAVAGE Bartholomew 173; Ezekiel 219; Isaac 252; John 250, 259; Zorabable 255
SAVETY Frederick 244
SAYES Samuel 242
SAYVERT William 203
SCAGGS John 176, 187; Richard 185; William 168
SCALLION Jonathan 161; Peter 159
SCANLAN Edward 192
SCANTLIN John 175
SCARBOROUGH Enclidus 175(2); John 175; Thomas 175; William 175
SCARFE James 147
SCARFF Benjamin 172; Henry 174
SCHARFF Henry 174
SCHLEY Thomas 168
SCHLIGO William 197
SCHNEBELY Henry 238
SCHNELBY John 238
SCHNERTZEL George 167
SCHOFEILD William 199
SCHOFF Jacob 240
SCHOFIELD Joseph 199
SCHOOLFIELD Benjamin 220; George 220; Henry 220; John 220, 251, 252; Joseph 257; Robert 252; Stephen 220
SCICELL Joshua 203
SCISSILL Archiabld 194; James 200; Joshua 197; Samuel 200; Thomas 194; William 194

INDEX TO APPENDIX B

SCOFIELD Thomas 215
SCOOLFIELD William 207
SCORE James 184; Joseph 181, 192
SCOTT Andrew 175, 184, 189; Aquila 173(2); Benjamin 173; Charles 193, 213; Daniel 173; David 163, 236; Henry 207; James 157, 158, 161, 162, 173(2), 174, 236; John 167, 180, 182, 242, 254, 256; John D. 158, 164; Lambert 180, 188; Matthew 145; Robert 163; Thomas 160, 200, 204; William 148, 149, 210, 236, 240
SCOWDRICK William 155
SCRIVENER Richard 149
SCROGGIN John 217; Walter 161
SCROGIN Joseph 217; Obediah 159
SCYSTER Henry 238
SEABURN John 195
SEAGAR Thomas 210
SEAGER James 209; John 213
SEALE James 171; John 213
SEALY John 179
SEAMORE Henry 234; John 226, 234; Joseph 226, 234
SEAMOUR Henry 226
SEARES Henry 148
SEARLES Daniel 143
SEARS James 194, 195, 228; John 144; William 195, 228
SEAVNER Conrod 240
SEAYER William 206
SEDGE Simon 145
SEDGEWICK Benjamin 203; John 204; William 204
SEDWICK Benjamin 197; John 148; Thomas 149
SEERS John 252
SEFTON Edward 144
SEGO Benjamin 159
SELBY Benjamin 216; Daniel 250, 256, 259; Ezekiel 256; George 258; Henry 216; James 194, 250, 256, 257(2); Jesse 253; John 200, 205, 250, 256, 259; Joshua 255; Joshua Robert 208; Major 256; Parker 250, 253, 258; Philip 250, 259; Richard 195, 203; Samuel 196; Thomas 195(2), 203, 251; William 250, 256, 258; William Atkinson 256; Zachariah 195; Zadok 250, 252, 259
SELMAN Benjamin 207(2); William 143

SEMMES Edward 160; John 160; Joseph 164; Marmaduke 159; Thomas 159
SENER John 211
SENEY James 209
SERESHFIELD Joshua 167
SERGEANT William 168
SETH Charles 152; James 151, 223, 230
SEVERE Abraham 232; Peter 180; Vachel 231
SEVORAD William 152
SEWALL Nicholas 215; Nicholas H. 159; Thomas 185
SEWARD Charles 166; John 166; William 166
SEWEL Anthony 223; John 178, 235; Joseph 229, 235; Mark 227, 234; Nathan 225, 232; Richard 177; Samuel 226, 228; Thomas 225, 232; Thomas B. 234; Thomas Barnett 226; William 226
SEWELL Basil 233; Francis 159; Henry 215; James 148, 227; John 171, 226; Joseph 226; Lewis 159; Richard 185; Thomas 158; William 242(2)
SEWILL William 223
SEYBERT Henry 196; Nicholas 195
SHACKLER Frederick 247
SHACKLEY Martin 248; Michael 238
SHAD John 237
SHADDEN John 152
SHADNICK Thomas 214
SHADRICK John 214
SHAE John 237
SHAFFER Jacob 185, 192
SHAFTS James 203
SHAGHNASSEY Joseph 170
SHAHAN Edward 239
SHAKES George 183, 190
SHALLY Adam 237
SHAMWELL Jonathan 210; Joseph 211; William 211
SHANAHAN Elliott 234; John 234; Jonathan 225, 232
SHANEFIN Frederick 247; William 236
SHANK Christian 246(2); Jacob 238; Michael 246; Peter 237
SHANKS John 212; Joseph 213; Thomas 213
SHANTON Raymon 241
SHARER Isaac 248
SHARP Daniel 218; Samuel 223, 230

INDEX TO APPENDIX B

SHARPE George 218; Henry 152; James 154; John 154; William 154
SHASTO James 198
SHAT Melcher 249
SHAVER David 238; Jacob 238(2), 244; John 240; Paul 247; Peter 244, 247
SHAVES John 182
SHAW Basil 200; Benjamin 157, 159; David 238; Edward 184, 191; James 206; John 144, 162, 203; Joseph 162; Josias 207; Mathew (Matthew) 223, 230; Nathan 184; Thomas 198; William 162, 181, 182, 190, 208, 212, 229
SHAWHORN Daniel 187; Isaac 185; Thomas 185, 186
SHAWNESS Edward 244
SHAWS Samuel 168; Thomas 243
SHEAF Henry 144
SHEAFF Henry 145
SHEALD Benjamin 227
SHEAN John 149
SHEAPHEARD Thomas 242
SHEARBUT Benjamin Battee 143; Richard 143; Thomas 143
SHEARBUTT Samuel 195; Thomas 196
SHEARER Thomas 170
SHEARMAN John 155; Samuel 189
SHEARS John 189
SHEARWOOD John 202
SHEAVES Robert 226
SHECKELLS Richard 167
SHECKLES Richard 167
SHEEDY Roger 172
SHEETS Conroad 245
SHEGTEN Wendle 237
SHEHON David 199
SHEILD William 181
SHEIMER John 238
SHEKELL Abraham 197; John 198
SHEKELLS John 206
SHEKELS Abraham 203; Richard 203
SHEKLEWORTH Phill: 194
SHEKLY Michael 238
SHELL John 248
SHELLER John 145
SHELLERS William 240
SHELMAN John 168
SHELMERDINE Stephen 145
SHELTON William 219
SHEPARD John 179

SHEPHARD John 167, 243; Robert 242; Samuel 167, 242
SHEPHEARD James 243
SHEPHERD William 153
SHEPONE David 204
SHEPPARD Thomas 196
SHEPPERD Richard 176
SHERBOTT Thomas 201
SHEREDIN Thomas 173
SHERIDINE James 170
SHERLOCK James 204
SHERMANTINE Abintl. 215
SHERRARD Francis 180, 186
SHERWIN Abraham 224, 231; Thomas 225, 232
SHERWOOD Charles 227, 235; Daniel 228; Edward Man 228, 235; Francis 152; Hugh 227(2), 234; James 235; John 229; Jonathan 235; Joseph 155; Nicholas 225, 228, 232, 233; Nickson 153; Philimon 235; Robert 227; Samuel 228; Thomas 227, 229; William 227, 232
SHEW Peter 236
SHIELD John 189; William 189, 227
SHIELDS Benjamin 235; Caleb 145(2); Griffin 222, 228; Thomas 200, 205; William 225, 229
SHIFLER Nicholas 237(2)
SHILES Epaim 239
SHILLING Phillip 248
SHIPHAM George 220
SHIPLEY Richard 174
SHIPLY Henry 144
SHIRCLIFT Joseph 164
SHIRLEY George 215; Ignatius 214; Robert 212
SHNEBLEY Henry 246(2); John 246
SHNIDER John 246
SHOCK Christian 245
SHOCKEY Nicholas 238; Valentine 244
SHOCKLEY John 255
SHOCKLY Benjamin 256; Elijah 255; John 256; Jonathan 255, 257; Richard 255; Sampson 255; Saul 249, 254; Solomon 256; William 256
SHOEMAKER Gideon 143; Joshua 204
SHOEMAN Thomas 240
SHOLEY Luke 246
SHOMAKER Bolcher 236
SHOMATT John 165; John B. 165
SHONE Levin 219

INDEX TO APPENDIX B

SHOOP Adam 248
SHORE Alaner 256; Claner 256
SHORT Edward 170; George 200;
  Hezekiah 200; John 200; Samuel
  226, 232
SHOUTH Jacob 245
SHOWELL Bethewell 252; Eli 252;
  Elisha 254; John 252; Lemuel 254
SHRADER Conrad 168
SHRINEHART Frederick 238
SHRIVER Henry 236
SHRYER Frederick 169
SHRYOCK John 245; Leonard 245
SHUGANS James 243
SHULL Frederick 167
SHULTZ Martin 248
SHUMAN George 240; John 241
SHUP Jacob 247
SHURVIN William 184
SHY William 171
SIBBEY John 216, 238
SIBERT Peter 238
SIDES Christian 236; John 244
SIDNER Christopher 239; Frederick 240
SIEBERT Justice 144
SIGLER John 145
SILANCE John 212
SILBY William 239
SILENCES Thomas 213
SILL Benjamin 187; Joseph 184, 191
SILVER Benjamin 170; William 170, 175
SILVESTER David 222; John 226; Thomas
  222
SILWELL Jeremiah 242
SIMKINS George 238; John 238(2)
SIMM William 167
SIMMES Ignatius 163; James 161;
  Lambert 178
SIMMONDS John 181, 189; Noble 183;
  Robert 189
SIMMONS Archibald 187; David 188;
  Gilbert 178, 187; Isaac 146, 150;
  Jeremiah 178; Jonathan 244;
  Lambert 178, 187; Levy 244;
  Richard 244; Rigebel 178;. Samuel
  194; Thomas 149, 178; William 178,
  187
SIMMS Anthony 211; Elexious 198;
  Francis 160; Ignatious 239; Jo:
  198; Joseph 164; Joshua 164
SIMON James 187; John 245; Peter 236

SIMONS Ignatius 211; Jeremiah 180;
  Richard 188
SIMPERS Thomas 172
SIMPKINS Dickerson 167; Dickinson
  245; Silas 245; Syrus 167
SIMPSON Benjamin 144; Charles 160;
  Drummond 217; Elijah 155; Henry
  160, 164; Ignatius 160, 164; James
  160, 164(2), 185, 196; John 157,
  177(2); Joseph 165; Kendal
  (Kendall) 250, 259; Matthew 192;
  Sallamon 193; Thomas 150; William
  162
SIMS Elixus 206; Joseph 221; Smith
  219
SINCLAIRE Alexander 234; John 234;
  Jonathan 233; William 234
SINCLARE Alexander 226
SINCLEAR Duncan 195
SINGCLAIRE Peregrine 233
SINGCLARE John 226
SINGLETON John 171, 227, 235
SINN John 242
SINNET Samuel 182
SINNETT Robert 164
SINNOTT Samuel 189
SISK David 155; James 155
SISSILL Ralph 214
SIVER Michael 175
SKAGGS John 178
SKEGGS Richard 176
SKELES William 240
SKERVIN Francis 181; William 192
SKINNER Andrew 235; Capt 151; Clement
  150; Daniel 152; Edward 158, 164;
  Frederick 150, 152; George 162;
  James 148, 164(2); John 143, 152,
  224, 227, 231, 234; Joseph 228;
  Leonard 150, 203; Mordica 234;
  Phill 227; Richard 147, 227, 235;
  Robert 148, 150; Samuel 148;
  Thomas 152, 158, 164, 229; William
  164, 230, 242; Zebulon 234
SKIRVIN Francis 189
SLACK Jacob 170; William 225
SLADE Thomas 174
SLATER Ellis 147; James 163; John
  163; Nehemiah 163; Richard 163
SLATTER Battw. 254
SLAUGHTER Jacob 167; James 154; John
  154(2); Nathan 154
SLICER James 204

INDEX TO APPENDIX B

SLICK Jacob 169
SLIPPER William 177
SLOCAM Robert 250; Thomas 250; William 250
SLOCOMB Riley 257
SLOCUMB Thomas 259; William 259
SLOUSER Peter 240
SLUBEY William 189
SLUBY William 182
SLY John 147; Patience 147; Robert 160; Samuel 147
SMALL James 224; Robert 170; Theofilus 224; Theophilus 231
SMALLWOOD Bayne 158, 163; Hezekiah 158, 163; James 165; James Boyden 165; John 163; Keabard 158; Luke 165; Lyde Stone 165; Major 168; Pryor 163; Samuel 165; Thomas 163(2); William 196
SMART Richard 212; William B. 214
SMASHEY James 253
SMEN James 187
SMISAR Mathias 246
SMITH Adam 245; Alexander Lawson 170; Anthony 144; Archabald (Archibald) 193, 217,223, 230, 249, 254; Basil 160, 174, 196, 202, 210, 212; Benjamin 170, 249; Capt 151; Charles 233; Charles S. 161; Clem. 164; Daniel 149, 150, 176, 198, 203; David 170, 241, 248; Edward 181, 189, 210, 219, 228, 235; Edward Barton 212; Elias 210; Elijah 226, 249, 256; Elisha 234; Ezekiel 156; Francis 145; Gavin H. 147; George 149, 153, 177, 179, 185, 186, 245, 248, 249, 254, 256; Gerrard 201; Gilbert Hamilton 143(2); Henry 165, 228, 235, 236, 240(2); Ichabod 170; Isaac 156, 177; Isaiah 249; Jacob 248; James 150, 161, 177, 181, 182, 184, 186, 188, 210, 215, 216, 217, 239, 243, 258; James Edward 205; Jehu 254; Jeremiah 150; Jesse 150, 252, 254; Job 153; John 144(2), 146, 150(2), 153, 160, 161, 165, 169, 170, 175(2), 176, 177, 179, 182, 184, 186(2), 187, 188, 199, 200, 202, 209, 211(2), 215(3), 216, 217, 218, 229, 245, 249, 252(2), 253(2),; John H. 148; Joseph 149, 150(2), 164, 171, 174, 207, 246; Joshua 155, 220; Josias 171; Lambert 178, 179, 186, 187; Levi 252; Levin 156(2), 249(2), 254; Mathew (Matthew) 160, 177, 186; Michael 152, 168; Milby 252; Mordicay 150; Nat. 179; Nathan 149, 152, 193; Nathaniel 175; Nicholas 160, 180, 186, 197, 246; Oliver 177; Peter 240, 248; Phillip 241; Purnell 253; Ralph 155, 170; Ralph 170; Richard 148, 156, 184, 193, 253; Robert 170, 239, 242; Samuel 144, 170(2), 182, 184, 196, 220, 249, 254, 258; Simon 184; Solomon 254; Southey 155; Stephen 184; Sutton 184; Thomas 149, 155, 156, 158, 162, 173, 176, 177, 184, 186, 188, 196, 197, 202, 203, 216, 228, 240, 252; Thorogood 146; Vernon 215; Walter 148, 163, 199, 207; William 146, 150, 152, 155, 169, 171, 173, 174, 175, 177(4), 179, 181, 183, 184, 186(3) 187, 202, 210, 215, 219, 230, 244, 254 258; Zachariah 174
SMITHE Robert 144
SMITHSON Nathaniel 173; William 173; William E. 159
SMOCK Brittingham 251; Holland 257; John 253; McKemmy 253; Powell 251; Stephen 251
SMOOT Cuthbert 215; Isaac 160; John 162(2), 215; Josias 165; Kendly 160; Thomas 162, 215; William 163, 215; William B. 160
SMOOTE William B. 159
SMULLEN Edmond 220; Samjel 255; William 255, 257
SMULLIN William 220
SMULLING John 219
SMYLEY Samuel 250, 258
SMYTH George 192; Hynson 185, 192; James 189(2), 192; John 190, 192; Michael 192; Richard 181, 192; Samuel 191; Simon 191; Stephen 192; Thomas 190, 192; William 189, 191
SNATSELL George 168
SNEAD John 258
SNEED Henry 251
SNEIDER Valentine 145

INDEX TO APPENDIX B

SNELL George 198, 206
SNELLING Acquila 219; Henry 229; William 225
SNIDER Adam 237; Casper 246; Jacob 246; John 238, 242; Martin 238; Peter 242, 243
SNIDIKER Christan 167
SNIDWAR Christian 242
SNIVELEY Michael 243
SNOAK Mathias 247
SNODGRASS William 175
SNOW William 156
SNYDER Henry 236, 238; Henry John 246; Jacob 247; John 240, 247
SOAPER Basil 194; James 193
SOLERS James 149
SOLWAY William 181
SOMERVELL Alexander 149; James 145; Thomas 148
SONE William 163
SOOK Henry 240
SOPER Zadock 199
SORAT Alphonsus 161
SOTHORAN Leven 209; Richard 209; Samuel 209
SOTHORON John Johnson 209; Richard 209
SOTSSER Henry 237
SOUTH Benjamin 239
SOUTHERLAND Ignatius 162; Robert 163
SOUTHERN Alexander 205
SOWEL Anthony 230
SOYL John 199
SPALDING Benedict 211; Bennit 211; Clarke 211; Edward 212; Elezius 211; Enoch 213; George 213; Henry 211; Michael 212; Philip 211, 215; Ralph 214; Richard 160, 213; Thomas 211; William 163
SPANGLE Henry 244
SPARKS Richard 155; William 175
SPARLING Andrew 246
SPARROW Benjamin (Benn.) 200, 201; Jonathan 199, 201; Thomas 144; William 196, 201
SPARROWE Thomas 196
SPATES Robert 194
SPEACE Daniel 239
SPEAK Hezekiah 204; Ignatius 200; Martin 200; Richard 200

SPEAKE George 158; Henry 165; Lawson 158, 163; Richard 158, 163; Thomas 162
SPEAKS Hezekiah 199; Ignatius 205; Martin 206; Nicholas 195
SPEAR James 178; John 145, 146
SPEARMAN John 178, 179, 187; William 178
SPECE Zadok 203
SPECER Michael 238
SPECKNALL Bazil 147; John 147; Robert 148
SPECKNELL Leonard 147
SPEDDING Levin 232; Robert 232
SPEER William 256
SPENCE George 151; Patrick 156; Pearce 154
SPENCER Elisha 232; Francis 149; Hugh 183, 190; Isaac 177, 186; James 187; John 220; Jonathan 183, 234; Marmaduke 227, 233; Pere 183; Perry 235; Richard 183(2), 234; William 145
SPENDER Daniel 183
SPINK William 210
SPIRE Jeremiah 239
SPIRES William 257; Zachariah 248; Zapheniah 244
SPONG Leonard 242
SPRIGG Frederick 194; Joseph 245; Osborn 236; Thomas 194, 245
SPROUTS William 247
SPRY Christopher 228, 233; Francis 186, 234; John 226, 235
SPURRINGER George 240
SPURRY John 153
SRAKAN William 225
SRONG William 189
ST. CLAIR Cambel 177; Vernon 210; William 176, 177
STACK John 238; Thomas 156; William 225
STACY Levin 222, 228
STAFFORD Abram 156; James 156; Jervis 156; John 156(2)
STAINS Moses 226
STAINTON Benson 152
STAIR Casper 238; Frederick 238(2)
STAKE Martin 240
STALINGS Henry 149; William 149
STALLET John 191

INDEX TO APPENDIX B

STALLING Absolem 147; Isak 146; Joseph 193
STALLINGS Benjamin 147, 148, 150; Griffith 200; Isaac 150; James 149; John 149; Lancelot 143; Newman 147; Phenus 150; Richard 147, 148; William 148
STALLINS Samuel 174
STALLIONS Samuel 161; Thomas 206
STAMBURGH Phillip 244
STAMP Thomas 147; William 203
STAMPS William 197
STANDFIELD Richard 227, 235
STANDIFORD Samuel 172
STANDLERS Michael 193
STANDLEY James 224, 231
STANFORD David 218; Jesse 255; Jonathan 255; Joshua 218; Obediah 216; Stephen 255; Thomas 216; William 216
STANFORTH James 150; John 147, 148; Richard 150
STANLEY Christopher 168; Ebenezer 176, 187; Isaac 176, 187; John 176, 187; Joseph 176
STANLY Eben 178; Isaac 178; John 178; Joseph 178
STANT James 222, 229; John 151; Peter 156
STANTON Benjamin 245; John 155; Michael 245
STAPLE James 185
STAPLEFORD Andrew 157; Thomas 182, 189
STAPLETON Josiah 175; Thomas 175
STAR Henry 193
STARK Joseph 156
START John 223; Richard 235
STASMAN Adam 245
STATES James 186
STATSMAN Daniel 247; David 247; Henry 248
STATTET John 191
STAUFER Mathias 237
STAVELY James 176; John 176; Joseph 176, 185
STEAL William 204
STEALL Arther 195; James 194; William 199
STEEDHAM Thomas 154
STEEL James 173, 188; Joseph 171
STEELE George 162

STEEN James 183, 190; William 190
STEER Michael 238
STEIN Jacob 242
STELL James 180
STENNET Benjamin 150
STENNETT John 147
STENSON William 209
STEPHENS Benjamin 196; Edward 193; Hugh 165; John 193; Lewis 195; Richard 196; William 148, 173, 179
STEPHENSON Joseph 158; Thomas 175
STERETT William 144
STERLING Aaron 215, 217, 221(2); Ephraim 221; Henry 221(2); John 216, 221, 257; Joseph 216; Josiah 221; Lill 221; Southey 257; Traves 221
STERN James 216
STERRETT Jonathan 175
STERRONTON George 242
STERTZMAN Adam 238
STEUART John 146; William Veal 199
STEVENS Archibald 217; Azell 156; Benjamin 218; Betel 155; Daniel 259; Edward 225, 232; Epp. 218; George 218, 224, 229, 231; James 213(2); John 154, 235, 251; Joseph 213; Joshua 251; Levi 218; Lewis 143; Oliver 201; Richard 147, 202; Stephen 217; Thomas 180, 188; William 156, 184, 191, 216, 220, 230(2), 231
STEVENSON Benjamin 258; George 258; Hugh 257; James 253(2), 257, 258; John 158, 170, 180; Jonas 171; Jonathan 258; Joseph 258; Samuel 255; William 251
STEVINS Benjamin 151
STEWARD Edward 150; George 163; Henry 158, 163; Ignatius 165; Isaac 163; James 162, 171; Walter 165; William 162(2)
STEWART Alexander 188; Andrew 225; Asa 180, 185; Athell 152; Caleb 144; Charles 196, 231; Edward 184, 188; Elisha 231; Hugh 172; James 149, 173, 225, 229, 241; John 159, 172, 177, 181, 186, 189; Major 181; Michal 157; Mordecai 197; Robert 144, 172, 176; Thomas 224, 231; William 152, 177, 185, 197,

INDEX TO APPENDIX B

201, 216, 217, 219(2); William V. 207
STIFFEE George 238
STIFFER Andrew 238; George 238
STILES Joseph 174; Stephen 213; William 204
STILLWELL Stephen 248
STIMAL Josiah 180
STINSON James 209; John 184
STIRGIS John 257; William 256
STIRGISS Joshua 250, 257
STIRKLAND William 147
STIRLING James 146
STOCK John 248
STOCKEY Jacob 247
STOCKSDALE Thomas 172
STOCKWELL Michael 243; William 240, 242
STODDARD Henelin Truman 158
STODDERT William 158
STOFSER George 237
STOKER Benjamin 232; Elijah 234; Ephraim 183; John 226, 234; Joshua 225, 232
STOKES Ephraim 190; Limuel 156; Peter 190; Robert 170; William 156
STONE Enoch 211; Haton 211; Ignatius 211; John 165, 211; Joseph 210, 211; Marshal 150; Matthew 159; Samuel 164; Thomas 146, 147, 164; William 145, 146, 148, 163, 211, 244; William B. 164; William H. 164
STONEBRAKER Gerrett 248; Michael 239; Valentine 240
STONECYFER John 240
STONEKING Henry 246
STONER Abraham 201; Jacob 197
STONES William 215
STONESIFER Daniel 237
STONESTREET Basil 163; Butler 199
STOONSTREET Butler 160; Leonard 160
STOOPS David 186; Nicholas 179, 186
STOREY Duke 156; John 153
STORK Richard 179
STORKE John 145
STORY Henry 197
STOSSER George 237
STOTHERD James 242
STOUT Richard 153
STOVER Christopher 244; Jacob 238; Michael 248

STRADLEY Griffith 153; James 154; Salathiel 154
STRAHAN John 183
STRANGE Silvester 214
STRATFORD Joshua 243
STRAWBRIDGE William 220
STRAWHAN Isaac 177; Samuel 177; Thomas 152, 177
STREET Mansfield 166; Richard 225, 232; Thomas 166; William 232
STRICKLAN John 148
STRICKLAND John 147; Joseph 147
STRICKLIN Joseph 150
STRIDER William 241
STRONG Edward 180; James 186, 190, 246; William 181
STROWD William 173
STUART George 236, 249; Thomas 240, 248
STUBBS Nicholas 155
STUCKEY Peter 236
STUDEBAKER Jacob 246
STUDHAM Thomas 154
STUN James 183, 190
STUP Joseph 247
STURGES Outton 258; Zadok 252; Abraham 258; Daniel 259; John 182, 189; John Outten 259; Joshua 258, 259; Levin 259; Outten (Outton) 250, 258; Outton John 250; Richard 250, 258; Thomas 257; William 250, 259(2)
STURGESS Levin 250; Stephen 250
STUTTS Henry 246
STYER George 244
SUDELEY William 197
SUDLER Thomas 182, 192
SUGART John 242
SUIT Benjamin 209; Dent 209; James 213; John Dent 210; Nathaniel 207; Samuel 209; Thomas 209; Walt. 159; William 160
SULF Jacob 241
SULGAR George 168
SULIVANE Jinkins 156
SULIVANT Dennis 149; Thomas 146, 150; William 146
SULLEMS Henry 238
SULLIVAN Cornelius 196; David 189; James 155, 176, 185; Jeremiah 179; John 156, 177, 178, 182, 184, 186;

INDEX TO APPENDIX B

Owen 156; Peregrine 177; Philip 150
SULLIVANE Daniel 155, 156; Darby 155; Fletcher 155; Florince 155; John 155; William 155
SULLIVANET William 150
SUMERHILL Charles 212; James 210; Philip 211; William 210
SUMERVILL John 148
SUMMERS Ben: 193; Caleb 193, 201; Clement 204; David 216; Elias 221; George 193, 216, 222; Hezekiah 204; Jacob 221; James 155, 157, 221; John 145, 193(2), 206, 221; Jonathan 216; Lazarus 216; Paul 199, 204; Richard 216; Robert 184, 191; Samuel 216; Stephen 221; Thomas 193(3), 216, 221, 230; William 152; William 157, 193(2), 220
SUNDERLAND Benjamin 146; John 146, 150; Josiah 150; Rezin 146; Thomas 146(2), 150
SUNDERLANE Josias 146; Thomas 146
SUNDERLING Thomas 146
SURMAN Charles 216; George 218; Nicholas 216
SURRELL Archibald 192
SUSEE James 178
SUTER George 206; James 201
SUTERS Charles 232
SUTES Alexander 197
SUTHERLAND Daniel 209
SUTOR John 197
SUTTON Benjamin 152; Edward 188, 189; James 152; John 152 181, 189, 199, 201, 214; Ozwain 171; Reuben 172; Robert 199, 207; Thomas 171
SWAIN Gabriel 172; Joshua 207; Nathaniel 172
SWAITS Francis 211; Robert 211
SWALES William 243
SWAN Ignatius 214; James 227, 235; John 144, 227, 235; Solomon 153; Thomas 153(2); Zach. 159
SWANK David 167, 245; Jacob 248; John 248
SWANN Bazel 158; Edward 212; Elkanah 210; Henry 210; James 161; Jesse 211; Jonathan 159; Samuel 161; Thomas 159(2); Zaphh. 161; Zed. 159; Zephaniah 193

SWANSTON Nicholas 216
SWART Samuel 170
SWATZEL Christian 248
SWATZELL John 249
SWEANY Matthew 173
SWEARENGAN Bennona 241
SWEARENGEN Joseph 167(2); Samuel 198; Thomas 198(2)
SWEARINGIN Van 194
SWEARINGON Obednigo 205; Samuel 205
SWEAT Aaron 229; Edward 229; William 228
SWEER Vachal 224
SWEREINGEN Samuel 249
SWETT Edward 222
SWIFT David 157; Gideon 154; James 153(2); John 153, 184, 191; Richard 153; Samuel 153; Thomas 153; Vincent 153
SWIGGATE Benjamin 157; Harmon 156; Henry 156; James 156; Johnson 156; William 156
SWIGGRT Robert 217
SWINGLE George 248; Leonard 248; Peter 248
S.INGLEY George 249; Nicholas 248
SWINGLY Michael 249
SWITCHFIELD Joshua 245
SWITZER Jacob 169
SWOOP Peter 238
SWYBERT George 196
SYLVESTER Bradbury 226; Cloudsberry 153; Herrington 151, 153; Isaac 229; James 153; Nixon 152; Purnall 153; William 151
SYVERT Jacob 247; John Jacob 247

TAILOR Robert 164
TALBERT James 239; Thomas 195; William 204
TALBOTT Benjamin 147; Daniel 147; Edward 150; George 195; James 173; John 147; Joseph 147; Notley 193; Philip 148; Richard 148; Thomas 147, 194; William 199
TALL Arther 193; Stephen 206
TALLBOY Robert 157; William 157
TALLMISE James 165
TALOR Robert 158
TANEY Charles 212; Raphael 211
TANGLER George 238
TANNEHILL William 200

INDEX TO APPENDIX B

TANNER Henry 148; John 237
TANT Bearnhard 247
TARLON Joshua 214
TARLTON Bennet 215; James 214; John 214; Stephen 212
TARR Azariah 259; Eli 250(2), 258, 259; Elijah 250, 259; Elisha 250; Israel 250, 259; James 256; John 209, 210, 250(2), 259(2); Jonathan 234; Joshua 259; Michael (Mickail) 250(4), 259(2); Nehemiah 250, 259; Phillip 244; Richard 226, 234; Samuel 250(2), 258, 259(2); William 250, 257
TARRING John 229; William 209
TARTER Nathaniel 242
TATE James 209; John 167; Timothy 174
TATOM John 186
TAWCH Robert 242
TAWNEY Joseph 149; Micael 150; Thomas 149
TAWNEYHILL John 147; Leonard 149; Malcham 206; William Harriss 206
TAWNYHILL James 150
TAWS John 221
TAYLOR William 183
TAYLER Alexander 251; Charles 251; George 251, 253; Sam 251; Stephen 252
TAYLO William 216
TAYLOR Abraham 173, 184, 188, 191, 219; Absolom 154; Amasa 172; Archibald 214; Asa 172; Austin 215; Barkley 217; Bryan 148; Coalbourn 216; Cornelious (Cornelius) 225, 232; David 251; Delah 150; Dennis 222; Edward 161; Elias 257; Elisha 250; Ezekiel 217; George 214; Height 192; Henry 179, 191, 210, 215; Hyth 184; Ignatious (Ignatius) 161, 210; Isaac 217, 251; Israel 172; Jacob 217, 250; James 144, 161(2), 172, 186, 193, 210, 214, 215; Jehu 258; John 147, 161(2), 172, 175, 176, 182, 187, 190, 191, 195, 214(2), 217, 220, 251 256; John Dixon 177; Joseph 215, 252; Joshua 217, 219, 250, 259; Levin 221; Littleton 257; Obed 250, 259; Philip 184; Richard 215, 250; Robert 172, 173, 183, 198, 215;

Samuel 184, 191 219, 220; Solomon 218; Staffd. 161; Stephen 172, 218; Thomas 172, 179, 187, 207, 249, 254, 259; Walter 171; William 146, 158, 188, 191 215(2), 217(2), 224, 228, 231, 255, 257; Zadock 218
TAYMAN Joseph 150; William 150
TEAGE Jacob 252
TEAGUE Samuel 250
TEBREW Richard 217
TEETER Isaac 247; Jacob 247
TELEFORTH John 188(2)
TEMPLEMAN Henry 156
TENANT James 188
TENGLEN George 246
TENNANT Samuel 233; William 183, 191
TENNISON Jesse 213; John 159, 210; Samuel 212; William 212
TENNISSON Benjamin 160
TERICH Leonard 160
TERUSH Abraham 236
THAIRMAN Thomas 245(2)
THAMAN Phillip 240
THARP James 183; John 184, 190, 192
THARPE John 151
THAWING William 199
THAWLEY Edward 151; John 151
THOMAS Allen 161; Andrew 241; Benjamin 175; Calib 161; Christian 237; Christopher 247; Clement 164; Daniel 172; David 173; Edward 166; Ellis 155, 163; George 220; Heathman 147; Henry 173, 192; Isaac 161; Jacob 237; James 166, 173, 195, 224, 227, 231, 235; Jerre 144; John 155, 161(2), 166(2), 173, 179, 187(2), 196, 198, 206, 215, 230(2), 237; Joseph Exel 182, 189; Leven 215; Martin 194, 218; Michael 237; Nathan 168; Nathan G. 167; Nathaniel 168; Nicholas 228; Notley 194; P. 169; Peter 237; Phil: 162; Philip 161, 167; Richard 154, 185(2), 192, 198, 206; Robert 155, 199, 204, 214; Samuel 182, 189(2), 198, 230; Sterling 185; Thomas 152, 160, 161, 174, 182; Tylor 215; William 161(2), 166(2), 195(2), 214, 215, 223 230; William A. 215; William Dawson 223, 230; Zacharia 210

INDEX TO APPENDIX B

THOMPSON Aaron 212; Andrew 174; Arthur 210(2); Athanasius 210; Babtis 194; Barnett 187; Barny 179; Basil 210(2), 213; Benjamnin 215; David 171; Edward 170; George 163, 202, 231; Ignatious 242; James 183, 196, 202, 210(2), 212; John 158, 162, 172, 196, 201(2), 207, 210, 227, 236; John B. 210(2), 211; John Basil 211; Joseph 207, 212, 213, 246; Joseph Green 163; Joshua 165; Leonard 163; Mark 210; Nathan 197; Oswel 213; Raphael 210(2); Richard 165, 199, 201, 212; Samuel 172; Thomas 162(2), 173, 210, 211; William 197, 201, 212, 248; Zachariah 197
THOMSON Charles 163; James 255; John 214; Williamson 164
THORIMAN William 175
THORN Absalom 161; Barton 159; Per. 159
THORNTON Brooks 222, 228; Jessea 213; John Vickers 222; Nathn. 223; Richard 225; Thomas 185; Vincent 212
THRELKIELD John 199
THRIFT John 177; Pere 176, 185
THURSTON Thomas 173
TIALL James 196
TIBBLES Henry 223, 229; John 223, 229
TICE Henry 247
TIGNOL Sothy 256
TILDEN Charles 183, 185, 189, 190; Marmadkue 183, 189; William Blay 177
TILGHMAN Aaron 220; Jabez 220; Joseph 220; Lloyd 228; Matthew 151; Philemon 185; Richard 223; Samuel 255; William 192, 221
TILHART Christopher 248
TILLARD Froget (Fragget) 180, 184; George 177; Samuel 184
TILLER Edward 180, 188; Jacob 248; John 182, 190; Jonas 186; Samuel 180
TILLEY John 207; Thomas 208
TILSON John 153
TIMMON Thomas 215
TIMMONS Benjamin 252; Elijah 252; Joseph 252; Lill. 219; Michael 219; Nehemiah 254; Sam 252; Stephen 252
TIMMS John 164, 183, 190; William 164
TIMONS Elisha 254; William 254
TIMS Charles 164
TINDAL Nehemiah 220
TINDALL John 250
TINGLE James 251
TINNY John 170
TINSLEY James 242
TIPPIT Jonathan 213; Notley 210
TIPTON Silvester 167
TISHE Samuel 183
TISHER Daniel 247; Jacob 247; John 248
TISUE Jacob 201, 237
TITLE John 185
TITSWORD Isaac 241
TITTEL Thomas 251
TITTER George 186
TITTLE James 244; John 191; Lazarus 185, 192
TIZZARD William 225, 229
TOADVINE Arnold 257; Henry 257; John 257; Stephen 218; William 256
TOBE Michael 237
TOBIN James 224, 231
TODD Benjamin 145; John 166; Michael (Michal) 156, 166; Nathan 156
TOICE George 237
TOLBERT Basil 195
TOLLENGER George 170
TOLLEY Edward Carvel 169; Zep. 172
TOLSON John 179
TOM Adam 238; George 244; Mathias 238; Michael 237
TOMERLSON Samuel 222
TOMKINS John 210
TOMLINSON Grove 193; Hugh 193; Humphrey B. 193; James 241, 243; Jessy 243; William 193, 232
TOMPSON Alexander 144; Richard 144
TON John Baptist 213
TONEY Isaac 187
TONNER Abraham 246
TOOL James 203
TOOLE James 197
TOON Bennit 210
TOOP Ephraim Chick 227, 234
TOOTWILER Henry 240
TORRY Benjamin 186

INDEX TO APPENDIX B

TOULSON Isaac 172; Nathan 185; Nathaniel 176; Samuel 191
TOWERS James 155; Solomon 155; Thomas 155
TOWNLY Joseph 160, 164
TOWNSAND John 255
TOWNSELY John 170
TOWNSEND Absolom 255; Alexander 250; Beletha 251; Charles 256; Danford 256; Dickson 255; Elias 256; Elijah 258; Ephraim 255; George 233; Israel 252; James 231, 254, 255, 256, 257; Jeremiah 252; John 250, 257, 259; Joshua 257; Lazarous 250; Levin 256; Solomon 255, 256; Thomas 227(2), 233, 252; Thomas Ogdin 231; William 251, 252, 255(3); Zadock 256
TOWNSHEND James 154; Thomas 153
TOWNSLEY John 170
TOWNSTIND Benjamin 152
TOWSEND Joshua 255; Rives 252
TRACEY Bazil 145; Charles 196, 201; Usher 172; William 203
TRACY Philip 200, 206; William 197, 201
TRADER Henry 218; James 217; Richard 218; Staten 258
TRAIL Archibald 195, 202; Basil 195, 203; David 195, 202; James 202(2); Orsban 202; William 196
TRAIN James 217
TRAMILL Phillip 243
TRAMMEL Nicholas 167; Philip 167
TRANOR John 159
TRANTLE Samuel 238
TRAPNELL James 145
TRASEY Timothy 241
TRAVERS John 259
TRAVIS Robert 172
TRAY Alexander 196
TREASSES Charles 189
TREDWELL Daniel 172
TREHEARN Cyrus 222; James 222; Obednigo 222; Samuel 222
TRENCHER Aaron 181, 189
TRESLEN Peter 237
TREVERE John 200
TREW Thomas 183, 184; William 181, 182, 189
TRIDLE Jacob 239

TRIPPE Edward 230; James 228; William 223, 229
TRISLER Jacob 199, 207
TROCKAM John 209
TROTH George 224, 231; Henry 181, 189, 225, 232; Samuel 189; William 229
TROTT Henry 196, 202; James 196; Samuel 148, 149; Thomas 149
TROTTER James 175; Lowden 245; Richard 175, 244
TROUP Adam 247; Alexander 227
TROUT Edmond 200
TROXELL Abraham 247; George 247
TROY Owen 223, 230
TRUE John Bladen 209
TRUETT William Powell 252
TRUITT --- 250; Benjamin 252; Eben. 254; Eli 252; G. 254; George 254, 256(2); Henry 257; Jacob 256; Jedediah 255; Nehemiah 251; Outton 253; Patty 252; Rounds 252; Samuel 254; Thomas 256; William 251, 252(2)
TRULOCK Henry 191; Jacob 184, 191; Philip 183, 191; Samuel 191
TRUMAN Edward 149; John 214
TRUMPOUR Leonard 246
TRUNDLE John 200, 206; Josiah 198, 206; Thomas 200
TRUPP Christopher 245
TRUSBY Richard 186
TRUTHS Richard 186
TUBB William 160
TUBBS David 252; John 251; Joseph 251
TUBMAN George 163; Richard 165; Samuel 159
TUCK William 144
TUCKER Alexander 199, 204; Benjamin 149; David 200; Edward 196; George 183, 192, 199; Gregory Page 195; Henry 200; Hezekiah 199; Isaac 143; Jacob 205; James 155; John 147, 148, 149(2), 176(2), 178, 196(2), 198; Jonathan 193; Joseph 199, 200, 206; N... 199; Nathaniel 209; Seaborn 143, 174; Stephen 195; Tempest 238; Thomas 148, 149(2), 200(2), 205; Walter 199, 204; William 143, 198, 199, 204(2), 223, 230
TUDERO Ruben 236

INDEX TO APPENDIX B

TUDEWILER Jacob 238
TUDEY Peter 180
TUELL Henry 208
TUFFEY Robert 226
TULL Benjamin 258; George 216, 221; Handy 257; Jacob 257; James 258; John 220, 221, 252; Jonathan 220; Levin 155, 221, 222; Thomas 221, 222; William 155, 221
TULLEY Benjamin 217; James 180; John 217; Joseph 219; Richard 217
TULLINGHAM Benajah 182
TULLY James 217
TUPLE Isaac 195
TURBOTT Samuel 231
TURBURT Peter 219
TUREY Lewis 187
TURK James 175
TURLEY Benjamin 202
TURNBULL George 146; John 208
TURNER Abraham 143; Alexander 150; Daniel 183, 191; Ebenezer 186; Edward 224, 226, 231, 232; George 256; Henry 155(2), 256; Jackson 255; James 235, 237; John 147, 148, 154, 158, 177, 183, 186, 191, 197, 212, 229; John Beall 159; Joseph 178, 187, 210, 226; Joshua 212; Levin 249, 254; Randolph 160; Richard 147, 148; Samuel 160; Thomas 143, 155, 223, 224, 231, 232; Valiant 229; William 143, 147, 148, 160, 178, 186, 187(2), 209, 250, 255; Zacharia 150; Zadock 256
TURNEY William 163
TURPIN Handy 218; John 221(2); Joshua 221; Neho. 220; William 217, 221
TUSH Samuel 172, 190
TUSSY Jacob 241
TUTER Francis 244; Jacob 244; John 244; Peter 244
TUTLE William 228
TUTTLE Baptist 204; William 235
TWIFORD Bartholomew 222; Brown 156
TWIGG Francis 243; John 243; Robert 243; William 255
TWILLEY George 217; Joseph 217; Stephen 217
TWILLY William 256
TWYFORD Charles 155
TYDINGS Cele 144

TYERS Charles 164
TYLER John 209; Richard 199; Robert 147; Spencer 221; Thomas 257
TYLOR David 221; Elijah 155; William 163
TYRE John 159; Joseph 159; Raphael 159; William 159
TYSOR Robert Clarke 212; William 209

UMBERSON Jacob 179
UMBLE George 205
UNDERHILL Michael 184
UNDERLIN Joseph 177, 186; Michael 192
UPP Nicholas 245
UPPERHOUR Harman 168
URVIN James 239
USELTON Francis 178
USILTON James 177
USLINGTON James 185
USSELTON Francis 186; Robert 186; William 186
USTLETON John 184; William 178
VALENTINE Frederick 245
VALGANOTE Joseph 242
VALIENT John 228, 235; Joseph 234; Richard 226, 234; William 226, 234
VALLIANT Daniel 155; John 155; Nicholas 144; Thomas 155
VANBIBBER Abraham 146
VANCE David 174; George 249; John 174; Peter 192; Samuel 174; William 256
VANDEGRIFT George 170
VANDERFORD Thomas 209
VANDIKE John 226, 235
VANGOVANTS Newcomb 179
VANHORN Ezekiel 170
VANSANT Benjamin 179; Christopher 179, 187; Ephraim 178; Garret (Garrett) 179, 187; George 177, 186, 187; Jacob 179, 187; James 180, 188; John 179, 188; John Clk 180; Joshua 177, 180; Lambert 186; William 180, 188
VANSICKLE Henry 171
VANSWERINGEN Joseph 148
VANTWORTH William 171
VASHON Simon 145
VASSET Henry 191
VAUGHN Charles 219
VAULX William 152
VAULZ Selathiel 156

INDEX TO APPENDIX B

VAYNE John 162; William 162
VEACH George 171
VEARD Elijah 193
VEARS John 193; William 193
VEASEY John 250; Sothey 250
VEATCH Ninian 195(2); Richard 195; Silas 195; Sollomon 195
VEAZY Charles 258; John 259
VEITCH Hezekiah 193; John 195; Thomas 193
VENABLES Benjamin 217; Ezekiel 161; Joseph 217; Lawrance 161; Samuel 161, 217; Theodore 161; Thomas 217; William 216
VENNABLES John 196, 202
VERDIN John 159; Richard 159
VERMILLION Giles 158; Hanson 204
VERNALL Henry 205
VESSELLS Eliger 215; Ephraim 213
VESSELS James 212; James C. 220
VESTRY Hugh 255
VICKERS Abner 184; Benjamin 192; Charles 227, 235; James 185, 189; Richard 225; Thomas 155; William 185, 192, 232
VICTOR James 256; John 256; Thomas 255
VIGEROUS Armwell 252
VILEY George 205
VINALL Richard 144
VINCEMOR Gambriel 179
VINCENT Benjamin 196, 201; Isaac 218; John 162; William 162(2)
VINEM Ray 144
VINEMAN Gabriel 176
VINING John 223, 235
VINSON David 152; Elisha 256; Jethrew 156; John 194; Rhods 162; William 196
VINTON Samuel 227, 233; Solomon 227, 233
VIRDEN James 258
VIRMIER John 213
VIRMILLION Edward 163; Francis 163; Giles 163; Guy 163; John 163
VOWLES Cyrus 210; John 210
VOWLS John 212

W... J... 213
W... John 200
W... William 199
WA... Robert 211

WADDELL Jesse 155; Rowland 156
WADDEY William 220
WADDLE Alexander 154; James 154; John 154; Robert 154
WADE Henry 239; John 239; Zachariah 158, 163, 164
WAGELEY John 248
WAGGENER Christopher 167
WAGGONER Christian 168
WAGONER Francis 240; John 236, 248(2); Martin 236; Peter 241, 245
WAILES James 234; Robert 232
WAILS Charles 217; Joseph 216; William 218
WAINRIGHT Cannon 255; George 253; James 230
WAINWRIGHT James 223; Richard 211
WAITE William 253
WAITS Robert 225
WAKEFIELD William 158
WAKELIN John 213; Thomas 213; William 213
WALE John 145
WALES Elijah 256; John 181, 189; Thomas 227, 234; William 233
WALKER Archibald 160; Christopher 248; Daniel 152, 223, 230; Francis 224, 231; George 203; Jacob 244; James 149, 170, 172, 213, 225, 232; John 144, 155, 156(2), 171, 172, 232, 253; Joseph 213; Moses 154; Nathan 223, 225, 230; Nicholas 241; Richard 195, 232; Robert 193; Roger 211; Stephen 213; Thomas 171, 195; William 155(2), 193, 200, 211, 225(2), 232(3), 240
WALLACE Alexander 204; David 219; Harbert A. 199; James 161, 199, 219; John 164, 188; Natt. 199; Richard 161, 219; Samuel 247; William 195, 199, 204; Zepheniah 199
WALLEN Quinton 229
WALLER Eben. 218; George 182, 189; Joseph 249; Thomas 217, 218; Will 216
WALLEY Charles 254
WALLING Delashmett 239
WALLINGS James 238
WALLIS David 176, 178; Francis 179, 188; George 182; Henry 180, 188;

INDEX TO APPENDIX B

Hugh 180, 188; John 177, 180(2), 188(3); Samuel 180, 182, 188; William 185, 192
WALLS Charles 259; George 161; John 178, 187, 217; William 176, 178, 187
WALLY Seth 254; Thomas 254
WALMORE Michael 239
WALSTON Boar 220; Boaz 220, 249, 256; Charles 221; Henry 219; Jesse 219; Joseph 219; Levin 221; Obediah 221; Peter 220; Thomas 221
WALTER Clement 194; Daniel 216; David 194; George 194; Jacob 241; James 216; John 194, 207, 237, 254; Levin 216; Levy 194; Robert 216; William 210
WALTERS Alexander 153; Isaac 180
WALTOM William 259
WALTON Capt. 258; Fisher 258
WAMPOLE Peter 243
WARBLETON Thomas 219
WARD Benjamin 143, 150, 193, 201; Cornelius (Cornelious) 215, 221, 241; David Linsy 163; Ed; 171, 194; Ezekiel 221; George 165; Henry 152, 158; Isaac 222; Jacob 216; James 149, 150, 171, 174, 216, 221(2), 255; Jesse 219, 220; John 158, 163, 198, 216, 221; Joseph 216, 219, 221; Joshua 174; Josiah 256; Levi 219, 222; Lloyd 197, 203; Matthew 219; Richard 150, 175; Samuel 158, 216; Solomon 219; Stephen 221(2), 222, 252; Thomas 163, 221; West 143; Will 220; William 158, 163, 187, 221
WARDEN Elijah 158
WARDER James 162; Jesse 163; John 162; Joseph 162; Philip 163
WARDIN Elijah 163
WARE Benjamin 146; Edward S. 159; Francis 159; Frederick 245; Jacob 159; James 183, 191; John 173
WAREHAM Valentine 189;
WAREMAN Francis 242
WARFIELD Alexander 168; James 144; Joseph 144(2); Philomen 144; Thomas 144
WARING Thomas 167
WARKMAN Jacob 245
WARMAN Henry 243; Stephen 194

WARNER Gary 223, 232; George 145; Hugh 149; Jacob 238; John 169, 235; Phillip 180; Robert 222; Thomas 195; William 227; Woolman 223
WARNOCK Philip 175
WARRAN Annanias 251; Isaac 251
WARREN Clark 152; Edward 162, 214; John 252; Sampson 229; Thomas 189; William 162, 214, 229
WARRICK Arthur 220; John 174; Josiah 220; William 174, 220
WARRIN James 197, 203
WARRING George 194; John 193, 225, 229; Solomon 156; Thomas 193; William 224
WARRINGTON Alexander 254; Nathaniel 154
WART Peter 246
WARTERS George 166
WARTHIN Ignatius 194
WARTON William 230
WARUM Valentine 181
WARWICK Andrew 173
WASEMAN James 160
WASH Daniel 150
WASHBOURN Ruben 218
WASHERBAUGH John 247
WATERBAGER George Frederick 242
WATERS ...immer 206; Basil 202; George 220; Hezekiah 145; Isaac 195, 202; James 187, 221; Jesse 252; John 217; John C. 160; Joseph 194, 213, 239, 251; Josephus 198, 207; Nacey (Nacy) 204; Nacy 197; Patrick 257; Richard 203; Thomas 196, 198, 207, 218; Tubman 221; Weaver 198, 207; William 160, 196, 258
WATHEN Barton 160; Bennett 160(2); Edward 213; Ignatious 159; James 212; James Waren 213; John 158, 213; John Baptist 160; John Baker 160; Joseph 213; Leonard 212; Martain 160; Nicholas 159; Richard 210; William 159
WATKINS Aaron 144; Capt. 144; Gassy 144; Gasy Chambers 144; John 144, 174, 185(2), 192; Joseph 156; Leonard 194
WATRON Benona 226
WATS William 149

INDEX TO APPENDIX B

WATSON Banoni 232; David 150; Edward 215; Elkahan 194; George 148; Henry 147, 150; James 246; Jesse 255; John 150, 184, 200, 209, 251, 258; Levin 250, 259; Major 258; Nathan 250; Parker 250; Peter 180, 188; Samuel 194; William 146, 183, 190
WATTERS Alexander 153; James 251
WATTS Alexander 214; Charles 180, 188; George 183, 190; Henry 214, 226; Hugh 234; John 187, 196, 202; Kenelon B. 212; Perry 232; Richard 171; Thomas 214, 228; William 187, 226, 234, 253; Willoughby 212
WATTSON Azariah 210; Henry 146; James 210; John 210
WAUGHOP James 214
WAYATT Caleb 254
WAYMAN Edmd. 194; Edward 234; Leonard 193; Thomas 193
WAYMON Edmond 226
WEATHERBURN John 145
WEATHERED Richard 190
WEATHERLY Abnor 155; Charles 217; Constant 217; Isaac 155; Isaiah 155; James 217; Jesse 155, 217; Job 155; John 155, 217; William 155
WEATHERTON Richard 159
WEAVER Thomas 182; Isaac 187; John 180, 186; William 223, 230
WEB John 225
WEBB Benjamin 180, 188; David 179; Elias 252; Elisha 252; Holland 178; Israel 258; James 176, 226; Jeptha 252; John 175, 178, 187, 223, 244, 252; Park 225, 232; Peter 223, 244; Robert 179, 187; Scarborough 252; Solomon 257; Thomas 190; William 175, 219, 222, 244, 252; Zepheniah 252
WEBBER John 151; Robert 194; Solomon 151
WEBSTER Richard 155; Henry 154; Jabez 219; James 169; John 155, 219; John Lee 170; Mesheck 219; Solomon 155; Thomas 156; William 154, 219
WEDDING John 162; Philip 159; Thomas 162(2)
WEDGE Jonathan 149
WEDGER John 253

WEEDEN Henry 234
WEEDON Richard 203
WEEMS David 148(2); James 147, 148(2); John 143, 147; Richard 143(2); William 146, 148
WEGG John 242
WEIGK Joseph 217
WELBY Jo. 195
WELCH Edward 164; George 164; James 180, 235; John 170; Lewis 179; Ossias 247; Roger 215; Thomas 223, 230
WELDER John 169
WELKER Andrew 244; Pall 244
WELLBARGER Mathias 246
WELLDEN David 187
WELLMAN Bennet 193; Jeremiah 202; John 193
WELLS Benjamin 143; Daniel 144; David 187; James 184, 191; Jeremiah 244; John 144, 255; Martin 147(2); Richard 143; Robert 243; Samuel 198; Thomas 147
WELSH Jacob 143; John 173; Thomas 180; William 171, 242
WELTMAN Bennett 196
WENNER Daniel 146
WEST Basil 197, 201; Benjamin 196, 197, 201, 234; Edward 197; Erasmus 195; Henry 224, 231; James 217; John 175; Jonathan 173; Joseph 194 195 197; Michael 171; Nathaniel 173; Nicholas 201; Osburn 197; Richard 196, 201; Robert 170; Samuel 196; Thomas 161, 171, 195, 201; William 173, 197, 201, 227
WESTERBARGER John 248
WESTLEY Humphrey 207
WESTLY Humphry 200
WETHERED John 182
WETHERHEAD John 186
WETHERTON Benjamin 159
WETZELL Frederick 207
WETZILL Frederick 199
WHALAND Edward 183, 190; John 183, 190; Matthew 206; Owen 184, 191; Thomas 183, 185, 190
WHALEN Mark 206
WHALING Daniel 194
WHALLEN Thomas 218

INDEX TO APPENDIX B

WHALY John 179; Nathaniel 255; William 216
WHARTON Revil 249; Robert 182; Thomas 182
WHEALER Charles 182; Jonathan 216
WHEAT Basil 198; Hezekiah 194; John 195, 202; Joseph 202; Martin 190; Zechariah 202
WHEATLEY Francis 211; John 214; Michael 222; William 213, 222
WHEATLY Sampson 215; John 156, 160, 161, 226; Nathan 152; Richard 161; Sampson 222; Thomas 161; William 215
WHEDON Oliver 144
WHEELER Benedict 164; Benjamin 164; Bennett 170; Charles 166, 190; Clement 164; Clems. 164; Elisha 252; Francis 210; George 149; Henry 244; Ignatius 164(2), 175; Isaac 174; John 252; Joseph 158, 164, 170; Josias 170, 173; Justinian 210; Leonard 164; Luke 158, 165; Richard 164; Samuel 208; Thomas 153, 165, 173; William 164; Zadock 220
WHEELOR Edward 205; William 205
WHELER Edward 200; Leonard 195; William 200
WHELOR Hanson 195
WHERRETT Thomas 214
WHERRITT Abner 214; John 214
WHETSTONE Christopher 247; Daniel 248; David 238
WHIGHT Isle 162; William 209
WHILEY George 150; Henry 150; James 147
WHITACRE Hezekiah 171; Isaac 173; John 171
WHITAKER Alexander 195; James 173
WHITBEY Joseph 153; Nathan 153
WHITBY Thomas 232; William 226, 232
WHITE Abednego 208; Alexander 199, 207; Barclay 255; Basil 200; Burgess 199; Charles 173; Edward 152; Eli 188; Francis 219; Henry 253; Isaac 218; James 152, 155, 200, 215, 225, 232; John 152, 179, 180, 187, 188, 197, 205, 215, 219, 240, 245, 253(2); Jonathan 161, 170; Joseph 153, 154, 200, 204; Joshua 256; Major 256; Philip 252;
Richard 163, 170; Samuel 157, 198, 223, 230, 257; Samuel Beall 206; Stephen 172, 174, 220, 253, 255; Thomas 157, 215, 219, 225, 256; Trewman 195; Walter 193; William 148, 161, 251, 255; William Bell 220; Zechariah 206
WHITEFORD Hugh 175; John 174; William 175
WHITEHOUSE Samuel 183
WHITELEY Nehemiah 166; William 151, 157
WHITELY Thomas 225
WHITEMAN Conrad 179
WHITEMIRE George 238; William 241
WHITFORD David 176
WHITHIM William 144
WHITLEY Benjamin 153
WHITLY William 154
WHITTINGHAM Heber 219
WHITTINGTON Abram. 179, 187; Benjamin 157; Francis 143(2), 150; James 149, 179, 222; John 149, 178, 187; Joseph 157; Samuel 148; William 143, 150, 222(2)
WHITTOCKS William 223, 229
WIATT Henry 180; Samuel 180; William 180
WICKERSHAM Thomas 223, 230
WICKES John 192; Joseph 182, 190(2), 191; Samuel 182, 190; Simon (Simeon) 182, 190
WICKLE George 240
WIETT Alexander 195; James 195; Thomas 156
WIGGINS John 242; Samuel 174; Thomas 242; Uriah 242; William 242
WIKERS Joseph 184
WILAN Peter 246
WILCOCK James 179
WILCOXEN Anthony 205; George 205; Jesse 204; John 205; Lewis 204
WILD John 173
WILDER James 162; John B. 162
WILDMAN Cornelius 211; John 211
WILES James 226; Thomas 240
WILEY John Woolf Elias 150
WILKERSON Alexander 165; Walter 165; William 211
WILKINS Bartus 189; Isaac 218; John 219, 242; Major 256; Samuel 190; Thomas 189

INDEX TO APPENDIX B

WILKINSON David 148; John 146, 148, 233; Joseph 146, 150; Richard 149; William 195
WILKISON Joseph 187
WILLABY William 228
WILLBERGER Mathias 247
WILLCOXEN Anthony 198; Henry 193; Jesse 199; John 198(2); Josias 200
WILLEN Clement 216; Edward 148; John 216; Levin 216; Thomas 148, 216
WILLETT Ambrose 258; Benjamin 201; Henry 259; Ninian 204; William 204
WILLEY Edward 166; William 166(2)
WILLIAM Richard 198
WILLIAMS Amos 195, 203; Andrew 195, 230; Aron 150; Arthur 216; B. 215; Baruch 157; Basil 244(2); Benjamin 195, 203, 221; Charles 195, 202; Charles N. 251; Christopher 177, 186; Clement 198, 207; Daniel 171, 200, 206; David 176, 180, 251; Dunbar 148; Edward 226, 232; Edward Owen 198; Eleven 244; Eli 188; Elie 248; Elisha 193, 199, 204; Esau 251; Francis 148, 150, 173; Gabriel 211; George 228; Hazel 193; Hudson 165; Hugh 211; Isaac 251, 253; Ismeal 251; Jacob 154, 196; James 153, 213, 214, 232, 238(2), 241, 256; Jesse (Jessee) 156, 251; Jestinian 160; John 144, 147, 149, 151, 159, 170, 171, 180, 183, 188, 191, 195(2), 198, 199, 200, 202, 206, 221(2), 252; Joseph 186, 238(2); Lawrance 244; Leonard 193, 206; Levin 221; Litt 221; Mathew 238; Moses 143; Osborn 208; Peter 243, 245; Planner 218; Richard 206, 217; Samuel 159, 200, 218 226; Shaderick 247; Simpson 214; Talbott 147; Tarott 244; Thomas 156, 208, 221; Vincent 153; Walter 208; William 144, 154, 155, 160, 170, 171, 187, 194, 195, 201, 202, 216; William N. 198; William P. 198; Zacariah 160; Zadock 244
WILLIAMSON Alexander 147; Bazil 147; Capt 151; Charles 147; George 172, 188; Henry 147; James 147, 184, 191; John 180, 188; Joseph 178; Robert 175

WILLIBY William 233
WILLIN Elijah 216; George 216; James 216; Levin 216; Samuel 216
WILLING John 196
WILLIS Abel 255; Benjamin 249, 255; David 253; Edward 161; Elijah 156; Ezekiel 156; Henry 155; Jabez 256; James 221; Jervis 154, 156; Joel 184, 191; John 155, 184, 191, 253; Joshua 155, 183, 190; Richard 155, 184; Robert 155; Samuel 228, 235; Shadrack 155; Thomas 155, 156; William 155, 254, 255, 256
WILLISON Cornelious 243; Edward 243; Jeremiah 243; John 243(2); Richard 243(2)
WILLIT Henry 250
WILLITT George 165; Griffith 193; Ninian 199; William 199
WILLMAN Jerre 196
WILLMER James 188
WILLMOR John Lambert 188
WILLMORE Robert 205
WILLMOT Robert 200; Thomas 200
WILLMOTT Thomas 205
WILLOBY Edward 156; Richard 152; Samuel 152; Solomon 152
WILLOUGBY John 154
WILLOUGHBY Job 166 William 154
WILLS John B. 163; Thomas 150
WILLSON Alexander 195; Christopher 152; Daniel 225, 232; David 192; Elisha 152; George 155, 189, 193, 225, 232; Gilbreath 245; James 152, 156. 188. 193, 194, 200, 225(2), 228; John 149, 156, 158, 194(2), 195, 200(2), 225, 232; Jonathan 155; Josiah 195; Mathew 193; Nathan 149; Richard 191; Robert 152; Solomon 152; Southy 225; Stephen 200; Thomas 200, 225, 232; William 152, 199, 200, 239; Zadock 197, 200
WILMAN Rhode 213
WILMER Blackiston 184; James 179, 182; John Lambert 180; William 180, 184
WILMORE John 181, 205
WILMOTT Richard 169; Samuel 173
WILON George 158
WILSON Abraham 161; Alexander 203; Andrew 170; Archibald 175;

INDEX TO APPENDIX B

Benjamin 146(2), 150, 171; Capt 151; Clement 208; David 208; Ephraim 217, 218; George 179, 181, 187(3), 201, 205, 218, 222; Helarey 150; Henry 143, 205, 206; Hiram 188; Ignatius 208; James 147, 179, 180, 182(2), 187(2), 190, 208, 209, 217, 220, 253; John 147, 158, 172(2), 179, 180(3), 187, 188(3), 205, 217, 220, 221(2), 222; John Maddox 206; Jonathan 206; Joseph 174, 175; Josias Sollers 208; Lewis 241; Matthew 203; Noah 207; Richard 167, 179, 182; Robert 172, 216; Samuel 180, 188; Stephen 205; Thomas 146, 150, 180, 203, 206; William 145, 179, 183, 187, 205, 221, 222, 257; William Alex 165; Wilson 206; Zadok 206
WILTEN Charles 216
WILTSHIRE Jonathan 144
WIMSATT Baptist 212; Henry 214; Ignatius 214; James 211; John 211; Joseph 212; Richard 211; Robert 211; Stephen 210; William 210
WINBEIGER George 207
WINBUGAR George 199
WINDERS James 248; John 238; Thomas 238
WINDHAM George 194; William 204
WINDLESS Daniel 239
WINDSOR Basil 198; Isaac 196; James 216; John 196, 219; John S. 198; Thomas 197; William 219
WINDSTANDLEY William 233
WINEMAN Gabriel 176
WINFIELD Jona 147; Richard 147
WINGATE Henry 210, 219(2); Phil 219; Philip 166
WINKENCOME John 245
WINLING Peter 244
WINN Sampson 244
WINNEL William 147
WINRIGHT Cannon 216; Evans 216; Solomon 216
WINSON John 230
WINSOR Basil 204; Ignatius 165; Isaac 201; John 202; Joseph 165; Thomas 203
WINSTANDLY Henry 227, 235; William 227

WINTER John 179; Walter 158; William 165
WINTERBOTTOM Daniel 234; John 226, 234; Robert 226, 234; Thomas 226, 234
WINTERS Elisha 183; George 238; James 245; John 258; Jonathan 227, 233
WIREY Jacob 240
WIRTMAN John 247
WIRY Adam 245
WISE Adam 212(2); Anthony 152; Caleb 212; Elijah 213; Elisha 211; George 245; James 179; John 240; Matthew 212, 215; Myre 213; Peter 241; Robert 215; Teter 242; Thomas 212; Valentine 237; William 171, 187, 212, 257
WISEMAN Richard 215
WISNER Jacob 236, 245
WISOGER Henry 247
WITHERINGTON James 210; John 210
WITMAN Andrew 207
WITRICK Jacob 239
WITTEN Thomas 168
WITZELL Peter 236, 239
WLS Robert 151
WOBREY Stephen 247
WOODBURN Jonathan 209
WOENS Joseph 213
WOLFHART Goodfree 244
WOLFKILL Jacob 238
WOLGAMAOT David 247
WOLGAMOT Samuel 241
WOLTZ Peter 240
WOLTZLAGER Valentine 248
WONNELL James 255
WOOD Aristarcus 193; Basil 168; Benjamin 148, 159, 161; Capt 151; Edward 147, 148, 167; Gerard 160; Henry 165; Hopewell 143; Ignatious 165; James 147, 170, 209; Jeremiah 149; Jesse 149; John 143, 147(2), 172, 201, 209, 210; Jonathan 148, 213; Joseph 148, 153; Joshua 170; Leonard 148, 150, 160, 209; Lunard 147; Misael 210; Morgan 143; Nathan 210; Peter 161; Robert Slye 211; Sabret 147; Samuel 149; Stephen 194; Thomas 200; William 143, 148(2), 150, 220; Zephaniah 193

INDEX TO APPENDIX B

WOODAL Allen 179; Edward 177; James 177(2) 184; John 176, 177; Thomas 177, 182; William 177(2)
WOODALL Edward 186; James 186(2); John 177, 185 186(2); Thomas 186, 189; William 186
WOODARD Benedict 204; Bennet 199; Francis 200, 202; Hezekiah 200; Joseph 201; Thomas 190, 200; Zechariah 206; Thomas 182
WOODBURN Daniel 209; John 209, 245
WOODEN Richard 172
WOODFIELD Thomas 150
WOODHOUSE David 244
WOODLAN Bryan 166
WOODLAND Abram. 187; James 179, 187; John 176, 179, 180, 188
WOODLEY Gavily 254
WOODS Edward 245; Samuel 229
WOODWARD Hezekiah 206; James 158; Jesse 164; John 173, 175; Joseph 212; Richard 164; Samuel 165; Thomas 171; William 212
WOODWORD Henry 163
WOODYARD William 195
WOOLASTON William 185
WOOLCUT Woolman 227
WOOLEN John 172; Major 172
WOOLF Jacob 238, 240; John 148, 238; Leonard 239
WOOLFHILL Conrod 237
WOOLFORD David 155; Godfrey 245; John 219
WOOLHEADER Adam 244
WOOLSLAYER Jacob 245
WOOLVERTOON Charles 166
WOOTEN Ignatius 214; John 214
WOOTERS Benjamin 151; Elijah 157; Lemuel 151; Solomon 157
WOOTON Thomas 212
WOOTTEN Richard 197
WOOTTERS Aaron 157; James 151; John 151, 157; Reuben 157; Richard 151; Thomas 151
WOOTTON Richard 208; T. S. 197
WORKMAN Andrew 243, 245; Isaac 243, 245; Jacob 243; John 243, 245; Joseph 243; Stephen 243, 245; William 245
WORKS Hugh 232
WORLEY Francis 166, 237; Thomas 247; William 247

WORMAN Francis 243
WORNELL William 202
WORRELL Benjamin 191; Edward 190; Simon 182; William 182, 190
WORTH Jonathan 176; William 180, 188
WORTHINGTON Charles 175; Henry 145; John 145; Nathaniel 144; Nicholas 144; Samuel 175
WORTON Robert 190; Thomas 190
WOULF (blank) 238
WRAINE William 172
WRENCH James 223
WRIDERWOOD Charles 215
WRIGHT Alexander 203; Archabald 179, 187; Edward 156, 192; Gowon 219; Handy 217; Hynson 177; Isaac 217; Isaiah 249, 254; Isle 162; Jacob 155; James 156(2), 203; John 175, 185, 187, 219; John L. 165; Joseph 202, 217; Joshua 156, 217; Lamuel 156; Levin 156(2), 217; Robert 165, 200; Samuel 165; Solomon 217; Stephen 217; Thomas 166, 196, 202, 207, 208; William 1 2 197(2)
WRIGHTSON James 228, 233; Joshua 228, 233
WROTH Benjamin 182, 189; James 183(2), 190(2); Kinsman 190; Kinvin 182, 183(2), 190
WUKLE George 240
WYANT Jost. 240
WYATT Edward 222; Henry 188; Samuel 188; William 188
WYKELL Henry 240
WYORY Jacob 238
WYVELL Edward 194

YARDLEY Nathaniel 172
YARDSLEY John 191; William 185
YATES Bennit 212; Henry 210; Ignatius 195; John 194, 249; Jonathan 162; Joseph 147, 207; Major T. 146; Martin 211; Thomas 195, 230; William 242
YEAMAN Thomas 174
YEARLY John 184; William 191
YEATES Donaldson 176, 181, 185; William 184
YEATS Thomas 176
YEWELL Solomon 152
YOE John 149; William 149, 174

INDEX TO APPENDIX B

YOST Lodowick 195, 202; Tobias 199, 207
YOSTY Peter 237
YOUNG Abraham 199; Balser 247; Benjamin H. 147; Daniel 149, 257; David 147; Ephraim 257; Ezekiel 257; George 148, 169, 245, 246; Hugh 145; Jacob 246; John 156, 169, 182, 190, 193, 200, 238, 257; John Abell 212; Ludwick 246; Michael 248; Milby 257; Peter 199, 204; Robert 143, 159, 180, 212; Samuel 245; William 169, 170, 194, 210, 258
YOUNGER Benjamin 149; David 147; George 147; John 147(3); Joseph 147; Margarett 147; Tiller 237, 240; William 147
YOUST Henry 248

ZACHARIAS Jacob 248
ZEALISON James 167
ZELIFSO John 187

Other books by F. Edward Wright:

Abstracts of Bucks County, Pennsylvania Wills, 1685-1785
Abstracts of Cumberland County, Pennsylvania Wills, 1750-1785
Abstracts of Cumberland County, Pennsylvania Wills, 1785-1825
Abstracts of Philadelphia County Wills, 1726-1747
Abstracts of Philadelphia County Wills, 1748-1763
Abstracts of Philadelphia County Wills, 1763-1784
Abstracts of Philadelphia County Wills, 1777-1790
Abstracts of Philadelphia County Wills, 1790-1802
Abstracts of Philadelphia County Wills, 1802-1809
Abstracts of Philadelphia County Wills, 1810-1815
Abstracts of Philadelphia County Wills, 1815-1819
Abstracts of Philadelphia County Wills, 1820-1825
Abstracts of Philadelphia County, Pennsylvania Wills, 1682-1726
Abstracts of South Central Pennsylvania Newspapers, Volume 1, 1785-1790
Abstracts of South Central Pennsylvania Newspapers, Volume 3, 1796-1800
Abstracts of the Newspapers of Georgetown and the Federal City, 1789-99
Abstracts of York County, Pennsylvania Wills, 1749-1819
Bucks County, Pennsylvania Church Records of the 17th and 18th Centuries Volume 2: Quaker Records: Falls and Middletown Monthly Meetings
Anna Miller Watring and F. Edward Wright
Caroline County, Maryland Marriages, Births and Deaths, 1850-1880
Citizens of the Eastern Shore of Maryland, 1659-1750
Cumberland County, Pennsylvania Church Records of the 18th Century
Delaware Newspaper Abstracts, Volume 1: 1786-1795
Early Charles County, Maryland Settlers, 1658-1745
Marlene Strawser Bates, F. Edward Wright
Early Church Records of Alexandria City and Fairfax County, Virginia
F. Edward Wright and Wesley E. Pippenger
Early Church Records of New Castle County, Delaware, Volume 1, 1701-1800
Frederick County Militia in the War of 1812
Sallie A. Mallick and F. Edward Wright
Inhabitants of Baltimore County, 1692-1763
Land Records of Sussex County, Delaware, 1769-1782
Land Records of Sussex County, Delaware, 1782-1789
Elaine Hastings Mason and F. Edward Wright
Marriage Licenses of Washington, District of Columbia, 1811-1830
Marriages and Deaths from the Newspapers of Allegany and Washington Counties, Maryland, 1820-1830
Marriages and Deaths from The York Recorder, *1821-1830*
Marriages and Deaths in the Newspapers of Frederick and Montgomery Counties, Maryland, 1820-1830

Marriages and Deaths in the Newspapers of Lancaster County, Pennsylvania, 1821-1830
Marriages and Deaths in the Newspapers of Lancaster County, Pennsylvania, 1831-1840
Marriages and Deaths of Cumberland County, [Pennsylvania], 1821-1830
Maryland Calendar of Wills Volume 9: 1744-1749
Maryland Calendar of Wills Volume 10: 1748-1753
Maryland Calendar of Wills Volume 11: 1753-1760
Maryland Calendar of Wills Volume 12: 1759-1764
Maryland Calendar of Wills Volume 13: 1764-1767
Maryland Calendar of Wills Volume 14: 1767-1772
Maryland Calendar of Wills Volume 15: 1772-1774
Maryland Calendar of Wills Volume 16: 1774-1777
Maryland Eastern Shore Newspaper Abstracts, Volume 1: 1790-1805
Maryland Eastern Shore Newspaper Abstracts, Volume 2: 1806-1812
Maryland Eastern Shore Newspaper Abstracts, Volume 3: 1813-1818
Maryland Eastern Shore Newspaper Abstracts, Volume 4: 1819-1824
Maryland Eastern Shore Newspaper Abstracts, Volume 5: Northern Counties, 1825-1829
F. Edward Wright and Irma Harper
Maryland Eastern Shore Newspaper Abstracts, Volume 6: Southern Counties, 1825-1829
Maryland Eastern Shore Newspaper Abstracts, Volume 7: Northern Counties, 1830-1834
Irma Harper and F. Edward Wright
Maryland Eastern Shore Newspaper Abstracts, Volume 8: Southern Counties, 1830-1834
Newspaper Abstracts of Allegany and Washington Counties, 1811-1815
Newspaper Abstracts of Cecil and Harford Counties, [Maryland], 1822-1830
Newspaper Abstracts of Frederick County, [Maryland], 1816-1819
Newspaper Abstracts of Frederick County, 1811-1815
Sketches of Maryland Eastern Shoremen
Tax List of Chester County, Pennsylvania 1768
Tax List of York County, Pennsylvania 1779
Washington County Church Records of the 18th Century, 1768-1800
Western Maryland Newspaper Abstracts, Volume 1: 1786-1798
Western Maryland Newspaper Abstracts, Volume 2: 1799-1805
Western Maryland Newspaper Abstracts, Volume 3: 1806-1810
Wills of Chester County, Pennsylvania, 1766-1778